# A Year in the Gospels with Martin Luther

## Sermons from Luther's Church Postil

VOLUME
1

CONCORDIA PUBLISHING HOUSE · SAINT LOUIS

Copyright © 2018 Concordia Publishing House
3558 S. Jefferson Ave., St. Louis, MO 63118-3968
1-800-325-3040 • www.cph.org

Manufactured in the United States of America

2   3   4   5   6   7   8   9   10            27   26   25   24   23   22   21   20   19

# Contents

## Volume I

## VOLUME 2

# INTRODUCTION

## About These Sermons

OF all the books that Martin Luther wrote, none were more widely read and used by common, everyday people than books containing his sermons, and no collection of Luther's sermons was printed in more editions—and distributed and read more widely during Martin Luther's lifetime—than the sermons in this collection. In fact, there were more than fifty editions printed and distributed during his life, an astounding number even in our own time, much less in Luther's time when printing and publishing was still in its relative infancy and public literacy was nowhere near what it is now.

Why is this? Because these sermons were intended to provide pastors with model sermons that would be for the edification of the people of God. Luther also wanted them to be read by laypeople. With this twofold purpose in mind, Luther was not preaching to entertain or amuse or indulge in lofty flights of philosophical academic speculation. His desire was to preach Christ and Him crucified (1 Corinthians 2:2). He wanted to open up the Bible to all so they would understand God's Word. Luther put forward the treasure of truth that had been for centuries obscured by layers of false doctrine and trust in human efforts to win God's favor. It was in the pulpit that God most powerfully used Luther to bring reformation to the Church, which through the Law and the Gospel is always being reformed by God the Holy Spirit.

Luther called this collection of sermons a "postil." The word *postil* comes from a Latin phrase meaning "after these words," referring to the sermon preached after the reading of portions of Holy Scripture. By Luther's time, the word *postil* had come to mean a collection of sermons for the whole Church Year. Luther regarded this sermon collection to be his chief devotional work during his life, and at one point Luther even said this was his "favorite book" he had written. He said that about others too, but he definitely looked on this collection fondly.

# WHAT IS THE HISTORIC CHURCH
# LECTIONARY AND CHURCH YEAR?

This collection of Luther's sermons follows the historic cycle of Gospel readings that all congregations used in Luther's day. Some Christians today are not accustomed to the idea of a "lectionary" or a "Church Year," so these brief remarks will help them understand what this is all about. Simply put, the use of a lectionary and a unique series of observances and days in a Church Year is intended to help people hear all the essential truths of God's Word and to be reminded of them, year in and year out. God Himself established for His people in the Old Testament a similar cycle of observances.

While Martin Luther preached straight through books of the Bible during midweek services, on Sundays he followed what we now call the "historic lectionary." Today, most liturgical churches that use a lectionary use a three-year series of readings, rather than this one-year series of readings. In either case, the philosophy behind repeating the same readings every year— or every three years—is rooted in the old saying "repetition is the mother of learning." The more often we have an opportunity to repeat and hear and listen to and meditate on a given portion of God's Word, the more deeply and richly we are able to make the truths in the readings our own. And so, over the centuries, the Church had developed a cycle of readings spread over one year of time, following a calendar that differs from the secular calendar. It is the year marked by the Church, known as the "Church Year."

The regular pattern of reading portions of Scripture during the worship services of the Church derives from the very earliest practice of the first Christians gathering early on Sunday morning. (At that time, Sunday was just a regular day of work!) They listened to readings from the Bible, heard sermons based on those readings, prayed, and celebrated the Lord's Supper. This basic pattern of worship continues to this day. We can trace the first known system of a fixed cycle of yearly readings all the way back to around AD 400, based on the custom of continually reading through the writings of the Old Testament, the Gospels, and the letters extant from the apostles, chiefly Paul.

The readings in the one-year lectionary flowed from and supported the Christian Church Year, which in turn developed from the practice of observing the great annual festival of the Resurrection of Jesus, preceded by observing the events during the last days of Jesus' life, known now as "Holy Week." Built around this core set of events, the Church Year expanded in both directions to form a complete annual cycle of observing various key events and teachings of Jesus. The Church Year usually begins in the month of November and starts with the season known as Advent. After Advent come the seasons of Christmas, Epiphany, Lent, Holy Week, Easter, and the Sundays following the Ascension. These seasons are known as the "festival half" of the Church Year and focus primarily on the major events of Christ's life; thus, the readings recount all these events. During the nonfestival half— which begins on the Festival of the Holy Trinity, the day on which the Church focuses on the doctrine of God the Holy Trinity—the concentration is on the public teaching and preaching of Christ, and thus you will hear His parables and parts of His major discourses, such as the Sermon on the Mount and so forth.

As you look at the table of contents of these sermons gathered from Luther's Church Postil, you will see how they follow the historic Church Year, beginning with Advent and ending with the Last Sunday after Trinity. You will also see some Latin words and phrases used to name some of the Sundays in the classical Church Year. In most instances, these terms were used to identify the Sundays before the start of Lent, the Sundays during Lent, and those after Easter, and they were taken from the appointed readings from the Psalms for these Sundays or other appointed readings or based on the numbering of the Sunday, again, in Latin. These Latin names became commonly used to identify these Sundays and even to mark secular time, so it is not uncommon to see correspondence from the time dated according to the Church Year calendar. Organizing life around the Church Year was typical in Luther's time.

Perhaps it should be said for those not familiar with the Church Year or a lectionary that in no way did Martin Luther, or do Lutherans to this day, believe or teach that it is necessary to follow a Church Year or lectionary, as if somehow our salvation depends on it or as if we are doing something to score "brownie points" with our Lord. No, neither is necessary, but generations of Christians from the first millennium forward have found these resources to be helpful tools to organize the life of the Church together, guide worship practices, and help structure preaching so that congregations will not be left to the mercy of the personal tastes and whims of their pastors; rather, they will always be hearing and covering the core teachings of the Bible every single year. The formal confessions of the Lutheran Church have this to say about why we use the historic calendar and lectionary of the Church:

> We gladly keep the old traditions set up in the church because they are useful and promote tranquility, and we interpret them in an evangelical way, excluding the opinion which holds that they justify. Our enemies falsely accuse us of abolishing good ordinances and church discipline. We can truthfully claim that in our churches the public liturgy is more decent than theirs, and if you look at it correctly we are more faithful to the canons than our opponents are (Apology XV 38, *Concordia*).

# About the New Translation
# of Luther's Church Postil

This is a translation of the mature version of Luther's Church Postil, the last one published during his lifetime. Never before has this edition of Luther's Church Postil been translated into English. That is more than a little ironic given it is the only edition the mature Martin Luther expressly approved and permitted. Previous versions of the Church Postil are based on less reliable texts and, in fact, based on editions of the Church Postil that Luther expressly rejected as going well beyond what he intended to be said or printed. Toward the end of his life, Luther finally had enough and undertook to publish his Postil in an improved and enhanced edition. He reviewed what had been previously published and revised it in line with his growing understanding of the Gospel. He was frankly quite outraged by the liberties that had been taken with earlier publications of the Church Postil. He then enlisted the help of a colleague, Caspar Cruciger, who had been a close associate of his for many years and one of the members of the team that worked with Luther on completing and improving the translation of the whole German Bible. The first half of this last, final, and best edition of Luther's Church Postil was published in 1540. Four years later, Cruciger finished his editorial work on the second half, and it was published in 1544 with Luther's approval.

We should also say something about the Bible translation used in this edition. We have provided the basis for each sermon, the appointed Gospel reading, simply quoting from the English Standard Version (ESV) of the Bible. Elsewhere, when you encounter quotes from Scripture, these are translations from the original German text, often from the Luther Bible translation, which was fully completed and published in full, for the first time, in 1534. Note that these translations may not match precisely any existing English translation, but we felt it important for the reader to encounter the Bible as Luther was actually quoting it, as close as possible in English translation. In addition, in Luther's time the Bible did not contain verse numbers. The Bible was only divided into books and chapters. That is why Luther himself and his colleagues did not cite Bible passages as "John 3:16" but would have simply written "John 3." So as not to burden the reader with brackets wherever the Bible is cited, distinguishing the citation to chapter, then the added versification, we have removed all such brackets; simply be aware that these verse numbers were not used in Bible translations until the late 1550s and eventually were used universally in all languages, as we have it today. And one more thing—when encountering Scripture references, if a book of the Bible appears in full, then Luther mentioned the book specifically. If the reference appears as an abbreviation or the verse is enclosed in brackets, then this is the editor's addition for clarity.

*Through the Gospels with Martin Luther* is an edition of Luther's sermons on the Gospels as contained in the scholarly translation published as volumes 75–79 in Luther's Works. The Luther's Works edition of Martin Luther's writing is the most extensive collection of Luther's writings translated into English. New volumes in this series continue to be added, adding to the previous fifty-four volumes published through the 1960s and 1970s. These volumes are available from Concordia Publishing House, which offers them for sale individually or by means of subscription, offering significant discounts as a result.

We are pleased to reintroduce to the English-speaking world these sermons on the Gospel lessons from the historic Church Year. Earlier English editions were based on defective original texts and used a style of English translation that made Luther sound like a British academic, rather than the lively, blunt, profound, and yes, even entertaining preacher that he actually was in the original German—characteristics brought forward into this superb English translation. We hope you will enjoy this collection from this new edition of the Church Postils, the sermons preached by Luther on the Gospel readings through the Church Year.

There are several extra sermons included with these sermons on the Gospel readings, based on readings from the Epistles that were included by Cruciger because he felt they were so good they should not be left out of the Postil, and so he inserted them along with the sermons on the appointed Epistle and Gospel lessons. Be aware that these were never included in the Church Postil, but they were included as an appendix in the new scholarly edition of the Church Postils, and we have included them here for you as well. Enjoy the bonus sermons! You will also enjoy Martin Luther's introduction to the Church Postil, "What Should Be Sought and Expected in the Gospels." It, along with Luther's remarks on how best to contemplate the sufferings and death of Christ, are particular gems in these books.

## ACKNOWLEDGMENTS

The chief translator of the new English edition of the Church Postil is Rev. James Langebartels, and the chief editor is Rev. Dr. Benjamin Mayes, the general editor for the ongoing extension of the American Edition of Luther's Works, with Dr. Christopher Brown, who lent his scholarly expertise to the Church Postil. Mrs. Dawn Mirly Weinstock, the production editor for Luther's Works, provided her painstaking attention to detail in bringing the Church Postil into print. Mr. Mason Vieth, now Seminarian Vieth, prepared the manuscript for publishing by sorting through the massive amount of footnotes and keeping only those most helpful to the lay reader. This edition of the Gospel sermons in the Church Postil was prepared by the undersigned, who alone bears responsibility for any errors or shortcomings in this publication.

May all those who read these sermons be richly blessed by a master pastor, preacher, and Bible teacher at work. May we all be strengthened by God the Holy Trinity to remain faithful disciples of our Lord and Master, Jesus Christ, the world's Redeemer, the one whose blood has cleansed us from all sin.

Rev. Paul T. McCain

PUBLISHER, CONCORDIA PUBLISHING HOUSE

THE FESTIVAL OF THE HOLY TRINITY, 2017

# ABBREVIATIONS

ARG            *Archiv für Reformationsgeschichte*

Concordia      *Concordia: The Lutheran Confessions.* 2nd ed. Edited by Paul T.
               McCain et al. St. Louis: Concordia, 2006.

DWB            Jacob Grimm and Wilhelm Grimm. *Deutsches Wörterbuch.* 16
               vols. in 32. Leipzig: S. Hirzel, 1854–1960.

$E^2$          *Dr. Martin Luther's sämmtliche Werke.* 2nd ed. 26 vols. in 27.
               Frankfurt and Erlangen: Heyder & Zimmer, 1862–85.

FC             *Fathers of the Church.* Edited by Ludwig Schopp. New York:
               Fathers of the Church, 1947–.

Kolb-Wengert   Robert Kolb and Timothy J. Wengert, eds. *The Book of Concord:
               The Confessions of the Evangelical Lutheran Church.* Minneapolis:
               Fortress, 2000.

Loeb           *Loeb Classical Library.* Cambridge, MA: Harvard University
               Press, 1912–.

LW             *Luther's Works: American Edition.* Volumes 1–30: Edited by
               Jaroslav Pelikan. St. Louis: Concordia, 1955–76. Volumes
               31–55: Edited by Helmut Lehmann. Philadelphia/Minneapolis:
               Muhlenberg/Fortress, 1957–86. Volumes 56–82: Edited by
               Christopher Boyd Brown. St. Louis: Concordia: 2009–.

LW             *Luther's Works: Contemporary Biography* (forthcoming)

$NPNF^2$       *A Select Library of the Christian Church: Nicene and Post-Nicene
               Fathers: Second Series.* Edited by Philip Schaff and Henry
               Wace. 14 vols. New York, 1890–1900. Reprint, Peabody, MA:
               Hendrickson, 1994.

PL             *Patrologiae cursus completus: Series Latina.* Edited by J.-P. Migne.
               221 vols. in 223. Paris: Garnier Fratres, 1844–64.

ST             Thomas Aquinas. *Summa theologiae.* Edited by Thomas Gilby
               et al. 61 vols. Oxford: Blackfriars, 1964–. Reprint, Cambridge:
               Cambridge University Press, 2006. Also Fathers of the English
               Dominican Province, trans. *Summa Theologica.* 3 vols. New York:
               Benziger, 1947–48.

| | |
|---|---|
| StL | Johann Georg Walch, ed. *Dr. Martin Luthers sämmtliche Schriften: Neue revidirte Stereotypausgabe.* 23 vols. in 25. St. Louis: Concordia, 1880–1910. |
| WA | *D. Martin Luthers Werke: Kritische Gesamtausgabe.* 73 vols. in 85. Weimar: H. Böhlau, 1883–. |
| WA DB | *D. Martin Luthers Werke: Deutsche Bibel.* 12 vols. in 15. Weimar: H. Böhlau, 1906–. |
| WA TR | *D. Martin Luthers Werke: Tischreden.* 6 vols. Weimar: H. Böhlau, 1912–21. |
| Wander | Karl Friedrich Wilhelm Wander. *Deutsches Sprichwörter Lexikon.* 5 vols. Leipzig: Brockhaus, 1867–80. Reprint, Darmstadt: Wissenschaftliche Buchgesellschaft, 2007. Cited by volume and page, then word and number, e.g., Wander 2:212, "Gott" no. 22. |

# SHORT INSTRUCTION

## WHAT SHOULD BE SOUGHT AND
## EXPECTED IN THE GOSPELS

P EOPLE are strongly accustomed to count the Gospels according to
their books and to say, "There are four Gospels." That is why people do
not know what St. Paul and Peter say in their Epistles, and why their
doctrine is regarded only as an appendix to the doctrine of the Gospels, as
also can be heard in the prologue of Jerome. It is a still worse custom that
people regard the Gospels and Epistles as law books in which we are taught
what we are to do, and the works of Christ are described in no other way than
as examples for us. Where these two erroneous opinions remain in people's
hearts, they can read neither the Gospels nor the Epistles in a useful and
Christian way; they remain mere heathen, as before.

Therefore, we should know that there is only one Gospel, though written
by many apostles. Each Epistle of Paul and Peter, along with Luke's Acts, is
a Gospel, even though they do not report all the works and words of Christ,
but one has it shorter and less than another. There is not one of the four
great Gospels which includes all the words and works of Christ, nor is that
necessary. The Gospel is and should be nothing else than a report and history
about Christ. Similarly, it happens that someone writes a book about what
a king or a prince has done and said and experienced in the days of his life,
which can be described in many ways—some longer, some shorter.

Thus the Gospel should be and is nothing else than a chronicle, history,
and reading about who Christ is, what He has done, said, and experienced,
which some write short, some long, some this way, some another way. Most
briefly, the Gospel is a report that Christ is God's Son who became a human
being for us, died, rose again, and was made Lord over all things. St. Paul says
as much in his Epistles and emphasizes it, though he omits all the miracles
and acts which are described in the four Gospels. Yet he includes enough of
the whole, full Gospel, as can be seen clearly and beautifully in the greeting
to the Romans, where he tells what the Gospel is and says: "Paul, a servant
of Christ Jesus, called as an apostle, set apart to preach the Gospel of God,
which He promised beforehand through His prophets in the Holy Scripture,
concerning His Son, who was born from David according to the flesh and

was proved to be God's Son in power according to the Spirit who sanctifies, since the time of His resurrection from the dead, Jesus Christ our Lord" [Rom. 1:1–4].

There you can see that the Gospel is a history about Christ, God's Son and David's Son, died and risen and made Lord, which is the sum total of the Gospel. Since there is not more than one Christ, there is and can be no more than one Gospel. Because also St. Paul and Peter taught nothing else than Christ in that way, their Epistles can be nothing else than the Gospel. Because also the prophets proclaimed the Gospel and spoke about Christ—as St. Paul reports here and as everyone well knows—their doctrine when they speak about Christ is nothing other than the true, pure, correct Gospel, as if Luke or Matthew had written it. When Isaiah says that He will die for us and carry our sins (Isaiah 53), he has written the pure Gospel. Indeed, I say that whoever does not grasp this belief about the Gospel can never be enlightened in the Scriptures or find the correct basis [for understanding them].

Second, [you can see] that you should not make a Moses out of Christ, as if He did no more than teach and set an example, as the other saints do, as if the Gospel were a doctrinal or law book. Therefore, you should grasp Christ—His Word, works, and suffering—in two ways. First, as an example that you should follow and do, as St. Peter says, "Christ also suffered for us, leaving us an example" (1 Peter 2 [:21]). As you see Him pray, fast, help people, and show love, so you should also do for yourself and for your neighbor. But that is the least part of the Gospel, for which it cannot even be called "Gospel," for in that way Christ is of no more use to you than any other saint. His life remains with Him and does not help you at all. In short, that way does not make any Christians, but only hypocrites. You must go much higher than that—though now for a long time this has been regarded as the best way, even an extraordinary way, to preach.

The main point and basis of the Gospel is that before you grasp Christ as an example, you first receive and apprehend Him as a gift and present given to you by God to be your own. When you see or hear that He has done something or suffered something, do not doubt that Christ Himself with His doing and suffering is yours. You can rely on Him no less than if you had done it—indeed, as if you were Christ. That is truly apprehending the Gospel, that is, the superabundant goodness of God, which no prophet, no apostle, no angel has ever fully expressed, which no heart can ever sufficiently be amazed at and comprehend. That is the great fire of God's love for us by which the heart and conscience become happy, certain, and at peace; that is what preaching Christian faith means. Such preaching is called the Gospel, which means in German as much as a cheerful, good, comforting message, for which reason the apostles are called the twelve messengers.

Isaiah says, "To us a Child is born, to us a Son is given" (Isaiah 9 [:6]). If He is given to us, then He must be ours; then we must also receive Him as our own. [Paul writes]: "How has He not given us everything with His Son?" (Romans 8 [:32]). When you grasp Christ in that way as your gift, given to you as your own, and do not doubt, then you are a Christian. Faith frees you from sin, death, and hell and causes you to conquer all things. No one can sufficiently express that. Rather, the complaint is that even though the Gospel is praised every day, this kind of preaching is suppressed in the world.

When you now have Christ in that way as the basis and chief blessing of your salvation, then the second part follows, namely, that you take Him as an example and devote yourself to serving your neighbor, just as you see that He devoted Himself to you. Then faith and love are both active, God's commandment is fulfilled, and the person is cheerful and fearless to do and suffer anything. Therefore, just look at this: Christ as a gift nourishes your faith and makes you a Christian. But Christ as an example uses your works, which do not make you a Christian, but rather they come from you who have already been made a Christian. Now as far as gift and example are separate, so far are faith and works separate. Faith has nothing of its own, but only Christ's works and life. The works do have something special from you, but they should also not be your own, but belong to your neighbor.

Therefore, you see that the Gospel is not properly a book of laws and commands which demand our activity from us, but a book of divine promises in which He promises, offers, and gives to us all His blessings and benefits in Christ. That Christ and the apostles gave much good instruction and explained the Law is to be counted among the benefits as a second work of Christ, for correct teaching is not the least benefit. Therefore, we also see that He does not dreadfully force and drive us, as Moses does in his book and as is the nature of a command. Rather, He teaches us in a pleasing and kind way, and only tells us what to do and not to do, and what will happen to evildoers and benefactors. He drives and compels no one. He teaches in such a tender way that He entices us more than commands us as He begins to say: "Blessed are the poor. . . . Blessed are the meek," etc. [Matt. 5:3, 5]. The apostles commonly use the words "I admonish," "I ask," "I implore," etc. But Moses says, "I command," "I forbid," and then threatens and frightens with dreadful punishments and torments. With this instruction, you can read and listen to the Gospels beneficially.

Now, when you open, read, or hear the book of the Gospel, as Christ comes here or there or someone is brought to Him, then you should learn the preaching or the Gospel through which He comes to you or you are brought to Him. To preach the Gospel is nothing other than bringing Christ to us or us to Him. But when you see how He works and helps everyone to whom He comes and who is brought to Him, then you will know that faith works this in you, and He offers this help and kindness to your soul through the Gospel. If you submit and let Him do good to you—that is, if you believe that He does good to you and helps you—then you certainly have it; then Christ is yours and is given to you as a gift.

Accordingly, it is necessary that you follow this example and also help and do for your neighbor, also to give him a gift and an example. Isaiah says about this: "Comfort, comfort My people, says your God. Speak tenderly to Jerusalem, and preach to her that her warfare has an end, for her iniquity is pardoned, for she has received from the Lord's hand double for all her sins" (Isaiah 40 [:1–2]). The twofold blessing is these two parts in Christ: the gift and the example. They are also signified by the two parts of the inheritance (which the Law of Moses attributes to the first son [Deut. 21:17]) and by many other figures.

It is sin and a shame that we Christians have gotten to the point that we not only do not understand but also first need someone to show us with other books and explanations what is to be sought and expected in it. The Gospels and the Epistles of the apostles were written so that they themselves would be such pointers and lead us into the writings of the prophets and of Moses, that is, the Old Testament, so that there we ourselves could read and see that Christ was wrapped in swaddling cloths and laid in the manger, that is, that He is contained in the writings of the prophets. Then our studying and our reading should lead us to see who Christ is, why He was given, how He was promised, and how all Scripture points to Him, as He Himself says, "If you believed Moses, you would believe Me; for he wrote of Me" (John 5 [:46]). Likewise: "Seek and search the Scriptures, for it is they that give testimony about Me" (John 5 [:39]).

That is what St. Paul meant when he said at the beginning of his greeting to the Romans that the Gospel was promised by God through the prophets in the Holy Scriptures (Romans 1 [:1–2]). For that reason the evangelists and apostles always show us in the Scriptures and tell us: "Thus it was written" or "This happened so that the writings of the prophets might be fulfilled." Luke says that the Thessalonians heard the Gospel with all joy and studied and examined the Scriptures day and night to see if these things were true (Acts 17 [:11]). So St. Peter writes at the beginning of his first letter: "Concerning this, your salvation, the prophets who prophesied about the grace that was coming to you searched and inquired carefully, inquiring what person or time the Spirit of Christ in them was indicating and predicting the sufferings that are in Christ and the glory thereafter. It was revealed to them, for they were serving not themselves but us, in the things that have now been announced to you through those who proclaimed the good news to you by the Holy Spirit sent from heaven, things into which angels long to look" (1 Peter 1 [:10–12]).

What else does St. Peter want here than to lead us into Scripture? It is as if he were saying: We preach and open the Scriptures to you through the Holy Spirit, so that you yourselves can read and see what is in them and what time the prophets have written about, as [Peter] also said, "All the prophets who have spoken, from Samuel on, also proclaimed these days" (Acts 3 [:24]). Therefore, Luke also says that Christ opened the understanding of the apostles so that they understood Scripture (Luke 24 [:27]). Christ says that He is the door through whom people must enter; and whoever enters through Him, to him the porter opens so that he may find pasture and salvation (cf. John 10 [:9]). Finally, it is true that the Gospel itself is the pointer and instructor in the Scriptures, just as I would gladly point to the Gospel with this preface and give instruction.

But look at what fine, tender, godly children we are! So that we might not need to study the Scriptures and learn Christ there, we regard the whole Old Testament as nothing, as that which is expired and of no value. Nevertheless, it alone has the name of being called "Holy Scripture." The Gospel ought properly not be writing, but the oral Word which produces Scripture, as Christ and the apostles did. Therefore, even Christ did not Himself write [anything], but only spoke and called His doctrine not Scripture but Gospel, that is, a good message or proclamation which is to be promoted not with the pen but with the mouth. Then we go ahead and make out of the Gospel a law book, a doctrine of commands; we make out of Christ a Moses, out of the helper only a teacher. What penalty should God not impose on such stupid, wrongheaded people? It is fair that He has abandoned us to the pope's doctrines (that is, human lies) because we have abandoned His Scriptures; now, instead of Holy Scripture, we have to learn the decretals of a lying fool (that is, a wicked scoundrel). Would to God that the pure Gospel were still known among Christians and that this work of mine were not needed or useful at all; then there would definitely be hope that the Holy Scriptures would again have their worth restored. That is enough for a preface and a short instruction; in the exposition we will say more about it.

# GOSPEL FOR THE
# FIRST SUNDAY IN ADVENT

*Matthew 21 [:1–9]*

*Now when they drew near to Jerusalem and came to Bethphage, to the Mount of Olives, then Jesus sent two disciples, saying to them, "Go into the village in front of you, and immediately you will find a donkey tied, and a colt with her. Untie them and bring them to Me. If anyone says anything to you, you shall say, 'The Lord needs them,' and he will send them at once." This took place to fulfill what was spoken by the prophet, saying, "Say to the daughter of Zion, 'Behold, your king is coming to you, humble, and mounted on a donkey, and on a colt, the foal of a beast of burden.'" The disciples went and did as Jesus had directed them. They brought the donkey and the colt and put on them their cloaks, and He sat on them. Most of the crowd spread their cloaks on the road, and others cut branches from the trees and spread them on the road. And the crowds that went before Him and that followed Him were shouting, "Hosanna to the Son of David! Blessed is He who comes in the name of the Lord! Hosanna in the highest!"*

1. In the preface, I said that there are two things to be noted and considered in the Gospel readings: first, the work of Christ presented to us as a gift and kindness, to which our faith is to cling and in which it is to be exercised; second, the same work offered as an example and model for us to imitate and follow. Thus all the Gospel lessons first teach faith and then works. We will therefore divide this Gospel into three parts: first, faith; second, good works; and third, something of the history and secret meaning.

## First, concerning Faith

2. This Gospel especially encourages and requires faith, for it presents Christ in His gracious coming, whom none may receive or accept unless he believes Him to be the one and agrees with the way this Gospel portrays Him. Nothing but grace, gentleness, and kindness are here shown to be in Christ, and whoever believes this about Him and thinks of Him in this way is saved. See that He rides not on a stallion, an animal of war, nor does He come in great pomp and power, but He sits on a donkey, a peaceful animal fit only for burdens and labor as a help to man. The way He comes shows that He is

not coming to frighten or force or oppress people, but to help them, to carry their burdens, and to take responsibility for them. And though it has always been the custom of the country to ride on donkeys and to use horses for war, as the Scriptures often tell us, yet all of this is done to make known to us that the entrance of this King is gentle and kind.

3. Second, it also shows the pageantry and conduct of the disciples toward Christ. They brought the donkey and the colt to Christ, put their clothes over the donkey, and set Him on it. It also shows the conduct of the people who spread their clothes and branches from the trees on the road. This shows that there was no fear or terror there, but only cheerful confidence in Him as one with whom they got along very well. He received these things cheerfully from them and was completely pleased with it.

4. Third, there is no armor present, no battle cry, but only singing, praising, rejoicing, and glorifying God.

5. Fourth, Christ weeps over the city of Jerusalem, as Luke writes [19:41–42], because it neither recognizes nor receives this grace. Their injury was very painful for Him, to say nothing of Him dealing with them in stringency and terror.

6. Fifth, [Christ's] kindness and gentleness are best shown when [Matthew] introduces the words of the prophet [Zech. 9:9] and tenderly invites us to believe and receive Christ. It was because of this prophecy that this part of this Gospel took place and the story was written, as the evangelist himself testifies. Therefore, let us regard this passage as the chief part of this Gospel, for in it Christ is pictured for us and we are told what to expect from Him, what to seek in Him, and how to benefit from Him and make use of Him.

7. First, he says, "Say to the daughter of Zion" [Matt. 21:5]. That is said to the preachers, and thereby they are given a new sermon to preach, namely, nothing other than what is given in the following words, that is, a true and saving knowledge of Christ. Whoever preaches anything else is a wolf and a deceiver. This is one of the verses of which Paul speaks (Romans 1 [:2]), in which the Gospel is promised, for the Gospel is a sermon about Christ, as He is here depicted, that we should believe.

8. I have often said that there are two kinds of faith. The first is that you certainly believe that Christ is the kind of man described and proclaimed here and in the entire Gospel, but you do not believe that He is such a man for you, and you doubt whether you have and will have this from Him, and you think: "Yes, He is such a man to the others, such as St. Peter, Paul, and the godly saints. But who knows whether He is such to me and whether I may expect the same from Him and may confide in it, as these saints did?"

9. See, this faith is nothing. It never receives Christ nor tastes Him. It cannot feel any desire or love from Him or for Him. It is a faith about

Christ and not toward or in Christ, a faith which the demons also have, as well as all evil men. For who does not believe that Christ is a gracious King for the saints? This wicked and vain faith is now taught by the accursed synagogues of Satan. The universities, together with the monasteries and all Papists, say that this faith is sufficient to make Christians. That is really nothing other than to deny the Christian faith and to make heathen and Turks out of Christians, as St. Peter proclaimed about them, saying, "There will be false teachers among you, who will deny the Lord who bought them" (2 Peter 2 [:1]).

10. Second, he says "the daughter of Zion" [Matt. 21:5]. In these words he refers to the other, true faith. For if he commands that the following words be spoken about Christ, then there must be someone who hears, receives, and clings to them in firm faith. He does not say, "Say *of* the daughter of Zion," as if someone should otherwise believe that she had Christ, but: "You yourselves should say to her that she is to believe it regarding herself and think it true, without any doubt that it will happen to her as these words read." That is the faith that alone is called "Christian faith," when you believe without any wavering that Christ is such a one not only for St. Peter and the saints but also for you, and even more so for you than for all the others. Your salvation does not depend on the fact that you believe Christ to be Christ for the godly, but that He is Christ for you and is your own.

11. This faith causes you to delight in Christ so that He tastes sweet in your heart. Then love and good works will follow naturally. But if they do not follow, then faith is surely not present; for where faith is, there the Holy Spirit must be present and must work love and goodness in us.

12. This faith is now condemned by apostate and rebellious Christians, the pope, bishop, priests, monks, and the universities. They call this faith arrogance, wanting to make oneself equal to the saints. Yet by doing this, they fulfill St. Peter's prophecy when he says of these false teachers: "Through them the way of truth will be blasphemed" (2 Peter 2 [:2]). For this reason, when they hear faith praised, they think love and good works are being pro-hibited. In their great blindness they do not know what faith, love, and good works are. But if you want to be a Christian, you must let these words be spoken to you, to you, to you, and cling to them and believe without any doubt that it will happen to you just as the words say. You must not consider it arrogance that in this you are like the saints, but rather a most necessary humility and despair—not of God's grace but of yourself. Under penalty of the loss of eternal salvation, God wants such arrogance toward the grace He offers. If you do not want to be like the saints, and even holy yourself, where will that leave you? It would be arrogance if you wanted to be holy and saved through yourself and your own work, as the apostate Papists are

now teaching. They call that which is faith "arrogance," and that which is arrogance they call "faith"—the poor, deluded people!

13. But when you dare to be holy in faith in Christ and through His coming, that is the true praise and glory of God, by which you confess, love, and praise His grace and work in you, and cast aside and condemn yourself with your works, and despair of yourself. That is being a Christian. For we say, "I believe [there is] one holy Christian Church, which is a communion of saints."[1] If you want to be a part of the holy Christian Church and the communion of saints, then you must also indeed be holy as the Church is, but not through yourself nor from yourself, but from Christ alone, from whom others are holy too.

14. Third, he says: "Notice" or "See" [Matt. 21:5]. With these words he would awaken us as from sleep and unbelief, as though he were asserting something great, strange, or remarkable, something we have long wished for and should receive with joy. Such awakening is certainly necessary because of this: reason and nature despise all that concerns faith and are completely unsuited to it. For example, how can nature and reason comprehend that the King of Jerusalem should be such a one, who comes forth in such poverty and humility and rides on a donkey borrowed from someone else? How does such an entrance tally with being a great king? But it is the nature of faith that it does not judge or reason by what it sees or feels, but by what it hears. It clings to the Word alone, and not at all to sight or appearance. For this reason Christ here was received as a king only by those who followed the words of the prophet, who believed in Christ, who judged and received His kingdom not with their eyes but with their spirit—these are the true daughter of Zion. For it is impossible for those who follow their sight and feeling and who do not adhere firmly to the plain, pure Word not to take offense at Christ.

15. Let us first of all receive and hold fast this picture in which the nature of faith is depicted for us. For just as the appearance and object of faith as here presented is nothing at all, and preposterous to all reason and nature, so also the same ineffectual and preposterous appearance is to be found in all articles and instances of faith. It would not be faith if it appeared and acted as faith regards it and as the words indicate. Just for that reason it is faith, because things do not appear and act the way faith and the words say.

If Christ had entered magnificently, like a worldly king, then the appearance and the words would have conformed suitably to reason and nature, and it would have looked to the eyes just as the words say. But then no faith would have remained there. Thus it happens that whoever believes in Christ must perceive riches in poverty, honor in dishonor, joy in sorrow, life in death, and hold fast to them in that faith which clings to God's Word and expects this.

1 I.e., in the Third Article of the Apostles' Creed (Kolb-Wengert, p. 22; *Concordia*, p. 16).

16. Fourth: "your King" [Matt. 21:5]. Here he separates this King from all other kings. "He is your King," he says, "who was promised to you, to whom you belong, who alone shall rule you, yet in the spirit and not according to secular government. He it is whom you have desired from the beginning, for whom your dear fathers have sighed with a heartfelt longing and for whom they have cried. He will deliver and free you from all that has so far burdened, oppressed, and held you captive."

Oh, this is a comforting word for a believing heart, for without Christ a person is subjected to many raging tyrants who are not kings but assassins, at whose hands he suffers great misery and fear. These tyrants are, for example, the devil, the flesh, the world, sin, as well as the Law and death with hell. By all of these the troubled conscience is oppressed, is severely imprisoned and leads a bitter and anxious life. For where there is sin, there is no good conscience; where there is no good conscience, there is only an insecure life and an inextinguishable fear of death and hell. In the presence of these, no joy and pleasure can exist in the heart securely, but as Leviticus 26 [:36] says, "Such a heart is terrified even by a rustling leaf."

17. When a heart receives this King with a strong faith, then it is secure and fears neither sin, death, hell, nor any other evil; for he well knows and does not doubt that this King is a Lord over life and death, sin and grace, hell and heaven, and that all things are in His hand. For this reason He became our King and came to us: to deliver us from all such oppressive tyrants and to rule over us Himself alone. Therefore, whoever is under this King and regards Him in firm faith cannot be harmed by sin, death, hell, devil, men, or any creatures. Instead, just as his King lives without sin and is blessed, so through Him he shall be kept living and blessed forever without death and without sin.

18. See, such great things are contained in these little words: "See, your King" [Matt. 21:5]. Such boundlessly great treasures are brought by this poor, neglected King who rides on a donkey. Reason does not see any of this, nor does nature comprehend it, but faith alone does. Therefore, He is properly called "your King"—yours, yours, you who are driven and tormented by sin, devil, death and hell, the flesh and the world—so that you may be governed and led lovingly under Him in grace, in the Spirit, in life, in heaven, in God.

With this word, therefore, he requires faith in order that you may consider it certain that He is such a King to you, has such a kingdom, and comes and is proclaimed for this purpose. If you do not believe this of Him, you will never attain it by any work of your own. As you regard Him, so you have Him. What you expect of Him, you will find in Him. And as you believe, so shall it be to you [cf. Matt. 8:13]. Yet He remains immovably who He is—a King of life, of grace, and of salvation—whether people believe it or not.

19. Fifth: He "is coming" [Matt. 21:5]. Without a doubt, you do not come to Him and fetch Him; He is too high and too far from you. With your effort, pains, and work you cannot reach Him, lest you boast that you had brought Him to yourself by your own merit and worthiness. No, dear friend, all merit and worthiness is defeated here, and there is nothing on your side but demerit and unworthiness; on His side, nothing but grace and mercy. The poor and the rich here meet together, as Proverbs 22 [:2] says.

20. By this are condemned all the shameful teachings about free will, which come from the pope, the universities, and the monasteries. For all their teaching is that we are to begin and lay the first stone. By the power of our free will we are first to seek God, to come to Him, to run after Him, and to gain His grace. Beware, beware of this poison! It is nothing but the doctrine of the devil, by which all the world is led astray. Before you can call on God or seek Him, God must first have come to you and have found you, as Paul says: "How can they call on Him unless they first believe? And how can they believe in Him unless there first is someone preaching? And how can they preach unless they are first sent?" etc. (Romans 10 [:14–15]). God must lay the first stone and begin in you, if you are to seek Him and to pray to Him. He is present already when you begin and seek Him. If He is not present, then you are beginning nothing but sheer sin, and the greater and holier the work you attempt, the greater the sin will be, and you will become a hardened hypocrite.

21. You ask: "How shall we begin to be godly, or what shall we do that God may begin His work in us?" Answer: Didn't you hear that there is no work or beginning in you that will make you godly, as little as the increase and the completion is in you? The beginning, the advance, and the completion is God's alone [cf. Phil. 1:6]. Everything you begin is sin and remains sin, no matter how brightly it shines. You can do nothing but sin, no matter what you do. Therefore, the teaching of all schools and monks is deception, when they teach people to begin, to pray, to do good works, to contribute money, to give, to sing, to become clergy—and to seek God's grace through those things.

22. But you say, "Then I must necessarily sin, if I work and live without God, only from my free will, and I could not avoid sin, no matter what I do?" Answer: Truly it is so. You must remain in sin, no matter what you do, and it is all sin what you alone do out of your free will. For if out of your own free will you could not sin, or could do what pleased God, what would you need Christ for? He would be a fool to shed His blood for your sin, if you by yourself were so free and mighty that you could do something which is not sin.

23. Learn, then, from this Gospel what takes place when God begins to make us godly and what the beginning of becoming godly is. There is

no other beginning than that your King comes to you and begins to work in you. It takes place in this way: The Gospel must be first of all. It must be preached and heard. In it you hear and learn how all you do is nothing before God and that everything you do or begin is sin. Your King must first be in you and rule you. See, here is the beginning of your salvation. You fall away from your works and despair of yourself, because you hear and see that all you do is sin and amounts to nothing, as the Gospel tells you, and you begin to receive your King through faith, to cling to Him, to appeal to His grace, and to find consolation only in His goodness.

It is not by your power that you hear and accept this, but by God's grace, which renders the Gospel fruitful in you so that you believe Him. For you see how few there are who accept it, so that Christ for that reason weeps over Jerusalem [cf. Luke 19:41]. Now our Papists not only don't accept it but also condemn this doctrine,[2] for they will not allow all they do to be sin and nothing; they want to lay the first stone; they rage and fume against the Gospel.

24. Furthermore, it is not in your power or merit to cause the Gospel to be preached and your King to come; God must send Him out of pure grace. Therefore, no greater wrath of God exists than where He does not send the Gospel; there can be only sin, error, and darkness there, no matter what they do. Again, there is no greater grace than where He sends His Gospel, for there fruit and grace must follow together, even if not all, or even only a few, accept it. Thus the most terrible wrath of God is in the pope's government, so that St. Peter dares to call them "the children of execration" [cf. 2 Pet. 2:1–3], for they teach no Gospel, but only human doctrine about their own works.

25. See, that's what "your King is coming" means. You do not seek Him; He seeks you. You do not find Him; He finds you. For the preachers come from Him, not from you. Their preaching comes from Him, not from you. Your faith comes from Him, not from you. And everything that faith works in you comes from Him, not from you. Where He does not come, you remain outside; and where there is no Gospel, there is no God there, but only sin and perdition, no matter how free will can or wants to do, suffer, work, and live.

26. Sixth: He "is coming to you" [Matt. 21:5]—you, you! What does that mean? Is it not enough that He is your King? If He is yours, why does he need to say that He "is coming to you"? But all this is stated by the prophet in order to present Christ in a most delightful way and to draw us to faith. It is not enough that Christ redeems us from the tyranny and dominion of sin, death, and hell and becomes our King, but He gives Himself to us for our very own, so that all He is and has may be ours, as St. Paul writes: "He did not spare His

---

2 The Paris theological faculty stated that Luther was heretical because he said good works come entirely from God and not at all from human free will; see *Judgment of the Paris Theologians* (1521), WA 8:288 (LW 71).

own Son but gave Him up for us all, so how will He not also with Him give us all things?" (Romans 8 [:32]).

27. Thus the daughter of Zion has two kinds of possessions from Christ. The first is faith and the Spirit in the heart, by which she becomes pure and free from sins. The second is Christ Himself; there she may boast of the possessions given by Christ, as though all Christ is and has were her own, that she may rely upon Christ as upon her own inheritance. Of this St. Paul says that Christ is our Mediator (cf. Romans 8 [:34]). He receives us, and we in turn receive Him as our own, for "God made Christ to be for us wisdom, righteousness, sanctification, and redemption" (1 Corinthians 1 [:30]). About the two kinds of possessions Isaiah says: "Comfort, comfort My people, says your God. Speak tenderly to Jerusalem, and preach to her that her warfare is ended, for her iniquity is pardoned, and she has received from the Lord's hand double for all her sins" (Isaiah 40 [:1–2]).

See, here this is called "He is coming to you" for your good, for your very own. Since He is your King, you receive grace from Him in your heart, so that He helps you from sin and death and thus becomes your King and you, His subject. But by coming to you, He becomes your own, so that you gain mastery of His possessions, just as a bride becomes mistress of her bridegroom's possessions in addition to the jewelry that he puts on her. Oh, these are pleasant and comforting words! Who can despair and be afraid of death and hell when he believes in these words and wins Christ as his own?

28. Seventh: "gentle" [Matt. 21:5]. This word is to be especially noted, and it greatly comforts the sin-burdened conscience. Sin naturally makes a timid conscience, which is terrified of God and hides, as Adam did in Paradise [cf. Gen. 3:8], and cannot endure the coming of God, since it knows and naturally feels that God is the enemy of sin and severely punishes it. For that reason it flees and is terrified when God is even named, and is anxious that He will immediately hit him with the club. In order that such thoughts and timidity may not pursue us, he gives us the comforting promise that this King comes humbly.

It is as if he said: "Do not flee, and do not be afraid, for He does not now come as He came to Adam, to Cain, to the flood, to Babylon, to Sodom and Gomorrah, nor as He came to the people of Israel on Mount Sinai. He does not come in wrath; He does not want to call you to account nor to affix blame. All wrath is laid aside; nothing but gentleness and kindness remain. He indeed wants to deal with you in such a way that your heart will have pleasure, love, and full confidence in Him, that from now on you will cling to Him and find refuge in Him much more than you before were terrified and fled from Him. See, He is nothing but gentleness toward you. He is a different man completely. He acts as if He were sorry ever to have terrified you and to have caused you to flee by His punishment and wrath. For that reason He wants to make you bold again and to comfort you and kindly bring you to Himself."

See, I think this is what it means to speak consolingly to the heart of a sin-burdened conscience; this is what it means to preach Christ correctly and to proclaim the Gospel. How is it possible that such words should not make a heart glad; and drive away all fear of sin, death, and hell; and establish a free, secure, and good conscience that henceforth gladly does and leaves undone all and more than is desired from it?

29. The evangelist, however, altered the words of the prophet slightly. The prophet's words read: "Rejoice greatly, O daughter of Zion! Shout aloud, O daughter of Jerusalem! Behold, your King is coming to you; righteous and having salvation is He, poor and riding on a donkey and on a young colt of the donkeys" (Zechariah 9 [:9]). The evangelist expresses the exhortation to joy and shouting directed toward the daughter of Zion and the daughter of Jerusalem briefly in these words: "Say to the daughter of Zion" [Matt. 21:5]. Likewise, he leaves out the words "righteous and having salvation." Likewise, where the prophet says, "He is poor," the evangelist says, "He is gentle." Likewise, when the prophet says "on a colt, the foal of the donkeys," he specifies many donkeys in the plural. The evangelist says "on a colt, the foal of a worker," or "a beast of burden," that is, a donkey that is used daily for carrying burdens and working. How shall we harmonize these accounts?

30. First, we should know that the evangelists were not compelled to quote all the prophets' words exactly. It was enough for them to give the same meaning and to show the fulfillment, directing us to the Scriptures so that we ourselves should read further what they omit and see that nothing at all was written that has not been abundantly fulfilled. It is also natural that whoever has the reality and the fulfillment does not pay so much attention to the words as to the fulfillment. Thus we often see that the evangelist quotes the prophets somewhat altered, yet all of that happens without detriment to the understanding and meaning, as was said.

31. When the prophet exhorts the daughter of Zion and the daughter of Jerusalem to joy and shouting, he is making it abundantly clear that the coming of this King is most comforting and pleasant to every sin-burdened conscience, since He removes all their terror and fear so that they do not flee from Him and tremble, as if He would be their strict judge and would press them with the Law, as Moses did. Thus He also terrified them; they could not have a cheerful and consoling confidence in God, since the knowledge and perception of sin naturally come from the Law. But [the prophet] would arouse them most strongly with this first word so that they look to Him and expect from Him every grace and kindness. For what other reason should

he exhort them to rejoice and command them not only to rejoice but also to shout and be very happy? He says this by divine command and on behalf of God to all who are in sorrow, fear, and anguish before God. Thus he shows that it is God's will and full intent, and by doing this he commands that they should, contrary to their natural fear and terror, have a joyful confidence toward Him. And this really is the natural voice of the Gospel, which the prophet here begins to proclaim, just as Christ always speaks in the Gospel and as the apostles everywhere exhort people to rejoice in Christ, as we will often hear afterward.

The evangelist does not incite to joy in the same way the prophet does, but simply says, "Say to the daughter of Zion." He does that to express how the joy and shouting will happen, so that no one expects a bodily joy, but rather a spiritual joy, a joy derived only from saying and hearing by the faith of the heart. According to bodily appearance, there was nothing joyful in Christ's poor entrance; for that reason His spiritual entrance must be preached and believed, that is, His gentleness, which makes us joyful and glad.

33. That the prophet gives Christ three titles—"poor, righteous, and having salvation"—while the evangelist has only one—"gentle"—is done for the sake of brevity; he wants to show more than explain. It seems to me that the Holy Spirit let the apostles and evangelists abbreviate passages of the Scriptures in order to keep us close to the pure Scriptures, and not in order to set an example for future interpreters who speak copiously apart from the Scriptures and thereby draw us secretly from the Scriptures to human doctrines. It is as if the Holy Spirit said: "If I extend the Scripture, everyone will follow that example. Then it will happen that people will read more in other books than in My book, as the chief book, and there would be no end to the writing of books [cf. Eccles. 12:12], so that people would go constantly from one book to the next, until they finally lose the Scripture, as it has indeed happened." Therefore, with this abbreviating of passages He wants to draw us only to the original book where they are contained at greater length and in totality, so that there is no need for everyone to make a separate book and leave this first one.

34. Thus we also see that it is the intention of all the apostles and evangelists in the whole New Testament to chase and drive us into the Old Testament, which alone is what they call "Holy Scripture." For the New Testament by its nature was supposed to be only physical, living words and not writing. For that reason also Christ did not write anything but gave the command to preach and promote the Gospel orally, which previously had been hidden in the Scriptures.

35. Nevertheless, in the Hebrew language the two words "poor" and "gentle" do not sound very different and mean the sort of poor man who

is not lacking in money and property, but one who in his heart is miserable and humbled, in whom one certainly finds no anger or haughtiness but only gentleness and sympathy. And if we want to have the full meaning of this word, we may best take it out of the Gospel of Luke, where he describes that, when Christ entered, He wept and lamented over Jerusalem [cf. Luke 19:41].

As you now see, Christ's conduct shows the meaning of the words "poor" and "gentle." What is His conduct? His heart is full of sorrow and compassion toward Jerusalem. There is no anger or vengefulness, so that out of His great gentleness He even weeps over the destruction of His enemies. No one was so evil that He would have harmed him or wished to. His sorrow makes Him so mild and gentle that He doesn't at all think of anger, haughtiness, threatening, or revenge, but presents only compassion and goodwill. See, this is what the prophet calls "poor" and the evangelist, "gentle." Blessed is he who knows and believes Christ in this way, for he cannot ever be afraid of Him, but must have an open and comforting confidence in Him and access to Him. He is not disappointed, for as he believes, so he finds it [cf. Matt. 8:13]. These words do not lie or deceive.

36. The word "righteous" [Zech. 9:9] ought not be understood here of the righteousness with which God judges, what people call the "strict righteousness of God." For if Christ came to us with that, who would remain before Him? Who could receive Him, since even the saints cannot endure it? In that way the joy, delight, and love of His entrance would be changed into the greatest fear and terror. Rather, it means the grace by which He justifies us. I wish that the little words *justus* ["just, righteous"] and *justitia* ["justice, righteousness"] had never been brought into use in German for the strict, judicial righteousness, for they properly mean "godly" and "godliness." When we say in German that he is a godly man [*ein fromm Mann*], Scripture says that he is *justus*, "just" or "righteous." But Scripture calls God's strict righteousness "severity," "judgment," or "rightness."

Therefore, the prophet should be understood here to say: "Your King is coming to you righteous," or "godly" [*fromm*]; that is, He comes to make you godly through Himself and His grace. He knows well that you are not godly. Your godliness should consist not of your deeds, but of His grace and gift, so that you are righteous, or godly, from Him. This is how St. Paul speaks: "He alone is righteous and the justifier" (Romans 3 [:26]). Likewise: "In the Gospel the righteousness of God is revealed" (Romans 1 [:17]); that is, in German, the godliness of God—namely, His grace and mercy, by which He makes us godly before Him—is preached in the Gospel. You see the same in this saying of the prophet, that Christ is preached to us for godliness, that He comes to us godly and righteous, and we through Him are to become godly and righteous in faith.

37. Note this point diligently, that whenever you find in Scripture the words "God's righteousness," you are not to understand them of the self-existing, intrinsic righteousness of God, as the Papists and many of the holy fathers have erroneously held, of which you would otherwise be frightened. But know that, according to the usage of Scripture, it means the grace and mercy of God poured into us through Christ, from which we are considered godly and righteous before Him. And it is called God's righteousness or godliness because not we but God graciously works it in us, just as "God's work," "God's wisdom," "God's strength," "God's Word," "God's mouth" signifies what He works and speaks in us. All this St. Paul clearly demonstrates: "I am not ashamed of the Gospel, for it is a power of God" (note: which works in us and strengthens us) "for salvation to all who believe in it. For in it the righteousness of God is revealed, as it is written: 'The righteous lives by his faith'" (Romans 1 [:16–17]). Here you see that he speaks of the righteousness of faith and calls it the "righteousness of God" preached in the Gospel, since the Gospel teaches nothing else but that whoever believes has grace and is righteous before God and will be saved.

The word "Savior" compels us to accept this as the meaning of the little word "righteous." For if Christ came with His strict righteousness, He would not save anyone but would condemn all, since they are all sinners and unrighteous. But now He comes not only to make godly and righteous but also to save all who accept Him, so that He alone is the righteous one and the Savior, offered graciously to all sinners out of unmerited gentleness and righteousness.

38. When the evangelist calls the donkey a "beast of burden" [Matt. 21:5], he is describing the kind of donkey about which the prophet is speaking. It is as though he said, "The prophecy is fulfilled in this donkey that is capable of bearing a burden." It was not a special donkey trained for this purpose, as customarily in that land donkeys were trained for riding, so very humbly was this prophecy fulfilled. And when the prophet speaks of "the donkeys," as if it were the colt of many donkeys, he means it was the kind of colt donkeys have, not the colt of a horse.

## [SECOND,] CONCERNING GOOD WORKS

39. That is enough for the first part, on faith. We now come to the second part, to good works. We receive Christ not only as a gift by faith but also as an example through love toward our neighbor, to whom we are to give service and do good as Christ does to us. Faith brings and gives Christ to you as your own with all His possessions. Love gives you to your neighbor with all your possessions. These two things constitute a true and complete Christian

life; then follow suffering and persecution for such faith and love; and out of these grows hope in patience.

40. You ask, perhaps, what are the good works you are to do for your neighbor? The answer is that they have no name. Just as the good works Christ does for you have no name, so the good works you do for your neighbor neither can nor should have any name.

41. How are you to know them? Answer: They have no name so that there may be no distinction made and they may not be divided, so that you leave some undone. Rather, you should altogether give yourself up to [your neighbor] with all you have, just as Christ did not only pray or fast for you. Prayer and fasting are not the works He did for you, but He gave Himself wholly to you, with praying, fasting, all works and suffering, so that there is nothing in Him that is not yours and was not done for you. Thus it is not your good work that you give some alms or that you pray, but that you surrender yourself completely to your neighbor and serve him, wherever he needs and wherever you can, be it with alms, prayer, work, fasting, counsel, comfort, instruction, admonition, rebuke, pardon, clothing, food, and finally even with suffering and dying for him. Tell me, where now are such works to be found in Christendom?

42. All the world sings, speaks, writes, and thinks about good works. Every sermon is about good works. All monasteries, all convents, the whole world claim good works. Everyone wants to be occupied with good works. And yet good works are by no means done; indeed, no one knows anything about them. Oh, that all such pulpits in all the world were on fire and burned to ashes! How they mislead people with good works! They call good works what God has not commanded, such as pilgrimages; fasting to honor the saints; building and decorating churches; endowing Masses and vigils; praying rosaries;[3] much prattling and howling in church; becoming a monk, nun, or priest; using special food, clothes, or places—who can enumerate all the horrible abominations and deceptions? This is the pope's government and holiness.

43. If you have ears to hear and a mind to observe, listen and learn for God's sake what good works are and mean. A good work is good because it is useful and benefits and helps the one for whom it is done. Why else should it be called good? For there is a difference between good works and great, high, numerous, and beautiful works. When you throw a big stone a great distance, that is a great work, but for whom is that useful and good? If you can jump, run, and joust well, that is a fine, beautiful work, but for whom is

---

3 The rosary, a sequence of prayers associated with a string of beads, was a form of Marian devotion introduced and promoted by the Dominicans in the late fourteenth century.

that useful and good? For whom is it helpful when you wear a costly robe or build a beautiful house?

44. I come to our Papists' work: For whom is it helpful when you spread silver or gold over the walls, stone, and wood in the churches? Who would be made better if each village had ten bells as big as the one at Erfurt?[4] Who would be helped if all houses were nothing but convents and monasteries as costly as the temple of Solomon? Who is helped if you fast for St. Catherine, for St. Martin, or for this or that saint? For whom is it useful if you are shorn whole or half, if you wear a gray or a black cowl? Who would be helped if all people held Mass every hour? What benefit is it if in one church, as at Meissen, they sing day and night without interruption?[5] Who would be made better if every church was full of silver, pictures, and jewels? That is altogether folly and deception. Human lies invented these things and called them good works; they claim to serve God with these things and to pray for the people and their sins, just as if God were helped by our property or as if His saints were in need of our work. Sticks and stones are not as ignorant and mad as we are. A tree bears fruit not for itself, but for the good of people and animals, and these fruits are its good works.

45. Therefore, hear how Christ explains good works: "Whatever you want others to do to you, do that to them, for this is the Law and the prophets" (Matthew 7 [:12]). Don't you hear what the contents of the whole Law and of all the prophets are? You are not to do good to God and to His deceased saints—they are not in need of it. Still less should you do it to wood and stone—to which it is of no use nor is it needed—but to people. Do you not hear? To people you should do everything that you want done to you.

46. Without a doubt I would not want you to build me a church or a tower or to cast bells for me. I would not want you to construct for me an organ with fourteen stops and ten ranks of pipes. I can neither eat nor drink those things, neither support my wife nor child, neither keep my house nor land. You may feast my eyes with these things and tickle my ears with them, but what shall I give to my children? What about my necessities? Oh, madness, madness! Moreover, the bishops and princes, who should hold back such things, are the first in such folly, and one blind person leads another [cf. Matt. 15:14]. Such people remind me of young girls playing with dolls and of boys riding on sticks. Indeed, they are nothing but children who play with dolls and ride on sticks!

4 Known as the *Maria Gloriosa*, the large bell cast by Geert van Wou (1440–1527) in 1497 for the Erfurt cathedral of St. Mary (*Mariendom*) was, at the time, the world's largest free-swinging bell and is still admired for its beautiful, pure tone.

5 Luther is referring to the so-called "eternal choir" (*ewiger Chor* or *laus perennis*), i.e., continual choral prayer in the Meissen Cathedral. See LW 25:450 n. 24.

47. Keep in mind that you need not do any good for God and His deceased saints, but only get, seek, ask, and receive good from Him in faith. Christ has done and accomplished everything for you, paid for your sins, secured grace, life, and salvation. Be content with Him, and only think how you can bring Him more and more into yourself and strengthen this faith. Therefore, direct all you can do and your whole life to this end: that it be good. It is good when it is useful to other people and not to yourself. You don't need it, since Christ has done and given for you all that you might seek and desire for yourself, here and hereafter, whether it be forgiveness of sins, merit of salvation, or whatever it may be called. If you find you have a work that you do for the benefit of God or of His saints or of yourself and not only for your neighbor, know that such a work is not good.

48. A man is to live, speak, act, hear, suffer, and die for the love and service of his wife and child, the wife for the husband, the children for the parents, the servants for their masters, the masters for their servants, the government for its subjects, the subjects for their government, each one for his fellow man, even for his enemies, so that always one is the other's hand, mouth, eye, foot, even heart and mind. These are truly Christian and naturally good works, which can and should be done unceasingly at all times, in all places, toward all people. Therefore, see that the Papists' works in playing organs, singing, clothes, ringing [bells], burning incense, sprinkling [holy water], going on pilgrimages, fasting, etc., are really beautiful, great, numerous, high, wide, and bulky works, but there is no good, useful, and helpful work in them, so that one may well speak the proverb about them: "It is beautifully evil."

49. But beware of their acute subtleties, when they say, "If these works are not good or useful to our neighbor in his body, they are spiritually useful for his soul, since they serve God and propitiate Him and secure His grace." Here it is time to say, "You are telling lies as wide as your mouth is." God is served not with works, but with faith. Faith must do everything that is to be done between God and us. He who has faith can pray for his fellow man. He who has no faith can pray for nothing.

Therefore, it is a truly devilish lie to regard such outward pomp to be spiritually useful and good. A miller's maid, if she believes, does more good, accomplishes more, and I would trust her more if she only takes the sack from the donkey than all the priests and monks [do] if they sang themselves to death day and night and tormented themselves until they bleed. You big, stupid fools, do you want to help the people with your faithless life and distribute spiritual goods, though there is on earth no more miserable, needy, godless people than you are? You should be called not "spiritual,"[6] but "spiritless."

50. See, Christ teaches these good works here by His example. Tell me, what does He do to be useful and good for Himself? The prophet directs it all to the daughter of Zion and says, "He is coming to you" [Matt. 21:5; Zech. 9:9], and His coming as righteous, Savior, and gentle is all for you, to justify and save you. No one had asked or called Him. He comes freely, of Himself, out of pure love, just to do good and to be useful and helpful.

Now His work is not of one kind but of all kinds, namely, it embraces all that is necessary to justify and save her. But justification and salvation include that He delivers her from sin, death, and hell, and does it not only for His friends but also for His enemies—yes, mere enemies—yet He does it so tenderly that He weeps over those who won't let Him do such good work for them and will not accept Him. Therefore, He risks everything He has and is so that He may blot out their sin, conquer death and hell, and justify and save them. He retains nothing at all for Himself and is content that He already has God and is blessed. Thus He serves only us according to the will of His Father, who wanted Him to do that.

51. See, then, whether He keeps the Law: "Whatever you want others to do to you, do that to them" [Matt. 7:12]. Is it not true that everyone sincerely wishes that another might step in front of his sin, take it upon himself, and blot it out, so that it would no more sting his conscience, and in addition free him from death and deliver him from hell? What does everyone desire more deeply than to be free from death and hell? Who would not gladly be without sin and have a good, joyful conscience before God? Do we not see how all people have striven for this with praying, fasting, pilgrimages, contributing money, monasticism, and priestcraft? Who forces them? It is sin, death, and hell, from which they would like to be safe. And if there were a physician at the end of the world who could help with this, all lands would become deserted, and everyone would run to this physician and risk property, body, and life to make the journey.

And if Christ Himself were surrounded by death, sin, and hell, as we are, He would wish that someone would free Him from it, take His sin away, and give Him a good conscience. Since He would have others do this for Him, He proceeds and does it for others, as the Law says. He steps into our sin, goes into death, and overcomes for us both sin, death, and hell, so that henceforth all who believe in Him and call upon His name shall be justified and saved, be without sin and death, and have a good, joyful, secure, fearless, and blessed conscience forever, as He says: "If anyone keeps My Word,

---

6 *geistlich*, literally, "a spiritual one," a general term for those who, according to medieval ecclesiology, belonged to the "spiritual" as opposed to the "secular" estate.

he will never taste death" (John 8 [:51]); and "I am the resurrection and the life. Whoever believes in Me shall never die, and though he die, yet shall he live" (John 11 [:25–26]).

52. See, this is the great joy, to which the prophet exhorts when he says: "Rejoice greatly, O daughter of Zion! Shout aloud, O daughter of Jerusalem!" [Zech. 9:9]. This is the righteousness and the salvation for which this Savior and King comes. These are good works done for us by which He fulfills the Law. Therefore, the death of Christian believers is not death but a sleep, for they neither see nor taste death, as Christ says here.

53. But the Papists and their disciples, who want to escape death, sin, and hell by works and satisfaction, must keep doing them eternally. For they presume to do from themselves what Christ alone did and could do, from whom they should have waited for it by faith. Therefore, they are misled, foolish people who do works as a service to Christ and His saints, which they should do for their neighbors. Again, they want to find in themselves what they should have awaited from Christ by faith, and they have gone so far finally that they spend on stone and wood, on bells and incense what they should spend on their neighbors. They go on and do much good for God and His saints, they fast for them and endow hours[7] [of prayer] for them, and at the same time leave their neighbor as he is, thinking only: "Let us first help ourselves!" Then comes the pope and sells them his trifles and letter[8] and leads them by the mouth into heaven—not into God's heaven, but into the pope's heaven, that is, the abyss of hell. See, this is the fruit of unbelief and ignorance of Christ; this is our reward for having left the Gospel in obscurity and setting up human doctrine in its place.

54. See, now you know what good works are. Think of it and act accordingly. As to your sin, death, and hell, take care that you do not add to them, for you cannot do anything here; your good works will avail nothing; you must let someone else do the work for you. Such works properly belong to Christ, and they are His own to do. You must leave this verse to Him, that He is the King of Zion who is coming, that He alone is the righteous Savior [cf. Zech. 9:9]. In Him and through Him you will blot out sin and death through faith. Therefore, if anyone teaches you to blot out your own sin by works, beware of him.

55. If they quote some passages of Scripture against this, such as Daniel [4:27]: "Free yourself from your sins with alms," and the like, then be wise. For such passages do not mean that the works could blot out or make satisfaction

---

7 *Horas*, the canonical prayer hours, such as Matins, Lauds, Vespers, and Compline. People were encouraged to give money to endow benefices; the duties attached to many benefices included the recitation of the canonical prayer hours.

8 I.e., indulgences.

for sin, for this would rob Christ of this passage and His entire entry and would deny all His works. Rather, such passages mean that these works are a sure sign of faith, which from Christ receives victory over all sins and death. For it is impossible for him who believes in Christ as his righteous Savior not to love and do good. If, however, he does not do good or does not love, then it is certain that faith is not present. Therefore, you can know by the fruits what kind of a tree it is, and love and works show what kind of Christ is in him and that he believes in Christ.

56. Thus faith blots out sin in a different way than love. Faith blots it out with its own deed alone, while love or good works prove and demonstrate that faith has done so and is present, as St. Paul dares to say, "If I had all faith, so as to move mountains, but had not love, I would be nothing" (1 Corinthians 13 [:2]). Why? Without doubt because faith is not present where there is no love; they do not stay separated from each other. Therefore, see to it that you do not let yourself be confused and led away from faith to works.

57. We must do good works, but our confidence must not be built on them, but on Christ's work. We should not attack sin, death, and hell with our works, but send them away from us to the righteous Savior, to the King of Zion, who rides on the donkey. He knows how to treat sin, death, and hell: He kills sin, chokes death, and devours hell. Let that man take care of such matters, and apply your works to your neighbor, so that you have a sure testimony of faith in the Savior who kills death. But more of this later.

## [Third,] the History and the Secret Meaning

58. In the story of this Gospel reading, we must first look to the meaning and reason the evangelist quotes the words of the prophet, which described long ago and clearly (with very excellent and wonderful words) the bodily, public coming and entrance of our Lord Christ to His people of Zion or Jerusalem (as the text says). By doing so, the prophet wanted to show and explain to his people and to all the world who the Messiah would be and how and in what way He would come and show Himself, and he offers a publicly visible sign of that when he says, "Behold, your King is coming to you, poor and riding on a donkey," etc. [Zech. 9:9], so that we would be certain of it and not miss the promised Messiah or Christ, nor wait for another.

With his words he takes action to refute the mistaken notion of the Jews, who thought that, because there were such glorious things written and said about Christ and His kingdom, He would show Himself in great public, worldly pomp and glory, as a King against their enemies, especially the Roman Empire, under whose power they were held captive, and would overthrow its power and mighty men and in its place set up the Jews as lords and princes. They thus hoped for and expected nothing from the promised

Christ but a worldly kingdom and deliverance from bodily captivity. Even today they cling to such a dream, and therefore they do not want to believe in our Christ, because they have neither seen nor attained to such bodily deliverance and worldly power. They were led to this notion and strengthened in it by their false preachers, the scribes and the priests, who distorted the Scriptures about Christ and interpreted them according to their own fleshly understanding as referring to bodily, worldly things, because they would like to be great worldly lords over others.

59. But the dear prophets plainly prophesied against this and faithfully gave warning that they should not have thought of such an earthly kingdom or of bodily deliverance, but should have looked back and paid attention to the promises of the spiritual kingdom and of a deliverance from the awful fall of the human race in Paradise. There it was said, "In the hour that you eat of the forbidden tree, you shall surely die" [Gen. 2:17]. Also against this is the first promise given about Christ, that the Seed of the woman shall trample the serpent's head, etc. [cf. Gen. 3:15], that is, deliver us from the power and prison of the devil, in which he forcibly holds the whole human race under sin and eternal death, and instead shall bring us to eternal, divine righteousness and eternal life. Therefore, the prophet also calls Him "righteous and having salvation." This truly is a different deliverance than any bodily freedom, power, and glory, which end with death, under which everything must remain eternally.

They ought to have considered this and rejoiced in it, since the dear prophets had with great heartfelt desire sighed and prayed for it, and this prophet exhorts to such great joy and shouting. But they and their shameless preachers made only a bodily thing out of this misery and unhappiness, as if it were a joke about sin and death or the power of the devil, and considered it the greatest misfortune that they lost their bodily freedom and were made subject to the emperor and required to pay taxes to him.

60. The evangelist therefore quotes this saying of the prophet to rebuke the blindness and false notions of all those who seek bodily and temporal things in Christ and the Gospel, and to convince them by the testimony of the prophet, who shows clearly what kind of a king Christ is and what they should seek in Him. He calls Him "righteous and having salvation," and yet adds this sign of His coming by which they are to know and receive Him: "He is coming to you poor, and sitting on a young donkey," as if he would like to say: "A poor, miserable, almost beggarly rider on someone else's borrowed donkey, one kept by the side of the old, working donkey not for ostentation but only to carry." He does this to tear them away from gazing and waiting for the gloriously magnificent entrance of a worldly king. And he gives them such a sign just so that they would not have doubts about Christ nor take

offense at His poor appearance. All pomp and splendor are to be removed from sight, and the heart and the eyes directed and pinned to this poor rider, who comes forth as so poor and miserable and empties Himself of all kingly form, that they might not seek in Him bodily and temporal things but eternal things, as indicated by the words "righteous and having salvation."

61. This verse, first, clearly and powerfully strikes down the Jewish dream and notion about a worldly reign of the Messiah and about bodily deliverance. It takes away any reason and pretext that would excuse them for not accepting Christ, and cuts off all hope and expectation for another, because it clearly and distinctly announces and exhorts them that He would come in that way and that He has fulfilled everything. Thus against the Jews we Christians have a firm ground and sure evidence and proof from their own Scripture that this Messiah, who thus came to them, is the true Christ predicted by the prophets, and that no other shall ever come, and that in the vain hope of another's coming they miss out on both their temporal and eternal deliverance.

62. That is enough about the history. Now let us also look at its hidden or spiritual meaning. Here we are to know that all Christ's bodily journeying and traveling signify His spiritual traveling. His bodily walking therefore signifies the Gospel and faith. For just as with His bodily feet He walked from one town to another, so by preaching He came into all the world. Hence this lesson shows well what the Gospel is and how it is to be preached, what it does and effects in the world. This history is at the same time a fine, pleasing image and picture of how this occurs in the kingdom of Christ through the preaching office. We will consider this point by point.

*Now when they came near to Jerusalem, toward Bethphage, to the Mount of Olives. [Matt. 21:1]*

63. All the apostles say that Christ became man at the end of the world and that the Gospel would be the last thing preached. "Dear children, it is now the last hour, and as you have heard, the antichrist will come," etc. (1 John 2 [:18]). Again: "These things were written down for our warning, on whom the end of the ages has come" (1 Corinthians 10 [:11]). Therefore, just as the prophets came before the first coming of Christ in His humanity, so the apostles are the last messengers of God, sent before the final coming [of Christ] and the Last Day, so that they might diligently proclaim the same thing (which is what they also do). Christ indicates this by not sending out His disciples to fetch the donkey until He drew near to Jerusalem, where He was now supposed to enter. Thus the Gospel is brought into the world by the apostles shortly before the Last Day, when Christ will enter with His own into the eternal Jerusalem.

65. And the sending out shows that the kingdom of Christ exists in the public and oral preaching office, which should not stop and remain at one place—as it was hidden up till now only among the Jews in the Scripture and was promised in the future by the prophets—but goes publicly, free and unhindered, into all the world.

66. "The Mount of Olives" signifies the great grace and mercy of God, from which the apostles were sent and the Gospel was brought. For "oil" in Scripture signifies the grace and mercy of God, by which the soul and the conscience are comforted and healed, just as oil soothes, or softens and heals, the wounds and injuries of the body. And from what was said above, we see what unspeakable grace it is that we know and have Christ, the righteous Savior and King. Therefore, He does not begin sending them on the level plain, nor on a barren, rocky mountain, but on the Mount of Olives, to show to all the world the mercy which prompted Him to send such grace. There is not simply a drop or handful of it, as formerly, but because of its great abundance it might be called a "mountain." The prophet also calls such grace "God's mountain" and says, "Your righteousness is like the mountains of God" (Psalm [36:6]), that is, "great and overwhelming, abundant and overflowing." This can be easily understood when one considers what it means that Christ bears and conquers our sin, death, and hell and does everything for us that is necessary to our salvation. He does not let us do anything for it but practice it toward our neighbor, and to test whether we have such faith in Him or not. Thus the Mount of Olives signifies that the Gospel was not preached nor sent until the time of grace came. From this time on, the great grace goes out into the world through the apostles.

*Jesus sent two disciples, saying to them: "Go into the village that lies before you." [Matt. 21:1–2]*

67. These "two disciples" represent all the apostles and preachers who have been sent into the world. This is because the evangelical preaching stands firm with two witnesses, as Paul says, "Now the righteousness of God is manifest, and the Law and the prophets bear witness to it" (Romans 3 [:21]). Thus we see how the apostles, too, always introduce the Law and the prophets, who prophesied of Christ, so that what Moses and Christ said would be observed: "Every speech shall stand firm in the mouth of two or three" (Matthew 18 [:16; cf. Deut. 19:15]).

68. But when He says, "Go into the village in front of you," not mentioning the name, this signifies that the apostles are not sent to one nation alone, as the Jews previously were separated by God from the Gentiles and alone bore the name "people of God," and they alone had God's Word and promise of the coming Christ. But now that Christ is coming, He sends His

preachers out into all the world and commands them to go straight forward and preach of Him everywhere, to all the heathen and whoever comes before them, and to reprove, teach, and exhort without distinction, no matter how great, learned, wise, and holy they may be.

69. The Lord here comforts and strengthens the apostles and all preachers. It is as if He said: "I am sending you into the world, which is over against you and seems to be something great, for there are many kings, princes, learned, rich, and everything that is great in the world and amounts to anything. But don't be afraid. Go on. It is but hardly a village. Do not be moved by great appearances. Preach sharply against it, and fear no one." For it is impossible to preach the Gospel truth if the preacher fears the great lords and does not despise all that the world esteems highly. The Lord will have no flatterer as a preacher. He does not say, "Go around the village or to one side of it." Go inside to them, and tell those sharply, who are doing to you whatever they want, what they do not want to hear.

*And soon you will find a donkey tied, and a colt with her. Untie them and bring them to Me. [Matt. 21:2]*

71. This is also said as consolation for preachers, that they should not be concerned about who believes or receives them. For it is decreed: "My Word that goes out from My mouth shall not return to Me empty" (Isaiah 55 [:11]). Paul says, "In the world the Gospel is bearing fruit" (Colossians 1 [:6]). Therefore, it is not otherwise possible. Where the Gospel is preached there will be some who grasp and believe it. This is the meaning of the mystery that the apostles so immediately find the donkey and the colt with her, if they only go. It is as if He said: "Only go—that is, only preach. Do not be concerned about who they are who will hear. Let Me be concerned about that. The world will be against you; don't let that trouble you. Nevertheless, you will find those who will hear and follow you. You do not know them yet, but I already know them in advance. You preach, and let Me be in charge."

72. See, in this way He consoles them that they should not cease to preach against the world; no matter how harshly they are contradicted and opposed, it will not be without fruit. You find people now who think that, because it is impossible to convert the world, we should be silent so that there is not a tumult. "It is all in vain," they say. "Pope, bishops, priests, and monks do not accept it and do not change their lives. What is the use of preaching and storming against them?"

But the Lord rightly refutes this and says: "Only go; only preach. What does it matter if it is over against you? For all that, you will find there whatever I want you to find there." We should now do likewise. Although the great lords storm against the Gospel and there is no hope that they will improve, yet we must preach. There will yet be found those who listen to it and improve.

73. Why does He have them bring two donkeys, or why are not both the same, two young or two old ones, if it was not enough for Him to ride on one? Answer: Just as the two disciples represent the preachers, so the two donkeys represent their disciples and hearers. The preachers shall be Christ's disciples and be sent by Him; that is, they should preach nothing but Christ's doctrine. Nor should they go to preach unless they are called to this, as the apostles have kept both of these. But the students are the old and the young donkey.

74. Here we need to know that man is divided into two parts, an inner and an outer man. He is called "outer" according to his outer, visible, bodily life and conduct; he is called "inner" according to his heart and conscience. One can compel the outer man with laws, punishment, pain, and shame—or entice him with favor, money, honor, and reward—to do the good and refrain from the bad. But no one can compel or entice the inner man to do willingly, out of pure pleasure, and gratuitously what he should do, unless the grace of God changes his heart and makes it willing.

For that reason Scripture concludes that all men are liars [cf. Ps. 116:11], since no one does good and refrains from evil of his own free will, but everyone seeks his own and does not do it out of love for virtue. For if there were no heaven or hell, no disgrace or honor, no one would do good. If there were as great an honor and praise in committing adultery as in honoring marriage, you would see adultery committed with much greater pleasure than marriage is now honored. All other sins would be done with greater zeal than virtue is being practiced. Therefore, all good conduct without grace is mere glitter and semblance, for it touches only the outer man, without the pleasure and free will of the inner man.

75. See, these are the two donkeys. The old donkey is the outer man. He is tied with laws and fear of death, with hell and shame, or with enticements of heaven, of life, of honor, just as the donkey is tied up. He goes forward with the external appearance of good works and is a pious villain, but he does it unwillingly and with a reluctant heart and a heavy conscience.

Therefore, the evangelist calls the donkey "a beast of burden" [Matt. 21:5], a donkey capable of bearing a burden, who works hard under a burden. It is a miserable, pitiable life, which is extorted out of the fear of hell, death, and shame. Hell, death, and shame are his yoke and burden, heavy beyond measure, from which he has a burdened conscience and is secretly an enemy of both the Law and God. Especially the Jews were such people, and such are all who work at fulfilling God's commands and earning heaven with their works and their own powers. They are tied by their consciences to the Law.

They must do it, but they would rather not. They are carriers of sacks, lazy donkeys, and yoked rogues.

76. But the colt, the young donkey (of which Luke [19:30] and Mark [11:2] write that no one had ever yet ridden on it), is the inner man, the heart, the spirit, the will, which can never be subject to the Law, even if it is tied by conscience and feels the Law. But he has no desire or love for it until Christ comes and rides on him. As this colt was never ridden by anyone, so man's heart has never been subject to the good; but, as Moses says, it is "always inclined toward evil from his youth" (Genesis 6 [:5]; 8 [:21]).

77. When Christ tells them to "untie" them, it means that He is telling them to preach the Gospel in His name, in which is proclaimed grace and pardon of all sins and how He fulfilled the Law for us. The heart is here untied from the fetters of conscience and receives grace, which makes his heart and inner man free and happy, willing and joyous to do and not to do all things. Thus man is untied, not from the Law, that he should do nothing, but from the reluctant, heavy conscience that he had from the Law, with which he was the enemy of the Law and which threatened him with death and hell. Now he has a good conscience under Christ, is a friend of the Law, never fears death and hell, does freely and willingly what before he did reluctantly. See, in this way the Gospel unties the heart from all evil, from sin, from death, from hell, and from a bad conscience, through faith in Christ.

78. When He commands them to bring them to Him, that is said against the pope and all sects or rabble-rousing preachers, who lead the souls from Christ to themselves. But the apostles bring them to Christ; that is, they preach and teach nothing but Christ, and not their own doctrine or human laws. For the Gospel teaches us to come only to Christ and to know Christ rightly. In this the spiritless prelates take a hard hit on their government, with which they bring souls to themselves, as Paul says: "I know that after my departure fierce wolves will come in among you, not sparing the flock; and from you will arise corrupt talkers, to draw away the disciples to themselves" (Acts 20 [:29–30]). But the Gospel converts men to Christ and to no one else. Therefore, He has the Gospel go out and sends preachers, that thereby He may draw us all to Himself, that we may know Him, as He says, "When I am lifted up, I will draw all people to Myself" (John 12 [:32]).

*If anyone says anything to you, you shall say, "The Lord needs them," and he will leave them to you at once. [Matt. 21:3]*

79. St. Paul compares the Law to "guardians and schoolmasters" (Galatians 4 [:2]), under whom the young heir is brought up in fear and constraint. The Law forces us with threats so that we externally abstain from evil works because of the fear of death and hell, though the heart does not

become good through that. There were, as Luke writes, owners of the donkey and the colt who said to the apostles: "What are you doing, untying the colt?" (Luke [19:33]). For where the Gospel begins to untie the conscience from its own works, it sounds just as though it were forbidding good works and the keeping of the Law. Therefore, all teachers of the Law, or (as the Gospel calls them) writers and scribes, say: "If all our works are nothing and if the works done according to the Law are evil, well, then, we will never do good. You forbid good works and repudiate God's Law. You heretic, you untie the colt and want to make people free and bad." Then they go right to work and hinder it, so that the colt and the conscience can't be untied and brought to Christ. They claim that people must do good works, and they keep the people tied up with laws.

80. This text shows how the apostles are to act toward these people. They are to say, "Their Lord needs them"; that is, they are to instruct them in the works of the Law and the works of grace and thus say: "We do not forbid good works, but we untie the conscience from false good works, not so that they live free to do evil, but so that they come under Christ, their true Lord, and under Him do truly good works. For this He needs them and wants to have them." St. Paul presents this beautifully in Romans 6, where he teaches that through grace we are free from the Law and its works, not so that we should do evil, but truly good works.

81. It all amounts to this: that the scribes and Law enforcers do not know what good works are. They therefore don't want to set the colt free, but they drive it with merciless human good works. However, where instruction is given concerning good works, they let it pass, if they are at all sensible and true teachers of the Law, as they are here represented. The mad tyrants, who rave with human laws, have nothing in this Gospel reading. It speaks only of the Law of God and of the very best teachers of the Law. For without grace, even God's Law is a fetter and makes captive consciences and hypocrites whom none can help until other works are preached, which are not ours but Christ's, and until He works in us with grace. Then all constraint and coercion of the Law is ended, and the colt is soon untied.

*All this took place to fulfill what was spoken by the prophet, who says, "Say to the daughter of Zion," etc. [Matt. 21:4–5]*

82. This prophecy has already been sufficiently explained. The evangelist cites it so that we may see how Christ has come not for the sake of our merit, but for the sake of divine truth. For He was promised long ago before we, to whom He comes, existed. Therefore, just as God promised the Gospel out of pure grace, so He has also fulfilled it to demonstrate His truth—that He keeps

what He promises—in order to stir us to build confidently on His promise, for He will fulfill it.

And this is one of the Scriptures in which the Gospel was promised, of which Paul says, "God promised the Gospel beforehand through His prophets in the Holy Scripture, concerning His Son, Jesus Christ," etc. (Romans 1 [:2]). We have now heard how, in this verse, the Gospel, Christ, and faith are pointed out with the utmost excellence and consolation.

*The disciples went and did as Jesus had commanded them. They brought the donkey and the colt and put on them their cloaks, and He sat on them. [Matt. 21:6–7]*

83. These are the preachers who by the Gospel have untied consciences from the Law and its works and brought them to the works of grace, who made completely good saints out of hypocrites, so that Christ henceforth rides upon them.

84. The question arises here whether Christ rode upon both donkeys. Matthew reads as if the disciples put Him on both donkeys, while Mark, Luke, and John speak only of the colt. Some think He sat first on the colt, but because it was too wild and untamed He then sat on the donkey. These are fables and dreams.

We should take it that He rode only on the colt, and not on the donkey. Yet He had both of them brought on account of the spiritual significance mentioned above. When Matthew says He sat on them as though He rode on both, it is said according to Scripture's characteristic and its common way of speaking, called "synecdoche," where a thing which applies only to some of them is ascribed in general to a whole group. For example, Matthew writes that the robbers reviled Christ on the cross [Matt. 27:44], while, as Luke writes, only one did [Luke 23:39–42]. So also Christ says that the city of Jerusalem stones the prophets, while only some from the city did it (Matthew 23 [:37]). People say, "The Turk killed the Christians," though he only killed some of them. Thus Christ rode on the donkeys, though He only rode on the colt, because both donkeys are taken together. People say that what happened to one happened to all.

85. Now consider the spiritual riding. Christ rides on the colt; the donkey follows. That is, when Christ dwells through faith in our inner man, then we are under Him in His government. But the outer man, the donkey, goes alone. Christ does not ride on it, though it follows after. That is, as St. Paul says, the outer man is unwilling, he does not yet carry Christ—indeed, he struggles against the inner man, as he says: "The desires of the flesh are against the spirit, and the desires of the spirit are against the flesh, for these are opposed to each other, to keep you from doing the things you want to do"

(Galatians 5 [:17]). Yet because the colt carries Christ, and the spirit is willing by grace, the donkey (that is, the flesh) must be led after by the reins, for the spirit crucifies and chastises the flesh, so that it must be subject.

86. See, this is the reason Christ rides upon the colt and not upon the donkey, and yet wants to have both for His entrance, for body and soul must be saved. Although here on earth the body is unwilling, incapable of grace and of carrying Christ, it must endure the spirit on which Christ rides. The spirit pulls the body and leads it along by the power of grace received through Christ.

87. What does it signify that the apostles, without command, put their cloaks on the colt? Here again not all the disciples put all their cloaks on the colt, as it sounds, but perhaps only a coat of one disciple. But it is written for the spiritual meaning, as if it were all the cloaks of all the disciples, or at least of the two. To be sure, it was a poor saddle and attire, but it was rich in meaning. I think that [the cloaks] are the good example of the apostles, with which the Christian Church is covered and adorned and Christ is praised and honored, namely, their preaching and confession, suffering and dying for the Gospel's sake, just as Christ said that Peter would glorify Him by his death (cf. John 21 [:19]). Paul says in today's Epistle [Rom. 13:11–14] that we should put on Christ, by which he doubtless wants to show that good works are the cloaks of the Christians, by which Christ is honored and glorified in us before all people. Now, the examples of the apostles are the highest and nearest [to Christ] above all the saints. They instruct us best and teach Christ most clearly. Therefore, they should not, like the other cloaks, lie on the road, but on the donkey, so that Christ may ride on them and the donkey walk under them. We should follow these examples of the apostles, and praise Christ with our confession and life, and embellish and adorn the doctrine of the Gospel, as Titus 2 [:10] says.

88. Hear how Paul lays his cloak on the colt: "Be imitators of me, as I am of Christ" (1 Corinthians 10 [11:1]); and "Remember your leaders, those who spoke to you the Word of God. Consider their end, and imitate their faith" (Hebrews 13 [:7]). No saint's example is pure in faith except that of the apostles. All the other saints after the apostles have an addition of human doctrine or works. Therefore, Christ sits on their cloaks to show that they are truly Christian and faithful examples above others.

89. That they "set Him on [the colt]" must also signify something [cf. Luke 19:35]. Could He not mount it Himself? Why does He pretend to be so delicate? As I said above, the apostles did not want to preach themselves nor to ride on the colt themselves. St. Paul says: "We do not want to lord it over your faith" (2 Corinthians 1 [:24]) and "What we proclaim is not ourselves, but Jesus Christ as Lord, with ourselves as your servants" (2 Corinthians 4 [:5]). Likewise: "You should not domineer over them" (1 Peter 5 [:3]), as if it were

your inheritance. They preached the pure faith to us and also offered their example and let it serve us for this alone: that Christ might rule in us and faith remain pure, so that we don't receive their word and work as if it were their own, but that we learn Christ in both their words and works. But all of this has been corrupted by the pope and his sects.

> *Much of the crowd spread their cloaks on the road, and others cut branches from the trees and spread them on the road. [Matt. 21:8]*

92. Spreading the cloaks on the road means that we should, according to the example of the apostles, honor, adorn, and embellish Christ also with our confession and all our life, so that we divest ourselves of all praise for wisdom and holiness and submit to Christ alone with our pure confession; likewise, that we should apply all we have—honor, property, power, body, and life—to the honor and furtherance of the Gospel, and for its sake, if necessary, risk everything for it.

So kings and lords and whatever is great, powerful, and rich should have served Christ with their property, honor, and power in order to further the Gospel, and should have risked everything for the sake of the Gospel. The holy patriarchs, prophets, and godly kings in the Old Testament did that with their example. But now all of that is turned upside down, especially among the papistic crowd, which against Christ seizes all honor and power for itself, and by doing so has oppressed the Gospel.

93. But when they "cut branches from the trees and spread them on the road," this also signifies the preaching office and the testimony of Scripture and the prophets about Christ. (One of those is the prophecy of Zechariah cited here [9:9].) Thus people should establish and adorn the preaching about Christ, and the whole preaching office should be directed toward making Christ known and confessed.

St. John writes that they cut branches off palm trees and went out to meet Him (John 12 [:13]). Some add that, because this happened on the Mount of Olives, there were also olive branches, and that is not implausible, though the Gospels don't report it.

94. There is also a reason palm branches and olive branches are mentioned. They testify what the confession is and what is to be preached and believed about Christ. It is the nature of the palm tree that when it is made into a beam, it does not bend under any load but holds itself up against the load.

96. For this reason they carried palm branches before kings and lords when they had gained a victory and held a triumphal procession. So also the carrying of olive branches was a sign of submission, especially by those who desired and asked for grace and peace, as was commonly done among the ancients.

Thus, with this pageantry [of spreading palm branches] toward Christ, they indicated that they accept Him as their Lord and King given by God (as they then testify with their shouts and congratulations), as a victorious and invincible Savior, confessing themselves submissive to Him and seeking grace from Him. This was how Christ was supposed to be preached and confessed in all the world: as the victorious, invincible King against sin, death, and the power of the devil and of all the world, for those who are oppressed and tormented by them, and as a Lord in whom sheer grace and mercy are to be found and sought, as their faithful Priest and Mediator before God.

The Word of the Gospel about this King is a word of grace and mercy that brings us peace and reconciliation from God, besides being an invincible power and strength, as Paul calls the Gospel "a power of God for salvation to everyone who believes" (Romans 1 [:16]). "The gates of hell shall be unable to prevail against it," as Christ says (Matthew 16 [:18]).

*And the crowds that went before Him and that followed Him were shouting and saying: "Hosanna to the Son of David! Blessed be He who comes in the name of the Lord! Hosanna in the highest!" [Matt. 21:9]*

97. St. Paul says, "Christ yesterday and today and forever" (Hebrews 13 [:8]). All who are saved from the beginning of the world to the end are and must be Christians and be saved through the Christian faith. Therefore, St. Paul says, "Our fathers ate the same food and drank the same drink" (1 Corinthians 10 [:1–4]). And Christ says, "Your father Abraham saw My day and was glad" (John 8 [:56]).

98. Thus the multitudes going before signify all Christians and saints before Christ's birth. Those who follow signify all the saints after Christ's birth. They all believe and cling to the one Christ. The former expected Him in the future; the latter received Him in past times. Therefore, they also, all together, sing one song and praise and bless God in Christ. For we can give God nothing other than praise and thanks, since we receive everything else from Him, be it grace, Word, work, Gospel, faith, and all things. That is also the only true Christian worship, to praise and give thanks, as the psalmist says, "Call upon Me; then I will hear you and I will help you, and you shall glorify Me" (Psalm 50 [:15]).

99. What does "Hosanna to the Son of David" mean? They took the word "Hosanna" from Psalm 118 [:25–26], which says: "Hosanna, [save us] O Lord! O Lord, help us and give us success! Blessed be He who comes in the name of the Lord!" They applied this verse to Christ. It is a good wish, as in German one wishes a new ruler success and health. Thus here also the people thought Christ would be their physical king, and for that reason they wish Him success and health. For in German "Hosanna" would be: "Oh, give

health" or "Beloved, save" or however else you might express such a wish. Now they add "to the Son of David," and thus mean: "O God, give health to the Son of David! O God, give success, blessed be," etc. All of that we say in German: "Oh, dear God, give success and health to this Son of David for His new kingdom! Let Him enter in God's name so that it is blessed and succeeds," etc.

100. Mark [11:10] proves clearly that they meant His kingdom when he writes that they said, "Blessed is the coming kingdom of our father David, who comes!" When all churches now read it as "Osanna," that is incorrect. It should be "Hosanna." Accordingly, they made a woman's name out of it, and the one they should call "Susanna" they call "Osanna." "Susanna" is a woman's name and means "a rose." In the end, after making a farce out of Baptism, the foolish bishops baptize bells and altars, which is a great nonsense, and call the bells "Osanna." But away with the blind leaders! We should learn here also to sing "Hosanna" and "Hatslihanna"[9] to the Son of David together with those multitudes, that is, to wish success and health to the kingdom of Christ, to holy Christendom, that God would abolish human doctrine and let Christ alone be our King, who governs only by His Gospel, and let us be His colts! God grant it. Amen.

9 As "Hosanna" (הוֹשַׁע־נָּא) is the Hebrew for "save," so "Hatslihanna" (הַצְלִיחָה־נָּא) is the Hebrew for "give success" (Ps. 118:25; Neh. 1:11).

# GOSPEL FOR THE SECOND SUNDAY IN ADVENT

*Luke 21:25–33*

*"And there will be signs in sun and moon and stars, and on the earth distress of nations in perplexity because of the roaring of the sea and the waves, people fainting with fear and with foreboding of what is coming on the world. For the powers of the heavens will be shaken. And then they will see the Son of Man coming in a cloud with power and great glory. Now when these things begin to take place, straighten up and raise your heads, because your redemption is drawing near." And He told them a parable: "Look at the fig tree, and all the trees. As soon as they come out in leaf, you see for yourselves and know that the summer is already near. So also, when you see these things taking place, you know that the kingdom of God is near. Truly, I say to you, this generation will not pass away until all has taken place. Heaven and earth will pass away, but My words will not pass away."*

## THE SIGNS [OF THE LAST DAY]

1. The first thing for us to understand is that though the signs preceding the Last Day are of different kinds and great, they will all be fulfilled, even though none or very few take note of them or regard them as such. For two things will and must happen together, and are both proclaimed together by Christ and the apostles: first, that many and great signs will come; second, that the Last Day will come unexpectedly, so that the world from the beginning never expects it, even though that time is at the door. Although they will see these signs—yes, even hear that they are signs of the Last Day—still they will not believe, but laugh at them and confidently say: "You fool! Are you worried heaven is falling and that we shall live to see that day?"

2. Some, indeed, must live to see it, and it will be those who least expect it. There will be such security and contempt among men, as we will prove from the words of Christ and the apostles. Christ says: "Watch yourselves, lest your hearts be weighed down with gorging and drunkenness and worry about your livelihood, and that day come upon you suddenly. For it will come like a trap upon all who dwell on the face of the whole earth" (Luke 21 [:34–35]). From these words it is clear that people will exceedingly give themselves over to gorging and drunkenness and their earthly livelihood;

drowned in gorging and drunkenness, they will sit securely and dwell on the earth as if [the day] were still very far away. For if there were not such great security and contempt, that day could not unexpectedly break in so suddenly. But now, He says, it will come like a trap by which birds and beasts are caught, just when they are after nourishment and least expect the trap. Thus He sufficiently shows that the world will live riotously—it will eat and drink, build and plant, and diligently and skillfully strive for earthly things, and think that the Last Day won't come for more than a thousand years, when in an instant they will stand before the terrible judgment of God.

3. The words of Christ say the same: "For as the lightning flashes from heaven above and lights up everything under heaven, so will the Son of Man be in His day" (Luke 17 [:24]). See here again that the day will fall on the world with the utmost suddenness. Further, He says: "Just as it was in the times of Noah, so will it be in the days of the Son of Man. They were eating and drinking and marrying and being given in marriage, until the day when Noah entered the ark, and the flood came and destroyed them all. Likewise, just as it was in the times of Lot—they were eating and drinking, buying and selling, planting and building, but on the day when Lot went out from Sodom, fire and sulfur rained from heaven and destroyed them all—so it will be on the day when the Son of Man is revealed" [Luke 17:26–30]. These words testify sufficiently that people will be so secure and will be so deeply choked by the cares of this life that they will not believe the day is at hand.

4. There is now no doubt that Christ did not proclaim these signs so that no one would note or recognize them when they should appear, though few indeed will do so, just as in the times of Noah and Lot few recognized the punishment in store for them. Otherwise, He would have admonished and said in vain: "When you see these things, you know that it is before the door" [Luke 21:31]. Again: "Raise your heads, for your redemption is drawing near" [Luke 21:28]. Therefore, there must certainly be some who do that and recognize the signs, and raise their heads and wait for their redemption, though they do not really know on what day that will come. Therefore, it is necessary for us to pay careful attention to whether the signs are being fulfilled now or have been or will be.

5. I will not force or press anyone to believe as I do; neither will I permit anyone to deny me the right to believe that the Last Day is not far away. Just these signs and words of Christ move me [to that belief]. For the history of the centuries that have passed since the birth of Christ nowhere reveals conditions like those of the present. There has never been such building and planting in the world. Such dainty and varied eating and drinking has not been as common as it now is. Clothing has become so costly that it cannot become more so. Who has ever heard of such commerce as now encircles

the world and swallows the world? There arise and have arisen all kinds of art, painting, embroidery, and engraving, which has not been equaled since Christ's birth.

6. In addition, there are such keenly intelligent people who let nothing be hidden, so that now a boy of twenty knows more than twenty doctors formerly knew. There is such a knowledge of languages and all kinds of wisdom that, it must be confessed, the world has reached such great heights in the things that pertain to the body—or, as Christ calls them, "cares of this life": eating, drinking, building, planting, buying, selling, keeping wife and child— that everyone must see and say either ruin or a change must come. It is not easy to think of either improvement or ruin. Dawn breaks and there is a new day, whatever it may be; it cannot be otherwise. There was never such wit, reason, and understanding among Christians in temporal and bodily things as now—to say nothing of the new inventions, such as printing, firearms, and other implements of war.

7. Moreover, not only have such great strides been made in worldly commerce but also in spiritual matters. There has never been greater error, sin, and falsehood on earth from the beginning as there has been in the last century. The Gospel was publicly condemned at Constance,[1] the pope's lies were adopted as law in all the world, and he now flays to the bone the whole world. The sacrifice of the Mass is celebrated many hundred thousand times a day in the world; no sin may equal that. By confession, sacrament, indulgence, and laws, countless souls are driven to hell, so that it seems God has given the whole world over to the devil. In short, it is impossible that there should be greater lies, more heinous error, more dreadful blindness, and more obdurate blasphemy than have ruled in Christendom through the bishops, monasteries, and universities. As a result, Aristotle, a dead, blind heathen, taught and ruled Christians more than does Christ.

8. Moreover the pope has blotted out Christ and become his vicar.[2] That is true, and all too true: he sits in Christ's place; would to God he sat in the devil's place. I won't mention here the coarse sins, such as unchastity, murder, infidelity, covetousness, and the like, which are all practiced without shame or fear. Unchastity has taken forms against nature and has drowned no estate

---

1 The Council of Constance (1414–18), at which, among other things, John Hus was burned at the stake; cf. Luther's *Circular Disputation against the Council of Constance* (1535), WA 39/1:13–39 (LW 72).

2 The bull of Boniface VIII (r. 1294–1303), Unam sanctam (1302), asserted that the pope is the vicar of Christ and that all authority, temporal and spiritual, has been entrusted to him. See Tanner 1:640–45.

as much as the spiritual estate—if I should call them "spiritual,"[3] when they are more than flesh and completely spiritless.

9. However it may be with other signs, I am certain of this sign of which Christ speaks: that eating and drinking, building and planting, buying and selling, taking wife and husband, and other cares of this life will prevail before His coming. I am just as certain that He speaks of "the abomination of desolation" (Matthew 24 [:15]), the Antichrist, under whose rule the worst error, blindness, and sin shall flourish, just as they now flourish under the pope in the most tyrannical and shameless form. This above all else compels me to believe that Christ will soon come; for such sins are too great. Heaven cannot long endure them; they greatly provoke and defy the Last Day. It must fall on them before long.

If it were only the unchastity of the world before the flood or the worldliness of Sodom, I would not believe that the Last Day would come because of that. But to destroy, root out, condemn, and blaspheme God's worship, God's Word, God's Sacrament, God's children, and everything that belongs to God; and to put the devil in His place and worship and honor him, to regard his lies as God's Word—that makes an end to the matter. That leaves me with no doubt [that the Last Day will come] before we are aware of it. Amen.

10. The apostles also prophesied about this human security before the Last Day. St. Paul says: "The day of the Lord will come like a thief in the night. While people are saying, 'There is peace, and there is no emergency,' then sudden destruction will come upon them" (1 Thessalonians 5 [:2–3]). Now we know that a thief never comes but when one feels most secure. And we read: "Scoffers will come in the last days with scoffing, following their own lusts. They will say, 'Where is the promise of His coming? For ever since the fathers fell asleep, all things are continuing as they were from the beginning of creation.' But the day of the Lord will come like a thief in the night; and then the heavens will pass away with a roar," etc. (2 Peter 3 [:3–4, 10]).

Who are those who follow their own sinful desires but the Papist clergy? They want to be subject neither to God nor to man, but insist before all the world that they are free to live and do what they want. They are the ones who say: "Where is His coming? Do you think that the Last Day will come soon? Things will continue as they have in the past."

11. We read in the history of the destruction of Jerusalem that many signs were fulfilled, yet they would not believe that they applied to their destruction until they experienced it.[4] Finally, from the beginning of the world it has ever been so, that the unbelieving could not believe that calamity

---

3  *geistlich*, literally, "a spiritual one," a general term for those who, according to medieval ecclesiology, belonged to the "spiritual" as opposed to the "secular" estate.

4  Cf. Josephus (ca. 37–ca. 101), *Jewish War* 6.4.310–15 (Loeb 210 [1928/1990], pp. 268–71)

was near—they always experienced it before they believed it. This is as the psalmist says, "Bloodthirsty and deceitful men shall not live out half their days" (Psalm 55 [:23]), for they always mismeasure [the time] and never fear; therefore, their hour must come unexpectedly. So here people put off the Last Day for a thousand years when it is coming the next night. Those are the first signs. Now we will look at the second.

### And there will be signs in the sun. [Luke 21:25]

12. This sign in the sun is that it will lose its brightness, as has often happened, as Jesus says, "The sun will lose its shining" (Matthew 24 [:29]). I will not conceal but will express my opinion. Some think that the sun will become dark so that it no longer shines. That is incorrect, for day and night must continue to the end, as God promises: "As long as the earth stands, fruit and harvest, cold and heat, summer and winter, day and night, shall not cease" (Genesis 8 [:22]). Therefore, this sign must not interfere with day and night and must happen before the Last Day, because it is a preceding sign. Therefore, it cannot be otherwise than that the sun loses its brightness, as usually happens.[5]

13. Now at all times such a sign in the sun has signified a great disaster that followed, as history shows. Thus in recent years we have had so many eclipses that I do not think there have ever before been so many so close together. God has been silent about them, and no great evil has followed them; for that reason they have been despised and disregarded. In addition, the masters of the stars have told us—and this is true—that such things occur in the natural course of the heavens, with the result that the despising is strengthened and carnal security increased. Nevertheless, God, in carrying on His work in silence, lets us be secure and moves forward in His plans. Whatever the natural course of the heavens may be, these signs are always signs of His wrath and predict sure disaster for the future. If these are not seen, shall God make other suns and moons and stars and show other signs in them?

14. The course of the heavens has been so arranged from eternity that before the Last Day these signs must appear. The heathen write that a comet arises from natural [causes], but God has created none that do not signify a definite disaster. In short, you should know that what wanders through the heavens in the usual way God causes to be seen as a sign of His wrath.

5 I.e., in an eclipse.

### And moon. [Luke 21:25]

15. This sign is, as Matthew reports, that "the moon will not give its light" (Matthew 24 [:29]); that is, it will lose its brightness. The same is to be said of this as of the signs in the sun, no matter how natural it may be. This sign has frequently occurred in recent years. Is it not true that scarcely a year has passed of late in which sun or moon or both have not been eclipsed, sometimes one of them twice a year? If these are not signs, then what are signs? It may be that previously this happened more, but not so many and so nearly together. When Jerusalem was to be destroyed, some signs preceded which had occurred before, but they were still new tokens.

### And stars. [Luke 21:25]

16. That is, as Matthew says, "the stars will fall from heaven" (Matthew 24 [:29]). This sign can be seen daily;[6] whether it happened as frequently in former days, I do not know. Aristotle makes natural, useless things out of this; but in short, the Gospel is God's Word and wisdom, and it calls the falling of the stars a sign. Let us remain there. Therefore, if the stars fall, or the sun and moon lose their brightness, know that these are signs, for the Gospel does not lie to you. But because in these years they are so many and close together, and yet nothing special has happened, you have to think that these are signs of the Last Day, of which Christ is speaking here; for they must appear often in order that the great day may be abundantly pointed out and proclaimed. These signs appear and have appeared for a long time, but no one considers them; so it shall be that they will wait for other signs, just as the Jews are waiting for another Christ.

### And on earth the nations will be distressed and will tremble. [Luke 21:25]

17. This is not to be understood that all nations or a large part of them will suffer this; for you must note that these are to be signs. Stars do not fall from the heavens at all times; the sun does not lose its brightness for a whole year or a month, but for an hour or two, more or less; the moon also does not lose its brightness for a whole week or a whole night, but, like the sun, for an hour or two—that all these may remain signs without turning everything upside down. Hence not many will endure distress and anxiety, but only a few, and not continuously, so that they remain signs for the others who despise them and say on the advice of the physicians that it is the fault of temperament or melancholy or [the influence of] the planets in the heavens or some other natural cause. Meanwhile, such obvious signs pass by such

---

6 I.e., meteor showers.

blind people unobserved, and it happens that with seeing eyes we see the signs but do not perceive them, as happened to the Jews with Christ (cf. Matthew 13 [:14]).

18. The "nations being distressed" is not bodily. For, as we heard, enough peace and property will remain that they will eat and drink, build and plant, buy and sell, marry and be given in marriage, dance and leap, and entangle themselves in this present life as if they wanted to remain here forever. I take ["nations being distressed"] to be great torment of conscience. For since the Gospel, by which alone the conscience can be comforted, is condemned and human doctrines are set up, which teach us to lay aside sin and earn heaven by works, this must result in a heavy, difficult, and distressed conscience, which never has any rest, which would gladly be godly, do good, and be saved [but] is afraid and does not know how to do that. Sin and conscience oppress him and produce the difficulty, and however much is done, no rest is found, so that he doesn't know what he should do. This is the source of so many vows and pilgrimages, so much worship and honor of the saints. From this has grown the foundation of so many Masses and vigils. Some scourge and torment themselves, some become monks; or so that they may do more, they become Carthusian monks.

These are all works of distressed and perplexed consciences and are in reality the trouble of which St. Luke here speaks. He uses two words which suggest that first a man gets into need and difficulty and it becomes narrow, as if he were thrown into a narrow prison cell; second, he becomes anxious and does not know what to do to get out of the difficulty; he becomes bewildered and attempts this and that, and yet nothing helps. That means, the way I speak German, to become distressed. This is what happens with these consciences: their sin has taken them captive; they are bound by a strict conscience which greatly oppresses and frightens them. They want to escape, but another grief overtakes them; they are anxious, for they know not where to begin—they try everything, but nothing helps.

19. Now the great, vulgar masses do not fall into this distress, but only the few—generally the most sensible, sensitive souls, and good-hearted people who have no desire to harm anyone and would live honorable lives, but they have something secret about them, which is usually unchastity. This consumes them day and night so that they never are truly happy. And this is just like roast venison for the monks and priests, for here they can flay [consciences], especially with women: here people confess, are taught, absolved, and go wherever the holy father confessors direct. Meanwhile, the poor people become our Lord God's sign of the Last Day. To such the Gospel is life and comfort, while the others condemn it.

20. See, no one can deny this sign, which has been especially common the past hundred years, so that many have become insane and crazy over it, as also Gerson writes. Although at all times there have been such people, it was formerly not so common in the world. From the beginning of the world no human doctrine has ruled a tenth part or even a hundredth part as far and as horribly, and tortured and murdered so many consciences, as the doctrines of the pope and his disciples, the priests and monks. Such [troubled] hearts come especially from the rules about confession, which previously were not commanded or driven as much. Therefore, this has never been a sign of the Last Day until now. There must be many and great signs, and yet they are despised by most.

### *And the sea and the waves shall roar. [Luke 21:25]*

21. This will take place through the winds, for all roaring of the waters comes from the winds. Therefore, the Lord shows with these words that there will be many and great winds. By "sea," however, is not to be understood only the ocean, but all standing, still waters, according to the language of Scripture, which says, "The waters that were gathered together God called seas" (Genesis 1 [:10]), whether they were seas, lakes, or ponds. Rivers, on the other hand, are changeable, flowing waters.

22. You must not think that all waters, streams, ponds, lakes, seas, and whatever is wet in the world will, at the same time at once, roar and become windy. The sign is that some seas and rivers roar and are windy, and this happens often and close together. For just as not all stars fall and not all people are anxious, so not all water roars and is windy at all places at the same time.

23. Here Lady Hulda,[7] heathen learning, sits in the universities, throws open her mouth, and says, "Have you never seen the wind or heard the water roaring? My Aristotle teaches that it just naturally happens." Let that go; we well know that God's Word and sign must be despised by the cunning idols. Hold onto the Gospel, which teaches you to believe that all great winds and water sprays are signs. And though such signs have repeatedly occurred in the past, they shall nevertheless be many and great before the Last Day.

24. I think that within the space of ten or twelve years we have had and heard such roaring and spraying, without considering what will be, that I scarcely believe that previous times have heard so much wind and spray. We should also consider that, though in former times some of these signs occurred rarely and singly, now they come in heaps together, not rarely but many of them and frequently. Our time sees sun and moon together lose

---

7  That is, human reason or human learning.

their brightness, stars fall, people become anxious, great wind and water sprays, and whatever more—it all comes at once.

25. We have also seen so many comets and so many crosses fallen from heaven.[8] Also, how many signs and wonders have been seen for some years in the heavens, such as sun, moon, stars, rainbows, and many other strange sights. Let them be signs, great signs, which mean much, which even the masters of the stars and Lady Hulda cannot say come from the natural course [of things], for they knew nothing of them before nor did they prophesy of them.

26. No astronomer can say that the course of the heavens foretold the coming of the terrible beast which the Tiber threw up a few years ago: a beast with the head of a donkey, the breast and belly of a woman, the foot of an elephant for its right hand, with the scales of a fish on its legs and the head of a dragon in its hinder parts, etc. This beast typifies the papacy and the great wrath and punishment of God. Such a heap of signs presages greater results than the mind of man can conceive.

*And people will faint with fear and with expectation of what is coming on the world. [Luke 21:26]*

27. This is not the great profligate mass, which despises God's signs and ascribes them all to nature, but the best and most excellent, who take these things to heart and ponder them. The fainting or withering means that they are scared to death, or the next thing to death, so that fear consumes them and makes them weak. What do they fear and wait for? Christ says, "What is coming on the world," that is, the Last Day, the terrible judgment, hellfire, eternal death, and what comes with them. Why do they fear and wait for these things, on whom they perhaps won't come, instead of the world on whom they will come? [They do this] so that they can be God's signs who must be despised by the whole world.

28. I am not yet able to say who these people are, unless it should be those who have to deal with the extreme trial of death and hell, concerning whom Tauler writes. For such temptations consume flesh and blood, even bone and marrow, and are death itself. No one can endure them unless he is miraculously sustained. Some of the patriarchs have tasted them, such as Abraham, Isaac, Jacob, Moses, David; but at the end of the world they will be more common. This sign will then perhaps still increase, though there have been many and still are, of which few people know. There are individuals who

---

8  Mysterious appearances of crosses on clothing were reported repeatedly in the sixteenth century. See Philip M. Soergel, *Miracles and the Protestant Imagination* (Oxford: Oxford University Press, 2012), p. 75; Percy Stafford Allen, *The Age of Erasmus* (Oxford: Clarendon, 1914), p. 214.

are in the perils of death and are wrestling with death; they feel that which will come over the whole world and fear that it will also remain upon them.

It is to be hoped, however, that such people are in a state of grace. For Christ speaks as if He would separate the fear and the thing which they fear—and so divides these that He gives to them the fear, but He gives to the world the thing that they fear. We are to expect that by this fear and anxiety they have their hell and death here, while the world, which fears nothing, will have death and hell hereafter.

*For the powers of heaven will be shaken. [Luke 21:26]*

29. By "the powers of heaven" some understand the angels of heaven. But since Christ speaks of signs, and says we shall see them and in them recognize the coming of the Last Day, they must surely be visible and be perceived with the bodily senses. For even those people whose consciences are in distress and whose hearts are fainting from fear, even though this affects the soul, yet it is recognized in the body externally by word and visage. Thus these powers of heaven must be shaken and perceived bodily and externally.

30. But the Scriptures speak in two ways about the powers of heaven. First, "the powers of heaven" are the "powerful heavens" or the heavens which are the most powerful of all creatures, as is written: "God called the heaven 'firmament'" (Genesis 1 [:8]), that is, "fortress or strengthening"; for every creature under heaven is ruled and strengthened by the light, heat, and movements of the heavens. What would the earth be without the heavens but a desolate darkness? In the same way Scripture calls the princes and nobles in the world powerful because they rule over and have an effect on their subjects.

31. Second, "the powers of heaven" signify the hosts of heaven, as the psalmist says: "By the Word of the Lord the heavens were made, and by the breath of His mouth all their powers" (Psalm 33 [:6]), that is, "all their hosts." And Genesis reports: "Thus the heavens and the earth were finished, and all the powers of them" (Genesis 2 [:1]), that is, "all the hosts of them." This way of speaking about the powers of heaven is the common way in Scripture. And it is clear from these passages that the hosts or powers of heaven include all that is in them: in the heavens, the sun, moon, stars, and other heavenly bodies; on earth, man, animals, birds, fish, trees, herbs, and whatever else lives upon it.

32. The passage before us may therefore mean the powers of heaven in both senses, but chiefly the hosts of heaven. Thus Christ means to say that all creatures will be shaken and serve as signs of that day: sun and moon with darkness, the stars with falling, the nations with wars, men with anxiety and fear, the earth with quaking, the waters with winds and roaring, the air with pestilence and poison, and thus also the heavens with their hosts and shaking.

33. I still do not know what is meant by the shaking of the heavenly hosts, unless it is the great conjunction of the planets which happened in 1524. For the planets are certainly the chief of the powers and hosts of heaven, and their strange gathering is a definite sign for the world. Christ does not say that all the hosts of heaven will be shaken, but some of them; for not all stars are shaken, just as it was said above that not all people endure difficulty and fear, not all waters always roar and thunder, sun and moon are not dark every day; for these are all to be only signs, which can only occur in some few places, so that they may be something special compared to the other places which are not signs. Therefore, I am convinced that this shaking of the heavenly host is the conjunction of the planets.

34. You should not be led astray here into thinking that this conjunction happens because of the natural course of heaven. Christ calls it a sign. It is to be well noted because it does not happen alone, but with other signs and at the same time. Let the unbelievers doubt and despise God's signs and say they are [only] natural; you hold onto the Gospel.

35. There are still more signs described elsewhere, such as earthquakes, pestilence, famine, and wars (cf. Luke 17 [:20]; Matthew 24 [:7]). We have seen much of these, even though they also happened previously; but they are not for that reason any less signs, especially since they occur at the same time as the others. It is a known fact also that wars at the present time are of such a character as to make former wars appear as mere child's play—so very horrible is what is done with guns, armor, and munitions. But since this Gospel does not speak of these, let us not consider them further. Only let us consider them as signs, great signs, signifying great things; but they are already forgotten and despised.

*And then they will see the Son of Man coming in the cloud with great power and glory. [Luke 21:27]*

36. Here "power" may again signify the hosts of angels, saints, and all creatures that will come with Christ to judgment. (I believe this is the correct interpretation.) Or it may mean the power and strength that make this coming of Christ so much more powerful than the first, which was weaker and inferior. He says not only that He will come but also that they shall see Him come. At His birth He came also, but was seen by no one. He comes now daily through the Gospel, spiritually, into believing hearts; no one sees that either. But this coming will be public, so that all must see Him, as Revelation 1 [:7] says, "And every eye will see Him." And they shall see that He is none other than the bodily man Christ, in bodily form, as He was born from Mary and walked on earth.

He could have said, "They will see Me," but that would not have clearly indicated His bodily form. But when He says, "They will see the Son of Man," He clearly indicates that it will be a bodily coming, a bodily seeing in bodily form yet in great power, with the great host of angels and all glory. He will sit on a bright cloud, and all the saints with Him. The Scriptures speak much of that day, and everything is pointed to it.

Let that be enough concerning the signs. What comes next deals with comfort for Christians against these signs.

## THE SECOND PART

*When these things begin to take place, look up and lift up your heads, because your redemption is drawing near. [Luke 21:28]*

37. Here you may say, Who can lift up his head in the face of such terrible wrath and judgment? If the whole world is terrified at that day, and hangs its head and looks down out of terror and fear, how are we to lift up our heads and raise them, which without a doubt means joy and longing? Answer: All of this is spoken only to Christians who are truly Christians, and not to heathen and Jews. But true Christians suffocate in great temptations and persecutions from sin and all kinds of evil, so that this life becomes bitter and loathsome to them. Therefore, they wait and long and pray for redemption from sin and all evil—as we also pray in the Lord's Prayer: "Thy kingdom come" and "Deliver us from evil" [cf. Matt. 6:10, 13]. If we are true Christians, we will earnestly and heartily pray this prayer. But if we do not pray heartily and earnestly, we are not yet true Christians.

38. If we pray correctly, then we must regard these signs, however terrible they are, with joy and longing, as Christ exhorts: "When these things begin to take place, look up." He does not say, "Be filled with fear or hang your heads," for what we have prayed for so earnestly is coming. If we earnestly want to be freed from sin, death, and hell, we must desire and love this coming.

St. Paul also says, "He will give the crown of righteousness not only to me but also to all who have loved His appearing" (2 Timothy 4 [:8]). What will He give to those who hate and dread it? Without doubt, [He will give] hell, as to His enemies. Again: "We should wait for the coming of the glory of our great God" (Titus 2 [:13]). Again: "Be like people who are waiting for their lord, when he comes home from the wedding feast" (Luke 12 [:36]).

39. But what do those do who are filled with fear and do not want Him to come when they pray: "Thy kingdom come; Thy will be done; deliver us from evil"? Do they not stand in the presence of God and brazenly tell Him lies against themselves? Do they not strive against the will of God, who wants to have this day for the redemption of His saints? Therefore, we should be

careful not to hate or dread that day. Such dread is a bad sign and belongs to the damned, whose hard minds and hardened hearts must be terrified and broken, if they are to improve.

40. But to believers that day will be comforting and sweet. That day will be at the same time the highest joy and safety to the believer and the deepest terror and flight to the unbeliever; just as also in this life the truths of the Gospel are exceedingly sweet to the godly and exceedingly hateful to the wicked. Why should the believers fear and not rather exceedingly rejoice, since they trust in Christ who comes as judge to redeem them and is their portion [cf. Ps. 16:5]?

41. But you say, "I would indeed await and love this coming if I were godly and without sin." Answer: Well, then, how does fearing and fleeing help you? It would not redeem you from sin even if you were afraid for a thousand years. The damned are eternally afraid, but this does not take away their sin; in fact, this fear only increases sin and prevents you from being without sin, and yet you cannot escape that day. Fear must depart and be replaced by a desire for righteousness and for that day. But if it is true that you would gladly be godly and without sin, then give thanks to God and continue to desire still more to be without sin. Oh, that such desire were so powerful in you as to bring you to your death!

42. There is no one so well prepared for the Last Day as he who desires to be without sin. If you have such a desire, what do you fear? You are then in perfect accord with that day. It comes to set free from sin all who desire it, and you also are of the opinion that you will be set free in that way. Thank God; remain and continue in that opinion. Christ says His coming is for our redemption. But see to it that you do not deceive yourself by saying that you would like to be without sin and not to fear that day. Perhaps your heart is false and you do fear it, not because you would like to be without sin, but because in the face of that day you cannot sin freely and securely. See to it that the light within you is not darkness [cf. Matt. 6:22–23]. For a heart that truly wants to be free from sin will certainly rejoice in the day that fulfills its desire. If the heart does not so rejoice, there is no true desire to be free from sin.

43. Therefore, we must above all things lay aside all hatred and aversion of this coming and exercise diligence, that we would earnestly and gladly be free from sin. When this is done, we may not only calmly await the day, but with all our desire and joy pray for it and say, "Thy kingdom come; Thy will be done." In this you must let go of your own way of thinking and feelings, hold fast to the comforting words of Christ, and rest in them alone.

44. How could He exhort, comfort, and strengthen you in a more delightful way? First, He says, "You will hear of wars, but you should not be frightened." When He tells you not to be frightened, what else is that than His

command that you be of good cheer and discern the sign with joy? Second, He tells you joyfully to look up; third, to lift up your heads; and fourth, He calls it your redemption. What can comfort and strengthen you if such a word does not? Do you think He would lie to you or would deceive you into a false confidence? Dear friends, don't let such a word be spoken in vain; thank God and trust in it—there is no other remedy or comfort if you cast this word to the winds. It is not your condemnation but your redemption of which Christ speaks comfortingly. Will you turn His words around and say, "It is not your redemption but your condemnation"? Will you flee from your own salvation? Will you not greet God who comes out to meet you, nor thank Him who greets you?

45. Without a doubt, He has spoken this comforting word also for the fainthearted, who, though they are godly and prepared for the Last Day, are yet filled with great anxiety and [thus] hinder their desire for this coming, which is especially found at the end of the world; therefore, He calls it their redemption. For at the end of the world, when sin will so terribly hold sway, and along with sin the second part (the punishment for sin with pestilence, war, and famine) will also hold sway, it is necessary that believers have a strong confidence and comfort against both afflictions: sin and its punishment. Therefore, He uses the sweet word "redemption," which all hearts gladly hear. What is redemption? Who would not gladly be redeemed? Who would desire to remain in such a desert, both of sin and of punishment? Who would not wish an end to such misery, such danger for souls, such ruin for man—especially when Christ so sweetly allures, invites, and comforts us?

46. The godless preachers of dreams [cf. Jer. 23:25–28] should be censured; in their sermons they hide these words of Christ from the hearts of people and turn faith away from them, who want to make people godly by terrifying them, and who afterward prepare [people] for this day with their own good works and satisfaction for their sins. Here despair, fear, and terror must remain and grow—and with it, hatred, aversion, and abhorrence for the coming of the Lord—and enmity against God must be established in the heart. Meanwhile, they teach people to picture Christ as nothing but a stern judge whom they are to appease and expiate by their works, and never regard [Him] as the Redeemer, as He calls and offers Himself, of whom we are to expect in firm faith that out of pure grace He will redeem us from sin and all evil.

47. See, this is the way it always happens. When people do not preach the Gospel correctly, and only pursue hearts with commands and threats, they only drive them farther from God and only make them angry at God. They ought to terrify, but only the obstinate and hardened; but afterward, when people have become fearful and fainthearted, they are to strengthen and comfort them again.

48. From all this we see how few there are who pray the Lord's Prayer correctly, even though it is prayed unceasingly in all the world. For there are very few who would not prefer it if that day never came. This is nothing else than: "May God's kingdom not come"! Thus their heart prays against their mouth, and while God judges according to the heart, they judge according to the mouth. For this reason they institute so many prayers, fill all the churches in the world with their bawling, and say they've prayed it all. In reality their prayer is nothing other than: "Thy kingdom not come, or not yet." Tell me, is not such a prayer blasphemy? Is it not of such a prayer that the psalmist speaks: "Let his prayer become sin" (Psalm 109 [:7])? All the world's property and money is going to fill every corner full of such blasphemy, and then they call it worship!

49. Yet he who feels such fear ought not despair, but rather use it wisely. One uses it wisely if he permits such fear to drive and exhort him to pray for grace, which takes away his fear and gives him joy and delight in that day. For Christ promised: what we ask for we shall receive (cf. Matthew 7 [:8]). Therefore, those who are fearful are nearer their salvation than the infamous and hard-hearted, who neither fear nor find comfort in that day. For even if they do not have joy and delight in that day, they do have a driving that exhorts them to pray for such joy and delight.

50. On the other hand, one uses fear unwisely if he only increases it and remains in it, as though he wanted to be cleansed from sin through it; but this leads to nothing good. Not fear, which must be cast out, as John says [1 John 4:18], but love, which must abide, as St. Paul says [1 Cor. 13:13], will remain on that day. Fear should drive us to seek such love and pray God for it. Where fear does not end, it opposes the will of God and your own salvation; that, then, is a sin against the Holy Spirit.[9] It is unnecessary that he be altogether without fear, for we still have human nature abiding in us, which is weak and cannot exist without the fear of death and the judgment; but the spirit is to be uppermost, as Christ says, "The spirit is willing, but the flesh is weak" (Matthew 26 [:41]).

> *And He told them a parable: "Look at the fig tree and all trees. As soon as they come out in leaf, you see from them and notice that the summer is near. So also, when you see these things beginning, know that the kingdom of God is near." [Luke 21:29–31]*

51. These are pure words of comfort. He does not give a parable about fall or winter, when all the trees become bare and the dreary days begin, but about spring and summer, which is a happy, joyous time, when all creation

---

9  That is, despair of God's mercy. See also LW 59:192–93 n. 31.

buds forth and is happy. By this He teaches quite clearly that we are to look forward to and take comfort in the Last Day with as much joy and delight as all creation shows in spring and summer. What else is the meaning of this parable, if in it He does not teach us this? He could have found others that were not so joyous.

52. Moreover, He does not say that your hell or condemnation is near, but the kingdom of God. What else does it signify that the kingdom of God is near than that our redemption is near? The kingdom of God is we ourselves, as Christ says, "Behold, the kingdom of God is within you" (Luke 17 [:21]). Therefore, [the time] approaches when we are to be redeemed from sin and evil. In this life it begins in the spirit; but since we must still battle with sin and suffer much evil, and since death is still before us, the kingdom of God is not yet complete in us. But when once sin and death with all evil are taken away from us, then it will be complete. The Last Day will do this, and it will not happen in this life.

53. Therefore, dear man, examine your life; probe your heart to ascertain how it is disposed toward this day. Do not put your trust in your own good life, for that would soon be put to shame; but think of and strengthen your faith so that you are not frightened of this day as the condemned and crooked are, but long for it as for your redemption and the kingdom of God in you. Then when you hear [that day] named or think of it, your heart will dance for joy and ardently long for it. If you will not direct yourself toward this, do not think that you otherwise will endure, even if you had the works of all the saints.

*Truly, I say to you, this generation will not pass away until all has taken place. Heaven and earth are passing away, but My words do not pass away. [Luke 21:32–33]*

54. Why does the Lord make His words so firm and precious, and sternly confirm them beyond measure with comparisons, oaths, and tokens of the generation that shall remain with them, and also that heaven and earth shall pass away before [His words pass away]? This all happens, as was said above, so that all the world would become so secure and with open eyes despise the signs to such a degree that no words of God have been so despised as these which proclaim and characterize the Last Day. It will appear to the world that there are no signs; and even though they see them, they will still not believe them. Even the elect of God might doubt such words of God and signs, in order that the day may come at a time when the world has never before been so secure and be suddenly assaulted in the greatest security, as we heard from St. Paul above.

55. Therefore, Christ wants to make us certain and wake us up so that we await the day when the signs appear with certainty. In fact, even if the signs were uncertain, those are not in danger who regard them as certain, while those are in danger who despise them. Therefore, let us deal with certainties and consider the above-named signs as correct, so that we do not run with the unspiritual. If we are mistaken, we have at least hit the mark; if they are mistaken, they will remain mistaken [forever].

56. He calls the Jews "this generation." This passage clearly proves that the common saying that all Jews are to become Christians is not true. The passage "There will be one shepherd and one sheepfold" (John 10 [:16]) was fulfilled not when the Jews went over to the Gentiles, but when the Gentiles went over to the Jews and became Christians at the time of the apostles, as St. Augustine often explains. Christ's words say the same: "I have other sheep that are not of this fold. I must bring them also, and they will listen to My voice. So there will be one shepherd and one sheepfold" (John 10 [:16]). Here you clearly see that He is speaking about the Gentiles who have come to the Jewish fold; therefore, the passage has been long since fulfilled. But here He says, "This generation will not pass away" until the end; that is, the Jews who crucified Christ must remain as a token. And though many are converted, their generation and kind must survive.

57. Some have also been troubled about how heaven and earth will pass away, and they take the blind heathen Aristotle as their aid. He must interpret the words of Christ for them, and he says that heaven and earth will not pass away as to their essence but only as to their form. They think much of what they say! If they so understood it that heaven and earth will continue to be something, they would indeed be right. But let the blind go, and know that just as our remains will be changed according to essence, and yet be made the same again also according to essence, so heaven and earth on the Last Day, with all the elements and everything else, will be melted with fire and become dust, together with all human bodies, so that there will be nothing but fire everywhere. When everything is again most beautifully created anew, our bodies will shine brightly like the sun [cf. Matt. 13:43], and the sun will be seven times brighter than it now is [cf. Isa. 30:26]. Peter speaks of this day: "The day of the Lord will come in which the heavens will pass away with a roar, and the elements will dissolve because of heat, and everything built on the earth will be turned to dust. But we are waiting for new heavens and a new earth, and what He has promised us, in which righteousness shall dwell" (cf. 2 Peter 3 [:10, 13]).

St. Paul also testifies that the Last Day "will be revealed by fire" (1 Corinthians 3 [:13]). And Isaiah writes: "And the light of the moon will be as the light of the sun, and the light of the sun will be sevenfold brighter than now, at that time when the Lord binds up the brokenness of His people and heals their wounds" (Isaiah 30 [:26]). Likewise: "For behold, I create new heavens and a new earth, and the former ones shall not be remembered or come into mind. But they shall be glad and rejoice forever in that which I create" (Isaiah 65 [:17–18]). Therefore, this passing away is not only according to form but also according to essence—unless you do not want to call it "being destroyed" when things turn to dust which cannot be found or seen, such as when burned bodies become ashes and nothing.

58. But where do our souls remain when all of creation is on fire and there is nothing to stand on? Answer: Tell me, where are they now? Or where are they when we sleep and are not aware of what happens outside our bodies and to all bodily creatures? Do you think that God cannot preserve souls in His hand so that they will never perceive how heaven and earth become dust? Or do you think that He must have a physical stall, as a shepherd does for his sheep? It is enough to know that they are in God's hands and not in the body or home of any creature. Although you do not know how it happens, do not be led astray. Since you have not yet learned what happens to you when you fall asleep or awaken, and can never know how near you are to waking or sleeping, though you daily do both, how do you expect to understand this? What counts is: "Father, into Your hands I commit My spirit" [Luke 23:46]; stay with that. Nonetheless, heaven and earth become new, and our bodies also, and become alive again to eternal salvation. Amen. If we knew how souls were maintained, faith would be at an end. But now we journey and know not where; we trust in God and put it in His hands, and faith retains its value.

59. Finally, we must also look at a little of the secret meaning in this Gospel. The sun is Christ, the moon is the Church, the stars are Christians, the powers of heaven are the prelates or planets in the Church. Now these physical signs surely signify what has long since taken place and is now taking place in Christendom, for they follow the wages of sin and threaten and manifest the punishment resting upon them.

60. That the sun loses its brightness no doubt signifies that Christ does not shine in Christendom—that is, that the Gospel is not preached and faith is expiring so that there is no longer any worship. This has happened and is happening through human teachings and works. The pope sits in the churches in the place of Christ and shines like crap in a lantern—he with his bishops, priests, and monks. They are the ones who have darkened the sun for us, and instead of the true worship of God, they have set up the worship of idols and ghosts with their tonsures, hoods, vestments, pipes, ringing, singing, chiming, etc. Oh, what darkness! What darkness!

61. From this it necessarily follows that the moon also does not give any light; that is, when faith expired, love also had to expire, so that no Christian works are seen anymore, no example is found in which one serves another. But the people have been led to works for idols and ghosts, and into instituting Masses, vigils, altars, chapels, chalice, bells, and that sort of nonsense. Again, what darkness!

62. I interpret the falling of the stars to mean [the falling of a] man who has been baptized and become a Christian and then became a cleric or monk. Whoever wants to believe me, may; whoever does not want to need not do so, but I know what I am talking about. I do not say that they will all be lost; God can preserve in the fire whomever He will. But I say that whoever becomes a cleric or monk under the pretext of taking up a holy estate steps from Christian faith into unbelief; for the falling of the stars does not signify the gross falls—such as murder, adultery, theft—but a falling from faith. Clerics and monks (unless God does special wonders) are, with respect to their estate, rebellious and apostate Christians; there are no worse people on earth.

63. The Turks also are non-Christians; but in two ways they are better than these. First, they have never been Christians; they have never left [the] faith. Second, they do not sin against the Sacrament. But these people make a sacrifice and good work out of the Mass, which they do daily and innumerably. This is certainly the most abominable perversion on which the sun has shone. In short, whoever wants to be godly and saved by works and a spiritual estate leaves the faith and falls from heaven; for the blood of Jesus Christ alone must make us godly and save us. Therefore, whenever you see a star fall, know that it means to become a cleric, a monk, or a nun.

64. "People fainting for fear" signifies the torments which the pope's saints and fallen stars suffer, for while they do great things, their consciences never have peace. All Scripture calls them essentially labor and work.

65. The storming winds and roaring waters are the secular estates, both high and low. There is no prince or land at peace with the other, no faith or trust in one another; everyone is looking only to his own interests. There is also no punishment or discipline or fear upon the earth; and the whole world is so engaged in gorging, drunkenness, unchastity, and all lusts that it blusters and storms.

66. The "powers of heaven" are our planets: our spiritual squires and tyrants, popes, bishops, and their companions, the universities, which are all so deeply stuck in worldly affairs, property, honor, and pleasures that they think they are not planets, that is, wanderers (for "planet" in Greek means a wanderer, one who does not travel on the right way but travels backward and to both sides, as the planets also do in the heavens). The Germans express that with a proverb: "The more learned, the more crooked"; that is, the

spiritual government is only planets. But now the Gospel dawns and points out to them what virtue is and colors them with their own hue. It shows that they are unlearned idolaters and soul-deceivers; when they get angry, they move to form a conjunction. They gather together, shelter themselves behind bulls and other pieces of paper, and threaten a great flood. But it will do them no good. The dawn comes, which cannot be placed under a bushel like a candle [cf. Matt. 5:15].

67. The comparison with the fig tree seems to me to signify the Holy Scriptures which have so long been hidden in obscurity, but now are bursting forth and gaining leaves; that is, the Word breaks forth. For twelve centuries it has not spread so far, nor have its languages been so well-known. I have no doubt that Scripture is a fig tree, which is easily proven. It was fig leaves with which Adam and Eve covered themselves; for the old Adam always uses Scripture to adorn himself. Therefore, the Book must come forth, its leaves must become green, and it does not help that the planets move much. But the summer is not far distant, God willing, and the fruit will also follow the leaves. I fear that there will be nothing but leaves, for we talk much about true faith but do nothing.

68. That is enough for the explanation; if anyone wants to go further, he can start here. But the planets with their gangs will not believe any of this, so that Scripture remains true, which assigns these people great security and contempt for all of God's Word, works, and signs.

# GOSPEL FOR THE THIRD SUNDAY IN ADVENT

## Matthew 11:2–10

*Now when John heard in prison about the deeds of the Christ, he sent word by his disciples and said to Him, "Are You the one who is to come, or shall we look for another?" And Jesus answered them, "Go and tell John what you hear and see: the blind receive their sight and the lame walk, lepers are cleansed and the deaf hear, and the dead are raised up, and the poor have good news preached to them. And blessed is the one who is not offended by Me." As they went away, Jesus began to speak to the crowds concerning John: "What did you go out into the wilderness to see? A reed shaken by the wind? What then did you go out to see? A man dressed in soft clothing? Behold, those who wear soft clothing are in kings' houses. What then did you go out to see? A prophet? Yes, I tell you, and more than a prophet. This is he of whom it is written, 'Behold, I send My messenger before Your face, who will prepare Your way before You.'"*

## THE HISTORY

1. The biggest point that I find treated on this Gospel reading is: Did John the Baptist know that Jesus was the true Christ? This is an unnecessary question, since not much depends on it. St. Ambrose thinks John asked this question neither in ignorance nor in doubt, but in a Christian spirit. Jerome and Gregory write that John asked whether he would be Christ's forerunner also into hell, an opinion that has not the least foundation, for the text plainly says, "Are You the one who is to come, or shall we look for another?" [Matt. 11:3]. This looking, according to the words, refers to His coming on earth to the Jewish people; otherwise John ought to have said, "Or do those in hell look for You?" And since with His works Christ answered that He had come, it is certain that John asked about Christ's bodily coming, as Christ Himself thus understood it and answered accordingly, though I do not deny that Christ also descended into hell, as we confess in the creed.[1]

2. Thus it is certain John knew very well that Jesus was the one who should come, for he had baptized Him and testified that Christ was the Lamb of God who takes away the sin of the world [John 1:29], and he had also

---

1 That is, the Apostles' Creed (Kolb-Wengert, p. 22; *Concordia*, p. 16).

seen the Holy Spirit descending on Him in the form of a dove and heard the voice from heaven: "This is My beloved Son, with whom I am well pleased" [Matt. 3:17]. All is related fully by all four evangelists [cf. Matt. 3:13–17; Mark 1:9–11; Luke 2:21–22; John 1:32–34]. Why, then, did John ask this question? Answer: It was not done without good reasons. First, it is certain that John had it asked for the sake of his disciples, as they did not yet hold Christ to be the one He really was. And John did not come in order to draw the disciples and the people to himself, but to prepare the way for Christ, to lead everybody to Christ, and to make them subject to Him.

3. Now the disciples of John had heard from him many excellent testimonies concerning Christ, namely, that He was the Lamb of God and the Son of God, and that Christ must increase while he must decrease [John 3:30]. His disciples and the people did not yet believe all this, or they could not yet understand it. Rather, the disciples and all the people thought more of John than of Christ. For this reason they clung so strongly to John, even to the extent that they became zealous for his cause and indignant toward Christ when they saw that He also baptized, made disciples, and drew the people to Himself. They complained to John about this because they feared that their master would become unimportant, as John [the evangelist] describes it (John 3 [:26f.]).

4. They were led to this delusion for two reasons. First, Christ had not yet been called by the people, but only by John; He had not yet done any signs, and He had no reputation, but only John did. Therefore, it appeared so strange to them that he should point them and everybody else away from himself and to another, since there was no one present except John who had a name and reputation. Second, Christ appeared so very humble and common, being the son of a poor carpenter and of a poor widow.[2] Besides, He did not come from the priesthood nor from the learned, but was only a layman and a common laborer. He had never studied, but was brought up in carpentry just like other laymen. They could not harmonize John's excellent testimony and the humble layman and laborer Jesus.

Therefore, though they certainly believed that John told the truth, they still thought: Perhaps it will be someone other than this Jesus. And they looked for one who would trot in among them, like a highly learned chief priest or a mighty king. John could not lift them from that delusion with his words. They clung to him and regarded Jesus as being much inferior, meanwhile looking for the glorious entrance of the great man of whom John spoke. And if it really were Jesus, then He had to assume a different attitude; He must saddle a steed, put on yellow spurs, and burst in like a lord and king

---

2 Since Joseph is not mentioned after the account of the twelve-year-old Jesus in the temple (Luke 2:41–52), it is often assumed that Joseph had died and that therefore Mary was a widow.

of Israel, as kings previously did. As long as He did not do that, they would cling to John.

5. But when Jesus began to perform miracles and was talked about, then John thought he would point his disciples away from himself and lead them to Christ, so that they would not establish a new sect after his death and become Johnites. Rather, so that all might cling to Christ and become Christians, John sends them to Christ, so that from now on they might learn not only from His testimony but also from the words and deeds of Christ Himself that He was the one of whom John had spoken. For His works and entrance should not be awaited with drums and trumpets and other worldly display, but by spiritual power and grace; not by riding and walking on the pavement and carpets, but by making the dead alive, making the blind to see, making the deaf to hear, and removing all kinds of bodily and spiritual evil. That should be the pomp and entrance of this King, the least of whose works could not be performed by all the kings, all the learned, and all the rich in the world. This is the meaning of the text.

> *Now when John in prison heard about the deeds of the Christ, he sent two of his disciples and had them say to Him: "Are You the one who is to come, or shall we wait for another?" [Matt. 11:2–3]*

6. It is as though John were saying to his disciples: "There you hear of His works, which I have never done nor anyone else before Him. Now go to Him and ask Him whether or not He is the one. Put away the gross worldly delusion that He will ride on a steed in armor. He begins to become great, but I must decrease. My work must cease, but His must continue. You must leave me and cling to Him."

7. It is easy to see how necessary it was for John to point his disciples away from himself to Christ. For what benefit would it have been to them if they had followed John's holiness a thousand times and had not attained to Christ? Without Christ there is no help or remedy, no matter how holy people may be. So at the present day, what benefit is it to the monks and nuns to observe and follow the rules of St. Benedict, Bernard, Francis, Dominic, and Augustine, if they do not embrace Christ alone and depart also from their John? All Benedictines, Carthusians, barefooted friars,[3] Preachers,[4] Augustinians, Carmelites, all monks and nuns are surely lost, and only Christians are saved.[5] Whoever is not a Christian cannot be helped even

---

3  That is, Franciscans.

4  That is, Dominicans.

5  On these religious orders and their founders, see Luther's preface and afterword to *Papacy with Its Members* (1526), LW 59:138–47.

by John the Baptist, who indeed, according to Christ, was the greatest of all saints.

8. However, John deals kindly with his disciples and has patience with their weak faith until they become strong. He does not condemn them because they do not firmly believe him. Thus we should deal with the consciences of men ensnared by the examples and regulations of holy men, until they are freed from them.

*Jesus answered and said to them: "Go and tell John what you hear and see: the blind see, the lame walk, lepers are cleansed and the deaf hear, and the dead are raised up and the poor have the Gospel preached to them. And blessed is the one who is not offended at Me." [Matt. 11:4–6]*

9. Christ answered John also for the sake of his disciples. He answers in a twofold way: first, with works; second, with words. He did the same thing when the Jews surrounded Him in the temple and asked Him: "If You are the Christ, tell us plainly" (John 10 [:24]). But He pointed them to His works and said: "I am preaching to you, and you do not believe. The works that I do in My Father's name bear witness about Me" (John 10 [:25]). Again: "If you do not want to believe Me, believe the works" (John 10 [:38]). So here Christ first points them to the works, and then also to the words, when He says, "Blessed is the one who is not offended by Me." With these words He not only confesses that He is the one but also warns against being offended. If He were not the Christ, then he who is not offended by Him would not be saved. For one can dispense with all the saints, but one cannot dispense with Christ. No saint helps, but only Christ helps.

10. The answer through works is more certain, first, because such works were never before accomplished either by John or by anyone else; and second, because these works were predicted by the prophets. Therefore, when they saw that it happened just as the prophets had said, they could and should be certain. For Isaiah said of this: "The Spirit of the Lord God is upon Me, because the Lord has anointed Me to preach the Gospel; to the poor He has sent Me, to bind up the brokenhearted, to proclaim redemption to the captives and recovery of sight to the blind, to proclaim the year of the Lord's favor" (Isaiah 61 [:1–2; Luke 4:18–19]). When He says, "He has anointed Me," He understands that He is the Christ and that Christ should do these works, and He who is doing them must be the Christ. For the Greek word "Christ" is "Messiah" in Hebrew, *Unctus* in Latin, and *Gesalbter* ["anointed"] in German. But kings and priests used to be anointed for the kingdom and priesthood. But this anointed King and Priest, Isaiah says, shall be anointed by God Himself, not with earthly oil but with the Holy Spirit who is upon Him, as He says, "The Spirit of the Lord God is upon Me." "That is My

ointment with which He anointed Me." Thus He preaches the good news, gives sight to the blind, heals all kinds of sickness, and proclaims the year of the Lord's favor, the time of grace, etc.

Again Isaiah says: "Behold, our God Himself will come and help you. Then the eyes of the blind shall be opened, and the ears of the deaf unstopped; then shall the lame man leap like a deer, and the tongue of the mute be loosed" etc. (Isaiah 35 [:4–6]). Now, if they compared Scripture with these works and these works with Scripture, then they could recognize John's testimony of Christ, that He must be the true man. And Luke writes that "in that hour" when John's disciples asked Him, Christ "healed many people of diseases and plagues and spirits, and on the blind He bestowed sight" (Luke 7 [:21]).

11. But here we must take to heart the good example, that Christ appeals to His works and wants the tree recognized by its fruits, thus rebuking all false teachers, the pope, bishops, clerics, and monks who will come in the future under His name, saying, "We are Christians," just as the pope boasts that he is the vicar of Christ. Here we have it stated that where there are no works, there is also no Christ. Christ is someone living, active, and fruitful, who does not rest but works unceasingly wherever He is. Therefore, those bishops and teachers who are not doing the works of Christ we should regard and avoid as wolves.

12. But they say that it is unnecessary for everyone to do these works of Christ. How can all the saints give sight to the blind, make the lame walk, and do other miracles like those of Christ? Answer: Christ did also other works, such as patience, love, peace, meekness, and the like, which everybody should do. Do these works, and then we also shall know Christ by His works.

13. Here they reply: "Christ says, 'The scribes and the Pharisees sit on Moses' seat, so practice and observe whatever they tell you—but not what they do. For they preach, but do not practice' (Matthew 23 [:2–3]). Here Christ commanded people to look at the doctrine, not the life." Answer: What do I hear? Have you now become Pharisees and hypocrites, and confess it yourselves? If we would say this about you, then you would indeed become angry. Well, then, if you are such hypocrites and apply these words to yourselves, then you must also apply to yourselves all the other words Christ speaks against the Pharisees. However, as they wish to shield themselves by these words of Christ and put to silence the ignorant, we will regard these words highly, for even the murderers of Christians at the Council of Constance attacked John Hus with this passage, claiming that it granted them liberty for their tyranny, so that no one dared to oppose their doctrine.

14. Therefore, it must be noted that teaching is also a work, even the chief work of Christ, because here among His works He mentions that the

Gospel is preached to the poor. Therefore, just as the tyrants are known by their works, so are they known by their teachings. Where Christ is, there surely the Gospel will be preached; where the Gospel is not preached, there Christ is not present.

15. Now, in order to grant to our Pharisees that not the life but the doctrine should be observed, well, let them teach, and we will gladly be lenient toward their lives. But now [our Pharisees] are much worse than the Pharisees who taught Moses' doctrine, though they did not practice it. But our blockheads, that is, idols, neither do nor omit; there is neither life nor doctrine. They sit on Christ's seat and teach their own lies and are silent about the Gospel. Therefore, these words of Christ will not shield them; they must be wolves and murderers, as Christ calls them in John 10 [:1].

16. Thus Christ here wants them to hear the Pharisees, but no further than [when they sit] on Moses' seat, that is, when they teach the Law of Moses, the commandments of God. For in the same place where He forbids to do according to their works, He counts their teachings among their works, saying, "They tie up heavy and unbearable burdens and lay them on people's necks, but they themselves are not willing to move them with their finger" [Matt. 23:4]. See, He wants their teachings, which are hard to bear, to be forbidden as first among their works, so that finally the meaning of the passage is: All that they teach from Moses, you should observe; but whatever they teach and do otherwise, you should not observe. Much more we should listen to our Pharisees only on Christ's seat, when they preach the Gospel to the poor, and not hear nor observe what they otherwise teach and do.

17. Thus you see how artfully the crude Papists have made this passage the basis for their doctrine, lies, and power, even though no passage is more strongly against them and more severely condemns their teachings than this one. Christ's words stand clear and firm: "Do not do according to their works." But their doctrine is their own work, and not God's. They are a people raised only to lie and to falsify the Scriptures. Where a person's life is not good, it is rare that he preaches correctly; he would always have to preach against himself, which he will hardly do without additions and foreign doctrines.

In short, you should know that whoever does not preach the Gospel does not sit either on Moses' or on Christ's seat. For this reason you should act neither according to his words nor according to his works, but flee, as Christ's sheep do: "My sheep hear My voice. They do not hear the voice of strangers, but they flee from them" (John 10 [:27, 5]). But if you want to know what the seat is, then listen to David: "Blessed is the man who walks not in the counsel of the godless, nor stands in the way of sinners, nor sits in the seat of scoffers" (Psalm 1 [:1]). Again: "You will never be allied with the seat of iniquity, which interprets the Law badly" (cf. Psalm 94 [:20]).

18. But what does it mean when He says, "The poor have the Gospel preached to them"? Is it not preached also to the rich and to the whole world? Or how is the Gospel such a great thing, that He calls it a great benefit, since so many people are hostile to it? Here we must know what "Gospel" is, otherwise we cannot understand this passage. We must, therefore, diligently observe that from the beginning God has sent two kinds of word or preaching into the world: the Law and the Gospel. These two preachings must be carefully distinguished and recognized, for I tell you that outside of the Scriptures there never has been a book written to this day, not even by a saint, in which these two preachings are correctly and distinctly treated, and yet so very much depends on knowing this.

## The Difference between the Law and the Gospel

19. The Law is that word by which God teaches and demands what we are to do and not do, such as the Ten Commandments [cf. Exod. 20:1–17]. Now, if human nature is not aided by God's grace, it is impossible to keep the Law for the reason that man, since the fall of Adam in Paradise, is depraved and has only the evil desire to sin and cannot find heartfelt pleasure in the Law, which we all experience in ourselves. For there is no one who does not prefer that there were no Law, and everyone finds and feels in himself that it is difficult to be godly and do good and, on the other hand, that it is easy to be wicked and do evil. But this difficulty or unwillingness to do the good is the reason we do not keep the Law of God. Thus the Law of God convicts us, even by our own experience, that by nature we are evil, disobedient, lovers of sin, and hostile to God's laws.

20. From all this must follow either overconfidence or despair. Overconfidence follows when a man strives to fulfill the Law by works, by trying hard to do as the words of the Law command. He serves God, doesn't swear, honors father and mother, doesn't kill, doesn't commit adultery, and the like. But meanwhile he does not look into his heart, does not realize with what motives he leads a good life, and conceals the old rogue in his heart with such a fine life. For if he would truly examine his heart, he would realize that he is doing everything with aversion and under compulsion, that he fears hell or seeks heaven, if he does not seek much less, namely, honor, property, health, and fear of disgrace, hurt, or afflictions.

In short, he would have to confess that he would rather live differently if the consequences of such a life did not restrain him, for he does not act purely for the sake of the Law. But because he does not realize his bad motives, he lives securely, looks only at his works and not into his heart, presumes that he is keeping the Law of God perfectly, and thus Moses' face remains covered to him [cf. Exod. 34:33–35; 2 Cor. 3:13–15]; that is, he does not understand the intent of the Law, namely, that it must be kept with a happy, free, and joyous will.

21. Similarly, if you ask an unchaste person why he does that, he can answer nothing other than for the sake of the carnal pleasure he finds in it. For he does not do it for reward or punishment, for gain or to escape from some evil. The Law requires such a desire in us that, if you ask a chaste person why he is chaste, he should answer: "Not for the sake of heaven or hell, not for the sake of honor, but for the sole reason that it seemed good to me and gives me heartfelt pleasure, even if it were not commanded." See, such a heart loves God's Law and keeps it with pleasure. Such people love God and righteousness; they fear and hate nothing but unrighteousness. However, no one is thus by nature. But the others love reward and gratification, fear and hate punishment and pain; therefore, they also hate God and righteousness, love themselves and unrighteousness. They are dissemblers, hypocrites, dishonest, liars, and conceited. So are all people without grace—but above all, the works-righteous. For this reason the Scriptures conclude: "All men are liars" (Psalm 116 [:11]). "All men are in vain" (Psalm 39 [:5]). "There is none who does good among the children of men" (Psalm 14 [:3]).

22. Despair follows when the man becomes aware of his motives and realizes that it is impossible for him to love the Law of God, for he finds nothing good in himself, but only hatred of the good and desire for the evil. He realizes that with works he cannot do enough [to satisfy] the Law; therefore, he despairs of works and pays no attention to them. He should have love, but he finds none, nor can he have any by or from himself. Now he must be a poor, miserable, humbled spirit whose conscience oppresses and frightens him through the Law. It commands and demands, but he has not a penny to pay. For such a person only the Law is useful, for it was given for the purpose of working such knowledge and humility; that is its proper work. These persons well know that the work of hypocrites and false saints is nothing but lies and deception. David was at this point when he said, "I said in my trembling: 'All men are liars'" (Psalm 116 [:11]).

23. For this reason Paul calls the Law a "law of death" (Romans 7 [8:2]) and a "power of sin" (1 Corinthians 15 [:56]). He says, "The letter kills, but the Spirit gives life" (2 Corinthians 3 [:6]). All this is as much as to say: If the Law and human nature rightly meet together and know each other, then first conscience and sin will appear. Then the man sees how deeply wicked his heart is, how great his sins are, even what he formerly considered good works and not sin. So he must himself judge that of himself he is nothing other than a child of death, wrath, and hell. Then there is trembling and terror; all overconfidence vanishes; there is fear and despair. Thus man is crushed, destroyed, and truly humbled. Now, because only the Law works all of this,

St. Paul is right to call it the "law of death" and a "letter that kills," and a law which makes sin powerful and works wrath (Romans 7 [:13; 4:15]). For the Law does not give or help at all; it only demands and drives and shows us our misery and destruction.

24. The second word of God is neither Law nor command and demands nothing of us. But when the first word of the Law has worked misery and poverty in the heart, then He comes and offers us His blessed and life-giving Word. He promises and binds Himself to give grace and help so that we can come out from such misery, and all sins are not only forgiven but also blotted out, and, in addition to this, love and delight in keeping the Law are given [to us].

25. See, this divine promise of grace and forgiveness of sin is properly called the Gospel. And I say here again, once and for all, that you should understand the Gospel as nothing other than the divine promise of His grace and the forgiveness of sins. For that is why it happened that previously Paul's Epistles were not understood and could not be understood, because they did not know what the Law and the Gospel really mean. For they regarded Christ to be a lawmaker, and the Gospel a mere doctrine of new laws. That is nothing else than locking up the Gospel and concealing all things.

26. The word "Gospel" [*Evangelium*] is Greek and signifies "joyous news," because it proclaims the wholesome doctrine of life by divine promise and offers grace and forgiveness of sin. Therefore, works do not belong to the Gospel, for it is not Law; rather, only faith [belongs to the Gospel], for it is altogether a promise and an offer of divine grace. Whoever now believes the Gospel receives grace and the Holy Spirit. This causes the heart to rejoice and find delight in God, and [the heart] then keeps the Law voluntarily, gratuitously, without fear of punishment, without seeking reward, since the heart is perfectly satisfied with God's grace, by which the Law has been fulfilled.

27. But all these promises from the beginning of the world are founded on Christ; God promises no one this grace except in Christ and through Christ, who is the messenger of the divine promise to the whole world. For this reason He came and through the Gospel brought into all the world these promises, which before this had been proclaimed by the prophets. Therefore, there is nothing that anyone (like the Jews) should expect of the divine promises apart from Christ. Everything is drawn together and enclosed in Christ. Whoever does not hear Him hears no promises of God. For just as God acknowledges no law besides the Law of Moses and the writings of the prophets, so He makes no promises except through Christ alone.

28. But you might say, "Isn't there also much Law in the Gospels and in the Epistles of Paul, and again many promises in the books of Moses and the prophets?" Answer: There is no book in the Bible in which both are not

found. God has always placed side by side both Law and promise. For He teaches by the Law what is to be done and by the promises where we are to receive that.

29. But the New Testament is especially called "Gospel" above the other books because it was written after the coming of Christ, who fulfilled the divine promises, brought them to us, and publicly proclaimed them by oral preaching, which previously were concealed in the Scriptures. Therefore, hold to this distinction, and no matter what books you have before you, whether of the Old or of the New Testament, read them with this distinction so that you observe that when promises are made in a book, it is a Gospel book; when commandments are given, it is a Law book. But because in the New Testament the promises are found so abundantly, and in the Old Testament so many laws are found, the former is called "Gospel" and the latter, "the Book of the Law." We now come back to our text.

### *The poor have the Gospel preached to them. [Matt. 11:5]*

30. From what has just been said, it is easily understood that among all the works of Christ none is greater than that the Gospel is preached to the poor. This means nothing else than that to the poor the divine promise of grace and consolation in Christ and through Christ is preached, offered, and applied, so that whoever believes has all his sins forgiven, the Law is fulfilled, the conscience is freed, and at last life eternal is given. What more joyful news could a poor, sorrowful heart and a troubled conscience hear than this? How could the heart become more bold and courageous than by such consoling, abundant words and promises? Sin, death, hell, the world and the devil, and every evil are scorned when a poor heart receives and believes this consolation of the divine promise. To give sight to the blind and to raise up the dead are but insignificant deeds compared with preaching the Gospel to the poor. Therefore, He mentions it last as the greatest and best among these works.

31. But it must be observed that Christ does [not] say, "The Gospel is not preached except only to the poor," by which He would without doubt mean for it to be a sermon only for the poor. For it has always been preached to the whole world, as He says, "Go into all the world and preach the Gospel to the whole creation" (Mark 16 [:15]). Thus these poor are certainly not the beggars and the bodily poor, but the spiritually poor, that is, those who do not covet and love earthly goods, but rather those poor, brokenhearted ones who in the agony of their conscience seek and desire help and consolation so ardently that they covet neither riches nor honor. Nothing will be of help to them, unless they have a merciful God. Here is true spiritual poverty. They are those for whom such a message was intended and whose hearts it delights. They feel that they have been delivered from hell and death.

32. Therefore, though the Gospel is heard by all the world, yet it is not accepted other than only by such poor people. Moreover, it is to be preached and proclaimed to all the world that it is a preaching only for the poor and that the rich cannot grasp it. Whoever would grasp it must first become poor, just as Christ says that He came "not to call the righteous, but sinners" (Matthew 9 [:13]), even though He called the whole world. But His calling was such that He could be received only by sinners, and all He called should become sinners; but they would not do it. So also those who heard the Gospel should all become poor, so that they would be fit for it; but they would not. Therefore, the Gospel remained only for the poor. So also God's grace was preached before all the world to the humble, so that they all might become humble; but they would not.

33. Now you see who the greatest enemies of the Gospel are, namely, the works-righteous saints, who are overconfident, as was said above. For the Gospel cannot at all agree with such people. They want to be rich in works, but the Gospel wants them to be poor. If they will not yield, the Gospel also cannot yield; it is the imperishable Word of God. Thus they clash and take offense at each other, as Christ says, "And whoever falls on this stone will be broken to pieces; and on whomever it falls, it will crush him" (Matthew 21 [:44]).

Again, they condemn the Gospel as error and heresy; and it happens, as we see daily and as it has happened from the beginning of the world, that between the Gospel and the works-righteous saints there is no peace, no grace, no reconciliation. But Christ must let Himself be crucified, for He and His must be in this pinch between the Gospel and works, and thus be oppressed and crushed like wheat between two millstones. The lower stone is the quiet, peaceful, immovable Gospel; the upper stone is the works and their masters, who are ranting and raging.

34. With all this [John] contradicts strongly the fleshly and worldly opinion [his disciples] had about Christ's coming. They thought that the great King, about whom John preached so nobly that he was not worthy to untie His shoe [cf. John 1:27], would enter in such splendor that everything would be gold and costly ornaments, and even the streets would be paved with pearls and silks. As they lifted up their eyes so high and looked for such splendor, Christ pulls down their eyes and holds before them the blind, lame, deaf, dead, dumb, poor, and everything that to external appearances conflicts with such splendor, and presents Himself in a form in which no one would look for a hospital orderly, to say nothing of such a great King that the great man John is not worthy to untie His shoe. This was as if Christ said to them: "Abandon that idea, and look not at My person and form, but at the works I do. Worldly lords, because they rule by force, must be accompanied by rich,

high, sound, strong, wise, and able men. With them they have to associate, and they need them, or their kingdom could not exist; therefore, they can never attend to the blind, lame, deaf, dumb, dead, lepers, and the poor.

"But because My kingdom does not seek profit from others but only gives profit, has enough in itself and needs no one's help, therefore I cannot be surrounded by such as are already sufficient of themselves, sound, rich, strong, pure, alive, godly, and able in every respect. To such I am of no benefit; they obtain nothing from Me. They would even be a disgrace to Me, because it would seem that I needed them and was benefited by them, as worldly rulers are by their subjects. Therefore, I must do otherwise and keep to those who can be benefited by Me; I must associate with the blind, the lame, the dumb, and all kinds of sick people. The character and nature of My kingdom demand this. Therefore, I must also act in such a way that such people can be around Me."

35. And now very aptly follow the words: "Blessed is the one who is not offended at Me" [Matt. 11:6]. Why? Because these two things seemed to be so far from each other: Christ's despised appearance and John's excellent testimony. Nature cannot make sense of them. Now, all the Scriptures pointed to Christ, and there was danger of misinterpreting them. So nature spoke: "Can this be the Christ, of whom all the Scriptures speak? Should this be the one, whose shoe John does not think he's worthy to untie, whom I scarcely consider worthy to scrape my shoes?" Therefore, it is surely true that it is a great grace not to be offended at Christ, and there is here no other aid or help than to look at His works and compare them with the Scriptures. Otherwise it is impossible to prevent the offense. His form and appearance are just too low and despised.

## TWO KINDS OF OFFENSES

36. Here note that there are two kinds of offenses: one of doctrine and the other of life. These two offenses must be carefully noted. The offense of doctrine comes when one believes, teaches, or thinks of Christ differently than is to be believed, taught, and thought, just as here the Jews thought of and taught about Christ differently than He was, mistaking Him for a worldly king. Scripture mostly deals with this offense, with which Christ and Paul always deal, scarcely mentioning any other. Note well that Christ and Paul speak of this offense.

37. It is not without reason that I exhort you to note this. For under the reign of the pope this offense has been hushed entirely, so that neither cleric nor monk knows of any other offense than that caused by open sin and wicked living, which Scripture does not call an offense; but they thus construe and twist this word. On the other hand, regarding their whole way

of life (which they think to be the best) and all their teachings (by which they think they are helping the world), they do not consider these to be an offense, but an improvement. And yet these are poisonous offenses, the likes of which have never been [seen] under the sun. For they teach the people to regard the Mass as sacrifice and a work in order to become godly, atone for sin, and be saved by works. All of this is nothing else than rejecting Christ and destroying faith.

38. Thus the world today is filled with offenses up to the very heavens, which is terrible to contemplate. For no one now seeks Christ in poverty, blindness, death, etc.; but all want to enter heaven in a different way, which must surely fail.

39. The offense of life is when one sees an openly wicked work done by another and teaches it. But it is impossible to avoid this offense, since we have to live among the wicked. Nor is it so dangerous, since everybody knows that it is evil, and no one is deceived by it but wantonly follows the known evil; there is no dissimulation or pretense. But the offense of doctrine is that there should be the most beautiful religious ceremonies, the noblest works, the most honorable life, and that it is impossible for common reason to censure or discern it; only faith knows through the Spirit that it is all wrong. Christ warns against this offense when He says, "Whoever offends one of these little ones who believe in Me, it would be better for him to have a millstone fastened around his neck and to be drowned in the depth of the sea" (Matthew 18 [:6]).

40. Therefore, watch out! Whoever does not preach Christ to you, or who preaches Him otherwise than as one associating with the blind, the lame, the dead, and the poor, as this Gospel teaches—flee from such a person as from the devil himself, because he teaches you how to become foolish and to take offense at Christ, as now the pope, the monks, and their universities do. All their doings are an offense from head to foot, from the skin to the marrow, as snow is scarcely anything but water; nor can these things exist without causing great offense, since offense is the nature and essence of their doings. Therefore, to undertake to reform the pope, the monasteries, and the universities and still maintain them in their essence and character would be like squeezing water out of snow and still preserving the snow. But what it means to preach Christ among the blind and poor we shall see at the end of our text.

*As they went away, Jesus began to speak to the crowds concerning John: "What did you go out into the wilderness to see? Did you want to see a reed shaken by the wind? What, then, did you go out to see? Did you want to see a man in soft clothing? Behold, those who wear soft clothing are in kings' houses. What, then, did you go out to see? Did you want to see a prophet? Yes, I tell you, he is more than a prophet." [Matt. 11:7–9]*

41. Inasmuch as Christ thus praises John because he is not a reed nor wears soft clothing and because he is more than a prophet, He gives us to understand by these figurative words that the people were inclined to look upon John as a reed, as wearing soft clothing, and as a prophet. Therefore, we must see what He means by that and why He censures and rejects their opinion. I have said enough about it: John is to bear witness of Christ, so that they might not take offense at Christ's coming.

42. Now, as it was of great importance for them to believe John's witness and acknowledge Christ, He praises John first for his steadfastness, thus rebuking their wavering, on account of which they would not believe John's witness. It is as though He would say: "You have heard John's witness concerning Me, but now you do not adhere to it, you take offense at Me, and your hearts are wavering. You are looking for someone other than Me, but know not who, when, or where, and thus your hearts are like a reed shaken to and fro by the wind. You are sure of nothing and would rather hear something else than from Me. Now do you think that John should also turn his witness from Me, throw your thoughts to the winds, and speak of another whom you would be pleased to hear? Not so. John does not waver, nor does his witness; he does not follow your wavering delusion. But you must fix your wavering by his witness, and thus remain with Me and think of no other."

43. Second, He praises him because of the harshness of his clothing, as though to say: "Perhaps you might believe him [when he says] who I am as to My person, but you expect him to speak differently about Me, saying something soft and pleasant to hear. It is indeed harsh and severe that I come so poor and despised. You desire Me to break in with pomp and flourish of trumpets. Had John said that about Me, he would not be so coarse and harsh. But do not think only of that. Whoever is to preach about Me must not preach differently than John is doing. It is to no purpose; I will assume no other form or appearance. Those who teach differently are flatterers who are in kings' houses, not in the wilderness. They are rich and honored by the people. They teach man-made doctrines from themselves, not from Me."

44. Third, He praises him because of the dignity of his office, namely, that he is not only a prophet but even more than a prophet, as though to say: "In your high-soaring, wavering thoughts, you take John for a prophet who speaks of the coming of Christ, just as the other prophets have done, and thus again your heart goes to a different time when you expect Christ to come, according to John's witness, so that you do not accept Me. But I say to you that your thoughts are wrong. For just as he forbids you to be like a shaken reed and to expect someone else than Me, and he also does not allow you to

expect a different appearance than I have, so also he forbids you to look for another time. Rather, his witness points to this person, this appearance, and this time, and it opposes your slippery thoughts at every point and binds you firmly to Me."

45. Now, if you want to do him justice, then you must simply follow his witness and believe that this is the person, the appearance, and the time that you should accept, and abandon your delusion about waiting for another person, appearance, and time. For it is decreed that he should be no shaken reed, no man of soft clothing, and, above all, not a prophet pointing to future times, but a messenger of present events. He will not write, as did the other prophets, but will point out and orally announce Him whom all the prophets have described, as follows:

*This is he of whom it is written: "Behold, I send My messenger before You, who will prepare Your way before You." [Matt. 11:10]*

46. "What else can this mean than that you dare not wait for another or for Me to act differently or for another time? Here, I am present, the one of whom John speaks. For he is not a prophet but a messenger, and not only a messenger who is sent by the Lord who stays at home but also a messenger who goes before the face of his Lord and brings the Lord along with him, so that there is but one time for the messenger and for the Lord. Now if you do not accept him as such a messenger, but take him for a prophet who only proclaims the coming of the Lord, as the other prophets have done, then you miss out on Me, the Scriptures, and everything else."

47. Here we see that Christ is mainly acting so that they regard John as a messenger and not as a prophet. To this end Christ quotes the Scriptures and the passage of Malachi 3 [:1], which He does not do in reference to the other points, namely, His person and appearance. For to this day it is the error of the Jews that they look for another time; and if they then had believed that the time was at hand and had let John be a messenger and not a prophet, then everything could easily have been adjusted as to the person and appearance of Christ, since they at last had to accept His person, at least after the time had passed. There was to be no other time than the days of John, the messenger and servant of his Lord. But when they let the time pass and look for another time, it is much less possible for them to regard His person and appearance. They remain reeds looking for soft clothing as long as they regard John as a prophet and not as a messenger.

48. We must accustom ourselves to the Scriptures, in which "angel" really means a messenger—not an errand boy who carries letters, but one who is sent to deliver the message orally. Thus in the Scriptures this name is common to all messengers of God in heaven and on earth, whether they

are holy angels in heaven or the prophets and apostles on earth. For thus Malachi speaks of the office of the priest: "The lips of a priest should guard knowledge, and people should seek instruction from his mouth, for he is an angel of the Lord of hosts" (Malachi 2 [:7]). Again: "Then Haggai, the angel of the Lord, spoke to the people with the Lord's message" (Haggai 1 [:13]). And again, Jesus "sent angels" (that is, messengers) "ahead of Him, who went and entered a village of the Samaritans" (Luke 9 [:52]). Thus all who proclaim His Word are God's angels who win people for His message. From that also comes the word "Gospel" [*Evangelium*], which means "a good message." But the heavenly spirits are especially called angels because they are the highest and most exalted messengers of God.

49. Thus John is also an angel or orator,[6] and not only such a messenger, but one who also prepares the way before the face of the Lord in such a way that the Lord Himself follows in his footsteps, which no prophet ever did. For this reason John is more than a prophet, namely, an angel or messenger and forerunner, so that in his day the Lord of all the prophets Himself comes with this messenger.

50. "Prepare" here means to get the way ready, so that whatever interferes with the course of the Lord is out of the way, just as the servant clears the way before the face of his master by removing wood, stones, people, and all that is in the way. But what was it that blocked the way of Christ and that John was to remove? Sin, without a doubt, but especially the good works of the haughty saints; that is, he should make known to everybody that the works and deeds of all men are sin and ruin and that all need the grace of Christ. He who knows and acknowledges this thoroughly is himself humble and has well prepared the way for Christ. Of this we shall treat further in the following Gospel.[7] Now is the time to apply this Gospel to ourselves.

## THE DOCTRINE OF FAITH AND GOOD WORKS

51. As we have said on the other Gospels—that we should take from them the two doctrines of faith and love, or accepting and bestowing good works—so we should also here praise faith and exercise love. Faith receives the good works of Christ; love bestows good works on our neighbor.

52. First, our faith is strengthened and improved when Christ is presented to us in His own natural works, namely, that He associates only with the blind, the deaf, the lame, the lepers, the dead, and the poor—which is pure love and kindness toward all who are in need and in misery—so that finally Christ is nothing else than consolation and a refuge for all troubled

---

6 *Mundbote*, a word Luther used to explain what "apostle" means.

7 See sermon for Fourth Sunday in Advent on John 1:19–28.

and weak consciences. Here faith is necessary, which is based on this Gospel and relies on it, never doubting that Christ is just as He is presented to us in this Gospel, and does not think of Him otherwise nor lets anyone persuade us to believe otherwise. Then surely we have Christ as we believe and as this Gospel speaks of Him. For as you believe, so you will have it [cf. Matt. 8:13]. And blessed is he who is not offended by Him.

53. Guard yourself here diligently against offense. Who are those who offend you? All who teach you to do works instead of to believe; those who make Christ into a lawmaker and a judge and won't let Him be a helper and a comforter; who frighten you into acting with works before God and toward God in order to atone for your sins and to merit grace. Such are the teachings of the pope, priests, monks, and universities, who close up your mouth with their Masses and worship, and lead you to another Christ, and take away from you the real Christ.

For if you want to believe correctly and truly obtain Christ, then you must put aside all works with which you would act toward God and before God. They are only an offense which leads you away from Christ and away from God. No works are valuable before God except Christ's own work. You must let His work act for you toward God, and do no other work before Him than to believe that Christ is doing His work for you and places it toward God. In this way your faith remains pure, does nothing other than keep quiet, lets Him do good and accepts Christ's work, and lets Christ practice His love on you. You must be blind, lame, deaf, dead, leprous, and poor, or you will take offense at Christ. The Gospel does not lie to you which shows Christ doing good only among the needy.

54. See, this means correctly to acknowledge Christ and to receive Him. That is to believe in a truly Christian way. Those who want to atone for sins and to become godly by their works miss the present Christ and look for another, or at least they believe that He is to do otherwise, that first of all He will come and accept their works and consider them godly. These are, like the Jews, lost forever. There is no help for them.

55. Second, He teaches us to apply the works correctly and shows us what good works are. All other works, except faith, we are to direct toward our neighbor. For God demands of us no other work that we should do for Him than only faith in Christ. With that He is satisfied, and with that we give honor to Him, as to one who is gracious, merciful, wise, kind, truthful, and the like. After this think of nothing else than to do to your neighbor as Christ has done to you, and let all your works with all your life be directed to your neighbor. Look for the poor, sick, and all kinds of needy; help them, and let it be the practice of your life that they are benefited by you, helping whoever needs you, as much as you possibly can with your body, property, and honor.

Whoever points you to other good works than these, avoid him as a wolf and as the devil, because he wants to put a stumbling block in your way, as David says, "In the path where I walk they lay snares for me" (Psalm 142 [:3]).

56. But this is done by the crooked people of the Papists, who with their worship set aside such Christian works and teach the people to serve God only and not mankind. They establish monasteries, Masses, vigils, become spiritual, do this and that. And these poor, blind people call "worship" what they themselves have chosen. But you know that to serve God is nothing else than to serve your neighbor and do good to him in love—whether your neighbor is a child, wife, servant, enemy, friend—without making any difference, whoever needs your help in body or soul, and wherever you can help in temporal or spiritual matters. This is worship and good works. O Lord God, how we fools go out into the world and neglect to do such works, even though in every corner there are more than enough on whom we could practice [our good works]! No one looks after them nor cares for them. But look to your own life. If you do not find yourself among the needy and the poor, where the Gospel shows us Christ, then you may know that your faith is not right and that you have not yet tasted of Christ's benefit and work for you.

57. Therefore, see what important words these are: "Blessed is the one who is not offended at Me" [Matt. 11:6]. In both parts we take offense. In faith, because we undertake to become godly in a different way than through Christ and go our way blindly, not acknowledging Christ. In love we take offense because we are not mindful of the poor and needy, do not look after them, and yet we think we will satisfy faith with other works. Thus we come under the judgment of Christ, who says, "I was hungry and you did not feed me." Again: "Whatever you did not do to the least of My people, you did not do it to Me" (Matthew 25 [:42, 45]).

Why is this judgment right, if not for the reason that we have not done to our neighbor as Christ has done to us? He has given us needy ones His great, rich, eternal benefit, but we will not do our meager service to our neighbors, thus showing that we do not truly believe and that we have neither accepted nor tasted His benefit. Many will then say, "Did we not prophesy in Your name, and cast out demons in Your name, and do many mighty works in Your name?" But He will answer them: "Depart from Me, you evildoers" (Matthew 7 [:22–23]). Why? Because they did not retain true faith and love.

58. Thus we see in this Gospel how difficult it is to acknowledge Christ. There is a hindrance, and one takes offense at this, another at that. There is no headway, not even with the disciples of John, though they plainly see Christ's works and hear His words.

59. This we also do. Although we must see, hear, understand, and confess that the Christian life is faith in God and kindness or love to our needy

neighbor, yet there is no progress. This one clings to his worship and his own works; that one is hoarding all to himself and helping no one. Even those who gladly hear and understand the doctrine of pure faith do not proceed to serve their neighbor, as though they expected to be saved by faith without works. They do not see that their faith is not faith, but a pretense of faith, just as the picture in the mirror is not the face itself but only a reflection of it, as St. James so beautifully writes: "Be doers of the Word, and not hearers only, deceiving yourselves. For if anyone is a hearer of the Word and not a doer, he is like a man who looks at his face in a mirror. When he has seen it, he goes away and forgets what he was like" (James [1:22–24]). Thus they see within themselves a reflection of true faith when they hear and speak [of the Word], but as soon as the hearing and speaking are done, they are concerned about other affairs and are not doing according to it, and thus they always forget about the fruit of faith, namely, Christian love, of which Paul also says, "The kingdom of God does not consist in words but in deeds" (1 Corinthians 4 [:20]).

# GOSPEL FOR THE FOURTH SUNDAY IN ADVENT

*John 1:19–28*

*And this is the testimony of John, when the Jews sent priests and Levites from Jerusalem to ask him, "Who are you?" He confessed, and did not deny, but confessed, "I am not the Christ." And they asked him, "What then? Are you Elijah?" He said, "I am not." "Are you the Prophet?" And he answered, "No." So they said to him, "Who are you? We need to give an answer to those who sent us. What do you say about yourself?" He said, "I am the voice of one crying out in the wilderness, 'Make straight the way of the Lord,' as the prophet Isaiah said." (Now they had been sent from the Pharisees.) They asked him, "Then why are you baptizing, if you are neither the Christ, nor Elijah, nor the Prophet?" John answered them, "I baptize with water, but among you stands one you do not know, even He who comes after me, the strap of whose sandal I am not worthy to untie." These things took place in Bethany across the Jordan, where John was baptizing.*

1. The evangelist describes and magnifies the testimony of John with many words. Although it would have been sufficient if he had written about John: "He confessed," he repeats it once again and says, "He did not deny, but confessed" [John 1:20]. Without a doubt he is praising the beautiful steadfastness of John in a great temptation, when he was tempted to commit a great apostasy from the truth. And now consider the particular circumstances.

2. First, those sent to him are not servants or ordinary citizens, but priests and Levites from the highest and noblest class, who were Pharisees, that is to say, the leaders of the people. That was a distinguished embassy to such a common man, who might justly have felt happy and haughty at such an honor, since the favor of lords and princes is highly esteemed in this world.

3. Second, they sent to him not common people, but citizens of Jerusalem (the capital), the Sanhedrin, and the leaders of the Jewish nation. So it was as if the entire people came and did honor to him. What a wind that was and how it would inflate, if it met a vain and worldly heart!

4. Third, they do not offer him a present nor ordinary glory, but the highest glory of all, the kingdom and all authority: they are ready to accept him as the Christ. That is a high and sweet temptation! For if he had not perceived that they wanted to regard him as the Christ, he would not have said,

"I am not the Christ" [John 1:20]. And Luke also writes that, when everybody thought he was the Christ, John spoke: "I am not who you think I am, but I am sent before Him" (cf. Luke 3 [:15–17]).

5. Fourth, when he did not want this honor, they tempted him with another and were ready to take him for Elijah. For they had a prophecy of Malachi, where God says: "Behold, I will send you Elijah the prophet before the great and terrifying day of the Lord comes. And he will turn the hearts of fathers to their children and the hearts of children to their fathers, lest I come and strike the land with the ban" (Malachi 4 [:5–6]).

6. Fifth, when he does not want to be Elijah, they tempt him further and offer him the common honor of a prophet, for since Malachi they had not had a prophet. John, however, remains firm and unshaken, though tempted by so much honor knocking at the door.

7. Sixth and last, since they knew no more honors, they let him choose who or as what he wished to be regarded, for they greatly desired to do him honor. But John does not want their honor and answers no more than that he is a voice calling to them and to everybody. This they do not heed. What all this means we shall hear later on. Let us now examine the text.

> *This is the testimony of John, when the Jews sent priests and Levites from Jerusalem to ask him: "Who are you?" [John 1:19]*

8. They sent people to him; why did they not come themselves? John had come to preach repentance to each one of the Jewish people. They did not pay attention to this preaching. It is clear, therefore, that they did not send to him with good and pure intentions, offering him such honor. They also did not believe from their hearts that he was Christ or Elijah or a prophet; otherwise they would have come themselves to be baptized, as did the others. What, then, did they seek of him? Christ explains this: "You sent to John, and he bore witness to the truth. He was a burning and shining lamp, and you were willing to rejoice for a short while in his light" (John 5 [:33, 35]). From these words it is clear that they looked for their own honor in John, desiring to make use of his light, that is, of his highly famous name, in order to adorn themselves before the people.

For if John had joined them and accepted the honor they offered, then they also would have become great and glorious before all the people, as being worthy of the friendship and honor of so holy and great a man. But by doing so, would not all their avarice, tyranny, and wickedness have been confirmed as a purely holy and precious thing? Thus John with his holiness would have become the greatest possible cover for their dishonor; and the coming of Christ would justly have been regarded with suspicion, as being opposed to the doings of the priests and tyrants, with whom John, this great and holy man, would have taken sides.

9. Thus we see what wickedness they practice and how they tempt John to deny Christ and become a Judas Iscariot, in order that he might justify their vice and they might share his honor and popularity. Are they not fine operators, seeking to bring John's honor to themselves? They offer him an apple for a kingdom and would exchange chips for coins. But he remained solid, as follows:

*He confessed, and did not deny, but confessed: "I am not Christ."*
*[John 1:20]*

10. John's confession has two parts: first, he confesses, and second, he does not deny. His confessing is his confession about Christ, when he says, "I am not the Christ." To this same confession belongs also his confession that he is not Elijah or a prophet [John 1:21]. His not denying is his admission that he says what he is: he is the voice in the wilderness, which with its cry prepares the way of the Lord. Thus his confession is a free confession, which not only confesses what he is not but also what he is. For the part of confession in which someone confesses what he is not is still obscure and incomplete, since one cannot know what is really to be thought of him. But here John openly says what is to be thought of him, and what not; he makes this certain when he confesses that he is not the Christ and does not deny that he is the voice before His coming [John 1:23].

11. Yet someone might say: The evangelist reverses his words in that he calls it a confession when John says that he is not the Christ, which is rather a denial, for he denies that he is the Christ. To say no is to deny, and the Jews wish him to confess that he is the Christ, which he denies; yet the evangelist says that he confessed. And again, it is much more a confession when he says, "I am the voice in the wilderness." But the evangelist considers this matter and describes it as it is before God, and not as the words sound to men. For they are occupied with him denying [to be] Christ and not confessing what he was. But since he remains firm and confesses what he is and is not, his act is a precious confession before God and not a denial.

*And they asked him: "What then? Are you Elijah?" He said, "I am not."*
*[John 1:21]*

12. As said above, the Jews had a prophecy that Elijah was to come before the day of the Lord (Malachi 4 [:5]). It is therefore also among Christians a current belief that Elijah is to come before the Last Day. Some add Enoch; others, John the evangelist. So we will say a little bit about this.

13. First, it all depends on whether the prophet Malachi is speaking about the second coming of the Lord on the Last Day or about the first coming in the flesh and through the Gospel. If he is speaking about the Last Day, then we are certainly to expect Elijah, for God does not lie. The coming of Enoch and John, however, has no foundation in Scripture and is therefore to be considered as a fable and tomfoolery. But if he is speaking about Christ's coming in the flesh and through the Word, then no further Elijah is to be expected; rather, John is that same Elijah announced by Malachi.

14. I am of the opinion that Malachi spoke of no other Elijah than John, and that Elijah the Tishbite, who went up to heaven with the chariot of fire (cf. 2 Kings 2 [:11]), is not at all to be expected. I am especially forced to this opinion by the words of the angel Gabriel, who says to John's father, Zechariah: "He will go before Him in the spirit and power of Elijah, to turn the hearts of the fathers to the children, and the unbelievers to the wisdom of the righteous" (Luke 1 [:17]). With these words we see that the angel is pointing to the prophecy of Malachi and cites the same words of the prophet, who also says that Elijah is to turn the hearts of fathers to children, as cited above. If there were another Elijah prophesied about by Malachi, without a doubt the angel would not have pointed to John.

15. Second, the Jews themselves always understood that Malachi was speaking about Christ's coming in the flesh. Therefore, they here ask John whether he is the Elijah who is to come before Christ. But they erred in think-ing of the original and bodily Elijah. For though the text requires that Elijah is to come first, it does not require that it be the former Elijah. [Malachi] does not say that Elijah the Tishbite is to come, as Scripture calls him (1 Kings 17 [:1]; 2 Kings 1 [:3, 8]), but merely Elijah, a prophet. The angel Gabriel explains this as "in the spirit and power of Elijah" (Luke 1 [:17]), as if to say that he will be a true Elijah. In the same way we now say in German of one who is and acts like another that he is truly that other, as when I say: the pope is a true Caiaphas, or John Hus is a true Paul. Thus, through Malachi, God promises one who is to be a true Elijah; but that is John.

16. Nevertheless, I would not believe the interpretation of the Jews alone, if Christ had not confirmed it. When the disciples saw Elijah and Moses on Mount Tabor, they said to the Lord: "Then why do the scribes say that Elijah must come beforehand?" (Matthew 17 [:10]). It is as if they would say, "You have already come, and Elijah did not come before, but only now, after You appeared; and yet they say that he must come before." Christ did not reject this understanding, but rather confirmed it and said: "Elijah shall indeed come, and he will restore all things. But I tell you that Elijah has already come, and they did not recognize him but did to him whatever they pleased." Matthew explains: "Then the disciples understood that He was speaking to

them of John the Baptist" (Matthew 17 [:11–13]). Mark adds: "I tell you that Elijah has already come, and they did to him whatever they pleased, as it is written of him" (Mark 9 [:13]).

17. Now there is no other prophecy concerning Elijah's coming other than this one of Malachi, and Christ applies it to John. And if someone suggests that Christ says, "Elijah shall indeed come, and he will restore all things," it proves nothing, for He Himself explains it in the following words: "But I tell you that Elijah has already come," etc. He means to say: "What you have heard about Elijah, that he comes and will restore all things, is correct and true, for it is so written and it must happen. But they do not know of which Elijah this is said, for he has already come." With these words, therefore, Christ confirms the Scriptures and the interpretation concerning the coming Elijah, but He rejects the false interpretation concerning an Elijah other than John.

18. But Christ most strongly asserts that no other Elijah is coming when He says: "All the prophets and the Law prophesied until John, and if you are willing to accept it, he is Elijah who is to come. He who has ears to hear, let him hear" (Matthew 11 [:13–15]). Here it is made clear that only one Elijah was to come. Had there been another, He would not have said, "John is Elijah who is to come," but He would have had to say, "John is one of the Elijahs," or simply: "He is Elijah." But by calling John that Elijah whom everybody expects, who without a doubt was announced to come, He makes it sufficiently clear that the prophecy of Malachi is fulfilled in John and that after this no other Elijah is to be expected.

19. Therefore, we insist that the last preaching before the Last Day is the Gospel, through which Christ has come into all the world; before this preaching and advent [of Christ], John came and prepared the way. Also all the prophets and the Law prophesy until John; it is not allowed, then, for someone to stretch them beyond John to another Elijah who is yet to come. Thus the prophecy of Malachi must also fit John's time. For because He applies all of the prophets to John's time, He does not let any of them pass him by. And so we conclude with certainty that no other Elijah is to come, but that the Gospel will endure to the end of the world.

*"Are you the Prophet?" And he answered: "No." [John 1:21]*

20. Here some think that the Jews asked about that prophet of whom Moses writes: "I will raise up a prophet like you from among their brothers," etc. (Deuteronomy 18 [:18]). But Peter (Acts 3 [:22]) and Stephen (Acts 7 [:37]) apply this passage to Christ Himself, which is the correct interpretation. The Jews also certainly identified this prophet, like Moses, as being above Elijah. Therefore, they understood Him to be Christ and asked John

whether he was an ordinary prophet, like the others, since he was neither Christ nor Elijah. For they had had no prophet since the days of Malachi, who was the last and concluded the Old Testament with the above-mentioned prophecy concerning the coming of Elijah. John therefore is the nearest to and first after Malachi, who in finishing his book points to him. Thus they asked whether he was one of the prophets, as also Christ says of him: "What did you go out to see? A prophet? Yes, I tell you, one who is also more than a prophet" (Matthew 11 [:9]). And Matthew writes: "They all considered John a prophet" (Matthew 21 [:26]).

21. Now the question arises: How did John confess the truth when he denied that he was Elijah or a prophet, and yet Christ Himself called him Elijah and more than a prophet? Did he not himself know that he had come in the spirit and power of Elijah and that the Scriptures called him Elijah? If someone says that he did not confess himself to be a prophet because he was more than a prophet, that is simply disgraceful, as if he would exalt and praise himself. Therefore, it is to be held that in all simplicity he confessed the truth, namely, that he was not the Elijah about whom they asked nor a prophet. For the prophets commonly led and taught the people, who sought advice and help from them. John was not that kind of prophet and did not want to be, for the Lord was present, and they were to cling to Him and follow Him. Thus he did not want to draw the people to himself, but to lead them to Christ, as it must necessarily happen until Christ Himself came.

[John said this] also because a prophet foretells the coming of Christ, but John shows the present [Christ], which is different from the prophet's task. In the same way a priest in the bishop's presence points the people away from himself to the bishop, saying, "I am not the priest; he is your priest"; but in the bishop's absence he rules the people as the bishop.

22. Thus John points the people away from himself to Christ. And though this is a higher and greater office than that of a prophet, yet it is not so on account of his merit but on account of the presence of his Lord. Praising John as being more than a prophet does not announce his own worthiness but that of his Lord, who is present. For it is customary that a servant is greater, more worthy, and more honorable in the absence of his master than in his presence.

23. Thus the rank of a prophet is higher than that of John, though his office is greater and more immediate. For a prophet rules and leads the people, and they adhere to him; but John does no more than point them away from himself to Christ, the present Lord. Therefore, in genuine simplicity he denied being a prophet, though abounding in all the qualities of a prophet. He did all this for the sake of the people, in order that they might not accept his testimony as the promise of a prophet and expect Christ still to

be coming at another time, but that they might recognize him as a forerunner and guide, and follow his guidance to the Lord, who was present. That is what the following words say:

> *So they said to him: "Who are you? We need to give an answer to those who sent us. What do you say about yourself?" He said, "I am a voice crying in the wilderness: 'Make straight the way of the Lord,' as the prophet Isaiah said." [John 1:22–23]*

24. This is the second part of his confession, in which he declares what he is, after having denied that he was Christ or Elijah or a prophet. It is as though he were to say: "Your salvation is much too near for a prophet to be required. Do not stretch your eyes so far out into the future, for the Lord of all the prophets is Himself here, so that no prophet is needed.

"The Lord is coming this way, whose forerunner I am; He is treading on my heels. I am not prophesying of Him as a prophet, but crying as a forerunner to make space and room for Him so that He may enter. I do not say, 'See, He is coming,' as the prophets did; but I say, 'See, He comes and is here.' I do not speak words about Him but point to Him with my finger. This is what Isaiah proclaimed long ago, that such a crying to make room for the Lord should go before Him. That is who I am, and not a prophet. Therefore, step aside and make room; permit the Lord Himself to be present and walk among you, and do not look for any more prophecies about Him."

25. Now this is an answer which no learned, wise, and holy man can endure, and John must literally be possessed of the devil and be a heretic. Only sinners and fools think him a holy, godly man; give way to his crying; and make room for the Lord, removing the obstacles from His way. The others, however, throw logs, stones, and dirt in His way; they even kill both the forerunner and the Lord Himself for daring to say such things to them. Why? John tells them to prepare the way of the Lord. That is to say, they do not have the Lord nor His way in them. What do they have then? Where the Lord is not, nor His way, there must be man's own way, the devil, and all that is evil. Judge, then, whether those holy, wise people are not justly angry at John, condemn his word, and finally slaughter both him and his Master! Should he be so bold as to consign such holy people over to the devil and label all their doings as false, wicked, and damnable, claiming that their ways are not the Lord's ways, that they must first of all prepare the Lord's ways, and that they have lived all their holy lives in vain?

26. Moreover, if he secretly wrote it on a tablet, they might perhaps have patience with that. But he gives voice to it; and not only a voice, but he cries it aloud; and not in a corner either, but openly under the sky, in the wilderness, before all the world; and publicly, before all people, he makes these saints

into sinners and a disgrace with all their doings, so that no one is deceived by their pretense. Thus they lose all the honor and profit which their holy life formerly brought them. That is not to be endured by such holy people, but for the sake of God and justice they must condemn that false doctrine, in order that the poor people may not be misled or the service of God corrupted; and for the love and service of God the Father, they will have to kill John and his Master.

27. This, then, is the preparation of Christ's way and John's proper office. He is to humble all the world and proclaim that they are all sinners—lost, damned, poor, needy, miserable people; that there is no life, work, or estate (however holy, beautiful, and good it may appear) that is not damnable unless Christ our Lord dwells therein, unless he works, walks, lives, is, and does everything through faith in Him; that they all need Christ and should desire to share His grace.

See, where it is preached that all people's work and life is nothing, that is the true voice of John in the wilderness and the pure and clear truth of Christian doctrine, as Paul says, "They are all sinners and lack the glory that they should have had toward God" (Romans 3 [:23]). This is truly humbling and cutting out and destroying overconfidence. That is truly to prepare the way of the Lord, to give room, and to make way.

28. Now here are found two kinds of people: some believe the crying of John and confess that it is true for them. These are the people to whom the Lord comes. In them His way is prepared and made ready, as Peter says that God "gives grace to the humble" (1 Peter 5 [:5]). The Lord Himself says, "Whoever humbles himself will be exalted" (Luke 18 [:14]). Here you must learn well and understand spiritually what the way of the Lord is, how it is prepared, and what prevents Him from finding room in us. The way of the Lord, as you have heard, is that He does all things within us, so that all our works are not ours but His, which happens by faith.

29. But the preparation does not consist in you making yourself worthy by praying, fasting, mortifying yourself, and your own works, as now all preaching during Advent foolishly urges. Rather, as has been said, it is a spiritual preparation, consisting in a thoroughgoing knowledge and confession of your being unfit, a sinner, poor, damned, and miserable, with all the works you can do. The more a heart is thus minded, the better it prepares the way of the Lord, even if meanwhile it drinks nothing but malmsey, walks on roses, and does not pray a word.

30. The hindrance, however, which does not give way for the Lord is not only the coarse, bodily sins of unchastity, wrath, haughtiness, avarice, etc., but rather also spiritual opinion and pharisaical pride, which thinks highly of its own good life and works, feels secure, does not itself condemn them,

and in addition refuses to let them be condemned. Such, then, is the other class of men, namely, those who do not believe John's voice but say it is of the devil, since it forbids good works and condemns the service of God. These are the people to whom most of all and most urgently it is said, "Prepare the way of the Lord," and who least of all accept it.

31. Therefore, John speaks to them with cutting words: "You brood of vipers! Who taught you to flee from the wrath to come? Bear fruits of repentance that are genuine" (Luke 3 [:7–8]). But, as said above, the more people are urged to prepare the Lord's way, the more they obstruct it and the more unreasonable they become. They will not be told that their doings are not the Lord's until they, to the glory and honor of God, destroy the truth and the word of John, with him and his Lord as well.

32. Now see whether it was not a great confession of John when he dared to open his mouth and freely say that he was not Christ, but a voice to which they did not like to listen, chiding the great teachers and leaders of the people because their doings are not right and not the Lord's. And as it went with John, so it still goes, from the beginning of the world to the end. For such proud holiness cannot hear that it must first prepare the way for the Lord, since it thinks it sits in God's lap and lets itself be flattered that it has long ago finished the way, before God even thought of seeking a way into them—those precious saints! The pope and his followers have also condemned John's voice: "Prepare the way of the Lord." In short, it is an intolerable voice—except to poor sinners and troubled consciences, in whose hearts it is pleasant.

33. But is it not a wrong and strange way of speaking when he says, "I am the voice of one crying"? How can a man be a voice? He ought to have said, "I am one crying with a voice"! But that is speaking according to the manner of the Scriptures. God told Moses: Aaron "shall be your mouth" (Exodus 4 [:16]); that is, he will speak for you. Job says, "I was an eye to the blind and a foot to the lame" (Job 29 [:15]). Similarly, we say in German about a miser that gold is his heart, and money is his life.

So here "I am the voice of one crying" means: "I am one who cries and have received my name from my work. Just as Aaron is called a mouth because of his eloquence, I am a voice because of my crying." And that which in Hebrew reads "the voice of one crying" would be translated into Latin and German as "a crying voice." In the same way, Paul speaks of "the poor of the saints" instead of "the poor saints" (Romans 15 [:26]), and of "the mystery of godliness" instead of "the godly mystery" (1 Timothy 3 [:16]). Just as when I say "the language of the Germans," I would say better "the German language." So here "a voice of one crying" means "a crying voice." The Hebrew tongue speaks this way much more.

*(Now they had been sent from the Pharisees.) They asked him: "Then why are you baptizing, if you are neither the Christ nor Elijah nor a prophet?" John answered them: "I baptize with water, but among you stands one you do not know, even He who comes after me, who was before Me, the strap of whose shoe I am not worthy to untie." [John 1:24–27]*

34. It seems as though the evangelist omits something in these words and that the complete words would be: "I baptize with water, but among you stands one who baptizes with fire," just as Luke has: "I baptize you with water, but He will baptize you with fire" (Luke 3 [:16]); and again: "John baptized with water, but you will be baptized with the Holy Spirit" (Acts 1 [:5]). But, though he here is silent about this other Baptism, he sufficiently indicates that there is to be another Baptism, since he speaks of another who is coming after him and who without a doubt will not baptize with water.

35. Now begins the second onset, whereby John was tempted on the left side. For since they could not move him with the enticement [of honor], they attack him with threats. And here their false humility breaks out and reveals that it is sheer pride. They would also have done that if John had followed them, after they had had enough of him. Therefore, learn here to be on your guard against men, particularly when they act friendly and gently; as Christ says: "Beware of men. Be wise as serpents and without falsehood like doves" (Matthew 10 [:17, 16]). That is to say: Do not trust those who are gentle, and do no evil to your enemies.

36. See, these Pharisees, who professed their willingness to accept John as the Christ, when things didn't happen as they desired, turn and censure John's Baptism. It is as if they would say: "Since you are not Christ nor Elijah nor a prophet, you should know that we are your superiors according to the Law of Moses, and you therefore must conduct yourself as our subordinate. You are not to act independently, without our command, knowledge, and permission. Who has given you the right to introduce something new among our people with your baptizing? You will get into trouble with your wickedness and disobedience."

37. John, however, just as he had despised their hypocrisy, so he despises their threats, remains firm, and confesses Christ as before. Moreover, he rudely attacks them and charges them with ignorance, saying, as it were: "I do not baptize with water because of your command, for nothing depends on that. There is another present from whom I have a command; you do not know Him, but He is more than enough for me. If you did know Him or wanted to know Him, you would not ask about my right to baptize, but you would come to be baptized yourselves. For He is so much greater that I am not worthy to untie the strap of His sandal."

38. John's words "He is the one who comes after me, who was before me," three times quoted by the evangelist in this chapter [John 1:15, 30], have been misinterpreted and obscured by some who referred them to Christ's divine and eternal birth, as though John meant to say that Christ had been born before him in eternity. But what is remarkable about the fact that He was born before John in eternity, since He was also born before the world and all things? Thus He was also to come not only after [John] but also after all things, since He is the first and the last (cf. Revelation 1 [:17]). Therefore, both His future and His past agree. But John's words are clear and simple and speak about Christ when He already was a man. The words "He will come after me" cannot be taken to mean that He would be born after him, since John at the time he spoke was about thirty years old, as also Christ was.

39. Thus the understanding is certainly that he is speaking these words about the preaching office, with the meaning: "I have come, that is, I have begun to preach, but I shall soon stop, and another will come and preach after me." Thus Luke writes that Christ began "from the Baptism of John" (Acts 1 [:22]) and "Jesus was thirty years of age when He began" (Luke 3 [:23]). "Are you the one who is to come" (Matthew 11 [:3]), that is, the one who will begin to preach? For Christ's ministry began first after His Baptism, when His Father glorified Him and testified about Him [cf. Matt. 3:17]. Even the New Testament and the time of grace did not begin at the birth of Christ, as He Himself says, "The time is fulfilled, and the kingdom of God has come" (Mark 1 [:15]). For if He had not begun to preach, His birth would have been of no use; but when He did begin to act and to teach, then also began all prophecies, all Scripture, a new light, and a new world.

40. So we have what he means by saying, "He will come after me." But it is not yet clear what the words mean: "He has been before me; He was before me," which they refer to His eternal birth. We maintain in all simplicity that those words were spoken about the preaching office, with the meaning: "Although He is not yet preaching, but is first coming after me, and I am preaching before Him, nevertheless He is already at hand, and so close by, that before I began to preach He has already been there and has been appointed to preach." The words "before me" therefore point to John's office, and not to his person. Thus: "He is before me, that is, before my preaching and Baptism, namely, for about thirty years; but He had not yet come and had not yet begun." John thereby indicates his office, that he is not a prophet foretelling the coming of Christ, but one who precedes Him who is already present, who is so near that He has already been in existence so many years before His beginning and coming.

41. Therefore, he also says, "Among you stands one you do not know." He means to say: "Do not let your eyes look into future times. He of whom the

prophets speak has been among you in the Jewish nation for about thirty years. Take care and do not miss Him. You do not know Him; therefore, I have come to point Him out to you." The words "among you stands one" are spoken after the manner of the Scriptures, which say: A prophet will arise or stand up. Jesus says, "False prophets shall arise" (Matthew 24 [:24]), or stand up or spring up. And God says, "I will raise up a prophet from among their brothers" (Deuteronomy 18 [:18]). John wants to show that this raising, rising up, standing up, and wakening was fulfilled in Christ. He has already come forward from among their brothers, as God had promised, and they did not know Him.

42. This, then, is the second office of John and of an evangelical preacher: that he not only makes all the world sinners, as we have heard above, but also gives comfort and shows how we may get rid of our sins. He does that by pointing to the one who is to come. Thus he points us to Christ, who is to redeem us from our sins when we receive Him in true faith. The first office says, "You are all sinners and lack the way of the Lord." When we believe this, the other office follows and says: "Look to and receive Christ. Believe in Him; He will free you of your sins." If we believe this, we have it. We will say more of this later.

> *These things took place in Bethabara[1] across the Jordan, where John was baptizing. [John 1:28]*

43. The evangelist John describes this testimony so carefully that he even mentions the place where it happened. The confession of Christ is greatly dependent on the testimony, and there are many offenses in the way. Undoubtedly, however, he wished to allude to some spiritual mystery of which we shall now speak.

## The Secret Meaning of This Gospel Reading

44. This is the sum of it: This Gospel reading depicts the preaching office of the New Testament, what it is, what it does, and what happens to it.

45. First, it is the voice of one calling, not a piece of writing. The Law and the Old Testament are dead writings, put into books, but the Gospel is to be a living voice. Therefore, John is a figure and an image and also an author, the first of all preachers of the Gospel. He writes nothing but calls out everything with his living voice.

46. Second, the Old Testament or the Law was preached among the tents at Mount Sinai to the Jews alone. But John's voice is heard in the wilderness, freely and openly, under the heavens, before all the world.

---

1 Luther's reading follows the *Textus Receptus*, which has "Bethabara" instead of "Bethany" (Desiderius Erasmus, ed., *Novum Instrumentum omne* [Basel: Johannes Froben, 1516], p. 193.

47. Third, it is a calling, clear, and loud voice, that is, one that speaks confidently and fearlessly and fears no one, neither death, hell, life, world, devil, men, honor, disgrace, or any creature. Thus Isaiah says: "A voice says, 'Preach!' And I said, 'What shall I preach?' All flesh is grass, and all its beauty is like the flower of the field. The grass withers, the flower fades, but the Word of our God will stand forever." Again: "Get you up to a high mountain, O Zion, preacher; lift up your voice with strength, O Jerusalem, preacher; lift it up, fear not" (Isaiah 40 [:6–9]). The world cannot endure the Gospel; therefore, there must be a strength which despises it and can cry out against it fearlessly.

48. Fourth, John's clothes are of camel's hair, and he has a leather belt (Matthew 3 [:4]). Although this signifies the strict and chaste life of preachers, it above all signifies the nature of the preaching or of the Gospel. It is a voice, but not embellished with soft clothes; it does not dissemble or flatter. It is a preaching about the cross—a hard, rough, sharp speech for the old man—and it girds the loins for spiritual and bodily chastity. This is taken from the life and words of the dead patriarchs, who like camels have borne the burden of the Law and of the cross. He ate wild birds [*sic*] and wild honey—not the wild birds of this land, but there were other animals in that land. This means those who receive the Gospel, namely, the humble sinners, who take the Gospel to themselves and in themselves.

49. Fifth, John is on the other side of the Jordan. "Jordan" means the Holy Scriptures, which have two sides. The left side is the bodily understanding, which the Jews have. John is not there, for that [understanding] does not produce sinners, but saints, arrogant about their works. The right side is the true spiritual understanding, which rejects and kills all works in order that faith alone may remain in all humility. The Gospel brings this [understanding], as Paul does when he says, "The Scripture concludes that they are all sinners" (Romans 3 [cf. Rom. 3:23; Gal. 3:22]).

50. Sixth, here begins the dispute between true and false preachers. The Pharisees cannot endure John's voice, they despise his teaching and Baptism and remain obdurate in their doings and teachings. But on account of the people they pretend to think highly of him. But because he does not want what they want, he must be possessed of the devil, and finally he must be beheaded by Herod.

So it is now, and so it has always been. No false teacher wants people to say that he preaches without or against the Gospel, but, on the contrary, that he thinks highly of it and believes in it. Nevertheless, he does violence to it, making it conform to his meaning. This the Gospel cannot permit, for it stands firm and never lies. Then [the Gospel] is reviled as heresy and error, as the doctrine of devils, until they do violence to it and forbid it and cut off its head so that it may nowhere be preached or heard. This was done by the pope in the case of John Hus.

51. Thus he is a truly Christian preacher who preaches nothing but that which John proclaimed, and firmly insists upon it. First, he must preach the Law so that the people may learn what great things God demands of us, which we cannot do because of the powerlessness of our nature which has been corrupted by Adam's fall, and thus baptize with the Jordan. The cold water means the teaching of the Law, which does not kindle love, but rather extinguishes it. For through the Law man learns how difficult and impossible the Law is. Then he becomes hostile to it, and his love for it cools; he feels that he hates the Law from the bottom of his heart. That is then a grievous sin, to be hostile to God's commands.

Then man must humble himself and confess that he is lost and that all his works are sins along with his whole life. Then John's Baptism has been accomplished, and he has been not only sprinkled but also baptized. Then he sees why John says, "Repent." He understands that John is right and that everyone must mend his ways, or repent. But Pharisees and those holy in their own works do not arrive at this understanding, nor do they permit themselves to be baptized. They think that they do not need repentance, and therefore John's words and Baptism are foolishness in their eyes.

52. Second, when the first teaching of the Law and Baptism are over, and man, humbled by the knowledge of himself, must despair of himself and his powers, then begins the second part of the teaching, in which John points the people away from himself to Christ and says, "Behold, the Lamb of God, who takes on Himself the sin of the world!" [John 1:29]. By this he means to say: "First, I have by my teaching made you all sinners, condemned all your works, and told you to despair of yourselves. But in order that you may not also despair of God, I will show you how to get rid of your sins—not that you can take off your sins or make yourselves godly through your works; another man is needed for this. I cannot do it, but I can point Him out. It is Jesus Christ, the Lamb of God. He—He, and no one else either in heaven or on earth—takes our sins on Himself. You yourself could not pay for the very smallest of sins. He alone must take on Himself not only your sins but also the sins of the world, and not just some sins of the world but all the sins of the world, be they great or small, many or few." This, then, is preaching and hearing the pure Gospel and recognizing the finger of John, who points out to you Christ, the Lamb of God.

53. Now, if you can believe that this voice of John is true, and if you can follow his finger and recognize the Lamb of God carrying your sin, then you have gained the victory, then you are a Christian, a master of sin, death, hell, and all things. Then your conscience will rejoice and become heartily fond

of this gentle Lamb of God. Then will you love, praise, and give thanks to our heavenly Father for this unfathomable wealth of His mercy, preached by John and given in Christ. You will become willing to do His divine will, as best you can, with all your strength. For what more comforting and delightful message can be heard than that our sins are not ours anymore, that they no more lie on us, but on the Lamb of God? How can sin condemn such an innocent Lamb? [Sin] must be vanquished and blotted out by Him, and likewise death and hell (the reward of sin) must also be vanquished. See what God our Father has given us in Christ!

54. Take care, therefore; take care, lest you presume to get rid of the smallest of your sins through your own merit before God, and lest you take the title away from Christ, the Lamb of God. John testifies and says, "Mend your ways, or repent." But he does not mean for us to mend our ways and to take off our sins by ourselves. He declares this powerfully by adding: "Behold, the Lamb of God, who takes away the sin of the world!" As we have said above, he means that each one is to know himself and his need for correction; yet he is not to look for this in himself, but in Jesus Christ alone.

Now may God our Father, according to His mercy, help us come to this knowledge of Christ, and may He send into the world the voice of John, with many evangelists! Amen.

# GOSPEL FOR CHRISTMAS DAY

*Luke 2:1–14*

*In those days a decree went out from Caesar Augustus that all the world should be registered. This was the first registration when Quirinius was governor of Syria. And all went to be registered, each to his own town. And Joseph also went up from Galilee, from the town of Nazareth, to Judea, to the city of David, which is called Bethlehem, because he was of the house and lineage of David, to be registered with Mary, his betrothed, who was with child. And while they were there, the time came for her to give birth. And she gave birth to her firstborn son and wrapped Him in swaddling cloths and laid Him in a manger, because there was no place for them in the inn. And in the same region there were shepherds out in the field, keeping watch over their flock by night. And an angel of the Lord appeared to them, and the glory of the Lord shone around them, and they were filled with great fear. And the angel said to them, "Fear not, for behold, I bring you good news of great joy that will be for all the people. For unto you is born this day in the city of David a Savior, who is Christ the Lord. And this will be a sign for you: you will find a baby wrapped in swaddling cloths and lying in a manger." And suddenly there was with the angel a multitude of the heavenly host praising God and saying, "Glory to God in the highest, and on earth peace among those with whom He is pleased!"*

## THE HISTORY

1. Haggai records God's words: "I will shake heaven and earth when He whom all nations desire shall come" (Haggai 2:7). This is fulfilled today, for the heavens were shaken; that is, the angels in the heavens sang praises to God. And the earth [was shaken], that is, the people on the earth, so that everyone had to get up and make a journey, one to this city, another to that, throughout the whole land, as the Gospel tells us [Luke 2:1–3]. It was not a violent, bloody uprising, but rather a peaceful one awakened by God, who is the God of peace.

It is not to be understood that all countries upon earth were so shaken, but only those under Roman rule. "All the world" signifies only the world of the Roman Empire, which had not even half of the whole world under it. However, no land was shaken so much as was the Jewish land, which had

90

been divided in an orderly way among the tribes of Israel, though at this time the land was inhabited mostly by the tribe of Judah, since the ten tribes led into Assyria never returned.

2. "This taxing," says Luke, "was the first" [Luke 2:2]; but we find in the Gospels and elsewhere that it continued always, that they even demanded tribute of Christ (Matthew 17 [:24]) and tested Him with the tax (Matthew 22 [:17]). On the day of His suffering, they accused Him of forbidding the payment of taxes [cf. Luke 23:2]. The Jews did not like to pay tribute and unwillingly endured this tax at the emperor's command, maintaining that they were God's people and free from Caesar. They had great disputes as to whether they were obliged to pay the tribute, but they had to and could not protect themselves against it even with force. For this reason they would have been pleased to drag Jesus into the discussion and bring Him into the power of the Romans. This taxing was therefore nothing else than a tax common in all lands, that every individual should annually pay a penny, and the officers who collected and stored away this and other tribute and taxes were called "publicans," which people translated incorrectly as "manifest sinners."

3. Observe how exact the evangelist is in his statement that the birth of Christ occurred in the time of Caesar Augustus and when Quirinius was governor[1] of the Roman Empire in the land of Syria. The Jewish land is a part of Syria, just as Austria is a part of the German land.[2] And this occurred during the very first taxing; this tribute was never before paid until just at the time when Christ was to be born. By this He shows that His kingdom was not to be worldly, nor would He rule over worldly power in a worldly way, but that He and His parents were subject to it. And because He comes at [the time of] the first taxing, He leaves no doubt about it, for if He had desired to leave it in doubt, He might have been born later, at another taxing, so that people would have to say that it was accidental and by chance, without any other deliberation.

4. If He had not wanted to be subject, He might have been born before that taxing. But all His works are precious teachings; therefore, He has things turn out so that by divine counsel and purpose He does not rule in a worldly way, but is subject. And that is the first blow against the pope's government and all he has, which fits with Christ's kingdom as night does with day.

5. This Gospel is so clear that it requires very little explanation, but it should be well considered, regarded, and taken deeply into the heart. No one will receive more benefit from it than those who keep quiet, banish everything, and diligently look into it. In the same way, the sun is seen reflected in

---

1 *Hauptmann*, literally, "captain." In his Bible translation, Luther used *Landpfleger* for "governor" in Luke 2:2 (WA DB 6:216–17).

2 I.e., part of the Holy Roman Empire.

calm water and gives warmth, but cannot be seen nor give warmth in water that is roaring and running.

Therefore, if you want to be enlightened and warmed, to see the divine grace and miracle, so that your heart is kindled, enlightened, devout, and joyful, then go where you are quiet and take this picture deep into your heart, and you will find miracle upon miracle. But to give the simple a start and a motive [to do so], we will illustrate it in part, and afterward may enter into it further.

6. First, see how plainly and simply things happen on earth, and yet how high they are regarded in heaven. On earth it happens this way: Here is a poor young woman, Mary of Nazareth, regarded as nothing at all and thought of as one of the least citizens of the city. No one is aware of the great miracle she carries; she is silent, keeps her own counsel, and regards herself as the least in the city. She starts out with her husband, Joseph; very likely they had no servant, so he is master and servant, and she is mistress and maid. They abandoned their home or entrusted it to others.

7. Now they may have had a donkey on which Mary sat, though the Gospel does not mention it, and it is probable that she went on foot with Joseph. Imagine how she was despised at the inns along the way, though she was worthy of being brought there in a golden carriage and all pomp.

How many wives and daughters of prominent men at that time lived in comfort and respect, while the mother of God takes a journey in midwinter on foot while pregnant! How unfairly things happen! Now it was more than a day's journey from Nazareth in Galilee to Bethlehem in the land of Judea. They had to journey either by or through Jerusalem, for Bethlehem is south of Jerusalem, while Nazareth is north.

8. The evangelist shows how, when they arrived at Bethlehem, they were the most insignificant and despised, so that they had to make room for others until they were shown to a stable, where they had to receive common lodging, common table, common bedroom and bed with the cattle, while many a wicked man sat at the head [of the table] in the inn and was honored as lord. No one noticed or recognized what God was doing in that stable. He lets the large houses and costly apartments remain empty, lets their inhabitants eat, drink, and be merry; but this comfort and treasure are hidden from them. Oh, what a dark night this was for Bethlehem, which was not conscious of that glorious light! See how God shows that He utterly disregards what the world is, has, or desires—and, furthermore, that the world shows how little it knows or notices what God is, has, and does.

9. See, this is the very first picture with which Christ puts the world to shame and shows us that all it does, knows, and is, is objectionable, that its greatest wisdom is foolishness, its best action is injustice, and its greatest

good is misfortune. What did Bethlehem have when it did not have Christ? What do they now have who at that time had enough? What do Mary and Joseph lack now, though at that time they had no room to sleep appropriately that night?

10. Some have commented on the word *diversorium* ["inn" (Luke 2:7)], as if it meant the archway over a street, through which everybody could pass, where some donkeys stood, and that Mary could not get to an inn. This is not right. The evangelist wants to show that Joseph and Mary had to withdraw to the stable, because there was no room in the inn and in the rooms where the guests generally lodged. All the guests in the inn were provided with room, food, and bed, except these poor people who had to creep into a stable out back where it was customary to house cattle.

This word *diversorium*, for which Luke has *katalyma*, means nothing else than a room for guests, which is proved by the words of Christ: He sent the disciples to prepare the [Last] Supper and said, "Tell the master of the house: 'The Teacher says to you, "Where is the guest room (*katalyma*) where I may eat the Passover with My disciples?"'" (Luke 22 [:11]). So also here Joseph and Mary had no room in the *katalyma*, the inn, but only in the stable in the landlord's backyard. That landlord was not worthy to shelter and honor such a guest. They had neither money nor power, so they had to stay in the stable. O world, how stupid you are! O man, how blind you are!

11. But the birth is still more pitiful. No one took pity on this young woman who was giving birth for the first time; no one took to heart her pregnancy; no one saw that in a strange place she had not the least thing necessary for a delivery. There she is, alone, without any preparation, without light, without fire, in the middle of the night, in the darkness. No one offered her any service as is customarily done for pregnant women. Everyone was dead drunk in the inn, a crowd of guests from all places; no one thinks of this poor woman. I think that she did not expect the birth so soon, or she would probably have remained at Nazareth.

12. Just imagine what kind of cloths they were in which she wrapped the child, possibly her veil or some article of her clothing she could spare. But that she should have wrapped Him in Joseph's trousers, which are exhibited at Aachen, appears entirely too false and frivolous. These are fables, of which there are many more in the world. Is it not at all inappropriate that Christ should be born in the cold of winter, in a strange land, in the open country, in such a despised and miserable way?

13. Some debate about how this birth took place, whether she was delivered of the child in prayer, in great joy, before she was aware of it, without any pain. I do not reject that opinion, possibly invented for the sake of the simple. But we must abide by the Gospel, which says that she gave birth to Him, and

by the Apostles' Creed, which says, "Born of the Virgin Mary."[3] There is no deception here, but, as the words read, a true birth.

14. It is well-known what is meant by giving birth and how it happens. It happened to her just like other women, with good reason and the assistance of her body parts, as happens at a birth, so that she is His natural mother and He is her natural Son. Therefore, her body did not lose its natural function in giving birth, except that she gave birth without sin, without shame, without pain, and without injury, just as she had also conceived without sin. The curse of Eve did not come on her, which reads: "In pain you shall bear children" [Gen. 3:16]; otherwise it happened to her the same as with every woman who gives birth.

15. Grace does not shatter or interfere with nature and its work, but rather improves and promotes it. Likewise, she also fed Him with milk from her breasts in the natural way; without a doubt it was not someone else's milk, nor did it come from another body part than the breasts. Nevertheless, God supernaturally filled them with milk without injury or impurity, as we sing of her: *ubere de coelo pleno* ["with breast full from heaven"]. I mention this that we may be grounded in the faith, and know that Christ was a natural man in every respect just as we, and not separate Him from our nature, except where it concerns sin and grace. In Him and in His mother nature was pure in all the members and in all the operations of those members. No female body or member ever performed its natural function without sin, except in this one virgin; here, once, God honored nature and its operations. We could not draw Christ so deeply into our nature and flesh [without] this being still more comforting for us. Therefore, we are not to take away from Him or from His mother anything that is not in conflict with grace, for the text clearly says that she gave birth to Him, and the angels said that He is born.

16. How could God have shown His goodness more than that He sank Himself so deeply into flesh and blood, that He did not even despise the natural privacy but honored nature most highly where Adam and Eve brought it most miserably into shame? From now on even that can be regarded as godly, honorable, and pure, which in all men is the most ungodly, shameful, and impure. These are real miracles of God, for in no way could He have given us stronger, more forcible, and purer pictures of chastity than in this birth. When we do no more than look at this birth, and reflect on how the sublime Majesty works with earnest and boundless love and goodness upon the flesh and blood of this virgin, we see how here all evil lust and every evil thought, no matter how strong they are, is banished.

17. No female can inspire such pure thoughts in a man as this virgin; nor can any male inspire such pure thought in a woman as this Child. When

---

3 That is, in the Second Article (Kolb-Wengert, p. 21; *Concordia*, p. 16).

we look at this birth and recognize the work of God in it, only modesty and purity flow from it.

18. But what happens in heaven concerning this birth? As much as it is despised on earth, so much and a thousand times more is it honored in heaven. If an angel from heaven came and praised you and your work, would you not regard it of greater value than all the praise and honor the world could give you and for which you would be willing to bear the greatest humility and contempt? What kind of honor is it when all the angels in heaven cannot restrain themselves from breaking out in rejoicing, so that even poor shepherds in the fields hear them preach, praise God, sing, and pour out their joy without measure? Were not all [other] joy and honor at Bethlehem— yes, that of all the kings and nobles on earth—nothing other than filth and abomination, of which no one likes to think, when compared with the joy and glory here displayed?

19. See how superabundantly God honors those who are despised by men, and that very gladly. Here you see that His eyes look into the depths of humility, as is written: "He is enthroned above the cherubim" [Ps. 99:1] and looks into the depths or the abyss [cf. Ps. 95:4]. The angels could find no princes or rulers, but only unlearned laymen, the most lowly people on earth. Could they not have addressed the high priests, the learned in Jerusalem, who knew so much about God and angels? No, the poor shepherds, who were nothing on earth, must be worthy to have such great grace and honor in heaven.

20. See how utterly God overthrows that which is high! And yet we rant and rage for nothing but this empty height, since we receive no honor in heaven; we continually step out of God's sight into the depths, so that He won't see us, but He alone looks there.

21. That's enough for the simple for the purpose of pondering. Let each one ponder it further for himself. If every word is properly grasped, it is as fire that sets the heart aglow, as God says, "My words are like fire" (Jeremiah 23 [:29]). And as we see, the divine Word is such that it teaches us to know God and His work, and to see that this life is nothing. For as He does not live according to this life and does not have goods, honor, and temporal power, He does not regard these things or speak of them, but teaches only the opposite. He works in a contradictory way, looks with favor on what the world turns away from, teaches that from which it flees, and takes up that which it leaves behind.

22. And though we do not gladly endure such acts of God and do not want to receive good things, honor, and life in this way, yet it must be so, for nothing different will happen. God teaches and acts no differently. We must turn to Him; He will not turn to us. Whoever does not regard His Word, His

work, or His comfort has assuredly no good evidence of being saved. In what more delightful way could He have shown how gracious He is to the obscure and despised on earth than through this poor birth, over which the angels rejoice and make it known to no one but to the poor shepherds?

23. Let us now look at the mysteries or secret things set before us in this history. In all the mysteries two things are especially set forth: the Gospel and faith, that is, what is to be preached and what is to be believed, who are to be the preachers and who are to be the hearers. This we will now consider.

## THE TEACHING ABOUT FAITH

24. The first is faith, and it is right that we recognize it as the first in all the words of God. It is of no value only to believe that this history is true as it reads; for all sinners, even the condemned, believe that. Scripture and God's Word do not teach that faith is a natural work without grace. Rather, the right and gracious faith which God's Word and work demands is that you firmly believe that Christ is born for you, and that this birth is yours and occurred for your benefit. The Gospel teaches that Christ was born because of us, and that He did and suffered everything because of us, as the angel says: "I proclaim to you great joy that will be for all the people. For unto you is born this day in the city of David the Savior, who is Christ the Lord" [Luke 2:10–11]. In these words you clearly see that He is born for us.

25. He does not simply say, "Christ is born," but "Unto you, to you He is born." Likewise, he does not say, "I bring joy," but "To you, to you I bring good news of great joy." Likewise, this joy does not remain in Christ but is for all the people. No condemned or wicked man has, or can have, this faith. For that is the true basis of all salvation; it unites Christ and the believing heart, so that all they have on both sides is held in common. But what do they have?

26. Christ has a pure, innocent, and holy birth. Man has an impure, sinful, condemned birth; as David says, "Behold, I was begotten from sinful seed, and in sin did my mother conceive me" (Psalm 51 [:5]). Nothing can help this except the pure birth of Christ. Thus Christ's birth cannot be distributed in a bodily way nor would that help; therefore, it is distributed spiritually through the Word to everyone, as the angel says that it is given to all who firmly believe so that no harm will come to them because of their impure birth. That is the way and manner to become pure from our miserable birth from Adam. For this purpose Christ wanted to be born, that through Him we might be born in a different way, as He says in John 3 [:3]. This takes place through faith; as James says, "He willingly gave us birth by the Word of truth, that we should begin to be His new creatures" (James 1 [:18]).

27. See, in this way Christ takes our birth away from us and absorbs it into His birth, and gives us His, that in it we might become pure and new, as

if it were our own, so that every Christian may rejoice and glory in Christ's birth as if he also, like Christ, had been born bodily of Mary. Whoever does not believe this, or doubts it, is no Christian.

28. That is the great joy of which the angel speaks. This is the comfort and exceeding goodness of God that, if a man believes this, he can boast of the treasure that Mary is his true mother, Christ his Brother, and God his Father. For all these things are true and happen when we believe. This is the principal thing and the principal treasure in every Gospel, before any doctrine of good works can be taken out of it. Christ must above all things become our own, and we become His, before we can take hold of works.

But this cannot occur except through the faith that teaches us rightly to understand the Gospel and properly to lay hold of it. This is knowing Christ correctly, so that the conscience is happy, free, and satisfied. Out of this grow love and praise to God, who in Christ has given us such superabundant gifts free of charge. This gives courage to do, avoid, and suffer everything as is well pleasing to God, whether in life or in death, as I have often said. This is what Isaiah means: "To us a Child is born, and to us a Son is given" (Isaiah 9 [:6])—to us, to us, to us is born, and to us is given.

29. Therefore, see to it that you do not find pleasure in the Gospel only as a history, for that does not last long; also not only as an example, for that does not stick without faith. But see to it that you make this birth your own and trade places, so that you are freed from your birth and receive His. This happens when you believe. So sit in the lap of the Virgin Mary and be her dear child. But you must exercise this faith and ask for it, because while you live you cannot establish it too firmly. This is our foundation and inheritance, on which good works must be built.

30. If Christ has now thus become your own, and you have by such faith become pure through Him and have received your inheritance without any personal merit, only through the love of God who gives to you as your own the blessing and work of His Son, then the example of good works follows, that you will also do for your neighbor as you have seen that Christ has done for you. Here good works are their own teacher. What are the good works of Christ? Is it not true that they are good because they have been done for your benefit, for God's sake, who commanded Him to do the works on your behalf? In this, then, Christ was obedient to the Father, in that He loved and served us.

31. Therefore, since you have received enough and have become rich, you have no other commandment in which to serve and be obedient to Christ than so to direct your works that they may be good and useful for your neighbor, just as the works of Christ are good and useful for you. For that reason He said at the Last Supper: "A new commandment I give to you,

that you love one another just as I have loved you" [John 13:34]. Here you see that He loved us and did everything for us in order that we may do the same, not for Him—for He does not need it—but for our neighbor. This is His commandment, and this is our obedience. Therefore, faith makes Christ ours, and His love makes us His. He loves, we believe, thus we are united into one cake. Again, our neighbor believes and expects our love; we are therefore to love him also and not let him want and expect it in vain. One is the same as the other: as Christ helps us, so we help our neighbor, and all have enough.

32. From this you can note how far those who have bound good works to stone, wood, clothing, eating, and drinking have gone out of the way. What would it help your neighbor if you could build a church entirely out of gold? What help to him is the ringing of many large bells? What help to him is the great glittering appearance of the churches, Mass vestments, relics, silver pictures and vessels? What help to him are the burning of many candles and incense? What help to him is the noise, muttering, and singing of vigils and Masses? Do you think that God will let Himself be bought off with the ringing of bells, the smoke of candles, the glitter of gold, and such nonsense? He has commanded none of these. But if you see your neighbor going astray, sinning, or suffering in body, property, or soul, there, there you are to rush in, leave everything else, and help him with all you are and have. If you can do nothing else, then help him with words and gestures. Thus has Christ done to you and given you an example for you to follow.

33. See, these are the two things that a Christian is to practice. The one is toward Christ, that he draws Him into himself and through faith he makes Him his own, clothes himself in Christ's blessings, and boldly builds on them. The second is toward his neighbor, that he lowers himself [to serve] him and lets him rule over his possessions as he rules over the possessions of Christ. He who does not practice these two things will not be helped even if he fasts to death, tortures himself or lets himself be burned, and does all miracles, as St. Paul teaches (1 Corinthians 13 [:1–13]).

## The Secret Meaning
## of the Doctrine of This Gospel Reading

34. The other mystery, or secret teaching, is that in the church nothing more than the Gospel should be preached. Now the Gospel teaches nothing more than the two previous things: Christ and His example; and two kinds of good works, the one belonging to Christ by which we are saved through faith, the other belonging to us by which our neighbor receives help. Whoever teaches anything other than the Gospel leads people astray; and whoever does not teach the Gospel according to these two parts leads people all the more astray and is worse than the one who doesn't teach the Gospel, because

he desecrates and cheats with God's Word, as St. Paul complains about some [2 Cor. 2:17].

35. Now nature could not have discovered such a doctrine, nor could all human ingenuity, reason, and wisdom have devised it. Who would fathom from himself that faith in Christ makes us one with Christ and gives us for our own all of Christ's blessings? Who would devise that no works are good except those done for our neighbor or instituted for him? Nature teaches no more than to act according to the letter of the Law. Therefore, it falls back upon its own works, such as monasteries, fasting, clothing, pilgrimages; one in this way, another in another way thinks he is fulfilling the commandment, and yet they are nothing more than self-chosen, useless works by which no one is helped. Now unfortunately the whole world is blinded and is going astray through the doctrines and works of men, so that faith and love along with the Gospel have perished.

36. Therefore, the Gospel properly understood is a completely super-natural preaching and light that points only to Christ. This is signified first by the fact that it was not a man who made it known to others, but an angel came down from heaven and made the birth of Christ known to the shepherds; no human being knew anything about it.

37. Second, it is signified by the fact that Christ was born at midnight, by which he indicates that all the world is in darkness as to its future and that Christ cannot be known by mere reason, but He must be revealed from heaven.

38. Third, it is signified by the light that shone around the shepherds, which teaches that here there must be an entirely different light than all reason is. And St. Luke here says "glory of God" [Luke 2:9]—that is, the brightness of God—shone around them; he calls that light a brightness or the glory of God. Why does he say that? [He says that] to point to the mystery and to show the nature of the Gospel. For while the Gospel is a heavenly light that teaches nothing more than Christ, in whom God's grace is given to us and what we do is entirely rejected, it exalts only the glory of God, so that henceforth no one may be able to boast of his own power but must give God the glory. It is of His love and goodness alone that we are saved through Christ.

See, the divine honor and the divine glory is the light in the Gospel which shines around us from heaven through the apostles and their succes-sors, who preach the Gospel. The angel was in the place of all the preachers of the Gospel, and the shepherds in the place of all the hearers, as we shall see. For this reason the Gospel can tolerate no other teaching besides its own. For the teaching of men is earthly light and human brightness—it exalts the honor and praise of men, and makes arrogant souls [who trust] in their own works—while the Gospel teaches [us] to dare to praise and rely on Christ, on God's grace and goodness.

39. Likewise, fourth, this is signified by the names "Judea" and "Bethlehem," where Christ chose to be born. "Judea" in German means "confession" or "thanksgiving"—as when we confess, praise, and thank God that all we possess are His gifts. One who so confesses and praises is called *Judaeus* ["Jew"]. Such a king of the Jews is Christ, as the expression is: *Iesus Nazarenus Rex Iudaeorum* ["Jesus of Nazareth, King of the Jews"].[4] So in German we say of someone who is thankful or unthankful that "he acknowledges it" or "he doesn't acknowledge it." This shows that no teaching can make such a confession except the Gospel, which teaches Christ.

40. Likewise, *beth* means "house"; *lehem* means "food" or "bread"; and *Bethlehem* means "a house of bread." The city had that name because it was situated in a good, fruitful country, abounding in grain, so that it was the granary for the neighboring towns. We call such a city a "breadbasket."[5] Formerly it was called "Ephrata," which means "fruitful." Both names had the same cause, that it had fruitful and abundant soil. This signifies that without the Gospel this earth is a wilderness, and there is no confession of God nor thanksgiving.

41. But where the Gospel and Christ are, there is the Bethlehem abounding in grain and the thankful Judea. There everyone has enough in Christ, and there is thanksgiving for divine grace. But human doctrines thank themselves and leave a barren land and deadly hunger. No heart is satisfied unless it hears Christ rightly proclaimed in the Gospel. The heart comes to Bethlehem and finds Him; it also comes and remains in Judea and thanks its God eternally. Here he is satisfied; here God receives His praise and confession. Apart from the Gospel there is nothing but thanklessness, and we would have nothing but starvation.

42. But with his words the angel shows the Gospel most clearly and that nothing else is to be preached in Christendom. He takes on himself the office and words that conform to the Gospel and says, *Evangelizo*. He does not say, "I preach to you," but: "I speak a gospel to you"; "I am an evangelist; my word is a Gospel." Thus the word "Gospel" (as said above during Advent) means a good, joyful message which is to be preached in the New Testament. How does the Gospel read? Listen, he says: "I bring you good news of great joy," "My Gospel speaks of great joy." Where is it? Hear again: "For unto you is born this day in the city of David the Savior, who is Christ the Lord" [Luke 2:11].

43. See here what the Gospel is, namely, a joyful preaching concerning Christ, our Savior. Whoever preaches Him rightly preaches the Gospel and

4 The inscription on the cross, commonly abbreviated INRI, is found most fully in John 19:19.

5 *Schmalzgrube*, literally, a "larder," but used figuratively for a rich, fertile region.

pure joy. How can a heart hear of greater joy than that Christ is given to him as his own? He not only says that Christ is born, but he also makes His birth our own by saying "your Savior."

44. Therefore, the Gospel not only teaches the history of Christ but also makes Him our own and gives Him to all who believe it, which is the true and proper nature of the Gospel (as was said above). What would it help me if Christ had been born a thousand times, and it were sung daily in a most lovely manner, if I were never to hear that He was born for me and was to be my very own? If the voice gives a sound, no matter how furtive and bad it may sound, my heart listens with joy, for it penetrates and sounds sincere. If now there were anything else to be preached, the evangelical angel and the angelic evangelist would have touched on it.

## THE MEANING OF THE SIGNS

45. The angel says further: "This will be a sign to you: you will find the child swaddled and laid in a manger" [Luke 2:12]. The cloths are nothing other than the Holy Scriptures, in which the Christian truth lies wrapped, in which faith is described. For the entire Old Testament contains nothing else than Christ as He is preached in the Gospel. Therefore, we see how the apostles appeal to the testimony of the Scriptures and with them prove all that is to be preached and believed about Christ. Thus Paul says that the faith of Christ through which we become righteous is witnessed by the Law and the prophets (cf. Romans 3 [:21]). And Christ Himself, after His resurrection, opened to them the Scriptures and showed how they speak of Him [Luke 24:27].

Likewise, when He was transfigured on Mount Tabor, the two, Moses and Elijah, stood with Him (cf. Matthew 17 [:3])—that is, the Law and the prophets as His two witnesses are signs pointing to Him. Therefore, the angel correctly says that the sign by which they can know Him is the cloths, for there is no other testimony on earth concerning Christian truth than the Holy Scriptures.

46. Accordingly, Christ's undivided tunic, which during His suffering was distributed and gambled away [John 19:23–24], signifies the Scriptures of the New Testament. That signifies how the pope, the Antichrist, would not deny the Gospel, but would mutilate it and play tricks with it by means of false glosses, until Christ is no longer to be found in it. Then the four soldiers who crucified the Lord are figures of all the bishops and teachers in the four quarters of the earth who mutilate the Gospel and kill Christ and His faith by means of their human teachings, as the pope with his Papists have long since done.

47. Thus we see that the Law and the prophets cannot be rightly preached and known unless we see Christ wrapped up in them. It is true that Christ does not seem to be in them, nor do the Jews find Him there. They are insignificant, unimportant cloths, mere words, which seem to speak of unimportant external matters, which could not be understood by themselves; but the New Testament, the Gospel, must point out, open, and enlighten them, as has been said.

48. First, the Gospel must be heard, and the appearance and the voice of the angel must be believed. If the shepherds had not heard from the angel that Christ lay there, they might have seen Him a thousand times and again a thousand times without ever knowing that the child was Christ. Thus St. Paul says that the Law remains dark and veiled for the Jews until they are converted to Christ (cf. 2 Corinthians 3 [:15–16]).

Christ must first be heard in the Gospel. Then it will be seen how the whole Old Testament is in such delightful harmony with Him, so that one must acknowledge being captive in faith and aware of how true Christ's saying is: "Moses wrote of Me; if you believed him, you would believe Me" (John 5 [:46]).

49. Therefore, let us beware of all teaching that does not teach Christ. What more do you want to know? What more do you need, if indeed you know Christ—as said above, if you walk through Him in faith toward God and in love toward your neighbor, and do to your neighbor as He has done to you? This is indeed the whole Scripture in its briefest form, so that no more words or books are necessary, but only to live and act in that way.

50. He lies in the manger. See that you are certain that nothing but Christ is to be preached in all the world. What is the manger but the gathering of the Christian people in the church for the sermon? We are the animals at this manger, where Christ is served to us, on whom we are to feed our souls; that is going to the sermon. Whoever goes to hear the sermon goes to this manger, but it must be a sermon about Christ! Not all mangers have Christ, nor do all sermons teach faith. There was only one manger in Bethlehem in which this treasure lay, and beside it there was an empty and despised manger in which there was no fodder.

Therefore, the preaching of the Gospel is empty of all other things; it has and teaches nothing besides Christ. But if it does teach something else, then it is not Christ's manger, but the manger of war horses full of temporal things and of fodder for the body.

51. But so that we may see how Christ in cloths represents faith in the Old Testament, we will here give several examples. We read that when Christ cleansed the leper, He said to him: "Go, show yourself to the priest and offer the sacrifice that Moses commanded, for a testimony to them" (Matthew

8 [:4]). Here you hear that the Law of Moses was given to the Jews for a proof, or sign, as the angel also here says, namely, that such Law represents something different from itself. What? Christ is the priest; all men are spiritual lepers because of unbelief. But when we believe in Him, He touches us with His hand, gives and lays on us His work, and we become clean and whole without any merit of our own. So we are to act toward Him, that is, be thankful and confess that we have become godly not by our works, but through His grace. Then our course will be right before God. In addition we are to offer our gift, that is, give of our own to help our neighbor, to do good to him as Christ has done to us. Thus Christ is served and an offering is brought to the true Priest, for it is done for His sake, in order to love and praise Him.

Do you here see how Christ and faith are wrapped up in the plain Scriptures and this figure? So you grasp that Moses in the Law gave only proof and application to Christ. The whole Old Testament should be understood in this way, and these cloths should be taken as signs pointing out and making Christ known.

52. Likewise, the fact that the Sabbath was so strictly commanded and no work was to be done on it shows that not our works but Christ's works are to be in us; for, as was said, we are saved not by our works but by the works of Christ. Now these works of Christ are twofold, as shown before. The first is what Christ has done personally without us, which are the most important and in which we believe. The second is what He works in us in love toward our neighbor. The first may be called the evening works and the second the morning works, so that evening and morning make one day, as it is written in Genesis 1 [:5], for the Scriptures begin the day in the evening and end it in the morning; that is, the evening with the night is the first half, the morning with the day is the second half of the whole natural day. Now as the first half is dark and the second half is light, so the first works of Christ are concealed in our faith, but the second, the love, are to appear in the day and be shown openly toward our neighbor. Thus the whole Sabbath is observed and sanctified.

53. Do you see how beautifully Christ lies in these cloths? How beautifully the Old Testament reveals the faith and love in Christ and His Christians? Now, swaddling clothes are commonly of two layers: the outside is coarse woolen cloth; the inside is more delicate linen. The coarse outer woolen cloth is the illustrations we are making from the Law, but the linen is the words of the prophets without illustrations. For example: "Behold, a virgin is pregnant and shall bear a Son, and shall call His name Immanuel" (Isaiah 7 [:14]), and similar passages which would not be understood of Christ if the Gospel had not pointed them out and shown Christ in them.

54. Thus we have pointed out that these two—faith and the Gospel—and nothing else is to be preached in Christendom. Let us now see who are to be the preachers and who, the learners. The preachers are to be angels, that is, God's messengers, who are to lead a heavenly life, are to be constantly engaged with God's Word so that they never preach the doctrine of men. It is a very inappropriate thing to be God's messenger and not to deliver His message. "Angel" means "messenger," and Luke calls him "the angel of the Lord," "God's messenger" [Luke 2:9]. More depends on his message than on his life. If he leads a wicked life, he injures himself, but if he brings a false message in the place of God's message, he leads astray and injures everyone who hears him, and causes idolatry among the people in that they accept lies instead of the truth, honor men instead of God, and worship the devil in place of God.

55. There is no more terrible affliction, misery, and misfortune on earth than a preacher who does not preach God's Word. Unfortunately, the world is now full of such [preachers], and they think they do well and are godly, and yet their whole work is nothing but murdering souls, blaspheming God, and setting up idolatry. It would be much better for them if they were robbers, murderers, and the worst scoundrels, for then they would know that they are doing evil. But now they go along under the name and pretense of beings priests, bishops, Papists, and clergy, and yet are ravenous wolves in sheep's clothing. It would be good if no one ever heard their preaching.

56. The learners are shepherds, poor people out in the fields. Here Christ keeps what He says: "The poor have the Gospel preached to them" (Matthew 11 [:5]) and "Blessed are the poor, for theirs is the kingdom of heaven" (Matthew 5 [:3]). Here are no learned, no rich, no mighty ones, for such people do not receive the Gospel. The Gospel is a heavenly treasure, which will not tolerate any other treasure and will not share the heart with an earthly guest. Therefore, whoever loves the one must let the other go, as Christ says, "You cannot serve both God and mammon" (Matthew 6 [:24]).

This is shown by the shepherds in that they were in the field under heaven and not in houses, and did not hold fast and cling to temporal goods. And besides, they are in the fields at night, despised by and unknown to the world, which sleeps in the night and by day gladly walks about and is seen; but the poor shepherds go about their work at night. They represent all the obscure who lead a poor, despised, and insignificant life on earth, and dwell only under the heavens in God's power; they are able to grasp the Gospel.

57. The fact that they were "shepherds" signifies that no one is to hear the Gospel for himself alone, but everyone is to tell it to others who do not know it. For he who believes for himself has enough and should endeavor to bring

others to such faith and knowledge, so that one may be a shepherd of the other, feed him, and wait on him in this world, during the night of this life.

At first the angel frightened the shepherds; for human nature is shocked when it first hears in the Gospel that all our works are nothing and are condemned before God, for it does not easily give up its opinions and arrogance.

58. Now each one should compare himself to the Gospel and see how close or far he is from Christ, and what is the character of his faith and love. There are many who are enkindled with dreamy devotion when they hear of this poverty of Christ; are almost angry with the citizens of Bethlehem, denounce their blindness and ingratitude; and think, if they had been there, they would have served the Lord and His mother and would not have let them be so miserable. But they do not look next door to see how many of their neighbors need their help, whom they ignore and leave as they are. Who is there on earth who has no poor, miserable, sick, erring, or sinful people around him? Why does he not exercise his love to them? Why does he not do for them as Christ has done for him?

59. It is untrue and false to think that you would have done much good for Christ, if you do nothing for them. If you had been at Bethlehem, you would have paid as little attention to Him as the others did. Because it has now been made known who Christ is, you want to serve Him. If He now came and laid Himself in a manger and told who He is, the one about whom you now know so much, you might do something. But previously you would not have done it. If the rich man in the Gospel had been told how great poor Lazarus would be in the future, so that he would be certain about it, he would not have let him lie there and perish [Luke 16:19–28].

60. Thus if your neighbor were now what he shall be in the future, and lay before you, you would surely wait on him. But now, since it is not so, you pay no attention to him and do not recognize your Lord in your neighbor; you do not do for him as He has done for you. Therefore, God permits you to be blinded, deceived by the pope and false preachers, so that you squander on wood, stone, paper, and wax that with which you might help your neighbor.

## EXPLANATION OF THE ANGELS' SONG

61. Finally, we must also discuss the angels' song, which we use daily in the Mass: "Glory to God in the highest" [Luke 2:14]. There are three parts in this song: the glory, the peace, and the pleasure or goodwill. They give glory to God, peace to the earth, and pleasure to people. The goodwill or pleasure might be understood as the divine goodwill and pleasure which He has toward men through Christ. But we will let it remain as the goodwill which people have from this birth, as the words read: *anthropis eudokia*, "goodwill to men" [Luke 2:14].

62. The first is the glory of God. We ought to begin here, so that in all things the praise and glory is given to God as the one who does, gives, and has all things, so that no one ascribes anything to himself or claims any merit for himself. For the glory belongs to no one but to God alone, who does not share or make it common with anyone.

63. Adam stole the glory through the evil spirit and appropriated it to himself, so that all men with him have come into disgrace, which evil is rooted in all mankind so deeply that there is no vice so deep in them as ambition. No one wants to be nothing; everyone is pleased with himself. From this comes all distress, strife, and war on earth.

64. Christ has brought back the glory to God in that He has taught us that all we do is nothing but wrath and displeasure before God, so that we may not be boastful and self-satisfied, but rather be filled with fear and shame in the greatest danger and shame, so that our glory and self-satisfaction may be crushed and become nothing, and we may be glad to be rid of it, in order that we may be found and preserved in Christ, as has been said.

65. The second is peace on earth. For just as strife must exist where God's glory is not found—as Solomon says, "Among the insolent is always strife" (Proverbs 13 [:10])—so also where God's glory is there must be peace. Why should they quarrel when they know that nothing is their own but that all they are, have, and can desire is from God? They let Him be in charge and are content that they have a gracious God. He knows that all he does is nothing before God, does not think very much of what he does, but thinks about another who is something before God, namely, Christ.

66. From this it follows that where there are true Christians, there is no dispute, quarreling, or strife among them. As Isaiah proclaims: "They shall not kill or harm one another on My holy mountain" (that is, in Christendom); and the reason follows: "For the land is full of the knowledge of the Lord" (Isaiah 11 [:9]). That is, since they know that all belongs to God and what we do is nothing, they can certainly have peace among themselves. Isaiah also says: "They shall beat their swords into plowshares, and their spears into pruning hooks; for no nation shall lift up sword against another nation, and they shall not learn war anymore" (Isaiah 2 [:4]).

67. Therefore, our Lord Christ is called a King of peace and is signified by King Solomon, whose name in German is Friedreich ["rich in peace"], so that He makes peace inwardly toward God in our conscience built through faith on Him and outwardly toward people in our bodily life through love, so that through Him there may everywhere be peace on earth.

68. The third is the goodwill of men. Here is meant not the goodwill that does good works, but the pleasure and peace of heart that is pleased with anything that happens, whether good or bad. The angels knew very well that

the peace of which they sang does not extend farther than to those who truly believe in Christ; such certainly have peace among themselves. But the world and the devil have no rest. They also let them have no peace, but persecute them to death, as Christ says: "In Me you have peace. In the world you have fear" ([cf.] John 16 [:33]).

69. Therefore, it was not enough for the angels to sing of peace on earth, but also [they sang] about pleasure of men, that is, that they take pleasure in everything, praise and thank God, regard all God's dealing with them as proper and good, do not murmur, but willingly remain under God's will. Because they know that God, whom they have received by faith in Christ as a gracious Father, does and works all things, so they exult and rejoice even under persecution, as St. Paul says, "We boast even of our sufferings" (Romans 5 [:3]). They regard all that happens to them as for the best, out of the abundance of the happy conscience they have in Christ.

70. See, such a goodwill, pleasure, good opinion in all things good or bad is what the angels mean in their song; for where there is no goodwill, peace will not long remain. He [who does not have it] puts the worst construction on everything, always magnifies the evil and doubles every mishap. Therefore, God's dealings with them do not please them; they want something different, and then it happens as the psalmist writes: "With the holy You are holy; with the blameless man You are blameless; with the pure You are pure" (that is, whoever has this pleasure in all things, You cause him to be pleasing to You and to all); "and with the crooked You are crooked" (Psalm 18 [:25–26]). That is, whoever is not pleased with all You do and work is not pleasing to You and to all that is Yours either.

71. Concerning the goodwill, St. Paul says: "Try to please everyone, just as I please everyone" (1 Corinthians 10 [:33]). How does that happen? If you let all things be good and pleasing to you, then you will in turn please everyone. It is a short rule: If you want to please no one, be pleased with no one; if you want to please everyone, be pleased with everyone—yet only so long as you do not abandon God's Word, for in that case all pleasing and displeasing ceases. But what may be given up without giving up God's Word may be given up, so that you may please everyone and let it seem good to you before God, and then you have this goodwill of which the angels sing.

72. We can learn from this song what kind of creatures the angels are. Do not consider what the natural philosophers dream about them. Here they have all been painted in such a way that they could not be painted better, such that even their heart and thoughts may be known. First, when they sing glory to God with joy, they show how full of light and fire they are, recognizing that all things belong to God alone and giving themselves nothing, so that they passionately give the glory only to Him to whom it belongs. Therefore,

if you want to think of a humble, pure, obedient, and joyful heart praising God, think of the angels. This is their first step, that by which they serve God.

73. The second is their love to us, just as above we were taught to do. Here you see what great and gracious friends we have in them, that they favor us no less than themselves; they rejoice in our salvation almost as if it were their own [cf. Luke 15:10], so that in this song they give us a comforting inducement to wish the best for them as for the best of friends. See, in this way you rightly understand the angels, not according to their substance, as the natural philosophers fruitlessly deal with them, but according to their inner heart, spirit, and mind, so that I don't know what they are, but rather what their chief desire and constant work is. By this you look into their heart. This is enough concerning this Gospel. What is signified by Mary, Joseph, and Nazareth will be explained in the Gospel from Luke 1.

## THE ARMOR OF THIS GOSPEL READING

74. This Gospel reading is the foundation for the words of the Apostles' Creed: "I believe in Jesus Christ, born of the Virgin Mary."[6] The same article is founded on more passages of Scripture, yet on none so clearly and abundantly as on this one. St. Mark says no more than that Christ has a mother; the same is also the case with St. John; neither say anything about the birth. St. Matthew says He is born of Mary in Bethlehem, but lets it remain at that, except that he gloriously preaches the virginity of Mary, as we will hear at its time. But Luke describes it clearly and diligently.

75. It was also proclaimed formerly by the patriarchs and prophets—as when God says to Abraham: "In your Seed shall all the nations of the earth be blessed" (Genesis 22 [:18]). Again He says to David: "The Lord swore to David a sure oath from which He will not turn back: 'From the fruit of your body I set a King on your throne'" (Psalm 132 [:11] and 89 [:4]). But those are obscure words compared with this Gospel.

76. Likewise, it is also signified in many figures, as in the almond staff of Aaron which bloomed in a supernatural manner, though a dry piece of wood (cf. Numbers 17 [:8]). So also Mary, apart from any natural and fleshly blood relation, power, and work, brought forth, in a supernatural manner, a true and natural Son from a natural mother, just as the staff bore natural almonds and remained a natural staff. Likewise, [her virginity is signified] by Gideon's fleece, which was damp from the dew of heaven, while the ground around it remained dry (Judges 6 [:37]), and many like figures which it is unnecessary now to enumerate. These figures do not conflict with faith, but rather they

6 In the Second Article of the Apostles' Creed (Kolb-Wengert, p. 21; Concordia, p. 16).

adorn it; for faith must first be believed and founded before I believe that the figure serves it.

77. Much depends on this article; in time of temptation let us not allow ourselves to be deprived of it, for the evil spirit attacks nothing so severely as our faith. Therefore, we must be equipped and know where in God's Word this faith is set forth; in time of temptation we point to that, and [the temptation] is already weak, for [the evil spirit] cannot stand against God's Word.

78. There are also many ethical teachings in this Gospel, such as humility, patience, poverty, and the like; but these are touched on enough and are not points of controversy, for they are fruits of faith and good works.

# GOSPEL FOR THE SECOND DAY OF CHRISTMAS

*Luke 2:15–20*

*When the angels went away from them into heaven, the shepherds said to one another, "Let us go over to Bethlehem and see this thing that has happened, which the Lord has made known to us." And they went with haste and found Mary and Joseph, and the baby lying in a manger. And when they saw it, they made known the saying that had been told them concerning this child. And all who heard it wondered at what the shepherds told them. But Mary treasured up all these things, pondering them in her heart. And the shepherds returned, glorifying and praising God for all they had heard and seen, as it had been told them.*

1. This Gospel reading is easily understood from the previous one,[1] for it shows an example and fulfillment of the doctrine given in the previous Gospel; that is, the shepherds did and found things, just as the angels had told them. Consequently, this Gospel teaches what the results and fruit of the Word of God are, and what the signs are by which we know whether the Word of God clings to us and works in us.

2. The first and chief point is faith. For if these shepherds had not believed the angel, they would not have gone to Bethlehem; in fact, they would have done none of the things reported of them in this Gospel.

3. Someone, however, might say, "Yes, I would certainly believe if an angel from heaven told me so." But that is saying nothing. Whoever does not receive the Word in itself will never receive it for the sake of the preacher, even if all the angels preached it to him. And whoever receives it because of the preacher does not believe in the Word, nor does he believe in God through the Word, but he believes the preacher and in the preacher. Therefore, his faith does not last long.

But whoever believes the Word does not care who the person is that speaks the Word and does not honor the Word for the sake of the person. On the contrary, he honors the person for the sake of the Word and always subordinates the person to the Word. And if the person perishes, or even falls from his faith and preaches differently, then he abandons the person before

---

1  See sermon for Christmas Day on Luke 2:1–14.

the Word. He remains with what he has heard, even if the person comes or goes, however he might.

4. That is also the correct distinction between divine faith and human faith. Human faith clings to the person. It believes, trusts, and honors the Word for the sake of the one who spoke it. But divine faith clings to the Word, which is God Himself. It believes, trusts, and honors the Word, not for the sake of the one who spoke it; rather, it feels that [the Word] is so certainly true that no one can ever tear it from him, even if the same preacher were to try to do it. This was proved by the Samaritans. First, they heard of Christ from the heathen woman, and on her word they went out of the city to Christ. When they themselves heard, then they said to the woman: "Now it is no longer because of what you said that we believe, for we ourselves now realize that this is the Savior of the world" (John 4 [:42]).

5. Again, all who believed Christ because of His person and His miracles fell away when He was crucified. So it is now and has always been so. The Word itself, without any regard for the person, must be enough for the heart; it must surround and lay hold of man, so that he feels captive by how true and right [the Word] is, even if the world, all the angels, all the princes of hell said differently, even if God Himself spoke differently. He does at times test His own elect and appears as if He would act differently than He had before said. This happened to Abraham when he was commanded to sacrifice his son Isaac [Gen. 22:2], and to Jacob when he wrestled with the Angel [Gen. 32:24–25], and to David when he was driven out by his son Absalom [2 Samuel 15], etc.

6. This faith persists in life and death, in hell and heaven, and nothing is able to overthrow it, because it rests upon nothing but the Word without any regard whatsoever to persons.

7. These shepherds possessed such faith, for they adhere and cling to the Word so fully that they forget the angels who declared it to them. They do not say: "Let us go and see the Word which the angels made known to us," but "which God has made known to us" [cf. Luke 2:15]. The angel was soon forgotten, and only the Word of God was grasped. St. Luke [2:19] speaks in the text in the same way about Mary, that she treasured and pondered the Word in her heart. Without doubt she did not let the humble appearance of the shepherds trouble her, but regarded it all as God's Word. And not only she but also all the others who heard these words from the shepherds and wondered (as the text says [Luke 2:18])—they all clung only to the Word.

8. It is an idiom of the Hebrew language that when it speaks of a historical fact, it says, "We would see the word," as St. Luke literally says here.[2] The history is grasped in the words and made known through the words.

---

2 Luke quotes the shepherds saying: ἴδωμεν τὸ ῥῆμα, "Let us see the word" (Luke 2:15).

Therefore, God has also provided that faith which clings to the Word and submits to the Word is expressed by what is said about the history. For if Christ's life and sufferings were not embodied in the words to which faith must cling, they would have been of no use, because all who saw them with their eyes received no benefit from them, or very little.

9. The second point is the unity in the spirit. For Christian faith is such that it unites hearts into one, so that they may be of one mind and of one will, as the psalmist says, "Behold, how good and pleasant it is when brothers dwell together in accord!" (Psalm 133 [:1]). St. Paul speaks about the unity of the Spirit in many places, such as: "Be diligent to be of one mind, of one will" (cf. Ephesians 4 [:3]; Romans 12 [:18]; 1 Corinthians 12 [:4]). Such unity is impossible apart from faith, for everyone is well pleased with his own ways, which is why the land, as people say, is full of fools. Experience shows how the orders, estates, and sects are divided among themselves. Everyone regards his order, his estate, his behavior, his work, his undertakings to be the best and the right road to heaven. He despises the others and does not accept them, as we see at present among the clerics, monks, bishops, and all that is spiritual.

10. However, those who have the true faith know that it depends indeed on faith, in which they harmoniously agree. Therefore, they are never divided and disunited because of any outward estate, conduct, or work. To them all external matters, however different they may be, are the same. Thus the shepherds here are of one mind, of one will, speak the same thought among themselves, use the same form of words, and say, "Let us go," etc.

11. The third [point] is humility, in that they acknowledge themselves to be human beings. Therefore, the evangelist adds "the men, the shepherds" [cf. Luke 2:15]. For faith teaches that everything which is human is nothing before God. Hence they despised themselves and thought nothing of themselves, which is true, fundamental humility and self-knowledge. Humility, then, includes that they ask nothing about things great and high in the world, but consider themselves to be unimportant, poor, and despised people, as St. Paul teaches when he says, "Do not think about things that are high, but associate with the lowly" (Romans 12 [:16]). Likewise, Psalm 15 [:4] says, "The righteous man despises a vile person and honors those who fear the Lord."

12. Out of all this, what follows is peace. For he who regards as nothing everything that is external and great easily lets them go and quarrels with no one about them. He experiences something better inwardly in the faith of his heart. Unity, peace, and humility are certainly also found among murderers, public sinners, even among hypocrites, but it is a unity of the flesh and not of the spirit, as Pilate and Herod became reconciled to each other and had peace and humility toward each other [Luke 23:12]. Likewise, the Jews, as

the psalmist says, "The kings of the earth set themselves, and the rulers take counsel together against Christ" (Psalm 2 [:2]). In the same way, the pope, monks, and priests are one when they contend against God, while at other times they are nothing but mere sects among themselves. Therefore, this is called a unity, humility, and peace of the spirit, in that it is above and in spiritual things, that is, in Christ.

13. The fourth [point] is love for your neighbor and disdain for yourself. The shepherds prove this in that they leave their sheep and go forth, not to the great and high lords in Jerusalem, not to the councillors in Bethlehem, but to the poor little group in the stable. They present themselves to the lowly, without a doubt willing and ready to serve and do whatever is required of them. If there had been no faith there, they would not have left the sheep and left their things lying about—if the angels had not before commanded them to do so. They did it of their own free will and of their own counsel, as the text says that they spoke with one another and "went with haste" [Luke 2:16] The angel did not command them, did not exhort them, did not advise them, but only pointed out what they would find, and left it to their own free will whether they would go and seek.

14. Love, too, acts in this way. It has no command, it does everything from itself, it hastens and does not delay. It is enough that its attention is called only to a thing. It needs and tolerates no taskmaster. Much could be said about that. A Christian ought to live freely in love, forget himself and his things, only think and hasten to his neighbor, as St. Paul says, "Let each of you look not at what is his own, but at what concerns another" (Philippians 2 [:4]). And: "Bear one another's burdens; so you will fulfill the law of Christ" (Galatians 6 [:2]).

15. However, the pope with his bishops and clerics have filled the world with laws and coercion, and there is nothing now in the whole world but mere driving and alarming. There are no voluntary orders or callings any longer, since it has been proclaimed that love will be extinguished and the world be ruined by human doctrines [cf. Matt. 24:11–12].

16. The fifth [point] is joy. This appears in the words that we gladly speak and hear about the things that faith in the heart has received. So here the shepherds chatter with one another joyously and pleasantly about that which they had heard and believed. They use very many words, as if they were chattering uselessly. They are not satisfied by saying, "Let us go over to Bethlehem and see this word that has happened," but they add "which God has done and has made known to us" [Luke 2:15]. Is it not chattering more than necessary that they say "which has happened, which God has done"? Could they not have easily spoken in fewer words: "Let us see this word which God has done there"?

17. But the joy of the spirit overflows with happy words, and they are not unnecessary; they are too few, and it cannot pour out as much as it would like to.

18. The sixth [point] is that they follow with deeds. For as St. Paul says, "The kingdom of God does not consist in words but in deed" (1 Corinthians 4 [:20]). So here the shepherds do not only say, "Let us go and see," but they also went—yes, they do more than they say. For the text says, "They went with haste," which is more than merely going, as they promised to do. So faith and love always do more than they say, and what they do is alive, busy, active, running over. So a Christian should use few words and many deeds, as he certainly will, if he is a true Christian. If he does not do this, then he is not yet a true Christian.

19. The seventh [point] is that they freely confess and publicly preach the word that was spoken to them about the child, which is the highest work in the Christian life. In this we are to risk our body and life, our wealth and honor. For the evil spirit does not attack so harshly those who believe correctly but live secretly and by themselves. He will not put up with it when we go forth and spread, confess, preach, and praise this for the good of others. Therefore, Luke says here that the shepherds did not only come and see, but they also preached what they heard in the field about this child, not only before Mary and Joseph but also before everybody.

20. Do you not think there were many who thought [the shepherds] were fools and insane in that they attempted, as coarse and unschooled laymen, to speak of the angels' song and sermon? How would one of them be received now, if he brought such stories and much more trifling ones before the pope, bishop, and scholars? But the shepherds, full of faith and joy, cheerfully were fools before men for God's sake. A Christian also does the same. For God's Word must be considered as foolishness and falsehood in this world.

21. The eighth [point] is Christian liberty, which is bound to no work. Rather, all works are alike to a Christian as they come to him. For these shepherds run to no desert, put on no hood, shave no tonsures, change neither clothing, time, food, drink, nor any external work, [but] return again to their sheepfolds and serve God there. For a Christian life consists not in outward conduct, nor does it change anyone as to his outward estate, but it changes him as to his inward estate; that is, it gives him another heart, another spirit, will, and mind which does the same work which any person without such a spirit and will does. For a Christian knows that it depends entirely on faith. Therefore, he walks, stands, eats, drinks, clothes himself, works, and lives as an ordinary man in his estate, so that one does not become aware of his Christianity. As Christ says: "The kingdom of God is not coming with signs

to be observed, nor will they say, 'Look, here it is!' or 'There!' Rather, the kingdom of God is within you" (Luke 17 [:20–21]).

22. The pope and his clergy fight against this freedom with their laws and chosen dress, food, prayers, places, and persons. They take themselves and everyone captive by their soul snares with which they filled the world, as St. Anthony saw in a dream. For they think salvation depends on their life and works. They call other people "worldly," though they themselves are seven times more worldly, since all they do is human works, concerning which God has commanded nothing.

23. The ninth and last [point] is praising and thanking God. For we are unable to give back to God any work for His kindness and grace, except praise and thanks which come from the heart, and have no need of many organs, bells, and blubbering. Faith truly teaches such praise and thanks as is here written about the shepherds, that they returned to their sheepfolds with praise and thanks. They are content, though they have not become wealthier, though they are not more highly honored, though they do not eat and drink better and do not have to do their work any better.

24. See, in this Gospel you have a picture of a true Christian life—first, according to its outward character, so that on the outside it appears to people to be nothing or very little, even falsehood and nonsense to most; but on the inside it is nothing but light, joy, and salvation. From this we see what the apostle means when he lists the fruits of the Spirit and says: "The fruit of the Spirit," that is, the works of faith, "is love, joy, peace, patience, kindness, goodness, faith, gentleness, and chastity" (Galatians 5 [:22–23]). Here there is no mention of persons, times, food, clothing, places, or similar choice human works as we see swarming in the life of the Papists.

## The Secret Interpretation

25. What it means to find Christ in such poverty, and what His swaddling clothes and manger signify, are explained in the previous Gospel.[3] His poverty teaches us to find Him in our neighbors, the lowliest and the most needy of them. His swaddling clothes are the Holy Scriptures. The result is that in our life of work we deal with the needy, but in our life of study and meditation we deal only with the Scriptures. Thus Christ alone is important for both lives; He stands before us in every purpose. We should shun the books of Aristotle, of the pope, and of all men, or read them in such a way that we do not seek to improve our souls through them, but for the time of this life, as one teaches a trade or civil law. However, it is not in vain that St. Luke places Mary before Joseph, and both of them before the child, and

---

3  See sermon for Christmas Day on Luke 2:1–14, paragraphs 45–46.

says that they "found Mary and Joseph, and also the baby in the manger" [Luke 2:16].

26. Now as we said before,[4] Mary is the Christian Church, Joseph is the minister, such as the bishops and pastors should be if they preached the Gospel. Here the Church is preferred before the prelates of the church, as Christ also says, "Whoever wants to be the greatest among you must be the lowest" (Luke 22 [:26]). That is now reversed, which is also no wonder, since they rejected the Gospel and exalted human babbling. The Christian Church retains now all the words of God in her heart and ponders them, comparing them with one another and with the Scriptures. Therefore, whoever would find Christ must first find the Church. How would someone know where Christ and faith were, if he did not know where His believers are? And whoever wants to know something about Christ must not trust himself nor build his own bridge to heaven by his own reason; but he must go to the Church, attend her, and ask her.

27. Now the Church is not wood and stone, but those who believe in Christ. One must hold to them, and see how those who certainly have Christ with them believe, live, and teach. For outside of the Christian Church there is no truth, no Christ, no salvation.

28. From this it follows that it is uncertain and false when the pope or a bishop wants alone to be believed and acts like a master; for they all err and may err. But their teaching should be subject to the crowd. The congregation[5] should decide and judge what they teach; their judgment should stand, in order that Mary may be found before Joseph, and the Church be preferred to the preachers. For it is not Joseph but Mary who keeps these words in her heart, ponders them, and compares them. The apostle also taught this when he says: "Let one or two explain the Scripture, and let the others judge. If something is revealed to someone sitting there, let the first be silent" (1 Corinthians 14 [:29–30]).

29. But now the pope and his followers have become tyrants, have reversed this Christian, divine, and apostolic order, have introduced a heathen and Pythagorean method, so that they may say any nonsense or deception that they want. No one is to judge them; no one is to contradict them; no one is to tell them to be quiet. And in this way they have quenched the Spirit so that among them one finds neither Mary nor Joseph nor Christ, but only the rats, mice, vipers, and snakes of their poisonous doctrines and hypocrisy.

4 Luther had not yet mentioned the secret meaning of "Mary" and "Joseph."

5 *Gemeine*, which Luther uses to mean either the Christian people as a whole or an individual congregation distinct from others.

30. This Gospel is not really a Gospel for disputing, for it teaches Christian morals and works; it does not so openly establish the point of faith. Although (as has just been stated) it is strong enough in mysteries, those are not of value in disputes. Rather, there must be open statements which clearly point to the articles of faith.

# GOSPEL FOR THE THIRD
# DAY OF CHRISTMAS

## John 1:1–14

*In the beginning was the Word, and the Word was with God, and the Word was God. He was in the beginning with God. All things were made through Him, and without Him was not any thing made that was made. In Him was life, and the life was the light of men. The light shines in the darkness, and the darkness has not overcome it. There was a man sent from God, whose name was John. He came as a witness, to bear witness about the light, that all might believe through him. He was not the light, but came to bear witness about the light. The true light, which gives light to everyone, was coming into the world. He was in the world, and the world was made through Him, yet the world did not know Him. He came to His own, and His own people did not receive Him. But to all who did receive Him, who believed in His name, He gave the right to become children of God, who were born, not of blood nor of the will of the flesh nor of the will of man, but of God. And the Word became flesh and dwelt among us, and we have seen His glory, glory as of the only Son from the Father, full of grace and truth.*

1. This is the highest of all the Gospel readings, and yet it is not, as some think, obscure or difficult. For here the high article of the deity of Christ is established most clearly, which all Christians should know and which they can certainly understand. Nothing is too high for faith. Therefore, we want, as much as we can, to treat it most plainly, and not as the scholastics, who have hidden it from the common man with their invented subtleties and frightened them away from it. There is no need of much pointed and sharp consideration, but only of plain, simple attention to the words.

2. First, we should know that all that the apostles taught and wrote they took out of the Old Testament, where all the things are proclaimed that were to be fulfilled later in Christ and were to be preached, as St. Paul says when he talks about "the Gospel of God, which He promised beforehand through His prophets in the Holy Scripture" (Romans 1 [:1–2]). Therefore, all their preaching is based on the Old Testament, and there is not a word in the New Testament that does not look back into the Old, where it had been foretold.

Thus we have seen in the Epistle how the deity of Christ is confirmed by the apostle from passages in the Old Testament. For the New Testament is nothing more than a revelation of the Old. Just as if someone had a sealed letter at first, and then broke it open, so the Old Testament is the testamentary letter of Christ, which He has opened after His death and caused to be read and proclaimed everywhere through the Gospel. This is shown by the Lamb of God who alone opens the book with the seven seals, which no one else could open, neither in heaven nor on earth nor under the earth [Rev. 5:1–5].

3. Now, so that this Gospel may be clearer and more easily understood, we must go back to the Old Testament, to the place on which this Gospel is founded—and that is when Moses writes at the beginning of his Book of Genesis: "In the beginning, God created the heavens and the earth. The earth was without form and void, and it was dark over the deep. And the Spirit of God was hovering on the water. Then God said, 'Let there be light,' and there was light" (Genesis 1 [:1–3]), etc. Then Moses relates how all the creatures were created in the same way as the light, namely, by the speaking or the Word of God. For example, God said, "Let there be an expanse"; or, again, God said, "Let there be sun, moon, and stars," etc.

4. From these words of Moses it clearly follows and is concluded that God has a Word, through which He spoke, before any creatures were created; and this Word may not and cannot be a creature, since all creatures were created through this divine speaking, as Moses' words clearly and forcibly state, since he writes: "God said, 'Let there be light,' and there was light." The Word must therefore have preceded the light, since light came by the Word; consequently, it was also before all other creatures, which also came by the Word, as Moses writes.

5. But let us go farther. If the Word preceded all creatures, and all creatures came into being and were created by the Word, then [the Word] must be of a different nature than a creature and was not made or created like a creature. It must therefore be eternal and without beginning. For when all things began it was already there, and [it] cannot be contained in time nor in creation, but is above time and creation; indeed, time and creation are made and have their beginning through [the Word]. Thus it is undeniable that whatever is not temporal must be eternal, and that which has no beginning cannot be temporal, and that which is not created must be God. For outside of God and His creation there is nothing—or no being. Thus we learn from these words of Moses that the Word of God, which was in the beginning and through which all creatures were made and spoken, must be the eternal God and not a creature.

6. Further, the Word and He who speaks [the Word] are not one person, for it is impossible that the speaker is Himself the Word. What sort of speaker would He be who is Himself the Word? He would have to be a mute, or the

Word would have to sound of itself without the speaker and speak itself. Scripture here speaks in strong and clear words: "God said," and thus God and His Word must be two.

If Moses had written "there was a saying" or "there had been a saying," it would not be as clear that there were two, the Word and the speaker. But when he says, "God said," and names the speaker and His Word, he forcibly states that there are two, that the speaker is not the Word and that the Word is not the speaker, but that the Word comes from the speaker and has its being not of itself but from the speaker. But the speaker does not come from the Word nor does He have His being from the Word, but from Himself. Thus Moses concludes that there are two persons in the Godhead from eternity before all creatures, that one has His being from the other, and the first has His being from no one but from Himself.

7. Again, Scripture confirms and establishes that there is only one God, since Moses begins by saying, "In the beginning, God created the heavens and the earth" [Gen. 1:1]. And later: "Hear, O Israel: Your God is only one God" (Deuteronomy 6 [:4]). See, Scripture proceeds with simple, comprehensible words, and teaches such high things so clearly, that everyone may well understand them, and so forcefully that no one can oppose them. Who is there that cannot here understand from these words of Moses that there must be two persons in the deity, and yet only one deity, unless he would deny the clear Scripture?

8. Again, whose thinking is so acute as to speak against this? He has to allow the Word to be something different from God, the speaker; and he must confess that [the Word] was before all creatures and that the creatures were made by [the Word]. Consequently, he must surely have [the Word] be God, for outside of creatures there is nothing but God. He must also confess that there is only one God. Thus Scripture forces the conclusion that these two persons are one complete God and that each one is the only, true, complete, and natural God, who has created all things; that the speaker has His being not from the Word, but that the Word has His being from the speaker; and yet all of this is eternal and from eternity, outside of all creatures.

9. The Arian heretics[1] wanted to draw a cloud over this clear passage and to bore a hole through heaven, since they could not overcome it. They said that this Word of God was indeed a god, not naturally, but by creation. They said that all things were created by [this Word], but it had also been created previously, and after that all things were created by it. They said this from

---

1 Followers of Arius (ca. 280–336), an Alexandrian presbyter, who taught that Christ, as the Word (John 1:1), was the highest creature but not true God. He was condemned at the Council of Nicaea in 325, but his numerous supporters regained the ascendancy under Emperor Constantine's sons.

their own dreams without any basis in Scripture, because they abandoned the simple words of Scripture and followed their own thoughts.

10. Therefore, I have said that he who desires to proceed safely on firm ground must have no regard for the many subtle and sharp words and fancies, but must cling to the simple, powerful, and clear words of Scripture, and he will be secure. We shall also see how St. John anticipated these same heretics and refuted them in their subterfuges and fabrications.

11. Therefore, we have here in Moses the real gold mine, from which everything that is written in the New Testament about the deity of Christ has been taken. Here you may see the source from which the Gospel of St. John flows and on which it is founded; and from [Moses] it is easy to understand.

See, it flows from the words "by the Word of the Lord the heavens were made" (Psalm 33 [:6]). And Solomon, when he describes in many beautiful words the Wisdom of God which was with God before all things, takes all of that from this chapter of Moses (cf. Proverbs 8 [:22]). All the prophets have worked in this mine and have dug their treasures from it.

12. But there are other words in this same Moses about the Holy Spirit, namely, when he says, "The Spirit of God was hovering over the waters" [Gen. 1:2]. Thus the Spirit of God must also be something different from the one who breathes Him, and yet He must be before all creatures.

Likewise, when [Moses] says [that] "God blessed" the creatures [Gen. 1:28]—considered them and was pleased with them—this benediction and kind consideration point to the Holy Spirit, since Scripture attributes life and kindness to Him. But these passages are not so well developed as those which refer to the Son; consequently, they do not glitter so brightly. The ore is still halfway in the mines, so that it is easy to believe—if reason is taken captive in such a way that it believes in two persons. If anyone has the time to compare the passages of the New Testament about the Holy Spirit with this text of Moses, he will find much light, pleasure, and joy.

13. Now we must open wide our hearts and understanding to look upon these words not as the insignificant, perishable words of man, but to think of them as being as great as He is who speaks them. It is a Word which He speaks in Himself, which remains in Him and is never separated from Him.

Therefore, we must think according to the apostle's thoughts of how God speaks with Himself and to Himself, and has a Word from Himself in Himself. However, this Word is not an empty wind or sound, but brings with it the whole essence of the divine nature. Reference has been made above in the Epistle to the radiance and image [Heb. 1:3]; the divine nature is imaged in such a way that it goes along into the image wholly and becomes the image itself, and the brightness gives off the radiance also in such a way that it goes into the radiance in essence. In the same way also God speaks His Word from

Himself in such a way that the whole deity follows the Word and remains in the Word by nature and is [the Word] in essence.

14. See, here we see where the apostle's words come from when he calls Christ an "image of the divine essence" and "the radiance of the glory of God" [Heb. 1:3], namely, from these words of Moses, when he teaches that God spoke the Word of Himself. This can be nothing else than an image that represents Him, since every word is a sign which signifies something. But here the thing signified is by its very nature in the sign or in the Word, which is not in any other sign. Therefore, he very properly calls it a real image or sign of His nature.

15. The word of man may also show some of this, for the human heart is known by the human words. People commonly say, "I understand his heart," or "his meaning," when they have only heard his words, since the heart's meaning follows from the words and is known through the words, as if it were in the word. Experience has taught the heathen to say, "Whatever kind of man he is, so he speaks." Likewise: "Speech is a likeness or sketch of the heart." When the heart is pure, it utters pure words. When it is impure, it utters impure words.

The Gospel agrees with this, where Christ says: "Out of the abundance of the heart the mouth speaks" and again "How can you speak good when you are evil?" [Matt. 12:34]. Also John the Baptist says, "He who is of the earth speaks of the earth" (John 3 [:31]). The Germans also have a proverb: "What the heart is full of flows out of mouth." "The bird is known by its song, for it sings as its beak has grown." Therefore, all the world confesses that no picture represents the heart so certainly as the words of the mouth, as though the heart were in the words.

16. The same is true with God. His Word is so much like Him that the deity is wholly in it, and whoever has the Word has the whole deity. But this comparison also falls short. For the human word does not bring with it the essence or the nature of the heart, but simply its meaning or sign, just as an engraving in wood or gold does not bring with it the human essence which it represents. But here, in God, the Word not only brings with it the sign and picture but also the whole essence, and is just as much God as the word or picture is. If the human word were pure heart or the intention of the heart, or if the heart's meaning were the word, then the comparison would be perfect. But this cannot be; consequently, the Word of God is above every word and is without equal among all creatures.

17. There have indeed been sharp disputations about the inner word in the heart of man, which remains within, since man has been created in the image of God. But it has remained so deep and obscure, and will remain so,

that it is impossible to understand it. Therefore, let us go on and come now to our Gospel, which is in itself clear and open.

*In the beginning was the Word. [John 1:1]*

18. What beginning does the evangelist mean except the one of which Moses says, "In the beginning God created the heavens and the earth" [Gen. 1:1]? That is the beginning in which the creatures began their essence. Other than this there was no beginning, for God has no beginning but is eternal. It follows, therefore, that the Word is also eternal, because it did not begin in the beginning, but in the beginning already was, as John says. It did not begin, but when all [other] things began, it already was; and its being did not begin when the being of all things began, but it was then already present.

19. How carefully the evangelist speaks, not saying, "In the beginning the Word became," but it was there and did not "become." There was a different origin of its being than "becoming" or "beginning." Furthermore, he says "in the beginning." If He had been made before the world, as the Arians maintain, He would not have been in the beginning, but He would have Himself been the beginning. But John is definite and clear: "In the beginning was the Word," and He was not the beginning. Where did St. John get these words? From Moses, as was said, "God said, 'Let there be light'" (Genesis 1 [:3]). From these words the other words follow clearly: "In the beginning was the Word." For if God spoke, there had to be a Word. And if He spoke it in the beginning, when the creation began, it was already in the beginning and did not begin with the creation.

20. But why does he not say, "Before the beginning was the Word"? That could be regarded as even clearer, since St. Paul often says "before the foundation of the world," etc. [Eph. 1:4]. The answer is that it is the same to be in the beginning and to be before the beginning; one follows from the other. St. John, as an evangelist, wanted to agree with the writings of Moses and to open them up in order to disclose his source, which would not have been the case had he said "before the beginning." Moses says nothing about what was before the beginning but describes the Word in the beginning, in order that he can the better describe the creation, which was made by the Word. For the same reason he also calls Him a Word, when he might well have called Him light, life, or something else, as is done later; for Moses speaks of a Word.

Now, "not to begin" and "to be in the beginning" are the same as "to be before the beginning." But if [the Word] had been in the beginning and not before the beginning, it must have begun to be before the beginning, and so the beginning would have been before the beginning, which would be a contradiction and would be the same as though the beginning were not the beginning. Therefore, it is put in a masterful way: "In the beginning was the

Word," so as to show that [the Word] did not begin and consequently must necessarily have been eternal, before the beginning.

### And the Word was with God. [John 1:1]

21. Where else should it have been? There never was anything outside of God. Moses says the same thing when he writes: "God said, 'Let there be light'" [Gen. 1:3]. If He is to speak, then the Word had to be with Him. But here he clearly distinguishes the persons, so that the Word is a different person than God with whom it was. These words of John do not allow [the interpretation] that God had been alone, because he says that something was with God, namely, the Word. If only one had been alone, why would he need to say, "The Word was with God"? To have something with Him is not to be alone or by Himself.

It is to be noted that the evangelist strongly emphasizes the little word "with," for he will say it again to express clearly the distinction of persons and to oppose natural reason and future heretics. Natural reason can understand that there is but one God, and many passages of Scripture confirm it—since it is true—but [natural reason] struggles against [the doctrine] that more persons than one are the same God.

22. That is the origin of Sabellius, the heretic, who said: The Father, Son, and Holy Spirit are only one person.[2] Again Arius, though he admitted that the Word was with God, would not admit that He was true God. The former confesses and teaches too great a simplicity of God; the latter, too great a multiplicity. The former mingles the persons with each other; the latter separates the natures from each other. But the true Christian faith takes the middle, and teaches and confesses unmixed persons and undivided natures. The Father is a different person from the Son, but He is not another God. It is correct that natural reason does not grasp this, for faith alone can grasp it. Natural reason produces heresy and error. Faith teaches and maintains the truth, for it clings to Scripture, which does not deceive or lie.

### And God was the Word. [John 1:1]

23. Since there is no more than one God, it must be true that God Himself is the Word, which was in the beginning before all creation. Some read and put the words in this order: "And the Word was God," in order to explain that this Word not only is with God and a different person but that

---

2 Sabellius (fl. ca. 217) taught that the Father, Son, and Holy Spirit were simply different external manifestations or modes of activity of the one God, not distinct persons. His teaching, called modal monarchianism, was opposed by bishop Calixt of Rome (d. 222) and by Tertullian (ca. 160–220). Cf. *Disputation on John 1:14* (1539), LW 38:262.

it is also in its essence one true God with the Father. But we shall leave the words in the order in which they now stand: "And God was the Word"; and this is also what it means. Since there is no other God than the one, only God, and this same God must also essentially be the Word, of which he speaks, so there is nothing in the divine nature which is not in the Word. It is clearly stated that this Word is truly God, so that it is not only true that the Word is God but also that God is the Word.

24. As firmly as these words are against Arius, who teaches that the Word is not God, so firmly do they appear to confirm Sabellius; for they sound as though the persons were mixed into each other, and thereby revoke or explain away the former words which separated the persons by saying, "The Word was with God."

But the evangelist wanted to arrange his words so that he would cast down all heretics. Here, therefore, he knocks Arius to the ground and attributes to the Word the true, natural deity by saying, "And God was the Word," as though he would say: "I do not say simply: 'The Word is God,' which might be understood as though the deity was only spoken about Him and He were not essentially so, as you, Arius, claim; but I say, 'And God was the Word,' which can be understood in no other way than that this one whom everyone calls God and regards as God is the Word. Again, lest Sabellius and reason think that I side with them and mingle the persons with each other and revoke what I have said on this point, I repeat it and say again:

*He was in the beginning with God. [John 1:2]*

25. With God, with God was [the Word], and yet God was the Word. Thus the evangelist fights on both sides that both are true: God is the Word, and the Word is with God; one nature of the divine essence, and yet not one person only. Each person is God complete and entire, in the beginning and eternally. These are the words on which our faith is founded and to which we must hold fast. For it is entirely above reason that there should be three persons and each one perfectly and completely the one God, and yet not three Gods but one God.

26. The scholastics have argued this back and forth with great subtleties, to make this comprehensible. But if you do not want to fall into the nets of the evil foe, then ignore their quibbling, opinions, and subtleties, and hold to these divine words. Enter into them and remain in them, like a rabbit in a cavern of the rocks [cf. Isa. 2:21]. If you go out of them and give yourself over to human chatter, then the enemy will lead you on and finally overcome you, so that you will not know where reason, faith, God, or even yourself are.

27. Believe me, as one who has experienced and tried it, and who does not speak in ignorance, Scripture was not given us in vain. If reason could

have handled things, Scripture would not have been necessary for us. Be afraid of Arius and Sabellius who, if they had remained in Scripture and told reason to take a hike, would not have originated so much trouble. And our scholastics would certainly be Christians if they left their nonsense with its subtleties and remained in Scripture.

*All things were made through Him. [John 1:3]*

28. Is this not said clearly enough? Who would be surprised if stubborn people do not let themselves be reproved of their error, no matter how clearly and plainly the truth is spoken to them? The Arians were able to evade this bright and clear passage by saying, "All things were made by the Word, but [the Word] was itself first made, and afterward all things were made by it." This is directly opposed to the words "all things were made through Him." There is no doubt that He was not made and is not counted among the things that were made. For he who mentions "all things" excludes nothing, as St. Paul also explains Psalm 8 [:6] when he says: " 'Putting everything in subjection under His feet.' Now in putting everything in subjection to Him, He left nothing outside His control" (Hebrews 2 [:8]); and: "But when it says, 'All things are put in subjection,' it is plain that He is excepted who put all things in subjection under Him" (1 Corinthians 15 [:27]).

So also the words "all things were made through Him" must without a doubt be understood to except Him by whom all things were made and without whom is nothing that is made. He also bases these words on Genesis 1, where Moses lists all the creatures God made and always says, "God said, and it was so," in order to show that they were all made by the Word. But St. John continues and explains himself still more fully when he says:

*Without Him nothing was made that was made. [John 1:3]*

29. If nothing was made without Him, much less is He Himself made without whom nothing was made, so that Arius' error should have produced nothing, though it has helped nothing. There is need of no explanation that this Word is God and the real Creator of all created things, since without Him nothing was made that ever was made.

30. Some have been in doubt about the order of the words in this text and want to join the words "that was made" to the following words in this way: "What was made was in Him life." That was the opinion of St. Augustine. But the words properly belong to the preceding words as I have given them, thus: "And without Him was not anything made that was made." He means to say that none of the things that were made were made without Him, so that he may the more clearly express that all things were made through Him

and that He Himself was not made. Thus [the evangelist] directly and firmly maintains that [the Word] is true God, though not from Himself but from the Father. Therefore, he says "made through Him" and "made by the Father."

### In Him was life. [John 1:4]

31. This passage is commonly cited in the high speculation and difficult understanding about the twofold nature of creatures for which the Platonic philosophers are famous. They maintain that all creatures have their being first in their own nature and kind, as they were created, and second in the divine providence from eternity in which He decided to create all things. And thus as He lives, so all things in Him are also living; and this life of the creatures in God, they say, is nobler than the being in its own kind and nature. For in God things live which in themselves have no life, such as stones, earth, water, etc.

And therefore St. Augustine says that this Word is an image of all creation, like a treasury full of such images, which they call Ideas, according to which the created things were made, each one according to its own image. And John is supposed to have been speaking about this when he said, "In Him was life." [John was to have] joined these words to the previous ones in this way: What was made was life in Him; that is, all that was ever created, before it was created, had first lived in Him.

32. But this is going too far and is a forced interpretation of this passage. For John speaks very simply and plainly and does not intend to lead us into such pointed and subtle contemplations. I do not know that Scripture anywhere speaks of created beings in this way. They do say that all things were known, chosen, and even ready and living in the sight of God, as though creation had already taken place, as Christ says about Abraham, Isaac, and Jacob: "He is not a God of the dead, but of the living, for they all live to Him" (Luke 20 [:38]). But we do not find it written in this sense that all things live in Him.

33. These words also say something more than about the life of the creatures, which was in Him before the world. Rather, in a most simple way he means to say that He is the fountain and origin of life, that all things which live, live from Him and through Him and in Him, and outside of Him there is no life, as He Himself says, "I am the way and the truth and the life" (John 14 [:6]). Again: "I am the resurrection and the life" (John 11 [:25]). Consequently, John calls Him "the Word of life" (1 John 1 [:1]), and especially speaks about the life which people have from Him, that is, eternal life; because of this life, [John] began to write his Gospel.

34. The whole text proves this. For [John] himself explains which life he is speaking about when he says, "The life was a light of men" [John 1:4].

By these words he shows without a doubt that he speaks about the life and light which Christ gives to people through Himself. For this reason he also brings in John the Baptist as a witness of that light. Now it is obvious how John the Baptist preached about Christ, not in the high speculation of which they speak, but he taught plainly and simply that Christ is the light and the life of all men for their salvation.

35. Therefore, it is well to remember that John wrote his Gospel, as the historians tell us, because the heretic Cerinthus[3] arose in his day and taught that Christ did not exist before His mother, Mary, thus making a simple human being or creature of Him. To oppose this heretic, he begins his Gospel so highly and continues thus to the end, so that in almost every letter he preaches the deity of Christ, which is done by none of the other evangelists. [He also does that] with great diligence, so that he describes Christ treating His mother as a stranger and speaking harshly with her when He said to her: "Woman, what business do I have with you?" (John 2 [:4]). Were these not strange, harsh words for a Son to use in addressing His mother? So also on the cross He said, "Woman, behold your son" (John 19 [:26]). All this he does in order to prove thoroughly against Cerinthus that Christ is true God; and he puts the words in such a way that he not only opposes Cerinthus but also Arius, Sabellius, and all heretics.

36. We read also that this same holy John once saw Cerinthus in a bath-house and said to his disciples: "Let us flee quickly, lest we be destroyed with this man." And after John had come out, the bathhouse collapsed and destroyed this enemy of the truth. He thus sharpens and aims all his words against the error of Cerinthus and says: "Christ was not only before His mother, He was in the beginning the Word of which Moses writes in the very beginning, and all things were made through Him, and He was with God, and God was the Word and was in the beginning with God"—thus he strikes Cerinthus with nothing but thunderbolts.

37. Thus we take the meaning of the evangelist in this passage to be simply and plainly this: Whoever does not recognize and believe Christ to be true God, as I have so far described Him—that He was the Word in the beginning with God and that all things were made through Him—but wants to regard Him only as a creature who began in time, coming after His mother, as Cerinthus teaches, is eternally lost and cannot attain to eternal life; for there is no life apart from this Word and Son of God. In Him alone is life. The man Christ, if He were that alone and not God, would be of no help at

---

3 A Gnostic heresiarch, Cerinthus (fl. ca. 100) denied the divinity of Jesus and instead taught that Christ entered into the man Jesus at His Baptism, remained throughout His ministry, but returned to heaven to leave Jesus to suffer and die alone.

all, as He Himself says: "The flesh is no help at all. But My flesh is true food, and My blood is true drink" (John 6 [:63, 55]).

"Why is the flesh of no help at all, and yet My flesh is the only true food? Because I am not mere flesh and simply man, but I am God's Son. Thus My flesh is good not because it is flesh, but because it is My flesh." This is as much as to say: "Whoever believes that I, who am man and have flesh and blood like other men, am the Son of God and God, he properly feeds on Me and will live. But whoever believes that I am only a man, to him the flesh is of no help at all, for [to him] it is not My flesh nor God's flesh."

Thus He also says, "Unless you believe that I am He, you will die in your sins" (John 8 [:24]). Again: "So if the Son sets you free, you are free indeed" (John 8 [:36]). That is the meaning of the word "in Him was life." The Word of God in the beginning, who is Himself God, must be our life, food, light, and salvation. Therefore, that He makes us alive is not ascribed to the humanity of Christ, but the life is in the Word, which dwells in the flesh and makes us alive through the flesh.

38. See, this interpretation is simple and helpful. St. Paul often calls the doctrine of the Gospel a "doctrine of piety" [1 Tim. 6:3; Titus 1:1], a doctrine that makes men rich in grace. However, the other interpretation, which the heathen also have, namely, that all creatures live in God, does indeed make subtle babblers and is obscure and difficult; but it teaches nothing about grace, nor does it make men rich in grace. Therefore, Scripture casts off such people as "busybodies" [cf. 1 Tim. 5:13].

Just as we interpret the words of Christ "I am the life," so also should we interpret these words, not at all in a philosophical way about the life of creatures in God, but in the way that God lives in us and makes us partakers of His life, so that we live through Him, of Him, and in Him. For that is not to deny that even natural life comes through Him, which even unbelievers have from Him, as St. Paul says, "In Him we live and move and have our being, and are of His kind" (Acts 17 [:28]).

39. Yes, natural life is a part of eternal life, its beginning, but it ends through death, because it does not acknowledge and honor Him from whom it comes. Sin cuts it off so that it must die forever. On the other hand, those who believe and acknowledge Him from whom they live never die, but [their] natural life will be extended into eternal life, so that they will never taste death, as He says, "Truly, truly, I say to you, if anyone keeps My Word, he will never see death" (John 8 [:51]). And: "Whoever believes in Me will live, even if he dies" (John 11 [:25]). These and similar passages are well understood when we rightly learn to know how Christ has slain death and restored life.

40. But when the evangelist says "in Him was life" and not "in Him is life," as though he spoke of past things, the words must not be taken to mean

the time before the world or the time of the beginning; for he does not say "in the beginning life was in Him," as he has just before said of the Word, which was in the beginning with God. Rather, these words must be taken to mean the time of Christ's life or conduct on earth, when the Word of God appeared to men and among men, for the evangelist proposes to write about Christ and His life in which He accomplished all things necessary for our life.

This is said in the same way that he spoke of John the Baptist—"There was a man sent from God" and again "He was not the Light," etc. [John 1:6, 8]—as he afterward says about the Word: "And the Word became flesh and dwelt in us" [John 1:14], and "He came into the world" [John 1:10], and "He came to His own, and they did not receive Him" [John 1:11], and the like. In the same way Christ speaks about John the Baptist: "He was a burning and shining lamp" (John 5 [:35]).

41. So also here: "In Him was life," as He Himself says, "While I am in the world, I am the light of the world" (John 9 [:5]). The words of the evangelist are to be understood only of the past conduct of Christ [on earth]. For as I said at first, this Gospel is not as difficult as some think. They have made it difficult by their search for high, deep, and mighty things. He has written for all Christians, no matter how simple they are, and has made his words perfectly intelligible. For whoever ignores Christ's life and conduct, and wants to seek in his own way how He now sits in heaven, will always go astray. He must look for Him as He was and as He lived on earth, and there he will find life; there He has come as our life, light, and salvation; there all things occurred that we are to believe about Him. It has really been very properly said, "In Him was life," not that He is not our life now, but that He does not do now what He then did.

42. That this is the meaning can be seen from the words that John the Baptist "came as a witness, to bear witness about the light, that all might believe through him" [John 1:7]. It is sufficiently clear that John came solely to bear witness about Christ, and he was a forerunner of Christ, and yet he has said nothing at all about the life of the creatures in God according to that [philosophical] opinion. Rather, all his teaching and preaching were about the life of Christ on earth, in which He became the life and light of men. Now follows:

*And the life was the light of men. [John 1:4]*

43. Just as they have taken the evangelical understanding away from the word "life," so they have also done with the word "light." They invent subtle and high thoughts about how the Word of God in its deity is a light, which naturally shines and has always shone on the reason of men even among the

heathen. Therefore, the light of reason has been emphasized and based upon this passage of Scripture.

44. These are all human, Platonic, and philosophical thoughts, which lead us away from Christ into ourselves; but the evangelist wants to lead us away from ourselves into Christ. For he will not treat the divine, almighty, and eternal Word of God, nor speak of it, otherwise than as the flesh and blood which went about on earth. He will not distract us with the creatures which He has created, so that we run after, search for, and speculate about Him as the Platonic philosophers do; but he wants to gather us out of those rambling and long-winded thoughts into Christ.

[The evangelist] means to say: "Why do you run around and search so far away? Look, everything is in the man Christ. He has made all things. In Him is life. He is the Word by whom all things were made. Remain in Him and you will find everything. He is the life and the light of all men. Whoever directs you elsewhere than to Him deceives you. For He has offered Himself in this flesh and blood, and He wants to be sought and found there. Follow the testimony of John the Baptist, who shows you no other life or light than this man, who is God Himself." Therefore, this light must be understood as the true light of grace in Christ, and not the natural light, which also sinners, Jews, heathen, and devils have, who are the greatest enemies of the light.

45. But let no one reproach me for teaching differently from St. Augustine, who understood this text to mean the natural light. I do not reject that understanding and am well aware that all the light of reason was kindled by the divine light; and as I have said of the natural life, that it is a part and a beginning of the true life, when it has come to the right knowledge, so also the light of reason is also a part of the true light and a beginning of it, when it recognizes and honors Him by whom it has been kindled.

Now, it does not do this of itself, but remains in itself, becomes corrupted, and also corrupts all things. Therefore, it must be extinguished and perish. But the light of grace does not destroy the natural light. To the light of nature it is quite clear that two and three make five. That the good is to be done and the evil avoided is also clear to it; and thus the light of grace does not extinguish [the light of nature], but the natural light never gets to the point that it can distinguish the good from the evil. It happens with [natural light] as it does with one who should go to Rome but travels away from it. For he himself well knew that whoever would go to Rome must travel the right way, but he knew not which was the right road. So it is also with the natural light. It does not take the right road to God, nor does it know or recognize the right way, though it knows well enough that one should take the right road. Thus reason always takes the evil as the good. It would never do this if it did not fully realize with a clear vision that only the good should be chosen.

46. But this understanding is out of place at this place in the Gospel, because only the light of grace is preached here. St. Augustine was only a man, and we are not compelled to follow his understanding, since the text here clearly indicates that the evangelist speaks of the light of which John the Baptist bore witness, which is the light of grace, Christ Himself.

47. And since the opportunity allows it, we shall point out this false natural light, which causes all trouble and misfortune. This natural light is like all the other members and powers of man. Who doubts that man with all his powers has been created by the eternal Word of God like all other things and is a creature of God? But yet there is no good in him, as Moses says, "All his thoughts and mind with all his powers was inclined only to evil" (Genesis 6 [:5]).

48. Therefore, as true as it is that the flesh is a creature of God, yet it is not inclined to chastity but to unchastity. As true as it is that the heart is God's creature, yet it is not inclined to humility or to the love of the neighbor but to pride and selfishness, and it acts according to this inclination where it is not forcibly restrained. So also the natural light, though it is essentially so bright as to know that only good is to be done, yet it is so corrupted that it never finds what is good. It calls good whatever is pleasing to itself, gives its assent, and wantonly concludes to do what it has chosen as good. Thus it goes and always follows the evil instead of the good.

49. We shall also prove this by examples. Reason knows very well that we ought to be pious and serve God. It can babble much about that and thinks it can rule all the world. Very well, this is true and well said. But when it is to be done, and reason is to show how and in what way we are to be pious and serve God, it knows nothing, is stone-blind, and says one must fast, pray, sing, and do the works of the Law. It continues to act the fool with works, until it has gone so far astray as to imagine that people are serving God by building churches, ringing bells, burning incense, blubbering, singing, wearing cowls, having tonsures, burning candles, and other unspeakable tomfoolery of which all the world is now full and more than full. In this great blind error it continues, and the bright light always remains: one must be pious and serve God.

50. Now when Christ, the light of grace, comes and also teaches that we are to be pious and serve God, He does not extinguish this natural light, but opposes the way and manner of becoming pious and serving God as taught by reason. He says: "To become pious is not to do works, but to believe in God first without any works, and then to do works, for no works are good without faith."

51. Then begins the fight. Reason rages against grace and cries out against the light of grace, accuses it of forbidding good works, and will not

allow its way and standard of becoming pious to be rejected, but continually rages about being pious and serving God, and so makes the light of grace foolishness, even error and heresy, which must be persecuted and banished. See, this is the virtue of the light of nature, that it raves against the true light and constantly boasts about being pious, being pious, and is always crying: "Good works! Good works!" but it cannot and will not allow it to be taught what piety and good works are. Rather, what it thinks and asserts must be good and right.

52. See, here you have a summary of the origin and cause of all idolatry, of all heresy, of all hypocrisy, of all error, of which all the prophets have spoken, on account of which they were killed, and against which all of Scripture protests. All this deals with the stubborn, self-willed opinions and ideas of natural reason, which is self-confident and puffed up because it knows that we ought to be pious and serve God. It will neither listen to nor endure a teacher. It thinks it knows enough and will find out for itself what it is to be pious and serve God and how it may do so. You see, the divine truth cannot and should not endure that from it, for that is the greatest error and contrary to God's honor. Then strife and the cross begin.

53. See, I think it is clear that John does not speak here of the false light, nor of that bright natural light which rightly directs that we must be pious, for [that light] is already here. Christ did not come to bring [that light], but to blind and extinguish this false, self-willed opinion and to set in its place the light of grace, faith. The words themselves state that when they say, "The life was the light of men" [John 1:4]. If it is the light of men, it must be a different light than the one that is in men, since man by nature already has the natural light in him, and whoever enlightens man enlightens the natural light in man and brings another light, which surpasses the light that is in man.

He does not say that it is the light of irrational animals, but of man, who is a rational being. For there no man can be found in whom there is not the natural light of reason, from which cause he alone is called man and is worthy to be a man. For if [the evangelist] wanted this light to be understood as the natural light of reason, he should have said, "The life was a light of darkness," as Moses writes that "darkness was on the waters" (Genesis 1 [:2]). Therefore, this light must be understood as that which was revealed to the world in Christ on earth.

54. Notice the order of the words. [John] puts the life first, then the light. He does not say, "The light was the life of men," but, on the contrary: "The life was the light of men," because in Christ there is reality and truth, and not simply appearance, as in men. St. Luke says that externally Christ "was a prophet mighty in deeds and words" (Luke 24 [:19]), and again: "Jesus began to do and teach" (Acts 1 [:1]), where "doing" precedes "teaching." Otherwise it

is hypocrisy if the words are without works. He says that John the Baptist was burning and shining (John 5 [:35]), for to be shining and not first burning is deceptive. In order, therefore, that Christ may here also be recognized as the true and nondeceptive light, [John] first says that in Him was all life, and then that this same life was the light of men.

55. From that it follows that man has no other light than Christ, God's Son in the human nature. And whoever believes that Christ is true God, and that in Him is life, will be illuminated by this life and made alive. The light supports him, so that he may remain where Christ remains. As the deity is an eternal life, this same life is an eternal light; and as this same life cannot die, so also this light cannot be extinguished; and faith in this light shall not perish.

56. It is also especially to be noted that [the evangelist] assigns life to Christ as the eternal Word and not as man; for he says, "In Him" (understand the Word) "was life." Although He died as a man, yet He always remained alive; for life could not and cannot die. And consequently death was choked and overcome by that life, so much so that the humanity must soon again become alive.

This same life is the light of men, for whoever recognizes and believes such a life in Christ indeed passes through death yet never dies, as has been stated above. For this light of life supports him, so that death does not touch him. Although the body must die and decay, the soul does not feel this death, because it is in that light and through that light completely contained in the life of Christ. But whoever does not believe this remains in darkness and death. And though his body is united to him, even as it will be forever on the Last Day, yet the soul will nevertheless taste and feel death and will die eternally.

57. See, from this we realize how great was the harm desired by Cerinthus and all who believe and teach that Christ is only man and not true God. For His humanity would be of no help if the deity were not in it. Nevertheless, God will not and cannot be found other than through and in His humanity, which He has raised as a certain "signal" (Isaiah 11 [:12]), and thus gathered to Himself all His children from the world.

58. See now, if you will believe that in Christ there is such life that remains even in death and has overcome death, this light will properly enlighten you and will remain a light and life within you even at your death. It follows, then, that such life and light cannot be a creature, for no creature can overcome death, either in itself or in another. See how adequate and useful this understanding of the light is for our salvation, and how very far from those who make of it the natural light of reason. For [the natural light] does not improve anyone; it only leads away from Christ into the creature and false reason. We must enter into Christ and not look at the lights which come from Him, but

gaze at His light, from which the lights come. We must follow the streams which lead to the source, and not away from it. There follows:

*The light shines in the darkness, and the darkness has not comprehended it. [John 1:5]*

59. They have also dragged this passage into high thoughts and under-stood it to mean that reason has a natural light, as was said above, and that it is kindled by God; and yet [reason] does not recognize, comprehend, or feel Him or the light, by which it is kindled. Therefore, it is in darkness and does not see the light from which it has all its light and vision.

60. Oh, that this understanding were rooted out of my heart! How deeply it is settled there! Not that it is false or incorrect, but because it is out of place and unsuitable at this place in the Gospel, and it does not allow these blessed and comforting words [of the Gospel] to remain simple and pure in their correct understanding. Why do they not speak of reason only in this way: that it is kindled by the divine light? Why do they not speak of the natural life in the same way? The natural life is made alive by the divine life just as much as the rational light is enlightened by the divine light.

They might just as well say that life makes the dead alive and the dead do not comprehend it as to say that the light illumines dark reason and reason does not comprehend it. Likewise, I might also say that the eternal will makes the unwilling willing and the unwilling do not comprehend it, and so on about all the other natural gifts and powers. But how does reason and its light enter into such speculations? The Platonic philosophers with their useless and senseless babbling—though it glitters so charmingly that they were called the divine philosophers—first brought Augustine to this opinion on this text. Afterward, Augustine dragged us all in with him.

61. What more can their babbling teach than that reason is illumined by God, who is an incomprehensible light? In the same way life is given by God, who is incomprehensible life, and all our powers are made powerful by God, who is incomprehensible power. And as close as He is to the light of reason with His incomprehensible light, so close is He to life with His incomprehensible life and to the powers with His incomprehensible power, as St. Paul says, "In Him we live and move and are" (Acts 17 [:28]). And: "I fill heaven and earth. How, then, would I be a God far away and not near?" (Jeremiah 23 [:24, 23]).

Thus we have just heard in the Epistle reading that He upholds all things "by the word of His power" (Hebrews 1 [:3]). Therefore, He is not only close to the light of reason and illuminates it, but [He is also near] to all crea-tures, and flows and pours, enlightens and works in them, and fills all things. Accordingly we are not to believe that St. John speaks here of these things.

He only speaks to human beings and tells them what kind of light they have in Christ apart from nature and above nature.

62. It is also a blind and awkward expression when they speak about the natural light, saying that the darkness did not comprehend that light. What else would this be than to say that reason is enlightened and kindled by the divine light, and yet remains dark and receives no light? Where does their natural light come from? There can never be darkness where a light is kindled, though there is darkness from the lack of the light of grace. But they are not speaking of the light of grace, and so they cannot be speaking about the same darkness. Therefore, it is a contradiction of terms to say that the light illuminated the darkness and the darkness did not comprehend it, or remained dark, as also to say that life is given to a dead person and the dead person does not comprehend it or become aware of it, but remains dead.

63. But if someone should say, "We do not comprehend Him who gives light and life," then I would hear: "What angel does comprehend Him?" What saint comprehends the one who gives him grace? He remains hidden and incomprehensible. But this does not mean, as the evangelist says here, that the light is not comprehended by the darkness; but rather, as the words read, it means: "The light shines into the darkness, but the darkness remains dark and is not illuminated by it. It lets [the light] shine but does not see it, just as the sun shines on blind people, but they do not perceive it." See how many words I must spill out in order to remove this foreign understanding [of the text]!

64. Therefore, let us remain with the simple, unforced understanding of the words. All who are illuminated by natural reason comprehend the light, each one being illuminated accordingly. But this light of grace, which is given to men beyond the natural light, shines in darkness, that is, among the blind and God-forsaken people of the world; but they do not receive it, and they even persecute it. This is what Christ means when He says, "This is the judgment: the light has come into the world, and people loved the darkness more than the light" (John 3 [:19]).

See, before He was proclaimed by John the Baptist, Christ was among the people on earth, but no one took notice of Him. He was always the life and light of men. He also lives and enlightens. There was only the world of blind and dark people. If they had recognized who He was, they would have given Him due honor, as St. Paul says, "If they had recognized the wisdom of God, they would not have crucified the Lord of glory" (1 Corinthians 2 [:8]).

65. Thus Christ has always from beginning to end been the life and light, even before His birth. He shines at all times in all creatures; in Holy Scripture; through His saints, prophets, and preachers; in His works and words; and He has never ceased to shine. But wherever He shines, everything is dark, and the darkness does not comprehend Him.

66. St. John may have indeed directed these words against Cerinthus, so that he would see the clear Scripture and the truth that enlightened him, yet his great darkness did not comprehend it. So it is at all times and even now. Although Scripture is explained to blind teachers so that they may grasp it in truth, yet they do not comprehend it, and this remains true: the light shines in the darkness and the darkness does not comprehend it.

67. It is especially to be observed that the evangelist here says the light "shines" (*phainei*) [John 1:5]; that is, it is manifest and present to the eyes in the darkness. But he who has nothing more from it remains dark, just as the sun shines on the blind man, but he does not on that account see any better. So it is the nature of this light that it shines in darkness, but the darkness does not on that account become brighter. In believers, however, it not only shines, but it also fills them with light and sight, it lives in them, so that it may not be said that "the life is a light of men." On the other hand, light without life is a shining of darkness. Therefore, no shining helps unbelievers, for however clearly the truth is presented and shown to them, they still remain in the dark.

68. Thus we will understand all these sayings of the evangelist as common attributes and titles of Christ, which he wants to have announced in general as a preface and introduction to what he will write of Christ in his whole Gospel, namely, that He is true God and true man, who has created all things and has been given to man as life and light, though few among all those to whom He is revealed receive Him. This is what our Gospel reading contains and nothing more. Similarly, St. Paul has a preface and introduction to his letter to the Romans (Romans 1 [:1–17]). Now follows the actual beginning of this Gospel.

*There was a man sent from God; his name was John. [John 1:6]*

69. St. Mark and St. Luke also begin their Gospels with John the Baptist, and they should begin with him; as Christ Himself says, "From the days of John the Baptist until now the kingdom of heaven suffers violence" (Matthew 11 [:12]). And St. Peter says that Christ began from the Baptism of John, by whom He was also appointed and called to be a teacher (Acts 1 [:22]). St. John the Baptist himself shows this: "I saw the Holy Spirit descending on Christ as a dove, and I heard the Father's voice: 'This is My beloved Son, with whom I am well pleased'" (John 1 [:32; Matt. 3:17]). Then Christ was made a doctor,[4] and He began, and the Gospel went out through Christ Himself. For no one should begin the high, blessed, comforting words except Christ

---

4 *Doctor*, that is, an authorized teacher, not necessarily a physician.

alone. And for His sake John must first come and prepare the people for His preaching, so that they would receive the light and the life.

70. For, as we have heard, though Christ is everywhere the light which shines in the darkness and is not overcome [cf. John 1:5], yet He was especially and bodily in His humanity present among the Jews. He appeared to them, but He was not recognized by them. Therefore, His forerunner, John, came and preached about Him, in order that He might be recognized and received. This passage therefore agrees perfectly with the previous ones. Since Christ, the shining light, was not recognized, John came to open the eyes of men and to bear witness to the ever-present, shining light, which afterward was to be received, heard, and recognized itself without the witness of John.

71. Now I think that we are through with the most difficult and highest part of this Gospel, for what is said afterward is easy and is the same as that which the other evangelists write about John and Christ. Although, as I have said, this part is in itself not difficult, yet people have willingly made it difficult by natural and human glosses. It must become difficult when people take a word out of its [ordinary] meaning and give it a foreign one. Who would not think it a marvel, if he wanted to know what man is and would hear that man is something different from what all the world thinks? This is what happened here to the clear, simple words of the evangelist.

72. Still [John] uses his own style, since he always, because of Cerinthus, refers the testimony of John the Baptist to the deity of Christ, which is not done by the other evangelists, who only refer to Christ without emphasizing His deity. But here he says, "John came to bear witness of the light and to preach Christ as the life, the light, and as God," as we shall hear.

73. Therefore what was said about John the Baptist in Advent is also to be understood here, namely, that, just as he came before Christ and directed the people to Him, so the oral word of the Gospel is only to preach and to point out Christ. It was ordained by God for this purpose alone, just as John was sent by God. So we have heard that John was a voice in the wilderness, signifying by his office the oral preaching of the Gospel. Since the darkness was of itself unable to comprehend this light, though it was present, John must reveal it and bear witness of it. So also the natural reason is unable of itself to comprehend it, though it is present in all the world; the oral word of the Gospel must reveal it and proclaim it.

74. We see now that through the Gospel this light is brought to us, not from a distance, nor do we need to run far after it; rather, it is very near to us and shines in our hearts. Nothing more is needed than that it be pointed out and preached. And whoever hears it preached, and believes, finds it in his heart; for faith is only in the heart, and so this light is only in faith. Therefore,

I say it is near to us and in us, but of ourselves we cannot comprehend it; it must be preached and believed.

This is also what St. Paul means when he says, quoting Moses, that you do not need to cross the sea, nor climb up to heaven nor down into hell, for "the word is near: in your mouth and in your heart" (Romans 10 [:8]; cf. Deuteronomy 30 [:11–14]). See, that is the light shining in darkness and not being recognized until John and the Gospel come and reveal it. Then man is enlightened by it and comprehends it. And yet it changes neither time nor place nor person nor age, but only the heart.

75. Further, as John did not come of himself but was sent by God, so neither the Gospel nor any preaching about this light can come of itself or from human reason; but they must be sent by God. Therefore, the evangelist here sets aside all the doctrines of men; for what men teach will never show Christ, the light, but will only obstruct it. But whatever points out Christ is surely sent by God and has not been invented by man.

For this reason the evangelist mentions the name and says, "His name was John" [John 1:6]. In Hebrew "John" means "grace" or "favor," to signify that this preaching and message was not sent on account of any merit of ours but was sent purely out of God's grace and favor, and brings to us also God's grace and favor. St. Paul says, "How can they preach unless they are sent?" (Romans 10 [:15]).

76. From all this we see that the evangelist deals with Christ in such a way that He may be recognized as God. For if He is the light which is present everywhere and shines in the darkness, and this needs nothing more than to be revealed through the Word and recognized in the heart through faith, then He must surely be God. For no creature can shine so closely to all places and hearts. Again, He is God in such a way that He is nevertheless man and is preached among men by men. The words follow:

*He came as a witness, to bear witness about the light, that they all might believe through him. [John 1:7]*

77. See, it is now clear from what has been said that the Gospel proclaims only this light, the man Christ, and causes [the light] to overcome the darkness, yet not by reason or feeling but by faith. For he says, "That all might believe through him." Again: "He came as a witness, to bear witness." Now it is the nature of testimony to speak of that which others do not see, know, or feel; they must believe him who bears testimony. Thus the Gospel does not demand a rational decision and adherence, but a faith which is above reason, for in no other way can this light be recognized.

78. Enough was said above about how the light of reason fights and rages against this light, to say nothing of how it should comprehend it and adhere

to it. For it is established as fact: The darkness does not comprehend this light; therefore, reason with its light must be taken captive and blinded, as is said: "I will cover your sun," that is, your reason, "with a cloud" [cf. Ezek. 32:7], that is, with the Gospel or the Word of God or John's testimony, which requires faith and makes reason foolish. Again: "Your sun shall no longer enlighten you, and the light of your moon shall no longer be in you; but your God will be your everlasting light" (Isaiah 60 [:19]). For that reason, this light is testified through the Word, so that reason may turn away from itself and follow this testimony; then it will comprehend the light in faith, and its darkness will be illuminated. For if [reason] were able to comprehend or adhere to this light of itself, there would be no need for John or for his testimony.

79. Therefore, the aim of the Gospel is to be a witness for the sake of self-willed, blind, and stubborn reason, to restrain it, and to lead it away from its own light and opinion to faith, through which it can comprehend this living and eternal light.

*He was not the light but came to bear witness about the light. [John 1:8]*

80. Tell me why he says this and repeats once more the words that John was only a witness of the light? Oh, what necessary repetition! First, to show that this light is not a man, but God Himself; for, as I have said, the evangelist greatly desires to preach the deity of Christ in all his words. If John [the Baptist], the great saint, is not the light but only a witness to it, then this light must be much more than all that is holy, whether it be angel or man. For if holiness could make such a light, it would have made one of John. But it is above holiness and must therefore be above the angels, who also are not above holiness.

81. Second, to restrain the shameless preachers of men, who do not bear witness of Christ the light, but of themselves. For it is true, indeed, that all who preach the doctrines of men make a man the light, lead people away from this light to themselves, and put themselves in the place of this true light, as the pope and his followers have done. Therefore, he is the Antichrist; that is, he is against Christ and against the true light.

82. The Gospel endures no other doctrine alongside it; it will only testify of Christ and lead people to that light, to Christ. Therefore, O Lord God, these words "he was not the light" are truly worthy to be written in large letters and diligently noted against the men who point to themselves and want to give people doctrines and laws out of their own heads. They claim to be enlightening men but lead them with themselves into the depths of hell; for they do not teach faith and are unwilling to teach it. No one except the one sent by God, John, teaches the holy Gospel. Much could be said about this.

83. In short, whoever does not preach the Gospel to you, boldly reject him and do not listen to him. But he preaches the Gospel who teaches you to believe and trust in Christ, the eternal light, and not to build on any of your own works. Therefore, beware of everything told you apart from the Gospel. Do not put your trust in it. Do not regard it as a light that enlightens and improves your soul, but regard it as something external, as you regard eating and drinking, which are necessary for your body and which you may use at your pleasure or at the pleasure of another—but not for your salvation. For this purpose nothing is necessary or of use to you except this light.

84. Oh, these abominable doctrines of men, which are now so prevalent and which have so banished this light! They all want to be this light themselves, but not to be witnesses of the light. They teach themselves and their ideas but are silent about this light, or teach it in such a way as to teach themselves. This is worse than to be entirely silent; for by such teaching they make Samaritans who partly worship God and partly worship idols (cf. 2 Kings 17 [:33]).

*The true light, which enlightens everyone, was coming into the world. [John 1:9]*

85. Neither John nor any saint is the light. But there is a true light about which John and all evangelical preachers testify. For now enough has been said about this light, what it is, how it is recognized by faith, and how it supports us eternally in life and death, so that no darkness can ever harm us. But what is unusual is that he says, "It enlightens everyone coming into the world." If this were said about natural light, it would contradict his words that it is the true light. He had said before: "The darkness does not grasp it," and all his words are directed toward the light of grace. Then follow the words: "He came into the world, and the world did not recognize Him, and His own people did not receive Him" [John 1:10–11]. But whomever the true light enlightens is enlightened with grace and recognizes Him.

86. On the other hand, that he is not speaking about the light of grace is evident when he says, "It enlightens everyone coming into the world." This is clearly said about all people who are born. St. Augustine says it means that no man is enlightened except by this light. Similarly, people are accustomed to say about a teacher in a city (when there is no other teacher there): "This teacher instructs all the city"; that is, there is no other teacher in that city—he instructs all the pupils. It is not saying that he teaches all the people in the city but that he is the only teacher in the city, and none are taught by any other.

So here the evangelist would have us know that John is not the light, nor is any man nor any creature, but that there is only one light who enlightens everyone, and there is not a man on earth who is enlightened by anyone else.

87. And I cannot reject this interpretation; for St. Paul speaks in the same way: "For as by the one man's sin condemnation came to all men, so by the one man's righteousness justification has come to all men" (Romans 5 [:18]). Although not all men become righteous through Christ, He is nevertheless the only man through whom all justification comes.

So it is also here. Although not all men are enlightened, nevertheless He is the only light by which all enlightenment comes. The evangelist has used this way of speaking freely and had no fear that some might take offense because he says "all men." He thought he would help with such offense by explaining before and afterward: "The darkness has not comprehended it. The world did not know Him. His own people did not receive Him." These words are strong enough so that no one can say that [the evangelist] meant to say that all people are enlightened, but that He alone is the light that enlightens everyone, and without Him no one is enlightened.

88. If this were said of the natural light of reason, it would have little significance, since it not only enlightens all people who come into the world but also those who go out of the world, and even the demons. For this light of reason remains in the dead, in demons, and in the condemned; it only becomes brighter, that they may be all the more tormented by it. But since only human beings who come into this world are mentioned, the evangelist indicates that he is speaking of the light of faith, which enlightens and helps only in this life; for after death no one will be enlightened by it. [This enlightening] must take place through faith in the man Christ, yet from His deity. After this life we shall clearly see His deity, not through the humanity and in faith, but openly in itself.

89. Thus the evangelist chooses his words so that he does not reject the man Christ, and yet proclaims His deity. For this reason it was necessary for him to say "all men," so as to preach only one light for all and to warn us not to accept in this life the lights of men or any other lights. One man is not to enlighten another, but this light alone is to enlighten them. The preachers are to be only forerunners and witnesses of this light to men, that all may believe in this light.

Therefore, when he had said that He gives light to everyone, he saw that he had said too much, and so he added "who comes into the world," so that he might make Christ the light of this world. For in the world to come this light will cease and will be changed into eternal brightness, as St. Paul says that Christ will then hand over the kingdom to God the Father (1 Corinthians 15 [:24]). But now He rules through His humanity.

When He hands over the kingdom, He will also hand over the light—not as though there were two kinds of light, or as though we were to see something different from what we now see. But we shall see the same light and the same God we now see in faith, but in a different manner. Now we see Him hidden in faith. Then we shall see Him unhidden. It is as though I saw a golden picture through painted glass or otherwise veiled, and afterward pure and uncovered. So also St. Paul says, "Now we see through a mirror in a dark word, but then face-to-face" (1 Corinthians 13 [:12]).

90. See, you now know what the evangelist is speaking about when he says that Christ is the light of men through His humanity—that is, in faith, through which His deity is enlightened as through a mirror or colored glass, or as the sun shines through bright clouds, so that the light is attributed to His deity, not to His humanity, and yet His humanity, which is the cloud or curtain before the light, is not despised.

91. This language is sufficiently plain, and whoever has faith understands very well the nature of this light. Whoever does not believe does not understand it. Nor does that bother us. He is not supposed to understand it, for it is better that he knew nothing of the Bible and did not study it than that he deceive himself and others with his erroneous light. For he imagines it to be the light of Scripture, which, however, cannot be understood without true faith. For this light shines in the darkness but is not comprehended by it.

92. This passage may also mean that the evangelist wants the Gospel and faith preached in all the world, so that this light rises before all people of this world, just as the sun rises over all people. St. Paul says that the Gospel "has been preached in all creation under heaven" (Colossians 1 [:23]). [Christ] Himself said, "Go into all the world and preach the Gospel to the whole creation" (Mark 16 [:15]). Psalm 19 [:6] also says about [the sun]: "It rises from one end of the heaven, and runs back to the same end, and nothing is hidden from its heat." How this is to be understood was said above on the Epistle for Christmas night.

93. Thus it would be easier and simpler to understand that this light enlightens all people who come into the world, so that neither Jews nor anyone else should dare to set up their own light anywhere. And this understanding agrees well with the preceding passages. For before John or the Gospel bore witness of the light, it had shone in darkness and the darkness did not comprehend it. But after it has been proclaimed and publicly testified, it shines as far as the world extends, over all people, though not all receive it, as follows:

*He was in the world, and the world was made through Him, yet the world did not know Him. [John 1:10]*

94. All this is said of Christ as man and especially after His Baptism, when He began to give light according to John's testimony. Then He was in the midst of the world. But what place of the world knew it? Who received

Him? He was not even received by those where He was personally present, as follows:

*He came to His own possession, and His people did not receive Him. [John 1:11]*

95. This also is said about the coming of His preaching, and not about His birth. For His coming means His preaching and enlightening. The Baptist says, "After me will come one whose shoe strap I am not worthy to untie" (John 1 [:27]; Matthew 3 [:11]; Luke 3 [:16]; Mark 1 [:7]). On account of this coming, John is also called His forerunner, as Gabriel said to his father, Zechariah: "He will go on before Him to prepare His way" (cf. Luke 1 [:17]). For, as has been said, the Gospels begin with the Baptism of Christ. Then He began to be the light and to do that for which He came. He says that He came to His own people in the midst of the world and they did not receive Him. If this were not said of His coming through preaching and enlightening, [the evangelist] would not reprove them for not having received Him.

96. Who could know that it was He, if He had not been revealed? Therefore, it is their fault that they did not receive Him, even though He came and was revealed by John and by Himself. Therefore, John also says, "For this purpose I came to baptize, that He might be revealed in Israel" (John 1 [:31]). And He Himself says: "I have come in My Father's name, and you do not receive Me. If another comes in his own name, you will receive him" (John 5 [:43]). This is also clearly said about the coming of His preaching and revelation.

97. He calls the Jews "His own people" because they were chosen out of all the world to be His people, and He had been promised to them through Abraham, Isaac, Jacob, and David. For to us Gentiles there was no promise of Christ. Therefore, we are strangers and are not called "His own." But now through pure grace we have been adopted and have thus become His people; though, unfortunately, we daily let Him come through His Gospel and despise Him. Therefore, we must also put up with it when another, the pope, comes in His place and is received by us. We must serve the evil foe because we will not serve our God.

98. But we must not forget here that the evangelist refers twice to the deity of Christ. First, when he says, "The world was made through Him" [John 1:3]. Second, when he says, "He came to His own." For it is the nature only of the true God to have His own people. The Jewish people were God's own people, as Scripture frequently declares. If, then, they are Christ's own people, He must certainly be that God to whom Scripture assigns that people.

99. But the evangelist commends to everyone's consideration what a disgrace and shame it is that the world does not recognize its Creator and that

the Jewish people do not receive their God. In what stronger terms can you reprove the world than by saying that it does not know its Creator? What evil vice and names follow from this one point! What good can there be where there is nothing but ignorance, darkness, and blindness? What wickedness would not be present where there is no knowledge of God? What a horrible and frightful thing the world is! Whoever knew [the world] and properly considered this point should be all the more in hell—he could not be happy in this life, of which such evil things are written.

> *But however many did receive Him, to them He gave the power to become children of God, who believe in His name. [John 1:12]*

100. We see now what kind of a light [the evangelist] has been speaking about. It is Christ, the comforting light of grace, and not natural light or reason. For John is an evangelist and not a Platonist. All who receive natural light or reason receive Him according to that light—how else could they receive Him?—just as they receive the natural life from the divine life. However, that light and life do not give them the right to become children of God. Indeed, they remain enemies of this light, do not know it, do not receive it. Therefore, there can be no reference in this Gospel to natural light, but only to Christ, that He may be acknowledged as true God.

101. From now on this Gospel is well-known, for it speaks about faith in Christ's name, which makes us God's children. These are excellent words and powerfully refute the masters of works and the teachers of the Law. Good works never make a person different. Therefore, though the works-righteous think they are ever changing and improving their works, their person remains the same as before, and their works only become a mantle for their shame and hypocrisy.

102. But, as has often been said, faith changes the person and makes a child out of an enemy so secretly that the external works, rank, and way of life remain, when they are not by nature wicked deeds. Therefore, faith brings with it the entire inheritance and highest good of righteousness and salvation, so that these need not be sought in works, as the false corrupters teach us foolishly. For he who is a child of God already has God's inheritance through his sonship. So if faith gives this sonship, it is clear that good works should be done freely, to the honor of God, by those who already possess salvation and the inheritance from God through faith. This has been amply stated above on the second Epistle reading.

*Who were born not of blood nor of the will of the flesh nor of the will of a man, but of God. [John 1:13]*

103. To explain himself, [the evangelist] here tells us what faith does, and that everything apart from faith is useless. Here he forcibly puts down nature, light, reason, and whatever is not faith, to say nothing of praising them. The sonship is too high and noble to originate from nature or to be promoted by it.

104. John mentions four different kinds of sonship: one of blood, a second of the will of the flesh, a third of the will of man, a fourth from God. The first kind of sonship, that from blood, is easy to understand, since it is natural sonship. With this he refutes the Jews who boasted that they were of the blood of Abraham and the patriarchs, relying on the passages of Scripture in which God promises the blessing and the inheritance of salvation to the seed of Abraham. Therefore, they want to be the true people and children of God. But here he says there must be more than blood, or there is no sonship of God. For Abraham and the patriarchs themselves possessed the inheritance not because of blood but because of faith, as he teaches (Hebrews 11 [:8]). If the natural blood relationship were enough for this sonship, then Judas the betrayer, Caiaphas, Annas, and all the wicked Jews who in times past were condemned in the wilderness would have a proper right to this inheritance. For they were all from the blood of the patriarchs. Therefore, it is said, they were born not of blood, but of God.

105. The other two kinds of kinship or sonship—the will of the flesh and the will of man—are not yet sufficiently clear to me. But I see very well that the evangelist thereby wants to reject everything which nature is and can do, and to exalt only the birth from God. Therefore, there is no danger however we assign and divide these two parts in nature apart from grace. It is all the same. Some understand the sonship of the will of the flesh to come not from a blood relationship, but according to the Law of Moses. He commanded that the nearest kin must marry the wife of a deceased husband and raise a name and heir to the deceased one, so that the bloodline of his friend would remain. To this interpretation belongs also the step-relationship, which comes of the will of the flesh and not of blood relationship.

106. But [the evangelist] here calls man "flesh" (since he lives in the flesh), as Scripture usually calls him, which means: not as people have children outside of their bloodline, which is carnal and human and takes place in accordance with man's free will. But what is born from blood takes place without the free will, naturally, whether someone wants it or not.

107. The third kind [of sonship], the will of man, they take to mean the sonship of strangers, commonly called "adoption," when a man chooses and takes someone else's child as his own. Even if you were Abraham's or David's

real child, or stepchild, or you had been adopted, or you were a stranger, it does not help, for you must be born of God. Even Christ's own friends did not believe (John 7 [:5]).

108. If you wish, you can assign the kinship in this way: those of the blood are those who belong to the blood relationship, whether it be a full or a step-relationship. Those born of the will of the flesh may include all relatives who are not born of blood, such as those who have been adopted, as has been said. But those from the will of man are spiritual children, such as disciples are toward their teacher. Thus the evangelist puts down everything that might be accomplished by blood, flesh, nature, reason, skill, doctrine, law, free will, with all their powers, so that no one presumes to help another by means of his own doctrine, work, skill, or free will—or be allowed to help any man on earth—to the kingdom of God. Rather, after we have rejected everything, [we are to] strive for the divine birth.

Thus I think that "man" in Scripture usually means a superior who rules, leads, and teaches others. These are justly and most of all rejected, since no kinship dares more stubbornly and more insolently, and confides more in itself most strongly, to oppose grace at all times and to persecute it. In this respect let everyone have his opinion, as long as he bears in mind that nothing is useful which is not born of God. For if something else were useful, the evangelist (since he is so exact) would without doubt have put it next to the divine birth and would not have praised only this.

109. The divine birth is therefore nothing else than faith. How can this be? It has been explained above how the light of grace opposes and blinds the light of reason. If now the Gospel comes and bears witness to the light of grace—that man must not act or live according to his opinion, but must reject, kill, and abolish his natural light—if this man accepts and follows such testimony, gives up his own light and opinion, is willing to become a fool, allows himself to be led, taught, and enlightened, then he will be changed in the most important way, that is, in his natural light. His old light is extinguished and a new light, faith, is kindled. He follows [this new light] in life and in death, clings solely to the witness of John, or the Gospel, even if he is compelled to abandon all he had and could do before.

See, he is now born of God through the Gospel, in which he remains, and abandons his light and opinion, as St. Paul says, "I begot you in Christ Jesus through the Gospel" (1 Corinthians 4 [:15]); and as James says, "Of His gracious will He gave birth to us by the word of truth, that we should be firstfruits of His creatures" (James 1 [:18]). Therefore, St. Peter calls us newborn children of God (1 Peter 2 [:2]). Likewise, for this reason the Gospel is called God's womb, in which we are conceived, carried, and born.

Isaiah says, "Listen to Me, you remnant of a poor house, whom I carried in My body" (Isaiah 46 [:3]).

110. But this birth properly proves itself when there is temptation and death. There one sees who is newborn and who is old-born. Then the old light—reason—struggles and writhes and does not want to abandon what it thinks and wants, is unwilling to put up with and rely on the Gospel and abandon its own light. But those who are newborn, or are then becoming newborn, rely on [the Gospel] and abandon [their own] light, life, property, honor, and whatever they have, and trust and cling to the witness of John. Therefore, they come to the eternal inheritance as true children.

111. See, when this light, reason, and the old opinion are dead, dark, and changed into a new light, then the life and all powers of man must also follow and be changed. For where the reason goes, the will follows; where the will goes, love and delight follow. And thus the whole man must crawl into the Gospel, become new, and take off the old skin, as the snake does when its skin becomes old. It seeks out a narrow hole in the rock, crawls into it, sheds its old skin, and leaves it in the hole.

Thus man must also rely on the Gospel and God's Word and confidently follow its promises, which never lie. In this way he takes off his old skin— leaves behind his light, his opinion, his will, his love, his delight, his speech, his deeds—and becomes an entirely new man, who sees everything differently than before, judges differently, forms an opinion differently, thinks differently, wills differently, speaks differently, loves differently, desires differently, acts and conducts himself differently than before. He now understands whether all the conditions and works of men are right or wrong, as St. Paul says, "A spiritual man judges all things, and he is judged by no one" (1 Corinthians 2 [:15]).

112. Then he sees clearly what great fools they all are who want to become godly through works. He would not give one farthing for all the clerics, monks, popes, bishops, tonsures, cowls, incense, shining, burning of candles, singing, organs, prayers, with all their external things; for he sees how all this is simple idolatry and foolish hypocrisy, just as the Jews worshiped their Baal, Asherah, and the calf in the wilderness, which they looked upon as precious things in the old light of stubborn, self-conceited reason.

113. From this it is clear that no blood, no friendship, no command, no doctrine, no reason, no free will, no good works, no exemplary living, no Carthusian orders, no religious orders, even if they were angelic, are of any use or help to this sonship of God, but only a hindrance. For where reason is not first renewed and in agreement with these things, then it becomes hardened and blinded, so that it can scarcely, if ever, be helped. Rather, it thinks its doings and ways are right and proper, and then storms and raves

against all who despise and reject its doings. Thus it must remain the old man, the enemy of God and His grace, of Christ and His light. It beheads John, His witness—that is, the Gospel—and sets up human doctrines. This game storms on even now, in full splendor and power, in the doings of the pope and his clergy, who together know nothing of this divine birth. They stammer and drip doctrines and commandments about certain works with which they want to attain grace, and yet they remain in the old skin.

114. But what is here said certainly remains: This birth occurs not of blood, not of the will of the flesh nor of man, but of God. We must despair of our own will, works, and life—which have been poisoned by the false, stubborn, selfish light of reason—and in all things listen to, believe, and follow the voice and testimony of the Baptist. Then the true light—Christ—will enlighten us, renew us, and give us the right to become children of God. For this reason He came and was made man, as follows:

*The Word became flesh and dwelt among us, and we have seen His glory, glory as of the only-begotten Son of the Father, full of grace and truth. [John 1:14]*

115. By "flesh" we are to understand the whole human nature, body and soul. It is scriptural usage to call man "flesh," as above,[5] when he said, "Not of the will of the flesh" [John 1:13]; and in the Apostles' Creed we say, "I believe in the resurrection of the flesh," that is, of all men.[6] Likewise, Christ says, "If those days had not been cut short, no flesh would be saved" (Matthew 24 [:22]), that is, no man. The psalmist wrote: "He remembered that they were but flesh, like a wind that passes and comes not again" (Psalm 78 [:39]). Again: "You have given Him authority over all flesh, to give eternal life to all whom You have given Him" (John 17 [:2]).

116. I say this so carefully because this passage has endured much offense from heretics at the time when there were great and learned bishops. Some, such as Photinus and Apollinaris,[7] taught that Christ was a man without a soul and that the divine nature took the place of the soul in Him. Manichaeus taught that Christ did not have true, natural flesh but was only an apparition, passing through His mother, Mary, without assuming her flesh and blood, just as the sun shines through a glass but does not assume the nature of the

5 See above, paragraph 106.

6 In the Third Article (see Kolb-Wengert, p. 22; *Concordia*, p. 16).

7 According to Augustine, Photinus (d. 376) denied the preexistence of Christ, though he endorsed the virgin birth and the superhuman attributes of Jesus. Apollinaris (ca. 310–ca. 392), bishop of Laodicea, promulgated the first Christological heresy by claiming that the human spirit in Christ was replaced by the divine *Logos*. Both men and their teachings were formally condemned at the Council of Constantinople (381).

glass.[8] That is why the evangelist used a tangible word: "He became flesh," that is, a man like every other man, who has flesh and blood, body and soul.

117. Thus Scripture had to be tried and confirmed at that time, one part after another, until the time of the Antichrist, who suppressed it not partially but completely. For it has been prophesied that at the time of Antichrist all heresy will gather into one sludge and devour the world. That could not happen more than when the pope put down the entire Scripture and set up his own law. Therefore, bishops are now no more heretics, nor can they become heretics, for they have no part of the book by which heretics are made, that is, the Gospels. They have brought all heresy to themselves in a heap.

118. Formerly, heretics, as evil as they were, still remained in Scripture and left some parts intact. But what is left now, since this divine birth and faith are no more acknowledged and preached, but mere human laws and works are urged? What does it matter whether Christ is God or not God, whether He is flesh or an apparition, whether He has a soul or not, whether He came before or after His mother, or whatever errors and heresies there have been? We would have no more of Him than all those heretics, and would not need Him, and it would be as much as if He became man in vain, and all things were written about Him to no purpose, because we have made up a way by which we may come to God's grace: by our works!

119. Therefore, now there is no difference between our bishops and all heretics who have ever lived, except this: that we name Christ with our mouth and pen as a cover and a pretense. But we speak of Him so little, and are as little benefited by Him, as if He were the one of whom all heretics spoke foolishly, as St. Peter prophesied and said: "There will be false teachers among you, denying the Lord who bought them. Because of them the way of truth will be blasphemed" (2 Peter 2 [:1–2]).

120. What does it help if Christ is not the way the heretics have preached about Him, if He is no more to us and does no more for us than for them? What does it help if we condemn such heresy with our mouths and confess Christ correctly, if our hearts do not regard Him differently than they do? I do not see what Christ would be necessary for if I am able to attain God's grace by my works. It is unnecessary for Him to be God and man. In short, all that is written about Him is unnecessary; it would be sufficient to preach God alone, as the Jews believe, and then obtain His grace by means of my works. What more would I want? What more would I need?

8 Mani (216–277, typically referred to as Manichaeus at Luther's time), a Persian dualist and founder of Manichaeism, assigned to Jesus a place in his system as a heavenly messenger but denied that He had taken on a real body composed of evil matter. Cf. Luther, *Sermons on John 1–2* (1537–38/1565), LW 22:22–23.

121. Thus Christ and Scripture are not at all necessary, if the doctrine of the pope and his universities stands firm. Therefore, I have said that pope, bishops, and universities are not good enough to be heretics, but they surpass all heretics and are the sludge of all heresies, errors, and idolatries from the beginning, because they entirely crush Christ and the Word of God and only retain their names for appearance's sake. No idolater, no heretic, no Jew has ever done this—not even the Turk does this. And though the heathen were without Scripture and Christ before His birth, yet they did not oppose Him and Scripture, as these do. Therefore, they were far better than the Papists.

122. Therefore, let us be wise in this wicked, anti-Christian time and cling to the Gospel, which does not teach us that our reason is a light, as men teach us, but presents Christ as the one we may not do without, and says, "The Word, by which all things were made, is the life, and the life is the light of men" [cf. John 1:3–4]. Firmly believe that it is true that [Christ] is the light of men, that without Him all is darkness in man, such that man is unable to know what to do or how to act, to say nothing about being able to attain the grace of God by his own works, as the mad universities teach with their idol, the pope, and deceive all the world.

123. He came that He might become the light of men, that is, that He might become known. He showed Himself bodily and personally among men and was made man. He is the light in the lantern. The lost coin did not by its work and light go after and seek the lantern, but the lantern with its light sought the coin and found it. It has swept the whole house of this world with its broom and looked in every corner; and it continues to seek, sweep, and find even until the Last Day [cf. Luke 15:8–9].

124. But it is a high article [of faith] that the Word alone and not the Father was made flesh, and that nevertheless they are both one complete, true God. Yet faith comprehends it all, and it is proper that reason should not comprehend it. It happened and is written so that [reason] would not comprehend it, but become altogether blind, dark, and foolish, and so come from its false light into a new light.

125. Yet this article is not opposed to the light of reason, which says that we must serve God, believe, and be godly, which agrees with this article. But if [reason] is to guess and say who this God is, it jumps back and says, "This is not God," and wants to call God whatever it thinks [is God]. Therefore, when it hears that this Word is God and that the Father is the same God, it shakes its head, will not [look] up, and thinks [the article] is wrong and untrue, continues in its opinion, and thinks it knows better what God is and who He is than anyone else.

126. Thus the Jews continue in their opinion and do not doubt at all that God is to be believed and honored, but they retain the right themselves to

define who this God is. They want to be masters [over God], and He must Himself be lying to them and be in the wrong. See, this is the way reason acts in all God's works and words: it always cries out that it is honoring God's work and Word, but it is the pleasure [of reason] to form a verdict on what God's work and Word are. It wants to judge God in all His works and words but is unwilling to be judged by Him. What God is or is not is judged according to its caprice.

127. Now see: Isn't God justly hostile in Scripture to such immeasurable wickedness? Doesn't He justly prefer open sinners to such saints? What would be thought more annoying than such horrible impudence? I say this so that we may recognize what the delicate fruit is to which the pope and universities attribute so much, and which of itself and with its works, without Christ, attains to the grace of God. It is God's greatest enemy and would destroy Him in order that it might only and truly be God, since it attains to God's grace. I think that is surely darkness.

128. See, reason must in this way make idols and cannot do otherwise. It knows very well how to talk about God's honor, but always goes and gives that honor to what it thinks is God. That is certainly not God but their own opinion and error, of which the prophets in various ways complained. Nor does it improve the matter if anyone were to say, as the Jews do: "Yes, I mean the God who created the heavens and the earth; here I cannot be mistaken and must be right." God Himself answers: You "swear by the name of God and remember the God in Israel, but not in truth or righteousness" (Isaiah 48 [:1]). Again: "Though they say, 'By the living God!' yet they swear falsely" (Jeremiah 5 [:2]).

129. How does that happen? Whoever does not accept God in one point, especially in that one which He has had explained, will profit nothing if he afterward accepts God in the points which he has selected for himself. If Abraham would have said that it was neither God nor God's work that commanded him to sacrifice his son Isaac [cf. Gen. 22:1–19], but would have followed his reason and have said that he would not sacrifice his son but would otherwise serve the God who made heaven and earth, what would it have profited him? He would have lied, for he would in that very thing have rejected the God who created the heavens and the earth; and would have devised another god, under the name of the God who had created the heavens and the earth; and would have despised the true God, who had given him the command.

130. See, thus they all lie who say they mean the true God who created the heavens and the earth and yet do not accept His work and Word, but exalt their own opinion above God and His Word. If they truly believed in the God who created heaven and earth, they would also know that the same

God is a Creator over their opinion, and makes, breaks, and judges it as He pleases. But if they do not allow Him to be a Creator over themselves and their opinion even in such a small point, it cannot be true that they believe Him to be the Creator of all creation.

131. So you say: What if I am deceived, and He is not God? Answer: Be silent, for a heart which does not stand on its own opinion God will not allow to be deceived; for it is impossible that He should not come and dwell in such a heart, as the mother of God says, "He fills the hungry" [Luke 1:53]. Psalm 107 [:9] says, "The empty souls He fills." But if anyone is deceived, it is certain that he stood on his own opinion, whether secretly or openly. Therefore, a hungry soul always stands in fear of those things which do not certainly come from God. But the arrogant immediately stumble over that, thinking it sufficient that it glitters and seems good to them. Again, whatever is certainly from God, the hungry quickly accept it, but the arrogant persecute it.

132. Now there is no more certain sign that something is from God than that it is against or over our opinion. Thus the smart alecks think that there is nothing more certainly not from God than that which is against their opinion. Since they are creators and masters of God, whatever is correct according to their opinion must be God and of God. Thus all those who rely on themselves must be deceived, and all those who abandon themselves come to the right way; that is, they keep the true Sabbath. Where this opinion goes so far that it cites God's Word for its own wickedness, and thus judges Scripture according to its own light, there is no more aid or help. [This opinion] thinks that God's Word is on its side and must be preserved, but that is the last fall, truly Lucifer's calamity, of which Solomon speaks: "The righteous falls seven times and rises again, but the unbelievers fall into all calamity" [Proverbs 24:16].

133. That is enough about that. Let us return to the Gospel. [John] says, "The Word," who became flesh, "dwelt among us" [John 1:14]; that is, He walked among men on earth, as other men do. Even though He is God, He became a citizen of Nazareth and Capernaum and acted like other men, as St. Paul says: "Who, though He was in the form of God, did not count equality with God a thing to be grasped, but emptied Himself, taking the form of a servant, becoming just like another man. And being found in human form, He humbled Himself by becoming obedient to the point of death, even death on a cross" (Philippians 2 [:6–8]).

134. Therefore, this "equality" and "dwelling" is not to be understood according to His human nature, in which He had equality with men through His birth from Mary, through which He came into the human nature and had equality with men according to nature. Rather, these words are to be understood of His external being and mode of living, such as eating, drinking, sleeping, waking, working, resting, house and city, walking and standing,

clothing and dress, and all human walk and conduct, so that no one could have recognized Him as God, if He had not been so proclaimed by John and the Gospel.

135. He says further: "We have seen His glory" [John 1:14], or majesty, that is, His deity through His miracles and teachings. The word "glory" we have heard before in the Epistle, where it was said that Christ is "the radiance of God's glory" [Heb. 1:3], which means His deity. For what is *kabod* in Hebrew, *doxa* in Greek, *gloria* in Latin is *Herrlichkeit* ["majesty"] in German. We say about a ruler or a great man that he has done something majestically, and that it happened with great majesty, when it happened excellently, abundantly, and yet bravely.

Majesty does not only mean a great reputation, or far-famed glory, but also the things which are praised, such as costly houses, vessels, clothes, food, servants, and the like, as Christ says of Solomon: "Consider the lilies of the field, how they grow, yet I tell you, even Solomon in all his majesty was not arrayed like one of these" (Matthew 6 [:28–29]). It is reported that King Xerxes "gave a feast. He showed the majestic riches of his kingdom" (Esther 1 [:3–4]). Thus we say in German: This is a majestic thing, a majestic manner, a majestic deed, [and in Latin,] *gloriosa res*. This is also what the evangelist means here: "We have seen His glory, His glorious manner and deeds, which were not an insignificant, common glory, but the glory as of the only-begotten Son of the Father."

136. Here he expresses who the Word is, of whom he and Moses have spoken—namely, the only Son of God, who has all the glory that the Father has. Therefore, he calls Him the only, the only-begotten, so as to distinguish Him from all the children of God, who are not natural children as this one is. His true deity is shown in this way; for if He were not God, He could not be called the only-begotten Son compared to the others. This is as much as saying that He and no other is God's Son. This cannot be said of angels and saints, for none of them is God's Son but are all brothers and created creatures, children [of God] adopted by grace, not born by nature.

137. This seeing of His glory must not be applied only to bodily sight; for the Jews also saw His glory but did not regard it as the glory of the only-begotten Son of God. Rather, the believers have seen and believed it with their hearts. Unbelievers, whose eyes looked at the worldly glory, did not notice this divine glory. They do not tolerate each other. Whoever would be glorious before the world must be shameful before God. On the other hand, whoever is shameful before the world for God's sake is glorious before God.

*Full of grace and truth. [John 1:14]*

138. Scripture commonly uses these two words together. "Grace" means that all He is and does is agreeable before God. "Truth" means that all He is and does is completely good and right in itself, and thus that there is nothing in Him which is not agreeable and right. On the other hand, in man there is only disgrace and falsehood, so that all they do is disagreeable before God. They are fundamentally false and nothing but glittering, as the psalmist says, "All men are liars" (Psalm 116 [:11]). And again: "All men are as nothing at all" (Psalm 39 [:5]).

139. That is said against the presumptuous Papists and Pelagians,[9] who find something that is supposedly good and true outside of Christ, in whom alone is grace and truth. It is indeed true, as has been said above, that some things are true and agreeable, such as the natural light, which says that three and two are five, that God should be honored, etc.

But this light never accomplishes its end; for as soon as reason should act and bring this light into use and practice, it turns everything upside down and calls what is evil good, and what is good evil, calls something "the honor of God" which is His dishonor, and vice versa. Therefore, man is only a liar and vain and unable to make use of this natural light except against God, as we have already said.

140. It is unnecessary to look for the armor in this Gospel. It is all armor and the important point, on which is founded the article of faith that Christ is true God and man, and that nature, free will, and works are, without grace, nothing but lies, sin, error, and heresy, against the Papists and Pelagians.

9 Pelagius (ca. 354–ca. 418) taught that human beings are born innocent, without original sin, and are able to keep God's Law by their own free will. Augustine opposed him in the fifth century, and Luther regarded the scholastic soteriology of the medieval church as being essentially Pelagian: see, e.g., *Disputation against Scholastic Theology* (1517), LW 31:9, 11; *Heidelberg Disputation* (1518), LW 31:67–68; preface to Augustine, *On the Spirit and the Letter* (1533?), LW 60:35–44.

# GOSPEL FOR ST. STEPHEN'S DAY

*[December 26]*

*Matthew 23:34–39*

*Therefore I send you prophets and wise men and scribes, some of whom you will kill and crucify, and some you will flog in your synagogues and persecute from town to town, so that on you may come all the righteous blood shed on earth, from the blood of righteous Abel to the blood of Zechariah the son of Barachiah, whom you murdered between the sanctuary and the altar. Truly, I say to you, all these things will come upon this generation. "O Jerusalem, Jerusalem, the city that kills the prophets and stones those who are sent to it! How often would I have gathered your children together as a hen gathers her brood under her wings, and you were not willing! See, your house is left to you desolate. For I tell you, you will not see me again, until you say, 'Blessed is he who comes in the name of the Lord.'"*

1. This Gospel reading is harsh against the persecutors of faith. Yet the harsher it is against them, the more comforting it is to the believers who are persecuted. This Gospel teaches how obstinate the natural light, our own opinion, and reason are. When [reason] sinks into works and commands, then it no longer listens to anyone, as is said in the previous Gospel.[1] Rather, its work and opinion must be in the right, and it does not matter how much is preached or how many prophets God sends; all must be persecuted and put to death who oppose it, the great red murderess. St. John pictures her as "the great prostitute," Babylon, which "was arrayed in purple and scarlet," "sitting on a scarlet beast," and "holding in her hand a golden cup full of abominations and the impurities of her fornication" (Revelation 17 [:1–4]), that is, human teachings, by which she leads pure believing souls away from faith and puts them to shame; she slaughters all who oppose her.

2. This Gospel also shows the stubborn and murderous obstinacy, first, in that God tries everything with her and sends to her all kinds of preachers, who are mentioned by three names: prophets, wise men, and scribes.

3. The prophets are those who preach solely from the inspiration of the Holy Spirit, who have not obtained it from the Scriptures or through men.

---

1 See sermon for Third Day of Christmas on John 1:1–14, paragraph 45.

Such were Moses and Amos. These men are the highest and the best. They are wise, and they can make others wise. They write Scriptures and explain them. Such were nearly all the fathers before and at the time of Moses, and also many after him, especially the apostles, who were laymen and "uneducated, common men," as St. Luke says (Acts 4 [:13]).

4. The wise men are those who have [received their message] not only from God but also through the Scriptures and men. They are the disciples and followers of the prophets, but they themselves also preach and teach with their mouth and in living words. Such was Aaron, who spoke everything that Moses told him, as God said to Moses: "Put My Word in his mouth, and have him preach for you to the people, and you shall be God to him, but he shall be your mouth" (Exodus 4 [:15–16]). That is how all the priests are supposed to be, too, as Zechariah 11 says.[2]

5. The scribes are those who teach by means of writings and books where they cannot be present or teach orally. Such were also the apostles, and before them the evangelists and their followers, such as the holy fathers. Nevertheless, they did not write or deal with their own opinion, but God's Word, which they learned from the wise men and out of the Scriptures. These now are the three ways by which the truth may be revealed: by writing, by word, by thought—that is, by the writing in books, by the words of their mouth, by the thoughts of the heart. One cannot in any other way grasp the doctrine except with the heart, the mouth, and writings.

6. Now all this is of no value to obstinate reason, which does not listen to words, writings, as God tries it with her. [Reason] suppresses and burns the writings and books, as King Jehoiakim did with the books of Jeremiah (Jeremiah 36 [:23]). [Reason] forbids, silences, and condemns the Word. It expels and kills enlightenment together with the prophets. And it is strange that no prophet has been killed, expelled, or persecuted because he reproved coarse sins, except John the Baptist, whom Herodias had killed because he reproved her adultery [cf. Matt. 14:1–12]. Such a great man had to die for the most disgraceful reason. Although the Jews were not hostile to him for that reason, they did say that he had a devil because he would not let what they did be right.

7. Thus there have always been quarrels about true and false worship. Abel was slain by Cain so that his worship would not be of any value [Gen. 4:3–8; 1 John 3:12]. Thus all prophets, wise men, and scribes have reproved as idolatry the worship that springs from reason and human works without faith. Then the natural opinion came and said that [this worship] was done for the glory of God and should be right. Therefore, the prophets must die,

---

2 Perhaps Zech. 11:11 is meant.

as Christ says, "The hour is coming when anyone who kills you will think he is offering service to God" (John 16 [:2]).

Thus all the idolatry of the Old Testament was started not by those who wanted to worship wood and stone, but by those who wanted to worship the true God by so doing. Now, since God had forbidden this, and since it came from their own opinion without faith, it was certainly from the devil and not from God. Therefore, the prophets said that they served not God but the idols. But they could not endure this nor listen to it. Thus according to God's command they were not silent, and so they had to die, be expelled, and be persecuted.

8. Therefore, the whole dispute is that the false saints quarrel with the true saints about the worship of God and good works—the former saying this is divine worship; the latter saying, "No, it is idolatry and superstition." It has continued from the beginning and will continue to the end.

9. So also now. The Papists have invented good works and worship for themselves with their outward deeds and laws, but all of that is without faith, founded only on works and without God's command, mere human trifles. So we say that they do not serve God but themselves and the devil, as in all idolatry; and they only mislead the people away from their Christian faith and common brotherly love. But they will not put up with that, and so they cause the present misery.

Both sides agree that they are to serve God and do good works. But in defining what worship and good works are, they will never agree. For these people say that faith is [everything], but nature and reason with their works are lost. Those say that faith is nothing, but nature with its works is right.

Likewise, they also agree that coarse sins such as murder, adultery, and robbery are not right; but in the chief works that concern divine worship they are as separate as winter and summer. Those people hold to God and His mercy and fear Him. These run to wood and stone, food and clothing, days and seasons, and would win God over by building, founding, fasting, blubbering, and tonsuring. They fear nothing, are impudent and full of all arrogance. These holy, learned, wise people are not holy before God. They are not learned. They are not wise enough with all their prophets, wise men, and scribes.

10. There are several questions in this Gospel which we must look at. The first question is: Why does Christ say that all the righteous blood from Abel onward shall come on the Jews, since they have not shed it all [cf. Matt. 23:35–36]?

11. The answer is that the words of Christ are directed to the whole multitude and to the whole race of all those who from the beginning have persecuted the prophets. This is proved by the fact that He addressed not

only those of His own time but also all of Jerusalem: "Jerusalem, Jerusalem, you who kill the prophets and stone those who are sent to you! How often I have wanted to gather your children together," etc. [Matt. 23:37]. This applies not only to the people who were present but also to the previous inhabitants of Jerusalem.

Likewise, when He says: You murdered Zechariah "between the sanctuary and the altar," and yet this Zechariah was murdered by King Joash (2 Chronicles 24 [:21]) more than eight hundred years before Christ's birth, and still He says, "You have murdered him." So they also murdered Abel and will also murder the prophets and the wise men. It is as if He would say: "They are one people, of one kind, of one race; as the fathers, so also the children. For the obstinacy that opposed God and His prophets in the time of the fathers also opposes Him in their children. The mouse is like its mother." And when the Lord says that all the righteous blood shall come upon them, He means to say as much as that the people must shed all righteous blood. It is their nature to do so. They do not do otherwise. All blood that is shed, they shed. Therefore, all of it will come upon them.

12. But [the second question is] why does he cite only these two, Abel and Zechariah? Zechariah was not the last whose blood was shed, but after him Isaiah, Jeremiah, Ezekiel, Uriah, and Micah, and nearly all those who are named in the Scriptures. In fact, Zechariah is the first among the prophets reported in Scripture whose blood was shed. However, Christ does not speak here only of the prophets, but of the blood of all the righteous, of whom many were murdered under King Saul; likewise, many prophets under King Ahab, whose names are not mentioned.

13. In answer to this question I can say nothing except that Christ here holds to the usage of Scripture and sets us an example that we ought not to speak, hold, or mention what is not clearly founded in the Scriptures. For though Isaiah and other prophets have been murdered, yet we find no mention in the Scriptures of the manner of death of anyone after Zechariah. And thus, though he was not the last whose blood was shed, yet he is the last for whom there is a description of how he preached at his time and was murdered. Thus Christ cites the first and the last righteous persons mentioned in the Scriptures, and thus includes all other righteous blood that was not mentioned, yet was shed before and after them.[3]

It has indeed been written of the prophet Uriah that he was murdered by King Jehoiakim long after Zechariah (Jeremiah 26 [:23]); but this is told

3  The ordering of books in the Hebrew Old Testament differs from English Bibles. Abel's murder is described in the first book of the Hebrew Old Testament (Gen. 4:1–8); Zechariah's murder is described in the last book of the Hebrew Old Testament (2 Chron. 24:22). Thus all those murdered in between are included.

by others as a story which occurred long ago. At his time the Scriptures say nothing about him; they do not even mention that he ever lived, though they describe the time and history of the same king (2 Chronicles [36:4f.]; 2 Kings [24:1f.]). Therefore, the Lord does not cite him.

14. [The third question] is also asked: Why does Christ call him the son of Berekiah, since the Scriptures call him the son of Jehoiada? For these are the words: "The Spirit of God clothed Zechariah the son of Jehoiada the priest, and he stood above the people and said to them: 'Thus says God: "Why do you transgress the commandments of the Lord, so that you cannot prosper? You have forsaken the Lord, and so He has forsaken you."' But they conspired against him, and by command of the king they stoned him in the court of the house of the Lord. Joash the king did not remember the mercy that Jehoiada, Zechariah's father, had shown him, but killed his son. But when he was dying, he said, 'The Lord will see it and search it out!'" (2 Chronicles 24 [:20–22]). This happened because he reproved the worship they had established.

15. St. Jerome thinks he was called the son of Berekiah for spiritual reasons, because Berekiah means in Latin *benedictus*, "the one who is blessed." But others say more easily that his father, Jehoiada, was given the surname Berekiah perhaps because he did great good to the king and the people. Therefore, they called him "the blessed one," and after his death, out of gratitude, they murdered his son. This is the way of the world according to the saying: Whoever helps someone off the gallows will himself be helped back on by the same. Thus it happened to the Son of God. After God had done nothing but good for the whole world, they crucified His dear beloved Son, as is typified in this story.

16. Finally, [a fourth question] is asked: Since no one can withstand God's will, why, then, does He say, "How often I have wanted to gather your children together, and you were not willing" [Matt. 23:37]? This passage has been interpreted in various ways. Some have based it on free will and its ability, but it really appears that not free will but willfulness is reproved here, and that what is so severely condemned and reproved is a bad freedom that acts only contrary to God.

17. St. Augustine forces the words to apply to this understanding, as if the Lord means to say, "As many of your children as I have gathered, I have gathered against your will." But that is to do violence to these simple words. It would be much easier to say, "Christ speaks here as a man who has taken all human concerns on Himself." He did much according to His humanity that did not belong to His deity, such as that He had to eat, drink, sleep, walk, weep, suffer, and die. So one could say here that He spoke according to the human nature and its emotions: "I was willing, but you were unwilling."

18. For, as I have repeatedly said, we must give special attention to the words of Christ, some of which prove His divine nature, while others only prove His human nature. But, on the other hand, here He introduces Himself to us as God, since He says, "I send you," etc.—for sending prophets belongs to God alone. And He also said, "Therefore also the Wisdom of God says, 'Behold, I will send them prophets,'" etc. (Luke 11 [:49])—so His words sound as if He not only wanted to gather their children at that time but also previously and frequently, so that this is to be understood as referring to the divine will.

Therefore, we shall answer: These words are to be understood in the plainest and simplest manner as referring to the divine will, according to the usage of Scripture, which speaks of God as of a man for the sake of the simple, as it is written: "The Lord was sorry that He had made man" (Genesis 6 [:6]), and yet there is no sorrow in God. Likewise, it says that He was angry, yet there is no anger in Him. Likewise, the Lord came down to see the building at Babylon (Genesis 11 [:5]), yet He always remains sitting [on His throne]. And in the psalms, the prophet often says: "Awake! Why are You sleeping?" [e.g., Ps. 44:24]. Again: "Arise," come to me, and similar passages [cf. Ps. 9:19; 10:12]; and yet He does not sleep, does not lie down, is not far away. Again, God does not know "the way of the wicked" (cf. Psalm 1 [:6]), and yet He knows all things.

All these passages are uttered in harmony with our perception and way of thinking, and not according to the real state of the divine nature. Therefore, they are not to be used in lofty speculation about the heavenly utterances of the divine nature, but should be left here below, for the simple, and understood according to our feelings. For we do not perceive things any differently than if He did just as the words sound. This is a beautiful and comforting way to speak about God, which is neither terrifying nor high. Thus also here "how often I wanted" is to be understood as meaning that He acted in such a way that no one could think or feel otherwise than that He would gladly gather them, did gather them, as a man might do who eagerly wanted to do such a thing. Therefore, dismiss high things, and remain by the milk and simple meaning of the Scriptures [cf. 1 Pet. 2:2].

## THE DOCTRINE CONCERNING FAITH FROM THIS GOSPEL READING

19. In order, however, that we may take our doctrine from this Gospel reading, the Lord has given here a delightful picture and parable of what faith and believers are like, so that I do not know of a more delightful one in all the Scriptures. He spoke many harsh words to the Jews in this chapter out of His anger and indignation, and cried out His terrible "Woe!" on their unbelief

[cf. Matt. 23:1–31]. Therefore, He does as angry men are accustomed to do and speaks to those who were ungrateful for His kindness and goodwill in the strongest terms possible: "I would gladly have shared the heart in My body with them," etc. Thus also the Lord here, in the most heartfelt way possible, emphasizes His goodwill and kindness to the Jews and says He gladly would have been their mother hen if they had wanted to be His little chicks.

20. Note well how He pours forth these words and this parable with great earnestness and with His whole heart! In this picture you see how you are to conduct yourself toward Christ and what benefit He is to you, how you should make use of Him and enjoy Him. See the hen and her chicks, and there you see Christ and yourself painted and portrayed better than any painter can paint them.

21. First, it is certain that our souls are the chicks; the demons and evil spirits are the hawks in the air—except that we are not as clever as the chicks, to flee under our hen. The demons are more cunning in robbing us of our souls than the hawks are in stealing the chicks. Now it was said before in an Epistle reading that it is not enough for us to be godly, do good works, and live in grace. For our righteousness cannot stand before God's eyes and judgment, much less our unrighteousness. Therefore, I have said: Faith, if it is true faith, is of such a nature that it does not rely on itself nor on its believing, but clings to Christ, and takes refuge under His righteousness, and lets that be its shelter and refuge, just as the little chick does not rely on its own life and running, but takes refuge under the body and wings of the hen.

22. It is not enough for one who is to stand before God's judgment to say, "I believe and have grace," for all that is within him is not enough to protect him; but he opposes this judgment with Christ's own righteousness, which he lets deal with God's judgment and which stands gloriously before [God] forever. Under this [righteousness] he crawls, snuggles, and presses himself. He trusts and believes without any doubt that it will sustain him, and so it really happens that he is sustained by this faith, not because of him and his faith, but because of Christ and His righteousness under which he takes refuge. Moreover, faith that does not do this is not true faith.

See, that is what Scripture means when it says:

> He who sits under the shelter of the Most High and abides under the shadow of the Almighty will say to the Lord: "My refuge and my fortress, my God, in whom I hope." For He delivers me from the snare of the hunter and from the harmful pestilence. He will cover you with His pinions, and under His wings will be your refuge. His truth is a spear and shield, so that you need not fear the terror of the night, nor the arrow that flies by day, nor the pestilence that stalks in darkness, nor the plague that wastes at noonday. If a thousand fall at your side, and ten thousand at your right hand, yet it will not strike you. (Psalm 91 [:1–7])

23. See, all of this is said about faith in Christ, how it alone will stand and protect us from all danger and ruin, false doctrine, bodily and spiritual temptations from the devil, on the right hand and on the left, so that all others must fall and perish, because [faith] takes refuge under the wings and pinions of Christ and there finds refuge and confidence. So also Malachi says, "For you who fear My name, the sun of righteousness shall rise with healing under its wings" (Malachi 4 [:2]). Therefore, St. Paul calls Him *propitiatorium*, "the throne of grace" ([cf.] Romans 3 [:25]), and teaches everywhere how we must be sustained through Him and under Him. If, then, believers and saints are in need of such great shelter, what will become of those who proceed with their own free will and their own good works apart from Christ?

We must remain in Christ, on Christ, and under Christ, and not stray from our mother hen, or all is lost. St. Peter says, "The righteous is scarcely saved" (1 Peter 4 [:18]), so hard it is to remain under this hen. For many different temptations—temporal and spiritual—tear us from her, as the psalm above points out [Ps. 91:1–7].

24. Now see how the natural mother hen acts. Hardly any other animal takes such great interest in her young. She changes her natural voice and adopts a miserable and plaintive voice. She looks, she scratches [the ground], and calls her chicks. When she finds something, she does not eat it, but leaves it for the chicks. With all earnestness she battles and cries against the hawk, and willingly spreads out her wings and lets her chicks crawl under and on her, no matter what she suffers. This is indeed a delightful picture.

So also Christ has adopted a plaintive voice, has preached repentance to us, and from His whole heart pointed out to everyone their sin and misery. He scratches in the Scriptures and calls us to them and lets us eat them. He spreads His wings over us with all His righteousness, merit, and grace, and takes us lovingly under Him, warms us with His own natural heat—that is, with His Holy Spirit, who comes through Him alone—and fights for us against the devil in the air [cf. Eph. 2:2].

25. Where and how does He do this? Without a doubt He does it not bodily, but spiritually. His two wings are the two Testaments of Holy Scripture. They spread over us His righteousness and bring us under Him. This takes place when the Scriptures teach this and nothing else: that Christ is such a mother hen, that we are sustained in faith under Him and through His righteousness. Therefore, the psalm mentioned above [Ps. 91:1–7] itself explains the wings and pinions as "His faithfulness" or truth, that is, the Scriptures grasped in faith, "a breastplate and shield" against all fear and danger [cf. Eph. 6:13–15; 1 Thess. 5:8]. For we must grasp Christ in His Word and preaching and cling to Him with a firm faith that He is just as it says

about Him. Then we are certainly in Him, under His wings and truth, and shall be also well sustained under Him.

26. Therefore, His wings or truth is this Gospel, as well as all other Gospels, for they all teach Christ in this way—yet in some places more clearly than in others. Above, He was called a light and life,[4] also a Lord and helper. Now He is called a mother hen, and the emphasis is continually laid on faith. Thus His body is Himself, or the Christian Church. His warmth is His grace and the Holy Spirit.

27. See, that is the most loving hen, who would always gather us under her. She spreads her wings out and calls; that is, she preaches and has both Testaments preached, sends out prophets, wise men, and scribes to Jerusalem and into all the world. But what happens? We do not want to be chicks. Above all, the arrogant saints, who contend against her especially with their good works, have no desire to know that faith is so greatly needed and blessed, and that they are in danger, and they refuse to let what they do be called wrong. In fact, they themselves become hawks and swine. They devour and persecute the chicks along with the hens, tear their wings and bodies, murder prophets, and stone those sent to them. But what will be their reward? Listen, terrible things:

*See, your house shall be left to you desolate. [Matt. 23:38]*

28. That is a horrible punishment! We also see that in the Jews. They murdered the prophets so long that God sends them no more. He has now left them 1,500 years without preaching, without prophets; He has taken His Word from them and has drawn His wings back to Himself. And thus their house is desolate. No one edifies their souls. God no longer dwells among them. It has happened to them just as they wanted, as Psalm 109 [:17] says about them: "He wanted to have the curse; the curse will come upon him too! He did not want any blessing; it will stay far from him too!" (Psalm 109 [:17]). All the blood shed on the earth runs over them, and this Gospel is fulfilled in them.

29. Thus Isaiah said about them: "Well, then, I will show you what I will do to My vineyard. I will remove its wall, that it may be devoured; and its fence shall be torn down, that it may be trampled down. I will make it to lie wasted, that it may not be pruned or hoed; instead, thistles and thorns shall grow up. I will also command the clouds that they rain no rain upon it" (Isaiah 5 [:5–6]). Horrible words!

What does it mean that no rain shall come on them, except that they should not hear of the Gospel and faith? They shall be neither pruned nor

4  See sermon for Third Day of Christmas on John 1:1–14.

hoed—what does this mean, except that no one shall reprove them in their error and reveal their defects? Therefore, [the vineyard] is left to the doctrines of men, which tear and trample it so that it must remain desolate, so that it brings forth nothing but hedges and thorns, that is, work-saints who are without faith and bear no fruit of the Spirit. They grow and are prepared only for eternal fire, just like the hedges and thorns.

30. However, we Gentiles, too, can certainly take all of this to heart. It is just as bad with us, if not worse. We have also persecuted the mother hen and have not remained in faith. Therefore, it has also happened to us that [God] has left our house to lie desolate and our vineyard forsaken. There is no longer any rain in all the world. The Gospel and faith are put to silence. There is neither pruning nor hoeing; no one preaches against false works and the doctrines of men and prunes off such unnecessary things. Rather, He lets us be torn and trampled by the pope, bishops, priests, and monks, of whom the whole world is full, full, full; and yet they do no more than trample down and tear to pieces the vineyard. One teaches this, another that. One tramples this place, another that. Each wants to establish his sect, his order, his class, his doctrine, his theses, his works. By these we are so trampled that there is no longer any knowledge of faith, no Christian life, no love, no fruit of the Spirit, but mere fuel for the fire, hedges, and thorns—that is, dissemblers and hypocrites, who with their vigils, Masses, endowments, bells, churches, psalms, rosaries, saint worship, celebrations, cowls, tonsures, clothing, fastings, pilgrimages, and numberless other foolish works presume to be Christians.

31. O Lord God, we are too greatly torn to pieces, too greatly trampled. O Lord Christ, we miserable people are too desolate and forsaken in these last days of wrath. Our shepherds are wolves, our watchmen are traitors, our patrons are enemies, our fathers are murderers, and our teachers mislead us. Oh! Oh! When, when, when will Your severe wrath have an end?

32. Finally, comfort is spoken here to the Jews when He says, "For I tell you, from now on you will not see Me until you say, 'Praised be He who comes in the name of the Lord' " [Matt. 23:39]. Christ spoke these words on the Tuesday after Palm Sunday, and they form the conclusion and the last words of His preaching on earth; therefore, they are not yet fulfilled, but they must be fulfilled. They certainly did once receive Him on Palm Sunday, but these words were not then fulfilled. When He says, "You will not see Me again," this is not to be understood that they never saw Him afterward in the body, since they afterward crucified Him. But He means that they shall not see Him again as a preacher and as Christ, to which end He was sent; His office and He in His office were never seen again by them. In this preaching He gave them His last words, and His office, for which He was sent, was now concluded.

33. Now it is certain that the Jews will yet say to Christ: "Blessed is He who comes in the name of the Lord." Moses foretold this: "In the latter days, you will return to the Lord your God and obey His voice. For the Lord your God is a merciful God. He will not leave you or destroy you or forget the covenant with your fathers that He swore to them" (Deuteronomy 4 [:30–31]). Likewise, Hosea foretold this: "The children of Israel will be long without king or prince, without sacrifice or altar, without ephod or worship. Afterward the children of Israel shall return and seek the Lord their God, and David their king, and they shall honor the Lord and His goodness in the last time" (Hosea 3 [:4–5]). And Azariah said: "If you forsake [the Lord], He will forsake you. There will be many days in Israel without the true God and without a teaching priest and without Law. And when in their distress they turn to the Lord, the God of Israel, and seek Him, He will let Himself be found by them" (2 Chronicles 15 [:2–4]).

These passages cannot be understood other than of the present Jews. They have never before been without princes, without prophets, without priests, without teachers, and without the Law. St. Paul agrees and says: "Blindness has come upon Israel, in part, until the fullness of the Gentiles has come in. And in this way all Israel will be saved" (Romans 11 [:25–26]). God grant that this time may be near at hand, as we hope it is. Amen.[5]

---

5 Early in his career, Luther held out hope that large numbers of Jews would convert to Christianity. See *Lectures on Romans* (1515–16/1938–39), LW 25:429; *That Jesus Christ Was Born a Jew* (1523), LW 45:199–200; Mark Thompson, "Luther and the Jews," *Reformed Theological Review* 67, no. 3 (December 2008): 121–45, especially 128–30; and the introduction to *Four Sermons of Eisleben* (1546), LW 60:402 9.

The editions of the *Church Postil* after Luther's death (1546) have the following conclusion: "These passages all speak of the last times, when the Jewish kingdom and the true priesthood have ceased, but nevertheless many Jews will be converted to the true King and Priest, Christ, which happened after Christ's ascension through the apostles and later by the preaching of the Gospel. Amen" (E² 10:244 n. 82). Cf. sermon for Second Sunday in Advent on Luke 21:25–33, paragraph 56.

# GOSPEL FOR ST. JOHN'S DAY

*[December 27]*

*John 21:19–24*

*And after saying this He said to him [Peter], "Follow Me." Peter turned and saw the disciple whom Jesus loved following them, the one who also had leaned back against Him during the supper and had said, "Lord, who is it that is going to betray You?" When Peter saw Him, He said to Jesus, "Lord, what about this man?" Jesus said to him, "If it is My will that he remain until I come, what is that to you? You follow Me!" So the saying spread abroad among the brothers that this disciple was not to die; yet Jesus did not say to him that he was not to die, but, "If it is My will that he remain until I come, what is that to you?" This is the disciple who is bearing witness about these things, and who has written these things, and we know that his testimony is true.*

1. When Christ asked Peter three times whether he loved Him, and Peter answered three times, "Yes, I love you; You know this" [John 21:15], He three times commended His sheep to him and said, "Feed My sheep." Afterward He foretold Peter's death and said, "Truly, truly, I say to you, when you were young, you used to gird yourself and walk wherever you wanted, but when you are old, you will stretch out your hands, and another will gird you and lead you where you do not want to go" [John 21:18]. Then after this Gospel comes: "Follow Me," as if to say: "Because this will happen to you, keep this in mind and follow Me and yield willingly to death." It is clear enough that this "following" signifies his death, and all the disciples understood that, so that this is a clear and easy Gospel.

2. However, as some are greatly troubled about whether St. John died or is still alive, the evangelist shows clearly enough that Christ did not wish to have us know that; therefore, we should not seek it out. He says, "Jesus did not say he would not die, and He does not now say that he would die." He thus lets it be in doubt. If Christ had said, "I want him to remain until I come," it might have been understood that he would die on the Last Day. Because He says, "If it is My will that he remain," it is even more obscure, since He does not simply say whether it is His will or is not His will.

3. But in doing this Christ has given us an excellent and notable teaching, and for this reason Christ dismissed Peter with these words.

# THE TEACHING OF THIS GOSPEL READING

The teaching is as follows: irrespective of the example and lives of all the saints, everyone should attend to what is entrusted to him and pay attention to his calling. This is such a needed and beneficial teaching. It is a very common error that we look at the works of the saints and how they have lived and want to imitate them, thinking that what they did was precious and good. The useless babblers aid and urge this by preaching the lives of the dear saints and incorrectly presenting them to the people as examples.

4. Here Christ acts and speaks against this. Peter is a picture of such wild peddlers; when Christ had commanded him at once to follow Him, he turns about and looks at someone else and worries where the one Jesus loved is going. This is done also by those who ignore what has been commanded them and who look at the lives and works of those God loved, namely, His saints. Therefore, Christ leads Peter back and says, "What is that to you, where he goes? Follow Me, and let Me deal with him. If I wanted him to remain, would you also remain? Do you think I want the same from you as from him? No, not so. You attend to what is yours and to what I say to you. He, too, will find what is his. I want to have many kinds of servants, but they will not all do the same work."

5. See, there are many people who do everything except what is commanded them. Many hear that certain saints made pilgrimages, for which they are praised. So the fool starts off, leaves wife and children sitting, who are entrusted to him by God, and runs to St. James,[1] or here and there, and does not recognize that his calling and command are much different from that of the saint he is following. They do the same with their bequests, fastings, clothing, celebrations, priestcraft, monkery, and nunnery. All that is nothing but looking back at the disciple Christ loved and turning their backs to the command and calling to follow Christ. Then they claim they have done well, since they followed the saints.

6. Therefore, take heed that the way of God goes on the right road. First, it does not tolerate a human doctrine and way, or a command. Second, it does not tolerate self-sought or self-chosen works. Third, it does not tolerate the examples of the saints. Instead, it is directed toward paying attention to how God will lead us and what He wants from us. As the prophet says: "God teaches the way He has chosen" and "He teaches the humble His way" (cf. Psalm 25 [:8–9]).

7. Then you may reply: "But if I am not called, what shall I do then?" Answer: How is it possible that you are not called? You will always be in

1 That is, the shrine of Santiago de Compostela in Spain, one of the most popular pilgrimage sites of the Middle Ages.

some estate; you are a husband or a wife, or a son or a daughter, or a servant or a maid. Take the lowest estate for yourself. Are you a husband, and you think you do not have enough to do in that estate with governing your wife, children, domestics, and property so that all may be obedient to God and that you do no one any wrong? Even if you had four heads and ten hands, you would still be too little either to make a pilgrimage or to take some saint's work as your own.

8. Again, are you a son or daughter, and do you think you have not enough to do with being modest, chaste, and temperate during your youth, with obeying your parents, with not offending anyone by words or deeds? Yes, when someone gets out of the habit of honoring this sort of command and calling, he goes and prays the rosary and the like, things that do not serve his calling, and no one thinks about paying attention to his estate.

9. Again, are you a maid or servant, and do you think you would be idle if you were to serve your lord or mistress faithfully with all diligence in your estate and command, and keep your youth in check?

10. Again, are you a prince or lord, spiritual or secular? Who has more to do than you, in order that your subjects do right, peace is preserved, and wrong is done to no one? Where do you think the proverb comes from: "A prince or lord is rare game in heaven"? It comes from this: they leave their office, want to rule far and wide, and cannot rule themselves; afterward they come and want to make up for it with hearing Mass, bequests, rosaries, prayers, and indulgences, as if God dealt in secondhand clothes or like a child could be fooled with a penny.

11. So also now the bishops and spiritual prelates should feed the sheep of Christ and follow Christ, and even suffer death for it. Yet they observe their seven hours,[2] hold Mass, and have themselves called pious people. But if [even] one of the bishops enters heaven, then there must be a different heaven. All bishops at present are nothing but firewood for hell, since they administer not a bit of their office.

12. See, just as now no one is without some command and calling, so no one is without some kind of work, if he desires to do what is right. Everyone is to concentrate on remaining in his estate, looking to himself, looking after what has been commanded to him, and serving God and keeping His commandments. Then he will have so much to do that all time will be too short, all places too cramped, all strength too weak. For the evil spirit furiously attacks this way and makes it bitter for man so that only with difficulty can he continue in it. But if [Satan] brings one to the point of forgetting and abandoning his calling, then he no longer attacks him so hard. He has brought

---

2 The Divine Office, consisting of eight prayer services held at seven times throughout the day and night, to which all monks and clergy were obligated.

him off the highway, and he lets him at times find a path through the grass or a forest trail to nowhere,[3] that is, doing a minor good work that is not his own. Then the fool thinks he is on the right road and anticipates a great reward in heaven. The longer he wanders, the farther he strays from the highway, until he comes into the most pernicious delusion: that he thinks we are to deal with God by means of works, like King Saul did.

Oh no, dear man, with God it is not a matter of works, but of obedience, as Scripture says, "God does not want sacrifice, but obedience" (cf. 1 Samuel 15 [:22]). Therefore, it happens that a pious maid does what she is ordered and according to her office sweeps the yard or carries out the manure, or a servant in the same way plows and drives a team—they are walking straight toward heaven on the right road; while another who goes to St. James or to church, and ignores his office and work, is walking straight toward hell.

13. Therefore, we must close our eyes and not look at whether our works are great, small, honorable, contemptible, spiritual, temporal, or what kind of reputation and name they may have on earth; but look to the command and the obedience that is within it. If that is there, then the work also is right, precious, and completely godly, even if it were so insignificant as picking up a straw. However, if obedience and the command are not there, then the work is also not right but damnable, surely the devil's own work, even if it were so great as raising the dead.

For it is established: God's eyes do not look at the works, but at the obedience in the works. Therefore, it is His will that we look to His command and call. St. Paul says, "Each one should remain in the calling in which he was called" (cf. 1 Corinthians 7 [:17]). And St. Peter says, "Serve one another, each with the gift he has received, as good stewards of God's varied grace" (1 Peter 4 [:10]). See, here Peter says that the grace and gifts of God are not of one kind but varied, and each is to concentrate on his own, develop it, and with it be of service to others.

14. What a fine thing it would be if it were to happen that each attended to his own affairs and yet served others with them, and thus traveled together with one another on the right road to heaven. Thus St. Paul also writes that the body has many members, but the members do not all have the same function (Romans 12 [:4]; 1 Corinthians 12 [:12]). Since we have many members of one congregation, but all do not have the same function, no one should concentrate on someone else's work, but each should concentrate on his own, and all should live harmoniously in simple obedience to various commands in manifold works.

---

3 *Holzweg*, a path that is cut into the forest for the purpose of gathering wood but that does not connect to other towns or roads; a dead end.

15. If you then reply: "What? Should we not follow the lives and examples of the dear saints? Why, then, are they preached?" Answer: One should preach them so that God is praised in them, so that we are stirred up and take comfort in His goodness and grace and are shown not their works, but the obedience in their works. But now the obedience is left behind, and we are led so deeply into works that we have completely gotten away from obedience. We drop our jaws at works while despising our own command and calling. Therefore, there is no doubt that it is the instigation of the worst devil that has confined divine worship only to churches, altars, Masses, singing, reading, sacrifices, and the like, as if all other works were vain or of no use whatever. How could the devil have led us more completely from the right way than when he confines God's worship so narrowly, only to the churches and what is done in them?

16. Be on your guard. Look in front of you. Christ will not allow Peter to look around at the disciple whom He nevertheless loves. Do you think it was in vain that "the disciple whom Christ loved" more than all the other disciples was cited? It also did not happen in vain that he was not mentioned by name. He could have said: "Peter turned and saw John," rather than "the one Jesus loved," etc. But He wanted to oppose this vice and banish from their sight the works of the saints, so that pure obedience would remain, and no one would brag or use the excuse that he had followed the example of the saints.

17. See, we read in Scripture that God did not want David to build Him a church, even though David began to do so, because previously there had been no command for that. But He wanted Solomon to build it and gave him a command about it. All idolatry has come from regarding the works of the saints and not their obedience. They have seen how Noah, Abraham, Isaac, and Jacob sacrificed to God on altars. They went ahead and wanted to imitate them and produced idolatry. Scripture signifies such people by the name "apes," that is, an animal which looks only at the works and wants to imitate everything, even though nothing is commanded.

18. Therefore, let us grasp the words of Christ well: "You follow Me" [John 21:19]. You, you; let others attend to their affairs, you attend to yours; they will indeed come. For it is not in vain that in this Gospel it is stated that the disciple whom Peter looked at was also following, but he was following without Peter's looking. This whole Gospel lesson has been written for the sake of these words and their teaching; for it does not contain much on the doctrine of faith, but on the following and the works of faith. In the persona of Peter, Christ here addresses all spiritual prelates and instructs them in their office. The whole Gospel should treat this, but [these prelates] perhaps want to be left untaught by us. Therefore, we must pass it by and remain with our own duties.

# THE SECOND TEACHING

19. The second teaching from this Gospel is that everyone should be satisfied with his own part and not resent what someone else has nor murmur, though he is unlike him. For here, though John alone is called the disciple Jesus loves, still none of them murmured or resented that. Similarly, even though they thought that he would not die, that did not bother anyone, and there was no murmuring among them; but as the text says, "A saying spread abroad among the brothers" [John 21:23]. They (all the disciples and Christians) spoke of this as brothers and wished him well.

20. And this is no insignificant virtue. It breaks many great people, for even the holy patriarchs were lacking in this virtue and could not stand the superiority of Joseph, their brother.

21. It is a very common affliction that no one is satisfied with his own lot, so that even the heathen say, "How does it happen that there is always better fruit in another's field and that the neighbor's cow gives more milk than our own? Likewise, how does it happen that no one is satisfied with his life, that each thinks that another's life is better than his own?" Whoever is a merchant praises the craftsman who sits quietly at rest, while he must travel all over the countryside. On the other hand, the craftsman praises the merchant, because he is rich and is out among the people, and so on. Everyone is bored with his way of life and sighs for someone else's. If he is married, then he praises the one who has no wife; if he has no [wife], then he praises the married estate. If he is a minister, then he would prefer the secular estate; on the other hand, if he is secular, then he would prefer to be a minister. God cannot treat them in such a way that they would be satisfied. If they would serve Him in the life He has prepared for them, then [that life] would not be bitter or difficult for them. But now they are bored, and no one burdens them but themselves. Without the least need or cause, they themselves make their lives bitter.

22. And if God allowed someone to change his way of life according to his own wishes, in order to fix that boredom, then everything would stay the same, except that he would become more bored and finally [want to] remain with his [previous life]. Therefore, one must not think of changing his way of life but of changing his boredom. Cast aside and change the boredom, then one way of life will be like another for you, and all estates will have the same value when you realize you neither needed nor wished a change.

23. Thus some heathen have thought that if the sufferings of all people were all brought together and then evenly distributed, it would certainly happen that everyone would prefer to retain his own. God rules the world so very evenly that to every advantage there clings an equal disadvantage. Everyone sees no more than how well the shoe fits on someone else, but does not see where it pinches him. On the other hand, the one who wears the shoe

thinks not how well it fits, but how sorely it pinches. The world rushes on in this folly: everyone looks only at his own bad and at another's good; but if he should see only his own good and the other's bad, then he would thank God and be very satisfied, no matter how insignificant and bad his life is.

24. In order to avoid such unrest, discord, and boredom, faith is helpful and necessary, which believes with certainty that God governs all alike and places each one in the life which is the most useful and suitable for him, so that it could not turn out better, even if he had chosen it himself. This faith brings rest, satisfaction, and peace and banishes boredom. But where there is no faith, and one judges according to his own feelings, thoughts, and experiences, then boredom begins, for he feels only the complaints of his own life and not that of his neighbor. Again, he does not see the advantage of his life nor the suffering of his neighbor. That feeling then produces boredom, disgust, trouble, and labor in his life, and he becomes impatient and quarrelsome with God. Then praise, love, and thanks to God are silenced in him, and he remains his whole life a secret murmurer against God, like the Jews in the wilderness [cf. Deut. 1:27; Ps. 106:25]. Nevertheless, he has nothing more from it than that he makes his own life bitter and merits hell besides.

25. Therefore, you see how faith is necessary in all things, and how it makes everything easy, good, and sweet, even if you were in prison or in death, as the martyrs prove. And without [faith] all things are difficult, evil, and bitter, even if you had the pleasure and joy of the whole world, as all the great lords and wealthy prove, who always lead the most wretched lives.

26. Some say: "Yes, if I knew that neither my folly nor the devil had led me here, and I were certain that God Himself took care of me, I would gladly be joyful, satisfied, and contented." Answer: That is a foolish and unchristian assertion, which reveals an unbelieving heart. Christ says, "Look at the lilies of the field, how they grow" (Matthew 6 [:28]). Again: "Are not two sparrows bought for a penny? And not one of them will fall to the ground apart from your Father. But even the hairs of your head are all numbered. But you are better than many sparrows" (Matthew 10 [:29–31]).

27. If, then, your way of life is an estate which is not in itself sinful, though you have come into it through sin and folly, that way of life or estate will not therefore be any less pleasing to God; for God takes pleasure in all things except sin, as Moses says (Genesis 1 [:31]). Therefore, if you are in a calling that is not sinful in itself, you are certainly placed there by God, in a way of life that is well pleasing to God. Only take care that you do not sin in it. If you fall from a loft and break a bone in two, the room or the bed to which the fall brought you—and in which it forced you to remain—would not be any the worse or displeasing to God, even if someone else came there without such a fall.

28. I would even take it as a definite sign that you are in a truly God-pleasing estate if you feel boredom and disgust in it. God is surely present there, and lets the wicked foe attack and test whether you are fickle or steadfast, and gives your faith cause to battle and be strengthened.

29. When I speak of a calling which in itself is not sinful, I do not mean that we can live on the earth without sin. [People in] all callings and ways of life sin daily. But I mean the callings that God has instituted or whose institution is not opposed to God, such as marriage, servant, maid, lord, wife, sovereign, ruler, judge, officer, farmer, citizen, etc. I list as sinful callings robbery, usury, prostitution, and—as they are at present—the pope, cardinals, bishops, priests, monks, and nuns who neither preach nor listen to preaching. For these callings are certainly against God, where they only say Mass and sing and are not busy with God's Word, so that an ordinary woman may much sooner enter heaven than one of these.

30. To be clergy and not busy with God's Word, which should be your special work, is like being married and never together, but one fornicating here, the other there. In order to carry that out, many chapters and cloisters have become the devil's brothels and houses of prostitution: outwardly, in body, godly; but inwardly, in the soul, nothing but sin.

## Secret Meaning

31. Let us now be satisfied with these two doctrines. St. Augustine, however, strolls off to the side and interprets the two apostles, Peter and John, as two sorts of lives: St. Peter as the *active life* and St. John as the *contemplative life*. Therefore, he says that the active life must follow Christ and die, but the contemplative life remains forever. This is fine and easy, except that some have written so much about these two kinds of life that they have obscured the whole matter and no longer know what active or contemplative life is.

32. I, in my coarse manner of thinking, take it that the active life must not only cease and die bodily but also spiritually; that is, it must be rejected by the world, so that man does not rely on his works, even if they are good and must happen, but lives alone by faith and relies on Christ. That is the disciple whom Christ loves. Here the Gospel bursts open and shines forth its spiritual meanings, of which I do not perceive them all. For Christ's words and conduct emphasize works in such a way that they think only of faith.

33. Let us then take John to mean faith, or the inner life of the soul in faith, and St. Peter to mean works, or the outer life in works, yet in such a way that they are not separated from each other in one man. Thus we shall see the mysteries and what the active and contemplative life is with its dying and remaining.

34. First, he says, "This is the disciple whom Christ loved" [cf. John 21:20]. This means that faith alone makes people the truly beloved disciples of Christ, who receive the Holy Spirit through this very same faith, not through their works. Works also make disciples—not beloved disciples, but only temporary hypocrites who do not persevere. God's love does not keep them, because they do not believe.

35. Second, this is the disciple who at the Supper leaned back on Christ's breast [cf. John 21:20]. That is a great thing! Faith owns the heart of Christ; that is, it has all that Christ has and all right understanding. I have often said above, previously in the Epistle on Christmas Day, that faith makes Christ and the believer one, both having the same things in common. What Christ is and has becomes the property of the believer, and vice versa, as St. Paul says, "God did not spare His own Son but gave Him up for us all; how will He not also with Him give us all things?" (Romans 8 [:32]). Therefore, a Christian believer relies on Christ, takes comfort from Him, and leans on Him as on his own possession, given to him by God, just as St. John leans back on Christ's breast as on his couch, secure and certain.

36. See, faith in Christ brings with itself such a superabundant possession that one leans on Christ and rests securely and most tenderly, so that he fears nothing, neither sin, death, hell, the world, nor the devil; for he rests on life, on grace, and on salvation, possessing all things in heaven and on earth, yet only in faith, not yet manifestly. This is indicated by the fact that John leans back on Christ's breast not after His resurrection or in the morning, but before the resurrection and at supper, that is, still in this life, which is a supper, that is, at the end of the world, when souls are nourished by the Easter Lamb and the Gospel, which is prepared, served, and eaten by faith and through the preaching of the Word.

37. Third, he particularly mentions the breast, not the lap or the arms, indicating thereby that faith has all the wisdom of God and the correct understanding of all things. St. Paul says, "We have the mind of Christ," [and] again: "The spiritual man judges all things and is judged by no one" (1 Corinthians 2 [:16, 15]). Again: "When one turns to the Lord, the veil of Moses is removed" (2 Corinthians 3 [:16]), so that he knows all things. Therefore, the believer can rightly judge what is good and right in all estates, all works, all doctrines, all spirits, and never fails.

38. See, in this way man not only has all things through faith in Christ but also rightly, certainly, and wisely understands, knows, and judges all things. Moses saw this in the Law when he taught that from all animal sacrifices the breast is due to the priest and is to be his own (Leviticus [7:31]). But all believers and Christians are priests, as St. Peter says (1 Peter 2 [:9]). Therefore, faith brings him all property and all wisdom, so that through

property they are rich kings and have enough, and through wisdom they are great priests who can judge, order, and teach all the world.

39. Fourth, this is the disciple who said to Jesus: "Lord, who is it that is going to betray You?" [John 21:20]. What does that mean? Judas the betrayer was a figure of the pope, bishops, and clergy who abandon God's Word and introduce their own doctrines and works, by which they uproot Christian truth. Now their life has a fine appearance with their spiritual airs, ways, and works, so that natural reason cannot comprehend how they can be mistaken; natural reason even helps and praises it.

40. Now, since true faith and boasting about works never go together, and no one may rely on God's grace (that is, lean on Christ's breast) who relies on his works and doings, therefore grace and truth must sink as much as boasting about works rises. Thus it happens that truth unexpectedly and secretly sinks through these traitors, the clergy—so secretly, in fact, that the orthodox do not become aware of it, unless they diligently seek after truth. For Christ foretold that even the elect might be led astray (Matthew 24 [:24]). And therefore John is not content with leaning on the breast of Christ but anxiously goes on to ask who the betrayer is.

41. Thus the orthodox, by exploring Christian truth and considering grace, learn who this betrayer is; for since they notice that only grace (that is, Christ) and nothing outside of grace helps, and that nothing else is to be relied on, they easily see by this comparison of grace and nature that everything outside of grace is misleading. Then grace speaks to their heart so that they see that all who establish doctrine, life, and work apart from grace—and assert that they make people spiritual and godly in that way—are betrayers, murderers, and destroyers of grace.

42. Thus the betrayer of Christ is none other than the hypocrites who go on with the good appearance of a holy life and a spiritual estate, and yet annihilate Christian truth and the light of grace in themselves and in everybody else, so that nothing but human trifles remains with them. No one recognizes this except those who have true faith, and not even they do so before they pay special attention to it, investigate, ask, and compare one with the other; otherwise they also will allow such works to pass, thinking in their simplicity that they are being done correctly in faith because they so closely resemble genuine Christian works.

As a result, the betrayer's name is Judas Iscariot. Judas means "confessor," for all such saints confess Christ, do not openly deny Him, and even in their lives appear better than the true confessors. Iscariot, however, means "reward," for such saints are only pleasure-seeking, reward-seeking, and selfish. Everything that they do, they do for themselves, and nothing is done freely for the honor of God, just as Judas with his carrying of the moneybag sought and worked for nothing more than his own advantage. See, the world is full of spiritual people who basically are nothing but Iscariots, seeking their own advantage, who with their appearance lead all the world away from the right path of faith, and thus despise and sell Christ, that is, Christian truth and grace. More is to be said about this in the Passion.[4]

43. Now you see why St. John does not mention his own name. For faith neither makes sects and differences, as works do, nor does [faith] have any particular works by which it might be described. It performs all sorts of works, as they happen to be required, one as well as the other. But Judas Iscariot's kind is divided according to their works without faith. One is called a bishop because of his hat and staff, not because of faith; another is called a barefooted [Franciscan] because of his cowl and wooden shoes; a third is called an Augustinian because of his black cowl; and so on—one for this reason, another for that. But faith through all works and estates remains entirely nameless, and that is why it makes disciples whom Christ loves. Peter also has a name, for faith is not without works, but his is a name that Christ has given to him; it is not the cause of his being a beloved disciple.

44. Now we see what it means that this disciple is to remain and Peter is to follow, as said above. Faith remains until Christ comes, then it ceases; but works must sink and be despised. The world can take all things from us and destroy them, even our good works and good lives; but it must leave faith in our hearts, and [faith] will remain until the Last Day. From all this it can be understood that St. John has not written such things about himself for his own glory, as if he wanted to be regarded as something special above others. But he wanted to describe the secret and abundant virtue of faith. Only after the ascension of Christ did he understand that these things were done by Christ for that reason.

45. It is also a good sign that St. Peter turned to look at John, rather than St. John at Peter. For the works are to look to where faith stands, not faith to the works. Whoever has the time and desire to look can find many more meanings here.

---

4 When he composed the Lenten portion of his postil in 1525, Luther did not deal further with this theme. Instead of writing a new sermon on the Passion of Christ, he included *Sermon concerning Meditation on the Holy Suffering of Christ* (1519), of which see paragraph 1.

# GOSPEL FOR THE SUNDAY AFTER CHRISTMAS

*Luke 2:33–40*

*And His father and His mother marveled at what was said about Him. And Simeon blessed them and said to Mary His mother, "Behold, this child is appointed for the fall and rising of many in Israel, and for a sign that is opposed (and a sword will pierce through your own soul also), so that thoughts from many hearts may be revealed." And there was a prophetess, Anna, the daughter of Phanuel, of the tribe of Asher. She was advanced in years, having lived with her husband seven years from when she was a virgin, and then as a widow until she was eighty-four. She did not depart from the temple, worshiping with fasting and prayer night and day. And coming up at that very hour she began to give thanks to God and to speak of Him to all who were waiting for the redemption of Jerusalem. And when they had performed everything according to the Law of the Lord, they returned into Galilee, to their own town of Nazareth. And the child grew and became strong, filled with wisdom. And the favor of God was upon Him.*

1. The previous Epistle reading has apparently been prescribed for this Sunday by sheer misunderstanding. Whoever prescribed it thought that because it speaks of a young heir who is lord of all the property, it was spoken of the young child Christ. Many other Epistle readings and Gospel readings have been prescribed for unsuitable days from similar misunderstandings. Yet nothing depends on the series; it is the same whatever is preached at whatever time, if only the correct understanding remains in the series.

Thus this Gospel reading happened on the day of our Lady's Candlemas,[1] when she brought the child into the temple, and yet it is read on this Sunday. I say all this so that nobody may be confused by the chronological order or prevented from correctly understanding the Gospel. We will divide it into two parts: the one treating of Simeon, and the other of Anna. It is indeed a rich Gospel reading and well arranged: first, the man Simeon; second, the woman Anna, both aged and holy.

---

1 That is, the Feast of the Presentation of Our Lord, which is observed forty days after Christmas, on February 2.

## THE FIRST PART, ON SIMEON

*His father and His mother marveled at what was said about Him.*
*[Luke 2:33]*

2. What are those marvelous things, and through whom were they
spoken about Him? They are, of course, the things which St. Simeon had
spoken immediately before, when in the temple he took the child Jesus in
his arms and said: "Lord, now You are letting Your servant depart in peace,
according to Your Word; for my eyes have seen Your Savior, whom You have
prepared in the presence of all peoples, a light to enlighten the Gentiles,
and for the praise of Your people Israel" [Luke 2:29–32]. Luke says that they
marveled at these things, that this aged, holy man stood there before them
in the temple, took the child in his arms, and with joy spoke so gloriously
about Him, that He should be the light of all the world, a Savior of all people,
a praise of all Israel; and [Simeon] regarded Him so highly that he would now
gladly die since he had seen the child.

3. Now it was indeed marvelous that such things were said openly there
in that public and holy place by the great man, even though [he said them
about] a poor, despised baby, whose mother was poor and insignificant and
whose father, Joseph, was not wealthy. How could such a baby be considered
the Savior of all people, the light of all Gentiles, and the glory and honor of
all Israel? Now that it is known, it no longer seems so marvelous; but when
nothing as yet was known, they were very marvelous, and this poor infancy
was exceedingly unequal to the huge and great things Simeon said about Him.

But Joseph and Mary nevertheless believed it, and for that reason they
also marveled. If they had not believed it, it would have been despised by
them and not marvelous, but false and useless. Therefore, the fact that they
were marveling shows that Joseph and Mary had a high and great faith.

4. But someone might say: "Why, then, do they marvel at this? Had not
the angels told them before that He was Christ and the Savior, and had not
the shepherds also spoken glorious things about Him? It was also marvelous
that the kings or wise men had come from distant lands to worship Him with
their offerings. Mary knew well that she had conceived Him of the Holy Spirit
and had borne Him in an unusual way. Moreover, the angel Gabriel had said
that He should be great and be called God's Son [Luke 1:32]. In short, so far
[all] had been marvelous; now nothing was marvelous, but only those things
are announced and proclaimed concerning Him which have not happened
and are not yet seen."

5. I think that in this case we need not climb high nor seek far [for an
explanation]. The evangelist does not deny that they had marveled before
this, but here he simply wants to report what they did when St. Simeon spoke

such glorious things about the child. He means to say, "When Simeon spoke great things about the child, His parents did not despise that, but believed it firmly." Therefore, they stood there, listened to him, and marveled at his words. What else could they do? Thus it is not denied here that previously they marveled just as much, if not more.

6. We shall inquire later into the spiritual significance of this astonishment. Now we are concerned about the literal sense, which serves as an example for our faith, that we also should teach that God's works toward us are marvelous, that beginning and ending appear very much unlike. The beginning is nothing, the end is everything; just as here Christ, the child, appears to be nothing, and yet He finally became the Savior and light of all peoples.

7. If Joseph and Mary had judged according to what they saw, they would have considered Christ no more than a poor baby. But they disregard what they see and cling to the words of Simeon with a firm faith, and therefore they marvel at what he says. Thus we must also disregard all the senses when contemplating the works of God, and only cling to His words, so that our eyes and our senses may not offend us.

8. The fact that they were marveling at the words of Simeon is also written to show us that God's Word never goes out and is preached without fruit, as He says: "My Word, which goes out from My mouth" (i.e., from the mouth of God's messengers), "shall not return to Me empty, but it shall accomplish all that I want, and shall succeed in all for which I sent it" (Isaiah 55 [:11]). Thus the evangelist wants to say that Simeon made a heartfelt, beautiful speech, preaching the pure Gospel and God's Word. For what else is the Gospel but a sermon about Christ, declaring Him to be the Savior, light, and acclaim of all the world. Such preaching makes the heart happy and astonished at this great grace and comfort, if it is received in faith.

9. But though the words were beautiful and marvelously comforting, there were only a few who believed. Indeed, people despised it as being foolish. They went and stood in the temple—one prayed, another did something else—but they gave no [attention] to the words of Simeon. Yet because God's Word must produce fruit, there were indeed some who received it with joy and wonder, namely, Joseph and Mary. The evangelist here also secretly rebukes the unbelief of the Jews: many were there (for this happened publicly in the temple), and yet they would not believe, and all took offense at His infancy. Thus we learn here that we should hear God's Word gladly, for it does not go out [of God's mouth] without fruit.

# The Spiritual Meaning
## of This Gospel Reading about Simeon

10. From this follows the spiritual significance of this astonishment of Joseph and Mary. The temple is a place of God, therefore signifying every place where God is present; therefore, it also signifies the Holy Scriptures, where God may be found as in His proper place. To bring Christ into the temple means nothing else than to do what those did who received the Gospel with all eagerness: they ran into Scripture, daily examining them whether these things were so (Acts 17 [:11]).

11. Now in this same temple is Simeon. He represents all the prophets, who were full of the Holy Spirit, as Luke says about Simeon. They spoke and wrote from the Holy Spirit and waited for the coming of Christ, as Simeon did. They did not cease or end until Christ came, as St. Peter says that all the prophets spoke about the time of Christ (cf. Acts 3 [:24]). And Christ Himself says that the prophets and the Law continued until John, that is, until Christ's Baptism, when He began to be the Savior and light of all the world [cf. Matt. 11:13; Luke 16:16].

12. That is signified by Simeon, who was not to die until he had seen Christ [Luke 2:26]. For this reason he is called Simeon, that is, "one who hears," for the prophets had only heard of Christ as one who was still behind them and would come after them. Therefore, they had Him behind them and listened to Him. Now when someone comes into the temple with Christ and the Gospel and looks at Scripture, then the sayings of the prophets present themselves to Him so heartily, take Him in their arms, and all say with great joy: "This is the man. He, He it is of whom we have spoken, and now our words have come to an end with peace and joy." And they begin to give the most beautiful testimonies about how this Christ is the Savior, the light, the comfort, and the glory of Israel, and all that Simeon here declares and foretells.

St. Paul says that God promised the Gospel through the prophets in Holy Scripture (Romans 1 [:2]), which shows us what is meant by Simeon and by the temple. Likewise, Romans 3 [:21]. Christ said: "Search in the Scripture because it is what bears witness about Me. If you believed Moses, you would believe Me; for he wrote of Me" (John 5 [:39, 46]). This could be proved by examples, but it would take too long. Above, in the Epistle and Gospel for Christmas, we have seen examples of what beautiful and appropriate testimonies the apostles cited from Holy Scripture. Likewise, in the Christmas Gospel we spoke about the swaddling clothes in which the baby was wrapped.[2]

---

2 See sermon for Christmas Day on Luke 2:1–14, paragraph 53.

13. Now let the words of Moses, often quoted by the apostles, suffice, where he says, "The Lord your God will raise up for you a prophet like me from your brothers—to Him you shall listen" (Deuteronomy 18 [:15]; Acts 3 [:22]; 7 [:37]). Here Moses ends the people's listening [to him] and his public teaching about this prophet Christ, so that they should henceforth listen to Him. This is a testimony that Christ was to be a light and Savior after Moses, and without a doubt better than Moses; otherwise Moses would not have ended his teaching and leading and been quiet, but would have continued alongside Him. Likewise, Isaiah says: "Behold, I lay in Zion a foundation stone, a tested stone, a precious cornerstone, of a sure foundation: 'Whoever believes will not be terrified'" (Isaiah 28 [:16]). See how these and other passages agree with the Gospel, saying about Christ what the apostles preached about Him; all of Holy Scripture does that.

14. Therefore, Simeon had to be an old man in order to be the full and exact figure of the old prophets. He does not take the child in his hands nor in his lap, but in his arms. Although there is something deeper in this, it is enough for now that the prophecies and passages of Scripture do not keep Christ to themselves, but exhibit and offer Him to everybody, just as we do with those things we carry in our arms. St. Paul says that all was written not for his sake, but for our sake (Romans 4 [:23]; 15 [:4]). And Peter says that the prophets set forth what we have heard of Christ not for themselves, but for us [cf. 1 Pet. 1:10–12].

15. For this reason Luke does not say that [Joseph and Mary] were marveling at the words of Simeon, but "at what was said about Him" [Luke 2:33]. He is silent about Simeon's name, and deliberately pulls us away from Simeon to the spiritual meaning, so that thereby we would understand the statements of Scripture.

16. Only His father and mother were marveling at these things. Here the evangelist has given a sign in that he is silent about the names of Joseph and Mary, but calls them father and mother, in order to give us a reason for the spiritual meaning. Who is meant by the spiritual father and mother of Christ? He Himself names His spiritual mother: "Whoever does the will of My Father, he is My brother and sister and mother" (Mark 3 [:35]; Luke 8 [:21]).

St. Paul calls himself a father: "For though you have countless tutors in Christ, you do not have many fathers. For I became your father in Christ Jesus through the Gospel" (1 Corinthians 4 [:15]). Thus it is clear that the Christian Church—that is, all those who believe—are Christ's spiritual mother; and all apostles and teachers among the people who preach the Gospel are His spiritual father. As often as someone believes, so often is Christ born from them. These are the people who marvel at the sayings of the prophets: at how beautifully and vigorously they agree with Christ, how gloriously they speak of Him, [how] skillfully they testify to the whole Gospel, so that they have no greater desire in life than to see and experience these things in Scripture.

17. But the other [group], the great multitude of unbelievers, despise this Simeon, scoff at him, and twist his words as those of a fool. They promote their tricks and wantonness in the temple, and even put idols and the altar of Damascus there, as King Ahaz did [2 Kings 16:10–14]. These are the people who promote their wantonness with Scripture, but bring it into disgrace and interpret it in accordance with their human understanding. They introduce the anointed idol, reason, and make a doctrine of works and human laws out of [Scripture]. Finally, they completely desecrate and smash it and promote all sin and shame in it, as the pope does with his decrees and his universities with their Aristotle. Meanwhile, they are devout and consecrate and solemnize many stone and wooden churches, chapels, and altars. They are angry at the Turks for defaming and smashing these churches, but think that God ought to reward them for defaming and disturbing ten thousand times more badly His most precious temple, which is countlessly better and eternal. They are a blind, mad, crass people. Let them go, one blind person after another, into the eternal grave.

18. It might perhaps trouble a simple person that Luke calls Joseph Christ's father and does not show reverence to the virginity of Mary. But he speaks according to the usage which prevailed among the people and called him that. According to the custom of the Law, a stepfather is called a father, which is the usage throughout the world. Rather, he is properly called His father because he was the betrothed husband and bridegroom of His mother.

[The evangelist] had sufficient reason not to hesitate to speak this way, for he had previously described her virginity so plainly that he thought nobody would understand Joseph to be Christ's physical father. Therefore, since there was no danger because of his precautions, he could write this way without any hesitation. For the preceding narrative abundantly convinces us that Mary was His physical mother and Joseph was His customary father; and thus both are true, that He had father and mother.

### And Simeon blessed them. [Luke 2:34]

19. This blessing means nothing else than that he wished them happiness and prosperity, honor and all good. Luke reports that he blessed not only the child but all of them: child, father, and mother.

20. This blessing seems to be a rather insignificant thing, for people generally bless each other and wish [each other well]. But to bless Christ and His parents is a very high and unusual work, because Christ and nature are entirely opposed to each other. [Christ] condemns all that the world chooses; causes people to suffer the cross and all evil; deprives this world of all its

pleasures, possessions, and honors; and teaches that everything people are occupied with is foolish and evil. See, since nobody will or can endure that from Him, cursing, blaspheming, and persecuting of Christ and all His [disciples] begins, and there are very few Simeons who bless Him; but the whole world is full of those who curse Him and wish Him all evil, disgrace, and misfortune. For whoever does not intend willingly to despise all things and to suffer everything will not bless and praise Christ very long, but will soon take offense at Him.

21. There are indeed some who praise and bless Him because He does what they want and lets them do what they want. But then He is not Christ and does not do the works of Christ with them, but He is what they are and want. When, however, He begins to be Christ to them, and they are to forsake their works and to let Him alone be in them, then there is nothing but avoiding, blaspheming, and cursing.

22. Some similarly think that, if they were to see the baby Christ with His mother, as Simeon did, they also would joyously bless Him. But they lie; for they would certainly have been averted by His infancy and poverty and His contemptible appearance. They prove it by disregarding, hating, and persecuting such poverty and humble appearance in the members of Christ, among whom they might daily find the Head, Christ. Therefore, since they now avoid and hate the cross and contemptible appearance, they would certainly do the same thing if they were still to see Him with their eyes. Why are they not showing such honor to the poor? Why will they not honor the truth? But Simeon was of a different mind and was not offended at His appearance, but he confessed that [the Savior] was "a sign of opposition" [Luke 2:34] and is pleased that Christ rejects all high appearance and exhibits the form of the cross. Therefore, he does not bless [Christ] alone, but also His members, mother, and father.

23. Thus Simeon is here a preacher and lover of the cross and an enemy of the world; in blessing he gave a remarkable example of praising and honoring Christ in His despised, cursed, and rejected appearance which He had then in His own person and now still has in His members, who for His sake endure poverty, disgrace, death, and all kinds of cursing. Yet nobody does anything for them, receives, or blesses them; rather, they want to be godly people and Christians by praying and fasting, and by bequests and works.

## THE SIGNIFICANCE OF THE BLESSING ON CHRIST'S FATHER AND MOTHER

24. Here we find the spiritual significance: that the spiritual Christ, His spiritual father and mother—that is, the Christian Church with the apostles and their successors—are subjected on earth to all kinds of curses, and as

St. Paul says, they are like the rubbish, chaff, and scum of this world [cf. 1 Cor. 4:13]. Therefore, they must receive their blessing and comfort from some other source, from Simeon in the temple, that is, from the prophets in Holy Scripture, as St. Paul says, "Whatever was written previously was written for our instruction, that through endurance and through the comfort of Scripture we might have hope" (Romans 15 [:4]).

25. See here: a Christian must not think or undertake to arrange his affairs so that he is praised and blessed by the people of this world. No, it is already decided that he must expect shame and cursing, and submit to it and yield. He can expect no blessing other than from Simeon in the temple. Scripture is our comfort. It praises and blesses all who are cursed by the world for Christ's sake. This is the whole teaching of Psalm 37, also of Psalm 9 and many others, which tell us that God will rescue all those who suffer in this world.

And Moses writes that God took such a firm interest in godly Abel after his death that He, unasked, moved to revenge only by [Abel's] blood, did much more for him after his death than during his life [Gen. 4:10]. This shows that He cannot forsake even the dead—much less [could He forsake] the living who believe in Him. On the other hand, when Cain was slain, He was silent and took no interest in him.

26. These and similar passages of Scripture are our comfort and blessing, if we are Christians. To them we must cling and be satisfied with them. Here we see how blessed are those who endure cursing, and how wretched are those who curse. God cannot forget nor forsake the former; He will not think of or know the latter. What richer, greater comfort and blessing would we have? What is the blessing and comfort of this world compared with this comfort and blessing of Simeon in the temple?

> *And he said to Mary, His mother: "Behold, this child is appointed for the fall and rising of many in Israel, and for a sign that will be opposed (and a sword will pierce your own soul also), so that thoughts from many hearts may be revealed." [Luke 2:34–35]*

27. Why does he not say this also to the father, and why does he call the mother by name? He touches here on nature, and so names the natural mother and not the father. Therefore, what happened to her natural child would naturally hurt the mother alone. It probably also happened because Joseph did not live to see the time of Christ's suffering, which the mother would experience alone; and in addition to all this sorrow, she has to suffer as a poor and lonely widow, and Christ as a poor orphan. This is a situation unspeakably pitiable, and God Himself in Scripture takes good care of widows and orphans, calling Himself a judge of widows and a father of the orphans [cf. Ps. 68:5].

28. For Mary lived in all three estates—virginity, matrimony, and widow-hood—and the last is the most miserable, without any protection or support.[3] A virgin has her parents, a wife her husband, but the widow is alone. And Simeon foretold much suffering for her in that miserable condition. With that he showed and explained to her what he thought his blessing meant, namely, that it is a blessing before God and not before the world. For before the world it would be turned around, and [she] would not only be unblessed, but her child also would become the goal and mark at which everyone aims and curses, just as all bows and arrows are aimed at the target. See, this is what I think being blessed in the temple means. It was very necessary that she should be strengthened and comforted by a spiritual and divine benediction against the cannons of future execration, for she alone in her soul was to bear and endure this great storm of execration against her child.

29. First, [Simeon] says that Christ "is appointed for the fall and rising of many in Israel." This is the first comfort which His mother was to experience and realize in Him, that many would be offended at Him, even in Israel, the chosen people. In human eyes that is meager comfort, that she is the mother of the Son at whom so many are to be offended and fall, even in Israel.

Some have explained this text as follows: that many have been offended at Christ and their pride has fallen in a blessed way, so that they rise in humility, just as St. Paul fell and rose and all the self-righteous must fall, despair of themselves, and rise in Christ, if they would be saved. This is a good interpretation, but not enough here. Simeon says that many Jews would stumble on Christ and take offense at Him, by which they fall into unbelief, as has happened and still happens. That was a very sad picture and appearance, in addition to a terrible prediction to be heard in the ears of this holy mother.

30. Christ is not the cause of this fall, but the arrogance of the Jews is. It happened in this way: Christ came to be a light and Savior of all the world, as Simeon said, and everyone is justified and saved through faith in Him. For that to happen, all other righteousness which is sought in ourselves with works apart from Christ must be rejected. The Jews would not put up with that, as St. Paul says: "They do not recognize the righteousness that God gives" (through faith) "and seek to establish their own righteousness; therefore, they do not submit to God's righteousness" (Romans 10 [:3]). Thus they stumble on faith, fall ever deeper into unbelief, and become hardened in their own righteousness, so that they also persecute fiercely all who believe.

31. All the works-righteous must do the same thing: they depend on their works, they stumble against faith, they fall on Christ, so that they burn,

---

3 Since Joseph is not mentioned after the account of the twelve-year-old Jesus in the temple (Luke 2:41–52), it is often assumed that Joseph had died and that therefore Mary was a widow. See also below, paragraph 49.

condemn, and persecute all who reject their works or consider them useless, as we now see in the pope, the bishops, the doctors, and all the Papists. And they do this under the impression that they are doing God a service, in order to defend the truth and preserve Christianity, just as the Jews also alleged that they preserved the service of God and the Law of Moses when they killed the apostles and Christians and persecuted them.

32. Therefore, as Simeon here promises the mother of Christ that not all Israel will receive Him as their light and Savior, and that not only some or a few but many will stumble on Him and fall, so also the spiritual mother of Christ, the assembly of Christians, must not marvel when many false Christians, especially among the clergy, will not receive faith. For those are the people who rely on works and seek their own righteousness, who must take offense at Christ and faith and must fall, and who persecute and kill whatever speaks or acts against them.

This was prophesied long ago by the spiritual Simeon, namely, the prophets, who almost with one accord have spoken of this fall. Isaiah says: "The Lord speaks thus to me, as taking me by the hand, and instructs me not to walk in the way of this people, saying: 'Do not say, "Confederation." This people speaks of nothing but confederation. Do not fear what they fear nor be in dread. But sanctify the Lord of hosts. Let Him be your fear, and let Him be your dread. And He will become a sanctifying, but a stone of offense and a rock of stumbling to both houses of Israel, a trap and a snare to the inhabitants of Jerusalem. And many shall stumble on it. They shall fall and be broken; they shall be snared and taken'" (Isaiah 8 [:11–15]).

There are many more passages from which it is proved that Christ must be a rock against which the best and greatest will stumble, as Psalm 68 [:22] says, "The Lord says, 'I will bring back some from among the fat; I will bring back some from the depths of the sea.'" For Christ has been made a Savior and cannot yield or become different. But these arrogant people are stern and obstinate, will not yield their nonsense, and run their head against Christ, so that one of the two must break and fall. Christ, however, must remain and cannot fall; consequently, they must fall.

33. Again, as firmly as He stands against the works-righteous and will not yield to them, so firmly does He also stand for all who are founded on Him, as Isaiah says: "Behold, I lay in Zion a foundation stone, a tested stone, a precious cornerstone of a sure foundation: 'Whoever believes will not be terrified'" (Isaiah 28 [:16]). And He Himself says, "On this rock I will build My congregation; and the gates of hell shall not prevail against it" (Matthew 16 [:18]).

As now the falling and breaking is nothing other than unbelief and sinking into works, so the rising and being built upon this rock is nothing other than believing and withdrawing from works. These are the believers. Christ has been appointed for the rising of them and no one else. And as at Christ's time many in Israel rose in Him, so it will be until the end of the world, for nobody can rise through his works, or through the doctrines of men, but only through Christ. This is brought about by faith, as has often been said, without any works or merit. The works must first follow after the rising.

34. Therefore, you see how all of Scripture urges only faith and rejects works as incapable, even offensive and hindering justification and rising. For Christ only wants to be appointed for rising, or else He must lead to their fall. He lets nothing be appointed for rising in addition to Him. Is not the life of the Papists and the clergy abominable? They run their heads harshly and strongly against this rock, and their conduct is so contrary to the Christian life that it may indeed be called the behavior and government of the Antichrist.

The spiritual Simeon also speaks of this rising to the spiritual mother of Christ. For all the prophets teach Christendom that all people must persist only in Christ, as St. Paul quotes the prophet Habakkuk: "The righteous shall live by his faith" (Habakkuk 2 [:4]; Romans 1 [:17]; Hebrews 10 [:38; Gal. 3:11]).

35. So we see that this falling and rising by Christ is completely spiritual and that the falling and rising apply to different people. The falling applies only to those who are great, learned, mighty, and holy, and who trust too much in themselves. The Gospel does not show us Christ quarreling or in conflict with [those who confessed they were] sinners, but rather dealing with them in a most friendly way. But with the separatists, the scribes, and high priests He cannot make any progress, nor is He gracious to them. Therefore, just as the falling applies only to those who are already standing, so the rising applies only to those who are lying prone and have fallen. These are the spirits who long for grace, who know themselves, that they are nothing and Christ is everything.

36. It is noteworthy that Simeon adds the word "Israel." For Christ had been promised by all the prophets only to the people of Israel. At the same time it was foretold that many among that people would fall away only on account of their own righteousness. This is indeed terrifying for us Gentiles, to whom nothing has been promised. But out of pure grace, without forethought and unexpectedly, we have been added and have risen through Christ, as St. Paul says (Romans 15 [:9]) and as was said above in the Epistle for the Second Sunday in Advent. For this reason we should take Israel's fall to heart, as the apostle charges us (Romans 11 [:20]), so that we may not also fall, or unfortunately fall worse than the Jews and Turks and be misled by

the Antichrist, so that we would bear the name of Christ to the dishonor of God and our own harm.

37. Second, Simeon says that Christ is appointed "for a sign that will be opposed" [Luke 2:34]. Is it not a pity that the Savior and light of the world should be opposed, convicted, and condemned, who should be run after and sought from one end of the world to the other? But that teaches what the world is and what nature with its free will does: namely, it is the devil's kingdom and God's enemy, and not only acts against God's commandment but with senseless rage also persecutes and kills the Savior who would help them to keep God's commandment. But one sin leads to another. Those who stumble at Him must also oppose Him and cannot do otherwise. On the other hand, those who rise through Him must confess Him, speak well of Him, and preach Him, and they also cannot do otherwise. But a sword shall pierce through their souls, as we shall now see.

38. Now note the words. [Simeon] does not say that [Christ] shall be opposed, but that He is appointed for a sign that is always opposed, just as a goal or target is appointed for the marksmen, so that all bows and guns, arrows and stones may be aimed at it. Such a target is set up that the shots may be directed only at it and nowhere else. Thus [Christ] is appointed so that all the rounds go nowhere else but only at the mark. Thus Christ is the goal, and everyone is united so that all opposition is aimed at Him. And though the opponents are in the utmost disagreement with one another, yet they become united when they oppose Christ. This is proved since Pilate and Herod were mortal enemies, but became one in their opposition to Christ [Luke 23:12]. The Pharisees and Sadducees very much disagreed with each other, but they became united against Christ. David marvels and speaks about this: "Why do the nations rage and the peoples speak in vain? The kings in the land are outraged, and the rulers take counsel together, against the Lord and against His Anointed" (Psalm 2 [:1–2]).

39. Thus also all heretics, no matter how much they differed from each other and opposed each other, were nevertheless all united in their opposition against the one Christian Church. Even now, when no bishop, chapter, order, or monastery respects another, so that there are nearly as many sects and variations as heads, yet they are of one mind against the Gospel. The prophet Asaph writes that all the peoples gathered against the people of Israel: "Edom, Ishmael, Moab, the Hagrites, Gebal, Ammon, Amalek, the Philistines, Tyre, and Asshur" (Psalm 83 [:6–8])—yet not one of them agreed with the others. Malice and lies are certainly in disagreement with each other, but they must be united against truth and righteousness, so that every attack and opposition bursts against this mark and goal. They think they have just cause for this. For every faction fights against its own adversary: Pilate against Herod, the

Pharisees against the Sadducees, Arius against Sabellius, the monks against the priests. Moreover, every faction has its adherents and friends, and their discord or harmony is only partial.

40. But Christ is very impolite and unreasonable, rebuking them all. To Him Pilate counts as much as Herod, the Pharisees as much as the Sadducees, and He sides with neither party. Therefore, as He is against all of them, so they in turn all together fall upon Him. Thus truth is opposed to all lies and falsehoods, and therefore all lies are united against the truth and make of it "a sign that is opposed." It must happen that way. For Christ and the truth find no one who is godly and on their side, as the psalmist says, "All men are liars" [Ps. 116:11]. Therefore, [Christ] must rebuke them all without distinction and reject their works, so that they all may become needy and thirsty for His grace. Not all allow and want that—in fact, only the smaller part.

41. Thus we have here two Simeons. The physical Simeon proclaims to the physical mother that Christ in His own person is a sign appointed for those who oppose. Thereby he points to what the spiritual Simeon, the prophets, say to Christendom about Christian faith, namely, that this faith and Gospel, the living Word of truth, is a rock at which many will fall and rise, and that it finally is a sign that is opposed. Isaiah says with surprise: "Yet who believes our preaching?" (Isaiah 53 [:1]), as if he would answer: "Very few." Likewise, he says that so many will fall at this word that hardly the dregs and sludge of the people will be saved. This falling, rising, and opposition are described abundantly in the prophets.

42. Simeon has certainly stated before that Christ is the light and Savior of all the world, which the prophets also say. This shows us what Christ is—and His attitude toward the world. But when Simeon speaks of falling, rising, and opposition, he shows what Christ will achieve, what the world is, and what attitude it takes toward Christ. Thus it appears that Christ would have been willing and sufficient to be the light and Savior of all the world, and demonstrates that abundantly and extravagantly. But the world does not receive Him and becomes only worse, opposing and persecuting Him as much as it possibly can.

43. This shows us that this world is the devil's kingdom, not only full of wickedness and blindness but also a lover of wickedness and blindness, as Christ says, "The light has come into the world, and the world loved the darkness rather than the light" (John 3 [:19]). See, we are like that, as our walk on earth is among the devils and enemies of God, so that this life really ought to be dreadful for us.

44. From this we learn and become certain that we may take comfort and be happy even when many people take offense at our words and faith and oppose them, especially the great, the learned, and the spiritual. This is a sign

that our words and faith are correct, for they receive the treatment foretold by Simeon and all the prophets. They must stumble, fall, rise, and oppose; it cannot be otherwise. Whoever wants it otherwise must look for another Christ. This Christ is appointed for the falling and rising of many in Israel, and for a sign or mark that is opposed. Consequently, His members, every Christian, must be like Him on account of his faith and words. He is called *antilegomenos*, "one who is opposed" [Luke 2:34]. His ideas and faith must be condemned, banished, and cursed as the worst heresy, error, and foolishness. If that happens to Him, it has happened correctly; but when this does not happen, then we have neither Christ nor His mother nor Simeon nor the prophets nor faith nor the Gospel nor any Christians. For what does opposition mean other than denying, and also blaspheming, cursing, condemning, banishing, forbidding, and persecuting with all disgrace and humiliation as the worst heresy?

45. But these little words give still another comfort. [Simeon] says that [Christ] is a sign that is opposed, but not overthrown or destroyed. The whole world may condemn my faith and words, call them heretical, and misrepresent and corrupt them in the most shameful way, but they must let [my faith] remain and cannot take it from me. With all their rage and fury they accomplish no more than only to oppose, and I must be their mark and target. Nevertheless, they fall and I stand. Let them, as much as they want, oppose God, who opposes and fights with His deeds against their words. [We] shall see who will prevail. Here are works, and [there] are God's works; they establish, that is, they make the sign firm and solid on a good foundation. [If] a target is set up by God, who will abolish it? But there they have nothing more than fleeting words and a feeble breath from the mouth. The flies beat their wings and sharpen their beaks, but they do nothing more than dirty the wall and can do nothing more.

46. From this it follows that the doctrine and faith of the pope, the bishops, the religious establishments, the monasteries, and the universities are purely worldly and devilish, for there is no falling and no opposing. They will not permit that. Rather, there is only honor, power, riches, peace, and pleasure. They are our Lord God's true feeder pigs in His pigsty, except that someone among them may be tormented by the devil with spiritual temptations concerning faith and hope; for some like that are certainly found. For where Christ and faith in Him are, there must be opposition; otherwise it is not Christ. If people do not oppose openly, then the devils must do it secretly. These are severe temptations to unbelief, despair, and blasphemy. Such people may be preserved, but the other group lives without Christ, without Mary, without Simeon, without the least truth, but meanwhile they read many Masses, sing high and low, wear tonsures and spiritual vestments,

and are Solomon's apes and Indian cats [cf. 1 Kings 10:22; 2 Chron. 9:21].[4] While they do not want to endure opposition, and are not worthy of it, they have nothing and do nothing for which they would be opposed, yet they go and themselves become opponents. What else should they do? It is their proper work to condemn, forbid, curse, and persecute the truth.

47. I say this in order to do my duty sufficiently and to point out to every Christian his danger, so that all may know to guard against the pope, the universities, and the spiritual estate—where God's Word is not the driving force—as against the devil's own kingdom and rule. Cling to the Gospel and find out where there is opposition and where there is praise. Where you find no opposition, there Christ is not present; this sort of opposition is not from the Turks, but from our nearest neighbors. Christ was appointed a sign for the fall of many not in Babylon or Assyria, but in Israel, that is, among the people in the midst of whom He dwells and who boast to be His own.

48. Third, Simeon says to Mary, His mother: "A sword will pierce your soul" [Luke 2:35]. This is not said of a physical sword, but just as it is written about Joseph—"His body had to lie in irons" (Psalm 105 [:18])—similarly the Lord delivered "those who sat in darkness and shadow, imprisoned in affliction and in irons" (Psalm 107 [:10]). Likewise: "I have redeemed you from the iron furnace of Egypt" (Deuteronomy 4 [:20]). It is also often said that she would endure great sorrow and grief in her heart, though her body would not be tortured. Everybody knows how this happened. Thus we must take these words as a Hebrew figure of speech, expressing great sorrow and grief of the heart, just as we in German call such grief a heartbreak, as people say: "My heart is breaking" or "My heart is bursting."

49. We must save further speaking about this until Passiontide.[5] For now it is enough that we see how Simeon explains his blessing with a bitter gloss, in order that it might not be understood as a temporal blessing before the world. But what does it signify that Simeon here speaks only to Mary, His mother, by name, and not to Joseph? It signifies that the Christian Church, the spiritual Virgin Mary, remains on earth and is not destroyed, though the preachers and their faith and the Gospel, the spiritual Christ, are persecuted. Although Joseph died first and Christ was tortured, so that Mary was a widow deprived of her child, yet she remains, and this misery pierced her heart. Thus the Christian Church always remains a widow, and her heart is pierced because her Joseph, the holy fathers, died, and the Gospel is tortured. [The Church] must endure the sword, and yet always remain until the Last Day.

---

4 *indische Katzen*, that is, like part of Solomon's imported treasures.

5 *die Passion*, that is, the last two weeks of Lent. Or Luther may be referring specifically to the Passion history. See *Sermon for Meditation on the Holy Suffering of Christ* (1521), (LW 76), which was included in Luther's *Winter Postil* (1525ff.).

50. What can be more painful for a Christian heart than to see and experience how furiously the tyrants and unbelievers persecute and destroy the Gospel of Christ? This is done more at the present time under the pope than ever before. This happens according to their names, for "Mary" means "a bitter sea." This means that there is in her not only bitterness but also much bitterness, so that there is not only a drop, or a river, but also a whole sea of bitterness, for all sorrow inundated her, so that she may indeed be called "Mary," a bitter sea.

51. Finally, Simeon says that all this will happen "so that thoughts from many hearts may be revealed" [Luke 2:35]. What a blessed and necessary fruit of this falling and opposing! But in order to understand this, we must notice that there are two kinds of scandal and temptation among men. One is the temptation to coarse sins, such as being disobedient to parents, killing, unchastity, stealing, lying, and blaspheming, etc., which are sins against the Second Table of Moses.[6] Here it is not necessary that they actually stumble against the sign that is opposed; their thoughts are sufficiently revealed by their evil life. Scripture speaks little of this scandal.

52. But the second is Madame Cozbi, the pretty daughter of Prince Zur of Midian, because of whom 24,000 were slain in Israel, as Moses writes (Numbers 25 [:15]). This is the true scandal and temptation to the holy and beautiful sins of good works and worship, which bring misfortune on the whole world and against which nobody can guard sufficiently. These are sins against the First Table of Moses[7]—against faith, the honor of God, and His works.

53. For there is no greater, more dangerous, more pernicious scandal than an externally good life in good works and spiritual way of life. Those people are so upright, reasonable, honorable, and godly that scarcely a single soul could have been preserved or saved, if God had not appointed this sign and target against which they stumble and their hearts are revealed.

Here we see through their pretty words and beautiful works into their hearts, and find that these great saints and wise people are pagans and fools; for they persecute the faith for the sake of their works and don't want to be rebuked in their way of life. Thus their thoughts are revealed, and it can be seen that they build on their works and themselves, and thus not only sin continually against the first Commandments but also are enemies and endeavor to destroy and interfere with all that belongs to faith and God. Nevertheless, [they claim to do this] for no other reason than for the sake of God and to preserve the truth. See, such are the pope, the bishops, and almost all the clergy, who have filled the world full, full, full of traps and scandals

6 That is, Commandments 4–10 (Exod. 20:12–17).

7 That is, Commandments 1–3 (Exod. 20:3–8).

with the beautiful glittering and coloring of their spiritual life. Yet there is no faith but only works among them; the Gospel does not prevail, but only human laws.

54. All of Scripture speaks of this scandal, and God with all the prophets and saints contends against it. This is the true gate of hell and the broad highway to damnation [cf. Matt. 7:13]. Therefore, that prostitute is well called Cozbi [in Num. 25:15], *mendacium meum*, "my lie." All that glitters lies and deceives, but her pretty ornaments and jewelry deceive even the princes of Israel, and so she is not merely called "lie" but "my lie," because such deception pleases and entices almost everybody.

55. But in order to protect us, God has set up His Christ as a target (at which they stumble and fall, and which they oppose), so that we, not misled by their works and words, may not accept and follow their life as good. Before God no life is really good without faith; and where there is no faith, there is nothing but Cozbi, nothing but lies and deception. This becomes manifest as soon as we preach against them and consider their works worthless in comparison with faith.

See, then you must be a heretic with your faith. They step forth and unwillingly and unknowingly let you know their heart, so that you may see the horrible abomination of unbelief hidden under that beautiful life, the wolves hidden under wool, the whore hidden under the garland.[8] She is unashamed and wants her disgrace and depravity regarded as honorable and virtuous, or she will kill you. Therefore, God says to her: "You have the forehead of a whore; you refuse to be ashamed" (Jeremiah 3 [:3]); and "They do not conceal their behavior; they proclaim their sin like Sodom; they do not hide it" (Isaiah 3 [:9]).

Would she not be a mad and impudent prostitute who would have her adultery sung as honorable, even before her husband? But this is being done by all the preachers of works and unbelieving teachers, who shamelessly preach works and in addition condemn faith (the conjugal chastity). Their fornication is to be chastity, and true chastity is to be fornication. See, all this might remain hidden, and human nature and reason might not discover such vices, for their works are too pretty and their manners too polished. Indeed, human nature devises all this and delights in it; it thinks it is right and well-done, persists and becomes hardened in it.

Therefore, God appoints a sign on which nature stumbles so that everybody may learn how much higher is the Christian life than nature and reason. All [of nature's] virtues are sins, its light is darkness, its ways are errors. We need another heart, skin, and nature. This heart reveals that it is God's enemy.

---

8 The garland was a sign of virginity.

56. This is prefigured by the Philistines, whom God tormented so that their intestines went out below when they had God's ark with them [cf. 1 Sam. 5:6]. The intestines are the thoughts of the unbelieving heart, which break out when the ark of God comes to them, that is, when the Gospel and Christ are preached, which they will not tolerate. Thus it happens that the hearts of these saints, which otherwise could not be known, become revealed when Christ is held up before them. St. Paul says, "The spiritual person judges all things and is judged by no one" (1 Corinthians 2 [:15]), for he knows their disposition and the attitude of their hearts when he hears that they do not accept God's Word and faith.

## THE SECOND PART OF THE GOSPEL READING

*And there was a prophetess, named Anna, a daughter of Phanuel, of the tribe of Asher. She was advanced in years, having lived with her husband seven years after her virginity, and then as a widow at the eighty-fourth year. She did not depart from the temple, worshiping God with fasting and prayer day and night. [Luke 2:36–37]*

57. Here someone might say: From the example of Anna you see that good works are exalted, such as fasting and praying and going to church; therefore, they must not be rejected. Answer: Who has ever rejected good works? We only reject the false, glittering good works. Fasting, praying, and going to church are good works when they occur correctly. But the weakness is that these blind heads fall on Scripture, rush in blindly with boots and spurs, look only at the works and examples of the dear saints, and immediately want to teach and imitate them. Thus they become nothing but apes and hypocrites, for they do not perceive that Scripture speaks more of the person than of the works.

Scripture praises Abel's sacrifice and works, but first praises the person much more. They, however, disregard the person and only make use of the example. Thus they grasp at the works and miss the faith. They eat the bran and spill the flour. Likewise, the prophet Hosea says that they turn to other gods and love the grapeskins more than the grapes (cf. Hosea 3 [:1]). If you want to fast and pray with this holy Anna, well and good; but take care first that you imitate the person, and then the works: first become an Anna. But let us see what St. Luke says of her works and her person, so that we may correctly understand her example.

58. First, he says that she was a prophetess, and undoubtedly a holy, godly prophetess. Most assuredly the Holy Spirit was in her, and consequently the person, without any works, was righteous. Therefore, the works which she produced were also good and righteous. So you see that St. Luke

does not mean that she became godly and a prophetess through her works, but that she was a godly prophetess first, and then her works also became good. Why would you cut up and twist this example and the Gospel, and first and alone choose the works, while Luke describes first the person, and not only the works?

59. Second, he praises her as a widow who did works appropriate for her widowhood and remained in her calling. He depicts this, but does not separate these works, as if they were the only good works and worship and all others were rejected. St. Paul describes the life of widows: "Honor widows who are truly widows. But if a widow has children or nephews, let them first learn to govern their own household in a godly way and to repay their parents, for this is good and pleasing before God. She is truly a widow who is left all alone, who sets her hope on God and continues in supplications and prayers day and night. But she who lives in pleasures is dead while living" (1 Timothy 5 [:3–6]).

60. From this you see that Anna must have been a widow, alone [in the world], without any children or parents to take care of, otherwise she would have been serving the devil, not God, by not departing from the temple and neglecting her divine duty of governing her household. Luke indicates this when he writes that she had been a widow until her eighty-fourth year. Everybody may then easily calculate that her parents must have been dead and her children provided for, so that as an aged mother she was provided for by them, and she needed to do nothing more than to pray and fast and deny all lust. Luke does not say that all the eighty-four years of her life were spent in this way; but by the time that Christ was born and brought into the temple, she had begun to lead such a life, when all things, as well as her children and parents, were provided for and she was entirely alone.

61. It is, therefore, a very dangerous thing to look at only the works and look neither at the person nor at the estate or calling. It is very intolerable for God when anyone neglects the works of his calling or estate and wants [instead] to undertake the works of the saints. If, therefore, a married woman wanted to imitate Anna and leave her husband and children, her home and parents in order to go on a pilgrimage, pray, fast, and go to church, she would be doing nothing else but tempting God, mixing up the matrimonial estate with the state of widowhood, leaving her own calling, and clinging to the works of others. This would be the same as walking on your ears, putting a veil on your feet and a boot on your head, and turning all things upside down.

You should do good works, pray, and fast, as long as you do not thereby neglect or prevent the works of your calling and estate. The service of God is not bound to one or two works, nor is it expressed in one or two estates, but it is distributed into all works and estates. The work of Anna and all widows who, like her, are alone is praying and fasting, and here St. Luke agrees with St. Paul. The work of married women is not only praying and fasting but also governing their children and household well and caring for their parents, as St. Paul says [1 Tim. 5:4]. This also moved the evangelist to write about the works of this Anna, so that he might in many words diligently describe her estate and age, so that he might repel all those who would latch onto the works and suck poison from roses; and so he first points out her calling.

62. Third, the same reason prompts him to write that she lived with her husband seven years from when she was a virgin. Thus he exalts the state of matrimony and the works of that estate, so that nobody would think that he considers only praying and fasting as good works. For she did not do these things while she lived with her husband, or during the time of her virginity, but only after she had become an aged and lonely widow. Yet her virginity and her married life with its works are also praised, and they give us an example of truly good works. Why would you disregard them and cling only to the works of the widow?

63. It wasn't for nothing that the evangelist first praised her married estate and then her widowhood, for he abundantly stopped up the gaps for the blind works-righteous saints. She was a godly virgin, a godly wife, and a godly widow, and in all these three estates she attended to her appropriate works.

64. Do likewise. If you look at your estate, you will find enough good works to do if you would be godly. Everyone has enough works [to do] that he does not need to look for ones that are not his own. See, then we will truly serve God, just as St. Luke says that Anna served God with fasting and prayer night and day. But the works-righteous do not serve God, but themselves, and even the devil, since they do not attend to their works and they desert their own calling.

See, all the value of works depends on the persons and the calling, as we have said above in explaining the Gospel for the Day of St. John the Evangelist.[9] That is enough for now. Let us now see what Anna means spiritually.

## The Secret Meaning of Anna, the Prophetess

65. Simeon, as said above,[10] signifies the holy prophets, who have spoken about Christ in Holy Scripture. Therefore, Anna must signify those who stand by and listen to this message, confess and speak of it, as did Anna, who stood by when Simeon spoke about Christ. Thus Anna means nothing but the holy synagogue, the people of Israel, whose life and history are recorded in

---

9 See sermon for St. John's Day on John 21:19–24, paragraph 3 and paragraph 25.

10 See above, paragraphs 11–12; paragraph 32; paragraph 41.

the Bible. For Anna is found in the temple, that is, in Scripture. And as Mary signifies the Christian Church, the people of God after Christ's birth, so Anna signifies the people before Christ's birth. Therefore, Anna is old and near her death, while Mary is young and near to her birth. Thus the synagogue was at its end in the time of Christ, while the Church was in its beginning.

66. It has been said abundantly that the dear saints before Christ's birth understood and believed the prophets and were all preserved in Christ and His faith, as Christ Himself says about Abraham: "Your father Abraham rejoiced that he would see My day. He saw it and was glad" (John 8 [:56]). Likewise: "Many prophets and kings desired to see what you see, and to hear what you hear" (Luke 10 [:24]). Likewise, Paul wrote: "Jesus Christ is the same yesterday and today and forever" (Hebrews 13 [:8]). And still more clearly: "For you should know, dear brothers, that our fathers were all under the cloud, and all passed through the Red Sea, and all were baptized under Moses with the cloud and with the sea, and all ate the same spiritual food, and all drank the same spiritual drink. They drank from the spiritual Rock that followed them, which was Christ" (1 Corinthians 10 [:1–4]).

These and similar passages prove that all the saints before Christ's birth were saved in Christ, just as we are. Therefore, he tells many examples of their faith: of Abel, Enoch, Noah, Abraham, Moses, and others, who spent their lives in Christ and for Christ, whom they heard and (through the prophets) understood, believed, and waited for His coming (Hebrews 11).

67. For this reason all the narratives of the Old Testament so perfectly agree with Christ, and in fact all confess Him and stand around Him, just as Anna physically stood around Him, so that we greatly desire to read and hear how they all look and point at Christ.

Let us look at one example. Isaac was sacrificed by his father and yet remained alive; a ram, which Abraham saw behind him caught in the thicket by his horns, took [Isaac's] place [Gen 22:1–13]. That signifies Christ, God's Son, who in all things like a mortal man died on the cross. Yet the divine nature did not die; the human nature was sacrificed for them, just as the ram that by its horns (that is, by preaching, by which it butts up against and reproves the shaggy, bushy, disorderly people of the scribes and priests) was caught in the thicket was behind Abraham and came after him. Many other great things are buried in these narratives.

68. Likewise, Joseph was sold into Egypt and, after having been in prison, became the ruler of the whole land [Gen. 37:18–28; 39:1–23; 41:1–43]. That happened and was written because of Christ, who through His suffering became the Lord of all the world. But who has time enough to open up all these narratives and see how Samson, David, Solomon, Aaron, and others really and perfectly and seriously mean Christ alone?

69. St. Luke, therefore, here uses a powerful little word, that this Anna *epistasa*; that is, she stood over or beside or near that which happened to Christ in the temple. This is not the same as the Latin word *superveniens*, that she "came to there," though that would also be true; but this is better: that she stood over what happened. It sounds as if she got herself there and pressed forward intentionally to see Him, just as people say in German: "How the people press forward over the thing," etc. Thus all the histories of Holy Scripture make much of Christ in order to illustrate Him.

70. Yet they might not have been saved by this, and it might be that they did not know at the time that what they were doing agreed with Christ. For figures and interpretations are not a sufficient basis for our faith. Faith must first be based on clear Scripture, simply understood according to the sound and meaning of the words. Then, after the foundation for faith has been laid by the words [of Scripture], such interpretations of history can build up faith, in order to nourish and strengthen it. Therefore, as I have said, not only was their way of life a figure of Christ (the way of life that they led externally in works, through which nobody would have become holy), but rather they also believed from the heart in the coming Christ, having understood Him through clear passages and God's Word without figures.

71. For example, Adam and Eve received the promise after their fall, when God said to the snake: "I will put enmity between you and the woman, and between your seed and her Seed; He shall trample on your head, and you shall sting His heel" (Genesis 3 [:15]). Adam and Eve remembered this passage and promise and believed in the Seed of the woman who would trample on the snake's head, until Noah. He received another further promise when God said, "I will make My covenant with you" (Genesis 6 [:18]). Therefore, when Eve bore her first son, Cain, she rejoiced and thought he was the Seed God had spoken about. She joyfully said, "I have received the man of God" [cf. Gen. 4:1], as if she were to say, "This will be the man, the Seed, who is to fight against the snake." She would gladly have seen Christ, but it was not yet time. Afterward she saw that he was not the one, and she had to extend her faith further to another woman.

72. Afterward the clear promise came to Abraham when God said, "In your Seed shall all the nations of the earth be blessed" (Genesis 12 [:3]; 22 [:18]), of which we have spoken in the Epistle reading. The faith of all the saints before Christ's birth until the time of His coming was based on this passage, so that this passage may also be understood as "Abraham's bosom," of which Christ speaks (Luke 16 [:22]). Although this was further explained to David, yet all of that was still in the strength of this promise to Abraham.

This is the Seed of the woman, Mary's child, who fights against the snake in order to destroy sin and death. Therefore, the text says that the Seed will trample on the snake's head. Without a doubt He meant the snake that misled Eve, which was the devil in the snake, and Adam and Eve certainly understood that. Who will show us another Son or Seed who trampled on his head? If it had been said of a mere man, then Adam could have done the trampling as well as any of his children. Yet not Adam, nor a child of Adam, was to do it; but a woman's, a virgin's, child.

73. It is well stated that this Seed will trample on the devil's head, in which is all his life; but the devil will not trample on the head of the Seed, but His heel, or the sole of His foot. This means that the evil spirit profanes, destroys, and even kills the external, bodily life and works of Christ; but the head, the deity, remains alive and raises from death the sole of the foot, the humanity, which was trampled by the devil.

Thus in all Christians he tramples their soles, profanes and murders their life and works. But he must leave their faith—the head—alone, through which their works and life will also be restored. On the other hand, [Satan's] feet remain. Externally he is strong and rages, but inwardly his head—sin—is trampled. Therefore, his feet must also finally be trampled, and all of him must eternally die with sin and death. See, in this way God has redeemed all the old [believers] through His Word and their faith, and has kept them from sin and the power of the devil until the coming of Christ, signified by this holy Anna.

74. For this reason she does not take the child Christ into her arms, as Simeon did. She says nothing about Him, as Simeon did, but she stands by and speaks about Him to others. For the dear old fathers and the saints did not make prophecies about Christ, as the prophets did; they said nothing about Him, but held with firm faith and stood by what was said through the prophets. They brought it further to other people and grandchildren, just as Luke here says about Anna.

75. All her characteristics, of which Luke here tells, agree with this. First, she is a prophetess; that is, she understands the prophets. Thus all the old saints have understood Christ in the passages of Scripture by faith, and consequently they were all prophets.

76. Second, she is called "Anna," which in Latin is *gratia*, meaning "favor" or "grace." The two names Anna and John are almost one name in Hebrew. Anna means the one who is gracious, or one who is favored and pleasing. This signifies that the old fathers and saints did not have this faith and the promise of God by their own merit, but by the favor and grace of God, according to whose mercy they were [called] gracious and favorable. In the same way all people are agreeable and pleasing to God not on account of their worthiness, but only by God's grace. People are accustomed to say, since nature often throws its favor on an intolerable thing, that "favor and love may

as likely fall on a frog as on royalty"; likewise: "What is lovely to me no one makes disagreeable to me." Thus God loves us, who are sinful and unworthy, and we must all be His little Johns and Annas. There is nothing but Johns and Annas to Him.

77. Third, she is a daughter of Phanuel. After Jacob had struggled and wrestled with the angel, he called that place Pniel or Pnuel and said, "I have seen God face-to-face. From this my soul has been saved" (Genesis 32 [:30]). Thus Pniel or Pnuel means "God's face." Now the face of God is nothing but the knowledge of God, and no one knows God except by faith in His words. The words and promises of God give nothing but comfort and grace in Christ, and whoever believes them sees God's grace and goodness. This is the correct knowledge of God, which cheers and saves the heart, as David says, "Lift up the light of Your face upon us, O Lord, by which You put joy in my heart" (Psalm 4 [:6–7]); and again: "Comfort us, O God; let Your face shine, that we may be saved" (Psalm 80 [:3]). There is much in Scripture about the hiding and showing of God's face.

78. See, in this way all the old fathers and saints were spiritual children of Pnuel (of divine knowledge and wisdom), which made them joyful. Their faith in the divine promises brought them there and made them prophets. But nothing brought them to faith and the promise except that they were dear little Annas, that is, God's pure favor and mercy.

79. From this, there follows the fourth, that she was of the tribe of Asher. "Asher" means "blessed or saved" [cf. Gen. 30:13]. Thus faith makes us children of divine wisdom and blessedness. For faith destroys sin and redeems from death, as Christ says, "Whoever believes will be saved" (Mark 16 [:16]). Now blessedness is nothing other than redemption from sin and death.

80. Anna, then, is a daughter of Phanuel and Asher, full of wisdom and having a good conscience in the face of all sins and the terrors of death. Faith in the divine promise of His mercy gives all of this, and thus one quite properly follows the other: Anna, the prophetess, a daughter of Phanuel, of the tribe of Asher. This means that we obtain His promise by divine favor, and believe it, and in so doing we really know God and His goodness, which fills the heart with joy, security, and blessedness and frees us completely from sin and death.

81. Fifth, we go deeper into the spiritual interpretations. She was married with her husband seven years, and after that was a widow for eighty-four years, without a husband. If someone had the time and the skill, he might find and discover the whole Bible in this number. But in order that people may see that we Christians need nothing at all of Aristotle or human doctrine, but have in Scripture enough to study for all eternity, if we would want to, we will apply this number to the wonders of Scripture mentioned before.

The number seven is commonly taken to signify our temporal life, the life of this body, because all time is measured by the seven days of the week (Genesis 1), which is the first and chief measure of time found in Scripture. For in Genesis 1, Moses tells how God first created days and drew seven of them together; afterward weeks were gathered into months, months into years, years into a lifetime, etc. These seven years, therefore, signify the whole life of the saints of old, which they led in external and bodily conduct.

82. But who was her husband? St. Paul explains that a husband signifies the Law (Romans 7 [:1–4]). For just as a man is bound as long as he lives, so all who live under the Law are bound to it. Now the Law has been given to no people on earth except to this Anna, the Jewish people, as Paul says that the oracles of God were entrusted to them for all people (Romans 3 [:2]). And Psalm 147 [:19–20] says: "He declares His Word to Jacob, His statutes and judgments to Israel. He has not dealt thus with any other nation; they do not know His judgments"; and again: "He made known His ways to Moses, His acts to the children of Israel" (Psalm 103 [:7]). But He revealed the Gospel not only to this people but also to all the world, as the psalmist says, "Their line goes out to all lands, and their speech to the end of the world" (Psalm 19 [:4]), that is, the apostles'. Therefore, Anna, who lived seven years with her husband, signifies this people under the Law, in their outward conduct and bodily way of life.

83. Now we have heard in the Epistle for today that those who live under the Law do not live well, for they only do the works of the Law unwillingly and without delight, and are servants, not children. For no one keeps the Law correctly unless he does so willingly. But no one gives this willingness except faith in Christ, as has often been said. Where faith is present, it produces righteous works and fulfills the Law; for faith it is all the same whether it is under the Law or not under the Law, since Christ was also under the Law.

84. Therefore, in addition to the fact that St. Luke—or, more so, the Holy Spirit—threw this holy Anna, the holy people of old, under the Law and made slaves of them, he further shows that besides her life under the Law she also walked in the freedom of faith and the Spirit, and fulfilled the Law not only with works like a servant but rather also in faith. This is signified by the eighty-four years of her widowhood, meaning the spiritual life of faith led by the saints of old. For the widowhood, the life without a husband, signifies freedom from the Law.

And thus both lives were led together. According to their souls they were justified without the Law and its works, only through faith, and in this respect they were truly widows; but according to the body they were in the Law and its works. They did not, however, believe that they were justified by works, but having been justified by faith, they kept the Law freely, gratuitously, to the glory of God. Whoever lives in this way may also keep the Law, which will not harm him nor make him a slave, for Christ and the apostles also have kept the Law.

See, these are the people who at the same time live seven years with a husband and eighty-four years without a husband, who at the same time are free from the Law and yet under the Law, as St. Paul says of himself: "I was with those who were under the Law, though I myself was not under the Law" (1 Corinthians 9 [:20]).

85. How can he at the same time be under the Law and free from the Law? Namely, he externally and gladly kept the Law in order to serve others, but inwardly he clung to faith, by which he was justified without the works of the Law; for though he did the works of the Law, he did not want to be justified through them, which indeed is impossible.

In this way Anna, the holy people, has also kept the Law. For whoever believes and has been justified by faith may keep not only the Law of God but also the laws and works of the whole world, and they will not hinder him; for he keeps them freely, not thinking that he becomes godly through them.

But those who are only the married Anna for seven years, and not afterward the widow Anna for eighty-four years, only live under the Law, without the Spirit and without faith, as forced slaves. They believe that by doing the works of the Law they become godly. But in this way they can never become godly and justified, as today's Epistle sufficiently explains. This has been well arranged: first the seven years of wedded life, and then the eighty-four years of widowhood are mentioned, for St. Paul also says, "The first is not the spiritual man, but the natural, and then the spiritual" (1 Corinthians 15 [:46]).

86. If man is to become spiritual and receive faith, he must necessarily first be under the Law; for no one can know what he lacks without the Law, and he who does not know himself will not seek grace. But when the Law comes, it demands much, so that one feels and must confess that he cannot do it. Then he must despair of himself and in all humility sigh for God's grace. See, in that way the seven years come first, the Law precedes grace just as John [the Baptist] was the forerunner of Christ. The Law kills and condemns the natural, rational man [cf. 1 Cor. 2:14; James 3:15], so that grace may lift up the spiritual, inner man.

87. But no years are given to her virginity, which signifies the unfruitful life before the Law and before grace, and which is worthless before God. Therefore, virginity was totally despised and rejected in the Old Testament as an unfruitful estate.

94. Luke says that she never left the temple. What a salutary and necessary exhortation! We have heard that this temple is the Holy Scriptures. Now, among the Jewish people it was a particular trouble that they so liked to listen

to false prophets and human doctrines; they proved this by erecting many altars and much worship outside of the temple in high places and valleys. Moses sternly prohibited that and said: "Everything that I command you, you shall be careful to do. You shall not add to it or take from it" (Deuteronomy 5 [:32]; 12 [:32]). It is as if he would say, "I want you to be such an Anna, who does not leave the temple." They were, however, not all like Anna, but withdrew from the temple to their altars, that is, away from God's Law and beyond God's Law; they followed their own devices and false prophets.

95. But this was nothing compared with our present situation. We have not only been led astray from the temple by the pope and human doctrines, but we have also smashed and desecrated it with all kinds of sacrilege and abominations according to sheer self-chosen conduct, more than anyone can lament. But it truly ought to be, as St. Anthony so diligently taught his disciples, that nobody should undertake to do anything that God has not commanded or advised in Scripture, so that we might indeed remain in the temple. The psalmist speaks of this: "Blessed is the man who walks not in the counsel of the wicked, nor stands in the way of sinners, nor sits in the seat of scoffers; but his delight is in the Law of the Lord; and on His Law he meditates day and night" (Psalm 1 [:1–2]). St. Peter says, "The righteous is scarcely saved" [1 Pet. 4:18], who is in the temple. That is, the evil spirit also snatches to himself those who trust only in God's Word; nevertheless, they scarcely remain. Where, then, will those secure and wild people remain who base their lives on human doctrines?

96. A good life cannot endure human doctrines; they are offensive and dangerous, like a trap laid for you. We must remain in the temple and never leave it. The old saints did that, of whom St. Paul says that God spoke to Elijah: "I have kept for Myself seven thousand men who have not bowed their knees to Baal" (Romans 11 [:4; cf. 1 Kings 19:18]). Therefore, David complains about those hunters and tempters: "Preserve me, O Lord, from the hand of the godless; guard me from violent people who plan to trip up my feet. The arrogant hide a trap for me, and with cords they spread a net; on the way they set snares for me. Selah" (Psalm 140 [:4–6]). All this is said against human doctrines, which snatch us away from the temple. For God's Word and human doctrines will not at all get along with each other in the same heart. Yet these senseless murderers of souls—the Papists with their Antichrist, the pope—declare that we must have and keep more things than are in the Bible, and with their spiritual estates and orders they lead the whole world to hell.

97. Finally, [Luke] says that she "served God with fasting and prayer night and day" [Luke 2:37]. Now follow the works of faith. She must first be Anna, a prophetess, the daughter of Phanuel, of the tribe of Asher, married

seven years, a widow for eighty-four years, and always in the temple. Then her fasting and praying is right. Then the sacrifice of Abel is acceptable. Then God may be served with fasting and prayer day and night. But whoever starts with works turns everything upside down and obtains nothing. Thus, after St. Paul has taught faith to the Romans, he begins in chapter 12 to teach them many good works, and says they ought to present their bodies as a holy, living, acceptable sacrifice to God (Romans 12 [:1]). This happens when the body is mortified by fasting, watching, clothes, and labors. This is what Anna now does.

98. All the old saints did the same, for fasting means all kinds of mortification and chastisement of the body. Although the soul is just and holy by faith, [the body] is not yet entirely pure from sin and evil inclinations. Therefore, it must be forced and mortified and made subject to the soul, as St. Paul says of himself: "I chastise my body and keep it under control, lest I preach to others and myself be rejected" (1 Corinthians 9 [:27]). St. Peter also teaches that we should "offer spiritual sacrifices" (1 Peter 2 [:5]), that is, not sheep or calves, as in the Law of Moses, but our own bodies and ourselves, by the killing of sin in our flesh and mortification of the body. No one can do this who does not first believe.

99. Therefore, I have often said that works are to be done after faith, only not with the intention to merit much through them or to become godly—for that must be present before the works. Rather, [works are to be done] only to mortify the body and to be useful to our neighbor. And that is true worship in the works, when they are done freely and gratuitously for the honor of God. Why does He otherwise need your fasting, unless by doing so you suppress sin and the flesh, which He wants suppressed? When they fast for the saints or on special days and times, with no regard for mortifying the body, they only make an unprofitable work out of it.

100. But Anna does not fast only on certain special days—on Saturdays and Fridays, on the eve of apostles' days or ember days[11]—nor does she make any distinction about food. Rather, St. Luke says [she fasted] day and night and served God with it; that is, she continually deprives her body, not to do a work with it, but to serve God by suppressing sin.

101. St. Paul also teaches about this fasting and says, among other things, that with much fasting we commend ourselves as servants of God (2 Corinthians 6 [:4–5]). But our foolish fasting contrived by men is thought to be precious when it does not eat meat, eggs, butter, or milk for a few days.

---

11 Ember days were a Wednesday, Friday, and Saturday out of each quarter-year reserved for prayer and fasting. These days fell during: the week following the first Sunday in Lent, the week between Pentecost and Trinity Sunday, the week following the Feast of the Holy Cross (September 14), and the week following the Commemoration of St. Lucia (December 13).

It is not at all directed to the mortification of the body and of sin, that is, as a service to God; rather, we serve the pope and the Papists with that—and the fishermen.

102. She also prayed day and night—so she also certainly stayed awake. Nevertheless, we are not to understand that she continually prayed and fasted day and night, for she also had to eat, drink, sleep, and rest. Rather, such works were the mode of life she pursued day and night. What someone does during the day or at night must not be understood as being done all day and all night.

103. This is the second part of worship, in which the soul is offered up to God, just as the body is by fasting. And by prayer we do not understand only oral prayer but also the hearing, proclaiming, contemplating, and meditating on God's Word. Many psalms were spoken in prayers, in which scarcely three verses ask for something; the other verses teach something, rebuke sin, or speak with God, with ourselves, and with people. See, such works of worship were very dear to the fathers and old saints, with which they sought nothing but that God's honor and human salvation be accomplished. Thus we read in Scripture of much sighing and longing from the ancient fathers for Christ and the salvation of the world, as everyone sees that especially in the Psalms.

104. But our prayer now is only muttering the seven canonical hours, counting the rosary, and similar babbling of words. Nobody thinks seriously of asking and obtaining something from God, but they only perform it as an obligatory work and let it remain there. As a thresher beats with his flail, so they beat with their tongues, and merit only bread for the belly. Much less are they troubled to serve God with their prayers, that is, to pray for the general need of Christendom, but even the best among them think they have done well when they are godly and pray for themselves. Therefore, like the hypocrites, they merit only more hell with their prayers, for they serve neither God nor men, but only their belly and property. But if they were to serve God and their neighbor as they ought, they would have to abandon and forget the number of the words, and not think of how many psalms and words, but with all their hearts would seek God's honor and their neighbor's salvation, which is true worship. Then they would often pray the whole day for one thing, which they very much needed. This would be a true Anna prayer and worship.

For Luke did not write in vain that she served God with her prayers, but so that he might reject all the swarm and vermin of our foolish prayers, whereby we only increase and multiply our sins because we do not serve and seek God. Now let us return again to our text.

*She came up at that very hour and praised the Lord and spoke of Him to all who were waiting for the redemption of Jerusalem. [Luke 2:38]*

105. Our old Latin text reads "for the redemption of Israel," but the Greek has "who were waiting for the redemption of Jerusalem," [that is,] that Anna spoke to those who were in Jerusalem and were waiting for the redemption. Since she did not leave the temple, she could speak to no one except for those who were in Jerusalem, either to the inhabitants or to visitors. In the spiritual interpretation we have spoken sufficiently about the meaning of her standing about or near. For when we come with Christ into the temple of Scripture to present Him to God with thanksgiving, there is found at that very hour also this holy Anna, with all the saints of the whole synagogue, who unanimously look and point at Him with their faith and their whole life.

106. Moreover, the great worthiness of this holy woman is shown in a delightful way: ahead of many great people she had this grace that she recognized this poor child as the true Savior. There were undoubtedly priests present who received the sacrifice from Mary and Joseph but did not recognize the child and perhaps considered all they heard and saw from Simeon and Anna as old wives' tales. She must have been specially illumined by the Spirit, and been regarded as a great saint in God's eyes, who gave her that light more than all others.

107. And note that there were five persons there: the child Christ; His mother, Mary; Joseph; Simeon; and Anna. Yet this small number of people represent every station in life: husband and wife, young and old, virgin and widow, married and unmarried. So early [on] Christ begins to gather around Him people of every honorable estate and cannot be alone. Whoever, then, is not found in one of these estates is not in the state of salvation.

108. She praised the Lord. The Hebrew language uses the word "confess" with a wide meaning, which we can scarcely achieve with three words, such as: to confess sins, to confess faith, and to praise. Therefore, when the Hebrew language wants to praise, it says "confess," and very appropriately so. For to praise is nothing other than to confess the benefit received, the kindness of the benefactor, and the unworthiness of the needy person [who received it]. Whoever acknowledges and confesses this praises sincerely. Besides this, confessing is also admitting to something. Thus Christ says: "Everyone who confesses Me before men, I also will confess before My Father who is in heaven; but whoever denies Me before men, I also will deny before My Father who is in heaven" (Matthew 10 [:32–33]).

109. It was said above about the blessing of Simeon that it is an unusually high virtue to bless Christ, whom all the world curses. So also it is an unusually high work to give thanks to God for Christ. Those who recognize Him do that, but there are only few of them. The others blaspheme God, condemn,

persecute, and oppose Christ and His doctrine. What they do to His doctrine they also do to Him and to God, His Father, as He says, "Whoever despises you despises Me, and whoever despises Me despises Him who sent Me" (Luke 10 [:16]). It is a terrible thing that the world is so full of those who blaspheme and curse and that we must live among them. St. Paul predicts that in the last days there will be many blasphemers (cf. 2 Timothy 3 [:1–2]). This [prophecy] is now being fulfilled by the pope with the universities, chapters, and monasteries, which do nothing but condemn, persecute, and curse the Gospel of Christ.

110. Therefore, do not consider it only a little grace when you come to recognize Christ and give thanks to God for Him, when you do not regard Him as a condemned, cursed heretic and seducer and do not blaspheme, despise, and forsake God and His teaching, as is done by the great multitude. For with Christ it is not a matter of giving great honor to His person and name, as all His enemies do. Instead, He wants His doctrine to be honored, which is the real insight, as He says: "Why do you call Me 'Lord, Lord,' and not do what I tell you?" (Luke 6 [:46]); and "Whoever is ashamed of Me and of My words in this adulterous and sinful generation, of him will the Son of Man also be ashamed" (Mark 8 [:38]). Here you hear that He cares about His doctrine. The pope and his Papists also call Him "Lord," and then in His name, to His honor, and in His service they condemn His doctrine, slaughter his Anna, and persecute her throughout the world. It is terrible and unbearable to see the innumerable multitude which blasphemes God because of Christ, and in their raving go down to hell.

111. It is a sign that is opposed, against which more stumble and fall than ever before. It is common to say, "Thanks be to God!" but scarcely one in a thousand says it truthfully. At Elijah's time—still a time of grace—there were only seven thousand [believers] among so many Jews, who undoubtedly numbered more than a million. What will happen in the last times when the time of grace ends, which Daniel calls a time of wrath (cf. Daniel 11 [:36; 8:19])? We might well say to God with the psalmist: "Almighty God, where is Your mercy now, which was so great in times past? Have You then made all people for nothing?" (Psalm 89 [:49]).

112. [Anna] not only praised God but also spoke of Him to all who were waiting for redemption. Luke has a special reason for adding that Anna spoke of Christ only to those who were waiting for redemption. There were not many of them, and none at all among the highly educated priests. What could these high, holy, and learned people hear and learn from such an old, foolish woman! "We are the real leaders of the people." Without any doubt her words were regarded in the same way by those great lords. For God's Word, spoken about Christ, has the nature—and nothing else will come of

it—of being contemptible, foolish, heretical, sacrilegious, and presumptuous in these great, learned, and spiritual ears. Therefore, only the hungry, empty souls who are waiting for redemption grasp it, as Luke says here, that is, those who feel their sin, desire grace, light, and consolation, and know nothing of any wisdom and righteousness of their own.

113. Now faith and the knowledge of Christ cannot be silent. [Faith] breaks forth and speaks what it knows about Him, so that others are helped and His light is shared, as Psalm 116 [:10] says, "I believed; therefore, I spoke." [Faith] is much too kind and good to keep such treasures to itself. But when it speaks, it meets all kinds of affliction from the unbelieving saints; yet it does not care and goes right ahead. And who knows how Anna was treated! But perhaps they spared her on account of her age and gender, and simply despised her as a silly fool. Otherwise she would only have retained her life with difficulty, because she caused such error and heresy and spoke so many new and unheard-of things about Christ in opposition to all the doctrine and knowledge of the learned priests and teachers of the Law, who are satisfied and filled with wisdom and righteousness, who need no redemption but only the crown and reward for their works and merit.

For whoever wants to speak about the redemption of Christ is asserting that people are caught in sin and blindness. But that would offend such high saints, that they should be sinners and blind! Therefore, they cannot endure hearing about Christ and His redemption. Instead, they condemn it as a dangerous error and a diabolical heresy.

114. We now easily understand how it was that the spiritual Anna gives thanks to God and speaks of Christ to all who are waiting for the redemption of Jerusalem, for the dear saints of the Old Testament certainly recognized Christ. Therefore, she praises and thanks God all her life, speaks what is written in the Bible, and says nothing other than this redemption, how Christ was given only for the needy and the hungry. This is proven by all histories, for God never helped those who consider themselves strong and not forsaken; but on the other hand, He never forsook those who were needy and desired His help. In proof of this we might muster up many, even all, the examples of the Bible, but this is sufficiently clear and obvious to anyone who reads them.

*And when they had fulfilled everything according to the Law of the Lord, they returned into Galilee, to their own town of Nazareth. [Luke 2:39]*

116. As for the things that they accomplished according to the Law of the Lord, that will be given in the Gospel for Candlemas. The significance of Galilee and Nazareth is to be discussed in the Gospel for the Annunciation. Here it is to be noted, since St. Matthew writes it (Matthew 2 [:13]), that after

the Magi had found Christ in Bethlehem and offered Him gold, frankincense, and myrrh, and gone home, the angel appeared to Joseph in his sleep and told him to flee into Egypt with the child and His mother, which Joseph then did. How does this agree with what Luke says, that they returned home to Nazareth when the six weeks were over and they had performed everything according to the Law of God?

We must here hold to one of these ways [of understanding: either] that they first went into Egypt soon after the six weeks, and then returned home to Nazareth from Egypt in due time, or (what I think is correct) that they returned home immediately after the six weeks, as Luke says here. Then the appearance of the angel, of which Matthew speaks—that they should flee into Egypt—occurred at Nazareth, not at Bethlehem; and it certainly happened after the departure of the Magi, as Matthew says, but not so soon afterward. But [Matthew] says that it happened afterward because of the arrangement of his writing. For he writes about the flight into Egypt immediately after the Magi and omits what Luke writes here about the sacrifice in the temple. Thus it is clear that the two evangelists do not disagree.

117. The holy cross is depicted even better [in this second understanding]: the poor mother with her child, who had been on the road for seven or eight weeks and incidentally had given birth, had scarcely returned home to rest and to set up house again when they quickly had to be gone, leaving everything behind, and travel farther than before. The Lord Christ began His pilgrimages with His birth, and was always on a pilgrimage on this earth, with no certain place of His own. How differently from other children is this royal child reared and treated! How unfair and difficult this ought to seem to us! But the poor mother had to flee with the child into Egypt from the wrath of Herod. We shall speak more of this when this Gospel is explained.

*But the child grew and became strong in the spirit, filled with wisdom. And the grace of God was with Him. [Luke 2:40]*

118. Some have been inquisitive and were not satisfied with what Scripture says. They wanted to know what Christ did in His childhood and have received the reward for their inquisitiveness. Some fool or knave has distinguished himself by fabricating a book about the childhood of Christ, and has not been afraid nor ashamed to serve up his lies and deceptions about how Christ went to school and much more similar foolish and blasphemous tomfoolery. Thus he jests with his lies at the expense of the Lord, whom all the angels adore and fear and [before whom] all creatures tremble, so that this knave would have deserved "to have a millstone fastened around his neck and to be drowned in the deep sea" [Matt. 18:6] because he did not esteem the Lord of all more than to act as a cuckoo and ape toward Him. There are still

people who print this book, read, and believe it, which was what the knave wanted. Therefore, I say that such books would be burned by the pope, the bishops, and the universities, if they were Christians. But they do much worse and are and remain blind leaders.

119. Christ did not go to school, for no schools like ours existed at that time. He did not even learn any letters, as we read in the Gospel that the Jews marveled, saying, "How is it that this man knows the Scripture, when He has never studied it?" [John 7:15]. Similarly, they were astonished at His knowledge and said: "Why, isn't this Joseph's and Mary's Son? Don't we know His friends? Where did He get such wisdom and all of that?" [cf. Mark 6:2–3]. They thought it strange that a layman, the son of a carpenter, should be so learned when He had never studied. Therefore, they were offended at Him, as the Gospel says, and thought that He must be possessed by the evil spirit.

120. Let us therefore remain with the Gospel, which tells us enough about His childhood when Luke writes that He "grew and became strong, filled with wisdom," etc. Likewise, afterward, that He was submissive to His parents [Luke 2:51]. What else should he have written? It was not yet the time for Him to perform miracles. He was brought up like other children, except that, just as some children are more intelligent than others, so also Christ was an especially intelligent child compared to others. Therefore, nothing more is to be written about Him than Luke writes. If he had written what He ate, drank, and did every day, how He walked, stood, slept, and awoke, what kind of writing would that have been?

121. Therefore, it is also not necessary to believe—I think it is not true—that His knitted tunic, which those crucifying Him did not want to divide [cf. John 19:23–24], grew with Him from His youth.[12] Perhaps His mother did not make it for Him, but it was the common dress of the poor in that land. We should have a pure faith that believes nothing without a basis in Scripture. There is enough and more than enough in Scripture for us to believe, especially since Christ began to perform miracles and works only after His Baptism, as it is written (John 2 [:11–22]; Acts 10 [:37]).

122. Some hairsplitters are perplexed by the words of Luke according to which Christ, though He was always God, increased in spirit and wisdom. They grant that He grew, which is certainly a miracle, since they are so quick to invent miracles where there are none and despise them when there are [miracles]. They make this perplexity and question for themselves, for they have invented as an article of faith that Christ, from the first moment of His conception, was so filled with wisdom and the Spirit that no more could get in, just as a wineskin is filled so that no more can get in. They themselves

12 Such a miraculous tunic, supposedly knitted by Mary and growing to fit Jesus as He grew, is told of in *Von der kinthait*, p. 444. See WA 10/1.1:446 n. 1.

do not understand what they say or what they are talking about, as St. Paul writes (1 Timothy 1 [:7]).

123. Even if I could not understand what Luke means when he says that Christ increased in spirit and wisdom, I would honor his words as God's Word and believe they are true, though I might never find out how it could be true. And I should abandon my imaginary article of faith as human foolishness, which is far too worthless to be a measure and standard for divine truth. We must all indeed confess that Christ was not always cheerful, despite the fact that whoever is filled with the Spirit is also full of joy, since joy is a fruit of the Spirit (Galatians 5 [:22]). Likewise, Christ was not always sweet and gentle; He was angry and disgusted when He drove the Jews out of the temple (John 2 [:15–17]), and He was distressed in anger at their blindness (Mark 3 [:5]).

124. Therefore, we should understand the words of Luke most simply about the humanity of Christ, which was an instrument and house of the deity. And though He was always filled with the Spirit and with grace, yet the Spirit did not always move Him, but prompted Him now to do this, now something else, just as it happened. Although [the Spirit] was in Him from the beginning of His conception, yet just as His body grew and His reason naturally developed as in other men, so also the Spirit settled into Him more and more, and moved Him more and more as time went on. It is no delusion when Luke says that He became strong in spirit. Rather, just as the words plainly read, so it happened most simply: as He grew older, He truly grew larger; as He grew larger, He became more rational; and as He became more rational, He became stronger in spirit and more full of wisdom before God in Himself and before the people. No glosses are needed here. This is a Christian explanation which can be accepted without any danger, and it does not matter whether it overthrows their imaginary articles of faith.

125. St. Paul agrees with this when he says that Christ "emptied Himself of His divine form, taking the form of a servant, becoming just like any other man, and being found in the appearance of men" (Philippians 2 [:7]). St. Paul does not speak here of the likeness of Christ's human nature to our own, but he says: Christ, the man, after He was already a man, became just like other men and was found in appearance as a man. Now since all men grow naturally in body, reason, spirit, and wisdom, and there is no one who is otherwise, Luke agrees with Paul that Christ also increased in all parts, yet was a special child who increased specially more than others. For His bodily constitution was nobler, and God's gifts and graces were more abundant in Him than in others. Thus Luke's words have a very easy, clear, and simple understanding, if only these wiseacres would leave out their subtleties.—So much on this Gospel.

## Appendix: The Meaning of the Numbers

88. But how is it that faith or the spiritual life of the inner man, which without the Law is a widow without a husband, is signified by the number eighty-four? Here we will, as St. Augustine was accustomed to do, take a little walk and play around [with the number] spiritually. Everyone knows that the numbers seven and twelve are nearly the most glorious in Scripture. For there are many sevens and twelves [in Scripture], undoubtedly because there were twelve apostles who began and founded the faith in all the world; their doctrine and life was nothing but faith. Just as the one Moses received the Law from the angels, through which he is the married Anna and extorts works from the external man, so the apostles, who were twelve times more in number than Moses, received the Gospel not from angels but from the Lord Himself, through which widows, independently believing people, are justified without any works.

Now the saints of old, as we have said before, possessed this apostolic faith along with the Law. Therefore, they have not only acquired the number seven but also the number twelve, have not only possessed the one Moses but also the apostles who were twelve times more, and have lived both ways [under the Law and free from the Law], as we have heard before. Thus the number seven signifies the one Moses, and the number twelve signifies the apostles, who were twelve times as many as Moses. So it is determined that the number twelve signifies the apostles, the apostolic doctrine, the apostolic faith, the true widowhood, the spiritual life without the Law. So also the number seven signifies Moses, Moses' doctrine, the works of the Law, the real married estate.

89. The twelve apostles are signified by the twelve patriarchs [cf. Acts 7:8], the twelve precious stones on the breastpiece of Aaron [cf. Exod. 39:8–13], the twelve princes of the Israelite people, the twelve stones taken out of the Jordan [cf. Josh. 4:3–9], the twelve foundations and gates of Jerusalem [cf. Rev. 21:12–14], and many more. For all of Scripture urges faith and the Gospel, which were begun and established by the apostles. Thus this faith is also signified by these eighty-four years, which contain the number twelve in a wonderful way.

90. First, eighty-four is equal to twelve times seven. This signifies that the teacher of the Law is only one, Moses, being only one times seven, that is, the Law and the life under the Law. But the apostles are twelve, twelve times as many as Moses. Eighty-four bears the same relation to seven as twelve does to one. Now, as the Law was given through one and the Gospel through twelve, it is evident that seven signifies Moses and eighty-four, the apostles. So Moses' people are the married Anna, while the apostles' people are the

widow Anna—the former, externally in body and works; the latter, inwardly in Spirit and faith.

This also signifies that faith exceeds the works as much as twelve exceeds the number one, or as eighty-four exceeds the number seven. It comprises the whole sum and inheritance. The apostle calls it *holocleros*, the whole inheritance (1 Thessalonians 5 [:23]), just as the number twelve comprises all the people of Israel, divided into twelve tribes. For whoever believes has it all, is an heir, child, and saved. Notice also the divine arrangement here. As Anna was not a widow for twelve years nor a married woman for one year, God ordained this seven and eighty-four years so that they are like one and twelve. Besides this, there is thus also found, as we have seen, a greater spiritual significance in the number seven, in her wedded life and in the state of her widowhood.

91. Second, the mathematicians divide numbers and call it the quotient; that is, they look for how many times a number may be divided into equal parts. Thus twelve may be divided five times into equal parts. For twelve, first, is twelve times one, all equal parts; second, six times two; third, four times three; fourth, three times four; fifth, two times six. Beyond this there are no more which divide evenly. Seven and five are also twelve; likewise, three and nine, one and eleven, but the parts are unequal, so it is not an equal division. Now, they take the number of these equal parts and add them up to see how many they make. Thus here twelve is divided five times, so I take together $1 + 2 + 3 + 4 + 5$, which make fifteen, exceeding the number itself by three. Therefore, they call such a number the abundantly superfluous number, because the sum of the parts is more than the number itself. On the other hand, the division of some numbers is less than the number itself. For instance, eight divides three times evenly, namely, eight times one, four times two, two times four. But $1 + 2 + 4$ is only seven, one less than eight. This is called the deficient number. Between these two is the third number, in which the parts are equal to the number. Thus, six is six times one, three times two, and two times three; now one, two, and three added together make six.

92. Notice here also that Moses, the number seven, cannot be divided in that way, as all odd numbers cannot. For this equal division must have even numbers. But the apostles, the number eighty-four, is an abundantly superfluous number and can be divided eleven times into equal parts. Judas, the traitor, does not belong to the abundant number, though he is one of the number. He leaves a hole in the division, so that it is not twelve, and yet there are still twelve. He belongs to the number [of the apostles] in name, but not in reality. First, the number eighty-four is eighty-four times one; second, forty-two times two; third, twenty-eight times three; fourth, twenty-one times four; fifth, fourteen times six; sixth, twelve times seven; seventh, seven times

twelve; eighth, six times fourteen; ninth, four times twenty-one; tenth, three times twenty-eight; eleventh, two times forty-two. If you now add together the numbers from the division: 1 + 2 + 3 + 4 + 6 + 7 + 12 + 14 + 21 + 28 + 42, the result is 140, that is, 56 more than the number itself.

93. All this signifies that Moses undivided—the Law—like the number seven, remained by itself, having not passed beyond the Jewish people, much less having included other nations. But the apostles—the gracious, spiritual life and the Gospel—have broken out and overflowed abundantly over all the world. And just as the number one compared with twelve is very small and trifling, so that it could hardly look more unimportant, so also the number seven compared with eighty-four is very insignificant. For the Law with its works gives nothing at all to all its slaves but temporal possessions and worldly honor, a poor and wretched possession, which will not increase but surely decrease.

On the other hand, twelve compared to one is great and will increase and not decrease, for faith is blessed and overflows forever with possessions and honor.

We have dealt with this enough for now so that we can see that no dot of Scripture was written in vain. The dear old fathers have given us examples with their faith, and with their works have always pointed to that in which we should believe, namely, Christ and His Gospel. Therefore, we read nothing concerning them in vain, but everything about them strengthens and improves our faith. Let us now continue with Anna.

# GOSPEL FOR
# NEW YEAR'S DAY

*Luke 2:21*

*And at the end of eight days, when He was circumcised, He was called Jesus, the name given by the angel before He was conceived in the womb.*

1. On this day it is customary to dispense from the pulpit [good wishes for] the new year,[1] as if there were not enough other useful and salutary matters to preach, and it were necessary to present such useless fables in place of the divine Word and to make a game and a joke of so serious an office. The Gospel reading requires us to preach on the circumcision and the name of Jesus, and this we will do!

## OF THE CIRCUMCISION

2. First, let us ask the sophist, Lady Jezebel,[2] natural reason: Is it not a foolish, ridiculous, useless command when God demands circumcision? Could He find no other member of the body [to change] than this one? If Abraham had here followed reason, he would not have believed that it was God who demanded this of him [cf. Gen. 17:1–14]. For in our eyes it is such a foolish thing that there can scarcely be anything more foolish. In addition, the Jews had [to endure] great humiliation and disgrace, were despised by all the world because of it, and were regarded as an abomination. Moreover, there is no use in it. What benefit is it if the body is damaged? Man is made no better by it, for everything depends on the soul.

---

1 A custom is referred to here which arose in the latter part of the Middle Ages. On New Year's Day, the eighth day after Christmas, the preacher declared from the pulpit special new year's wishes to his hearers with reference to the eight different classes among them. For an example from 1573, see WA 10/1.1:504 n. 1. See E. Jane Dempsey Douglass, *Justification in Late Medieval Preaching: A Study of John Geiler of Keisersberg*, 2nd ed. (Leiden: Brill, 1989), p. 35. The custom introduced many absurdities and improprieties into the worship service. The practice was taken up in mockery by Jean Molinet (1435–1507); see Johan Huizinga, *The Waning of the Middle Ages* (Mineola, NY: Dover, 1999), p. 161.

2 Luther also used the name Lady Hulda to refer to human reason; see, e.g., the sermon for Second Sunday in Advent on Luke 21:25–33, paragraph 23.

3. But such are and ought to be all of God's commandments and works. In our eyes they appear most foolish, most contemptible, and most useless, in order that haughty Reason, who thinks herself clever and wise, may be put to shame and blinded and may surrender her opinion and submit to God, give Him honor, and believe that whatever He asserts is most useful, most honorable, and most wise, though she does not see it and thinks quite differently. If God had given a sign which would have been suitable to her and useful, wise, and honorable in her opinion, she would have remained in her old skin, would not have subordinated her haughtiness, would have continued in her custom of seeking only honor, gain, and wisdom, and living on earth—and so would have become ever more deeply rooted in worldly, temporal things. But now that He presents to her foolish, useless, and shameful things, He tears her away from seeking after gain, honor, and wisdom and teaches her to look only to the invisible, divine wisdom, honor, and gain—and for its sake willingly to suffer the lack of temporal honor, gain, and wisdom and to be foolish, poor, incompetent, and despised for God's sake. Therefore, God was not concerned about the circumcision, but about the humiliation of proud nature and reason.

4. So we also have Baptism in the New Testament, in order that we should go under the water and believe that we are thereby cleansed from sins and saved; also, that Christ's body is in the bread of the altar; also, that we worship the crucified man as Lord and God. All this is immeasurably far above and contrary to reason. So the works and words of God are all contrary to reason, and this, in turn, is also contrary to God and kicks against the "sign that is spoken against" [Luke 2:34].

People thought it was very foolish when Noah built the ark and said that the world would sink [Gen. 6:13f.]. So Lot had to be a fool when he said that Sodom and Gomorrah would perish [Gen. 19:14]. Moses and Aaron were fools before King Pharaoh [Exod. 5:1f.]. In short, God's Word and His preachers must be fools, as St. Paul says (1 Corinthians 1 [:21]). In all this God seeks nothing more than humility, that man bring his reason into captivity and be subject to divine truth. So this foolish circumcision was given to Abraham and his seed, in order that by it they should give glory to God and let Him alone be wise.

5. Now circumcision was an external mark by which God's people were distinguished from other nations. Similarly, we see that every prince gives his people and army his standard and watchword, by which they are known among themselves and by which foreigners can notice to what lord they belong. Thus God has never left His people without such a sign or watchword, by which it can be known outwardly in the world where His people are to be found.

The Jews were recognized by circumcision, which was their divine watchword. Our watchword is Baptism and the body of Christ. Therefore, the ancient fathers called these signs *characteres, symbola, tesseras,*[3] that is, "watchwords" or "standards," what we now call "sacraments," that is, holy signs. For where there is Baptism, there certainly are Christians, wherever they are in the world. It does not matter if they are not under the pope. He claims [that it does], for he would like to make of himself a sacrament and Christian watchword.

6. That is enough about the bodily reason for circumcision. We will now also look at the spiritual reason and its significance. First, why did He not command to circumcise a finger, hand, foot, ear, eye, or some other limb? Why did He select just that which in human life serves for no work or employment and which was created by God for birth and reproduction? If evil was to be cut off, then certainly the hand or the tongue, of all members, ought to have been circumcised, since by the tongue and hands all wickedness is perpetrated among men.

7. It is said that it was done for the reason that evil lust manifests itself most in that part of the body; therefore, also Adam and Eve felt the disobedience of their flesh there and sought a covering for their shame. That is all true, but in addition to that it also signifies, as we always say, that God does not condemn or save the person on account of his works, but his works on account of the person. Accordingly, our fault lies not in our works but in our nature. The person, nature, and our entire existence are corrupt because of Adam's fall. Therefore, no work can be good in us until our nature and the life of the person are changed and renewed. The tree is not good; therefore, its fruits are bad [cf. Matt. 7:17–18].

8. Thus in circumcision God quickly taught everyone that no one can become godly by works or laws, and that all works and labors for becoming godly or saved are in vain, as long as the nature and person are not renewed. You see now that if He had commanded to circumcise the hand or the tongue, this would have been a sign that the fault that needed changing lay in the words or works, and that He was favorable to the nature and person and hated only the words and works. But now in selecting that member which has no work, except that our nature and the life of the person come through it, He gives clearly to understand that the entire state of the nature is lacking, that its birth and all that comes from it are corrupt and sin.

This is original sin or the sin of the nature or the sin of the person, the truly chief sin. If this did not exist, there would be no actual sin. This sin is not done, like all other sins, but it exists, lives, and does all sins and is the

---

3 I.e., "marks, tokens, watchwords."

essential sin. It sins not for an hour or a while; but wherever and as long as the person exists, sin is also there.

9. God looks only at this natural sin. This [sin] can be driven away by no law, by no punishment, even if there were a thousand hells; only the grace of God, which makes the nature pure and new, can sweep it away. The Law only shows it and teaches how to recognize it, but does not save from it. [The Law] restrains only the hand or the limbs; it cannot restrain the person and nature from being sinful, for from birth already [the nature and person] has come before the Law and has become sin before the Law could forbid it.

As little as being born or receiving natural life depends on each person's power, so little does being without sin or being free from it depend on his ability. He alone who has created us must take it away. Therefore, He first gives us the Law, by which man recognizes this sin and thirsts for grace; then afterward He gives the Gospel and helps him.

10. Second, why does He command to circumcise males only, when nature and birth involve the woman also? The prophet also complains more about the mother than about the father when he says, "Behold, I was brought forth in iniquity, and in sin did my mother conceive me" (Psalm 51 [:5]). This was surely done on account of Christ and His mother, because it was going to happen, and could have happened, that a natural man and person could come from a woman without sin and the contribution of nature, but whatever is conceived from a man sins on both sides, the man and the woman, and this does not happen without sin on both sides. Therefore, Christ did not want to be conceived from a man, in order that His mother would not also have to sin and conceive Him in sin. Thus He made use of her womanly flesh and body for natural birth, but not for natural conception, and was conceived and born a true man without sin.

Because a pure, innocent birth, nature, and person may come from a woman—but from a man may come only a sinful birth, nature, and person—therefore circumcision was imposed upon males only, in order to signify that all birth from man is sinful and condemned, requiring circumcision and change, but that what comes only from a woman without a man is innocent and uncondemned, requiring no circumcision or change. If it were possible now that more women could bear [children] without men, these births would be altogether pure and holy; but this has been reserved for this one mother alone.

11. Third, why was it necessary to perform it on the eighth day? Here again the sin of nature is indicated. For the poor baby has no actual sin of its own; nevertheless, it must be circumcised and receive the sign for purification from sin. If He had commanded to circumcise after eight years, one might say it was done for sins committed and to avoid future sins. But

He puts down both ideas: He commanded to circumcise on the eighth day neither because of sins committed nor because of future sins, but without doubt because something greater than any actual sin is born and ingrained in human nature.

12. But here someone might point out that Abraham and his servants and household were circumcised when they were grown and old (cf. Genesis 17 [:23–27]); therefore, would not circumcision signify actual committed sins? The answer is: Scripture anticipates and abolishes the idea that Abraham was justified by circumcision, for he already was justified of his sins when he received circumcision. It is written that he was justified through his faith (Genesis 15 [:6]) before his circumcision, when he was eighty years old or a little more, and he received circumcision when he was ninety-nine years old, so that his circumcision came almost twenty years after his justification. From this St. Paul concludes against the Jews that not circumcision, but faith without circumcision justifies (Romans 4 [:11]), as Abraham's example shows.

Therefore, circumcision is not a putting off of sin, but a sign of such putting off, which is accomplished by faith alone, as was the case with Abraham. Therefore, as in Abraham, so in all men [circumcision] requires faith, which removes the sin of nature and makes the person righteous and accepted.

13. If now Abraham's faith had not been described before his circumcision, it would have been a sure sign of original sin in him, as it is in the case of children, whose faith is not described beforehand. Therefore, Scripture has so arranged it that Abraham first believed and afterward was circumcised, and others were first circumcised and afterward believed, in order to maintain both parts: first, that circumcision was only a sign of justification and nobody becomes godly through it; second, that only faith justifies without the cooperation of circumcision, and therefore faith—which opposes the arrogant righteousness of works—and its sign are clearly distinguished.

14. Perhaps the eighth day was appointed also for bodily reasons, in order that the baby might first grow stronger, lest it might appear that it had died from the circumcision, if it were circumcised directly after birth and then died from weakness.

15. But the spiritual significance is of greater importance. Seven days signify the time of this world until the Last Day, because this present time is described by weeks of seven days (Genesis 1). The eighth day is the Last Day after the present time, when weeks, months, and years will cease, and there will be only an eternal day. On that day circumcision will be fulfilled, when not only the soul but also the body, redeemed from sin, death, and all impurity, will shine like the sun [Matt. 13:43]. Meanwhile, by faith the soul is circumcised from sin and an evil conscience.

16. So we see that the Scriptures in all places urge faith, but only faith in Christ. Therefore, circumcision was not given by the Law of Moses, nor to the fathers before Abraham, but to Abraham, to whom Christ, his Seed, was promised for a blessing [Gen. 22:18], so that the bodily circumcision might everywhere agree with the spiritual circumcision.

17. Why, then, has [circumcision] ceased, if that same faith in Christ, to which it points, still remains? The answer is that God has always, from the beginning of the world to the end, maintained one faith in Christ, but He has not given only one sign of it. If all the signs which refer to faith remained, who could keep them? But since faith is inward and invisible, God has represented it to people by many external signs, in order that they might be incited to believe as by many examples, and has permitted each to continue for its time.

How many signs did Moses do in Egypt and in the wilderness, which have all passed away and lasted during their time and still were all signs of faith? So when God promised to Abraham the blessing in his Seed and gave to him a sign of it, namely, circumcision, it could not continue on the strength of that promise longer than the fulfillment of the promise. But when Christ, the blessed Seed, came, the promise was finished and fulfilled; it was no longer to be expected. Therefore, the sign also necessarily must be finished and cease. Why should it continue any longer, when the promise on which it depended was finished? But that which it signified—faith—remains always, whether the promise with its sign passes away or remains.

18. Yet circumcision is not finished in such a way that it is a sin to be circumcised, as St. Jerome[4] and many with him hold. But it has become free, so that whoever wishes may be circumcised or not circumcised, as long as he does not act in the belief that it is necessary and commanded, or that the promise of God to Abraham is unfulfilled and still to be expected, or presumes that he will become godly through [circumcision]—for faith cannot tolerate any of these beliefs.

Therefore, it does not depend on the work, but on the expectation and intention in the work. Whoever is circumcised in the same way that he cuts his hair, beard, or fingernails—in love and service to another—commits no sin, for he would do it unrestrained by the Law and as unnecessary for justification, not against the fulfilled promise of God, but from free choice and his own choosing, because the promise is fulfilled and the sign attached to it is finished.

---

4 In at least one place, Jerome actually held that circumcision is an indifferent thing, to be used only by those who intend to keep the Old Testament ceremonial law, but unnecessary for those who are saved through Christ; see *Commentary on Galatians* 2.5 (PL 26:394–400; FC 121:194–202).

19. Moreover, God has not had the custom of reestablishing a sign when once it has come to an end, but He has always instituted something new and different. So after the fulfillment of His promise, after the coming of Christ, Abraham's Seed, He set up a different and new sign, namely, Baptism. This indeed is the last sign to be instituted before the Last Day, because He Himself instituted it. Nevertheless, the same faith in Christ, which was in Abraham, always remains, for it does not know how to speak of either day or night, nor of any outward transformation. This Baptism has the same significance as circumcision, as is to be shown at the proper time.

20. Finally, it was the custom to name the child at circumcision, as we see here and with John the Baptist, who was also given his name at his circumcision [cf. Luke 1:59–63]. However, just as Christ was not obliged to be circumcised and the sign was empty in His case, so also His name had been given to Him before by the angel [Matt. 1:21], so that He did not obtain it by circumcision. This was done and is written so that He is everywhere free from the Law and from sin in contrast to all other men, and only serves us by putting Himself under the Law and becoming like us in order to redeem us, as St. Paul said that He was "under the Law, to redeem those who were under the Law" (Galatians 4 [:4–5]).

21. For when death fell on Him and killed Him, and yet had no right or case against Him, and He willingly and innocently submitted and let Himself be killed, then death became liable to Him, did Him wrong and sinned against Him, and itself spoiled everything, so that Christ has an honest claim against it. Now the wrong of which [death] became guilty toward Him is so great that death can never pay nor atone for it. Therefore, it must be subject to Christ and in His power forever, and so death is overcome and put to death in Christ [cf. 1 Cor. 15:54–57].

Now Christ did not do this for Himself but for us, and has given us this victory over death in Baptism [Rom. 6:4; 1 Pet. 3:21]. Therefore, all who believe in Christ must also be lords over death, and death must be their subject, even their criminal whom they are to judge and execute, even as they do when they die and at the Last Day. For by the gift of Christ death has also become obliged to all those who have received this gift from Christ. See, this is the sweet and joyous redemption from death through Christ; these are the spiritual conflicts of Joshua with the heathen of Canaan, such as the five kings on whose necks the princes of Israel put their feet at his command (Joshua 10 [:24]).

22. So also circumcision was unjustly done to Christ, since He was not obliged to have it. Therefore, it is justly subject to Him, and He has power over it, has conquered it, and has presented it to us, so that it must cease and has lost its right over those who believe in Christ. He has released us from

circumcision only by submitting to it innocently and by giving to us His right against it.

23. See, this means that Christ is "placed under the Law, to redeem those who were under the Law" [Gal. 4:5]. Moreover, He has subjected Himself to all other laws, to none of which He was obliged, since He is Lord and God over all. Therefore, they have all come into His power, have done Him wrong, and must now justly be subject to Him.

24. Now all this He has also given to us. Therefore, if we believe in Christ, and the Law would reprove us as sinners, and death would press in [on us] and drive the wretched conscience to hell, and if you then reproach them with their sin and wrong, which they have done to Christ, your Lord—do you not think that they also shall be put to shame and be more afraid of you than you of them? Death will feel its guilt and flee in disgrace; the Law will have to give up its fear and laugh pleasantly with Christ.

In this way, sin must be banished by sin. The sins which they have committed against Christ and now also against you on account of your faith are greater than those which you have committed against them. In this case, God, the just Judge, will not allow a great thief to hang a little one; on the contrary, if the great one is to be free, much more must the little one go free. St. Paul says about this: "O death, where is your sting? The sting of death is sin. But thanks be to God, who gives us this victory through Jesus Christ our Lord. For 'death has been swallowed up in victory'" (1 Corinthians 15 [:55–57, 54]). See, is not this a precious redemption from the Law through Him who innocently subjected Himself to the Law?

25. Praise God, what an exceedingly rich and mighty thing faith is! It even makes man into a god, for whom nothing is impossible, as Christ says: "'Can you believe'? All things are possible for one who believes" (Mark 9 [:23]). Therefore, Psalm 82 [:6] also says: "You are gods and children of the Most High, all of you."

26. His name is rightly called on this day "Jesus," which is [translated] "Savior," for Savior means one who helps, redeems, saves, and cures everyone. The Hebrew language calls this one "Jesus." So the angel Gabriel spoke to Joseph in sleep: "She will bear a Son, and you shall call His name Jesus, for He will save His people from their sins" (Matthew 1 [:21]). Here the angel himself explains why He is called Savior, "Jesus," namely, because He is help and salvation to His people. We have now heard how this happens through faith, to which He gives all His right and possession which He has over sin, death, and the Law. He makes [faith] righteous, free, and saved.

27. Now as circumcision signifies our faith, as we have heard, so the naming of children signifies that by faith we have a name and are known before God. For God knows none of those who do not believe, as Psalm 1 [:6]

says, "The Lord knows the way of the righteous, but the way of the godless perishes." "Truly, I say to you, I do not know you" (Matthew 25 [:12]).

What, then, is our name? Doubtless as Christ gives us all that is His, so He also gives to us His name. Therefore, all of us are called Christians from Him, God's children from Him, Jesus from Him, Savior from Him, and whatever is His name, that also is ours. As St. Paul writes: "In this hope you were saved" (Romans 8 [:24]), for you are "Jesus" or "Savior." See, there is therefore no limit to the dignity and honor of a Christian! These are the superabundant riches of His blessings, which He pours out on us, so that our hearts may be free, joyous, peaceful, and fearless. Then we keep the Law willingly and cheerfully. Amen.

# GOSPEL FOR [EPIPHANY,] THE DAY OF THE WISE MEN[1]

*Whom People Are Accustomed to Call the Three Holy Kings*

*Matthew 2:1–12*

*Now after Jesus was born in Bethlehem of Judea in the days of Herod the king, behold, wise men from the east came to Jerusalem, saying, "Where is He who has been born king of the Jews? For we saw His star when it rose and have come to worship Him." When Herod the king heard this, he was troubled, and all Jerusalem with him; and assembling all the chief priests and scribes of the people, he inquired of them where the Christ was to be born. They told him, "In Bethlehem of Judea, for so it is written by the prophet: "'And you, O Bethlehem, in the land of Judah, are by no means least among the rulers of Judah; for from you shall come a ruler who will shepherd My people Israel.' Then Herod summoned the wise men secretly and ascertained from them what time the star had appeared. And he sent them to Bethlehem, saying, "Go and search diligently for the child, and when you have found Him, bring me word, that I too may come and worship Him." After listening to the king, they went on their way. And behold, the star that they had seen when it rose went before them until it came to rest over the place where the child was. When they saw the star, they rejoiced exceedingly with great joy. And going into the house, they saw the child with Mary His mother, and they fell down and worshiped Him. Then, opening their treasures, they offered Him gifts, gold and frankincense and myrrh. And being warned in a dream not to return to Herod, they departed to their own country by another way.*

1. This Gospel reading agrees with the Epistle reading and speaks of the bodily coming of the heathen to Christ, by which their spiritual coming [to Christ], mentioned in the Epistle, is signified and begun. It is both a terrifying and a consoling Gospel: terrifying to the great, learned, holy, and mighty, who all despise Christ; consoling to the humble and despised, to whom alone Christ is revealed.

1 Luther usually calls them the "Magi"; cf. below paragraph 93, but also paragraph 11, where "Magi" is equated with "Wise Men."

# THE HISTORY

2. The evangelist first refers to Herod the king, in order to recall the prophecy of Jacob the patriarch, who said: "The scepter shall not depart from Judah, nor a master from his feet, until the Hero comes, and to Him the peoples shall cling" (Genesis 49 [:10]). From this prophecy it is evident that Christ must be present when the kingdom or government of the Jews has been taken from them, so that no king or ruler from the house of Judah would possess it. This was fulfilled now when Herod, who was not of the house of Judah, nor of Jewish descent, but of Edom—hence a foreigner—was made king over the Jews by the Romans, though at the great displeasure of the Jews. Hence for thirty years he broke them into pieces, spilled much blood, and killed the best of the Jews, before he overpowered and vanquished them.

3. Now when this first foreigner had ruled for thirty years, and had taken possession of the government so that he possessed it in peace, and the Jews had acquiesced so that they had no hopes of getting rid of him—thus the prophecy of Jacob was fulfilled—then was the time that Christ came and was born under this first foreigner and appeared according to the prophecy. It was as though He said: "The scepter has now ceased from Judah; a foreigner is ruling over My people; now is the time that I should come and become King; the government now belongs to Me."

4. These Wise Men are usually called the three kings, perhaps because of the number of the three gifts. However, it is unknown whether there were two, three, or how many there were. But they certainly came from the country of Arabia or Seba, which is evident from their gifts of gold, frankincense, and myrrh [Matt. 2:11], all three of which are precious in that country. It is certainly not to be thought that they had bought these elsewhere, for it is customary in the Orient to show respect with a present of the best fruits and goods of the country. Similarly, Jacob commanded his sons to carry presents of the best fruits of the land to Joseph in Egypt (Genesis 43 [:11]). If these were not the fruits of their own country, why should they have brought frankincense, myrrh, and gold—which are produced in that land—instead of silver and jewels or the fruits of some other country?

5. Therefore, these gifts were not presented to Christ as the artists paint it—that one offers gold, another frankincense, and the third myrrh—but they presented the three parts [of the gift] in common as for one person. And [probably] there was a small group of them, some of whom were the leaders, just as now a prince or a city sends a few brave men to the emperor as messengers with presents; that is the way it happened here.

6. Those whom the evangelist calls "Magi" we in German call "soothsayers," not in the same way that the prophets predicted, but like those whom

we call "wise men" and "wise women," who can tell people all kinds of things, who know a great deal about the occult arts and engage in dangerous things. The art of such people is called magic, and it is accomplished by the black arts sometimes, and by dealings with the devil; but not altogether as the witches and sorceresses do. For the Magi imitate the true prophets, though not from God's Spirit. For this reason they sometimes are correct, since their work is not, like that of the witches, altogether the devil's work, but rather a mixture of natural reason and the devil's help.

7. Similarly, their miracles are not altogether done by the devil's cunning, like the doings of the witches, but are mixed with natural works, and the Magi always imitate the real natural arts. For there is much that is secret in the working of nature; whoever knows how to apply them performs marvels in the eyes of those who know no better, just as the alchemists make gold out of copper.

8. Solomon knew much through the Spirit of God about this secret knowledge of nature and made good use of it when he judged between the two women concerning the living and the dead children, discovering the real mother by appealing to the deepest basis of nature (1 Kings 3 [:25]). Again, Jacob also made use of this same art when he used the striped sticks so that only striped sheep were born (Genesis 30 [:37–39]).

9. This is a fine and a truly natural art and is the source for all that physicians and others know, describe, and employ about the properties of herbs, plants, metals, stones, etc. The Scriptures also often cite them in comparisons of animals, stones, trees, herbs, etc. This art was especially practiced and studied among the Persians, Arabians, and in other countries of the Orient; it was an honorable art which made people wise.

10. But later on, swine and blockheads meddled with it, as happens with all arts and doctrines. They went too far astray and mixed this noble art with trickery and sorcery. They wanted to imitate [this noble art] and equal it. But when they could not do this, they abandoned the real art and became tricksters and sorcerers, prophesying and doing miracles through the devil's work, though sometimes through nature. For the devil has retained much of this art and at times uses it through the Magi. Thus "magus" has become a disgraceful name and means nothing more than those who prophesy and do miracles through the evil spirit. Nevertheless, sometimes it is helpful, because the works of nature, which cannot lie, are intermingled with it, which the evil spirit certainly knows.

11. Hence these Magi or Wise Men were not kings, but men learned and experienced in this natural art, though without doubt they were not completely pure but also used many tricks. Even to this day people from the Orient have great and diverse magic and, when the real art was despised and

had declined, this magic spread to all the world. Prior to this they devoted themselves to the course of the heavens and the stars. Thus presumptuous reason has always mixed and spoiled that which was good with its imitation and curiosity, attempting to ape everything it sees and hears. False prophets do the same thing to the true prophets, false works-righteous saints to the true saints, the falsely learned to the truly learned. If we look at the whole world, we will find that reason's work is nothing other than pure trickery by which it wants to imitate the good, but only perverts it and thus misleads itself and others.

12. Therefore, these Magi were nothing other than what the philosophers were in Greece and the priests in Egypt, and among us the learned in the universities. In short, they were the clergy and learned in the country of Arabia, just as if now learned clergy were sent from the universities to a prince with presents. For the universities also boast that they teach natural arts, which they call philosophy, while in reality they are teaching not only trickery but also poisonous error and mere dreams.

13. For the natural art, which was formerly called magic but now "natural philosophy," is to learn to recognize the forces and works of nature, such as that a stag will draw a snake out of its crevice with the breath of its nose, kill and eat it, and then on account of the great heat of the poison thirst for a cool spring, as Psalm 42 [:1] reports. Again, that a weasel will lure a snake out of its hole by wagging its tail, and when the snake, angered, slithers out, the weasel is lurking over the hole, so that when the snake looks at its enemy, the weasel fastens its teeth in the neck of the snake next to the poison, and thus kills its enemy in its own hole.

The Magi studied such arts, in which is hidden great wisdom concerning Christ as well as the conduct of people in their lives. If we would therefore properly translate this Gospel, we must say: the natural philosophers came from the Orient, or the naturalists from Fertile Arabia.

14. Some are also surprised that they could come such a long distance in so few days, for it is believed that they arrived on the thirteenth day after Christ's birth, and yet the geographers write that the capital city Saba in Arabia is a sixty-day journey from the Mediterranean Sea, which is not much over three German miles[2] from Bethlehem. But questions of this kind do not trouble me very much, nor is it an article of faith to believe that they arrived on the thirteenth day.

15. It is unnecessary that they came from the capital city Saba or from the remotest parts of the country. They may well have come from a place

---

2  The length of a *deutsche Meile* varied according to region. The Saxon *Meile* was approximately 6.06 miles or 9 km. It is about 29 km from Bethlehem to Haifa, on the Mediterranean Sea, which is slightly more than three German miles, as Luther says.

near the boundary of the country, and thus came at a convenient time in the natural way.

Mary had to remain inside at Bethlehem, unclean for six weeks according to the Law, just like any other woman [cf. Lev. 12:2–4], and might thus have been found there even more than twenty or thirty days. Nevertheless, I will not hinder the common delusion that it was a miracle, as long as no one is forced [to hold] as an article of faith how they made the journey and similar matters. It is unnecessary to have as an article of faith what the divine Scripture does not state.

16. So this is the meaning of the evangelist: When Christ was born under Herod, the first foreign king, and the time of the prophecy was fulfilled, this miraculous sign occurred. The one whom His own fellow subjects and citizens would neither seek nor acknowledge was sought by such strangers and foreigners after a journey of so many days. To Him whom the learned and the priests would not come and worship came the soothsayers and stargazers. It was indeed a great shame for the whole Jewish land and people that Christ was born among them, and they should first become aware of it through these foreign, heathen people living so far away. At least in Jerusalem, the capital city, they should have known about it. This gave them an earnest admonition to acknowledge and seek Christ. But their forehead was brass and their neck iron, as Isaiah says about them (Isaiah [48:4]).

*"Where is the newborn King of the Jews? We saw His star in the East and have come to worship Him." [Matt. 2:2]*

17. The text requires us to speak further about the naturalists or natural philosophers, because here the Magi recognized the birth of a king from the star, as they declared. It must be observed that every man knows a certain portion of the knowledge of nature. I know that a dog's tongue is good for healing wounds, that a cat will catch mice even when it is not hungry, that a hawk catches partridges, etc. One individual may know more than others about nature either by his own experience or through instruction. But God has not revealed to us all the facts about nature, but only a small portion of them. Yet reason is inquisitive and always wants to know more and more, and thus originated the study and investigation of nature.

18. But it is impossible that nature could be understood by reason after the fall of Adam, which blinded it, any further than experience or divine illumination allows. Yet restless reason will not remain silent and cannot be satisfied with this, but wants to know and see everything, like a monkey. For this reason it begins to speculate and to investigate farther than is commanded; it despises what has been given to it by experience or by God, and yet does not grasp what it seeks. Thus all its study and wisdom become only

error and nonsense. This is the reason why those who despise the natural arts or cannot acquire them are divided into innumerable parts and sects.

Some have written about the earth, others about water, some about this, and others about that, so that there was no limit to making books and study [cf. Eccl. 12:12]. Finally, when they were tired of the study of the earth, they ascended to the heavens and wanted to know the nature of the heavens and the stars, with which no one could ever have any experience. Thus they were entirely at liberty to dream, lie, deceive, and say whatever they wanted about the innocent heavens. People say: Those who lie about distant countries lie forcefully, because no one has had sufficient experience to contradict them.

19. So also here, because no one can reach up into the heavens and gain experience about their teaching or its error, they lie with full and sure power. Hence they teach that whoever is born in this or that sign must become a gambler, whoever is born under this or that star will become rich or wise. Again, this one must be struck dead [by lightning], or whoever builds, marries, or makes a journey on this or that day must fare so and so. They say it is the nature of the stars of heaven to affect human beings who are connected with such a time. God help us! How all things are subjected to this art! With full intent reason has fallen captive to it because they are great big lies and totally useless fables, in which [reason] in its blindness finds the greatest pleasure, for truth does not taste as good to it as do fables and lies.

25. When we return to the text, you might say: Yes, this Gospel tells how these Magi learned from the star about the birth of a king, and therefore proves that the art of the stars is to be taught and known, because God Himself helped them by causing a star to rise by which He stirred up and taught the Magi.

26. Answer: If you remain only with the example and learn as these Magi learned from the star, then you will do right and not fall into error, for there is no doubt that the sun, moon, and stars were created to be signs and to serve the earth with their shining, as Moses wrote (Genesis 1 [:14]). You learn from the sun that when it rises, the day begins; when it sets, the day has ended; and when it stands in the middle of the sky, that is noon, and so on. It has been fixed as a sign and measure of time and of the hours, so that your work and business is regulated according to it. So also the moon and the stars at night. Furthermore, you use the sun in plowing your fields and in caring for your animals; you can work according to whether it is hot or not hot.

27. Furthermore, you should also know that when the sun loses its brightness it is surely an evil sign, which will be followed by disaster—and likewise when a comet appears. This is taught by experience; and Christ says

that such signs will appear in the sun, moon, and stars and will signify the last distress of the world (Luke 21 [:25]).[3]

Great storms, lightning, floods, and fire in the air and on earth are also signs.[4] But how these things occur, or what kind of natural forces there are in all [these signs], or what is secretly at work in them, which the Magi investigate and speak of foolishly—all this is neither useful nor necessary for you to know. It is enough that you recognize in these the wrath of God and amend your life. In recent years there have been very many eclipses and many signs have been seen in many countries, for surely a great storm is at hand. Thus the darkness at the suffering of Christ signifies the calamity which rests upon the Jews to this day [cf. Matt. 27:45]. These are sure signs, for which purpose God created them, but those of which the charlatans dream are of an uncertain nature.

28. Thus these Magi had nothing else in this star than a sign and only used it as a sign, for which purpose God established it. Therefore, the stargazers and soothsayers cannot corroborate and glorify their false art from this Gospel. Although these Magi may also have been deluded by this same art, yet they used this star only as a sign. They do not at all say what Christ would be in the future and what would happen to Him, nor do they ask about it. They are satisfied that it was a sign of a great king and only ask where He is to be found.

29. And in order that Christ might forever fully shut the mouth of such babblers, He provided for His birth a special, new star, unsullied and untouched by their babbling. If they would say that He was born under the power of this star, He counters them beforehand and says: "This star is not like one of those about which your art invents things. If what will happen to all people in the future is in the stars, as you teach, then there must be none of those happenings in this star, which is of a new and different kind than the other stars, and you have known or heard nothing about it before." Again, if none of the other stars had any power over Christ, but He has His own new star, then it follows that they have no power over any human being, because He is equally a man like other men. Furthermore, if this new star had no power over other men, for it had not existed for long, it also certainly had no power over Christ, who is like all other men. Therefore, the natural philosophy of the stars is mere trickery.

30. I do not know how these Magi were certain in recognizing this star as a sign that signified a newborn king. Perhaps they found in their histories and chronicles that previously the birth of other kings had been shown in the heavens or through a star. For we find also in the Latin and Greek histories

---

3  Cf. sermon for Second Sunday in Advent on Luke 21:25–33, paragraphs 12–16.

4  Cf. sermon for Second Sunday in Advent on Luke 21:25–33, paragraphs 21–26.

that the coming or birth of some great princes and extraordinary men had been foretold by miracles and signs in the air and through signs in the heavens. These Magi knew quite well that these Jews were the specially chosen people of God, for whom God did much and had done much, above all other people. Therefore, as this was such a beautiful star, they certainly thought that God had given this people a new king. But the claim of some, that [these Magi] had the saying of Balaam: "A star shall rise out of Jacob" (Numbers 24 [:17]), is uncompelling, for it speaks more of the spiritual coming of Christ, and Christ Himself is the star. But whoever is unsatisfied with this may think whatever he wants; perhaps they had it by divine revelation.

31. At first they did not consider this King to be God, but one according to the usual manner of worldly kings, just as the queen from Fertile Arabia esteemed Solomon and came to him with presents from her land [1 Kings 10:1–13]. For this reason they also come to Jerusalem, the capital city, hoping to find Him in the royal palace in splendor. For the star that they saw over the Jewish country when they were yet at home in Arabia then disappeared, so that they did not see it on their journey until they traveled from Jerusalem to Bethlehem, as the Gospel says [Matt. 2:9].

32. But when they say, "We saw His star," they do not at the time think that Christ had created it, but that it was His because it is a sign of His birth, just as the masters of the stars still call each man's sign in which he was born "his sign," not as though he had created it himself. For Christ's deity remained hidden until His ascension, though it was often pointed out [cf. Phil. 2:8–9].

33. So also when they worshiped Him, they did it, as Scripture says, in the way that kings were worshiped in the Orient, not as though they considered them gods. Rather, Scripture calls the falling down before them and honoring them "worship," and it is applied equally to God and humans, just as the words "lord," "king," and even the name "God" [are used], as He said to Moses: "See, I have placed you as a god over Pharaoh" (Exodus 7 [:1]).

*When King Herod heard this, he was frightened, and all Jerusalem with him. [Matt 2:3]*

34. Why are they frightened by this? Were not the Jews waiting for Christ, who was promised them by God, as was said above (Genesis 49 [:10])? Were not Simeon and Anna and without doubt many more holy people at Jerusalem at that time looking for Christ's coming and rejoicing in it [cf. Luke 2:25–38]? There was an obvious reason for Herod to be frightened: He feared for his kingdom, because he was certainly conscious that he was a foreigner and had earned the ill will of the Jews. He also certainly knew that the Jews were waiting for Christ, who would redeem them as Moses had done. His

conscience had to worry that there would be an insurrection against him and that he would be driven from his kingdom.

On the other hand, the Jews feared Herod and the Romans, [believing] that it would cost them too much blood to have a new king. Before this they had opposed the Romans and Herod, to their own great misery, and they were just like the people of Israel in Egypt, who, when Moses was to lead them out and they were oppressed more than before, murmured against Moses [Exod. 5:20–21]. This was a sign of their weak faith, just as this fright of Jerusalem indicates unbelief, that is, that they looked more to human power than to divine power.

35. However, the holy people were not frightened, but rather were happy. And when the evangelist says that the whole city was frightened with Herod, he does not mean all the inhabitants and citizens of the whole city, but he speaks in conformity with the Scriptures: when it mentions a city only and not its inhabitants also, it means not all who are in it but the larger and greater part of them. Thus it is often written in the Book of Joshua that he destroyed this or that city, and then adds that he killed everything, whatever inhabitants lived in it [cf. Josh. 6:24; 8:24, 28].

> And assembling all the high priests and scribes of the people, he inquired of them where the Christ was to be born. They told him: "In Bethlehem of Judah, for so it is written by the prophet: 'And you, Bethlehem, in the land of Judah, are by no means least among the rulers of Judah; for from you shall come the Ruler who will be Lord over My people Israel.'" [Matt. 2:4–6]

36. Here we ask why Christ did not have these Magi led to Bethlehem by the star instead of having His birth, which was now known, investigated from the Scriptures? That happened so that we might learn to cling to the Scriptures and not to our own opinion nor follow the teaching of any man. He does not want to have given His Scripture for nothing; He wants to be found there, and nowhere else. Whoever despises and abandons it shall and will never find Him.

Thus we heard[5] that the angel also gave the shepherds a sign; it was not Mary or Joseph or any other people, no matter how holy they were, but only the swaddling clothes in which He was wrapped and the manger in which He was laid, that is, the writings of the prophets and the Law. In these He is wrapped, they contain Him, they speak only of Him and bear witness of Him. They are His certain sign, as He Himself says, "Search in Scripture, because you think that in it you have eternal life; and this is what bears

---

5  See sermon for Christmas Day on Luke 2:1–14, paragraph 45.

witness about Me" (John 5 [:39]). And Paul says: "The righteousness that avails before God has been revealed and testified by the Law and the prophets" (Romans 3 [:21]).

Furthermore, we have also heard that Simeon and Anna represent the Scriptures, which manifest Christ and carry Him in their arms.[6] And Abraham would not grant [the request] of the rich man in hell, that he send Lazarus to his brothers, but points to Scripture and says: "They have Moses and the prophets; let them hear them. If they do not hear Moses and the prophets, neither will they believe even if a dead man should rise" (Luke 16 [:29, 31]).

37. Against this faithful, divine doctrine our scholars have until now set up various ways to learn the truth. We must list a few of these so that we know to be on our guard against them. First, they have introduced innumerable laws, statutes, articles, and teachings invented by men, such as canon law[7] and the like, orders, rules, etc., which are without doubt not the swaddling cloths and manger of Christ, nor are they Simeon or Anna. St. Paul has earnestly warned us against such teachings, so that we remain in God's Word alone. For all human doctrines are dangerous and finally lead us away from faith, as Solomon was led astray by foreign women, which Paul interpreted, saying that human doctrines turn people away from the truth (Titus 1 [:14]).

38. However, if anyone were to use human doctrines in the same way that he eats and drinks and wears clothing, then they would be harmless. No one eats or drinks or puts on clothing for the purpose of becoming godly and saved. Such an intent or conscience would be crass folly for anyone. Rather, his intent and conscience to become godly is only that he strives firmly to believe in Christ, and thus he would become godly and saved. That intent is correct and that conscience is good.

Thus whoever fasts, labors, wears the clothes of monks or priests, or keeps the rules of his order, which he considers just as eating and drinking, is not godly because he does it, nor would he be evil if he did not do it. Rather, he knows that he is godly only through faith; he goes ahead and does well and is not harmed by human teachings any more than eating and drinking or the wearing of clothing harms him. But where are the ones who do this? Among a thousand there is scarcely one, for they all say in common: "If I do not become godly and saved by such a life, order, regulations, and work, what a fool I am to do them!"

---

6 See sermon for Sunday after Christmas on Luke 2:33–40, paragraphs 24–25, 41–42, 67–68.

7 *das geistlich Recht.* In scholarly parlance, the term "canon law" normally refers to the *Corpus iuris canonici,* the official codification of church law. Although that term was unknown in Luther's day, the compendium of law codes that it describes was already in existence, treated as a unity, and used as the basis of the teaching of canon law in the universities. See LW 75:116 n. 9; 59:338 n. 19.

39. It is therefore impossible for human doctrines not to lead away from the truth, as Paul says. For one of two things must happen: either they will be despised and abandoned when people hear that they do not make godly or save; or conscience and belief will be ensnared and killed when people believe that they do make us godly and must be kept, for then faith must perish and the soul must die. There is no help or rescue.

For faith cannot exist or tolerate that anyone should regard or have the conviction as though something else were useful and necessary for being godly other than [faith] alone. Therefore, whoever has [faith] cannot pay attention to human laws, but keeps them however and whenever he wants and is simply lord over them. But whoever has human laws without faith cannot recognize faith, but remains forever a slave of human teachings and never does a good work, as St. Paul says (cf. Titus 1 [:16]). For this reason we must cling to the plain Scripture, which teaches only Christ, that by faith in Him we become godly, and then freely do all good works to the good of our neighbor, as has often been said.

40. Second, they point us to the legends and examples of the saints in order to strengthen and promote their human teachings. And this truly impresses [many] and ruins innumerable souls. People do not notice how stealthily they are led away from Scripture and faith. They point to St. Benedict, Gregory, Bernard, Augustine, Francis, Dominic, and many greater saints;[8] no one dares to deny that they are holy men, and yet they lived in such human teachings and orders and became holy. Tell me, how can the simple heart withstand such blows and remain in faith? It would take an apostolic or evangelical spirit to remain [firm] against that. How sure they are! How they rush in blindly! When they have produced these examples of the saints, they think that they have lit the real lamp.

41. Now, if I say to them: These saints also ate, drank, slept, and wore clothing—would that not mean that we should establish an eat order, drink order, sleep order, and clothes order? They answer: "Well, these dear fathers did not do those things to become godly through them in the same way that they did the other things which they held to be good and holy ways." Here I answer: When you say that the dear fathers became godly through those things more than by eating, drinking, sleeping, and wearing clothing, you are obviously mistaken. For God has been careful to honor none of the saints with any miracles for the sake of the saint's works; rather, they were all full of the Spirit and faith. You abandon their Spirit and faith, and cling only to their

---

8 Of the men named by Luther, all founded a monastic order except Gregory ("The Great," r. 590–604), who was the first monk to be elected pope. For more on the orders associated with these individuals, see Luther's preface and afterword to *Papacy with Its Members* (1526), LW 59:138–49 and especially the footnotes there.

external deeds. That is the same as if a fool would do nothing more his whole life than sleep because he heard that St. Bernard had slept once, and wanted in that way to become godly and saved. Therefore, these saints are wronged when it is claimed that they observed these ordinances with the idea that they would make them godly and saved, and thus the people are deceived by the life and name of the dear saints.

42. But you say: "Yes, but they still kept them and did not reject them, nor did they attach as little value to them as you teach." I answer: It is not for you or me to judge their intention and their heart, but this is what we say: It is not impossible that they did attach all too high a value to them. But in doing so, they erred as men. For everybody must confess that the dear saints made mistakes and sinned. Therefore, God wants people to look only to His Word and to follow the example of the dear saints no further than where they follow the Word of God. But whenever they as human beings follow their own opinion or human teachings, then we should imitate godly Shem and Japheth, who covered the nakedness of their father, Noah, and not talk and babble about it with evil Ham [cf. Gen. 9:22–23]. Thus we should keep silent about the weaknesses of the saints and not spread them, so that we may imitate only their strengths.

It is no wonder that the dear saints have stumbled and erred in these things. The knowledge of Christ and of faith is such a high and great thing that God's grace alone must work it in us. Flesh and blood say nothing about this, but only the Father in heaven, as Christ says (Matthew 16 [:17]). Even greater saints than St. Augustine, Benedict, Gregory, and others like them have erred in these things. At the time of the apostles there already were such teachers, against whom St. Paul wrote all his letters in order to keep the faith altogether free from works and [human] doctrines.

43. And that you may marvel still more, the whole Christian church, when it was still new and at its best, erred in these things, so that only St. Peter, Paul, and Barnabas stood firm and held that no law or work is necessary and useful for making godly, as St. Luke clearly describes all of this (Acts 15 [:6–12]). There were great saints there, such as the apostles and their disciples; yet they insisted, and would have continued insisting, that the Law and works were necessary for salvation, if St. Paul and Peter had not resisted this. They themselves would not have known this if God had not, by miraculous signs from heaven, made them certain in this belief that only faith is useful and necessary to be saved, as it says in Acts 10 [:43].

44. Moreover, though St. Peter knew that and had himself helped to preserve it, yet at Antioch he also erred and made improper use of his freedom, so that only St. Paul withstood him (Galatians 2 [:11]). Not that St. Peter believed that he had to keep the Law, but he was not using freedom for

himself as he certainly knew he should, and he thought that he had to avoid them for the sake of others, which was wrong and was reproved by St. Paul.

Therefore, it amounts to nothing whatsoever when people set forth examples of the saints, what they did aside from or outside of Scripture. They are deceitful as much and even more than the errors of heretics and false teachers, because real and true holiness is all too much mixed up with their weaknesses. God arranges such things to keep us with His Scripture and doctrine, without which there is neither life nor light, even if all the angels were to teach such things [cf. Gal. 1:8].

45. Third, they introduce the saints' interpretations of the Scriptures, which are to be a light. They obstinately cling to them and believe that here they have something that no one could reject. They again and again restrain us from going to the pure Scripture. They say that Scripture is obscure and that many heretics come from it.

46. Is not this a chief part of all blasphemy? But who tells them that the fathers are not also obscure? Or who will guarantee us that the fathers did not err in their interpretations—since it is obvious that they did often err, often contradicted themselves, often contradicted each other, and very seldom were unanimous in their agreement? God arranges it this way and makes the interpretations of the fathers uncertain, and in this way restrains us from running away from His Scripture. We still go on slipping and refuse to be stopped.

Therefore, we should know that it is untrue when they say: "The fathers illuminate the obscure Scriptures." They are insulting the fathers and making liars out of them. The work of the fathers was not to illuminate Scripture with their own comments, but rather to set forth the clear Scripture and thus prove Scripture with Scripture alone, without any of their own additions.

47. However, it is true that heretics come from Scripture. From where else should they have come? There is no other book that teaches faith but Scripture. Therefore, just as no one can become a Christian except by Scripture, so also no one can become a heretic but by Scripture. Christ alone is "a sign that is opposed" [Luke 2:34], against which people stumble, fall, and rise.[9] Should we on that account reject Him or set up another Christ besides Him? If you are not lacking wine and bread, should people therefore leave their fields and vineyards alone or not cultivate others besides them? The evil spirit is the enemy of Scripture; therefore, he has made them infamous and doubtful with this outcry from his blasphemous mouth.

48. But what does this Gospel teach? First, these Magi did not ask for the chief priests and do not say: "Where is Annas or Caiaphas, or how did this or that man live?" But they say: "Where is the King of the Jews, who has been

9  Cf. sermon for Sunday after Christmas on Luke 2:33–40, paragraphs 37–40.

born?" [Matt. 2:2]. Yes, Christ does let them, as an example for us, rush off and make a mistake by seeking Him in Jerusalem, in the holy city, among the priests, the learned, and the leaders. He is not found in the holy place nor in the holy ceremonies. Nor did they receive as an answer any human glosses, but what Scripture alone says about Christ—that alone is to be sought among the holy people and in the holy places.

49. This example shows well that we should disregard all human works, teachings, comments, and life, and should pay attention only to the clear Scripture. As to the life and teachings of all the saints, we should retain the right of not snatching up everything that they teach or do, but rather pass judgment on these things and accept with discretion only what agrees with Scripture. But whatever is their own, without Scripture, we should consider as something human and let it be, as St. Paul teaches: "Test everything; hold fast what is good" (1 Thessalonians 5 [:21]).

Moses has also signified this in the Law, when he describes the clean and unclean animals, saying that all animals which are not cloven-footed and do not chew the cud are unclean (Leviticus 11 [:3]; Deuteronomy 14 [:6]). The people who are not cloven-footed are the ones who blindly rush in, snatch up whatever they find, and follow it. But the clean animals are those who act with the discretion of the Spirit in all external things and doctrines. They cling to whatever they see that agrees with Scripture, but they abandon whatever is a mere human invention without Scripture, no matter how great the saints are.

For there has not been a saint so perfect that he was not flesh and blood, who did not have a constant struggle with his flesh and blood, so that it is impossible to adopt what they do as pure Spirit and as our example. Nature and reason must often have gotten in under their guard, and they are not at all to be followed. Therefore, Moses commands us to cleave the feet, and Paul tells us to discern the spirits and not to accept all works and behavior.

50. Now in these three things—human teachings, examples of the saints, and the glosses of the fathers—they think (and many believe it) that they have done well, and no one dares to doubt or contradict them, so that they rule here in perfect safety. They imagine that no one except they alone have the Holy Scriptures, which they have so beautifully put in these three vessels.

51. In addition they sink still deeper into the abyss of darkness when they claim that the natural light and heathen arts are also good ways to discover the truth.[10] On this basis the universities are now so very deeply in error that they teach that no one can be a theologian—that is, the best Christian—without Aristotle.[11] Oh, blindness above all blindness!

10  See sermon for Third Day of Christmas on John 1:1–14, paragraph 45.

11  See sermon for Second Sunday in Advent on Luke 21:25–33, paragraph 7.

It could be tolerated if by "natural philosophy" they meant that fire is hot, that three and five are eight, and the like, which all natural reason certainly knows. But they go beyond that and invent idle dreams and useless thoughts about things that are nothing and of which they know nothing. It is grievous to think of their senseless, absurd studying, in which they go to so much expense and trouble that the evil spirit mocks them. God plagues them with this, as they have deserved, because they would not remain with the pure Scripture. For this reason they must devour the slime and stench of hell and perish.

52. They then fell in with the devil and followed the examples of the souls who appeared and asked for help. They believed everything that these spirits said, without alarm or fear. Thus the Mass has been so abused by soul Masses and trafficking[12] that it cannot be sufficiently lamented and pitied, even if the whole world shed tears of blood day and night.

Thus the devil has permitted himself to be conjured and constrained to reveal the truth, and by doing so he has turned our faith and Sacrament into mockery and sport, to his own liking. All this is the profit and reward of our curiosity, which has not been satisfied with God's Scripture and has regarded our faithful God and Father as a fool and a scarecrow, who presumes to teach us by His Scriptures, but does not teach us what we ought to know or is necessary for us to know. For this reason He serves us right by letting us become the devil's pupils, since we despised His school.

53. But you say: "Should we then not believe that wandering spirits go astray and seek for help?" I answer: Let wander what wanders, but you listen to what God commands. If you hold all these spirits in suspicion, you are not at all sinning; but if you regard one of them to be honest, you are already in danger of erring. Why? Because God does not want you to learn and investigate the truth from the dead. He Himself wants to be your living and all-sufficient teacher. You should cling to His Word. He knows best what to tell you about the dead and the living, for He knows all things. But whatever He does not tell you or want to tell you, you should not desire to know. Give Him the honor of believing that He knows what is not necessary, profitable, or good for you to know.

54. Therefore, you should freely and happily cast all such ghostly apparitions to the winds and be unafraid of them; they will then leave you in peace. And if sometime you have a poltergeist or noisy ghost in your house, then don't hold a dispute [with it], and know that it is not a good spirit and did

---

12  The commissioning of prayers and Masses to benefit the souls in purgatory had become, by the late Middle Ages, an important form of piety as well as a significant source of income for monasteries and churches; cf. *Smalcald Articles* (1537/1538) II II 1, 12–17 (Kolb-Wengert, pp. 301, 303–4; *Concordia*, pp. 264, 265–66); *To the Christian Nobility* (1520), LW 44:115–218; *Misuse of the Mass* (1521), LW 36:127–230; *Exhortation to All Clergy* (1530), LW 34:3–62.

not come from God. Make the sign of the cross and take your faith to heart. If God has inflicted him on you to chastise you, like godly Job, then be ready and endure it willingly. But if it is [the ghost's] own sport, then despise him by strong faith, and rely boldly on God's Word. He will not take a bite out of God's Word, have no doubt.

However, I hold that none of these poltergeists were appointed by God to chastise us, but it is their own mischief to terrify the people, in vain, because they no longer have any power to harm. If they had any power to harm, they would show themselves not with much noise, but would carry out their malice before you could be aware who had done it. But if a good spirit came to you, it would not happen in that way, with much noise and frivolity. If you try this and show such faith, you will find that such an apparition is not from God and will cease its work. If you do not believe, then he will have easy work, for then God's Word is not there, which is all he fears.

55. The Word of God on which you should place your confidence is what Abraham said to the rich man in hell when he desired the dead Lazarus to be sent to his brothers living on earth. Abraham refused him and said: "They have Moses and the prophets; let them hear them" (Luke 16 [:29]). From this text it is plain that God does not want us to be taught by the dead, but He wants us clinging to His Scriptures. Therefore, however and wherever a spirit comes to you, do not ask whether he is evil or good, but be bold and hit him quickly and scornfully in the nose with the words "They have Moses and the prophets," and he will soon feel what you mean. If it is a good spirit, he will only love you the more for adhering so freely and gladly to the Word of your and his God. If it is an evil spirit, as are all those that are noisy, he will soon bid you farewell.

Again, Moses says: "Israel, when you come into the land that the Lord your God will give you, you shall not learn to follow the abominations of those nations. There shall not be found among you anyone who causes his son or his daughter to pass through the fire, or a soothsayer, or a day-chooser, or one who regards the cry of birds, or a sorcerer, or a charmer, or a diviner, or an interpreter of signs, or one who inquires of the dead" (Deuteronomy 18 [:9–11]). Here you are told that it is a heathen abomination in the sight of God to ask the dead or the spirits, and it is strictly forbidden. Abraham was looking at these words of Moses when he did not let Lazarus go to the living. You can also use this passage against these spirits, saying, "You shall not inquire of the dead, says the Lord."

56. God has insisted on this so firmly that there is no example or story in the Scriptures in which the saints have asked the dead for something. This is the third hit that you can give to the spirits: No one ever heard or read of an

example in the Scriptures about asking such spirits for things; therefore, it is definitely to be despised and avoided as an apparition of the devil.

57. From this we may easily learn that the Samuel who was called up was an apparition (1 Samuel 28 [:8–20]), for all of it was contrary to this commandment of God. It is therefore not to be assumed that the real prophet Samuel was called up by the witch there. Scripture is silent there and does not say whether it was the real or false Samuel, because it demands that everybody know well that through Moses God has forbidden inquiring of the dead. And He never revokes His Word, as Job and Balaam said (Numbers 23 [:19; cf. Job 33:14]). How could the witch have any power over the saints, who are kept in God's hands alone?

58. However, if someone says, "In this way purgatory will also be denied," then I will answer: You are no heretic for not believing in purgatory, for there is nothing in Scripture about it. And it is better not to believe that which is outside of Scripture than to depart from that which is in Scripture. Let pope and Papists here rage as they please, who have made purgatory an article of faith,[13] because it has brought to them the wealth of the whole world and also brought countless souls to hell, souls who trusted when they were told to be redeemed from it with works. God gave no command concerning purgatory, but He did command us not to ask the dead nor to believe what they say. Consider Him more truthful and trustworthy than all angels, to say nothing of the pope and the Papists who, since all their work is false and deceiving, have little faith in purgatory.

But if anyone should here cite the sayings, comments, and examples of Gregory, Augustine, and other saints concerning purgatory, you have heard above[14] how far these saints are to be followed and believed. Who will assure us that they were not deceived and did not err, as in many other things?

59. Our faith must have a foundation, which is God's Word, and not sand or a bog, which is human delusion and works. Isaiah also agrees with this: "If they say to you: 'Inquire of the diviners and the sorcerers who mutter in their incantations,' should not a people inquire of their God alone, neither of the dead nor of the living, but according to His Law and testimony? If they will not, the morning light shall never come upon them" (Isaiah 8 [:19–20]). See, this is a clear passage that urges and compels us to seek in God's teaching and testimony for all that we want to know. And whoever does not do this shall be deprived of the morning light, which without a doubt is Christ and the truth itself. Note also that when [Isaiah] said we should inquire of God, lest anyone stare at the heavens and expect something extraordinary

---

13 The doctrine of purgatory had been formally defined beginning in the thirteenth century.

14 See above, paragraphs 40–41.

from God, he also shows where and how we should inquire of God, saying "according to His Law and testimony" [Isa. 8:20]. If [Isaiah] will not tolerate inquiring even of God Himself outside Scripture, how much less will he tolerate inquiring of others?

60. Meanwhile, Moses [Deut. 18:10–11] mentions many ways through which people inquire [about the future], namely, eight ways: [First,] the "soothsayers" are those who speak of the future, like the stargazers and false prophets, by inspiration of the devil. [Second,] the "day-choosers" are those who designate some days as unlucky and others as lucky for journeying, for building, for marrying, for wearing fine clothes, for battle, and for all kinds of transactions. [Third,] the "spirit friends"—I do not know what else to call them—are those who conjure the devil in a mirror, picture, stick, sword, glass, crystal, finger, nail, circle, rods, and the like, and in this way try to see secret treasures, events, and other things. [Fourth,] the "sorcerers," or "witches," are the devil's whores who steal milk,[15] cause storms, ride on goats and brooms, go about in cloaks, shoot the people, cripple, wither, torment infants in the cradle, bewitch the body parts, and the like. Fifth, the "charmers," who bless animals and people, bewitch snakes, speak a charm over steel and iron, see much and mutter and do signs. Sixth, the "diviners," who have the devil behind their ears[16] and can tell the people what they have lost, what they are doing, or what they will do, just as the Tartars[17] and Gypsies do. Seventh, "those who practice sorcery," who can give things a different form so that what looks like a cow or an ox is in reality a human being, and they drive people into love and fornication and many more such works of the devil. Last, also the "dead," the wandering spirits.

61. See, Moses did not forget anything, filling up every gap by which people would inquire and learn outside of God's Word. Thus he has often rejected private opinions and natural reason, especially: "You shall not do what seems right to you" (Deuteronomy 12 [:8]) and "Be not wise in your own eyes, and do not lean on your own understanding" (Proverbs 3 [:7, 5]). [He does this] so that we would see that God wants us to follow neither our own reason nor that which is above reason, but only His Word, as Isaiah said above, to inquire neither of the living nor the dead, but only of God in His Law.

15 Witches were believed to dry up the milk supply of nursing mothers, thus causing infant death; see Lyndal Roper, *Witch Craze: Terror and Fantasy in Baroque Germany* (New Haven: Yale University Press, 2004), p. 119.

16 That is, the devil is present with them secretly. Cf. WA 51:721, no. 438.

17 The Tartars (or Tatars) were a Central Asian people, associated in the medieval European mind with the thirteenth-century Mongol conquests.

St. Peter also says: "We have a firm, prophetic Word, and you will do well to pay attention to it as to a light shining in a dark place, until the day breaks and the morning star rises in your hearts" (2 Peter 1 [:19]). Does not St. Peter here agree nicely with Isaiah about God's Word and the morning light? And when St. Peter says that the Word alone is a light that shines in a dark place, does he not sufficiently show that there is only darkness where this Word is absent?

62. This digression was necessary in order to reply to the false teachers and doctrines of men and to preserve Holy Scripture in its purity. We now come back to our text and learn of these Wise Men to ask: "Where is He who has been born King of the Jews?" Let Herod inquire about the priests and scribes; we inquire only about the newborn king. Let the universities ask: "Where is Aristotle? Where is the pope? Where is natural reason? Where is Bernard? Where is Gregory? Where are the councils? Where are the doctors?" etc. We ask, "Where is Christ?" And let us not be satisfied or content until we hear the Scripture, which speaks about Him. Let us not be challenged by how great and holy Jerusalem is, nor how great and mighty Rome is. We seek neither Jerusalem nor Rome, but Christ the King in His Scripture. If we have this, then we leave Herod, the priests, and the scribes, along with Jerusalem and Rome, behind us and follow it until we find Him.

63. However, here we see that the Scripture and Christ have three kinds of disciples. The first kind are the priests and the scribes, who know Scripture and teach it to everyone, but do not themselves come to it. Is not this a great stubborn hardness [of heart] and contempt in the spiritually learned people? They hear and see that great and honest men come from a far country to seek Christ, and they are told that a star in the heavens testified to His birth. In addition they themselves produce testimony from Scripture. Since they were the priests and most learned men, they should have been in a hurry to run to Bethlehem joyfully and eagerly. Yes, if they had heard that Christ had been born in the Orient, they should by all means have run to Him, since all their hopes and consolation rested on Christ's coming.

64. But they feared Herod who would surely have killed them, if they had with a word confessed Christ and wanted to accept Him as their King, as he had previously killed Hyrcanus[18] for the same reason, and many others with him, and also had the innocent babies killed [Matt. 2:16]. Thus, because they feared death, they forsook their Lord and King and remained under the tyrant Herod and the devil.

18 Hyrcanus II, the Jewish high priest in the first century before Christ. Herod charged him with treason and killed him in 30 BC. Cf. Josephus (ca. 37–ca. 101), *Jewish Antiquities* 15.2 (Loeb 410 [1963], pp. 82–87).

65. Afterward, when Christ does not appear, and there is no worldly power connected with Him, they despised and forgot all of this, thinking that the Magi had been deceived. Thus Christ grew up among them entirely unknown, so that they no longer knew where He would come from, as St. John says (John [7:41–43]). These are the disciples of Christ who indeed know the truth, but dare not confess it nor defend it, and are therefore lost as Christ says: "Everyone who confesses Me before men, I also will confess him before My Father; whoever denies Me before men, I also will deny him before My Father" [Matt. 10:32–33].

66. The second kind of disciples are Herod and his people. Herod searched Scripture, believed it, and regarded it as the truth. He also believed that Christ was foretold there and had now been born; otherwise, he would have despised all this and not taken it seriously. Thus it is certain that he held that God's Word is in Scripture, and His Word must be fulfilled, and that God's work was fulfilled in the birth of Christ. Nevertheless, he determines intentionally and openly to run his head directly against God's Word and work. He thinks he can change what God says and does, even though he knows that God says and does it. Therefore, he searches and hears Scripture and Christ diligently, but only for the purpose of destroying and ruining it all. He was concerned that what God said (who cannot lie) would be true. Is not this incredibly foolish arrogance? Who would have thought that such intentions could have ever entered the human heart? And yet the world is always full of such people, and they are the highest and best in all places.

67. The third kind of disciples are the godly Magi who left their country, home, and possessions and neglected it all so that they might come and find Christ. These are the people who freely confess Christ and the truth. But Herod is those who persecute and destroy the Magi, and nevertheless he is God's servant, goes into the temple, and acts like other godly people.

## THE PROPHECY OF MICAH

68. Here we might also consider why the evangelist changed the words of the prophet and said: "And you, O Bethlehem, in the land of Judah, are by no means least among the rulers of Judah; for from you shall come the ruler who will be Lord over My people Israel" [Matt. 2:6]. And yet the prophet says: "But you, O Bethlehem Ephrathah, who are little among the thousands of Judah, from you shall come forth He who is Lord in Israel" (Micah 5 [:2]). Matthew says, "You are by no means least," but Micah says, "You are little." How do these two statements agree with each other?

69. The other difference—Matthew says "among the rulers of Judah," and Micah says "among the thousands of Judah"—can easily be reconciled. The Hebrew word *alphe* means "princes" and "thousand," so that whoever

wants may interpret the prophet with "princes" or with a "thousand." Just as if I say in German: "Here comes a *Herzog*," someone might interpret that about a prince or about an army, since *Herzog* in German means the one who leads the army or the military expedition—that is, the whole crowd and also the head or prince of that crowd—and whatever the crowd does, whether winning or losing, people say that the *Herzog* or prince has done it.

The Law of Moses also has a regulation that a prince should be placed over a thousand men (Exodus 18 [:21]), so that it means the same whether we say "among the princes" or "among the thousands." For the meaning is that there are many crowds, and each thousand into which the people are divided has its prince. And among those princes or thousands in the tribe of Judah he names the city of Bethlehem as little and small, just as if we were to say, "Among the cities of Saxony, Wittenberg is small." But it pleased the evange-list more to say "among the princes" rather than "among the thousands," since it was unnecessary that there should be just a thousand men; it is sufficient that there be a special government in which there might be a thousand men, and there is always a magistrate who rules over a thousand.

So we might call the mayor of each city (or even the county[19]) *aluph*, that is, a thousand or a county in which there may be about a thousand inhabit-ants who have an *aluph*, a prince or a mayor. In the same way we might trans-late the words of the evangelist and the prophet: "And you Bethlehem are a small and common city among the counties or cities of Judah." Compared to cities such as Hebron, Kiriath Sepher, and the like, it was a small city at that time.

70. When the prophet calls the city "Bethlehem Ephrathah" and the evangelist calls it "Bethlehem in Judah," this is the same thing, for both of them surely wanted to point to this Bethlehem that is a city, and which for-merly was called "Ephrathah" but now is called "Bethlehem in the land of Judah." We heard in the first Gospel lesson for Christmas[20] why this city was called "Ephrathah" and "Bethlehem," that is, a country rich in grain. Also the patriarch Caleb's wife, Ephrath [cf. 1 Chron. 2:19; Gen. 35:16, 19], was buried there and perhaps established the name. For Bethlehem means a "house of bread," and Ephrathah means "fruitful," so that it was a fruitful country with a good livelihood.

71. This, too, is easily reconciled: that the prophet says "a Lord in Israel," and the evangelist says "a ruler who will be Lord over My people Israel." In any case, the evangelist expresses how necessary the lordship is and how it rules the people.

19  *Gemein*, meaning here a small, local territory, such as a county in the United States.

20  See sermon for Christmas Day on Luke 2:1–14, paragraph 40.

72. But how can this be harmonized: the prophet calls the city "little" and the evangelist says "by no means least"? These are completely opposed to each other. It is insufficient if we wanted to say that the books were falsified. Indeed, there can be no other view but that the evangelist looks more at the spiritual greatness, which is also indicated by the prophet. It is as though he would say: "You, Bethlehem, are certainly little before men, but in truth you are not the least before God, since the Lord of Israel will come from you." Thus what the prophet meant, but did not express, the evangelist expresses and fulfills.

The figure of speech by which a certain thing is not directly mentioned but only indicated is also used in common speech. If I say, for instance, "You are certainly my friend, yet you side with my enemies," I really said, "You are not one of the least of my enemies." Again: "The beggars are poor, yet they have much money," that is, they are indeed not the poorest. So when Paul says, "You who abhor idols, do you rob temples?" (Romans 2 [:22]), that is, "You worship idols not a little precisely when you do not worship idols."

73. That is enough on that, for it is unpleasant to belabor this point very much, nor is it necessary for a right-believing person who gives all glory to God and does not doubt that everything is truly and correctly stated in Scripture, even though he does not know how to prove everything. It is useful for the learned so they can defend Scripture against the blasphemers and distorters.

Therefore, we arrive at the understanding of the meaning of the Scriptures, which do not speak here of a plain and common lord in Israel, such as there had been many before. This must be a very special [Lord] above all others whom the prophets so highly proclaimed and foretold. For the passage of Micah sounds as if there had been no lord in Israel before, because he says, "From Bethlehem shall come forth one who is to be Lord in Israel." That sounds as though he would say, "I will once and for all give the people of Israel a Lord, so that they may also have their own prince." So far the kings and princes have only been servants, and the people were not their own. This one, however, shall be a Lord to whom the people belong.

74. For this reason the ancients have always understood such passages to mean that Christ must be not only man but also God, and that His government would be without end, and that He would rule not bodily but spiritually. For no man, no angel, has a people of his own. God alone is the Lord of His own people, as David says: "The Lord Himself is the judge" (Psalm 7 [:8]). And when Gideon was asked by the people to rule them, he replied: "Neither I nor my children shall be your lord; God shall be your Lord" (Judges 8 [:23]). Therefore, when the people asked Samuel for a king, God said, "They have not rejected you, but they have rejected Me from ruling over them" (1 Samuel

8 [:7]). Not that it was a sin to have a king, for He gave them one; but they trusted more in human help and government than in God. And that was a great sin.

75. Now if Christ was to be a Lord over the people, as His own, then His government could be neither temporal nor bodily, but He must rule over the entire people past, present, and future. Therefore, He must be an eternal Lord. That must certainly happen only spiritually. But now if God gives Him His own government, He could not be a human being only. For it is impossible for God to give His glory, government, property, or people to another who is not true God, as He declares: "I will not give My glory to another" (Isaiah 42 [:8]).

76. Therefore, Micah continues: "His coming forth is from the beginning, before the days of the world" [Mic. 5:2], as if he would say: "I proclaim the Lord who will come from Bethlehem, but He does not begin then. He has been already in the beginning and from the [creation of the] world on, so that no day or beginning can be named in which He had not already come forth and had His being." Now from the beginning and before all the days of the world there has been nothing but the true, natural God alone. Thus the coming forth from the beginning could not be by one person only, for coming forth shows that there was someone from whom He came forth. Hence Micah proves that this Lord must be God's own natural Son, and that the one true God must be with Him eternally before all creatures.

77. On the other hand, if He is to come from Bethlehem in time, then He must be a true and natural man. And that is the chief article of the Christian faith. Those are His own people and the true Israel who acknowledge Him as such a Lord and permit Him to rule and work in them. But He is not the Lord of those who do not believe this, and they are not Israel.

78. From this we can further easily conclude why Christ had to die and rise from the dead, so that He could rule eternally and spiritually. For because the passage here proves that He had to become a true, natural, bodily man, it follows that He had to change this bodily life into a spiritual, invisible life, as it was impossible for Him to rule bodily as widely and as long as the prophet indicates.

79. [Micah] continues: "Therefore, He shall let them be tormented until the time when she who is to give birth has given birth; then the rest of His brothers shall return to the children of Israel. And He shall stand and shepherd in the strength of the Lord, in the victory of the name of His God. And they shall dwell secure, for at that time He shall be glorious to the ends of the earth" [Mic. 5:3–4]. From these words it is clear that Christ's kingdom should be increased to the ends of the earth by preaching and suffering, of which [Micah] says that in the victory of God's name He would preach and

shepherd [His flock], showing also that He would be persecuted on account of His preaching.

Therefore, [Micah] also says that a respite will be given the Jews in their temporal existence and government, until a new people had been born. She who gives birth is the assembly of the apostles, which during the sufferings of Christ was in the agony of the birth of a new spiritual people for this Lord of Israel, as He Himself proclaims (John 16 [:21–22]).

*Then Herod summoned the Wise Men secretly and carefully ascertained from them when the star had appeared. And he sent them to Bethlehem, saying, "Go and search diligently for the Child, and when you have found Him, tell me, that I, too, may come and worship Him." [Matt. 2:7–8]*

80. From this text we learn that these Magi were not kings or princes, but common, honest people, like the learned and the clergy. For Herod does not treat them magnificently, but has them journey to Bethlehem and attend to their business, and commands them to bring him word as if they were his subjects. He would not have done this if they had been kings or great lords; he would have invited them to his palace, journeyed with them, and treated them magnificently. For all historians agree that Herod was a pompous man, who knew how to treat people respectably according to the way of the world, and wanted to be seen before the world. Since, however, he calls them to himself secretly, without any show and pretense, they must have been of much lower rank than he was.

81. But why does he call them secretly? Was not the land his? Was he not powerful over all things? He did it for this reason: He knew quite well that the Jews were his sworn enemies and would gladly be rid of him. He was afraid, therefore, that if he called them publicly and the Jews became aware of it, they would anticipate him and instruct the Magi not to report it rightly, so that the new king may remain before him.

82. He asks them about the time of the star because of the same anxiety; he had already decided to kill the innocent babies. He thought in this way: "If the new king is born, the Jews will rejoice and will hide Him from me for a while until He is grown up, and then side with Him, exalt Him, and destroy me. Therefore, I must anticipate them and slyly investigate the time of His birth. Then if He is hidden from me, I will still find Him in the crowd when I have all the babies of that age killed, so that their hiding Him will not help." Nevertheless, on top of this clever plan, he alleges that he wants the new king made known to him and commanded the Magi to tell him. He feigned being completely spiritual and humble, as if he also wanted to worship Him.

83. If human wisdom had helped, he would have acted appropriately enough to kill Christ. But what Solomon says is true: "No wisdom and no

counsel avail against the Lord" (Proverbs 21 [:30]). Also: "God brings the counsels of the people to nothing; He frustrates the thoughts of the nations" (Psalm 33 [:10]). And: "The godless makes plans against the righteous and seeks how to put Him to death." But God laughs at him and "will not let Him come into his hand" (Psalm 37 [:32–33]). Here Herod must make such passages true, against his will, and be an example for our own comfort, so that we are free and secure and need fear none but God alone. If He is with us, neither guile nor force can harm us [cf. Rom. 8:31].

*When they had heard the king, they departed. And behold, the star that they had seen in the East went before them until it came to stand over the place where the Child was. When they saw the star, they rejoiced exceedingly. [Matt. 2:9–10]*

84. [Matthew] does not say that they promised the king, but that they heard his request to bring him word again. Yet it appears from the answer they received in sleep that in their simplicity they had been willing to return to Herod, since they did not know his malicious plan and regarded him to be a simple, just man. From this, we teach that the saints may well be deceived and err through the charming and glittering appearance of the unbelieving saints, so that they regard what is not good to be good. But in the end, they do not remain in it; they must first be instructed from heaven and delivered. The "hearing" mentioned by the evangelist may mean that they heard the words of the prophet about Him, that the new king about whom they had asked must be in Bethlehem; all their delight was to hear this.

85. This is an example of how the enemies of Christ may at times be of service and teach others correctly, as Caiaphas correctly taught that it was necessary for one man to die for the people (John 11 [:50]), and Balaam spoke many beautiful words about Christ (Numbers 24), though they do it sometimes in ignorance, against their will. So Christ taught the people to listen to the scribes and Pharisees and follow them when they sit on Moses' seat, but He forbade them to do their works (Matthew 23 [:2–3]). So these Magi acted correctly and gave us a good example when they listened to Herod, not for Herod's sake, not as said by him, but for the sake of the Scripture which he spoke to them, which is what they followed, not Herod's works.

From this, the good rule comes: we should listen to evil bishops and priests, as well as the godly ones, and should follow not their lives, but their teachings, provided their teaching is pure Scripture and not human inventions. For just as we should listen to the teachings of Scripture, even if spoken by Herod with the intention of committing murder, so we should not listen to human doctrine, even if spoken by St. Peter, Paul, or an angel, and it rains and hails nothing but miracles.

86. It was said above that the saints often err and give offense by human doctrines and works. Therefore, God does not want us to look to their examples, but to His Scripture. For this reason He permits it to happen that the saints often produce human doctrine and works. On the other hand, He causes the unholy often to teach the pure and clear Scripture, in order to guard us on both sides against offenses: on the left hand, in the evil life of the unholy; on the right hand, in the beautifully glittering lives of the saints. For if you do not look at Scripture alone, then the lives of the saints are ten times more harmful, dangerous, and offensive than those of the unholy. That is because they commit evil, crass sins, which are easily recognized and avoided, but the saints exhibit a subtle, pleasing appearance in human doctrines, so that even the elect might be led astray, as Christ says (Matthew 24 [:24]).

87. Now this offense of the saints is directly against the chief article of faith and doctrine; crass sins, however, do not contend against faith and doctrine. Although they may fall away, they do not storm against it, while human doctrine is nothing but storms against faith and doctrine, for they make people rely on themselves and their works. Christ preserves the saints from this in the midst of human doctrines and works, just as He preserved the three men Hananiah, Azariah, and Mishael at Babylon in the midst of the fiery furnace (1 Maccabees 2 [:59; cf. Daniel 3]). Therefore, the lives of the saints are not to be followed as an example, but rather are to be avoided, like miracles which are only to be admired and praised. For He does not want to do miracles in the fiery furnace for everyone; neither does He want to make everyone a Bernard, Francis, Gregory, Benedict, or Augustine.

88. The evangelist was considering this when he omitted Herod's name and said, "They heard the king" [Matt. 2:9]. He calls him by the name of his rank and authority, just as John says that Caiaphas uttered his prophecies not because his name was Caiaphas, but because he was the high priest (John 11 [:51]). The offices of king and priest are good and from God, though evil people make evil use of them, just as gold and silver and all creatures are good, and yet may be put to good or bad use.

Thus God here uses Herod—as he may be used, since he is God's creature—and lets the Magi also use him. Therefore, they did not look at or listen to Herod, but to the king. For them nothing depended on the fact that he was evil himself; they took from him what was of God and was good, just as the bee sucks the honey from the flower and leaves the poison to the spider.[21] They listened as he commanded them to go to Bethlehem and search diligently for the Child, as the prophet had foretold, which he had not from himself but from the priests. But they could not and would not know his evil

---

21 Cf. sermon for Sunday after Christmas on Luke 2:33–40, paragraph 61.

counsel and purpose—nor his evil life. Thus we are to learn to hate the vices of men but love the men, so that we separate the honey from the poison.

89. It is also stated here that this star could not be high in the heavens like the other stars, but must have hung near above them in the air; otherwise it would have been impossible for them to discover whether it stood over Jerusalem or over Bethlehem. For, according to the astronomers and experience, it is not easy because of their height to tell the town over which the stars of heaven really are, since two cities, ten or more miles apart, both think the star is above them. Moreover, you cannot perceive their course with eyesight, though they move more swiftly than a blink of the eye or lightning.

But they did not really see this star moving, but going on slowly before them, after which they walked or rode. A star in heaven moves much farther in the blink of an eye than ten journeys from Jerusalem to Bethlehem, for they move once around earth and heaven each day and night. All the stars move in the same way from their rising [in the east] to their setting [in the west], and in turn from their setting to their rising.

90. But this star, because it went with them from Jerusalem to Bethlehem, traveled from midnight [in the north] to midday [in the south]. This was clear proof that it was of a different kind, course, and position than the stars in the heavens. It was not a fixed star,[22] as astronomers call them, but rather a movable star that could rise and descend and move to any place. This once again shuts the mouth of the stargazers; the star had no special power over Christ's birth or life. It was probably not as large as the stars in the heavens, though it appeared larger on account of its nearness. In short, it was a servant of Christ and had no authority or power over Christ's birth.

91. It is strange, however, that the star now first reappears to them when they do not need it anymore, when they know the town where the Child is, while it was hidden before, when they needed it and did not know the town. But this happened in order to strengthen their faith through two witnesses, as the Law of Moses says, that every matter should be established by the evidence of two or three witnesses [cf. Deut. 17:6; 19:15]. Thus these Magi first heard the word of the prophet at Jerusalem as one witness of Christ's birth. The star, as the second witness, agrees with this and announces the same birth, so that they may be sure of the matter. The prophet speaks only of Christ at Bethlehem; so the star does not go any further than where the Child is at Bethlehem and remains over Him. They were right to rejoice at that.

---

22 *angehefter Stern*, that is, stars that do not seem to move in relation to other celestial objects in contrast to the planets, the sun, and the moon which "wander" or move over periods of time. For the role of the "fixed stars" in late medieval cosmology and early modern astronomy, see Ladina Bezzola Lambert, *Imagining the Unimaginable: The Poetics of Early Modern Astronomy*, Internationale Forschungen zur allgemeinen und vergleichenden Literaturwissenschaft (Amsterdam: Rodopi, 2002), pp. 2, 72–73.

*And going into the house they found the Child with Mary His mother, and they fell down and worshiped Him. Then, opening their treasures, they gave Him gifts: gold and frankincense and myrrh. [Matt. 2:11]*

92. These Magi were purposely prevented from finding Christ through themselves or men, but only through the writing of the prophet and the star of heaven, in order to reject all natural ability, all human reason, all light outside of the Spirit and grace, which now boasts and presumes to teach the truth and lead people aright, as the blind people now allege in the universities, as was said above. Here it is finally concluded that Christ, the saving truth, is not taught or found by human doctrine or assistance, but the Scripture and divine light must reveal Him, as He says: "Blessed are you, Simon, son of Jonah! For flesh and blood has not revealed this to you, but My Father in heaven" (Matthew 16 [:17]). With this, Christ distinctly rejects flesh and blood with its revelation—that is, man and all human understanding—which certainly cannot reveal Christ, since it is certainly only darkness.

He also says, "No one comes to Me unless My Father draws him" (John 6 [:44]). By this all the arrogance of our own human reason is condemned, since it cannot guide aright; all who follow it must go astray. God very zealously and forcefully restrains our natural opinion in all places and wants us to recognize that we are blind, to despair of our own light, to give Him our hand, and to let Him lead us on the ways which reason cannot know or follow.

## THE FAITH OF THE WISE MEN

93. These Magi here teach us the true faith. After they heard the sermon and the word of the prophet, they were not idle or slow to believe—and look at the obstacles and hindrance they faced! First, they made a mistake and came to Jerusalem, the capital, and did not find Him. The star disappeared. Do you not think they would have thought (or if they had had only human reason, would they not have thought): "Alas, we have traveled so far in vain! The star has misled us! It was a phantom! If a king had been born, He should of course be found in the capital and lie in the royal chamber. But when we arrived, the star disappeared, and we find no one who knows anything about Him. We foreigners are the first to speak of Him in His own country and royal city! Indeed, it must all be false!"

94. Moreover, they were frightened: "His own people were not glad to hear it and directed us out of the royal city to a little village. Who knows what we will find? They act so coldly and strangely; no one accompanies us to show us the Child; they do not believe themselves that a king is born to them and that we come for that reason and want to find Him. Oh, how unruly and disorderly everything appears at the birth of a king! If a young pup were born,

there would be a little noise. A king is born here, and everything is very quiet. Should not the people sing and dance, light candles and torches, and pave the streets with bouquets and roses? Oh, the poor king whom we seek! Fools we are to permit ourselves to be mocked and fooled in this way!"

95. Without a doubt they were still one part flesh and blood and were not free from such thoughts and notions. They underwent a good, strong battle for their faith. Natural reason could in no way have held its own here. If they had not found the king as they had expected, they would have at once pouted and become arrogant and said: "The devil led me here. A king cannot have been born here since everything is so quiet and wretched. There is more shouting when a child is born to our shepherd, and a calving cow is more talked about than this king."

96. See, reason and nature always do this; they go no farther than they can feel. If they no longer feel, they at once dare to deny God and say as the psalmist says of them: Here "there is no God" (Psalm 14 [:1]). The devil must be here. This is the light of the universities which is to lead them to God—indeed, into the abyss of hell! The light of nature and the light of grace cannot be friends. Nature wants to perceive and be certain before it believes. Grace believes before it perceives. For this reason, nature does not go further than her own light. Grace joyfully steps out into the darkness, follows the mere word of Scripture, no matter how it appears; whether nature holds it true or false, [grace] clings to the Word.

97. Because of the strife and struggle—that the dear Magi grasped the statement of the prophet and followed it into such a disorderly, shapeless appearance of a royal birth—God comforted and strengthened them by this star which went before them, and acted much more friendly toward them than before. Now they see it near, and it is their guide; they are certain of all things and have no more questions. Before, it was far from them, and they were uncertain where they would find the King.

98. So it is always with the Christian. After affliction has been endured, God becomes so sincerely dear to him and is so near and clearly seen that he not only forgets his anxiety and affliction but also obtains a desire and a love for greater affliction, and further becomes so strong that he no longer so easily takes offense at the insignificant, unattractive life of Christ. For now he experiences and realizes that this must happen to anyone who wants to find Christ: it must appear as if he would find nothing but disgrace.

99. Just as the Magi must have been ashamed of themselves if they mistakenly said, as perhaps they did say secretly in their hearts: "Ah, we were so successful; let us travel a little farther on and seek new kings."

This is, I think, real deception, as Lady Scarecrow, nature, usually acts toward all divine words and works. The fact that the Magi became so very happy when they saw the star indicates that they stood in such affliction and were very dejected when everything seemed to be so confused. Their joy indicates that they were carrying not a little shock and disgust and were severely attacked by unbelief. There was good cause for that, if they were to look at nature. Therefore, Christ says it well: "Blessed is the one who is not offended at Me" (Matthew 11 [:6]). "Blessed," to be sure, but it was difficult and grievous when it did not at all appear that Christ should be there.

100. When the Magi had come through the affliction and were at once newborn because of their great joy, they were now strong and no longer took offense at Christ; they had overcome this crash. Therefore, though they enter a poor house and find a poor, young wife with a poor baby, so very unlike the appearance of a king, so that their porter was more honorable and imposing—yet they are not at all afflicted by that. Rather, in great, strong, full faith they remove from their eyes and their minds whatever might attract and influence nature with its pretense, follow the words of the prophet and the testimony of the star in all simplicity, regard Him as a king, fall down before Him, worship Him, and give Him gifts. How powerful was their faith! How many things it despises, which would influence nature! How many there were then who thought: "Why, these are the biggest fools to worship such a poor Child. They must indeed be bewitched to make Him a king."

101. Now this is the heart of the Gospel, which teaches that the nature and character of faith is "the conviction of things unseen" [Heb. 11:1]. It clings to the bare Word of God and is guided by things which it does not see, which are pointed out in that same Word. Moreover, it sees many things which are enticing, as if what is said in the Word were nothing and in vain. Nature calls it "being deceived" and recoils from it, but faith calls it the true way and presses through. It lets nature be clever and wise, it remains [nature's] clown and fool, and thus comes to Christ and finds Him. Paul's words apply here: "The divine foolishness is wiser than men, and the divine weakness is stronger than men" (1 Corinthians 1 [:25]), for perceiving and believing do not stand together.

102. When they give three presents and worship Him, that is not to be understood that each gave a separate gift; rather, as said above, it was a common gift from the goods of their country, by which they confessed Him as a king. Nor was the worship like that due to God, for, in my opinion, they did not yet recognize Him as God; rather, in the usage of the Scriptures, kings and great people were "worshiped," which is nothing else than falling at their feet to honor them. In the same way now people bend the knee, and that happens without any words, but only with the movement of the body.

103. As for the conversation they had with Mary and Joseph, I let the idle concoct it. The languages in the Orient are not so far away and foreign from

the Hebrew language, so that they may easily have understood one another. In the same way that they spoke with Herod and the priests and the citizens of Jerusalem, they also spoke with Mary and Joseph. And even if they had had a different language, nevertheless the Jewish people were industrious and well-known at the Red Sea, so that in both countries both languages were always known, just as in German lands you find French and in France, German. Now the whole Red Sea has the country of Arabia on one side, and from there the Magi came.

*And God commanded them in a dream not to return to Herod, and they departed to their own country by another way. [Matt. 2:12]*

104. This shows that those who believe in God enjoy His special protection. For He pays particular attention to these Magi so that He takes care of their journey home and teaches them about it in their sleep.

105. And why did He not have them return to Herod, since He could have preserved the Child from all the world even if Herod had known and found Him? It is done for the purpose of teaching us not to tempt God. Whatever can be accomplished in an appropriate way and by ordinary means should not be despised. One should not say, "Yes, I will believe in God, and He will do it," such as when you do not want to work and say, "I will believe in God, and everything that is to grow will grow." Why should there be creatures, if you will not use them? In Genesis 1, He created and ordained all creatures with their works and indicated the use man shall make of them. He will never revoke this or make something specially for you.

106. Here you might ask: "How can I correctly believe and yet not test God, for you praise and preach faith alone and cannot extol it enough?" I answer: You should not believe before you have God's Word, nor believe any further than it. It is the character and nature of faith that it builds and relies on God's Word. Where God's Word is not, there cannot and shall not be any faith. Is this not stated with enough clarity and certainty? Therefore, the Word of God is called in Scripture "testament," "testimonies," "agreements," "covenants," which demand faith. He has never demanded us to believe any of His works without the Word.

107. But on the other hand, He has certainly confirmed His Word with works and miracles, so that people will believe the Word, as Christ says, "Even though you do not believe Me, believe the works" (John 10 [:38]). Wherever you do not have God's Word, you should continue to make use of your power, your goods, your friends, and all that God has given you, and thus remain in the order set up in Genesis 1. For He did not give it to you in vain, and He will not, for your sake, cause water to become wine or stone to become bread [cf. John 2:1–12; Matt. 4:3–4]. Rather, you should let each

thing be as He has created it and use it, until He compels you by word or work to use it differently.

108. But when the hour and place comes that the creature cannot help you any more and all your strength fails, then God's Word begins. For then He has commanded us to acknowledge Him as God, that is, to expect everything that is good from Him. The passages and the Word, though they always have authority, yet are first correctly recognized and made use of in need, when nothing else helps. He speaks of that in the words: "Call upon Me in need; I will deliver you, and you shall praise Me" (Psalm 50 [:15]). From this it is clear that it is impossible to test God when we are in need, for all His words and promises correspond to the time of need, when no one but He alone is able to help. Thus we read that when the devil tempted Christ to throw Himself down from the temple, He said: "No. It is written: 'You shall not test the Lord your God'" (Matthew 4 [:7]), as if to say, "I can certainly go down the steps; it is unnecessary to look for miracles."[23]

On the other hand, we read in the legends of the fathers that two brothers journeyed, and one of them died of hunger for God's sake (that is, he went to hell) for this reason: they came among evil people who gave them something to eat, and the one said that he would not take bread from these people but would expect his food from heaven above; but the other took and ate and remained alive. What did that fool do except despise God's order for creatures and test Him? No matter how evil those people are, they are still God's creatures as much as are thistles and thorns. If you use a thorn to prick open a boil or for some other purpose, will you for that reason ignore the fact that it is a bad, prickly brush?

Thus we read that Abraham and Isaac gave up their own wives and let them be taken from them in order not to test God. They let go what they could not keep. They did what they could [Gen. 12:10–20; 20:1–18; 26:1–11]. Therefore, God preserved them so that no harm was done to them or to their wives, while great kings were punished. From this it is quite clear that to test God is sheer malice and wickedness undertaken against God, except in time of need.

109. Beyond this testing, there is a second testing also in need, which was severely reproved among the people of Israel and which is unfortunately more common than the previous testing and is equally preposterous. This second testing occurs before someone has God's Word, in this way: Even though one knows that God has promised help in all need, he is not content with that, but goes forward and will not wait for and expect that promise. Instead, he prescribes the scope, place, time, and manner for His help. If He does not come as we expect and desire, then faith is gone. There [in the first

23  Cf. sermon for First Sunday in Lent on Matt. 4:1–11.

temptation] faith is too long; here it is too short. There it is too early; here it is too late. In both cases they fall away from the Word. Those have faith without the Word, which is not allowed; these have the Word without faith, which does not help. The good and blessed remedy is both Word and faith together, united in one, just as God and man in one Christ is one person.

110. Now, whoever clings to the Word alone, trusts, and waits for it does not doubt that what the Word says will certainly happen, does not prescribe the scope or determine the time or choose the measure and manner, but resigns it to God's will and pleasure that He will fulfill His Word when, how, where, and by whom He wants—his is an honest faith which does not and cannot test God.

111. Therefore, learn what it means to test God. It is easily understood; it is a deficiency of true faith. To faith belongs above all God's Word as the foundation and rock of faith. Therefore, to test God must mean nothing other than to deal with Him apart from His Word, that is, when someone believes what He did not command us to believe and gave us no Word, or when someone does not believe what He commanded us to believe and gave us His Word. Now He did not command you to believe that He would feed you when you have food before you or can find it without a miracle. But where you cannot find it, He has commanded that you firmly believe He will not forsake you. But you should not set a time or measure for Him, for He wants to be free, which is right, and will not forsake you, which is divine. What more could you want?

112. So it also happened with Christ. God could have preserved Him from the power of Herod. But since the matter could be resolved without the obvious need for a miracle, for our example He used ordinary means and creatures and led the Magi home by another way. It would have required an unnecessary miracle if they had returned to Herod and told him in which house the Child was to be found. But even this has its meaning, of which we will now speak further.

## THE SPIRITUAL MEANING OF THIS GOSPEL

113. Christ's natural birth everywhere signifies His spiritual birth, since He is born in us and we in Him, of which St. Paul says: "My little children, for whom I am again in the anguish of childbirth until Christ is formed in you" (Galatians 4 [:19]). Now two things are necessary for this birth: God's Word and faith, in which two things Christ's spiritual birth is accomplished. Therefore, this Gospel signifies spiritually nothing more than the nature of the divine Word and of faith—also, how they fare who are born spiritually, what temptations and conflicts faith must encounter.

114. First, by the fact that Herod, a foreigner, reigns over the people of God, He shows what kind of reign there was in their souls. They had rejected God, so that He no longer reigned in them by faith. [The Jews] had become nothing but a pharisaical, sadducean, hypocritical, and factious people, who wanted to make themselves godly and saved by human doctrines and outward works. They have no faith, as the entire Gospel and the life of Christ prove. Just as they, unbelieving in spirit, made for themselves a Herod in the place of Christ, so also they had to tolerate externally a bodily Herod instead of one descended from the royal line of David, and therefore in both relations there was purely a kingdom of Herod.

In the Greek language they call those who are noted for great clamor and deeds *heroes*, as were Hercules, Hector, Achilles, and the like. In German they are called *Riesen*, but in Saxon *Kerle*.[24] From this comes the name Charles, which means among us what "hero" or "Herod" does in Greek. "Herod" comes from "hero" and means "male," "gigantic," "doing great deeds," a Dietrich of Bern, a Hildebrand, a Roland,[25] or by whatever other name you may call these great murderers and man-eaters. They also existed before the flood. In Hebrew, Moses calls them *Nephilim* [Gen. 6:4; cf. Num. 13:33], which means "those who fall," that is, those who fall on others and with force suppress them. The people of Israel killed many of them in the Promised Land, who were called the *Anakim*, *Rephaim*, and *Emim* [Deut. 2:11]. *Anak* means "a golden chain"; therefore, they were called *Anakim* because they were the knights in the land and wore golden chains. *Rephaim* means "rescuers," because people regarded them as those who rescued the land and the people. *Emim* means "terrible and frightful," because the people were afraid of them.

115. Thus there have always been Herods, only under different names. Thus before the Last Day there must also be Herods, whom Christ at His coming will destroy. They are now called pope, cardinal, bishop, priest, monk, spiritual lords, and holy fathers, who must endure the great injustice of being called shepherds of the sheep of Christ, even though in truth they are ravenous wolves who flay and devour Christ's people in body, property,

24  At Luther's time, *Riesen* could mean both "giants" or "great men" in general. In modern German, *Kerl* often means a "guy" or "fellow," but at Luther's time it could mean "a brave man" or "hero."

25  On Dietrich of Bern, a heroic figure based loosely on the historical Ostrogothic king Theodoric the Great (454–526), see LW 69:378 n. 5. Many of the stories about Dietrich are not in the least historical; cf. *Large Catechism* (1529), Longer Preface 11 (Kolb-Wengert, p. 381; *Concordia*, p. 354). Hildebrand was the armorer, brother-in-arms, and fatherly friend of Dietrich of Bern in the *Nibelungenlied*. Roland was a Frankish warrior celebrated in a medieval epic for his heroism during an ambush by Muslim forces in Spain; see *The Song of Roland*, ed. and trans. Glyn S. Burgess (London: Penguin, 1990).

and soul [cf. Matt. 7:15]. They are the last and mightiest heroes, giants, man-eaters, and Herods, whom none but Christ from heaven can destroy.

116. Now Christ and Herod are entirely different and diametrically opposed one to the other. Christ is not characterized by great clamor and deeds. With Him there are no deeds of giants and heroes, but only pure humanity that thinks not of self, is despised, and lets God alone be and do all things and have the glory. On the other hand, what Herod does are great things, having all power and fame, as if he were the one who lacks nothing.

117. Now, since the Jews were inwardly true Herods, they thought much of themselves, of their deeds, and of their great reputation because of their splendid lives, so that Christ meant nothing to them. Therefore, God sent them a King Herod, who dealt with them in temporal things as they dealt with souls in spiritual things. They rejected Christ and God, and so He rejected their royal family. Since He could not reign in their souls, He did not allow their own flesh and blood to reign over their bodies and property. And as they killed and suppressed the people spiritually with their government and with human doctrines, so He permitted them to be killed, suppressed, and tormented bodily through Herod. Thus the physical Herod was a punishment and a sign of their spiritual Herod.

118. As it happens in all sins, that one perceives and hates the punishment but loves the sin and does not perceive it, so it also happened with the Jews. They indeed felt the physical Herod and hated him, but the spiritual Herod—their unbelieving, spiritual tyranny—they considered to be precious and good. Through their pharisaical, sectarian conduct, they presumed to deserve much from God for their human doctrines and works of the Law, and they could not see that just in that way they had deserved the rule of Herod, from which they were unable to free themselves no matter how much they wanted to. They considered themselves worthy on account of their great, spiritual, and holy conduct.

119. Thus we now also keenly perceive our Herod, who is flaying and choking us in body and property. But since we are not sincere Christians and do not permit Christ to be our King in a pure and free faith, but are pleased with the spiritual way of life that now holds sway and with our own works, we are unable to free ourselves from him, and there is no hope. We must let ourselves be devoured and ruined. There is no help. He must be our bodily and spiritual Herod.

120. Let it be established, first, that Herod signifies a governance not simply as worldly lords govern, since Herod was himself also a worldly lord; therefore, his governance must not signify a worldly governance and himself, but a different and spiritual governance. Thus the governance must not be over physical people and property, but spiritual people and property, that is,

their consciences and the things that belong to salvation, such as good works, a good life, the Sacraments, and God's Word.

121. Further, this spiritual governance may be governed in no more than two ways: first, in a blessed way, when Christ alone governs in the true faith and the pure Gospel; second, in a pernicious way, when man governs with works and human doctrines—just as the people of Israel were governed first by their own kings and second by Herod, a foreign king. Therefore, Herod signifies nothing else than such a spiritual governance which governs the people not through faith and the Gospel, but through works and doctrines of men; nevertheless, it has the name and the appearance of leading to heaven and of teaching the people correctly, though it is nothing other than the path and broad road to hell.

The sum of it all is that Herod is the pope with his spiritual governance. There we see no faith, no Gospel, but simply human doctrines and works, and he has an enormous Herod-like power and fame. The consciences of men should be guided, fed, and preserved through God's Word alone, but he leads and feeds them only with his own snot and spittle, with indulgences, orders, Masses, prayers, fasts, and the like, and in this respect is a mighty giant, a Roland, and a hero.

122. They say that if the Christian church were not sustained by this ruling she would founder, but faith and Christ alone should rule. Therefore, what the peasants say is true: Kunz Hildebrand,[26] the great whale, carries the world on his tail. That is, if it were not for what the pope did with his ruling, God would be entirely too weak, the apple of the world[27] would certainly fall out of His hand, and neither faith nor the Gospel could help. But now, since the pope comes to His assistance and lays the foundation with his many tonsures, caps, ropes, wooden shoes, bishop and cardinal hats; organs, peals, and smoke of incense; sounding of bells and candlewicks; blubbering in the churches; and growling in their bellies, particularly those who fast and do not eat milk, eggs, meat, and the like—in which the pope's holiness consists— then everything is preserved. And if the pope were in favor of doing away

---

26 *Kunz Hildebrand*, i.e., *concelebrant*. This corruption of the title of the one who assists at the celebration of the Mass was also used by the common people as the name of the legendary fish which, like Leviathan, surrounds or carries the earth; cf. *Commentary on Psalm 82* (1530), LW 13:56. See O. Brenner, *Kunz Hildebrand oder Sagen und Namen* (Augsburg: Bruckmann, 1912).

27 Holy Roman emperors had been portrayed holding the *Reichsapfel* ["imperial apple"] since Henry II (r. 1014–24); see J. M. Bak, "Medieval Symbology of the State," in *Viator*, Medieval and Renaissance Studies 4 (Berkeley: University of California Press, 1973), p. 56. Luther used the word *Weltapfel* ["apple of the world"] to describe God's power over all. See Albrecht Dürer's *Salvator Mundi*, an image of Christ with the orb of the world in His hand, in Katharine Baetjer, *European Paintings in the Metropolitan Museum of Art by Artists Born before 1865: A Summary Catalogue* (New York: Metropolitan Museum of Art, 1995), p. 219.

with such spiritual, orderly, holy governance, where would the world be? Here we have what Herod and Christ are: two kinds of spiritual governance, one unbelieving and the other believing.

123. Now, what is the star? It is nothing else than the new light, preaching, and Gospel, preached orally and publicly. Christ has two witnesses of His birth and rule. The one is the Scripture—words composed in letters. The other is the voice or the words proclaimed orally. St. Paul and St. Peter call that Word a light and lamp [2 Cor. 4:6; 2 Pet. 1:19].

124. Now, the Scriptures are not understood until the light rises, for the prophets become visible through the Gospel. Therefore, the star must first rise and be seen. In the New Testament, sermons must be preached orally, with living voices publicly, and that which formerly lay concealed in the letter and secret vision must be proclaimed in language to the ear.

The New Testament is nothing else than a making visible and a revelation of the Old Testament, as is testified when the Lamb of God opens the book with the seven seals (Revelation 5 [:9]). We also see that all the preaching of the apostles was nothing else than proclaiming Scripture and building on it. Therefore, Christ did not write down His doctrines Himself, as Moses did, but He taught them orally and commanded that they should be taught orally and gave no command to write.

Likewise, the apostles wrote very little, and then not all of them but only Peter, Paul, John, and Matthew. From the other apostles we have nothing except James and Jude, which many think are not writings of apostles. Those who have written do nothing more than direct us to the Scriptures of the Old Testament, just as the angel directed the shepherds to the manger and the swaddling cloths [Luke 2:12], and the star directed the Magi to Bethlehem.

125. Therefore, it is not at all a New Testament thing to write books on Christian doctrine, but rather, apart from books, there ought to be good, learned, spiritual, diligent preachers in every locality who can draw forth the living Word from the old Scriptures and without ceasing hold it before the people, as the apostles did. Before they wrote, they first preached to the people by word of mouth and converted them, which was their proper apostolic and New Testament work. This is the true star, which shows Christ's birth, and also the angelic message, which speaks about the swaddling cloths and manger.

126. Books had to be written, but this was a great detriment and an infirmity of spirit, which necessity compelled, and it is not the manner of the New Testament. For in the place of the godly preachers there arose heretics, false teachers, and all kinds of errors, who gave the sheep of Christ poison in the place of pasture, so that they had to try [writing books] in order to do what was necessary to rescue at least some of the sheep from the wolves. So

people began to write and through Scripture, as much as possible, to lead the lambs of Christ into Scripture, and thus provide that the sheep might feed themselves and be preserved from the wolves, if their shepherds would not feed them or became wolves.

127. For that reason, St. Luke also says in his preface [Luke 1:1–4] that he was moved to write his Gospel because of some who had presumed to write the history of Christ, without a doubt because he saw that they did not handle it correctly. All the Epistles of Paul only preserve what he had taught before; without a doubt he preached much more abundantly than he wrote. If wishing did any good, one could wish nothing better than that all books were simply done away with and that nothing remained in all the world, especially among Christians, other than the pure Scripture or the Bible. It contains more than enough of all kinds of knowledge and doctrine which is useful and necessary to know. But wishing is now in vain. Oh, that there were some good books besides Scripture!

128. Let it suffice for the present that this star is the bodily preaching and the bright revelation of Christ as He was concealed and promised in Scripture. Therefore, whoever sees the star certainly recognizes the King of the Jews, the newborn Christ. For the Gospel teaches nothing else but Christ, and therefore Scripture contains nothing else but Christ. But whoever does not recognize Christ may hear the Gospel—or, indeed, carry the book in his hands—but he does not yet understand it. Having the Gospel without understanding it is having no Gospel. And having the Scripture without recognizing Christ means having no Scripture and is nothing else than letting this star shine, and yet not seeing it.

129. This is what happens to the Herodians and the people of Jerusalem: the star was over their land and over their heads, but they did not see it. Thus, when the Gospel rose over the Jewish people, as Isaiah says in the Epistle [Isa. 60:1] that they let it shine but did not recognize it, of this Paul says: "If our Gospel is veiled, it is veiled in those who are perishing. In their case the god of this world" (that is, the devil) "has blinded the minds of the unbelievers, to keep them from seeing the bright light of the Gospel of the glory of Christ" (2 Corinthians 4 [:3–4]).

From this it is evident that unbelief alone is the cause of the blindness which does not see the Gospel, though it shines and is preached without ceasing. It is impossible for Christ and His Gospel to be recognized by reason; only faith recognizes them. And "seeing the star" signifies this faith.

130. These Magi signify and are themselves the first part of the Gentiles converted to faith through the Gospel. For the Gentiles were "Magi," that is, natural people who lived according to reason, who did not have the Law and the prophets, as the Jews did, but walked only according to nature, without

the divine Law and the Word. Now, the natural philosophers, like these Magi, generally go too far and turn natural philosophy into sorcery and the casting of spells, as stated above. Thus also nature, when left to itself and not assisted by the doctrines of God, most certainly takes the wrong path, on its own falls into error and blindness, and becomes a veritable witch, full of all kinds of unbelief.

131. Thus St. Paul says that though the Law of God had not been given to the Gentiles, nevertheless they had a natural conscience and they do the works of the Law naturally, which they found written in their hearts (Romans 2 [:14]). But though they were far from the Law and without God's Law, yet they are much closer and come to faith sooner than the Jews, because the Jews had the Law, depended on it, and thought they had sufficiently satisfied it by their works. Therefore, they despised the Gospel as something they did not need and as being false because it rejected works in which they took pride and lauded faith alone. The Gentiles had no reason to be so arrogant on account of being without the Law; therefore, they more easily adhered to the Gospel and recognized its benefit and their need for it.

132. That the Magi came to Jerusalem and inquired after the new King signifies nothing else than that the Gentiles, enlightened through the Gospel, come into the Christian Church and seek Christ. For Jerusalem is a figure of the origin of the Christian Church, in which God's people are gathered, which [translated] means "a vision of peace," because in the Christian Church peace is seen; that is, all who are in the Christian Church and are true Christians have a good conscience and peaceful confidence of heart from the forgiveness of sins through God's grace.

133. Now, in this peaceful place, Herod the man-eater reigns and always wants to reign. For all people and teachers of works have in them this affliction: that they naturally mislead, destroy, and oppress the true Jerusalem; ensnare good consciences and simple, godly hearts; and teach them to trust in themselves and in their works, so that faith perishes, peace and a good conscience is destroyed, while the rule of Herod with its great show and fame and works remains faithless and endless. This is the evangelist's goal when he tells us how Christ was born and sought at the time of Herod, in the very city of his governance.

You see, the Gospel truth wages all its warfare against the Herodian holiness. Whenever it comes, it finds Herodians, who rule the people with human doctrines and works. It also comes only to condemn these and to teach the pure grace of God instead of works, and pure faith instead of Law, and rescues the people of God at Jerusalem from the reign of Herod.

134. When Herod heard this, "he was frightened, and all Jerusalem with him" [Matt. 2:3]. Why? Because Herod was afraid of another king, the

true King, for he himself wanted to be the only king, with force. This was fulfilled when through the Gospel the Gentiles began to praise Christ and faith against the works and doctrines of men. The Jews became enraged, because they could easily perceive that if this should continue, what they were doing would be considered worthless, and their works and doctrines which appeared so great would be brought to shame. This they could not endure, and therefore they began to rage, as is shown in the Acts of the Apostles [i.e., Acts 6:8–8:3; 12:1–5]. For in this way their government, honor, power, and riches, which they had in such abundance under the spiritual reign of Herod, would receive a powerful blow.

135. Human works and doctrines at all times yield much money and property, while the doctrines of God and the work of Christ bring the cross, poverty, disgrace, and all kinds of hardship, which the holiness of Herod cannot endure. Thus it always happens that those who have ensnared and oppressed the poor people with an erring conscience and with human doctrines do not like to hear that the poor, miserable consciences receive the true understanding and instruction; and seek the simple, pure Word of God and faith; and speak much about wanting to have a new King and to see His star. [They do not like to hear that,] for then the pope, bishops, holy fathers, and spiritual lords could not fatten their bellies so well.

136. Therefore, the Herodian reign is neither interested nor pleased that the Magi, the unlearned, the laity, who know nothing, should begin to speak of the light of the Gospel and, disregarding the spiritual pomp of the Herodians, should inquire about another matter in the midst of Jerusalem. This indeed must have frightened Herod and his servants, because it concerned their pockets and their bellies. Indeed, all Jerusalem was frightened with him.

Many godly people, even though they hated the reign of Herod and wished that it did not exist, also were afraid that the truth might be brought to light inopportunely, that through it tumult and discord might be promoted in the world, that the government might be attacked, and that this could not be overcome without great harm. Therefore, they thought that it might be better to suppress the truth for a time or to bring it forth in such a manner that Herod would not be troubled nor aroused to cause great misery.

137. But the Magi do not ask about his fright and anger, but speak openly to Jerusalem about the star and the new king, and are not in the least concerned that the heavens might fall. For one must neither confess nor deny the Gospel on account of any particular person. It is God's Word. Herod must yield to it and follow it. But if he rages, then let him rage. Christ will yet remain before him.

138. But note that Herod at first does not think of using force, but of deceiving the new King with cunning. So he gathers together all the learned men and diligently searches the Scripture, as though he were anxious to learn the truth [Matt. 2:4]. And yet he thought that not Scripture but his own will and mind was right and would be accomplished. Here we arrive at the real character of Herod. Here we see the pope and his followers truly portrayed.

139. But so that no one may blame me for applying this to the pope and comparing the spiritual estate[28] with its governance so contemptuously to Herod, I want to stipulate here that I am doing it because it is my Christian duty and a debt of faithfulness which I am compelled by my conscience to furnish to everyone.[29] I force no one to believe me. If the truth and experience do not prove all that I say, then let anyone at all chastise me for lying; I will fulfill my brotherly office and be excused before God. If anyone despises my faithful warning, let him answer for it himself. I want to have said to him that Christ and His doctrine shall not tolerate the pope and his spiritual rule.

Therefore, let everyone guard himself against them, as against his eternal destruction, and cling firmly to Christ alone. Whether it brings the pope and the clergy any property or honor does not at all concern me. I must preach Christ, and not the property and honor of the pope and the clergy. What is said of the pope and the clergy is said of all those who oppress the people with their works and doctrines, and who do not teach the true faith, the pure Scripture, and the one Christ, as the Jews also did (but very little compared to the pope and his servants). Whoever will let himself be misled has heard my warning; I am innocent of his blood and destruction [cf. Ezek. 3:18].

140. The statement that "Herod assembled the rulers of the priests and scribes of the people and inquired about the birth of Christ" [cf. Matt. 2:4] is the same as what our spiritual governance, what all the unbelieving teachers of works, is doing. They want to keep the Scripture for themselves, and what they teach is supposed to be in the Scripture; yet their opinion comes first, and the Scripture is controlled accordingly. For their intention is to use Scripture only to suppress the truth and to confirm their doings, just as Herod searched in the Scripture only so that he might kill Christ.

141. Thus our Herod, the pope, with his Herodians, searches the Scripture and uses it, but he explains it only to destroy its true meaning and replace it with his ideas. With such show even the elect are deceived [cf.

28  *den geistlichen Stand*, i.e., "the clerical estate."

29  Luther regarded his public call as doctor of theology as the basis of his legitimacy as a reformer of the Church: see *Why the Books of the Pope and His Disciples Were Burned* (1520), LW 31:383; *On Translating* (1530), LW 35:193–94; *Commentary on Psalm 82* (1530), LW 13:66; *Infiltrating and Clandestine Preachers* (1532), LW 40:387–88. The doctorate was, in principle, the right to teach in any diocese in Christendom (the *ius ubique docendi*). See LW 69:169 n. 93 for a brief history of the authority of the university doctors of theology.

Matt. 24:24]; for there is no greater show, which frightens and deceives every conscience, than that which pretends to stand on God's name as if it would search and follow only God's Scripture and Word, and yet searches for only the opposite, to suppress Scripture with all its contents. Therefore, the Magi do not see the star of Jerusalem and do not know where they should go. And all who come among such glittering people will go astray and lose the true Christian understanding because of the great show of the unbelieving saints, unless they firmly grasp the pure Scriptures.

142. Although both Herod and the Magi received the Scripture here from the priests [cf. Matt 2:5–6], Herod grasped it with a false and evil intent. The Magi grasp it with a true and good intent. Therefore, they again see the star and are rescued from Herod's falsity, under which they had lost the star.

As here the conflict between Herod and the Magi is shown, so also [conflict] arises over Scripture between the true and the false saints, in that the true saints go astray a little and for a little while lose the true light, but they do not continue in [error]. They finally grasp the true sense of Scripture, come again to the clear light, and let the Herodians boast about their false sense of Scripture.

217. The statement that "Herod summoned the wise men secretly and learned from them what time the star had appeared" [Matt. 2:7] means that the spiritual Herodians do not deny the Gospel outwardly but learn it from the true Christians, with the intention, however, that they will use it for their own wantonness, just as Herod here intended to use the time the star appeared to kill Christ and confirm his own kingdom. Thus also now, when we hold up the Gospel to our spiritual people,[30] they do not deny that it is the Gospel, [but] hear and accept it. But they say that ours is not the correct understanding; there is a gloss and an interpretation which we shall get from no one but them, and everyone must agree with their interpretation. Thus they do not deny the Gospel, but they take away all its power, and under the name and appearance of the Gospel they advance their own dreams.

St. Paul calls this "having the appearance of godliness, but denying its power" [2 Tim. 3:5]. He does not say they do not have the power of godliness—though that is also true—but, much more harshly, that they deny it. Thus he states clearly that they are godless not only in their life and walk but also in their doctrine and government; they lead themselves with their lives and others with their doctrine away from the Gospel and salvation. The pope with his clergy now do that in all their sermons; they cry loudly "Gospel! Gospel!" and deny, condemn, and curse everything that is in the Gospel with all its contents, just as Herod learned of the star but wanted to destroy

---

30 *Geistlichen*, or "clergy."

everything the star signified. We will now consider a few of their doctrines in order to preserve ourselves from them.

218. (I) The Gospel teaches that salvation depends completely on faith. They hear that and do not deny it, but they take away from it all its power and say that faith without works is useless. Thus they secretly move away from faith to works, so that now they publicly condemn faith and ascribe everything to works. Thus they retain the little word "faith" only in appearance, and deny, condemn, and curse everything that has the nature of faith, and begin to divide faith into many parts. They speak of natural faith, spiritual faith, common faith, particular faith, unfolded faith, folded-up faith[31]— but they themselves, these blind leaders, know less of what they are blabbing about than any natural fool. The Gospel knows nothing of their many kinds of faith but has only the one which is founded on the pure grace of God, without any merit of works. They do not have even a spark of that, but condemn it as the worst heresy, and yet they say that they want to defend the Gospel and the Christian faith.

219. (II) Likewise, the Gospel says that Christ is our Savior. They hear that, but they undo and weaken every natural work, manner, and attribute of Christ, since they publicly teach that man can merit God's grace by his natural powers and works. Thus they condemn Christ with all His works, as St. Peter foretold about them: "There will be false teachers among you, even denying the Lord who bought them" (2 Peter 2 [:1]). For if nature of itself can attain God's grace, as now all universities, institutions, and cloisters teach and maintain in harmony with the pope, then Christ was born and died for nothing and in vain. Why did Christ need to shed His blood to acquire grace for us, when we through our nature can acquire it ourselves? Yet they want to be Christians, and lift high the name of Christ, but under that pretense they chide and condemn as heresy everything Christian.

220. (III) Likewise, the Gospel teaches that the Law of God is spiritual and cannot be fulfilled by nature; rather, the Spirit of God must fulfill it in us through faith (Romans 8 [:2–3]). Thus they deny neither the Spirit nor the Law; rather, they take away all its power and teach that man without the help of the Spirit can naturally fulfill God's Law in all its works, though by that he does not earn heaven. This is nothing other than denying the power of the Law and of the Spirit and only retaining their names.

31 Thomas Aquinas explained the Scholastic distinction between implicit and explicit faith by describing matters of faith as being more or less unfolded for simpler or more learned persons.

221. They go further and tear God's Law to pieces wherever they think it too difficult for nature, producing counsels[32] and superfluous, unnecessary things out of it. They teach that it is not necessary nor commanded that we love God with our whole heart [Matt. 22:37], nor that we give the cloak with the tunic [Matt. 5:40; Luke 6:29]; again, that we should not go to law [1 Cor. 6:1, 6], nor that we should lend and give to everybody without profit or interest [Luke 6:34–35], nor that we should endure injustice and do good to our enemies [1 Cor. 4:12; Matt. 5:44], etc. Thus they have put an end to the entire, true nature of the Christian estate, which consists alone in enduring injustice and doing good to everybody. Then, in the place of Christianity, they set up their own commands, namely, that they wear tonsures and cowls; eat no meat, eggs, butter, or milk; make much blubbering in the church. Thus nothing more remains of God's Commandments.

222. (IV) Likewise, the Gospel praises the pure grace of God which pardons and destroys sin. Now they do not deny the little word "grace," but hold it seemingly in high esteem. But in addition they teach all kinds of satisfactions for sin, institutions, orders, sects, and states of repentance, in order to purchase from God the forgiveness of sin and to pay Him for His grace. By that, the nature and work of grace are fundamentally destroyed and condemned; for grace is pure grace or nothing at all.

223. (V) Likewise, the Gospel teaches that through original sin all people are under wrath and disfavor, so that all their works are thereby rendered sinful. They do not deny the term "original sin," but take away its power by saying that nature is still good, and its works are not sinful and can also prepare it for grace. They also say that original sin did not harm nature in any way that is damnable, but only weakened it for doing good and inclined it to evil. If it does not follow that inclination, as it certainly can of itself, it does not deserve hell and can also earn the grace of God. See, this is as much as to say that original sin is not original sin, but under this name they deny the work and nature of sin.

224. (VI) Likewise, the Gospel teaches that love does not seek its own but serves others only. Now they indeed retain the little word "love," but separate its nature from it when they teach that ordinary love begins with itself and loves itself first and most. Then they say, "It is enough for love if you want something for another; you need not add the deed of serving

---

32 Scholastic theologians distinguished between the Commandments, binding upon all Christians for obtaining eternal life, and the "counsels of perfection" upon which monastic life was based, which might be observed to "render the gaining of this end more assured and expeditious" (Aquinas, *ST*, 1–2 q. 108 art. 4 [Blackfriars 30:60–65]). Cf. Luther's critique in *Explanations of the Ninety-Five Theses* (1518), LW 31:235; *Temporal Authority* (1523), LW 45:81, 87–92, 101–2; *Sermons on John 18–20* (1528–29/1557), LW 69:190–93; *Sermon on the Mount* (1530–32/1532), LW 21:3–4, 70, 74.

him." For it would be dishonest if the pope were to humble himself toward his subject; rather, he should make him kiss his feet.[33] It is enough that he imagines a thought toward him which says, "I wish everybody well—except my enemies." See, in that way all the nature and power of love perishes, and all that remains is the simple, empty, poor name.

225. (VII) Likewise, the Gospel teaches that hope is built purely on divine promises. They confess the little word "hope," but teach that hope does not rest on divine promises, but on its own merits.

226. (VIII) Likewise, the Gospel teaches that God's predestination is eternally sure, but they teach that it is based on the free will and is uncertain.

227. In short, they confess God and His names, but tear to pieces, destroy, and condemn as the worst heresy whatever God orders, wills, does, establishes, and executes, so that it is obvious how Christ's suffering is now spiritually fulfilled under the rule of the pope. See, thus in their teaching they have the appearance of faith, of hope, of love, of grace, of sin, of the Law, of Christ, of God, of the Gospel; yet they deny all of their strength and nature, and condemn it all as the worst heresy.

On this account the apostle spoke so harshly when he said, "They deny the power" of the whole divine worship and life, and have only the appearance of it [2 Tim. 3:5]. Lord God in heaven! Where are the streams of water, even streams of blood, that rightly should flow from our eyes in this last, terrible, and dreadful time of the unspeakable, immeasurable wrath of God on the world because of its sin and ingratitude?

228. Further: "Herod sends the Magi to Bethlehem and commands them to seek the Child diligently, pretending that he also wanted to come and worship Him" [cf. Matt. 2:8]. Here a second point is made about our Herodians, namely, that they live as they teach. For them, teaching and living are empty show and denial of the truth, for the life must be as the teaching directs. This is what the pope and the clerical estate now do: they certainly allow Christians to be godly and command them to seek Christ and the truth—yet with this addition, that they should be His betrayers and serve [the pope] when they seek [Christ].

For the pope now shamelessly and rashly asserts to all the world: "Anyone may seek Christ and live righteously; but if he does not also obey the pope's orders and command and serve him, subject in obedience to the pope with all his good life, then he cannot be saved." Thus he makes the people think

---

33 By the sixth century, it was customary that the emperor kissed the pope's feet when they met. Later this tradition expanded and prescribed that cardinals kiss the pope's feet upon his election and that individuals given a private audience with the pope greet him in this way. By the early eleventh century, the custom of foot-kissing had become an established ritual in the ceremony for the papal coronation of emperors. Cf. Luther's preface to Barnes, *How Popes Adrian IV and Alexander III Showed Good Faith to Emperor Barbarossa* (1545), LW 60:347–51.

that more, or at least just as much, depends on obedience to the pope as on God's commands.

229. See, this is Herod's addition: that he not only sends the Magi to Bethlehem but also holds them subject to himself and obliged only to treachery, to destroy Christ. For when people hold that obedience to the pope is necessary for salvation, and that whoever does not hold it is condemned, what are they all doing except betraying and surrendering Christ that Herod may find and kill Him? For Christian faith cannot exist beside such obedience or such a conscience, as has often been said. For faith alone must save, and such obedience must be regarded as not beneficial for salvation; or if it is regarded as beneficial and permitted, then faith must perish, and Herod must reign in Christ's stead. That means, then, really to surrender and betray Christ and faith in Him.

230. But when Herod says, "I also will come and worship Him" [Matt. 2:8], everyone sees that he is lying, that these are only words and an apparent pretense, under which he is thinking something much different, namely, to kill Christ and to upset His kingdom. Herod thus sets forth beautifully and briefly the image of all unbelieving saints. First, Herod does not pretend any simple thing; he does not say that he wants to give Him gold or myrrh, nor that he wants to help Him or to be His good friend. Rather, he undertakes the very highest and best work there is in the service of God, namely, humility and worship. He says, "I will come as a humble person and show the highest honor of worship."

231. This is what the Herodians, the spiritual ones,[34] now do: they do not undertake any ordinary work, but the very highest, the service of God. This they appropriate to themselves, exercise themselves in it, and dare to say that the life of other men is temporal and worldly but that they are in the service of God day and night. While others labor, they are praying and serving God for the poor people.

Do you not believe this? Well, then, ask the bells about it, which ring for their worship. They go into worship humbly, have themselves proclaimed God's servants before all men, fattening their bellies very well in the process, and seize for themselves all the property of the world and build houses as if they expected to live here forever. Therefore, we must here look at the difference between true and false worship, so that we may recognize and avoid the heart and mind of the villain Herod.

---

34 *Geistlichen*, or "clergy."

## True and False Worship

232. These cannot be distinguished better than by God's Word. That worship which is taught in God's Word must be the true worship; but that which is set up alongside or apart from God's Word, such as that made up by men, must certainly be the false Herodian worship. Now God's worship is written down nowhere except in His Commandments. For without a doubt he alone serves God who keeps His Commandments, just as a servant in the house is said to serve his master only when he does and attends to whatever his master tells him to do. However, if he does not do this, even if he otherwise does the will of the whole city, he is not said to serve his master. So, then, whoever does not do God's Commandments does not serve God, even though he keeps the teachings and commandments of all men.

233. Thus the worship of God means that you know, honor, and love God with your whole heart, put all your trust and confidence in Him, never doubt His goodness either in life or in death, either in sinning or in doing good, as the First Commandment teaches [cf. Exod. 20:3]. We can attain this only through the merit and blood of Christ, who has gained for us and gives us such a heart when we hear and believe His Word; for our nature cannot have such a heart of itself. See, this is the chief worship of God and the greatest thing, which we call a sincere Christian faith and love to God through Christ. Thus the First Commandment is fulfilled by us through Christ's blood, and God is very thoroughly served.

234. Second, when you honor God's name, call on it in need, and openly confess it before the tyrants and persecutors of this true worship, [then] do not be afraid, [but] reprove the Herodians and restrain them, as much as you can, from dishonoring God's name with their false life and teaching proclaimed under God's name—which is truly a great thing and loads the world onto itself. See, this is the second part of worship, kept in the Second Commandment [Exod. 20:7].

235. Third, when you bear the holy cross and must suffer much because of your faith and confession, so that you must risk body and life, goods and honor, friend and favor for it, this is correctly observing and keeping the Sabbath holy, since it is not you but God alone who works in you, for you are only a passive, persecuted man. This is the third part of worship, written down in the Third Commandment [Exod. 20:8]. See, here is the First Table with the first three commandments, which are summarized in the three parts: believing, confessing, and suffering. In this way we renounce this life and the world and live only for God.

236. Fourth, we come to the Second Table, and you further serve God when you honor father and mother [Exod. 20:12], are subject and obedient to them, and help them where they need it above all [other] people on earth,

so that without their will you will not enter the clergy if they need you first or want something else.

237. Fifth, you are to injure no one in his body [Exod. 20:13], but to do good to everyone, even to your enemies, visit the sick and prisoners, give help to all the needy, and have a good, kind heart for all people.

238. Sixth, you are to live chastely and temperately [Exod. 20:14], or always keep your marriage vow and help others to keep theirs.

239. Seventh, you are not to deceive or harm anyone, nor take advantage of anyone in temporal goods [Exod. 20:15]; but lend to everyone, give, exchange where you can, and preserve your neighbor from harm.

240. Eighth, you are to guard your tongue, and defame, slander, and lie to no one, but cover up, excuse, and spare everyone [Exod. 20:16].

241. Ninth and tenth, you are not to covet anyone's wife or property [Exod. 20:17].

242. See, these are the parts of the complete divine worship. He requires this from you, and nothing else. He pays no attention to whatever you do over and above that. This is also clear and easy enough for everyone to understand. Now you see that the true worship must be common to all estates and to all people, and this alone is to be found among God's people. And wherever another worship is found, it must certainly be false and misleading, such as that which is not common to all, but is confined to some special estates and people. That's enough about the true, common, and only worship.

243. Now let us look at the false, peculiar, factious, and diverse worship which is not commanded by God, but made up by the pope and his clergy. There you see many kinds of monasteries, orders, and cloisters, which have nothing in common with one another. One has a large tonsure, another a small one; one wears gray, another black, another white, another woolen, another linen, another a hair shirt; this one prays on certain days and times, another on different days and times; this one eats meat, that one fish; this one is a Carthusian, that one a barefoot monk.[35] This one has certain ceremonies, that one others; one prays with his stool facing Rome, another with his bench facing Jerusalem; this one conducts Mass in one way, that one differently; this one is bound to this monastery, that one to another; this one blubbers in the chancel here, that one in another, and the churches swarm full of their mutterings. They also live in celibacy and have all kinds of disciplines. And who can name all their countless, factious, extraordinary, and sectarian parts?

Now this worship has vomited forth another, still greater, born from it. There is neither limit nor measure to the building of churches, chapels, monasteries, and altars; to founding Masses and vigils; to establishing hours

---

35 I.e., a Franciscan.

of prayer;[36] and to generating vestments, surplices, chalices, monstrances, silver images and treasures, candlesticks, tapers, lights, incense, tables, and bells. What an ocean and a forest of these things there is! All of the laity's devotion, tribute, money, and property has gone into these things. They call this "multiplying the worship of God" and "providing for the worship of God," as the pope does in his spiritual laws.

244. Now compare these things with the true worship of God, and tell me where God has spoken a letter about any of these things? Do you still doubt, then, that the whole clerical estate under the pope is nothing but Herod's doings, glitter, and deception, which only hinders people and turns them away from the true worship? These are the altars and the groves over which the prophets lament regarding the people of Israel, that every town set up its own grove and altar and abandoned the only temple of God [cf. 2 Kings 17:9–13]. Thus this idolatrous, superstitious, papistic, Herodian worship has filled all the corners of the world and has banished and destroyed the true and correct worship of God.

245. Perhaps you look around and think: "What, could so many people be wrong all at once?" Beware, and do not let their number trouble you. Hold fast to God's Word, since He cannot lie to you [cf. Num. 23:19]. All people may lie, as Scripture says, "All men are liars" [Ps. 116:11]. Do not be astonished that so many are now in error. At Elijah's time there were only seven thousand godly men in all the people of Israel [1 Kings 19:18]. Tell me, what were seven thousand men compared to all Israel, of whom there were more than twelve hundred thousand[37] fighting men [cf. 2 Sam. 24:9; 1 Chron. 21:5], besides women and children? What was that whole people compared to the whole world, which was wrong all at once?

What, then, is to happen, since Christ and the apostles have spoken such terrible things of these times that even Christ Himself says, "When the Son of Man comes, will He find faith on earth?" [Luke 18:8]? There must be terribly great things, and many great people must be wrong, most of all those whom one would expect the least. Then the Antichrist will rule and lead the world astray. We want to be secure, not to pay attention to God's judgment, and not to take His wrath to heart, so that it would be unsurprising if He kept scarcely one man on earth godly.

246. This is the last and worst time, which all of Scripture has terribly threatened. Thank God, therefore, that you see in His Word what true and false worship are. Then see that you remain in it, and do not follow the crowd that proceeds without God's Word. If those scarcely remain who have God's

---

36 The Divine Office, consisting of eight prayer services held at seven times throughout the day and night, to which all monks and clergy were obligated.

37 I.e., 1.2 million.

Word and hold fast to it, where will those remain who follow their own nose apart from God's Word? Therefore, whoever wants to doubt, let him. God's Word and worship convince us sufficiently that the pope is the Antichrist and the clerical estates are his disciples who lead all the world astray.

248. See, this is the Herodian worship, which pretends to worship Christ and serve God, but there is nothing more there. It still glitters so prettily that it daily deceives many holy, godly people, and has often deceived them, as Christ says that they shall "lead astray even the elect" (Matthew 24 [:24]). This happened to St. Bernard, to St. Francis, and to St. Dominic and others, though they did not drown in error nor remain in it; for their correct faith kept them safe through such error and led them out.

249. This is what happened to these godly Magi. They had a good, true faith and intention, but they were still mistaken in Herod, regarded his assertions as correct, and believed his lies. They were even ready to follow him and be obedient to him, if they had not been instructed differently from heaven. So it happens today, and so it has happened, that many are obedient to the pope, and believe in simple faith that his behavior is right and good, and thus are mistaken. However their Christian faith helps them so that this poison does not in the end injure them, as Christ says, "If they drink any deadly poison, it will not hurt them" (Mark 16 [:18]), as long as they believe in My name. But what drink can be more deadly than such lies and hypocrisy of the false teaching about wrong worship?

250. Since we have now learned to know Herod's worship and perceived his false, malicious glitter, let us also now see his evil purpose and malice, in that he thought he could destroy not only the true worship but also Christ the King and His whole kingdom.

He ventures to do this in three ways: first, with the same glittering assertion of this false worship. For this pretext of worship is a strong enticement from true worship, which without special grace cannot be overcome, so that St. Paul does well in naming it *energiam erroris*, "a strong working of error" [2 Thess. 2:11]. The people cannot defend themselves against such seduction, unless there are valiant bishops and preachers who preach the only true worship, keep the people with the pure Word of God, and gainsay the false worship, as the prophets did in Israel and for that reason were all slaughtered. For this preaching costs one's neck and cannot be endured by Herod, the pope, and the spiritual, holy people. [This preaching] does great harm to their wallet, and to the souls of many godly people, which is intolerable to the devil, their teacher.

251. Second, Herod destroys [true worship] through his teaching, as was said above. Thus he teaches works instead of faith, contrary to the First Commandment about God's honor and work. He pushes aside the Second

and Third Commandments and teaches his own works and arrogance, and forbids [people] to confess the faith and God's name. He teaches disobedience to father and mother, against the Fourth Commandment, as said above. He teaches that it is unnecessary to love your enemies and to do good to them, against the Fifth. He tears marriage to pieces, against the Sixth. He robs and steals ill-gotten gain, and sanctions this, against the Seventh. He also teaches that it is unnecessary to lend and give. In summary, he teaches that it is unnecessary to love God and your neighbor from your heart [cf. Luke 10:27]. That means, to be sure, that he destroys the whole Scripture and worship of God.

252. Third, he is unsatisfied with such poisonous examples and deadly teachings, but goes ahead and exercises two kinds of force in them: spiritually, he excommunicates and curses the souls that do not follow him, and then bodily he burns, hunts, and persecutes their bodies, property, and honor in the most disgraceful way. What more could he do that is evil? I think he is a Herod; nevertheless, he must leave Christ alone and cannot carry out his will. He destroys many, but faith remains to the end of the world, though it is hidden, in flight, and unknown.

313. When the Magi came from Herod and turned to Bethlehem, the star appeared to them again, and they became very glad [Matt. 2:9–10]. This always happens when, after the error and deception of human teaching, the heart comes again to the knowledge of the pure truth and of the Gospel. Then at once it is free from Herod and sees how very certain and light the way of the truth is compared to the pretense of the Herodians; so the heart is made glad. For the Gospel is a comforting doctrine, which leads us out of human arrogance into confidence in the pure grace of God, as Psalm 4 [:6–7] says: "Lift up the light of Your face upon us, O Lord! Thereby You put joy in my heart."

314. Again, all who walk in the teachings of men and in their own ability lead a harsh, anxious life, and it still does not help them. What heart should not be glad to learn that the pope's rule is merely trouble and burdening of the conscience, and that it deceives the whole world with its pretense? Divine light and truth has this nature: that it lifts up the conscience, comforts the heart, and creates a free spirit—just as, on the other hand, the teaching of men naturally oppresses the conscience, tortures the heart, and quenches the spirit.

315. Moreover, the star thus goes before them and does not leave them until it brings them to Christ; it goes no farther, but remains over where the Child is. This is what the light of the holy Gospel does, which is like a bright lamp shining in the darkness, as St. Peter calls it (2 Peter 1 [:19]). It goes before us and leads us, if we only cling to it with a firm faith. It does not leave

us until it brings us to Christ and to the truth. But it goes no further, for apart from Christ it teaches us nothing.

316. Thus the nature and work of the Gospel is signified by this leading of a star, and all believers [are signified] by the Magi; just as the star led them bodily to Christ, and they followed it bodily, so the Gospel spiritually leads the hearts of men in this world, and believing hearts see it and follow it with joy until they come to Christ.

Thus St. Paul boasts: "I did not consider myself as knowing anything among you except Jesus Christ, the crucified" (1 Corinthians 2 [:2]). And he forbids us to follow any doctrine which does not teach Christ (Colossians 2 [:8]). What else is this than that the star points to Christ alone and nothing else, and goes no farther? Thus in this figure all human doctrines are condemned, and nothing should be preached to Christians other than the pure, clear light of the Gospel, and we should follow this star only. Therefore, pope, bishops, priests, and monks, with all their governance and teachings, are here condemned and are to be avoided as the tyranny of Herod.

317. Here, too, the mouth of the Papists and Herodians is closed, and their lies are properly punished, since they teach with wanton sacrilege that we should look for the Christian Church and faith with them, and whoever does not listen to them should be regarded as not listening to the Christian Church. They want to be the sign and the star that leads to Christ and the truth, but that is false and untrue. Do you want to know where Christ and the truth are? Learn that here from this history. Look not to the pope, not to the bishop's hat, not to the universities and monasteries. Do not be led astray by their abundant preaching, praying, singing, and holding of Masses. Do not care that they sit in the place of the apostles and brag about their spiritual office—that may deceive in everything and does deceive continuously—they are in error and teach error. There is only one sure sign by which you can recognize where Christ and His Church are, and that is this star, the holy Gospel. All else is false and wrong.

318. But where the Gospel is preached, there this star shines, there Christ certainly is, there you certainly find the Church, whether it is in Turkey, Russia, Bohemia, or anywhere else. If God's Word is heard, then it is impossible for God, Christ, and the Holy Spirit not to be there. On the other hand, it is impossible for God, Christ, the Holy Spirit, the Church, or anything blessed to be where God's Word is not heard, even if they worked all miracles. Rather, there must be only Herodians and the devil's rule there. Now everyone can see how the pope and the clergy are occupied only with human teachings apart from God's Word.

*And going into the house they saw the Child with Mary His mother, and they fell down and worshiped Him. [Matt. 2:11]*

319. This house is the Christian Church, the assembly of all believers on earth, in which alone you can find Christ and His mother; for in the Christian Church alone are those who, pregnant and fruitful by the Holy Spirit, bring forth in a Christian way and lead a Christian life. Everything that is outside of this house, however beautiful it may glitter, however reasonable it may be, has neither Christ nor His mother. That is, there is no Christian life there, for these cannot exist without faith and the Holy Spirit.

320. Therefore, when the pope, bishops, or anyone else demand that you should look to them if you want to see the Church, then think of this Gospel and look to the star. Be assured that if the star does not stand over a place, that is certainly not the house where Christ and His mother are to be found. That is, where the Gospel is not in the air, giving its light, there the Christian Church is certainly not found. This star will not fail you, and without it you will never arrive at the right place. It leads to this house and remains over this house. In the same way the Gospel brings you into the Church, and remains over the Church, is constant, and will not be driven away from it by any persecution. It is obvious and shines freely and clearly, aggravating all its enemies. We see all of that fulfilled in the apostles, martyrs, all saints, and still daily where it is preached.

*Then, opening their treasures, they gave Him gifts: gold and frankincense and myrrh. [Matt. 2:11]*

321. All bodily sacrifices in the Law of Moses, wherever they occurred, signify the spiritual sacrifice of which the Epistle to the Hebrews speaks: "Through Him, then, let us always offer up the sacrifice of praise to God, that is, the fruit of lips that confess His name" (Hebrews 13 [:15]). And Hosea says: "Return, O Israel, to the Lord your God, for you have fallen because of your iniquity. Take with you these words and return to the Lord; say to Him: 'Forgive us all sin, and do good to us, and we will offer to You the bulls of our lips'" (Hosea 14 [:1–2]), that is, praise and thanksgiving. These are the true calves that we should offer to You, of which also Psalm 51 [:18–19] speaks: "Lord, do good to Zion in Your grace; build up the walls of Jerusalem; then will You delight in the sacrifices of righteousness, in burnt offerings and whole offerings; then bulls will be offered on Your altar."

Likewise: "Hear, O Israel, I am your God. Not for your sacrifices do I rebuke you. Do you think I want to eat the flesh of bulls or drink the blood of goats? If I were hungry, I would not tell you, for the world is Mine. I know all the birds on the mountains, and all animals in the field are Mine. Offer to

God a sacrifice of thanksgiving, and pay your vows to Him, and call upon Me in need; I will deliver you, and you shall praise Me." Again: "The one who offers up thanksgiving praises Me; and there is the way that I show him the salvation of God" (Psalm 50 [:7–8, 13, 12, 11, 14–15, 23]). From these verses it is clear that sacrifice, if it is to be agreeable before God, should be praise and thanksgiving, or at least not without praise and thanksgiving. And where it is without praise and thanksgiving, He does not want it, as He says (Isaiah 1 [:11]): "What to Me is your sacrifice? I do not want your incense."

322. We cannot give God anything else, for it is already His, and we have everything from Him; we can give Him only praise, thanks, and honor. Psalm 116 [:12–13, 16–17] teaches: "How shall I repay the Lord for all His benefits to me? I will take the cup of salvation and call on the name of the Lord. You have burst my bonds. Therefore, I will offer up thanks to You and preach the name of the Lord."

Now "praise" is nothing else than confessing the benefit received from God and ascribing and referring this back not to ourselves, but to Him. And this praise and confession happens in two ways: first, before God alone; second, before men, and it is the proper work and fruit of faith.

St. Paul teaches about this: "Because if you confess Jesus with your mouth, that He is the Lord, and believe in your heart that God raised Him from the dead, you will be saved. For if one believes with the heart, he is justified, and if he confesses with the mouth, he is saved" (Romans 10 [:9–10]).

This is as though St. Paul were saying: That is not the true faith, that you believe in Christ secretly in your heart and praise Him in the corner; you must openly confess Him with your mouth before everyone, as you believe in your heart. That, then, immediately costs you your neck. For devils and men cannot listen to such confession, and the cross is closely connected to such confession, as you see that even now the pope, bishops, priests, and monks cannot listen to or tolerate Christ's Word, so that the prophet is right to say, "I will take the cup of salvation and preach the name of the Lord" [Ps. 116:13]. This is as though he were saying: "If I praise and confess God, they will afflict me and make me drink the cup of the martyrs. Well, then, I will accept it in God's name and not be quiet about God's praise. He will not harm me, but be beneficial to me and boldly help me to salvation." That is also what Christ means: "Whoever is ashamed of Me and My words in this adulterous and sinful generation, of him will the Son of Man also be ashamed when He comes in the glory of His Father with the holy angels" (Mark 8 [:38]).

323. Many have commented upon these three offerings, one in this way, another in that, yet all agree that it is a threefold confession. Therefore, we shall take from all what seems true to us. The offering of gold, they say, signifies that they confess that Christ is to be a King; the frankincense, that He

is to be a Priest; the myrrh, that He is to die and be buried. All three parts apply to Christ according to His humanity—yet in such a way that He is God and that such things have happened to His humanity because of His deity.

324. First, the Christian faith confesses and pledges that Christ is a King and Lord over all things, according to the words: "You will make Him Lord over the works of Your hands; You have put all things under His feet" (Psalm 8 [:6]). And again: "The Lord said to my Lord: 'Sit at My right hand, until I make Your enemies Your footstool'" (Psalm 110 [:1]). This confession of the true faith is the high and strong defiance and pride of all who believe in Christ against all that is against them, even though it be sword, hunger, cold, or any other creature (as St. Paul says, cf. Romans 8 [:35, 39]). Who can harm or terrify a Christian when he offers this gold, believes and confesses that his Lord Christ is Lord also over death, hell, the devils, and all creatures and has everything in His hands, even under His feet?

325. Whoever has a gracious prince is afraid of nothing that is under the power of this prince; he relies on him, boasts and confesses the grace and power of his lord. How much more does a Christian take confidence and boast against pain, death, hell, and the devil, and say confidently to them: "What can you do to me? Are you not under the feet of my Lord? Can you defy Him and devour me without His will?" See, a free heart makes this offering of gold. How rare that has now become! Therefore, it is very comforting, if anything terrifies or injures you, that your mouth burst out confessing Christ and saying: *Omnia subjecisti sub pedibus ejus*, "All things are under His feet"; who will then be against me [Ps. 8:6; Rom. 8:31]?

326. Second, they use incense in worship according to the Law of Moses to burn incense in the temple, which pertains to the office of priest. Therefore, to offer incense is nothing else than to confess that Christ is a Priest who is a Mediator between God and us, as St. Paul says that He speaks for us and is our Mediator before God, which is most necessary for us (cf. Romans 8 [:34]). For through His kingship and lordship He defends us in all things against all evil; but through His priesthood He defends us against all sins and God's wrath, steps forth and offers Himself to propitiate God for us, so that through Him we have confidence toward God and so that our conscience may not be terrified nor afraid of His wrath and judgment, as St. Paul says that through Him we have peace with God and access to His grace in faith (cf. Romans 5 [:1–2]).

327. Now it is a much greater thing that He makes us secure toward God and sets our consciences at peace, that God and we are not against each other, than that He makes creatures harmless to us. For guilt is much greater than pain, and sin is much greater than death, since sin brings death, and without sin there would be no death, or at least it would not be harmful. As Christ is

now Lord over sin and death, and has it in His power to give grace and life to all who believe in Him, so offering gold and incense is confessing these two offices and works of His and thanking Him, as St. Paul does: "'O death, where is your sting? O hell, where is your victory?' The sting of death is sin, and the power of sin is the Law. But thanks be to God, who has given us the victory through our Lord Jesus Christ" (1 Corinthians 15 [:55–57]).

328. That is a very high confidence, that a man can set this Priest against his sin, against his evil conscience, against God's terrible wrath and judgment, and with firm faith say and confess: *Tu es sacerdos in aeternum*, "You are an eternal Priest" [Ps. 110:4]. But if You are a Priest, then You intercede for all the sins [of those] who confess You as such a Priest. As little as God's judgment, wrath, sin, and an evil conscience can condemn or terrify You, so little do they condemn and terrify me, for whom You are such a Priest. See, this is truly offering incense, being stouthearted against all sin and God's wrath through faith in Christ.

329. Third, they use myrrh to anoint dead bodies so that they do not decay in the grave. Therefore, this records Christ's death and resurrection; for it is He alone who died, was buried, and did not decay, but rose again from the dead, as Psalm 16 [:10] says, "You will not abandon My soul to hell or let Your holy one see corruption." And this incorruptibility is signified through all who are preserved and kept through bodily myrrh. Accordingly, to offer myrrh is as much as confessing that Christ died and yet remained undecayed, that is, that death has been overcome by life [cf. 2 Tim. 1:10] and that He never died according to His deity and that His humanity again awoke from death.

330. This confessing is the most necessary of the three, though all three are necessary and must be undivided. For, since He has become a King and Priest for you, and given you so great a possession, you must not think that it has been done in vain or that it has cost little or come to you through your own merit. Sin and death have been overcome for you in Him and through Him, and grace and life have been given to you; but it was bitter for Him and cost Him much and has been bought for a high price with His own blood, body, and life. God's wrath, judgment, conscience, hell, death, and every evil thing could not be put away and all goodness acquired, for divine righteousness had to be satisfied, sin paid for, and death overcome with justice.

Therefore, it was St. Paul's practice, when he preached God's grace in Christ, to refer at the same time to His suffering and blood, so that he might show how all good things have been given to us through Christ, but not without His unspeakable merit and cost, as he says, "God put Him forward as a throne of grace through faith, in His blood" (Romans 3 [:25]). Also: "I did not consider myself as knowing anything among you except Jesus Christ, the crucified," etc. (1 Corinthians 2 [:2]). Therefore, offering myrrh is confessing the great expense and pains that it cost Christ so that He became our Priest and King.

331. See, these are the three parts for which we should praise and confess Christ, His three works which He has shown us and still daily shows us until the Last Day. The order also is beautiful. The evangelist lifts gold to the highest place. For He could not be King over all things for our good if He had not first reconciled us to God and assured our conscience, so that He could rule and work in us in peace and quiet, as in His own kingdom. Therefore, He must also be Priest for us. But if He is to be Priest and reconcile us to God according to His priestly office, He had to satisfy God's righteousness for us. But there was no other satisfaction; He had to give Himself to death, die, and thus overcome sin with death in Himself. Thus through death He came to the priesthood, through His priesthood to the kingdom, and received the myrrh before the incense, and the incense before the gold.

Nevertheless, Scripture always mentions the kingdom first, then the priesthood, then His dying, as Psalm 110 also does, which first describes His kingdom: "The Lord said to my Lord: 'Sit at My right hand, until I make Your enemies Your footstool'" (Psalm 110 [:1]). Then it speaks of His priesthood as follows: "The Lord has sworn and will not change His mind: 'You are a priest forever after the manner of Melchizedek'" (Psalm 110 [:4]). Finally, he concludes with His torment: "He will drink from the brook by the way; therefore, He will lift up His head" (Psalm 110 [:7]). Thus one might also say: He will taste the myrrh, therefore He will become a Priest; if He is a Priest, therefore He will also be King—so that one follows from the other, one is the cause of the other, and they follow one upon another.

332. I let the matter rest with these simple and plain interpretations and commend the lofty consideration of these things to people with nothing else to do. We should give most attention to not separating any of these three confessions, but offering them together. And though Isaiah in the Epistle reading speaks of gold and incense only, and is silent about the myrrh, that may perhaps have happened because Christ's kingdom and priesthood have always been from the beginning of the world, as St. Paul says, "Jesus Christ is the same yesterday and today and forever" (Hebrews 13 [:8]). For all the saints have been redeemed from death and sin through Him and through faith in Him. Nevertheless, at that time the third part—His suffering, the myrrh—had not yet been accomplished, which properly belonged to the evangelist to announce after its fulfillment.

333. However, the Herodians and Papists have not only separated these three offerings but also destroyed them with an unspeakable abomination. Nevertheless, they retain the names and confess in words that Christ is King,

Priest, and the one who died for us, but with other contradictory words they deny all this with the heart and their whole life, and condemn it in the most abominable way. Let us begin to note this with the myrrh, since they teach that man without God's grace, of himself and from the natural power of his reason and free will, can make himself worthy and receptive of divine favor. What else is this than desiring, without Christ's blood and suffering, to satisfy divine righteousness by one's own activity, to silence His wrath and judgment, and to give the conscience peace? This is indeed nullifying Christ's blood and all His suffering, even His whole humanity with all that He does, regarding them as useless and trampling them underfoot, of which St. Paul speaks: "For it is impossible, in the case of those who have once been enlightened and have tasted the heavenly gift, and have shared in the Holy Spirit and have tasted the kind Word of God and the powers of the world to come—if they fall away and crucify once again the Son of God to themselves and hold Him up to contempt—to restore them again to repentance" (Hebrews 6 [:4–6]). For without Christ there is no grace or repentance, but only wrath. The Papists still teach [people] to seek and find grace apart from Him. Thus the offering of myrrh is entirely done away with.

334. Then the previous offering of incense must be nothing. For how shall Christ be their Priest and Mediator, if they are so good and pure that they do not need His blood and mediation, but mediate through themselves, and step before God themselves to obtain grace and life through their natural ability? By doing so, they confess and teach that natural ability is pure and good, and so Christ need not be Priest. Who would ever have believed that Christians would come to such a point when anyone would teach or hear such things, which are dreadful to think of?

335. But now we see that all universities together with the pope and his clergy teach and hold nothing else, and if anyone teaches differently, that must be heresy. Peter hit on this precisely when he says, "There will be false teachers among you who will deny the Lord who bought them" (2 Peter 2 [:1]). He does not say, "They will deny Christ," but "the Lord who bought them." It is as if he said: "They will confess Christ with words, but they will not hold that He bought them with His blood. Rather, without His blood they want to redeem themselves, and through their own natural power obtain God's grace, which Christ alone has bought for us all with His blood." This is what they mean [when they say] that it costs nothing to obtain God's grace. Therefore, it happens that they want to obtain it themselves and cannot tolerate [to hear that] Christ bought them.

336. Now, where Christ is not acknowledged as Priest, He is much less acknowledged as King. For they are in no way subject to Him, they are their own masters, that is, the devil's own household. Although they do not want

Him to rule over them and alone to work in them, He is nevertheless a King, Priest, and Redeemer over all creatures, with no thanks to them. See, thus you recognize that now is the time when St. Peter denies Christ three times [Matt. 26:69–75]. Oh, that they had heard the cock's crow, had again come to themselves, had acknowledged their fall, had cried bitterly, and went out from the house of Caiaphas, that is, out from the hellish assembly of the pope, where the fire of worldly love has been kindled and the pope's household stands around warming itself! For divine love has grown utterly cold in them. Let this suffice on the spiritual offerings. There follows:

> *And God commanded them in a dream not to return to Herod, and they departed to their own country by another way. [Matt. 2:12]*

337. That is the final conclusion: that we are to shun human teaching and not again fall into it when we once have been redeemed from it, just as these Magi, once free from Herod, do not come to him again. Thus I also say that we are to shun the law and teaching of the pope and all Papists, at [the risk of] God's displeasure and our soul's salvation, since we have already recognized the correct evangelical truth. For they only teach us to come away from God so that we follow our own reason and works. Thereby the work of God is hindered, who should and would give us and work in us all things, and wants us also to expect that of Him, not from ourselves.

338. Human teaching, however, causes us first to begin all works, to want to be the first ones to seek God. He can come afterward and look over what we have begun. Let me give you this example: Those who seem to be the best teachers of young people say to them that they ought gladly to pray and to go to church, to live in celibacy and be godly. However, they do not tell them where they are to begin to seek all this. It is just as if it were enough that they had instructed them that they ought to be godly. Likewise, when after this they are to marry or to enter orders, they think it is enough that they themselves have begun. They do not regard God in order to speak to Him about it. Afterward, when they have begun, then God is to come and look at what they have made and be pleased and satisfied with it.

339. Yes, they train the young people in such a way that a girl is ashamed to ask God for a boy, and a boy to ask God for a girl. They consider it foolish to ask God for such a thing; they must themselves rush in blindly. That is why it happens that marriage rarely goes well. Ought not a girl be taught with all earnestness to step up to God and to say with all confidence: "See, dear God, I am now of age to marry. Be my Father, and let me be Your child. Give me a godly boy, and graciously help me into the married estate. Or, if it pleases You, give me a spirit to remain celibate."

Thus also a boy is to ask for a girl, and not begin things himself, but ask God to begin and lay the first stone. These would be true children of God, who begin nothing before they talk to God about it, no matter how insignificant it may be. Thus Christ would remain our King, and all our works would be His works and would be done well. But human teachings do not tolerate this; they rush in blindly as if there were no God, and as if they had to do whatever is to be done well. See, learn from this example that all human teaching is misleading and against God.

340. There are, however, three ways to shun human teachings: First, they can be avoided by the conscience only and not by the deed. For instance, this happens when I confess, pray, and fast according to the pope's laws, not with the thought that I must do these things or it is sin if I do not, but that I do them willingly of myself without necessity, and could omit them, if I wanted to. Here the work of the human teaching does happen, but the conscience is free, regarding the doing like the not doing. It is not sin if it is neglected; it is not good if it is done—for it is not furnishing obedience, but doing its own good pleasure. This is the best way.

341. Thus the Magi are still in Herod's land, they also travel under his governance, but they regard him as nothing, do not come to him, and do not furnish him any obedience. Thus now, whoever is and works under the pope so that he keeps his law not out of obedience but of his own free will (insofar as it is not against God's Word), how, when, where, and as long as he pleases, is not harmed by them. But this is a higher understanding, which few people have, and it is received only through God's Spirit in the heart, just as these Magi received it secretly in their sleep. No one can be persuaded with words from the outside if the heart itself does not perceive it from heaven.

342. The second way is to shun [human teaching] with both the conscience and with words, as those do who completely trample it underfoot and do the opposite [of what human teaching says] with a glad, secure conscience. And this way is the most necessary and best for weak consciences, so that they are liberated and made strong, perfect, and free. This cannot be done well with words and conscience alone, unless someone takes action and shows them the opposite with examples, just as Christ did, who had His disciples not wash their hands, contrary to the law of the Pharisees [cf. Matt. 15:2]. Thus it would be good for whoever now delays the prescribed confession and fasting at certain times to show with examples that the pope's laws are foolishness and deception, and to do all of this voluntarily at another time.

343. The third way is to shun [human teachings] with deeds alone and not with the conscience, as those do who boldly delay [observing human teachings] and nevertheless believe that they do wrong in not observing it. And unfortunately the common people in the world have such a conscience.

For this reason St. Paul calls this time a dangerous time [cf. 2 Tim. 3:1]. For such consciences sin continually whether they observe or do not observe, and the pope with his law is the murderer of their souls and the cause of such danger and sin. If they observe, they do it against faith, which should be free from all human teaching. If they do not observe, they do it against their conscience which believes that it must be observed. It is necessary that they be well instructed in the free Christian faith, and that they put aside this false conscience, or if they are unable to do this, that we should bear with their weakness for a time (as St. Paul teaches, Romans 15 [:1]) and allow them to follow and observe their conscience together with faith, until they also have become strong.

344. See, this is the other way to travel home and not to return to Herod. For every attempt to become godly generally happens through human teaching and outward holiness, but we must come out of this into pure faith and not afterward again fall away from faith into works. Thus we surely come into our fatherland, from which we have come, that is, to God, by whom we have been created; and the end comes together with the beginning like a golden ring. God grant this through Christ, our King and Priest, who is blessed to all eternity.[38]

---

38 Because this sermon concludes that part of the *Church Postil* which Luther completed in 1522, the editions of 1522 and 1525 add: "Here we will stop for a while so that this book does not become too large and boring to read. I hope to have abundantly pictured the Christian life in these twelve Epistles and Gospels, so that the Christian has been sufficiently instructed in what is necessary for salvation. If only God would grant that my interpretation and that of all teachers perish and that every Christian himself would take for himself the pure Scripture and the clear Word of God! You can see from my babbling how immeasurably different God's Word is from human words, and how no man with all his words is able sufficiently to attain to and elucidate a single Word of God. It is an infinite Word which must be grasped and contemplated with a quiet spirit, as the psalmist says, 'I will hear what God Himself speaks in me' (Psalm [85:8]). No one but such a quiet, contemplating spirit grasps it. Whoever could arrive at this without glosses and interpretations would have no need of my glosses and those of other men; indeed, they would only be in his way. Therefore, go in, go in, dear Christians, and let my interpretation and that of other teachers be only a scaffold for the true building, so that we may grasp and taste the pure, clear Word of God and remain there, for there alone God dwells in Zion. Amen."

# GOSPEL FOR THE FIRST SUNDAY AFTER EPIPHANY

*Luke 2:41–52*

*[Jesus'] parents went to Jerusalem every year at the Feast of the Passover. And when He was twelve years old, they went up according to custom. And when the feast was ended, as they were returning, the boy Jesus stayed behind in Jerusalem. His parents did not know it, but supposing Him to be in the group they went a day's journey, but then they began to search for Him among their relatives and acquaintances, and when they did not find Him, they returned to Jerusalem, searching for Him. After three days they found Him in the temple, sitting among the teachers, listening to them and asking them questions. And all who heard Him were amazed at His understanding and His answers. And when His parents saw Him, they were astonished. And His mother said to Him, "Son, why have You treated us so? Behold, Your father and I have been searching for You in great distress." And He said to them, "Why were you looking for Me? Did you not know that I must be in My Father's house?" And they did not understand the saying that He spoke to them. And He went down with them and came to Nazareth and was submissive to them. And His mother treasured up all these things in her heart. And Jesus increased in wisdom and in stature and in favor with God and man.*

1. Previously, under the blindness of the papacy, people knew how to teach and preach nothing else about the dear saints of God except to praise and glorify them excessively, and to extol their miraculous life and works of high devotion and heavenly joy, just as if they had not also been human beings on earth and had never suffered and felt any human distress, infirmity, and weakness, and as if people could not praise them enough but had to make them even into wood and stone. Then they strengthened this with false and shameful lies and fables, just as if the saints were highly honored when people only spoke of their miracles and should only see and learn those examples which no one could attain to in life or take comfort from. Then [the idea] prevailed to make them even into idols and to teach people to call on them as intercessors, mediators, and helpers in need instead of on the Lord Christ, to the shameful slander and denial of our dear Savior and High Priest, Christ.

2. So people have imagined that they were highly extolling the mother of Christ and knew of no greater honor for her than to fill and overload her with

graces and gifts, as if she had never suffered any temptation and had never stumbled or blundered in understanding or in anything else. On the contrary, Scripture and this Gospel show us how God deals with His saints in a very contradictory and (as Psalm 4 [:3] says) wondrous way [cf. Ps. 17:7]; and that the more highly He blesses, honors, and exalts them, the deeper He puts them both into cross and suffering—yes, into dishonor, shame, and abandonment.

3. Human reason without a doubt would teach and advise God that He should not treat His own Son so shamefully and disgracefully (as a murderer and a thief) and have His blood shed. Rather, He should provide [for Him] so that all the angels have to carry Him on their hands, all kings and lords have to fall at His feet and render Him all honor [cf. Matt. 4:5–10]. That is human wisdom, which sees, strives for, and desires nothing other than what is honorable, high, and precious and, on the other hand, shuns and flees from nothing more than from dishonor, contempt, suffering, and misery. So God reverses things and does the opposite: He deals with His dearest Son in a more unfriendly and angry way (according to human understanding and appearance) than with anyone else on earth, as if He were not God's, or a man's, but the devil's own child. He acted in the same way with His dearest servant John the Baptist, of whom Christ Himself says that no one has arisen like him among all those born of women [Matt. 11:11]; He gave [John] the honor of having his neck danced off by a prostitute [Matt. 14:6–11]. That was quite a dishonorable and shameful death.

4. He dealt similarly with His dear mother, so that she also had to experience and learn how He rules His saints in a wondrous way. The Gospels sufficiently show that He very seldom let her see and experience what was glorious, precious, and joyous, but for the most part she had to experience only suffering and anxiety, as the aged and holy Simeon had previously prophesied to her [Luke 2:34–35], as a model for all Christendom. Besides, He commonly spoke harshly and crossly with her and even unkindly sent her away, as we will hear afterward.[1]

5. So this Gospel first presents the mother of Christ as an example of the cross and great suffering which God allows to happen to His saints. Although the holy Virgin was greatly blessed with all grace and was a beautiful temple of the Holy Spirit, chosen above all for the great honor of being the mother of the Son of God—and without a doubt also had the greatest pleasure and joy in her Child, more than any other mother, as it naturally had to be—yet God so rules her that she had to have not paradise, but great distress, pain, and sorrow because of Him. The first misery which happened to her was that she had to give birth at Bethlehem, in a strange place, where she did not have

---

1 See below, paragraph 27; paragraphs 32–34; and sermon for Second Sunday after Epiphany on John 2:1–11, paragraphs 14–19.

a room with her Child other than to lay Him down in a public stable [Luke 2:7]. The second misery was that after six weeks she had to flee with the Child into a foreign country, until He was seven years old [Matt. 2:13–15].[2] Without a doubt she had much more misery which is not described.

6. One of these [miseries], and not the least, is this one which He hung around her neck: when He was lost from her in the temple and had her search so long and not find Him. He made her so terrified and distressed that she could have despaired, as she also confesses and says, "Your father and I have been searching for You in distress" [Luke 2:48]. Let us think a little how she must have been in her mind and heart. Every father and mother understands the misery and sorrow when a child they love leaves them unexpectedly, and they know nothing other than that the child is lost. If it lasts only an hour, how great is the sorrow, crying, and lamenting—there is no comfort, no eating, drinking, sleeping, or resting—and such misery that they would prefer to be dead. How much greater is it when it lasts a whole day and night, or even longer, when each hour is not one hour but a hundred years long?

7. Now, on the other hand, look at this mother who loses her first and only Son—neither she nor anyone else has or can have a Son like this one—who is only her Son, and she alone is His mother, without a natural father. Indeed, He is the true, only-begotten Son of God, and she has been especially commanded and entrusted by God with being His mother, tending to Him with all diligence, caring for Him, and looking after Him. So far she had raised Him, not without much trouble and concern, and defended Him among strangers and enemies. Now that He has grown a little, and she has her greatest joy and comfort in Him, she suddenly loses Him, when she thought she had Him most securely and need not be concerned as before. She lost Him not for one or two hours, not for a day and a night, but for three whole days, so that she can think nothing else than that she has lost Him finally and forever. Who can say or think how her motherly heart was anxious and troubled for three whole days, so that it was a miracle that she could live with such sorrow.

8. The affliction and suffering which she had to endure did not come accidentally and without her fault, but her own conscience struck her so that she had to think that God had entrusted the Child to her and that no one other than she had to answer for Him. Therefore, storms burst and thundered in her heart: "You have lost the Child; that is nobody's fault but your own. You should have tended and looked after Him and not let Him leave you for a moment. What will you say to God, since you have not attended to Him better? You have deserved that with your sins, and you are unworthy to

---

2  The *Glossa ordinaria*, Matt. 2:14–15 (PL 114:76), states that Christ hid in Egypt for seven years.

be His mother; you have deserved that He should condemn you before all people, because He showed you such great honor and favor when He chose you as His mother."

9. Should not her heart have fallen down and fainted from anxiety for two reasons? First, because she lost her Son and cannot find Him again. Second—which was the most difficult, which other mothers do not experience and which makes this suffering the worst—because she must defend herself before God, who is the only true Father of this Child. She had to think that He would no longer have or recognize her as His mother, and so she was more miserable and troubled in heart than any other woman on earth.

She now felt in her heart that she was in the same sin as our first mother, Eve, who brought the whole human race to ruin. What are all sins compared to this one, that she has so badly neglected and lost this Child, God's Son and the world's Savior? If He remained lost, or—because He could not be lost—if God had taken Him back to Himself, then she would be the reason the work of redeeming the world was prevented. These and, without a doubt, many other thoughts occurred to her and greatly frightened her heart, since even without that the conscience is a tender thing, and she as a godly child had a very tender heart and conscience.

10. Here you see how God deals with this most holy person, the mother of His Son. Even though she had been most highly honored by Him—and so her joy in her Son had been immeasurably great, such as no mother ever had—yet God assailed her so that she was stripped of her honor and comfort to that point that she cannot say, "I am my Son's mother." Previously she had been exalted to heaven, but now she suddenly lies in deep hell and in such terror and sorrow that she could have despaired and died, and could even have wished that she had never seen the Child or heard of Him. And thus she committed a greater sin than had any other person.

11. God can deal with His saints so that He takes their joy and comfort away from them whenever He wants, and precisely by doing so frightens them most by that from which they had their greatest joy. On the other hand, He can give the greatest joy from what terrified us the most. The greatest joy of this holy Virgin had been that she was this Child's mother, but now she has no greater terror and sorrow than just from this Son. We have no greater terror than from sin and death; yet God can comfort us in this, so that we even dare to boast, as St. Paul says, that sin must serve to make grace even greater and more abundant, and death, overcome by Christ, causes us to desire to be dead and to die with joy [cf. Rom. 5:20–21; Phil. 1:21].

12. On the other hand, when God has given us an excellent faith, so that we live in the strong confidence that we have a gracious God through Christ, then we are in paradise. But before we expect it, things can change so that

God causes our hearts to fall down and we think that He wants to tear the Lord Christ out of our hearts. He can be so concealed from us that we can have no comfort in Him. Rather, the devil inserts terrible thoughts about Him into our hearts, so that our conscience feels that it has lost Him. Then [our conscience] wavers and trembles as if we had merited only wrath and hostility from Him by our sins.

13. Even if you have no obvious sins, the devil can make sin out of what is not sin, and then drive and frighten your heart so that it tortures itself with the thought: "Who knows if God wants to have you or wants Christ to favor you?" So here the dear mother doubts whether He wants her as His mother any longer, and feels in her conscience that with her inattention she had neglected and lost her Son—even though she was not guilty, since He was not lost. So the heart speaks in such temptations: "Yes, God has so far given you an excellent faith, but perhaps He will no longer give you any, which you have deserved with this or that [sin]."

14. This is the hardest and greatest temptation and suffering with which God sometimes assails and trains His dear saints, which people customarily call *desertio gratiae* ["the desertion of grace"], when the human heart feels only that God along with His grace has forsaken it and does not want it anymore, and wherever it turns it sees nothing but wrath and terror. But not everyone undergoes such a great temptation, and no one understands it unless he has experienced it. Only strong spirits can endure such blows.

15. Yet these examples are presented to us so that we may learn from them how to behave and find comfort in our temptations, and to be prepared if God should want to assail us sometime with these or similar great temptations, so that we do not despair so quickly because of them. This was written not for the sake of this Virgin, the mother of Christ, but for our sakes, so that we can have both doctrine and comfort.

16. For that reason there are more similar examples in Scripture of such great temptations of the great saints, such as, without doubt, the holy patriarch Jacob, of whom it is written that he wrestled the whole night with the angel (Genesis 32 [:24]).

Likewise also Joshua, to whom God had made the great and powerful promise that he would destroy all the heathen who opposed him (Joshua 7 [:10–12]). Moreover, He Himself admonished him and told him only to "be strong and courageous," for He Himself would be with him, etc. [Josh. 1:5–6]. On the basis of this promise, [Joshua] courageously went up, defeated them, and gained a great victory.

But what happened? Just when he had such courage and faith and in that faith had acquired and defeated the city of Jericho, it happened that they marshalled no more than three thousand men from all the people against the city of Ai, which they should have acquired and defeated. They were haughty and proud, because the city was small and the enemy were few. But when they arrived, it suddenly turned against them, they despaired, turned their backs to the enemy, and fled, though not more than thirty-two were killed [cf. Josh. 7:3–5]. Joshua himself lost courage, sank to the ground, lay on his face all day, and lamented and cried to God: "Alas, O Lord, why have You brought us over the Jordan to give us into the hands of our enemies? Oh, that we had never come here" [Josh. 7:6–7].

There on the ground lies the great and valiant hero with his faith, who still had God's Word so strongly that God must again raise him up. Who has now put him in such despair? No one, except God who, in order to test him, hides and thus takes away his heart, so that he would learn from experience what man is and can do when God takes away His hand.

17. Such suffering is exceedingly difficult and intolerable to [human] nature; therefore, the saints cry out and lament anxiously and miserably. There is much of that lament in the psalms, such as: "I said in my trembling: 'I am cast away from Your eyes' " (Psalm [31:22]), that is, "I knew and felt nothing else than that my heart said to me: 'God does not want you.' " If God did not preserve them by His power and help them out of it again, they would have had to sink even to hell, as the psalmist says, "If the Lord had not been my help, my soul would already have been in hell" (Psalm 94 [:17]).

18. Therefore, this holy Virgin was a true martyr during these three days, and they were much harder for her than the external pain and torture was for any other saint. She was in such anxiety because of her Son that she could not have suffered a more bitter hell. The greatest torture and grief, beyond all suffering, is when the heart is assailed and tormented. Other sufferings that happen to the body are all the more bearable; the heart can even be joyful in such things when it despises all external suffering, as we read about St. Agnes and other martyrs.[3] That is a beautiful division and only half the suffering, since it happens only to the body, but the heart and soul remain full of joy. But when the heart alone carries it, then only great and high spirits, with special grace and strength added, can endure it.

19. Why does God let His loved ones experience this? To be sure, it does not happen without reason, nor from wrath or hostility, but from great grace

---

3 Cf. *Lectures on Genesis* (1535–45/1544–54), LW 8:191. St. Agnes (d. ca. 304) was martyred at the age of thirteen after speaking of her espousal to Christ. For Luther's frequent references to Agatha and Agnes, especially to the cheerfulness with which they faced death, see the sermon of February 7, 1546, LW 58:449, and the sermon of February 15, 1546, LW 51:392; a fuller list of citations is given in LW 69:113–14 n. 439. On Luther's frequent references to SS. Agatha, Anastasia, Lucy, Vincent, and others as models of an evangelical confidence in death, see Margaret Arnold, "To Sweeten the Bitter Dance: The Virgin Martyrs in the Lutheran Reformation," *ARG* 104 (2013).

and kindness. He wants to show us how He deals with us in a friendly and fatherly way in all things, and how faithfully He cares for His own people and guides them so that their faith is always trained more and more and becomes stronger and stronger. But He does this especially for the following reasons:

20. First, that He may preserve His people against arrogance, so that great saints, who have especially high grace and gifts from God, may not fall for it and trust in themselves. If they were always strong in spirit, and felt nothing other than only joy and pleasantness, they might finally fall into the devil's own pride, which despises God and relies on itself. Therefore, they must be seasoned and perplexed so that they do not always feel only strength of spirit, but from time to time their faith should struggle and their hearts be afraid, so that they may see what they are and have to confess that they can do nothing if God does not preserve them by His pure grace. So He keeps them in humility and knowledge of themselves, so that they do not become proud or secure in their faith and holiness, as it happened to St. Peter, when he thought he could lay down his life for Christ [John 13:37].

21. The prophet David confesses that he, too, had to learn the same thing: "I said in my prosperity: 'I shall never be defeated.' But when You hid Your face, I was terrified" (Psalm 30 [:6–7]). St. Paul laments the great suffering he endured in Asia when he says: "We do not want you to be ignorant, dear brothers, of the affliction we encountered in Asia. We were so utterly burdened beyond our strength that we gave up on life itself, and we had concluded that we had to die. But that happened so that we would not place our trust on ourselves but on God, who raises the dead" (2 Corinthians 1 [:8–9]). He says that a thorn was given him in the flesh, a messenger of Satan to beat him with fists, to keep him from becoming conceited because of the high revelation. God did not want to take that away from him, even though he pleaded three times about it, but he had to cling to the comfort of God's words that he should be satisfied with His grace and through it overcome his weakness (2 Corinthians 12 [:7–9]). Therefore, this testing of the saints is necessary, and even more necessary than eating and drinking, so that they may remain in fear and humility and learn to cling only to God's grace.

22. Second, God lets them experience this as an example for others, both to alarm the secure and to comfort the fearful and alarmed. The wicked and impenitent can see and learn from this to amend their ways and guard against sin, because they have seen how God deals with the saints so that they are in such anxiety that they feel nothing but wrath and hostility, and fall into such alarm as if they had committed the worst sin a person could commit.

So here the mother of Christ had to struggle with a heavy conscience into the third day, a conscience which accused her of losing God His dear Son, a sin the like of which no one on earth had committed, and so she feared nothing except the Most High. Yet it was truly not such a sin, and there was no wrath or hostility there.

23. If such heavy and almost unbearable alarm and anxiety overtakes godly hearts, what will become of the others who wickedly and securely persist in real sins, and who full well merit and amass God's wrath? How will they be able to stand when anxiety suddenly strikes them, which can happen at any hour?

24. On the other hand, such examples should serve to comfort alarmed and anxious consciences, when they see that God has assailed not only them but also the highest saints and caused them to suffer the same trials and alarm. If we had no examples in Scripture that this happened to the saints, then we could not endure it, and the fearful conscience would always lament: "I am the only one stuck in such suffering. When did God have the godly and the saints tested in this way? Therefore, this must be a sign that God does not want me." But now that we see and hear that God has dealt with all high saints in this way and did not spare His own mother, we have the doctrine and consolation not to despair in such suffering, but to keep still and wait until He helps us out of it, just as He has helped all His dear saints.

25. Third, we come to the true reason why God especially does this, namely, because He wants to teach His saints how to seek true comfort and prepare themselves to find and keep Christ. The main point in this Gospel lesson is to teach us how and where we are to seek and find Christ. As the text says, Mary and Joseph sought the Child Jesus for three days, and yet did not find Him, neither in the city of Jerusalem nor among their friends and acquaintances [Luke 2:44–45], until at length they came into the temple, where He sat among the teachers and where the Scriptures and God's Word are studied [Luke 2:46]. When they were astonished and began to lament how they had searched for Him in great distress [Luke 2:48], He answered them:

*"Why were you looking for Me? Do you not know that I must be in that which is My Father's?" [Luke 2:49]*

26. What does He mean: "I must be in that which is My Father's"? Do not all creatures belong to the Father? Everything is His; but He gave us the creatures for our use, so that we should manage them in our earthly life as we know how. But one thing He has reserved for Himself, which is called holy and God's own, which we must especially receive from Him. That is His holy Word, through which He rules hearts and consciences and sanctifies and saves them. Therefore, the temple is also called His holy place or His holy dwelling, because He is present and heard there through His Word. So Christ is in that which is His Father's when He speaks with us through His Word and by means of it brings us to the Father.

27. For that reason He rebukes His parents for running around and seeking Him in earthly and human things and affairs, among acquaintances and friends, and not thinking that He must be in that which is His Father's. By doing this, He wants to point out that His government and the whole Christian life exists only in the Word and in faith, not in other external things (such as the external, apparent holiness of Judaism), nor in temporal and worldly life or government. In short, He will not let Himself be found among friends or acquaintances, or in anything outside of the ministry of the Word. He does not want to be worldly, nor to be in that which is worldly, but in that which is His Father's, as He has always shown ever since His birth and in His entire life. He was certainly in the world, but He did not cling to the world, as He also said to Pilate: "My kingdom is not of this world" [John 18:36]. He was with friends and acquaintances and whomever He came to, but He did not take an interest in any of that whole worldly life, except that He traveled as a guest through it and used it for the necessities of His body. He attended only to that which is His Father's (that is, the Word's). There He wants to be found. There He must be sought by whoever wants to meet Him truly.

28. That is what I have said, that God will not tolerate that we should rely on anything else or cling with our hearts to something which is not Christ in His Word, no matter how holy and full of the Spirit it might be. Faith has no other ground on which it can stand. Therefore, the mother of Christ and Joseph experience that their wisdom, thoughts, and hope must fail and everything be lost when they seek Him for a long time from one place to another. They do not seek Him as they should, but as flesh and blood are accustomed, which always gape at some other comfort than the Word. It always wants to have something which it can see and feel, and to which it can cling with its thinking and reason.

29. Therefore, God has them sink and go astray, so that they must learn that all comfort in flesh and blood, in people and all creatures, is nothing and of no help or aid, unless it grasps the Word. Here everything must be abandoned: friends, acquaintances, the whole city of Jerusalem, all knowledge, understanding, and whatever they and all people are. All of that gives and helps to no true comfort, until people see Him in the temple, where He is in that which is His Father's. There He is certainly found, and the heart again obtains joy; otherwise it would have to remain hopeless from itself and all creatures.

30. So when God lets such a great temptation come to us, we should learn not to follow our own thoughts and human counsel, which send us here and there, to ourselves and others, but we should realize that we must seek Christ in that which is His Father's, that is, that we cling simply and alone to the Word of the Gospel, which truly shows us Christ and helps us to know

Him. If you learn this in all spiritual temptations, then you will truly comfort others or yourself and say with Christ: "Why do you run here and there and torture yourself with anxious and sorrowful thoughts, as if God had no more grace for you and as if there were no Christ to be found? Why will you not be satisfied unless you find Him by yourself and feel holy and without sin? Nothing will come from that; it is merely lost effort and labor."

Do you not know that Christ will not be present or let Himself be found except in that which is His Father's, and not in what you or all other people are or have? There is [certainly] no fault in Christ and His grace; He is not and never will be lost and can always be found. But the fault is in you when you do not seek Him correctly where He is to be sought, because you judge according to your senses and think you can grasp Him with your thoughts. You must come not where your or anyone's business and government are, but where God's is, namely, in His Word. There you will meet Him, and hear and see that there is no wrath or hostility there, as you feared and dreaded, but pure grace and heartfelt love for you. He speaks the most precious and best things as a friendly and dear Mediator for you to the Father. He does not send such temptations to you to push you away from Him, but so that you will learn to know Him all the better, cling all the more firmly to His Word, and rebuke your lack of understanding, so that you have to experience how loving and faithful He is to you.

31. That is the beautiful doctrine of this Gospel: how we are correctly to seek and find Christ. It shows the real comfort which makes the sorrowful conscience content, so that all terror and anxiety fall away and the heart again rejoices and becomes newborn. But [the heart] first becomes heavy before it comes to this point and grasps these things. It must first rush off and experience what it means that everything is lost and that Christ is sought in vain. Finally, there is no help left but, apart from yourself and all human comfort, to surrender only to the Word. In other bodily misfortunes and necessities you can seek comfort in the things that are ours, such as gold, possessions, friends, and acquaintances. But here, in these matters, you must have a different way, which is not human but God's own way, namely, the Word, through which He alone deals with us and we can deal with Him. But it is especially significant that the evangelist says:

*They did not understand the word that He spoke with them. [Luke 2:50]*

32. This shuts the mouths of vain babblers who too highly exalt the holy Virgin Mary and other saints as if they knew everything and could not err. In this place you hear that they err and blunder, not only by seeking Christ everywhere and not knowing where to find Him until they happen to come into the temple, but also by not understanding these words, with which He

rebukes their lack of understanding and says to them: "Did you not know that I must be in that which is My Father's?" [Luke 2:49]. The evangelist has intentionally pointed this out and will not conceal it, so that we will not allow such lying speech from foolish, inexperienced, and inflated teachers of works, who brag about the saints and even make them into idols.

33. The holy Virgin does not need such false, fictitious praise. God led her so that He concealed much from her, and then daily let her experience what she had not previously known, in order to keep her humble, so that she would not think herself better than others. The praise and glory she had were enough, in that He guided and sustained her with His grace and endowed her with many high gifts above others. And yet she, like others, had to learn and advance daily through all kinds of temptations and sorrows.

34. Such examples are very useful and necessary to show us that even in the saints, who are God's children and highly favored above others, weakness still remains, so that they often err and do wrong, have all kinds of infirmities, and sometimes even stumble coarsely—not intentionally or wantonly, but out of weakness or lack of understanding, as we see in the apostles now and then in the Gospel. We should learn not to build on any person or to rely on ourselves, but, as this Gospel teaches, to cling only to God's Word, and to take comfort from these examples so that we do not despair because of them, even though we are still weak and foolish. But we are not to become insolent and secure in this grace, as the proud, false saints do.

35. In summary, you have in this Gospel a strong example with which to knock down the common outcry of both the mad saints and the great know-it-alls—which they have so far promoted and still do promote, so that they can remain only with their worthless inventions against God's Word— namely, that they claim we must cling to the writings and doctrine of the holy fathers and to the decrees and resolutions of the church and councils, for (they say) they had the Holy Spirit and therefore cannot err, etc.

By doing so, they are trying to take us away from Scripture and the certain place to which Christ Himself points—where He can certainly be found—to uncertain ways, so that what happened to Mary, His mother, and to Joseph may also happen to us: that we seek Christ everywhere and find Him nowhere, unless we finally come to that place where He is. Until now this has been promoted powerfully in Christendom through the accursed government of the pope, who has hindered people from either seeking or finding Christ in Scripture, both with teaching and commanding, threatening and punishing.

36. As was stated above in the postil on the previous Gospel,[4] they have filled the world with a threefold doctrine by which people are led away from

---

4  See sermon for Day of the Wise Men (Epiphany) on Matt. 2:1–12.

God's Word. The first [doctrine] was very coarse, written by St. Thomas [Aquinas] (if he indeed is a saint) and other Scholastics, which comes from heathen learning and natural reason, about which they said: "The light of nature is just like a beautiful and bright tablet, and Scripture is like the sun shining on this tablet, causing it to glitter all the more beautifully. So the divine light also shines on the light of nature and illumines it."

With this comparison, they have brought heathen doctrine into Christendom. Afterward the universities taught and promoted this so much that they themselves even reversed the comparison, so that they wanted the art and doctrine of reason and of Aristotle to have illumined Scripture. Yet Scripture is the one true light, without which all the light of reason is simply darkness in divine things and in the articles of faith, as we have often said before.[5]

37. Second, they have filled the whole world full of human teachings and commands and of the so-called decrees and commands of the church about fasting, celebrating, praying, singing, clothing, monkery, etc., with which the whole swarm of the pope and the books of the Summists[6] are full; they have given the people hope of getting to heaven through such things. That has burst in like a flood and drowned the world; all consciences have been ensnared and captured by it, so that almost no one was saved from these jaws of hell. On this basis they have brought in the examples and lying legends of the saints, and confirmed them by the popes and councils, so that people had to regard them as equal to an article of faith. Therefore, like crazy people, they cry out without ceasing: "Ah, the holy councils have decided this, the church has commanded it, it has been done for a long time," etc.

38. Third, besides these two doctrines, they have also ignored Holy Scripture, but in such a way as to connect it to the writings and expositions of some of the fathers. Yet they have done this only so far as it pleased the pope and was not against his law. Thus no one can handle it otherwise than as it pleases the pope, who alone has the right to interpret Scripture, and everyone must comply with his knowledge and judgment. Nevertheless, they honor the fathers with words [by saying] that their interpretation and explanation must be followed. All the world has fallen into this and accepted all that the fathers said, as if they could not err. Again they cry out: "Ah, how should

---

5 Cf. sermon for Third Day of Christmas on John 1:1–14, paragraphs 56–58.

6 "Summists" [*Summisten*; Latin *Summistae*] are writers of summaries of theology or of casuistry, such as Angelus de Clavasio (1411–95), *Summa angelica de casibus Conscientiae* (Augsburg/Strassburg: Johann Rynmann/Johann Knobloch d. Ä, 1509); Raynerius de Pisis (d. ca. 1348), *Pantheologia sive Summa universae theologiae* ([Augsburg: Günther Zainer,] 1474); and, most famously, Thomas Aquinas, *Summa Theologica* (*ST*).

so many saints, scholars, and highly intelligent people not have understood the Scriptures?"

39. As was said, this should be answered from this Gospel. Whether they are called holy, learned, fathers, councils, or whatever else—even if they were Mary, Joseph, and all the saints together—it does not for that reason follow that they could not have erred and been wrong. Here we find that the mother of Christ, who had great understanding and enlightenment, was ignorant, since she did not think or know where to find Christ, and for that reason was rebuked by Him because she did not know what she should have known. If she blundered and through her ignorance came into such anxiety and sorrow that she even thought she had lost Christ, is it any wonder that other saints have often erred and stumbled when they went outside of Scripture and followed their own thoughts or dragged them into Scripture?

40. Therefore, it is wrong when people assert that we must believe and cling to what the councils have decided or to what the holy fathers have taught or written, for all these can and may be in error. Rather, people must point to a certain place where Christ is and wants to be found, namely, where He Himself points out and says that He must be in that which is His Father's.

41. It would be good if we Christians brought such examples from the Gospel into common usage, and even took a proverb from them against all teachings and whatever people produce which is not God's Word, and said that people should seek Christ not among friends and acquaintances, nor in anything which belongs to human beings, no matter how godly, holy, or great they may be. The mother of Christ herself erred and was wrong, since she did not know or understand this.

42. Therefore, the conscience can rely on no saint or creature apart from Christ alone. I will allow you to exalt and extol reason and the natural light as highly as you wish, but I reserve for myself the right not to depend on them. The holy fathers and councils have taught, complied with, decreed, and ordered whatever they wanted. I let all of that be as it is, but I will not be captured by them, as if I had to cling to such things or depend on them. In summary, let all these things have value and remain in esteem in our human affairs, where people arrange whatever and however they want. But we are not to meddle with Christ, that is, with the comfort of the conscience, or seek it there. Let the other things be for when we are among friends and acquaintances and deal with them, for they do not concern the conscience, but the external human life in the world.

43. If our Papists had been willing to grant this, as God's Word teaches them, then we would have been one with them for a long time, and would have been content that they establish and order whatever pleased them in such human affairs. But we would have retained the freedom of having to

cling to these things no further than it pleased us, not from necessity or as if they had any value before God. However, they obviously refused to do that, but made the addition that people are obliged to observe what they do as necessary for salvation. They call these things the commands of the Christian church, and they make it into a mortal sin if someone does not keep them. That is something we shall neither do nor tolerate.

44. "Yes," they say, "the church, the holy fathers, and the councils have decided and decreed many things in disputed articles against the heretics, which people have received everywhere, which everyone must believe and hold. Therefore, what the general church and councils have decided in other matters must also be binding."

45. Answer: Here again they must grant us free judgment, so that we must be bound not to everything without exception which was established by councils or taught by the fathers, but maintain this distinction: If they have established and decided anything according to God's Word, we will accept that, not for their sake but for the sake of the Word, on which they rely and to which they point us. Then they are not acting as men, but they are leading us to that which is God's. Then they are not among friends and acquaintances, but they sit among those who listen to Christ and consult with Him in Scripture. Then we rightly and gladly do them the honor of listening to them.

But when they go beyond this and apart from this rule establish something about other things, not from God's Word but according to their own opinion, this does not concern the conscience at all. Therefore, let these be human things to which we must not be bound or hold, as if Christian faith and life consisted in them. Rather, as St. Augustine has correctly said: *Totum hoc genus habet liberas observationes*, that is, we are free to keep or to omit whatever is of such things.

46. You say further: "Yes, the church and the fathers had the Holy Spirit, who did not let them err." That can easily be answered from what has been said: No matter how holy the church or the councils may be, they had no more of the Holy Spirit than Mary, the mother of Christ, who was also a member [of the Church], even at that time the most distinguished part of the Church. Even though she had been sanctified by the Holy Spirit, yet He sometimes let her err, even in the high matters of faith. For that reason it does not follow that the saints who have the Spirit cannot err and that everything they say must be correct. There still remains much weakness and ignorance even among the highest people. For that reason we must not judge doctrine and the matters of faith which come from the Holy Spirit according to personal holiness, for that can all be wrong. Rather, here you must come where God's Word is, for that is certain and does not err; there you certainly find

Christ and the Holy Spirit; there you can take your stand and remain against sin, death, and the devil.

47. Elsewhere in Scripture we have examples of when even the saints and the great multitude called "the church" erred, especially when, soon after the ascension of Christ—not more than eighteen years—the apostles and the multitude of those who were Christians came together at Jerusalem (Acts 15). Then some believers who were among the most distinguished and learned belonging to the party of the Pharisees rose up and said that the Gentiles should be compelled to be circumcised and to keep the Law of Moses, and they drew nearly the whole multitude to their viewpoint [Acts 15:5]. Then Peter, Paul, Barnabas, and James alone stood up, refuted them, and proved from Scripture that the Gentiles should be left unburdened by the imposition of the Law, because without it God had previously given them the Holy Spirit through the preaching of the Gospel, just as much as to the Jews [Acts 15:7–21].

There were many Christians who believed when the Church was still young and in her best condition, and yet all of them were in error, since they thought that the Law of Moses was necessary for salvation, except these three or four apostles, so that if they had not prevented it, an erroneous article and command against Christ would have been established and confirmed.

Likewise, St. Peter afterward, even though he himself had taught this, stumbled with Barnabas on the same article, so that they acted hypocritically with the Jews who would not eat with the Gentiles, and in that way gave offense to the Gentiles in the use of their freedom, so that St. Paul had to call them to account and rebuke them publicly, as he says in Galatians 2 [:11–14].

Therefore, let us learn from this example to be prudent in the matters that concern faith and Christ. Let us not allow ourselves to be pointed to people, but to remain only with the Word and to keep the rule St. Paul gives, that even if an angel from heaven should come and preach the Gospel differently, let him be accursed (Galatians 1 [:8]). We should remain with the fact that Christ can be found nowhere except in that which is God's.

48. We have also heard this above in many figures and examples, such as in the Gospel for Christmas (Luke 2 [:12]),[7] where the angel gave the shepherds no other sign by which they could find Christ than the manger (where they found Him lying) and the swaddling clothes (in which He was wrapped up), not at His mother's breasts or on her lap, which would have been more impressive. That is, God does not want to point us to any saint or other person, but to the mere word or Scripture, in which Christ is wrapped up as in cloths or swaddling, and in the poor manger (that is, the preaching

---

7  See sermon for Christmas Day on Luke 2:1–14.

of the Gospel), which is not at all impressive and serves no purpose at all except for the animals to take their feed from it.

Likewise, we have also heard that even though the holy patriarch Simeon had been promised by God that he would not die until he had seen Christ, he did not see Him until at the impulse of the Holy Spirit he came to the temple.[8] So also when the Wise Men from the East came to Jerusalem and no longer saw the star, they heard no other sign about where Christ was born and could be found than the Scriptures of the prophet Micah.[9] That is the chief point and principal doctrine of this Gospel. Finally, it is also significant that the evangelist says:

*His mother retained all these things in her heart. [Luke 2:51]*

49. This is also said for our admonition, so that we also endeavor to retain God's Word in our hearts, as the dear Virgin did. When she saw that she had erred and had not understood, since she had learned her lesson, she became all the more diligent to impress on her heart what she heard from Christ and to retain it there.

Again, she gives us an example that we should cling to the Word above all things and not let it out of our hearts, but always be occupied with it, and learn to strengthen, comfort, and improve ourselves in it, which is very necessary. When things become serious and we are assailed or tested, then it is soon forgotten or falls away, even among those who are diligent.

50. Whatever else could be said about this Gospel—such as how Christ went back home with His parents and was obedient and subject to them [Luke 2:51], etc.—is easily found. Likewise, how we are to understand that Christ increased in wisdom and in favor [Luke 2:52] was presented in the Gospel for the previous Sunday.[10]

8  See sermon for Sunday after Christmas on Luke 2:33–40.

9  See sermon for Day of the Wise Men (Epiphany) on Matt. 2:1–12.

10  See sermon for Sunday after Christmas on Luke 2:33–40, paragraphs 118–25.

# GOSPEL FOR THE SECOND SUNDAY AFTER EPIPHANY

*John 2:1–11*

*On the third day there was a wedding at Cana in Galilee, and the mother of Jesus was there. Jesus also was invited to the wedding with His disciples. When the wine ran out, the mother of Jesus said to Him, "They have no wine." And Jesus said to her, "Woman, what does this have to do with Me? My hour has not yet come." His mother said to the servants, "Do whatever He tells you." Now there were six stone water jars there for the Jewish rites of purification, each holding twenty or thirty gallons. Jesus said to the servants, "Fill the jars with water." And they filled them up to the brim. And He said to them, "Now draw some out and take it to the master of the feast." So they took it. When the master of the feast tasted the water now become wine, and did not know where it came from (though the servants who had drawn the water knew), the master of the feast called the bridegroom and said to him, "Everyone serves the good wine first, and when people have drunk freely, then the poor wine. But you have kept the good wine until now." This, the first of His signs, Jesus did at Cana in Galilee, and manifested His glory. And His disciples believed in Him.*

1. Enough has been written previously about marriage, so that we can let that be for now. We want to treat three points in this Gospel reading: first, the comfort married people have in their marriage from this history; second, the faith and love shown in this Gospel reading; third, the spiritual significance of this wedding.

## [COMFORT FOR MARRIED PEOPLE]

2. First, this estate is highly honored in that Christ Himself went to this wedding with His mother and disciples [John 2:2]. Moreover, His mother was there as the wedding planner, so that it seems that they were her poor friends or neighbors, and that she had to act as the mother of the bride; thus it was no more than a wedding, and not a pageant. Christ lived up to His teaching that He did not come to the rich, but to the poor [cf. Luke 4:18]; or when He does go to the great and the rich, He does it in such a way that He rebukes and scolds, so that He comes away from them in disgrace, meriting

not much thanks from them, to say nothing of honoring them with a miracle, as He does here.

3. The second honor is that He gives this poor wedding good wine with a great miracle [John 2:10], and becomes the bride's chief cupbearer; perhaps He otherwise had no money or present to give. He never showed such honor to the Pharisees. By doing this, He confirms that marriage is God's work and arrangement. No matter how much people want to despise it and regard it as insignificant, God nonetheless acknowledges His own work and loves it. Also our Caiaphas has himself often said and preached that marriage was the only estate instituted by God. Who, then, instituted the other estates? Without a doubt not God, but the devil by means of men! They still avoid, reject, and slander this [estate], and are so holy that they not only do not themselves marry—though they need it and ought to marry—but they also pursue an excessive holiness in that they do not want to be at any wedding.[1] So they are much holier than Christ Himself who went to the wedding as an unholy sinner.

4. Because marriage has the foundation and consolation that it was instituted by God and that God loves it [cf. Gen. 1:28; 2:22–24; Matt. 19:6], and that Christ Himself so honors and comforts it, it ought to be very dear to everyone and treasured in their heart, because they are certain that it is the estate God loves. Thus they can cheerfully endure everything that is difficult in it, even if it were ten times more difficult. That is why there is so much trouble and displeasure in marriage according to the outward man, because it must happen that everything which is God's Word and work must be troublesome, bitter, and difficult to the outward man, even if it is otherwise blessed.

For that reason [marriage] is also an estate which promotes faith in God and trains us to love our neighbor through all kinds of trouble, work, displeasure, cross, and all kinds of adversity. These things follow anything that is God's Word and work. The chaste fornicators, the holy onanists,[2] and the Sodomites are spared all of this, and serve God apart from God's estate by their own activity.

5. Christ shows that He wants to supply what is lacking in marriage by giving wine when it ran out, and making it out of water. It is as if He would say: "Do you have to drink water, that is, suffer affliction outwardly, which makes things bitter for you? Well, I will make it sweet for you and change the water into wine, so that your affliction will be your joy and delight. I will not

---

1 Members of the clergy were to avoid attending wedding feasts; see James A. Brundage, *Law, Sex, and Christian Society in Medieval Europe* (Chicago: University of Chicago Press, 1987), p. 191.

2 *Weichlinge*, Luther's translation for μαλακοὶ in 1 Cor. 6:9 (WA DB 7:100–101), where he understands it to mean men who practice onanism.

do this by taking the water away or having it poured out; it is to remain, but I will first add to it and make it full to the brim. I will not rid Christian marriage of affliction, but rather load it up." It happens in a wondrous way, so that no one understands it except those who experience it, namely, in this way:

6. God's Word will do it, by which all things are made, preserved, and changed. It is the Word of God which makes your water into wine and your bitter marriage into a delight. The heathen and unbelievers do not know that God created marriage (Genesis 2 [:24; 1:28]), and so their water remains water and never becomes wine. [God says:] "They do not perceive My good pleasure and delight in married life. If they did perceive it, they would have so much delight in My good-pleasure that they would not notice even the half of their affliction; they would notice it only outwardly and not inwardly. That would be the way to make wine out of water, to drown My good-pleasure into your displeasure in itself, and make good-pleasure out of it. But no one shows or gives to you My good-pleasure except My words: 'God saw everything that He had made, and it pleased Him very much' (Genesis 1 [:31])."

7. Here Christ also lets us see that He has no displeasure at the cost of the wedding nor with anything that pertains to the wedding, such as decorations, happiness, eating and drinking, as the usage and customs of the land require. These things can seem to be excessive and wasted expense and a worldly matter. [He has no displeasure with them], as long as they are in moderation and correspond to a wedding. The bride and groom must indeed be adorned; the guests must eat and drink, if they are to be happy. All this expense and behavior can be done with a good conscience, for Scripture now and again reports this, and it is written in the Gospel about bridal attire [Rev. 21:2], the wedding garment [Matt. 22:11], guests, and conviviality at weddings. Likewise, Abraham's servant gave Rebekah, the bride of Isaac, and her brothers "jewelry of silver and of gold" (Genesis 24 [:53]). No one should pay attention to the sour-faced hypocrites and self-made saints who are pleased with nothing but what they themselves do and teach, and will not endure a maiden wearing a garland or adorning herself a little.

8. God is unconcerned about such external things, as long as faith and love remain, and (as already said[3]) as long as it is in moderation and proper for each estate. This wedding, though it was poor and small, still had three tables, which is indicated by the word *architriclinus*, that "the master of the feast" [John 2:8] had three tables to provide for. Moreover, the groom did not himself attend to this, but had servants; and then, too, they had [to provide] wine to drink. All of that, if people did not want total poverty to follow, could have been omitted, as it sometimes happens among us. So also the guests did not merely quench their thirst with the wine, [but they drank more], for the

---

3 See above, paragraph 7.

master of the feast speaks about how people should give the good wine first, and then, when they were drunk, the poor wine [John 2:10].

Christ lets all this go, and we should also let it go and not make it a matter of conscience. They are not for that reason of the devil, if some drank a little more of the wine beyond [quenching their] thirst and became cheerful; otherwise, you would have to blame Christ for having given a cause [for sin] with His gift, which His mother asked for, so that both Christ and His mother are sinners, if the sour-faced saints should be the judges.

9. But the excess practiced at our time is not eating and drinking, but gorging and guzzling, carousing and boozing. They act as if it were a mark of skill or of strength to do a lot of gorging and guzzling, in which people do not seek to become cheerful but to be raving drunk. But these are pigs, not people. Christ would not give wine to them nor come to them. So also their clothing is not selected for the wedding, but for their own show and ostentation, as if those were the best and the strongest who wore gold and silver and pearls and used up much silk and other cloth, which even donkeys and sticks could do.

10. What, then, is moderation? Reason should teach that and take examples from other countries and cities where there is not such excess and ostentation. If I may give my opinion, I think that a farmer is well adorned when he wears to the wedding clothes twice as good as he daily wears at his work; a townsman, the same; a nobleman should be twice as well adorned as a citizen; a count, twice as well as a nobleman; a prince, twice as well as a count; and so on. So also eating and drinking and inviting guests should be guided by their social position, and the conviviality should be directed toward joy, not toward becoming raving drunk.

11. Is it a sin to sing and dance at a wedding, since people say that much sin comes from dancing? I do not know whether there was dancing among the Jews; but since it is the custom of the country, just as is inviting guests, decorating, eating and drinking, and being cheerful, I do not know that I should condemn it, except its excess when it is immodest or excessive. It is not the fault of dancing alone that there is sin, since that also happens at table or in the churches, just as it is not the fault of eating and drinking that some become pigs about it. Where [dancing] is modest, I leave to weddings their rights and usages; go on dancing. Faith and love are not danced away or sat away,[4] as long as you are modest and moderate in them. Young children dance without sin; do the same and become a child, then dancing will not harm you. Otherwise, if dancing were a sin in itself, then we must not permit children to dance. This is enough about weddings.

---

4  That is, by sitting at table to eat and drink.

## [Faith and Love]

12. Second, when we return to the Gospel, we see here the example of love in Christ and His mother. The mother serves as the mother of the family; Christ honors the household with His presence, miracle, and gift. All of that occurred for the good of the groom, the bride, and the guests, as is the nature of love and its works. Thus Christ invites all hearts to rely on Him as the one ready to help everyone, even in temporal things, and not to ignore them, so that all who believe in Him should not suffer any needs, whether temporal or eternal. Water must first become wine, and all creatures be transformed and changed into that thing His believer needs. Whoever believes must have enough, and no one can prevent it.

13. But the example of faith is even more wonderful in this Gospel. [Christ] lets it become an emergency, when the lack was felt by all and there was no other remedy or help. This shows how divine grace is. No one can partake of it who still has enough and has not yet felt his lack. [Grace] does not feed the full and satisfied, but the hungry, as we have often said. Whoever is still wise, strong, and godly, and finds something good in himself, and is not yet a poor, miserable, sick sinner and fool cannot come to the Lord Christ nor obtain grace.

14. But where the lack is felt, He goes ahead and does not immediately give what we need and want, but delays and tests our faith and trust, as He does here. What is still more bitter, He acts as if He does not at all want [to help], but speaks harshly and sternly. We can see this in His mother: she noticed the lack and complained to Him about it, desiring help and remedy from Him with a humble and modest request. She does not say, "Dear Son, make us some wine," but "They have no wine" [John 2:3]. Thus she only touches on His kindness, for which she completely relied on Him. It is as if she would say: "He is so good and gracious that He does not need my request; I will only point out to Him what is lacking, and then He will of Himself do more than was asked." That is the way faith thinks and pictures God's kindness, and does not doubt that it is so; therefore, it dares to ask and present its need.

15. But look at how harshly He dismisses the humble request of His mother, who speaks to Him with such great confidence [cf. John 2:4]. Now look at how faith is; what does it have in His presence? Absolutely nothing and darkness. It feels the lack but sees no help anywhere; in addition, God has become unfamiliar and angry at it, not recognizing it, so that absolutely nothing remains. It is the same as when the conscience feels sin and the lack of righteousness; or in the death throes, when we feel the lack of life; or in the fear of hell, when eternal salvation is lacking. Then there is certainly a humble longing and knocking [Matt. 7:7], asking and seeking to be free from

sin, death, and anguish. Then He acts as if now, first, there are truly sins, as if death remains and hell does not cease. He acts the same way toward His mother; by refusing, He makes the lack greater and more difficult than it was before she spoke to Him about it. Now it seems that it is completely lost, since the only comfort she was relying on for this lack is also gone.

16. Here her faith is in a real battle. Look at what His mother does and so teaches us. However harsh His words sound, however unkind He appears to be, in her heart she understands all of that not as anger or as against His kindness, but continues to think that He is kind, and does not let her hope be taken away by this blow. She will not disgrace Him in her heart and regard Him as unkind and ungracious, as do those who are without faith and fall away at the first attack and regard God no further than they perceive, like a horse and a mule (Psalm 32 [:9]). If [Christ's] mother had allowed those harsh words to frighten her, she would have gone away silently and upset; but instead she ordered the servants to do what He would tell them [John 2:5], and so proves that she has overcome the blow and still expects nothing but kindness from Him.

17. What kind of a hellish attack do you think it is, when the blow comes to a man in his distress, especially in the highest distress of conscience, that he feels that God is saying to him: *Quid mihi et tibi?* "What business do I have with you?" [John 2:4]? He must despair and give up hope, unless he knows and understands the nature of God's works and has been trained in faith. For he acts as he feels, and thinks nothing else about God than the way the words sound. He feels only wrath and hears only hostility, and so he regards God in no other way than as his enemy and angry judge. The way he regards God is the way he finds Him. Thus he expects nothing good from Him. That means that he renounces God with all His goodness. The result is that he flees from Him and hates Him, does not want God to be God, and blasphemes God, which is the fruit of his unbelief.

18. Therefore, the highest and most significant point of this Gospel is that we must give God the glory of being kind and gracious, even if He Himself acts and speaks differently, and all our mind and perception think differently. In that way our perception is killed and the old man perishes, so that only faith in God's kindness remains, and no perception remains in us. Here you see how His mother retains an untroubled faith and holds it out as an example for us. She is certain that He will be gracious, though she does not perceive it. It is also certain that she perceives differently than she believes. For that reason she lets it be free and committed to His kindness, and determines for Him neither time nor place, neither manner nor measure, neither person nor name. He will do it when it pleases Him. If it does not happen during the banquet, then at the end or after the banquet. [She thinks:]

"I will swallow this slap down: that He treats me with contempt and leaves me standing in disgrace before all the guests and speaks so unkindly to me, so that we all blush for shame. I know that He acts bitterly, but He is sweet." Let us do the same, if we are true Christians.

19. Note also how harsh He is to His own mother. By this He teaches us not only the example of faith mentioned above but also confirms, as Moses writes, that: "Whoever says to his father and mother: 'I do not know them,' observes Your words" (Deuteronomy 33 [:9]). Even though there is no higher authority on earth than that of father and mother, yet that is gone when God's Word and work begin. In divine matters, neither father nor mother—to say nothing of bishops or any other person—but only God's Word is to teach and lead. If father and mother would tell, teach, or even ask you to do something against God, and in the worship of God, which He has not clearly ordered and commanded, you should say to them: *Quid mihi et tibi?* "What do you and I have to do with each other?" [John 2:4]. So also here Christ does not want God's work done badly, as His own mother wanted to have it.

20. Father and mother are obliged—indeed, they were made father and mother by God for this very purpose—that they would teach their children and lead them to God not according to their own thoughts and opinions, but according to the command of God, as St. Paul says, "Fathers, do not provoke your children to anger, but bring them up in discipline and instruction to the Lord" (Ephesians 6 [:4]), that is, teach them God's commands and words, as you have learned them, and not your own things.

So you also see here in the Gospel that the mother of Christ pointed the servants away from herself to Christ and did not tell them: "Do whatever I say," but "Do whatever He tells you" [John 2:5]. Everyone is to be pointed only to His Word, if they are to be pointed in the right direction. So these words of Mary ("Do whatever He tells you") are and must be daily words for all of Christendom, and in that way all human doctrine and everything which is not properly Christ's Word will be knocked to the ground. We should firmly believe that whatever is commanded to us outside of and beyond God's Word is not, as they boast and lie, the commandment of the church. Mary says, "Whatever He tells you, do that, that, that, and nothing else," for there is enough to do here.

21. Here you also see that faith does not fail, and God does not let [it fail], but gives more and more gloriously than we ask. Not only wine is given here but also excellent and good wine, and an abundance of it. By this He again provokes and entices us to believe confidently in Him, even though He delays. He is truthful and cannot deny Himself [2 Tim. 2:13]. He is good and gracious—He must confess this about Himself and in addition prove it, unless we hinder Him and do not allow Him time and place and the means

to do so. Finally, He cannot omit it, as little as He can omit Himself, if we only wait for it.

## The Meaning of the Wedding

22. Third, we should touch briefly on the spiritual meaning. This wedding and every wedding signifies Christ, the true Bridegroom, and His Christendom, the Bride, as the Gospel sufficiently shows (Matthew 22 [:1–14]).

23. This wedding took place at Cana in Galilee; that is, Christendom began at Christ's time among the Jewish people and still continues among all who are like the Jews. The Jewish people are called "Cana" [John 2:1], which signifies "zeal,"[5] because they are ardently trained in the Law and cling to the works of the Law with great zeal, so that the Gospels, too, everywhere call them zealots, and especially St. Paul (Romans 9 [:31?]; 10 [:2]). It is natural that wherever Law and good works are, there will also be zeal and quarrels among people, when one wants to be better than the other; but especially [there will be zeal] against faith, which has no regard for their works and boasts only of God's grace. Wherever Christ is, there are always such zealots, and His wedding must be at Zeal City, for alongside the Gospel and faith you always find work-saints and Jewish zealots who squabble with faith.

24. "Galilee" [John 2:1] means "border" or "the edge of the country," where you step from one country into another. This signifies the same people as does Zeal City, those who dwell between the Law and the Gospel and ought to step out of works into faith, from the Law into Christian freedom, as some have done and now still do. But the greater part remain in their works and dwell on the borders, so that they attain to neither good works nor faith, and conceal themselves behind the pretense and glitter of works.

25. "Christ was invited to the wedding" [John 2:2] means that He was promised long before, in the Law and the prophets. People waited for Him lovingly and called Him to make water into wine, to fulfill the Law, to establish the faith, and to make true Galileans out of us.

26. "With His disciples" [John 2:2], because people expected Him to become a great King, and also because many apostles and disciples were needed so that His Word would be preached abundantly everywhere. Likewise, His mother [John 2:1] is the Christian Church taken from the Jews. She was there as one who especially belonged at the wedding, for Christ was properly promised to the Jewish people.

27. "The six stone water jars" [John 2:6], in which the Jews washed themselves, are the books of the Old Testament which by Law and commandment

---

5  Luther is identifying the city name Κανᾶ with the Hebrew word קַנָּא ["jealous, zealous"].

made the Jewish people only outwardly godly and pure. For that reason the evangelist also says that the water jars were there "for the Jewish rites of purification," as if he wanted to say: "This signifies the purification by works without faith, which never purifies the heart but only makes it more impure." This is a Jewish purification, but not a Christian or spiritual one.

28. The fact that there were six of the water jars signifies the labor and work involved in that purification for those who deal with works. The heart has no rest in them, since the Sabbath, the seventh day, is not there, when we can rest from our works and let God work in us. There are six workdays on which God created the heavens and the earth and commanded us to work. The seventh day is the day of rest [cf. Gen. 2:1–3], on which we are not to trouble ourselves with works of the Law, but let God work in us through faith, while we keep quiet and take a holiday from our works of the Law.

29. The water in them is the understanding and mind of the Law—according to which the conscience is guided—and is comprised of letters (as in the water jars).

30. [The water jars] are made of stone, as were the tablets of Moses [Exod. 24:12], but they signify the stiff-necked people of the Jews. Just as their hearts are against the Law, so the Law appears outwardly to be against them. It seems harsh and heavy to them, and therefore it is harsh and heavy. That causes their hearts to be hard and heavy to the Law. We all find, perceive, and experience that we are hard and heavy toward the good, and yielding and weak toward the evil. The wicked do not perceive this, but it is perceived by those who want to be godly and trouble themselves with their works. That is the two or three measures of these water jars.

31. To change water into wine is to make the understanding of the Law delightful. That happens in this way: Before the Gospel comes, everyone understands that the Law demands our works and that we must satisfy it with our works. That understanding produces either hardened, arrogant dissemblers and hypocrites, harder than any stone water jar, or anxious, troubled consciences. The water in the water jars always remains fearful and timid before God's judgment. This is the water-understanding. No one drinks from it; no one becomes cheerful from it. Rather, it is only for washing and purifying, but no one ever becomes truly pure inwardly.

The Gospel explains the Law in this way: It demands more than we can do and wants to have a different man than we are, one who can keep it. That is, it demands Christ and promotes Him, so that through His grace we become different people in faith, people like Christ, and then do truly good works. Thus the true understanding and meaning of the Law is to lead us to the knowledge of our inability and to drive us to seek grace and help not from ourselves, but from another—namely, from Christ.

32. Therefore, when Jesus wanted to make wine, He had them pour in still more water, up to the brim [John 2:7]. The Gospel comes and explains the understanding of the Law most fully (as was said). It explains how what we do is nothing but sin. For that reason we cannot get free from our sins through the Law. When the two or three measures hear this—namely, the good hearts who have troubled themselves with works according to the Law, and already themselves have a timid and troubled conscience—this understanding frightens them still more; the water threatens to overflow the brim of the jar. Before this they felt heavy and hard toward the good, but still thought they could measure up to it with their works. Now they hear that they are of no use at all and that it is impossible for them to measure up to it with their works. Then the jar is all too full of water, so that it can never hold more. Then the Law is most highly understood, and the result is only despair.

33. Then the comforting Gospel comes and makes the water into wine. When the heart hears that Christ fulfills the Law for us and takes our sin on Himself, then it no longer cares that impossible things are demanded by the Law and that we must despair and desist from our works. It is an excellent and delectable thing that the Law is so deep and so high, so holy and true and good, and demands such great things; it is loved and praised because it demands so many great things. The reason is that the heart now has in Christ all that the Law demands, and [the heart] would be utterly sad if it demanded less. Now the Law, which was previously hard, heavy, and impossible, is delightful and easy, because it now lives in the heart by the Spirit. There is no longer water in the water jars; it has become wine, it has been distributed, it has been drunk and has made the heart cheerful.

34. The servants [John 2:5, 7, 9] are all the preachers of the New Testament, such as the apostles and their successors.

35. The drawing [of the wine, John 2:8] and filling the glasses is taking this understanding from Scripture and preaching it to all the world, which is invited to the wedding of Christ.

36. The servants knew (the evangelist tells us) where the wine came from [John 2:9] and that it had been water. Only the apostles and their successors understand how the Law becomes delightful and pleasant through Christ, and how the Gospel fulfills the Law by faith but not with works; it has become entirely different than it was previously in works.

37. The master of the feast tastes that the wine is good but does not know where it came from. This master of the feast is the old priesthood among the Jews who knew only about works. Nicodemus was one of them (John 3 [:9]). He certainly is impressed by Christ but does not know how that happens or where it came from, since he still clings to works. Those who teach works cannot understand and recognize the Gospel and what is done from faith.

38. He summons the bridegroom and reproaches him for giving the good wine last, when everyone else gives the inferior [wine] last [John 2:10]. To this very day the Jews are astonished that the preaching of the Gospel was delayed so long and now first came to the Gentiles, while they so long had to drink bad wine and had to bear "the burden and heat of the day" [Matt. 20:12] so long in the Law, as is said elsewhere in the Gospel.[6]

39. Note that God and men proceed in contradictory ways. Men first give the best, and then the worse. God first [gives] the cross and suffering, and then honor and salvation. That is because men seek to preserve the old man; for that reason they teach us to keep the Law by works and make great and sweet promises. But it turns out flat and tastes bad, for the conscience becomes worse the longer it goes on, even if it does not feel this misery because it is so drunk on those great promises. But finally, after the wine has been swallowed and the false promises are gone, then [the misery] will find them. At first God causes the bad conscience and gives bad wine, even mere water; but afterward He comforts us in the Gospel with His promises, which endure forever.

---

6  See sermon for Septuagesima on Matt. 20:1–16.

# GOSPEL FOR THE THIRD SUNDAY AFTER EPIPHANY

*Matthew 8:1–13*

*When He came down from the mountain, great crowds followed Him. And behold, a leper came to Him and knelt before Him, saying, "Lord, if You will, You can make me clean." And Jesus stretched out His hand and touched him, saying, "I will; be clean." And immediately his leprosy was cleansed. And Jesus said to him, "See that you say nothing to anyone, but go, show yourself to the priest and offer the gift that Moses commanded, for a proof to them." When He had entered Capernaum, a centurion came forward to Him, appealing to Him, "Lord, my servant is lying paralyzed at home, suffering terribly." And He said to him, "I will come and heal him." But the centurion replied, "Lord, I am not worthy to have You come under my roof, but only say the word, and my servant will be healed. For I too am a man under authority, with soldiers under me. And I say to one, 'Go,' and he goes, and to another, 'Come,' and he comes, and to my servant, 'Do this,' and he does it." When Jesus heard this, He marveled and said to those who followed Him, "Truly, I tell you, with no one in Israel have I found such faith. I tell you, many will come from east and west and recline at table with Abraham, Isaac, and Jacob in the kingdom of heaven, while the sons of the kingdom will be thrown into the outer darkness. In that place there will be weeping and gnashing of teeth." And to the centurion Jesus said, "Go; let it be done for you as you have believed." And the servant was healed at that very moment.*

1. This Gospel teaches us two examples of faith and love: one in the leper, the other in the centurion. Let us look first at the leper. The leper would not have been so bold as to go to the Lord and ask to be made clean if he had not trusted and expected with his whole heart that Christ would be kind and gracious and would make him clean. Because he was leprous, he had reason to be afraid; moreover, the Law commanded the lepers not to go among the people [e.g., Lev. 13:45–46]. Nevertheless, he pressed forward [Matt. 8:2], not regarding the Law and the people, and how pure and holy Christ is.

2. See how faith acts toward Christ: it pictures for itself absolutely nothing but the pure kindness and free grace of Christ, without seeking or getting any merit. We certainly cannot say that the leper by his purity merited to approach Christ, speak to Him, and invoke His help. Just because he feels his impurity and unworthiness, he goes all the more and looks only

to Christ's kindness. That is true faith, a living confidence in God's kindness. The heart that does that believes correctly. The heart that does not do that does not believe correctly. They are the ones who do not keep their eyes only on God's kindness, but first look around for their own good works, in order to be worthy of meriting His kindness. They never become bold enough to invoke God in all seriousness or to come to Him.

3. Now this confidence or faith or knowledge of the kindness of Christ would not have arisen in this leper from his own reason if he had not first heard a good report about Christ, namely, how kind, gracious, and merciful He is, how He helps and gives, comforts, and aids everyone who only comes to Him. Without a doubt such a proclamation must have come to his ears, and from that proclamation he had taken courage and turned and interpreted the report to his own advantage. He applied that kindness to himself and thought with all confidence: "He will be so kind also to me, as the proclamation says about Him and as the good report sounds." So his faith did not grow out of his reason, but it came from that proclamation about Christ, as St. Paul says, "Faith comes from hearing, and hearing from the word or proclamation about Christ" (Romans 10 [:17]).

4. That is the Gospel which is the beginning, middle, and end of all good and of salvation. We have often heard that we must first of all hear the Gospel, and then believe and love and do good works, and not first do good works and so turn things upside down, as the teachers of works do. But the Gospel is a good report, talk, and proclamation about Christ, that He is nothing but kindness, love, and grace, as is said about no other person or saint. Even if there is a good report and proclamation about other saints, that is not the Gospel, unless it is only about Christ's kindness and grace. If it would speak at the same time about other saints, then it is no longer the Gospel. [The Gospel] builds faith and confidence only on the Rock, Jesus Christ.

5. So you see that this example of the leper fights for faith against works. Just as Christ helps this [leper] from pure grace through faith without any [of the leper's] works or merits, so He does for everyone, and wants us to regard Him the same and expect the same from Him. If this leper had come in such a way that he said, "Look, Lord, I have prayed and fasted so much; You should look at that and make me clean because of it," then Christ would never have cleansed him, since such a person does not rely on God's grace, but on his own merit. Then God's grace is not praised, loved, glorified, or desired, but our own works claim that glory and rob God of His. That means to kiss the hand and to deny God, as Job says: "Has my heart been secretly enticed, so that my hand kisses my mouth? This also would be an iniquity before the judges, for by doing so, I would have denied God above" (Job 31 [:27–28]). Isaiah writes: "They have worshiped the work of their hands" (Isaiah 2 [:8]);

that is, the glory and confidence they should have given to God's grace, they apply to their own works.

6. On the other hand, this example shows us Christ's love for the leper. You can see that love makes Him into a servant, so that He helps the poor man freely and gratuitously, and seeks neither profit, advantage, nor glory from it, but only the good of the poor man and the glory of God the Father. For that reason He also forbids him to tell anyone [Matt. 8:4], so that this would be a pure, sincere work of free and kind love.

7. This is what I have often said, that faith makes us into lords, and love into servants. Indeed, by faith we become gods and partakers of the divine nature and name [2 Pet. 1:4], as Psalm 82 [:6] says: "I said, 'You are gods, children of the Most High, all of you.'" But through love we become equal to the poorest of all. According to faith we lack nothing and have an abundance; according to love we serve everyone. Through faith we receive treasures from above, from God; through love we release them below, to our neighbors. In the same way, Christ according to His deity lacked nothing, but according to His humanity He served everyone who needed Him.

We have spoken about this quite often, that through faith we also must be born God's children and gods, lords, and kings, just as Christ was born as true God in eternity from the Father.[1] On the other hand, through love we burst forth and help our neighbors with good deeds, just as Christ became man to help us all. Just as Christ did not first deserve to be God through His works or acquire that through His incarnation, but has that by birth without any works, even before He became man, so we also have not deserved through works or love to be adopted by God, to have our sins forgiven so that death and hell do not harm us, but we received that through faith in the Gospel, by grace without any works and before our love. Just as Christ became man to serve us only after He is eternal God, so we also do good and love our neighbor afterward, only when we are already godly, without sins, being alive, saved, and God's children through faith. That is [enough] about the first example of the leper.

8. The second example is like it as far as faith and love are concerned. This centurion also has a wholehearted confidence in Christ and pictures before his eyes nothing but the kindness and grace of Christ; otherwise he would not have come to Him, or have sent to Him, as Luke [7:3] says. Thus he also would not have had such firm confidence, if he had not first heard

---

1 See. e.g., sermon for sermon for New Year's Day on Luke 2:21, paragraphs 25 and 27; the sermon for Third Day of Christmas on John 1:1–14, paragraphs 100–114; *[First] Lectures on Galatians* (1516–17/1519), LW 27:279; *Exposition of the Lord's Prayer* (1519), LW 42:28; *Sermons on 1 Peter* (1523), LW 30:33.

about Christ's kindness and grace. So also here the Gospel is the beginning and incentive of his confidence or faith.

9. Here we learn again that we must begin with the Gospel and believe it and not look at any merit or works, just as this centurion advanced no merit or work, but only his confidence in Christ's kindness. So we also see that all the works of Christ are examples of the Gospel, of faith, and of love.

10. So we also see the example of love, that Christ does good to him gratuitously, without any seeking for a gift, as was said above. Moreover, the centurion also shows an example of love, in that he cared for his servant as for himself, just as Christ cared for us. He did that good deed gratuitously, only for the benefit of the servant. He did that, as Luke [7:2] says, because that servant "was highly valued by him." It is as if [Luke] said: "The love and delight that [the centurion] had for [his servant] compelled him to see his need and to help him." Let us also do this, and make sure we do not deceive ourselves and let ourselves think that we now have the Gospel—but then pay no attention to our neighbor in his need. That is enough about those two examples. Let us now also look at some points of the text.

11. The leper softens his prayer and says, "Lord, if You will, You can indeed make me clean" [Matt. 8:2]. That is not to be understood as if he doubted Christ's kindness and grace, for that faith would be nothing, even if he believed that Christ was almighty and was able to do and know all things. Living faith does not doubt that God has a kind and gracious will to do what we ask. Rather, it is to be understood in this way: faith does not doubt that God has a good will toward the person and wishes and grants him every blessing. But we are unaware whether what faith asks and asserts is good and useful for us. God alone knows that. For that reason, faith asks in such a way that it leaves everything to the gracious will of God. If it serves His glory and our good, do not doubt that God will give it; or, if it is not to be given, then His divine will out of great grace does not give it, because He sees that it is better if not given. Nevertheless, faith remains certain and secure in God's gracious will, whether He gives it or not, as St. Paul also says that we do not know what or how we should pray (Romans 8 [:26]), and in the Lord's Prayer, He tells us to give preference to His will and to pray for it [Matt. 6:10].

12. That is, as we have often said, we ought to trust the divine kindness without doubt and without measure. But we ought to ask with the measure of what His glory, His kingdom, and will are, so that we do not dictate to His will the time, place, measure, or names, but leave all that freely to Him. For that reason the leper's prayer pleased the Lord so much and was soon granted. When we leave it to His will, and desire what pleases Him, then He cannot refrain from doing in return what pleases us. Faith makes Him favorable to us, and patient prayer causes Him to give us what we ask for.

We have spoken sufficiently about sending the leper to the priests (why it was done and what it signified) in the postil on the ten lepers.

13. His words—"With no one in Israel have I found such faith" [Matt. 8:10]—have been treated with concern, either so that Christ is not lying or so that the mother of God and the apostles are not less than this centurion. Although I could say here that Christ is speaking about the people of Israel where He had preached and to whom He had come, so that His mother and disciples were excluded as those who traveled with Him and came with Him to the people of Israel when He preached, nevertheless I will simply remain with the Lord's words and take them as they read, for the following reasons:

First, it is against no article of faith that the faith of this centurion had its equal neither in the apostles nor in the mother of God. Where Christ's words openly oppose no article of faith, we should take them as they sound, and not turn or deflect them with our explaining and interpreting, either for the sake of a saint, an angel, or God Himself. His Word is the truth itself, beyond all saints and angels.

14. Second, such interpreting and deflecting is derived from our fleshly mind and opinion, since we measure the saints of God not according to God's grace, but according to their person, worth, and greatness. This is against God, who measures them much differently, according to His gifts alone. He never allowed St. John the Baptist to do a miracle [cf. John 10:41], which many lesser saints have done. In summary, He often does through lesser saints what He does not do through great saints.

He hid from His mother when He was twelve years old and allowed her to be mistaken and ignorant [Luke 2:43]. On Easter Sunday He appeared to Mary Magdalene before He appeared to His mother and the apostles [John 20:11–18]. He spoke to the Samaritan woman (John 4 [:7]) and to the adulteress (John 8 [:10]) more pleasantly than He ever spoke with His own mother. Likewise, while Peter fell and denied [Luke 22:54–62], the murderer on the cross stood [firm] and believed strongly [Luke 23:40–42].

15. With these and similar marvels, He shows that He does not want to have His Spirit in His saints measured by us and that we are not to judge according to the person. He wants to give His gifts freely, as it pleases Him (as St. Paul says, 1 Corinthians 12 [:11]), not as it seems good to us. He even says about Himself that whoever believes in Him will do greater signs than He has done [John 14:12]. [He says] all of that so that no one will think himself above others, and so that no one will elevate one saint above the others and cause sects. Rather, we should let them all be equal in God's grace, no matter how unequal they are in His gifts. He wants to do through St. Stephen what He does not do through St. Peter, and through St. Peter what He does not

do through His mother, so that He is the only one who does everything in everyone, without any distinctions of person, according to His will.

16. So it should be understood that at the time He preached He did not find such faith either in His mother or in the apostles, whether or not He previously or afterward found greater faith in His mother and the apostles and in many others. It may well be that He gave His mother great faith at the time she conceived and bore Him, and afterward not or rarely so great, and sometimes let [her faith] diminish, as He did when she lost Him for three days (Luke 2 [:46]), as He does with all His saints. If He did not do that, the saints would certainly fall into arrogance and make themselves into idols—or we would make idols out of them, and look more at their worthiness and person than at God's grace.

17. From this we should learn how foolish and stupid we are about the divine works and marvels, when we despise the common Christian man and think that only the pointed hats and the learned can know and draw conclusions about God's truth. Yet here Christ elevates this Gentile with his faith above all His disciples. He does that because we cling to persons and estates, and not to God's words and grace. Therefore, we go along with persons and estates into every error, and then say that the Christian church and the councils have said such and such, and they cannot err[2] because they have the Holy Spirit. Meanwhile, Christ is present with those who are despised, and lets persons and councils go to the devil.

Therefore, note well that Christ elevates this Gentile so highly. He is of more value than Annas, Caiaphas, and all the priests, learned, and saints, all of whom should be students of this Gentile, to say nothing of them making resolutions or of imposing laws on him. God gives a great saint a small faith, and a small [saint] a great faith, so that each would always regard the other as higher than himself (Romans 12 [:3]).

### "Lord, I am not worthy." [Matt. 8:8]

18. The great faith of this Gentile knows that salvation does not depend on the bodily presence of Christ—for that does not help—rather on the Word and faith. The apostles did not yet know this, and probably not His mother either, but they clung firmly to His bodily presence and were unwilling for Him to leave them (John 16 [:17–18]). They did not cling only to His Word. But this Gentile is so fully satisfied with His words that he does not even wish His presence nor think himself worthy of it. Moreover, he proves his strong faith with a parable and says: "I am a man and can with a word do what I want with my people. Should You, then, with a word not do what You

---

2  Cf. sermon for First Sunday after Epiphany on Luke 2:41–52.

want? I certainly know, and You also demonstrate, that health and sickness, death and life are subject to You, just as my servants are to me." Therefore, his servant from that hour became healthy through the power of that faith.

## [INFANT BAPTISM AND FAITH THAT IS NOT ONE'S OWN]

19. Because[3] the season and this Gospel present it, we must say a little about faith that is not one's own and its power, since many are concerned about this, especially for the sake of young children, whom people think are saved in Baptism not through their own but through another person's faith. Here this servant became healthy not through his own faith but through the faith of his master. We have never yet treated this matter; therefore, we must treat it here in order to prevent, as much we can, future danger and error.

20. First, we must have the foundation firm and certain that no one is saved by another person's faith or righteousness, but through his own. On the other hand, no one is condemned for another person's unbelief or sins, but for his own unbelief, as the Gospel clearly and plainly says: "Whoever believes and is baptized will be saved, but whoever does not believe will be condemned" (Mark 16 [:16]). [Paul writes]: "The righteous shall live by his faith" (Romans 1 [:17]). [Christ says]: "Whoever believes in Him will not perish but has eternal life" [John 3:16]. Again: "Whoever believes in Him will not be judged, but whoever does not believe is judged already" (John 3 [:18]).

These are clear and open words that each must believe for himself, and he cannot be helped by another person's faith without his own faith. We must not yield these passages or deny them, no matter what happens; we should first let all the world be destroyed before we change this divine truth. If something is brought up which seems to be against this and which you do not know how to answer, you should confess that you do not understand it and leave it to God, rather than admit something against these clear passages. Let Gentiles, Jews, Turks, little children, and everything remain what it is and where it can, but these words should and must be right and true.

21. Now the question is where the young children remain who do not yet have reasoning abilities and cannot believe for themselves, because it is written: "Faith comes through hearing, and hearing through the preaching of God's Word" (Romans 10 [:17]). [Some say that] young children neither hear nor understand God's Word, and therefore they cannot have their own faith.

3 In 1529, Andreas Osiander (ca. 1496–1552) had paragraphs 19–46 specially printed against the Anabaptists, "because not everyone could buy the entire postil." This special printing was given the title *Infant Baptism and Faith That Is Not One's Own*: Martin Luther, *Von der kinder Tauff, un frembden glauben*, ed. Andreas Osiander (Nürnberg: Georg Wachter, 1529) [VD16 L3976]. (See E² 11:52.)

22. The sophists in the universities and the pope's rabble have invented the following answer to the question: "Young children are baptized without their own faith, namely, on the faith of the Church, which the sponsors confess at the Baptism. Accordingly, in Baptism sins are forgiven for the child from the power and might of Baptism, and its own faith is poured in with grace, so that it becomes a newborn child through water and the Holy Spirit [John 3:5]."

23. But if you ask them for the basis of this answer and where this is in Scripture, then it is found up the dark chimney, or they point to their cardinal's hat and say: "We are the highly learned doctors, and we say so; therefore, it is true, and you dare not ask any more about it." Nearly all their doctrine has no other basis than their own dreams and opinions. When they most specially arm themselves [with proof], then they drag in by the hair some passage from St. Augustine or another holy father. But that is not enough for us in these matters which concern the soul's salvation. They themselves and all the holy fathers are people and human beings. Who will guarantee and provide surety that they are speaking correctly? Who will rely on that and die for it, since they speak without Scripture or God's Word? As for the saints, here they don't matter—when it means losing or preserving my soul eternally, I cannot rely on all the angels and saints, to say nothing of one or two saints, if they do not show me God's Word.

24. From these lies they have advanced and come so far that they have taught and still hold that the Sacraments have such power that even if you have no faith and receive the Sacrament (as long as you do not have the intention of sinning), then you obtain grace and the forgiveness of sins without any faith.[4] They have introduced this from the previous opinion, namely, their dream that young children receive grace without any faith only from the might and power of Baptism. That is why they ascribe the same thing to adults and all people, because they are speaking these things out of their own heads. In that way they root out Christian faith in a masterful way, destroy it, and make it unnecessary; with the power of the Sacraments they establish only our own works. I have written enough about this in the article on the bull of Leo.

25. The holy ancient fathers have spoken somewhat more about this, though not clearly enough. They do not speak about this imaginary power of the Sacraments; rather, they speak as if the young children were baptized in the faith of the Christian Church. But because they do not explain thoroughly

---

4 Luther refers to the scholastic doctrine that the sacraments were effective "just by doing the work" (*ex opere operato*), regardless of the faith or merit of the minister and regardless of the faith or preparation of the recipient, provided only that the minister intended to perform a sacrament of the church and that the recipient did not willfully impose an obstacle to the sacrament. See Oberman, *Harvest of Medieval Theology*, pp. 146–60, 467.

how this Christian faith benefits the children, whether they receive their own faith through it or whether they are only baptized on the Christian faith, without their own faith, the sophists have gone ahead and explained the words of the holy fathers to mean that children are baptized without their own faith and receive grace only in the Church's faith. They are enemies of faith; if only they can elevate works, then faith must endure it. They do not once think that the holy fathers might have erred or that they themselves have incorrectly understood the fathers.

26. Guard yourself against this poison and error, even if it were the explicit opinion of all the fathers and councils; for it does not last, there is no basis in Scripture for it, but only the human opinions and dreams. Moreover, it is directly and openly against the chief passage, where Christ says, "Whoever believes and is baptized," etc. [Mark 16:16]. In short, the conclusion is that Baptism helps no one and is to be given to no one unless he believes for himself; without faith no one is to be baptized. St. Augustine himself says, "It is not the Sacrament which justifies, but faith in the Sacrament."

27. Besides these there are some others, called the Waldensians,[5] who hold that each one must believe for himself and must receive Baptism or the Sacrament with his own faith; if he does not, then for him Baptism or the Sacrament is good for nothing. So far they speak and teach correctly. But when they go ahead and nevertheless baptize young children whom they regard as not having their own faith, that is a mockery of Holy Baptism, and they sin against the Second Commandment when they consciously and wantonly take God's name and Word unnecessarily and in vain. There is no help for them in their excuse that children are baptized on the basis of their future faith, when they will think for themselves. Faith must be present before or in Baptism; otherwise the child is not freed from the devil and sins.

28. Therefore, if their opinion were correct, then everything that is done with the child in Baptism would have to be mere lies and mockery. The baptizer asks whether the child believes, and people answer for the child: "Yes." He asks whether [the child] wants to be baptized, and people answer for the child: "Yes." Nevertheless, no one is baptized for the child, but [the child] himself is baptized. Therefore, [the child] must himself believe, or the sponsors must be lying when they say in his place: "I believe." Likewise, the baptizer declares that [the child] is born anew, has forgiveness of sins, is freed from the devil, and as a sign of this he puts on him a white shirt and treats him in all things as a new, holy child of God. All of that would have to be false

---

5 Luther often called the Bohemian Brethren or Unity of Brethren "Waldensians." Cf. Luther's preface to *Account of the Faith of the Brethren* (1533), LW 60:17–23; and preface to *Confession of the Barons and Nobles of Bohemia* (1538), LW 60:214–19. With this title Luther also could be referring to Anabaptists.

if his own faith were not there. It would be better never to baptize children than to act foolishly and deceptively with God's Word and Sacrament, as if He were an idol or a fool.

29. It also does not help that they divide the kingdom of God into three parts: first, the Christian Church; second, eternal life; third, the Gospel. Then they say that children are baptized into the kingdom of heaven in the third and first ways; that is, they are baptized not to be saved and to have the forgiveness of sins, but they are received into Christendom and brought to the Gospel. All of this is saying nothing and is invented out of their own opinions. It is not coming into the kingdom of heaven when I come among Christians and hear the Gospel. Even heathen can do that, even without Baptism. It is not coming into the kingdom of heaven when you say about the kingdom of heaven in the first, second, or third ways whatever you want; rather, being in the kingdom of heaven means that I am a living member of Christendom, and not only hear the Gospel but also believe it. Otherwise a man would be in the kingdom of heaven in the same way that I might throw a stick or a log among Christians, or as the devil is among them. Therefore, that [way of being among the Christians] is worthless.

30. It also follows from this that the Christian Church would have to have two kinds of Baptism, and that children would not have the same Baptism as adults. Nevertheless, St. Paul says there is only "one Baptism, one Lord, one faith" (Ephesians 4 [:5]). If Baptism does not do and give to children what it does and gives to adults, then it is not the same Baptism; indeed, it is no Baptism, but playing at and mocking Baptism, since there is no other Baptism than that which saves [cf. 1 Pet. 3:21]. If you know or believe that it does not save, then you should not give it; but if you do give it, then you do not give Christian Baptism, for you do not believe that it accomplishes what Baptism should accomplish. Therefore, it is a different and foreign baptism. For that reason it would almost be necessary for the Waldensians to have themselves baptized again, as they baptize our people again, because they not only received Baptism without faith but even against faith. In mockery and dishonor of God they give a different, foreign, unchristian baptism.

31. If we cannot answer this question better and prove that young children themselves believe and have their own faith, then it is my sincere counsel and judgment that we immediately desist—the sooner the better—and never baptize a child, so that we do not mock and slander the blessed majesty of God with such tomfoolery and trickery which has nothing behind it.

Therefore, we here speak plainly and conclude that in Baptism the children themselves believe and have their own faith, which God works in them when the sponsors intercede for them and bring them into the faith of the Christian Church. We call that "the power of someone else's faith": not that anyone can be saved by that [kind of faith], but that through it, as through its intercession and help, he can himself obtain from God his own faith by which he is saved.

It happens the same way as my natural living and dying. If I am to live, then I must myself be born, and no one can be born for me so that I live through them; however, my mother and the midwife can through their living help me to my birth, so that I live in that way. So if I am to die, then I must myself suffer death, and no one can die for me so that I die; but he can certainly help me to my own death, such as when he frightens me, falls on me, chokes or crushes me, or suffocates me with stench. Likewise, no one can go into hell for me; but he can mislead me by false doctrine and life, so that I go into [hell] by my own error, brought onto me by his error. So no one can go to heaven for me; but he can help me to get there by preaching, teaching, governing, praying, and obtaining faith from God [for me], through which I can go to heaven. This centurion was not healed of the paralysis of his servant, but he acquired having his servant obtain health.

32. So here we also say that children are not baptized in the faith of the sponsors or of the Church, but the faith of sponsors and of the Church prays for and gains for them their own faith in which they are baptized and believe for themselves. We have strong and firm passages about that (Matthew 19 [:13–15]; Mark 10 [:13–16]; Luke 18 [:15–16]). When some brought little children to the Lord Jesus so that He could touch them and the disciples hindered them, He rebuked the disciples, embraced the children, laid His hands on them, blessed them, and said, "To such belongs the kingdom of God" [Matt. 19:14; Mark 10:14; Luke 18:16]. No one will take these passages away from us nor overcome them with good reasons. It says here that Christ does not want people to forbid the little children to be brought to Him; He even commands that they be brought to Him, blesses them, and gives them the kingdom of heaven. Let us note that well.

33. Without a doubt this was written about natural children, and it is wrong when people want to explain Christ's words as if He had meant spiritual children, who are small because of their humility. These were bodily small children, whom Luke calls "infants" [Luke 18:15]. On them His blessing was placed, and about them He says that the kingdom of heaven is theirs. What do we want to say here? Do we want to say that they were without their own faith and that the other passage is false: "Whoever does not believe will be condemned" [Mark 16:16]? Then Christ is also lying or dissembling when He says that the kingdom of heaven is theirs, and is not speaking seriously about the true kingdom of heaven.

Interpret these words of Christ as you please, we have [to conclude] that children are to be brought to Christ and are not to be hindered; when they are brought to Him, then He compels us to believe that He blesses them and gives them the kingdom of heaven, as He does for these children. It is proper for us to act and believe in no other way, as long as the words stand: "Let the little children come to Me and do not hinder them" [Matt. 19:14]. No less is it proper for us to believe that when they are brought to Him, He will embrace them, lay His hands on them, bless them, and give them heaven, as long as this text stands that He blessed and gave heaven to the children who were brought to Him. Who can ignore this text? Who, on the other hand, will be so bold as not to allow little children to come to Baptism or not to believe that He blesses them when they come to Him?

34. He is just as present in Baptism now as He was then. Because we Christians certainly know this, we dare not keep Baptism away from children. So also we dare not doubt that He blesses all who come to Him, just as He blessed those [children]. Thus nothing more remains than the thoughts and faith of those who brought the little children to Him. By bringing them, they cause and help the little children to be blessed and to obtain the kingdom of heaven, [but] that could not be if [the children] did not have their own faith for themselves, as has been said.

So we also say here that the little children are brought to Baptism by the faith and work of another; but when they get there and the priest or baptizer deals with them in Christ's place, then He blesses them and gives them faith and the kingdom of heaven, for the priest's word and deed are the word and work of Christ Himself.

35. St. John also agrees with this when he says: "I am writing to you, fathers"; "I am writing to you, young men"; "I am writing to you, children" (1 John 2 [:13]). He is not satisfied to write to the young men; he also writes to the children—and writes that they know the Father. From this it follows that the apostles also baptized children and held the view that they believe and know the Father, just as if they had begun to reason and could read. Although someone could explain the word "children" as referring to the adults, as Christ sometimes calls His disciples [e.g., John 13:33], yet here it is certain that he is speaking about those who are younger than the young men, so that it sounds like he is speaking about the young crowd, those who are under fifteen or eighteen years, and excludes nobody down to the first year, for all these are called "children."

36. But we want to look at their reason for thinking that the children do not believe. They say that it is because they have not yet begun to reason and so cannot hear God's Word; but where God's Word is not heard, there can be no faith: "Faith comes from hearing, and hearing comes from God's Word" (Romans 10 [:17]). Tell me, is it Christian to judge God's works according to our opinion and to say, "Children have not begun to reason, and therefore

they could not believe"? How is it, then, that through your own reasoning you have already come away from faith, and the children by their unreasoning have come to faith?

Dear friend, what good does reason do for faith and God's Word? Is it not [reason] which most strongly opposes faith and the Word of God, so that no one can come to faith because of [reason]? It will not tolerate God's Word unless it is blinded and disgraced, so that we must die to [reason] and become fools, as unreasonable and unwise as a little child, before we believe and receive God's grace. Christ says: "Unless you turn and become like children, you will never enter the kingdom of heaven" (Matthew 18 [:3]). How often does Christ tell us that we must become children and fools? How often does He condemn reason?

37. Likewise, tell me what kind of reason the little children had whom Christ embraced and blessed and to whom He gave heaven? Were they not still without reason? Why, then, does He command them to be brought to Him and bless them? Where did they get the faith which makes them children of the kingdom of heaven? Yes, just because they are without reason and foolish, they are better adapted for faith than adults and the wise, for whom reason is always in the way and refuses to push its big head through the narrow door. If we are talking here about faith and God's work, then we must not look at reason or its works. Here God works alone, and reason is dead, blind, and like a stupid log in this work, so that Scripture is right when it says, "God is astonishing in His saints" [cf. Ps. 68:35 (67:36 Vg)]. Likewise: "As the heavens are higher than the earth, so are My ways higher than your ways and My thoughts than your thoughts" (Isaiah 55 [:9]).

38. But since they are stuck so deep in their reason, we must attack them with their own cleverness. Tell me, why do you baptize a person when he has begun to reason? You answer: "He hears God's Word and believes." I ask: How do you know that? You say, "He confesses it with his mouth." What shall I say? What if he lies and deceives? You cannot see his heart. Well, then, you baptize on no other basis than what the man shows outwardly. You are uncertain of his faith and must think that if he does not have more on the inside in his heart than you perceive on the outside, then his hearing, his confessing, and his faith will not help, for it may be sheer delusion and not true faith. Who are you, then, to say that external hearing and confessing are necessary for Baptism? [You say that] where these are not, we should not baptize, and where they are, we should baptize. But here you yourself confess that such hearing and confessing are uncertain and are not enough for a person to receive Baptism. Why do you baptize? How will you continue, when you have so thrown Baptism into doubt?

Is it not true that you must come and say that it is improper for you to do or know any more than that you should baptize whoever is brought to you and asks for Baptism? You must believe or commit to God whether or not he inwardly, truly believes; in that way you are excused and baptize correctly. Why, then, will you not do that for the children, whom Christ commands to be brought to Him and whom He wants to bless? Rather, you first want to have the outward hearing and confessing, which you confess is uncertain and insufficient for the Baptism of the one to be baptized. You abandon the sure words of Christ (when He commands that little children be brought to Him) for the sake of your uncertain external hearing.

39. Moreover, tell me, where is the reason of a person who believes in Christ while he is asleep, since his faith and God's grace never leave him? If faith can remain without the help of reason, so that [reason] is unaware of it, then why should [faith] not also begin in children before reason knows anything about it? I could say the same thing about all the estates in which a Christian lives and is busy or otherwise occupied, that he is unaware of his faith and reason, and yet his faith does not on that account cease. God's works are secret and wonderful, where and when He wants; on the other hand, they are quite obvious, where and when He wants, so that they are too high and too deep for us to judge about them.

40. Because He commands us here not to hinder little children from coming to Him so that He may bless them, and we are not required to be certain about the internal state of faith (external hearing and confessing are not enough for the one baptized), we are to be content that, for us who are doing the baptizing, it is enough to hear the confession of those to be baptized, who themselves come to us. [We are to hear their confession] so that we do not give the Sacrament against our conscience to those from whom no fruit is to be expected. But when they assure our conscience with their seeking and confessing that we may give it to them as a Sacrament which gives grace, then we are excused. If his faith is not true, we leave that to God; we have not given it as a useless thing, but with the consciousness that it is beneficial.

41. I say all of this so that we do not baptize thoughtlessly, as those do who give it with wanton knowledge that it does nothing and is not beneficial. Those baptizers sin by deliberately using God's Sacrament and Word in a useless way, or consciously thinking that it cannot do anything. That is treating the Sacrament in an unworthy way; it tempts and slanders God. That is not giving the Sacrament but mocking the Sacrament. But if the person baptized lies and does not believe—well, you have still done right and have given the true Sacrament with a good conscience, as something that ought to be useful.

42. As for those who do not come of themselves but are brought (as Christ commands us to bring the little children [Matt. 19:14]), you should commit their faith to Him who commands us to bring them and baptize them on His command, and say: "Lord, You bring them here and command me to baptize them, so You will certainly answer for them. I rely on that. I dare not drive them away or hinder them." If they have not heard the Word, by which faith comes, as adults hear it, they hear it like little children. Adults grasp [the Word] with their ears and reason, [but] often without faith. [Little children] hear it with their ears, without reason and with faith. Faith is all the closer the less reason there is. [The faith] which brings them is stronger than the will of adults who come of themselves.

43. What troubles these writers most is that in adults there is reason, which acts as if it believes the Word it hears; they call that "believing." On the other hand, they see that in children there is as yet no reason, for they act as if they do not believe. But they do not see that faith in God's Word is a much different and deeper thing than what reason does with God's Word. [Faith] is God's work alone beyond all reason. The child is closer than the adult—yes, much closer—and the adult is farther away than the child—yes, much farther away.

44. But this is a human work, made by reason. It seems to me that if any Baptism is certain, the Baptism of children should be most certain, just because of the words of Christ telling us to bring them, while the adults come on their own. There can be deception in adults because of their reason, but there can be no deception in children because their reason is hidden. Christ makes His blessing effective in them, as He has commanded that they be brought to Him. These very striking words are not to be disregarded, when He tells us to bring the children to Him and rebukes those who hinder it [Matt. 19:14].

45. But in so doing we do not want the preaching office weakened or set aside. To be sure, God does not have these things preached for the sake of rational hearing, since no fruit comes from that, but for the sake of spiritual hearing, which, as was said, children also have, as well as and even better than adults. So they, too, indeed hear the Word. What else is Baptism than the Gospel to which they are brought? Even if they only hear it once, they hear it all the more powerfully because Christ, who has commanded them to be brought, welcomes them. The adults have the advantage here in that they hear it often and can reflect back on it. Nevertheless, it also happens with adults that even many sermons do not penetrate to spiritual hearing; but then it may hit home once in one sermon, and he has enough forever. What he hears afterward either improves what he heard first or destroys it again.

46. In summary, the Baptism and comfort of children is in these words: "Let the children come to Me; do not hinder them, for of such is the kingdom of God" [Mark 10:14]. He has said this and does not lie. So it must be right and Christian to bring little children to Him. That cannot happen other than in Baptism. So it must also be certain that He blesses them and gives the kingdom of heaven to all who come to Him, as the words read: "Of such is the kingdom of God." That is enough about this for now.

47. Here at the end we should treat what leprosy and paralysis signify spiritually. But much is said about leprosy in the postil of the ten lepers. Therefore, it is not treated at length here.

# GOSPEL FOR THE FOURTH SUNDAY AFTER EPIPHANY

### *Matthew 8:23–27*

*And when He got into the boat, His disciples followed Him. And behold, there arose a great storm on the sea, so that the boat was being swamped by the waves; but He was asleep. And they went and woke Him, saying, "Save us, Lord; we are perishing." And He said to them, "Why are you afraid, O you of little faith?" Then He rose and rebuked the winds and the sea, and there was a great calm. And the men marveled, saying, "What sort of man is this, that even winds and sea obey Him?"*

1. This Gospel reading, according to its history,[1] presents us with an example of faith and unbelief, so that we may learn how great the power of faith is and that it must deal with great and terrible things and accomplish even miracles; and that unbelief is such a despondent, timid, and frightened thing, which can do nothing at all. Experience lets us see this in the hearts of the disciples. First, when they entered the boat with Christ, it was calm, and they perceived nothing; had anyone then asked them if they believed, they would have said, "Yes." But they did not see how their heart trusted in the calmness and in the fact that there was no storm, and thus was based on visible things. When the bad weather came and the waves fell over the boat, then their faith was gone, for the calmness and the peace to which they clung were gone; therefore, they sailed along with nothing but unbelief.

2. But what does this unbelief do? It sees nothing more than it perceives. It does not perceive life and security, but the waves [coming] over the boat and the sea which offers them death and every danger. Because they perceive that and pay attention to it and do not turn away from it, their terror, fear, and trembling do not cease. Indeed, the more they look at it and sense it, the more severely death and fear work at them and will devour them at any moment. Unbelief cannot abandon such perceiving and cannot think differently even for a moment, for it has nothing else to which it clings and from which it can take comfort; therefore, it cannot have peace or be calm even for a moment. That is what happens in hell, where there is nothing but fear, trembling, and terror, with never an end.

---

1 As opposed to the spiritual meaning, which is discussed below, paragraphs 10–17.

3. But if faith had been there, it would have happened in this way: [faith] would have put the wind and the waves of the sea out of their minds, and pictured before their eyes God's power and grace, promised in His Word, instead of the wind and tempest. And it would have relied on that [Word] as if it sat on a hard rock and did not float on the water, and as if the sun shone brightly and it was calm and there was no storm. It is the high art and power of faith that it sees what is unseen and does not see what is still perceived, which even pushes and presses on us. In the same way, unbelief sees only what it perceives and cannot at all cling to what it does not perceive.

4. God gives faith not so that it can deal with insignificant things, but [so that it can deal with] things the whole world cannot handle, such as death, sin, world, and devil. All the world cannot stand against death, but flees from it and is terrified of it and also is overcome by it; but faith stands firm, opposes death (which consumes all the world), prevails over it, and even swallows that which insatiably consumes life [cf. 1 Cor. 15:54].

So also all the world cannot constrain or suppress the flesh; rather, it rules over all the world, and what it wants must happen, so that all the world becomes fleshly through it. But faith attacks it, subjugates it, and bridles it, so that it must serve.

Likewise, no one can endure the world's raging, persecuting, slandering, desecrating, hatred, and jealousy. Everyone yields and becomes weak, while [the world] conquers and wins. Except faith mocks them and tramples them with its feet and turns them into joy and delight.

5. So, who could overcome the devil with his innumerable, cunning insinuations with which he hinders the truth, God's Word, faith, and hope and starts so many errors, sects, temptations, heresies, doubts, superstitions, and abomination without measure? Compared to him, all the world is like a spark of fire compared with a fountain of water. In this all must be subject to him, as we also see, hear, and understand. But it is faith that keeps him busy and remains not only untempted before him but also reveals his craftiness and puts him to shame, so that his deception has no force, becomes weak, and collapses, as now happens with his indulgences and his papacy.

So no one can quiet and silence even the least sin. Rather, it bites and devours the conscience, so that nothing helps. Even if all the world were to comfort and assist such a person, he must go down into hell. Here faith is the hero who quiets all sins, even if they were as many as all the world had done.

6. Is it not almighty and inexpressible that faith can withstand such powerful enemies and obtain the victory? As a result, St. John says, "This is the victory that has overcome the world—our faith" (1 John 5 [:4]). This does not happen in peace and calm rest, for it is a battle which does not end without wounds and blood. Indeed, in this battle the heart perceives sin, death, flesh,

devil, and world so harshly that it thinks nothing else than that it is lost, that sin and death have won, and that the devil has prevailed. It perceives little of the power of faith. That is characterized in this story when the waves not only hit the boat but even swamped it, so that now it was to be wrecked and sunk, while Christ lay there and slept [cf. Matt. 8:24]. When there was no hope of life, death had prevailed and won, and life was defeated and lost.

7. As it happened here, so it happens and must happen in all the other attacks of sin, the devil, etc. We must perceive that sin has taken captive the conscience, that nothing but wrath and hell remain, and that we must be eternally lost. The devil must cause so much with his error and false teaching that it appears God's Word must be defeated and the world must surrender to error. So the world must also rage and persecute so that it appears no one can withstand it or be saved or confess faith. Rather, Cain wants to rule alone and to have his brother dead, so that he is no more [Gen. 4:1–16]. However, we must judge and act not according to appearance and perception, but according to faith.

8. Therefore, this Gospel is a comforting example and doctrine of how we should act so that we do not despair in the distress of sin, in the agony of death, and in the raging of the world, and so that we know that we are not lost, even if the waves swamp the boat; that we will not go to hell, even if we perceive sin, wrath, and hostility in an evil conscience; that we will not die, even if all the world hates and persecutes us, even if it opens its jaws as wide as the sunrise. These are all waves that fall over your little boat and cause you to despair and force you to cry out: "We are lost, O Lord, help!" [cf. Matt 8:25]. Thus you see here the first point of this Gospel, which is what the nature of faith should be, and then how incapable and despondent unbelief is.

9. The second point, love, is shown by Christ when He rose, cut short His sleep for their sake, took an interest in their need as if it were His own, and helped them due to unrestrained love without their merit. He neither takes nor seeks anything for it, but has them benefit from and use His goodness. We have often heard how Christian love is, that it does everything freely and gratuitously, to the praise and glory of God, so that a Christian lives on earth for the sake of such love, just as Christ lived only for the purpose of doing good. He Himself says, "I came to serve, not to be served" (Matthew 20 [:28]).

## SPIRITUAL MEANING OF THIS ACCOUNT

10. Christ here represents the Christian life, especially the preaching office. The boat signifies Christendom. The sea signifies the world. The wind signifies the devil. Christ's disciples are the preachers and godly Christians. Christ is the truth, the Gospel, and faith.

11. Before Christ entered the boat with His disciples, the sea and the wind were calm. But when Christ entered it with His disciples, then the storm began, as He Himself says, "I have not come to bring peace on earth, but the sword" [Matt. 10:34]. So if Christ had left the world in peace and not rebuked its works, then it would indeed have been calm. But since He preaches that the wise are fools, that the saints are sinners, and that the rich are lost, they become mad and wild. Similarly now, some know-it-alls think it would be excellent if we merely preached the Gospel and let the clerical estate continue doing what it is doing, for they would tolerate that. But that everything they do should be rebuked and be all wrong, that is what they call "preaching strife and insurrection," and they say it is not Christian doctrine.

12. But what does this Gospel say? There was a great storm on the sea when Christ and His disciples were in the boat. The sea and the wind left other boats in peace, but this boat must suffer distress because Christ is in it. The world can tolerate all preaching except Christ's preaching. That is because whenever He comes and wherever He is, He preaches so that He alone is right and rebukes all others. As He says, "Whoever is not with Me is against Me" [Matt. 12:30]; and again: "The Spirit will convict the world concerning sin and righteousness and judgment" [John 16:8]. He does not say that He will only preach, but that He will convict the whole world and whatever is in it. This rebuking causes the storm and dangers to this boat. If He was supposed to preach so as to let them and their deeds remain unrebuked, He would all the more have been silent beforehand and would have remained outside [the world]; for if the world were good and not to be rebuked, then people would have no need for Him.

13. It is a comfort for Christians, and especially for preachers, when they are certain and confident that when they present and preach Christ, they must suffer persecution; nothing else will come of it. It is a truly good sign that the preaching is truly Christian when they are persecuted, especially by the great, holy, learned, and clever people. On the other hand, when they are praised and honored, [then their preaching] is not upright, as He says: "Woe to you, when all people speak well of you, for so their fathers did to the false prophets. It is good for you when people hate you and spurn your name as evil on account of the Son of Man; for so their fathers did to the prophets" (Luke 6 [:26, 22–23]). Look at how the doctrine of our spiritual clergy is regarded: they have the world's goods, honor, and power among them and want to be Christian teachers; whoever praises and preaches their ideas is their glory and delight.

14. Therefore, we also have here the example of where they are to seek their comfort and help. They are not to seek that from the world, for human skill and power will not protect them. Rather, they are to seek that from

Christ Himself and from Christ alone, to whom and on whom they are to depend in every need with all faithfulness and confidence, as the disciples do here. If they had not believed that He would help them, they would not have awakened Him and called on Him. Yet their faith was still weak, and they still had much unbelief, so that they did not fully yield themselves and stake their lives on Him, nor did they believe that He could rescue them in the midst of the sea and snatch them from death.

Thus it is determined that the Word of God has no master or judge and also no protector other than God Himself. It is His Word. Therefore, just as He issued it without any human merit or advice, so He will also Himself maintain and defend it without any human help and strength. Whoever seeks from men protection and comfort in these things will fall and lack both, forsaken by God and by men.

15. By sleeping He shows [first] the status of their hearts, namely, that they had a weak, sleepy faith. But He especially shows that at the time of persecution Christ withdraws and acts as if He is sleeping, and gives neither strength nor power, neither peace nor rest, but lets us be anxious and labor in our weakness. This leads us to see that we are nothing at all and that everything depends on His grace and power, as Paul confesses that he had to suffer such great affliction so that we would learn to "rely not on ourselves but on God who raises the dead" (2 Corinthians 1 [:9]). David often felt that God was sleeping and reports it in many places, such as when he says: "Rouse Yourself, O Lord, and stand up! Why are You sleeping and forgetting us?" (Psalm 44 [:23]).

16. In summary, this Gospel gives us two comforting and defiant maxims. [First,] when persecution arises because of God's Word, we can say: "Yes, I know well that Christ is in the boat, and for that reason the sea and wind rage, and the waves fall on us and want to send us to the bottom. But let them rage, for it is determined that the wind and sea are subject to Him. The persecution will not continue further or longer than He wants [cf. 1 Cor. 10:13]. Even if they overtake us, they must still be subject to Him. Since He is Lord over everything, nothing will harm us. May He help us so that we do not despair in unbelief. Amen."

17. [Second,] the men marveled and praised the Lord that the wind and sea obeyed Him [Matt. 8:27], and this signifies that through persecution the Gospel and God's Word only advance and become stronger, and faith increases. This contradicts the way things work with worldly possessions, which decrease in misfortune and adversity and increase in prosperity and peace. Christ's kingdom increases in affliction and decreases in peace and luxury, as St. Paul says, "My power is made stronger in weakness," etc. (2 Corinthians 12 [:9]). May God help us! Amen.

# GOSPEL FOR THE FIFTH SUNDAY AFTER EPIPHANY

*Matthew 13:24–30*

*He put another parable before them, saying, "The kingdom of heaven may be compared to a man who sowed good seed in his field, but while his men were sleeping, his enemy came and sowed weeds among the wheat and went away. So when the plants came up and bore grain, then the weeds appeared also. And the servants of the master of the house came and said to him, 'Master, did you not sow good seed in your field? How then does it have weeds?' He said to them, 'An enemy has done this.' So the servants said to him, 'Then do you want us to go and gather them?' But he said, 'No, lest in gathering the weeds you root up the wheat along with them. Let both grow together until the harvest, and at harvest time I will tell the reapers, "Gather the weeds first and bind them in bundles to be burned, but gather the wheat into my barn."'"*

1. The Lord Himself explained this parable in the same chapter at the instigation of His disciples and said: "The one who sows good seed is the Son of Man. The field is the world. The good seed are the children of the kingdom. The weeds are the children of evil. The enemy who sowed them is the devil. The harvest is the end of the world. The reapers are the angels" [Matt. 13:37–39]. These seven points of the Gospel clearly comprehend what He meant with this parable. But who could have found this explanation, since in this parable He calls the seed "people" and the field "the world," but in the previous parable[1] He called the seed "the Word of God" and the field "the people" or "the hearts of the people"? If He had not Himself explained it, everyone would have imitated the previous parable and had the seed be God's Word, and thus lost the [correct] understanding.

2. Therefore, let us note [something] here for the benefit of the intelligent and learned who are to discuss Scripture. Imitating or conjecturing is not right in Scripture; rather, one should and must be certain of his case. Similarly, Joseph explained the two dreams of the cupbearer and the baker—which seemed to be the same—differently, and not one in imitation of the other (Genesis 40 [:12–19]). Even though there would not have been a great

---

1 The parable of the sower, Matt. 13:3–9, 18–23.

danger if people had explained the seed as God's Word, it still would not have been correctly understood.

3. Thus this Gospel teaches us what happens in the world with the kingdom of God (that is, with Christendom), especially on account of its doctrine. Specifically, it is not to be expected that there should be only orthodox Christians and the pure doctrine of God on earth; rather, there must also be false Christians and heretics, so that the true Christians would be approved, as St. Paul says [1 Thess. 2:4; 1 Cor. 11:19]. This parable speaks not about false Christians who are so only outwardly in their lives, but about those who are unchristian in their doctrine and faith under the Christian name, who glitter beautifully but are harmful. It is a matter of the conscience, not of the actions. There must be spiritual servants who can identify the weeds among the wheat. In summary, we should not be surprised or frightened when all kinds of false doctrine and faith arise among us [cf. Matt. 24:24]. The devil is always "among the sons of God" (Job 1 [:6]).

4. Second, [this Gospel reading teaches] how we should act toward these heretics and false teachers. We are not to uproot or destroy them. He plainly says that we should "let both grow together" [Matt. 13:30]. We should deal here only with God's Word, for it happens in these matters that whoever goes astray today can get on the right path tomorrow. Who knows when the Word of God will touch his heart? But if he is burned [at the stake] or otherwise slaughtered, then he has been prevented from getting on the right path; thus the Word of God is taken away from him, so that he who could otherwise have been saved must be lost. That is why the Lord says here that the wheat would be rooted up if they gathered the weeds [Matt. 13:29]. That would be a very horrible thing before God, for which we could never answer.

5. Note what mad people we have been for such a long time! We wanted to force the Turks to believe with the sword, the heretics with fire, the Jews with killing, and so we rooted out the weeds by our own power, just as if we were the people who could rule over hearts and spirits, and we could make them godly and right, which God's Word alone must do. But we separate people from the Word with murder, so that [the Word] cannot work on them, and thus at once bring a double murder on ourselves, as far as it depends on us, namely, that we murder the body for time and the soul for eternity. Afterward we say we have done God a service and want to merit something special in heaven.

6. Therefore, this passage should justly frighten the inquisitors and executioners (if they did not have iron foreheads), even if they had real heretics in front of them. But now they burn the true saints and are themselves heretics. What is that otherwise than that they root out the wheat and allege that they are gathering the weeds, like crazy people?

7. This Gospel reading with its parable also teaches that free will is nothing, because the good seed was sown only by Christ, and the devil could sow nothing but evil seed. We also see that the field produces nothing itself except weeds, which the animals eat, even if [the weeds] make the field green and even take it over, as if it were their own. So the false Christians are good for nothing among the true Christians except to support the world and to be food for the devil. They become green and glitter so prettily, as if they alone were the saints, and take over in Christendom as if they were the lords, and as though the government and the seats at the head of the table must be theirs. They have no other reason for that than their own boast that they are Christians and are among Christians in the Church of Christ, even though they themselves see and confess that they live unchristian lives.

8. The Lord depicts the devil as casting seed while the people sleep, and then going away so that no one sees who did it. Thus He shows how the devil can deck himself out and conceal himself so that he is not regarded as a devil. We experience that in Christendom when [the devil] first smuggles in false teachers, who go about beautifully, as if there were nothing but God and the devil were far more than a thousand miles away. No one sees anything other than that they expound God's Word, name, and work. It is cunningly camouflaged. But when the wheat comes up, then we see the weeds. That is, when we want to treat God's Word correctly and teach faith so that fruits will come from it, then they step out in opposition to it: they want to possess the field; they are anxious, lest only wheat grow in the field and their interests are omitted.

9. Then the servants, the preachers, are surprised. They do not yet pass judgment on them, but want to interpret everything for the best, since [the false teachers] do bear the Christian name. But they see that there are weeds and bad seeds. They step away from faith and fall into works, and think about rooting them out. They lament about this to the Lord through wholehearted prayer in the Spirit. He again says that they should not root it out; that is, they should have patience, endure the slander, and commend it to God. Although [the weeds] hinder the wheat, yet they make [the wheat] appear all the more beautiful compared to the weeds, as St. Paul also says, "There must be sects, so that those who are approved may be recognized" [cf. 1 Cor. 11:19; 1 Thess. 2:4]. This is enough about that.

# GOSPEL FOR
# SEPTUAGESIMA SUNDAY

*Matthew 20:1–16*

*[Jesus said,] "For the kingdom of heaven is like a master of a house who went out early in the morning to hire laborers for his vineyard. After agreeing with the laborers for a denarius a day, he sent them into his vineyard. And going out about the third hour he saw others standing idle in the marketplace, and to them he said, 'You go into the vineyard too, and whatever is right I will give you.' So they went. Going out again about the sixth hour and the ninth hour, he did the same. And about the eleventh hour he went out and found others standing. And he said to them, 'Why do you stand here idle all day?' They said to him, 'Because no one has hired us.' He said to them, 'You go into the vineyard too.' And when evening came, the owner of the vineyard said to his foreman, 'Call the laborers and pay them their wages, beginning with the last, up to the first.' And when those hired about the eleventh hour came, each of them received a denarius. Now when those hired first came, they thought they would receive more, but each of them also received a denarius. And on receiving it they grumbled at the master of the house, saying, 'These last worked only one hour, and you have made them equal to us who have borne the burden of the day and the scorching heat.' But he replied to one of them, 'Friend, I am doing you no wrong. Did you not agree with me for a denarius? Take what belongs to you and go. I choose to give to this last worker as I give to you. Am I not allowed to do what I choose with what belongs to me? Or do you begrudge my generosity?' So the last will be first, and the first last."*

1. Some of the fathers have applied this Gospel reading to the preachers from the beginning to the end of the world, so that the first hour is Adam's time; the third, Noah's time; the sixth, Abraham's; the ninth, Moses'; and the eleventh, the time of Christ and His apostles. Such babbling is good for killing time, if you have nothing else to preach. It makes little sense that the denarius should be eternal life, with which the first [group]—Adam and the holy patriarchs—was not satisfied, or that such holy people should grumble in the kingdom of heaven and further be reprimanded by the father of the house and regarded as the last (that is, condemned).

2. Therefore, we abandon such fables and remain with the simple teaching and meaning of Christ, who wants to show with this parable how things happen in the kingdom of heaven, that is, in Christendom on earth. God

here directs and works in an unusual way, namely, in making the first last and the last first. All of this is said to humble those who are something, so that they would trust in nothing but God's pure goodness and mercy. On the other hand, [this is said] so that those who are nothing will not despair, but also trust in God's goodness, just like the others.

3. Therefore, we must not look at this parable in all the details, but rather note the main point He wants to make. We should not pay attention to what the penny or denarius means, nor to what the first or the last hour is. Rather, [we should pay attention] to what the father of the house has in mind, that His goodness should be regarded alone, higher than all works and merit. Similarly, in the parable of the dishonest manager (Luke 16 [:1–8]), what is presented to us is not the whole parable, so that we should also cheat our Lord, but only the shrewdness of the manager, that he provided so well and wisely for himself and found what was best for himself, even though it harmed his lord. Whoever would seek in detail and preach about the debtors—and what the account books, the oil, the grain, and the measurements signify—would miss the true meaning and follow his own imagination, which would be good for nothing.

Such parables were not told so that we would cling to every detail. St. Paul compares Adam and Christ and says that Adam was a prototype of Christ, even though Adam handed sin and death down to us, while Christ handed down life and righteousness (Romans 5 [:12–21]). The comparison consists not in the inheritance, but in the result of the inheritance: just as sin and death cling to and, by inheritance, follow those who are born of Adam, so life and righteousness cling to and, by inheritance, follow those who are born of Christ. Similarly, one could refer to an unchaste woman, who adorns herself with love for the world and sin, as a pattern of a Christian soul, which also adorns itself before God, but not with sins as she does.

4. Thus the focus of the parable in this Gospel is not on what the denarius is, or on the different [hours], but on the earning and acquiring, that is, how we can earn the denarius. Those who were [hired] first thought they had acquired the denarius, and something more, by their own merit, and yet the last ones [hired] acquired it by the lord's goodness. So God wants to show that what God gives us is pure goodness, and no one should think himself above others. Therefore, He says here: "I am doing you no wrong. Is not the money Mine and not yours? If I were giving away your money, then you should grumble. Am I not allowed to do what I choose with what belongs to Me?" [Matt. 20:13–15].

5. So here Christ is alarmed first of all at the arrogance (similar to today's Epistle) of those who want to fight their way into heaven with works—just

as the Jews did and wanted to be closest to God. So far our clergy[1] have also done the same. They all labor for set wages; that is, they take no other interest in God's Law than that they should fulfill it with the works listed for the specified reward. They never understand the Law correctly and do not know that they must have pure grace before God. That means that they hire themselves out and agree with the Lord [to work] for a denarius as their day's wage. Consequently, their lives become bitter, and they live in a difficult order.

6. Now when the Gospel comes and equalizes everything, as St. Paul does (Romans 3 [:23])—so that those who have done many works have no more value than public sinners, and must also become sinners and put up with the words "all have sinned" (Romans 3 [:23]), and that no one is justified before God by works [Rom. 3:20]—then they look around and despise those who have done nothing at all, because their great trouble and work count for no more than the idleness and careless life of the others. Then they grumble against the father of the family, think it is not right, slander the Gospel, and become hardened in their ways. So they lose the favor and grace of God; they must take their temporal wages and trot away with their denarius and be condemned, for they served not for the eternal favor but for pay. And that is what they get, and nothing more.

But the others must confess that they have deserved neither the denarius nor the favor, but more is given to them than they thought was promised to them. They remain in grace and are saved; moreover, here in this life they have enough, for it all depends on the goodwill of the father of the family.

7. Therefore, if we want to explain this literally, then the denarius must be the temporal gift, and the favor of the father of the family is the eternal gift. The day and the heat must apply not to the time but to the conscience, so that [it means that] the work-saints work long and hard; that is, they work with a heavy conscience and a reluctant heart, forced and driven by the Law. The short hour [worked by those hired last] is the light conscience led by grace, which lives willingly and well, without the driving of the Law.

8. Thus they have the same denarius; that is, a temporal gift is given to both. Those [hired] last did not seek it, but it came to them because they sought first the kingdom of God (Matthew 6 [:33]), and besides have grace for eternal life and are happy. Those [hired] first seek the temporal, haggle and serve for that; therefore, they must lose grace and deserve hell for their hard life. Those [hired] last do not think and presume to deserve the denarius, and yet obtain it all; when those [hired] first see it, they presume to obtain more and lose everything. Therefore, we clearly see, if we look into their hearts, that those [hired] last do not pay attention to their merit but enjoy the Lord's goodness; those [hired] first do not pay attention to the

1 *Geistlichen*, or "spiritual people"

Lord's goodness but look at their own merit, and think that it is owed to them and grumble about it.

9. We must apply these two words "last" and "first" to two sides: first, before God, and, second, before people. Those who are the first before people—that is, those who consider themselves and let themselves be considered as the closest and first before God—are just the opposite before God in that they are the last and the farthest away from Him. On the other hand, those who are the last before people—that is, those who consider themselves and let themselves be considered the farthest away and the last before God—are just the opposite in that they are the closest and the first before God. Whoever wants to be secure should cling to the words "Whoever exalts himself will be humbled" [Matt. 23:12]. For this is what it says: The first before people is the last before God; the last before people is the first before God. On the other hand, the first before God is the last before people; the last before God is the first before people.

10. This Gospel does not speak simply of ordinary first and last people—as in the world the exalted are nothing before God more than the heathen who know nothing of God—but it means those who imagine that they are the first or the last before God. Hence it acts very boldly and strikes very admirable people, so that even the greatest saints are frightened. Therefore, Christ even reproaches the apostles themselves about this [cf. Matt. 18:1-4]. Here it happens that one who is poor, weak, despised before the world, and even suffers for God's sake—so that there is no sign that he is anything—and yet in his heart he is secretly full of his own good-pleasure, so that he imagines that he is the first before God, just for that reason is the last. On the other hand, if someone is so despondent and bashful that he thinks he is the last before God—even though before the world he has money, honor, and property—just for that reason he is the first.

11. One also sees how the highest saints have been afraid and how many have fallen from a high spiritual estate. David laments: "When I did not calm and quiet my soul, my soul was weaned like [a child] is weaned from its mother" (Psalm 131 [:2]). Likewise in another place: "Let not the foot of arrogance come to me" [Ps. 36:11]. How often he rebukes the impudent, the shameless, and the proud (Psalm 119 [:21]). Likewise St. Paul says: "To keep me from becoming exalted because of the high revelation, the thorn was given me in the flesh" (2 Corinthians 12 [:7]). We heard in the Epistle what very admirable people have fallen—all of whom without doubt experienced this loathsome, secret trap: They became secure and thought: "We are so close [to God] that there is no need for us to know God, because we have done this and that." They do not themselves see how they have made themselves the first before God. See how Saul fell [1 Samuel 15]! [God] let

David fall [2 Samuel 11]! How Peter had to fall [Mark 14:66–72]! How some disciples of Paul fell [e.g., 1 Tim. 1:20]!

12. Therefore, it is also very necessary that this Gospel be preached in our times to those who know the Gospel, such as me and those like me, who can teach and point out fault with all the world and who think they are the closest [to God] and have eaten up the Holy Spirit with his feathers and bones.[2] Why is it that so many sects have already arisen, one taking up this, another that, in the Gospel? Without a doubt because none of them thought that these words—"the first are the last" [Matt. 16:16]—concerned or applied to them; or, if the words did apply, then they were secure and without fear because they thought themselves to be the first. Therefore, according to these words, it must happen that they become the last and go ahead proclaiming such shameful doctrines and blasphemies against God and His Word.

13. Has this not also happened with the pope? He and his people think no differently than that he is God's representative[3] and the closest of all [to God], and he has persuaded the world of this. But in doing so he became the devil's representative and the farthest away from God of all, so that no one under the sun has ever so raged and raved against God and His Word. Nevertheless, he did not see the horrible trap, for he was secure and was unafraid of this subtle, sharp, high, and striking judgment: "The first are the last." This strikes the deepest part of the heart, their own spiritual opinion, which thinks it is the first even in poverty, dishonor, and misfortune; indeed, that is when it does so most of all.

14. So here is the summary of this Gospel: no one is so high, or will get so high, that he does not have to be afraid that he may become the very lowest [cf. 1 Cor. 10:12]. On the other hand, no one has fallen so deeply, or can fall so deeply, that he cannot hope to become the highest, because all merit is abolished and only God's goodness is praised. It is has been determined most surely: "The first shall be the last, and the last shall be the first." When He says, "The first shall be the last," He takes away all your arrogance and forbids you to exalt yourself above any prostitute, even if you were Abraham, David, Peter, or Paul. But when He says, "The last shall be the first," He prevents all your despair and forbids you to cast yourself below any saint, even if you were Pilate, Herod, Sodom, and Gomorrah.

15. Just as we have no reason to be arrogant, so we also have no reason to despair. The middle path is established and preserved by this Gospel, that we should not look at the denarius but at the goodness of the Father of the family, which is one and the same toward high and low, first and last, saints

2 An allusion to the dove, symbol of the Holy Spirit.

3 The bull of Boniface VIII, *Unam sanctam* (1302), asserted that the pope is the vicar of Christ and that all authority, temporal and spiritual, has been entrusted to him.

and sinners. No one can boast or take comfort or be arrogant about this more than another. He is not only the God of the Jews but also of the Gentiles, of all at the same time, no matter who they are or what they are called.

# GOSPEL FOR
# SEXAGESIMA SUNDAY

*Luke 8:4–15*

*When a great crowd was gathering and people from town after town came to Him, He said in a parable, "A sower went out to sow his seed. And as he sowed, some fell along the path and was trampled underfoot, and the birds of the air devoured it. And some fell on the rock, and as it grew up, it withered away, because it had no moisture. And some fell among thorns, and the thorns grew up with it and choked it. And some fell into good soil and grew and yielded a hundredfold." As He said these things, He called out, "He who has ears to hear, let him hear." And when His disciples asked Him what this parable meant, He said, "To you it has been given to know the secrets of the kingdom of God, but for others they are in parables, so that 'seeing they may not see, and hearing they may not understand.' Now the parable is this: The seed is the word of God. The ones along the path are those who have heard; then the devil comes and takes away the word from their hearts, so that they may not believe and be saved. And the ones on the rock are those who, when they hear the word, receive it with joy. But these have no root; they believe for a while, and in time of testing fall away. And as for what fell among the thorns, they are those who hear, but as they go on their way they are choked by the cares and riches and pleasures of life, and their fruit does not mature. As for that in the good soil, they are those who, hearing the word, hold it fast in an honest and good heart, and bear fruit with patience."*

1. This Gospel speaks about the students and the fruits which the Word of God has in the world. It does not speak about the Law or about human ordinances, but, as He Himself says, about the Word of God which He Himself, Christ the sower, preaches. The Law produces no fruit, just as little as human ordinances do. He establishes four groups of students of the Word of God.

2. The first group are those who hear, but do not understand or pay attention to it [Luke 8:12]. These are not the common people on earth, but the greatest, wisest, and holiest—in short, they are the majority. He is not speaking here about those who persecute the Word or who do not listen to it, but about those who hear it and are students of it, who even want to be called true Christians, who live with us in the Christian congregation, and who partake of Baptism and the Sacrament with us. But they are and remain

fleshly hearts who do not accept the Word, for it goes in one ear and out the other.[1] Similarly, the kernel fell on the path and not on the ground, and remained lying out on the path, for the path was trodden hard by human and animal feet [cf. Luke 8:5].

3. That is why He says that "the devil comes and takes away the Word from their hearts, so that they may not believe and be saved" [Luke 8:12]. This power of the devil not only means that hearts which were hardened through a worldly mind and life lose and abandon the Word, so that they never understand or know it, but it also means that instead of God's Word the devil sends false teachers, who trample it down with human doctrines. It says here both that the seed was trampled on the path and [that it was] eaten up by the birds.

Christ Himself explains the birds as the devils who take away the Word and devour it. That happens when he turns their hearts away and blinds them so that they do not understand or pay attention to it, as St. Paul says, "They will turn away from listening to the truth and turn aside into myths" (2 Timothy 4 [:4]). He understands "trampling" as the human doctrines which rule in our hearts. He also says that salt which has lost its taste is "thrown out and trampled under people's feet" (Matthew 5 [:13]); that is, as St. Paul says, they must "believe what is false" (2 Thessalonians 2 [:11]) because they did not obey the truth [Gal. 3:1; Rom. 2:8].

4. Thus all heretics, sects, and fanatics belong to this group, who understand the Gospel in a fleshly way and explain it however they want according to their own mind. They all hear the Gospel but produce no fruits. Rather, they are ruled by the devil and more harshly oppressed by human ordinances than they were before. It is a terrible thing when Christ says that the devil takes the Word away from their hearts [Luke 8:12], by which he proves that the devil rules powerfully over their hearts, even if they are called "Christians" and hear the Word.

Likewise, it is miserable to hear that they are trampled and must be placed beneath men in their pernicious doctrines. Under the appearance and name of the Gospel, the devil subtly takes the Word from them, so that they never understand it and are never saved, but must be eternally lost, as now our fanatics do in all lands. Where this Word does not remain, there is no salvation, and great works and holy lives do not help, for when He says that they are not saved because the Word was taken away from them [Luke 8:12], He proves quite strongly that not works but faith alone saves through

1 *es gehet zu eim Ohr ein, zum andern wieder aus.* This expression has the same meaning in German as in English: to hear something without attention and without letting it have any effect on one's attitude.

the Word, as St. Paul says, "It is a divine power to save all who believe in it" (Romans 1 [:16]).

5. The second group are those "who receive it with joy" [Luke 8:13], but they do not persevere. This is also a large group who understand the Word correctly and grasp it purely, without any sects, divisions, or fanatics. They rejoice that they know the real truth and are able to know how they may be saved without works through faith, and, in addition, that they are free from imprisonment by the Law, their conscience, and human doctrines. But when it comes to the point of suffering harm, insults, disgrace, and loss of life or property, then they fall away and deny it, for they do not have enough root and are not [planted] deeply enough. Therefore, they are like the seed on a rock, which quickly springs forth and sprouts, which is good to look at and holds promise; but when the sun shines hot, it withers, for it lacks soil and moisture and has only rock [Luke 8:6]. These do the same. In a time of persecution, they deny the Word or keep quiet about it. They do, speak, and suffer everything their persecutors command or want. Yet formerly they sprang forth quickly and cheerfully spoke and confessed when there was still peace and no heat, so that there was hope they would produce much fruit and advantage for people. These fruits are not only the works but also much more the confessing, preaching, and spreading of the Word, so that many others are converted through it and the kingdom of God is increased.

6. The third group are those who hear and understand, but then fall off on the other side, namely, into the pleasures and laziness of this life, so that they do nothing at all with the Word [Luke 8:14]. This group is also rather large, for though they do not produce heresies like the first group but always have the pure Word [and] though they are not attacked on the left side with adversity and persecution like the second group, they fall off on the other side, for their ruin is that they have peace and good days. For that reason they do not take the Word seriously, but become lazy and absorbed in the cares, riches, and pleasures of this life, so that they are good for nothing. Therefore, they are like the seed which fell among the thorns. Although there is no rock, but good soil; though there is no path, but deeply plowed ground—yet the thorns will not let it grow, but choke it [Luke 8:7]. Thus they have everything necessary for salvation in the Word without using it, and so they rot in carnal pleasures in this life. This is where those people belong who hear but do not restrain their flesh; those who know but do not act accordingly; those who teach but do not follow it themselves. They remain this year as they were last year.

7. The fourth group are those who grasp it and retain it with "a fine and good heart" [Luke 8:15] and produce fruit with patience, that is, those who hear the Word and continually cling to it, so that they would risk everything

and leave everything for it. The devil does not take it away from them or mislead them; the heat of persecution does not do away with them; the thorns of pleasure and the greed of this age do not hinder them. Rather, they produce fruit: teaching others the same thing, increasing the kingdom of God, and then also doing good to their neighbor in love.

That is why He says "with patience" [Luke 8:15], for they must suffer much on account of the Word: insult and disgrace from the sects and heretics, hatred and jealousy with injury to body and property from their persecutors, not to mention what the thorns and the temptations of their own flesh do. It is well called "the Word of the cross" [1 Cor. 1:18], for whoever will cling to it must bear the cross and misfortune with patience and triumph.

8. He says "in a fine and good heart" [Luke 8:15]. Just as a field that lacks thorn and brush and is level and spacious is a beautiful, clean place, so also a heart is fine and pure, wide and spacious that is without worry and greed for temporal sustenance, so that there is room for the Word of God there. But a field is good not only when it is fine and level but also when it is fertile and fruitful, so that it has good ground which abounds in grain, not like a stony or gravelly field. So a heart which has good ground with a full spirit is strong, fertile, and good to retain the Word and to produce fruit with patience.

9. Here we see why it is unsurprising that there are so few true Christians, for the seed does not fall only on good ground, but only the fourth and smallest part does. Those who boast that they are Christians and praise the teaching of the Gospel are not to be trusted, such as Demas, St. Paul's disciple, who finally deserted him [2 Tim. 4:10], or those disciples of Christ who withdrew from Him (John 6 [:66]). He Himself calls out and says, "He who has ears to hear, let him hear" [Luke 8:8], as if He would say: "Oh, how few true Christians there are. One cannot believe all who are called Christians and hear the Gospel; more is required than that."

10. All this is said for our instruction, so that we do not go astray, since so many misuse the Gospel and few grasp it correctly. It is frustrating to preach [the Gospel] to those who treat it so shamefully and even work against the Gospel. This preaching [of the Gospel] should be common, so that it is proclaimed to the whole creation, as Christ says, "Proclaim the Gospel to the whole creation" (Mark 16 [:15]); and Psalm 19 [:4]: "Their line goes out to all lands, and their speech to the end of the world." What does it matter to us if many despise it? Nevertheless, it must be that "many are called and few are chosen" [Matt. 22:14]. For the sake of the good ground that produces fruit with patience, the seed must also fall in vain on the path, on the rock, and among the thorns. We are certain that God's Word does not go away without fruit, but it always finds the good field, as He says here that some seed of the sower also falls on the good field, and not only on the path, among

the thorns, and on the stony ground. Wherever the Gospel goes, there are Christians: "My Word shall not come empty" (Isaiah 55 [:11]).

11. It is to be noted that Mark [4:8] and Matthew [13:8] say the seed produced some thirtyfold, some sixtyfold, and some a hundredfold. According to the explanations of all [previous commentators], this is to be understood of the three kinds of chastity—that of virgins, married people, and widows. The hundredfold fruit is ascribed to virginity; thirtyfold, the least of all, to the married estate; and sixtyfold to widows. But that is such coarse, worthless babbling that it is a sin and a shame that it has remained so long in Christendom and has been taught by so many high teachers, and no one has noticed it. In this we can see how many valiant, vigorous, and diligent teachers there have been, how one blindly believed the other, and how God let such great saints and people be so coarsely foolish in these great matters of the soul. In that way He warns us to believe no teacher, no matter how holy and great he is, unless he brings God's pure Word [cf. Gal. 1:8].

12. First, it would be an insult to the Word of God if there were to be no more fruits [from it] than chastity, since St. Paul mentions many others (Galatians 5 [:22–23]). In summary, the Word of God accomplishes everything good and makes us wise, intelligent, clever, prudent, godly, good, patient, faithful, discreet, chaste, etc. For that reason alone, this comment about three kinds of chastity is totally unchristian.

Likewise, the heathen and wicked people who do not have the Gospel or even persecute it still have virgins, widows, and married people. Without a doubt, Annas and Caiaphas were honorably married people [John 18:13, 24]. Likewise, people have virginity, in addition to widowhood and marriage, before they have God's Word, for they are born as virgins. When the Gospel comes, it finds them as virgins, widows, and married people and does not first make them into virgins, widows, or married people.

13. Second, marriage, virginity, and widowhood are not fruits or virtues or works, but three estates created and ordered by God; they are not in our power, but are divine works and creations, as are all other creatures. If it were right to make the estates into fruits, then we would have to say that lordship, servitude, maleness, childhood, and the offices of all were only fruits of the Gospel. In that way no fruits at all would be left for the Gospel, since such estates are found completely apart from the Gospel. Chastity has been elevated because of its great prestige, to the great danger and injury of souls, just as if there were no other virtues to adorn a Christian than virginity.

14. I will say further that chastity is a different and much higher thing than virginity, which is nothing else than that a female has been guilty of no

man.[2] Nevertheless, it also happens that virgins, because of the nature of their female bodies, not only have desire and passion for men but must also be full of seed and blood in order to bear children and multiply, as God created them, and that creation is not their work but God's alone. They cannot hinder that, but it must happen as God created it to happen naturally, whether children are born or not. But chastity [in a woman] must be the kind of attitude which has no or little desire for men, and has in her body no or little seed [to bear] fruits or children.

15. Now it commonly happens that a wife often does not feel this desire and passion, this flow or seed, for she is freed from that by and through her husband. Moreover, while a virgin has sheer desire with the thoughts in her heart and has seed in her body, a wife has much displeasure mixed in from her husband, so that, as it is commonly said, the highest and best chastity is in the married estate, because there is less passion and desire in that estate, and there is the least chastity in virginity, because there is much more passion and desire in that estate. Therefore, chastity is a virtue far above virginity, for we can still call a bride a virgin, even though she is full of passion, desire, and love for her bridegroom. Chastity soars high over all three estates—over marriage, over widowhood, and over virginity. But if God does not work a miracle, it sinks, and it is greatest in marriage and least in virginity. There are not three kinds of chastity, but three estates of chastity.

16. It is true that if we consider virginity according to its outward appearance, it seems great that she refrains and does not satisfy her desire with a man. But what if someone bears his desire without a husband or wife longer, and [then] satisfies it better than with a husband or wife? Is there not more unchastity where there is greater passion, love, lust, and stimulation than where there is less? Therefore, if it is considered according to passion and stimulation, as unchastity ought to be considered, virginity is more unchaste than marriage. That can be seen easily in the young girls who are virgins, and yet are full of lust and curiosity and think it much greater than it really is. In short, I would be glad to see a virgin twenty years old who had a healthy, normal female body.[3]

2 In German and Latin, the words for "virgin" (*Jungfrau, virgo*) are feminine and thus were used only for women. For male virginity, other terms, such as "chaste" or "celibate" (*keusch, castus, caelebs*), were used.

3 That is, a body not tormented with lust, "flow," "seed," and the like. In sixteenth-century Germany, the average age at first marriage, which had been increasing since the late fourteenth century, was in the early twenties for women and the middle to late twenties for men. Luther urged marriage by twenty for men and eighteen for women: see Steven E. Ozment, *When Fathers Ruled: Family Life in Reformation Europe* (Cambridge, MA: Harvard University Press, 1983), pp. 37–38.

17. That is enough about chastity, now that we know that these fruits of the Word must be understood differently and in a wider sense than about chastity. And we know specifically that these fruits are that many people are converted through them and come to the knowledge of the truth. Although works are also called fruits, yet He is speaking here especially about the fruits which are produced in hearts when they are enlightened, believing, confident, and wise in Christ. St. Paul wrote: "In order that I might reap some fruit among you, just as among other Gentiles" (Romans 1 [:13]), and "The Gospel is bearing fruit in the whole world, as it also does among you" (Colossians 1 [:6]); that is, many become alive, freed from their sins, and saved through it. It is the proper work of the Gospel—as the Word of life, grace, and salvation—to release us from sin, death, and the devil. In harmony with this fruit, the fruits of the Spirit then follow, works such as patience, love, faithfulness, etc. [cf. Gal. 5:22–23].

18. That some produce fruit thirtyfold, some sixtyfold, and some a hundredfold is the same as saying that more people are converted in one place than in another, and one apostle and preacher preaches in a wider area and more than another. People everywhere are not equally numerous, they do not produce as many Christians, and the preachers do not [all] preach as widely and as much, but this happens as God has provided and ordered. We can certainly attribute a hundredfold fruit to St. Paul's words, which were preached in the widest area and were preached the most, even though he was no virgin.

19. But what does it mean when He says, "To you it has been given to know the mystery of the kingdom of God" [Luke 8:10]? What is the mystery? If we are not to know it, why, then, is it preached? "Mystery" means a hidden, concealed thing, which we do not know. "The mystery of the kingdom of God" is the things hidden in the kingdom of God, such as Christ with all His grace which He shows to us, as Paul describes Him [cf. Eph. 2:7], for whoever truly knows Christ also knows what God's kingdom is and what is in it. It is called "mystery" because it is spiritual and secret, and it certainly remains that way, if the Spirit does not reveal it. Although there are many who see and hear it, yet they do not understand it. Similarly, there are many now who preach Christ and hear how He was given for us; but that is all still on their tongues and not in their hearts, for they themselves do not believe it or sense it, as St. Paul says, "The natural man understands nothing of the Spirit of God" (1 Corinthians 2 [:14]).

For that reason He says here "to you it has been given" [Luke 8:10]. That is, the Spirit gives it to you, so that you not only hear and see it but also recognize and believe it with your heart; therefore, it is no longer a mystery to you. But the others who hear it as well as you, but do not have faith in their hearts, do not see and understand it; to them it is a mystery and remains unknown to them. Everything they hear is nothing else than hearing a parable or a dark saying. This is also proved by our fanatics, who know how to preach much about Christ; but because they themselves do not sense it in their hearts, they rush ahead, leave the true basis of the mystery behind, and are occupied with questions and peculiar things that they have made up. But when things become serious, they know nothing at all about trusting God and finding the forgiveness of sins in Christ.

20. But St. Mark says that Christ spoke to the people in parables so that they could understand it, each according to his ability [cf. Mark 4:33]. How does that agree with St. Matthew, who says that He spoke in parables so that they would not understand it [Matt. 13:13–14]? It must be that St. Mark wants to say that parables serve so that ignorant people can grasp them externally, even if they do not understand them. Afterward, they can be taught, and then understand them. Parables are naturally pleasing to the simple people, and they retain them easily, because they are taken from the common things people deal with. St. Matthew means to say that these parables are of the kind that no one can understand them, no matter how often he grasps and hears them, unless the Spirit makes them known and reveals them. I do not mean that they are preached so that no one will understand them, but that it naturally follows that if the Spirit does not reveal them, no one understands them. Christ took these words from Isaiah (6 [:9–10; Luke 8:10]), where the high understanding of divine providence is mentioned, that He conceals and reveals to whomever He will and has determined from eternity.

# GOSPEL FOR THE VIGIL
# OF THE LORD'S FAST OR
# QUINQUAGESIMA SUNDAY

*Luke 18:31–43*

*Taking the twelve, He said to them, "See, we are going up to Jerusalem, and everything that is written about the Son of Man by the prophets will be accomplished. For He will be delivered over to the Gentiles and will be mocked and shamefully treated and spit upon. And after flogging Him, they will kill Him, and on the third day He will rise." But they understood none of these things. This saying was hidden from them, and they did not grasp what was said. As He drew near to Jericho, a blind man was sitting by the roadside begging. And hearing a crowd going by, he inquired what this meant. They told him, "Jesus of Nazareth is passing by." And he cried out, "Jesus, Son of David, have mercy on me!" And those who were in front rebuked him, telling him to be silent. But he cried out all the more, "Son of David, have mercy on me!" And Jesus stopped and commanded him to be brought to Him. And when he came near, He asked him, "What do you want Me to do for you?" He said, "Lord, let me recover my sight." And Jesus said to him, "Recover your sight; your faith has made you well." And immediately he recovered his sight and followed Him, glorifying God. And all the people, when they saw it, gave praise to God.*

1. This Gospel also presents us with the two points, faith and love, both in Christ, who says that He must go to Jerusalem and let Himself be tormented, and in the blind man whom Christ serves and helps. The first point, faith, proves that Scripture will not be fulfilled except by Christ's suffering and that Scripture speaks about nothing other than Christ; everything has to do with Christ, who must fulfill [Scripture] by His death [Luke 18:1]. But if His death must do this, then our death will add nothing, for our death is a sinful and cursed death. But if our death, which is the highest and severest suffering and misfortune, is sin and cursed, what else should our suffering and torment merit? If our suffering is nothing and useless, what should our good works do, since suffering is always nobler and better than works? Christ must here be all alone, and faith must cling to this.

2. He spoke these words [Luke 18:31–33] before He had completed His suffering, when He was on the way, traveling to Jerusalem and to the

Passover. The disciples did not at all expect His suffering and thought that they would be happy at the festival. He did this so that afterward they would become even stronger in faith, when they realized that He said these things beforehand, then willingly went to His suffering and was crucified, but not by the power and cleverness of the Jews, His enemies. Long before, Isaiah had prophesied that He would willingly and gladly give Himself as a sacrifice (Isaiah 53 [:7]). On Easter Sunday the angel admonishes the women to remember these words which He had spoken to them [Luke 24:6], so that they would know and even more firmly believe that He suffered this willingly for our good.

3. The right basis for knowing Christ's suffering is to know and understand not only His suffering but also His heart and will for that suffering. Whoever looks at His suffering without seeing His will and heart in them must be terrified at it rather than rejoice in it. But if we see His heart and will in [His suffering], this produces true comfort, confidence, and joy in Christ. For this reason Psalm 40 [:7–8] praises this will of God and of Christ in suffering: "In the book it is written of Me that I should do Your will, O My God, and I do it gladly." The Epistle to the Hebrews says: "By that will we all have been sanctified" (Hebrews [10:10]). He does not say "through the suffering and blood of Christ" (which is certainly true), but "through the will of God and of Christ," because they both were of one will: to sanctify us through the blood of Christ.

Here in the Gospel He points out His will for suffering when He first prophesies that He will go to Jerusalem and be crucified [Luke 18:31–33], as if He would say: "Look into My heart, and see that I do this willingly, freely, and gladly, so that you will not be frightened or shocked when you see it, and so that you will not think that I do this reluctantly, that I have to do it, that I am forsaken, and that the Jews are doing this with their power."

4. But the disciples did not understand these words (he says), and the words were "hidden from them" [Luke 18:34]. That is as much as to say: Reason, flesh, and blood cannot understand or grasp that Scripture had to speak about how the Son of Man must be crucified. Much less does it understand that this is His will and that He does it gladly. It does not believe that this is necessary for us, but it wants to deal with God on the basis of its works. Rather, God must reveal this in the heart through His Spirit, even after it is proclaimed externally in words in their ears. Even those to whom the Spirit reveals it scarcely believe it, but struggle with it. It is a great and wonderful thing that the Son of Man is crucified willingly and gladly to fulfill Scripture, that is, for our good. It is a mystery and remains a mystery.

5. As a result of this, how foolish are those who teach that people should patiently bear their sufferings and death in order to do penance and obtain

grace! Those are especially [foolish] who comfort those who should be executed by the judgment of the court or otherwise should die. They assert that if they bear it willingly, then for that reason all their sins will be forgiven them. They mislead the people, for they hide Christ and His death on which we trust and lead the people to false trust in their own suffering and dying. This is the very worst thing a man can experience at the end of his life; by it he is led directly into hell.

But you should learn to say: "What death! What patience! My dying is nothing; I will not have it or hear of it for my comfort. Christ's suffering and death are my comfort on which I trust, and through it my sins are forgiven. Freely I will endure my death for the praise and glory of my God and for the advantage and service of my neighbor, but I will not at all rely on it."

6. It is one thing to die boldly or to endure death patiently, or otherwise to bear pain willingly, and it is a completely different thing to blot out sin and obtain grace before God by such dying or suffering. The first has certainly been done by the heathen, and many worthless scoundrels and rough people still do it. However, the second, like all other lies, is a poisonous, deadly addition devised by Satan, by which he has caused our confidence and comfort to be in our own doings and works. We must guard against this.

Just as much as I should resist anyone who teaches me that I should enter a monastery if I want to be saved, so much should I also oppose anyone who would set up my own dying or suffering for my comfort and hope in my last hour, as if that would be useful to me for washing away my sins. Both of these things deny God and His Christ, slander His grace, and turn His Gospel upside down. Those who hold a crucifix before the dying and remind them of the death and suffering of Christ do much better.

7. I must relate an example and experience that serves well here and is not to be despised. There was a good hermit, who had been educated in this faith in human merit, who had to comfort a dying man, so he boldly went ahead and comforted him in this way: "My friend, only endure your death patiently and willingly, and I will pledge my soul that you will be a child of eternal life." Well, he promised he would, and then died patiently with this comfort. Three or four days later, the hermit also became mortally sick, and the true master, Remorse, came and opened his eyes so that he saw what he had done and taught. He lay there until he died and lamented the advice and comfort he had given that man: "Alas, what have I advised him!" Frivolous people laughed at him, that he did not do what he had taught another to do. On his soul he told another to die cheerfully, and he himself now despairs, not only because of death but also because of the advice he had given so confidently and now so publicly rebuked and retracted.

But God surely said to him what is written in Luke 4 [:23]: "Master, now help yourself," and another passage: "So it happens to one who is not rich toward God" [Luke 12:21]. Here for sure one blind man led another, and both fell into the pit [Luke 6:39], and both were condemned: the first, because he passed on into death [trusting] in his own patience; the second, because he despaired of God's grace, did not acknowledge it, and then thought that if he had not committed the sin, he would have passed on into heaven. Christ remained unknown and denied by both of them.

So some books went astray [on this point], in which St. Augustine and others emphasized statements that death is a door to life and a medicine against sin. People did not see that these words are to be understood about Christ's death and suffering.

As insignificant as this example is, it teaches us in a masterly way that no work, no suffering, no death can help or stand the test before God. Here we cannot deny that the first man did the greatest work, namely, he underwent death with patience, in which his free will did its best; and yet he was lost, as the second man confesses and proves with his despair. Whoever does not believe these two men will have to find it out for himself.

8. We have been discussing faith in the suffering of Christ. Just as He has now willingly given Himself for us, so we also, according to His example of love, should give ourselves for our neighbor, with all that we have. We have spoken sufficiently elsewhere on the fact that Christ is to be preached in these two ways.[1] But these are words which no one wants to understand; the Word is hidden, for "the fleshly man does not understand what is divine," etc. [Luke 18:34; 1 Cor. 2:14].

9. The second part is the blind man, in whom we see shining brightly both love in Christ for the blind man and faith in the blind man toward Christ. We want to look briefly at the faith of the blind man.

10. First, he hears people saying that Christ "is passing by" [Luke 18:37]; previously, he had heard that Jesus of Nazareth was a good man who helps everyone who calls on Him. His faith and confidence in Christ grew out of what he heard, so that he did not doubt that He would also help him. He could not have had such faith in his heart if he had not heard and known about Christ, for faith does not come except by hearing [Rom. 10:17].

11. Second, he believes firmly and does not doubt that what he heard about Him was true, as the following signs prove. Even though he recognized Him, he still does not see or know Christ, and could not see or know whether Christ had the heart and will to help him; rather, he believed exactly what he had heard about Him. He based his confidence on [Christ's] reputation and on these words, and therefore was not disappointed.

1 See *Short Instruction* (1522), LW 75:8–9.

12. Third, in accord with this faith he calls and prays [Luke 18:38–39], as St. Paul describes the order: "How will they call on Him if they do not believe?" Likewise: "Whoever calls on the name of the Lord will be helped" (Romans 10 [:14, 13]).

13. Fourth, he also freely confesses Christ and fears no one. Because of his pressing need, he does not ask for anyone else. True faith is such that it confesses Christ as the one who can and will help, while others are ashamed of Him and afraid of the world.

14. Fifth, he struggles not only with his conscience, which without a doubt agitated him because he is unworthy, but also with those who threatened him and told him to be quiet [Luke 18:39]. They wanted to terrify his conscience and make him fearful, so that he would look at his unworthiness and Christ's worthiness and then despair. Wherever faith begins, struggle and strife also begin.

15. Sixth, he stands firm, prevails, and wins. He does not let the whole world tear him from his confidence, not even his own conscience. Therefore, he maintains his request and overcomes Christ, so that He stops, tells them to bring him, and offers to do whatever he wants [Luke 18:40–42]. So it happens with all who only hold firmly to the Word of God; close their eyes and ears against the devil, the world, and themselves; and act just as if they and God were alone in heaven and on earth.

16. Seventh, he follows Christ [Luke 18:43]; that is, he walks on the way of love and of the cross, on which Christ walks, does righteous works, is in a good estate and way of life, and is not occupied with foolishness, as the work-saints are.

17. Eighth, he thanks and praises God [Luke 18:43] and offers a righteous sacrifice which is pleasing to God. "The one who offers thanksgiving praises Me; and there is the path, that I show him the salvation of God" (Psalm 50 [:23]).

18. Ninth, he causes many others to praise God [Luke 18:43], seeing him,[2] for a Christian is useful and helpful for everyone, and besides praises and honors God on earth.

19. Finally, let us see how Christ encourages us with works and words to believe. First with works, in that He takes such a firm interest in the blind man, makes it clear how pleasing faith is to Him, so that He is captivated, stops, and does what the blind man desires in his faith. Second, He praises his faith in words and says, "Your faith has made you well" [Luke 18:42]. He throws the honor of the miracle away from Himself and attributes it to the

---

2 *an ihm*, i.e., seeing what God had done to him.

faith of the blind man. In summary, faith is granted what it asks, and it is moreover our great honor before God.[3]

20. This blind man signifies the spiritually blind, that is, each person born from Adam who does not see or know the kingdom of God; it is grace when he feels and knows his blindness and desires to be freed from it. Those are the holy sinners who sense their faults and sigh for grace.

He sits along the road and begs [Luke 18:35]; that is, he sits among the teachers of the Law and desires help. Begging means that he must struggle with works alone and have recourse only to them. The people pass by and leave him sitting there; that is, the people of the Law are noisy and let their doctrine of works be heard. They want to precede Christ and Christ can follow them.

He hears Christ; that is, when a heart hears about the Gospel and faith, it calls and cries and has no rest until it comes to Christ. Those who would silence and scold him [Luke 18:39] are the teachers of works, who want to suffocate and quiet the doctrine and reputation of faith, but they stir up hearts all the more. The Gospel is such that the more it is restrained, the more it increases. After he received his sight, all his work and life are nothing but the praise and honor of God. He follows Christ with joy, which surprises and improves the whole world [Luke 18:43].

---

3 What follows is the spiritual interpretation of the miracle.

# GOSPEL FOR THE FIRST SUNDAY IN LENT

*Matthew 4:1–11*

*Then Jesus was led up by the Spirit into the wilderness to be tempted by the devil. And after fasting forty days and forty nights, He was hungry. And the tempter came and said to Him, "If You are the Son of God, command these stones to become loaves of bread." But He answered, "It is written, 'Man shall not live by bread alone, but by every word that comes from the mouth of God.'" Then the devil took Him to the holy city and set Him on the pinnacle of the temple and said to Him, "If You are the Son of God, throw Yourself down, for it is written, 'He will command His angels concerning you,' and 'On their hands they will bear you up, lest you strike your foot against a stone.'" Jesus said to him, "Again it is written, 'You shall not put the Lord your God to the test.'" Again, the devil took Him to a very high mountain and showed Him all the kingdoms of the world and their glory. And he said to Him, "All these I will give You, if You will fall down and worship me." Then Jesus said to him, "Be gone, Satan! For it is written, 'You shall worship the Lord your God and Him only shall you serve.'" Then the devil left Him, and behold, angels came and were ministering to Him.*

1. This Gospel is read today at the beginning of Lent so that we can imprint the example of Christ on Christians and so observe the fast, which is completely a farce. [It is a farce,] first, because no one can follow that example and fast without any food for forty days and nights, as Christ did. On the contrary, Christ followed Moses' example, who also fasted forty days and nights when he received the Law of God on Mount Sinai [Exod. 24:18]. So Christ also wanted to fast when He was bringing and issuing to us His new command. [It is a farce,] second, because our fasting is upside down, instituted by men. Although Christ fasted forty days, yet His word is not there, and He does not command us to fast the same way. He certainly did more things that He does not want done by us; rather, whenever He tells us to do and not to do something, then we should recognize that we have His word.

2. But the worst of all is that we have taken up and promoted fasting as a good work, not to constrain the flesh, but rather as a merit before God, in order to blot out sins and obtain grace. This point has made our fasting stink so slanderously and shamefully before God that no drinking and eating, no

gluttony and drunkenness, could be as bad and stink as much. It would even be better to be dead drunk day and night than to fast in this way.

Moreover, even if everything was good and correct, so that this fasting was directed only to the chastisement of the flesh, it would still be useless and for nothing, because this was not free and was not left to each one willing to take it up themselves, but was extorted by human commands, so that it was done unwillingly. I will not mention how much other harm has resulted from this—that pregnant women and their babies, along with sick and weak people, are damaged by it—so that it would be better to call it not a holy fasting but a devilish fasting. Therefore, we will pay closer attention to this Gospel, which teaches us true fasting in the example of Christ.

3. Scripture presents us with two kinds of good fasting: one, when we willingly take it up in order to suppress the flesh in the spirit, of which St. Paul says, "By labors, wakefulness, fasting" (2 Corinthians 6 [:5]). The second is when we must endure it—and yet willingly do so—because of scarcity and poverty, of which St. Paul says: "To the present hour we suffer hunger and thirst" (1 Corinthians 4 [:11]); and "The time will come when the bridegroom is taken away from them; then they will fast" (Mark 2 [:20]). Christ teaches us this kind of fasting when He is alone in the wilderness and has nothing to eat, and yet gladly bears this scarcity. The first kind of fasting we can stop whenever we want and can make up for it with food; the second kind we must observe and wait until God Himself changes it and makes up for it. For that reason the second is much more noble than the first, because it happens with greater faith.

4. That is also the reason why the evangelist intentionally says at the start that He was driven by the Spirit into the wilderness so that there He would fast and be tempted [Matt. 4:1], so that no one would imitate this example of his own choice and make a self-serving, self-willed, and chosen fast out of it, but rather would wait for the Spirit, who will send him plenty of fasting and temptation. Whoever rushes headlong into the danger of hunger or some other temptation, without being led by the Spirit, when he can have eating and drinking and other comforts from God's blessing, is putting God to the test.

We should not seek scarcity and temptation, for they will certainly come by themselves. When they come, we should do our best and act bravely. It says, "Jesus was led by the Spirit into the wilderness" [Matt. 4:1], and not "Jesus Himself chose [to go] into the wilderness." "All who are led by the Spirit of God are sons of God" (Romans 8 [:14]). God wants to give His blessings so that we use them with thanksgiving, and not leave them lying, and thus put Him to the test. This is what He wants, and He compels us to it through His Spirit or through necessity, which we cannot circumvent.

5. This history was written for us, both for doctrine and for admonition. First, for doctrine, so that we would know how Christ has served and helped us with His fasting, hunger, temptation, and victory. Whoever believes in Christ will suffer from no scarcity, and no temptation will harm him; rather, he will have enough in the midst of scarcity and be secure in the midst of temptation, since his Lord and Head has overcome all of that for his good. He is certain of that because [Christ] says, "Take heart; I have overcome the world" (John 16 [:33]). If He can nourish Christ for forty days without any food, then He can also nourish His Christians.

6. Second, [this was written] for admonition, so that, according to this example, we would gladly suffer scarcity and temptation in service to God and for the good of our neighbor, as often as necessity requires it, as Christ has done for us. That will certainly happen when we teach and confess God's Word. Therefore, this Gospel is an excellent comfort and strength against the unbelieving, shameful belly, in order to support and strengthen our conscience, so that we do not worry about bodily nourishment but are certain that He can and will nourish us.

7. How this temptation happens and how it is overcome is all very beautifully pictured for us here in Christ. First, He was led into the wilderness [Matt. 4:1]; that is, He was left alone by God, angels, humans, and all creatures. What kind of a temptation would it be if we were not forsaken and left alone? It does hurt when we feel that there is no way out, such as when I must nourish myself but have no money—not a shred, not a twig—and I sense no help from others, and there is no aid. That is what it means to be led into the wilderness and left alone. Then I am in a real school and learn how weak my faith is, how great and rare true faith must be, and how deeply shameful unbelief lies in every human heart. But whoever has his pockets, cellar, and granary full has not yet been driven into the wilderness or left alone. Therefore, he also does not feel the temptation.

8. Second, the devil steps up and attacks Christ with this same worry about the belly and with unbelief in God's goodness and says, "If You are the Son of God, command these stones to become bread" [Matt. 4:3]. It was as if he would say: "Yes, trust in God, and do not cook anything; just wait until a roasted chicken flies into Your mouth. Now tell me how You have a God who cares for You. Where now is Your heavenly Father, who cares for You? I think He has abandoned You. Eat and drink now from Your faith, and let us see how fat You become. If only there were stones [to eat]! What a wonderful Son of God You are! How fatherly He treats You, since He sends You not even a crust of bread and lets You be so poor and needy. Do You now still believe that You are His Son and that He is Your Father?" With similar thoughts he truly attacks all of God's children. Christ certainly felt this, for He was no

stick or stone, even though He was and remained pure and without sin, as we cannot remain.

9. Christ's answer—"Man does not live by bread alone" [Matt. 4:4]— proves that the devil attacked Him with worry about His belly, or unbelief and greed. That sounds as if He were saying, "You want to point Me only to bread and to deal with Me as if I thought only about bodily nourishment."

This temptation is very common also among godly people, and is especially felt by those who are poor, who have a child and a house with nothing in it. For that reason St. Paul says that the love of money is a root of all evil [1 Tim. 6:10], for it is a fruit of unbelief. Do you not think that such unbelief, worry, and greed are the reason people are afraid of married life? Why do people refrain from it and remain in unchastity, unless they are worried that they will have to die of hunger and suffer scarcity? Here we should look at Christ's work and example. He endured scarcity for forty days and nights, and yet in the end He was not forsaken, but even angels provided for Him [Matt. 4:11].

10. Third, look at Christ's attitude toward this temptation of His belly and how He overcame it. He saw nothing but stones and what was inedible, but He went ahead and clung to the Word of God, strengthened Himself, and knocked the devil down with it. All Christians should valiantly make use of this saying when they see that there is lack and scarcity and everything has become stones; when their spirit then fidgets, they should say: "What would it be if the whole world were full of bread? Nevertheless, man does not live on bread alone, but still more is required, namely, the Word of God." These words are so beautiful and powerful that we must not rush past them, but emphasize them even more.

11. Christ takes these words from Moses, who says: "Your God humbled you and let you hunger and fed you with manna, which you and your fathers did not know, that He might make you know that man does not live by bread alone, but man lives by all that comes from the mouth of the Lord" (Deuteronomy 8 [:3]). That is as much as to say: "Since He let you hunger and yet you remain alive, you should certainly catch on that God nourishes you without bread through His Word, for if you lived and were nourished only with bread, then you would certainly have to be full of bread all the time." The Word which nourishes us is what He has promised and foretold to us, [namely,] that He is our God and wants to be our God.

12. What Moses and Christ mean is that whoever has God's Word and believes it certainly has the two points: First, if he lacks and does not have, but must suffer hunger, then that [Word] will preserve him, so that he will not die or perish from hunger, just as if he had plenty to eat. The Word which he has in his heart nourishes and preserves him, even without eating and

drinking. But if he has a little to eat, then a morsel or pieces of bread will feed and nourish him as much as if he had a royal meal, for not the bread but the Word of God nourishes also the body naturally, just as it creates and preserves all things (Hebrews 1 [:3]).

The second point is that there will certainly be bread at last, no matter where it comes from, even if it should rain from heaven as the manna did, where nothing grows or can grow. Everyone can confidently rely on these two points: that either he must obtain bread to eat in the midst of hunger, or, if not, then hunger must become so tolerable and bearable that it nourishes him just as much as bread does.

13. Now, what has been said about eating and nourishing should be understood also about drinking, clothing, house, and all our necessities. He may indeed let us become destitute and suffer from a lack of clothing, house, etc., but, in short, there must finally be clothing, and the leaves of the trees will rather have to become coats and robes [Gen. 3:7]; or, if not, then the coat and robe we wear will never become old, just as it happened to the children of Israel in the wilderness: their clothing and shoes did not wear out [Deut. 8:4]. So also the wild wilderness had to become their houses, there had to be a path where there was no path, there had to be water where there was no water, and stones had to become water [Exod. 17:1–7; Num. 20:1–13]. God's Word stands firm, which says, "He cares for us" [1 Pet. 5:7]. St. Paul [writes]: "God richly provides us with everything to enjoy" [1 Tim. 6:17], and [Christ says]: "Seek first the kingdom of God, and all these things will be added to you. Only do not be anxious," etc. (Matthew 6 [:33–34]). Such words must remain true and continue forever.

14. We can certainly have all of this from our daily experience. People think—and I also believe it—that not as many sheaves grow as there are people alive; rather, God daily blesses and increases the wheat in the sack, the flour in the bin, the bread on the table and in the mouth, as Christ did (John 6 [:5–13]). We also commonly see that poor people and their children are fatter and their food reaches farther and is better for them than all the provisions among the rich. It is a special affliction, like pestilence or war, when the godless sometimes suffer need, or in time of famine many die of hunger. In other ways we see in everything that not food, but God's Word nourishes everyone.

15. God nourishes all the world through bread, and not just through the Word without the bread, because He conceals His work under [the bread] in order to train our faith. Similarly, though He commanded the children of Israel to arm themselves and to fight, yet He did not want the victory to come through their swords and deeds; rather, He Himself wanted to defeat and overcome the enemy by means of their swords and through their deeds.

Here He could also say: "The soldier does not win through his sword alone, but by every word that comes out of the mouth of the Lord." Similarly, David also sings: "Not in my bow do I trust, nor can my sword help me" (Psalm 44 [:6]); and similarly: "The king is not helped by his great might; a giant is not delivered by his great strength. War horses also do not help," etc. (Psalm 33 [:16–17]). Nevertheless, He uses the man and the warhorse, the sword and the bow, though not because of the strength or might of the man and the warhorse; rather, under the curtain and cover of the man and the warhorse, He fights and does everything. This is proved by the fact that He has often done this without the man and the warhorse, and daily does it, where there is need and He is not being put to the test [Matt. 4:7].

16. He also does the same thing with the bread. When there is [bread] on hand, then He nourishes us through it and by means of it, so that we do not see it and think that the bread does it. But where there is no [bread] on hand, He nourishes us without bread, only through the Word, as He does by means of the bread. Thus the bread is His assistant, just as St. Paul says, "We are God's assistants" (1 Corinthians 3 [:9]); that is, through and by means of our outward preaching office, He inwardly gives grace, which He also could certainly give without our office and does give. Because the office is there, we should not despise it nor put God to the test. Thus God nourishes us outwardly by bread; but only inwardly does He give us the growth and digestion, which the bread cannot give.

In summary, all creatures are God's masks and disguises, which He wants to have work with Him and help Him do all kinds of things, which He otherwise can do and does do without their cooperation, so that we may simply cling to His Word alone. Thus, when there is bread, we should not trust any more on account of it, and when there is no [bread], we should not despair any more on account of it. Rather, we should use it when it is there and do without it when it is not there, certain that we will still live and be nourished both times through God's Word, whether there is bread or not. With this faith we can properly overcome greed and worries about our belly and temporal nourishment.

17. The second temptation is opposed to the first and contrasts with it. What takes place is that the devil teaches us to put God to the test. He tells Christ to fall down from the pinnacle of the temple [Matt. 4:6]. This was unnecessary, since there were surely good stairs which He could walk down. This was a temptation to put God to the test, as is shown by Christ's answer when He says, "It is written: 'You shall not put the Lord your God to the test'" [Matt. 4:7]. So He points out that the devil wanted to incite Him to put God to the test.

18. This temptation very appropriately follows the first one. When the devil finds a heart which trusts God in scarcity and in need, then he soon ceases his temptation of the belly and of greed and thinks: "Wait, if you want to be completely spiritual and believing, then I will help you out." Then he goes ahead and attacks them on the other side, so that they also believe what God does not command them to believe nor want them to believe.

For example, if God has provided bread in your house, as He does every year throughout the world, and you would not use it, but instead would cause yourself need and scarcity and say: "We are supposed to believe God! I will not eat bread, but wait until God sends me manna"—that would be putting God to the test, for He does not tell us to believe where something is at hand that we can and should obtain. How can we believe when we already have it?

19. So you can see how he pretends that Christ is facing a scarcity and a need when there is no scarcity or need; rather, there was a good way at hand for Him to come down from the temple without such a newly invented and unnecessary way of descending. For that reason he also led Christ to the temple "in the holy city" [Matt. 4:5] (the evangelist says) and placed Him in a holy place. He gives man such precious thoughts that he thinks he is full of faith and on the true, holy path—and yet he is not in the temple, but is only on the outside of the temple; that is, he is not in the true and holy attitude of faith, but only outwardly in the appearance of true faith. Yet he is in the holy city; that is, such people are found only in Christendom and among Christians, who hear much preaching about faith. He applies the passages of Scripture to these people, for such people learn Scripture by hearing it daily, but apply it no further than to their own delusions and false faith.

He quotes from the psalms, that God has commanded the angels to guard God's children and "bear them on their hands" (Psalm 91 [:11–12]). But the scoundrel omits what is there, namely, that the angels are to guard God's children "in their ways," for the psalm reads: "He will command His angels concerning you to guard you in all your ways," etc., so that according to God's command the protection of the angels stretches no further than the way on which God has commanded us to walk. When we walk in these ways of God, then the angels protect us. But the devil omits the way of God and explains and applies the angels' protection to all kinds of things, even to what God has not commanded. That is wrong, and it puts God to the test.

20. Now, this temptation rarely happens in coarse, outward things, such as bread, clothing, house, etc. There are many foolhardy people who endanger their body and life, their property and honor without any need of doing so—as do those who rush headlong into a fight or jump into water or gamble for money or otherwise put themselves into danger. About them the wise man [Sirach] says, "Whoever loves danger will perish by it" [Ecclus. 3:26],

for in the way that you strive, in that way it will turn out, and good swimmers easily drown and good climbers easily fall. Nevertheless, it rarely happens that those with false faith in God abstain from bread, clothing, and other necessities when they are at hand. We read about two hermits who would not accept bread from the people but [thought that] God should send them bread from heaven. One of them died and went to the devil, his father, the one who taught him such faith and told him to fall from the pinnacle of the temple.[1]

21. In spiritual matters, where we deal with the nourishment not of the belly but of the soul, this temptation is powerful. Here God has set up a method and way in which we can nourish our souls eternally in the richest way without any scarcity, namely, Christ our Savior. But no one wants this way, this treasure, this provision. Everyone seeks other ways and another provision to help their souls. Those are the right ones, the people who believe they can be saved through their own works; the devil puts them on the top of the temple. They follow him and descend where there is no way; they believe and trust in God with their works where there is no faith or trust. They do not know where they are going, and they break their necks. In addition, he quotes Scripture and persuades them to believe that the angels guard them, and that their way, works, and trust are pleasing to God, and that He has told them through Scripture that they should do good works—but they do not look at how falsely Scripture was explained to them.

22. We have identified who these people are enough and more than enough, namely, the work-saints and unbelieving hypocrites under the name and number of the Christian life and people. This temptation must take place in the holy city and is in strange contrast to another [temptation]. In the first temptation, scarcity and hunger are the reason that people do not believe, and they would gladly have more than enough, so that they would not need to believe. In this [second temptation], the abundance is the reason that they do not believe, since they are satiated with the common treasure, and each one undertakes something of his own to take care of his soul. This is the way it happens with us: if we have nothing, then we doubt God and do not believe; if we have an abundance, then we become tired of it and want to have something else, and again do not believe. There we flee and hate the scarcity and seek to have plenty; here we seek scarcity and flee from plenty. No, whatever God does for us is never right. This is the bottomless wickedness of our unbelief.

23. The third temptation is to temporal honor and power, as the words of the devil clearly state. He shows Christ all the kingdoms of the world and offers to give them, if He would worship him [Matt. 4:9]. This applies to those who fall away from faith for the sake of honor and power, so that they

---

1 For this anecdote, see sermon for Epiphany on Matt. 2:1–12.

may have good days here, or who believe no more than what allows their honor and power to remain. This is how the heretics are who cause sects and factions among Christians in matters of faith, so that they may be haughty before the world and live in honor. This third temptation can be placed on the right side, just as the first [temptation] is on the left side. The first is the temptation of misfortune, by which we are incited to anger, impatience, and unbelief. The third and last is the temptation of prosperity, by which we are incited to pleasure, honor, joy, and whatever is high. The second and middle [temptation] is completely spiritual and uses hidden snares and error to lead reason away from faith.

24. Whomever the devil cannot overcome with poverty, scarcity, need, and misery, he attacks with riches, favor, honor, pleasure, power, and the like, and fights on both sides against us. St. Peter says that he prowls around and around [1 Pet. 5:8]. Those he cannot overthrow with suffering or love— that is, neither with the first [temptation] to the left side nor with the third [temptation] to the right side—he goes beyond this again and attacks us with error, blindness, and a false understanding of Scripture. If he wins there, then things go well neither on the left nor on the right. Rather, whether we suffer poverty or have abundance, whether we fight or acknowledge our defeat, all is lost. In error, neither patience in misfortune nor steadiness in prosperity help, since both points often describe the heretics, and the devil gladly pretends to be vanquished (even though he is not vanquished) in the first and last [temptations] when he has won only in the middle or second [temptation]. [The devil] has his own people suffer much and be patient, even despise the world, but none of that happens with a true heart and faith.

25. Now these three temptations taken together are difficult and severe, but the middle one is the greatest, for it attacks in the spirit the doctrine of faith itself, and is spiritual and in spiritual matters. The other two temptations attack faith in external things, such as prosperity and misfortune, love and suffering, etc., though both test us profoundly. It hurts when we are to cling to heaven and always be in want and eat stones where there is no bread. On the other hand, it hurts to despise and abandon the advantage, honor, possessions, friends, and companions we already have. However, faith, grounded in God's Word, can do all things [cf. Phil. 4:13]; if faith is strong, then these things are light.

26. The order in which these temptations met Christ, one after another, cannot be known with certainty, for the evangelists do not agree. The one that St. Matthew places in the middle is placed last by St. Luke [Luke 4:9–12], and the one that [St. Luke] places in the middle [Luke 4:5–8] is placed last by St. Matthew, as if not much depended on the order. But if we want to preach and speak of this, the order of St. Luke would be the best. It sounds good

to recite and relate that the devil first attacks with scarcity and misfortune. If that does not work, then [he attacks] with prosperity and honor. Finally, when all of that does not help, he attacks with all his might and hits us with error, lies, and other spiritual tricks.

However, because they do not happen this way in practice and experience, but it turns out that a Christian is attacked sometimes with the last [temptation] and other times with the first, St. Matthew did not give attention to the order, which would be appropriate for a preacher to point out. Perhaps it was also the same with Christ throughout the forty days: that the devil held to no order with Him, but today attacked Him with this one, tomorrow with the second one, and then for ten days with the first one, and so on, as it happened.

27. At the end, the angels came and served Him [Matt. 4:11]. This must have happened bodily, so that they appeared bodily and brought Him food and drink, and likewise all other needs. This serving happened externally to His body, just as also the devil, His tempter, without doubt appeared in bodily form, perhaps also as an angel. In order to put Him on the pinnacle of the temple and to show Him all the kingdoms of the world in a moment, [the devil] must have been something higher than a man, as he then identifies himself as something higher when he offers Him all the kingdoms on earth and wants to be worshiped. But he obviously did not come in the form of the devil, for he becomes very beautiful when he wants to lie and deceive, as St. Paul says that he pretends to be "an angel of light" [2 Cor. 11:14].

28. This was written for our comfort, so that we would know how many angels serve us when one devil attacks us, if we fight valiantly. And if we stand firm, God does not let us suffer scarcity, but angels must first come from heaven and become our bakers, cellarers, and cooks and serve us in all our needs. This was not written for Christ's sake, for He does not need it. If the angels served Him, then they can and should serve us too.

# GOSPEL FOR THE SECOND SUNDAY IN LENT

## Matthew 15:21–28

*And Jesus went away from there and withdrew to the district of Tyre and Sidon. And behold, a Canaanite woman from that region came out and was crying, "Have mercy on me, O Lord, Son of David; my daughter is severely oppressed by a demon." But He did not answer her a word. And His disciples came and begged Him, saying, "Send her away, for she is crying out after us." He answered, "I was sent only to the lost sheep of the house of Israel." But she came and knelt before Him, saying, "Lord, help me." And He answered, "It is not right to take the children's bread and throw it to the dogs." She said, "Yes, Lord, yet even the dogs eat the crumbs that fall from their masters' table." Then Jesus answered her, "O woman, great is your faith! Be it done for you as you desire." And her daughter was healed instantly.*

1. This Gospel reading presents us with a true example of a steadfast, perfect faith. This woman withstands and overcomes three great and intense contests, and beautifully teaches us the true character and virtue of faith, namely, that it is a heartfelt confidence in the grace and goodness of God, which is learned and revealed through the Word. St. Mark [7:25] says that she had heard the report about Jesus. What kind of a report? Without doubt a good report and reputation that Christ was a godly man and gladly helped everybody. This report about God is a true Gospel and word of grace. This is the source of this woman's faith, for if she had not believed, she would not have run after Him. So we have often heard how St. Paul says that faith comes through hearing and that the Word must precede and be the beginning of salvation (Romans 10 [:17]).

2. But how does it happen that many more heard this good report about Christ, and yet they did not run after Him and paid no attention to this good report? Answer: The physician is helpful and welcome to the sick, but the healthy pay no attention to him. This woman perceived her need, and for that reason she ran after the sweet fragrance (Song of Solomon 1 [:3; 4:11]). So also Moses must come first and teach us to perceive our sins so that grace may become sweet and welcome.

Therefore, all is lost, no matter how kindly and delightfully Christ is portrayed, if one is not first humbled by knowledge of himself and is not eager for Christ, as the Magnificat says: "He fills the hungry with good things, and the rich He sends away empty" [Luke 1:53]. All of this is said and written for the comfort of the miserable, poor, needy, sinful, and despised people, so that in all of their need they know to whom they should flee for comfort and help.

3. But see how Christ drives and pursues faith in His people so that it becomes strong and firm. First, she runs after His good reputation and cries out with sure confidence that He would deal graciously with her according to what was reported about Him. But Christ pretends to be completely different, as if He would let her faith and good confidence be wrong and what was reported about Him be false [Matt. 15:23–24]. Thus she could have thought: "Is this a good and kind man?" Or: "Are these the good words which I have heard about Him, on which I have relied? It must not be true; He is your enemy and does not want you; He could at least speak a word and say to me: 'I do not want you.' He is as silent as a stump."

It is a very hard blow when God appears to be so stern and angry and hides His grace so very deeply. This is well-known by those who feel and experience it in their hearts and think that He will not do what He has said and will let His Word be false. This happened to the children of Israel at the Red Sea [Exod. 14:10–12] and otherwise to many other great saints.

4. Now, what does the woman do about this? She turns her eyes away from His unfriendly appearance, is not misled by all of that, does not dwell on it, but clings steadily and firmly to her confidence in the good report she had heard and grasped about Him, and does not cease [Matt. 15:25–27].

We must also do the same and learn to cling firmly to His Word alone, even if God with all His creatures would act differently than this Word says about Him. How it hurts nature and reason when, in destitution, she takes off, and leaves behind everything that she senses, and clings to the bare Word alone, even when she senses the opposite. May God help us in time of need and of death to such courage and faith!

5. Second, when her outcry and faith do not help, the disciples step forward with their faith and plead for her; they think that they will certainly be heard [Matt. 15:23]. When they think that He should become gentler, He becomes all the more harsh and lets both their faith and their plea miss their goal, as she sees and senses. He is no longer silent and does not let them doubt, but rejects their plea and says, "I was not sent except to the lost sheep of the house of Israel" [Matt. 15:24].

This blow is still harsher, since not only our own person is repudiated but also that comfort is rejected which we still have, namely, the comfort and intercession of godly and holy people. When we feel that God is ungracious to us or we suffer some other need, our last resort is to go to godly, spiritual people and seek advice and help from them, if they are willing [to help] as love demands. Yet nothing comes of that—even they are not heard, and things are only worse with us.

6. Here we could reproach Christ for all the words in which He has promised to hear His saints, such as: "If two are gathered to ask for something they agree on, it will be done for them" [Matt. 18:19]; and "Whatever you ask, if you believe, it will be yours" [Mark 11:24]; and many more. Where are those promises now? He quickly answers and says, "Yes, it is true. I hear every plea, but I have made that promise to the house of Israel."

What do you think? Is that not a thunderbolt that dashes both heart and faith into a thousand pieces, when we feel that God's Word, on which we build, was not spoken to us but applies [only] to others? Here all saints and intercession are at a standstill, and the heart must abandon the Word, if it would stick with its own perceptions.

7. But what does the woman do? She does not give up. She clings to the Word, even though it is being forcefully torn out of her heart. She does not turn away from His stern answer, but still trusts firmly that His goodness is still hidden behind it. She still does not think that Christ is or can be ungracious. That is what "firmly clinging" means.

8. Third, she runs after Him into the house—as Mark [7:24–25] writes—perseveres, falls down before Him, and says, "Lord, help me!" [Matt. 15:25]. There she gets the final deathblow, when He says directly to her (as the words read) that she is a dog and unworthy to share the children's bread [Matt. 15:26]. What will she say to this? He simply asserts that she is one of the damned and lost, who is not to be numbered among the elect.

9. That is an answer that can never be contested, one that no one can get past. Yet she does not cease, but concedes His judgment and grants that she is a dog. She desires also no more than a dog, namely, to "eat the crumbs that fall from their masters' table" [Matt. 15:27].

Is not that a masterpiece? She clutches at Christ's own words. He compares her to a dog; she grants that and asks nothing more than that He would let her be a dog, as He Himself had judged her to be. Where could He go? He is captured. We let a dog have the crumbs under the table; that is its right. Therefore, He now completely opens His heart to her and yields to her will, so that she is now not a dog, but a child of Israel [Matt. 15:28].

10. This was written for all our comfort and instruction, so that we may know how deeply God hides His grace from us, so that we would not consider Him according to our perception and thinking but strictly according to His Word. Here you see that though Christ pretends to be harsh, yet He gives no final judgment when He says, "No." Rather, all His answers sound like no, but they are not no—they are undecided and pending.

He does not say, "I will not listen to you," but is silent and says neither yes nor no. So also He does not say that she is not of the house of Israel, but that He was sent only to the house of Israel [Matt. 15:24]. Thus He leaves it undecided and pending between no and yes. So He does not say, "You are a dog, and we should not give you the children's bread"; rather, "It is not right [to take the children's bread and throw it to the dogs]" [Matt. 15:26]. Again, He leaves it undecided whether she is a dog or not. Nevertheless, all three points sound more like no than yes, even though there is more yes there than no. In fact, there is only yes there [cf. 1 Cor. 1:19–20], but it is very deep and secret, and it looks only like no.

11. This points out the condition of our heart in temptation. As it perceives, so Christ acts. [Our heart] thinks there is nothing else but only no, and yet that is untrue. Therefore, it must turn away from this perception and with a firm faith in God's Word grasp and hold onto the deep, secret yes under and above the no, as this woman does. When we grant that God is right in His judgment against us, then we have won and caught Him in His own words.

For example, when we feel in our conscience that God reproaches us as sinners and judges us unworthy of the kingdom of heaven, then we experience hell and think that we are eternally lost. Whoever has this woman's ingenuity should catch God in His own judgment and say: "Yes, Lord, it is true. I am a sinner and unworthy of Your grace. Nevertheless, You have promised forgiveness to sinners, and You 'came not to call the righteous' [Mark 2:17; Luke 5:32] but (as also St. Paul says) 'to save sinners' [1 Tim. 1:15]." Then, by His own judgment, God has to have mercy on us.

12. When King Manasseh repented, as his prayer shows, he granted that God was right in His judgment, confessed his guilt as a great sinner, and made use of God's promised forgiveness of sinners [2 Chron. 33:12–13, 18–19]. So also David says, "Against You only have I sinned and done what is evil in Your sight, so that You may remain just in Your words and not be faulted in Your judgment" (Psalm 51 [:4]).

When we do not endure God's judgment and cannot say yes when He considers and judges us to be sinners, then all hostility comes down on us. If the condemned could do it, they would be saved in a moment. We certainly say with our mouths that we are sinners, but when God Himself says this in our hearts, then we no longer stand, and we desperately desire to be godly and regarded as the godly, as long as we would be free from His judgment. But it must be so; if God is to be just in His words [Ps. 51:4] that you are a sinner, then you can make use of the right which God has given to every sinner, namely, the forgiveness of sins. Then you not only eat the crumbs under the table like the dogs, but you also are a child [of God] and have God as your own, just as you want.

13. That is the spiritual meaning of this Gospel, together with the scriptural explanation. Just as it happened for this woman in the physical sickness of her daughter, whom she healed miraculously through her faith, so it also happens to us when we are to be healed of sin and spiritual sickness, which is a truly wicked devil. She must become a dog, and we must become sinners and fuel for hellfire, and then we have already recovered and are saved.

14. Whatever more is to be said on this Gospel reading, such as that one can obtain grace and help through the faith of another without his own faith, as happened here to the woman's daughter, has been sufficiently treated elsewhere.[1] It is also clear enough and easy to find more about the example of love given us here in this Gospel reading by Christ and His disciples, together with this woman, since none acts, prays, and cares for himself, but each for another.

---

1  See sermon for Third Sunday after Epiphany on Matt. 8:1–13.

# GOSPEL FOR THE THIRD SUNDAY IN LENT

## Luke 11:14–28

*Now He was casting out a demon that was mute. When the demon had gone out, the mute man spoke, and the people marveled. But some of them said, "He casts out demons by Beelzebul, the prince of demons," while others, to test Him, kept seeking from Him a sign from heaven. But He, knowing their thoughts, said to them, "Every kingdom divided against itself is laid waste, and a divided household falls. And if Satan also is divided against himself, how will his kingdom stand? For you say that I cast out demons by Beelzebul. And if I cast out demons by Beelzebul, by whom do your sons cast them out? Therefore they will be your judges. But if it is by the finger of God that I cast out demons, then the kingdom of God has come upon you. When a strong man, fully armed, guards his own palace, his goods are safe; but when one stronger than he attacks him and overcomes him, he takes away his armor in which he trusted and divides his spoil. Whoever is not with Me is against Me, and whoever does not gather with Me scatters. When the unclean spirit has gone out of a person, it passes through waterless places seeking rest, and finding none it says, 'I will return to my house from which I came.' And when it comes, it finds the house swept and put in order. Then it goes and brings seven other spirits more evil than itself, and they enter and dwell there. And the last state of that person is worse than the first." As He said these things, a woman in the crowd raised her voice and said to Him, "Blessed is the womb that bore You, and the breasts at which You nursed!" But He said, "Blessed rather are those who hear the word of God and keep it!"*

1. This is a beautiful Gospel reading. In it we learn many different things. Nearly everything is set forth here about what Christ, His kingdom, and the Gospel are—both what they do and how they fare in the world. First, as all the Gospel readings do, it teaches us faith and love, for it presents Christ to us as a Savior and Helper in every need because of His great love. Whoever believes that is saved. Here we see that He had nothing to do with the healthy, but with this poor man who had a fourfold problem. He was blind, as Matthew says [Matt. 12:22], mute, and possessed, as Luke says [Luke 11:14]. Now all who are mute are also deaf, so that in Greek "deaf" and "mute" are the same word. In this way He attracts us to Himself, so that we should expect all good from Him and run to Him in every need. Then again also, according to the nature

of love, [this Gospel reading teaches us] to treat others as He has treated us. This is the common and most delightful doctrine of this and all the Gospel readings throughout the whole year.

This poor man did not come to [Christ] without the Word, for those who brought him to Christ must have heard tell about this love of Christ, by which they were moved to trust Him. Thus we learn that faith comes through the Word; but there has been enough about this elsewhere.[1]

2. Second, it is pointed out here how Christ and the Gospel fare in the world, namely, that there are three kinds of hearers. [First,] some are astonished at Him; these are the godly and true Christians, who regard Him as so great that they are amazed at Him. [Second,] some slander Him, as did the Pharisees [Matt. 12:24] and scribes [Mark 3:22], who were annoyed because they could not do as much, and who worried that the people would regard Him as higher than themselves. [Third,] some tempt Him and want to have a sign, so that He would do what they want and so make it into an amusement, just as Herod desired from Christ [Luke 23:8].

But He answers both—first, the slanderers in this Gospel reading, and then the tempters—saying that no sign will be given to this evil generation except the sign of Jonah, the prophet, which is not part of this Gospel reading [Luke 11:29]. He answers the slanderers in a kind way and deals with five points against them.

3. First, with honest and reasonable arguments He concludes from two comparisons that one demon cannot cast out another, for if that were so, the demons would have to be divided against themselves, and Satan's kingdom would certainly not stand [Luke 11:17–18]. It is the nature of things that if a kingdom is divided against itself and is driving its citizens away, it is unnecessary to go to war against it, for it will go to ruin much quicker than through war. So also when a house is divided against itself, it does not need to be overthrown. So also the heathen Sallust, taught by nature and experience, says: "Great possessions fall to pieces through disunity, but through unity small possessions become great." If the demons were divided against themselves so much that one was casting out another, then his kingdom would be nothing, and we would have peace from them.

4. What could these slanderers have said to such clear arguments? Their mouth had been stopped, but their hearts were still hard, so that they did not ask about that. A hard heart will not be instructed, no matter how distinctly and clearly the truth is presented; but the faith of the godly is strengthened when they see that the basis of their faith is right and good. Just for that reason we must answer the hardened and shut their mouths. Even though they will not be converted nor keep quiet, it still serves the purpose of making

---

1 See sermon for Quinquagesima on Luke 18:31–43.

their hardened folly obvious, for the longer they talk, the more foolish they become, so that we can understand that what they say does not retain even the appearance of being good and right. Solomon says, "Answer a fool, lest he be wise in his own eyes" (Proverbs 26 [:5]); that is, answer him "according to his folly," so that [his folly] is confounded for the sake of others, so that they do not follow him and are not deceived, as if he were right. Otherwise, where you have no argument, it is better to keep quiet, as Solomon also says, "Answer not a fool according to his folly, lest you be like him yourself" (Proverbs 26 [:4]).

5. It also cannot be said here that the demons pretend to be divided against themselves and to yield to each other in order to deceive the people, for it is openly seen how they resist and defend themselves, cry out and rage, break loose and rave when they see how serious it is that they will be driven out. Then one must confess that they are opposed to Christ and His Spirit and not united with Him; to Him they yield unwillingly, but must yield. Therefore, nothing remains here but the openly slanderous lie—in which they are caught and confounded—when out of their poisonous hatred and jealousy they attribute God's work to the devil.

From that we learn not to be surprised when our doctrine and deeds are slandered and when hard hearts are not satisfied or converted, even though they are overcome by obvious truth and their mouths are shut. It is enough that their hardened folly is exposed, acknowledged, and shown to be nothing by our answer before the godly, so that they are not misled by its good appearance. Then let them go where they want, for they have their condemnation, as St. Paul says (Titus 3 [:11]).

6. Second, [He answers the slanderers] with an obvious example and a similar work when He says, "By whom do your sons cast them out?" [Luke 11:19]. It is as if He would say: "Is this not an obvious tyranny? Just what you praise in your sons, you condemn in Me. When your sons do it, it is of God; but when I do it, it must be of the devil." It must happen that way in the world. What Christ does is of the devil; if someone [else] were to do it, it would be correct. Our tyrants and enemies of the Gospel now do the same thing. They condemn in us what they themselves do and confess and teach. They must do that so that their judgment is publicly approved, though they are condemned with all justice.

These "sons," whom Christ says cast out demons, were (I think) certain exorcists among the people, for God had given this people various spiritual gifts from the beginning. He calls them their "sons" as if He would say: "I am God's Son and must be of the devil, but these who are your sons, born from you, do the same things and must not be of the devil."

7. "Therefore, they will also be your judges" [Luke 11:19]. That is, "I appeal to them. They will have to judge that you have unjustly slandered Me, and thus condemned yourselves." If one demon does not cast out another, then some other power must do it which is neither devilish nor human, but divine. For that reason He adds: "If it is by the finger of God that I cast out demons, then the kingdom of God is coming upon you" [Luke 11:20]. Matthew explains this "finger of God" as the Holy Spirit, for he has "if it is by the Spirit of God that I cast out demons" (Matthew 12 [:28]).

In summary, Christ wants to say: "If the kingdom of God is to come to you, then the devil must be cast out, for his kingdom is against God's kingdom, as you yourselves must confess." Now, people do not cast out the devil with the devil, much less with men or through human power, but only through God's Spirit and power.

8. The result is that wherever God's finger does not cast out the devil, the devil's kingdom is still there, and wherever the devil's kingdom is, God's kingdom is not. The unavoidable conclusion, then, is that as long as the Holy Spirit does not come into us, we are not only incapable of any good but also are, of necessity, in the devil's kingdom. But if we are in his kingdom, then we can do nothing other than what pleases him—otherwise it would not be called his kingdom. St. Paul says to Timothy that the people were captured in the snare of the devil to do his will [2 Tim. 2:26]. How could he tolerate one of his own people undertaking a thought to do something which is against his kingdom and not for his kingdom?

These are extremely dreadful words! Christ here grants to the devil a kingdom which cannot be avoided without the Spirit of God, and God's kingdom cannot come unless his kingdom is cast out of us with divine, heavenly power.

9. This is proved also by this poor man, who was possessed bodily by the devil. Tell me, what could he do, even with [the help of] all people on earth, to get free from the devil? Without a doubt, nothing. He would have to do and suffer whatever the devil, his master, wanted, until Christ came with God's power. Now look, if he could not free himself bodily from the devil, how could he free himself spiritually through his own power? The soul is the reason that the body is possessed as a punishment, because [the soul] is possessed through sin, and it is more difficult to get free of sin than from the punishment [of sin], and the soul is always more firmly possessed than the body. This is proved by the fact that the devil leaves the possessed body its natural powers and works, but he robs the soul of reason, judgment, common sense, understanding, and all its powers, as we can see in possessed people.

10. Third, [He answers the slanderers] with a comparison taken from our own experience, namely, when a strong man is overcome by someone

stronger, and his armor and goods are taken away [Luke 11:21–22]. Thus He testifies that no one can overcome the devil except God alone, and again that no one can boast that he himself can cast out either sin or the devil. Look at how he depicts the devil: He calls him a strong giant who guards his land and house. That is, the devil not only possesses the world as his own kingdom, but he also has preserved and established it, so that no one can take it from him. He possesses it also in peace, so that it does whatever he wants.

As much as a house or land can oppose the tyrant or restrain the one who possesses them, so much can free will and human power oppose both sin and the devil—namely, not at all. [The man] must be under them. As the house must be conquered by the stronger one and won from the tyrant, so man must also be redeemed through Christ and won from the devil. We see here again that our activity and righteousness helps nothing at all for our redemption, but it is only God's grace.

11. Fourth, [He answers the slanderers] with beautiful sayings and teachings, such as: "Whoever is not with Me is against Me, and whoever does not gather with Me scatters" [Luke 11:23]. "The devil is not with Me, for I cast them out; thus he must certainly be against Me." But this saying applies not only to the devil but also to the slanderers whom He here convicts and condemns of being against Him because they are not with Him.

To be "with Christ" means to have the same mind and view as Christ, that is, to believe that Christ's works and not our works help us, for this is what Christ holds and teaches. But to "gather with Christ" means to do good through love and to become rich in good works. Whoever does not believe is by himself through his own works; he is not with Christ but against Christ, for he denies Christ by building on his own works. So also, whoever does not love does not gather with Christ, but does useless works through which he only becomes worse and goes further away from faith.

12. Fifth, [He answers the slanderers] with the threat that "the last state is always worse than the first" [Luke 11:26]. Therefore, observe that we should not only leave the Gospel and Christ unslandered—since He does such great things for us and casts the devil out of us—but also seriously and fearfully keep them, so that afterward seven worse demons do not possess us when only one did before [Luke 11:26]. This is what happened to the Jews, who had never been so bad as they were after the Gospel was proclaimed to them. Under the papacy we became seven times (that is, many times) worse heathen under the name of Christ than we had ever been before. St. Peter says that their "last state has become worse for them than the first" (2 Peter 2 [:20]). If we neglect this great light which we now have, then we also will become worse than we were before, for the devil does not sleep. We have been sufficiently warned.

13. Finally, when the woman cries out and praises Christ that the mother who bore such a Son is blessed [Luke 11:27], He opposes her carnal devotion and teaches us all the summary of this Gospel reading, namely, that we should not gape at the works or merits of the saints, but much rather hear and keep the Word of God [Luke 11:28]. Nothing depends on how holy and worthy the mother of this Son is, nor are we helped by it, not even by how exalted the Son and the fruit is. Rather, [we are helped by] what this Son has done for us: that He has redeemed us through grace from the devil without our assistance and merit. This is proclaimed to us through the Word of God, which we should hear and hold in firm faith. Then we, too, will be blessed, like this mother and her Son.

Although this Word and work must be slandered, we should tolerate this and answer it with meekness, as St. Paul teaches, for the improvement of others.

## ALLEGORIES

14. This mute, deaf, blind, and possessed man represents all the children of Adam, who through their flesh are possessed by the devil in original sin, so that they must be his own and act according to his will. Therefore, they are also blind; that is, they do not know God. They are deaf, since they do not hear God's Word and are not obedient or subject to it. They are also mute, for they thank, praise, speak, and preach nothing about Christ and God's grace.

But they are all too talkative about the devil's teachings and worthless human inventions. There they see all too sharply and are more shrewd in their undertakings, opinion, and pleasure than the sons of light [Luke 16:8]. There they hear with both ears and accept everything flesh and blood think about. Thus all of our works, words, and life, both in body and soul, whether they are external holiness or sin, are of the devil and must be redeemed through God's work. He possesses us for His kingdom so that we will know Him; see, hear, and follow Him; and praise and preach Him. All of this happens through the Spirit of God in the Word of God, which casts out the devil with his kingdom.

15. The Jews call the chief demon "Beelzebub" [Luke 11:15]. "Zebub" in Hebrew means a fly, and "Baal" or "Beel" means a man or sovereign, such as a master of the house. When they come together as "Beelzebub," it means the archfly or the chief fly, or in plain German: the lord of the flies or the large horsefly. They gave Satan such a contemptible name, as if they were entirely free and secure before him and even his lords. That is what all secure, lazy hypocrites do, who think they are so pure and holy that the devil is a helpless, weak fly compared to them, so that they do not need Christ's grace and God's Word. Yet they think that [the devil] is strong enough for others—in

fact, that whatever God-fearing people teach and do must be from the devil. They regard him to be as helpless as if he were a weak fly. The devil can also gladly tolerate such contempt, under which he is yet higher in their hearts than the true God.

16. The tyrant in the yard or house is the devil, as was said. He sits there in peace, if God's Word and finger do not come against him through Christ. People do what he wants, for they do not know any better, just as this mute and deaf man did. His weapons and defense are the carnal opinions, doctrines, and principles with which he holds consciences and protects himself.

17. But when the stronger one, the Gospel, comes, his peace is over. He rages and becomes mad and does not want to be condemned, unmasked, punished, or pointed out. Then he rouses up his armor: the powerful, shrewd, rich, and holy people, whom he stirs up against God's Word, as we see in the persecution of the evangelical teachers. Such raging and persecution mean that the devil does not like to be cast out, and he rages in the whole body [cf. Luke 9:39, 42]. The way he acts in a body with its members when he is cast out is the way he acts in the whole world when he must yield to the Gospel: he stirs up all his powers, but it does not help him, for he must leave.

18. The stronger one who overcomes him is Christ. He takes away his armor, that is, He converts some of the persecutors [Acts 9:1–19], and so makes him weaker and His own kingdom stronger. He also divides the spoil [Luke 11:22]; that is, those He converts He uses for various offices, graces, and works in Christendom, about which Paul writes in Romans 12. He is also in the yard or on the porch, for the devil's kingdom exists in the outward appearance and glittering of wisdom, holiness, and strength; but when it is taken up by the Gospel, it is found to be only folly, sin, and without any strength.

19. "After the unclean spirit has gone out, it passes through dry places, seeking rest" [Luke 11:24]; that is (as people say), the devil does not take a vacation and does not sleep, but again seeks how he can capture people. "Dry places" are not godless hearts, for in them he rests and dwells like a strong tyrant, as the Gospel here says; rather, they are dry and desolate places here and there in the country where no people live, such as the wild and wildernesses. In malice and wrath he rushes to such places when he is cast out, just as the devil found Christ in the wilderness [Luke 4:1–13]. Now in the Jewish land there is not much water; He speaks about that here because it has a lot of dry wilderness. In other lands which are well watered, such as ours, the demons dwell in the waters and swamps, and sometimes drown people who bathe or travel in them. Likewise, in some places there are water nymphs, who entice children into the water and drown them; those are all demons.

20. "When it comes again, it finds the house swept and adorned" [Luke 11:25] (St. Matthew adds "idle" [Matt. 12:44]); that is, the man is sanctified and adorned with beautiful spiritual gifts, so that the evil spirit sees that he can do nothing more with his old tricks, since they are known. Similarly, after idolatry was cast out among the Gentiles, he no longer attacks the world with that. But what does he do? He undertakes something different, goes out, brings back seven worse spirits, goes in, and dwells there, so that "the last state is worse than the first" [Luke 11:26].

He has also done the same with us. When Christ had become known in the world and the devil's former kingdom with its idolatry had been destroyed, he undertook a different thing and attacked us with heresy, until he introduced and established the papacy, in which Christ was completely forgotten, and so people became worse heathen under the name of Christ, as we can see with our own eyes. So it also happened to the Jews after the destruction of Jerusalem, and to the Greeks under the Turks, and it happens to all who hear God's Word and then become secure and lax in it, as St. Matthew says that he finds the house idle (Matthew [12:44]). He throws bad seed among the wheat at night when the people are sleeping (Matthew 13 [:25]). For that reason it is necessary that we be watchful, as the apostles everywhere admonish us to be, especially St. Peter: "Brothers, be sober-minded; be watchful. Your adversary the devil prowls around like a roaring lion, seeking someone to devour" (1 Peter 5 [:8]). Wherever he abolishes faith, he easily restores all former vices.

# GOSPEL FOR LAETARE SUNDAY [FOURTH SUNDAY IN LENT]

## John 6:1–15

*After this Jesus went away to the other side of the Sea of Galilee, which is the Sea of Tiberias. And a large crowd was following Him, because they saw the signs that He was doing on the sick. Jesus went up on the mountain, and there He sat down with His disciples. Now the Passover, the feast of the Jews, was at hand. Lifting up His eyes, then, and seeing that a large crowd was coming toward Him, Jesus said to Philip, "Where are we to buy bread, so that these people may eat?" He said this to test him, for He Himself knew what He would do. Philip answered Him, "Two hundred denarii worth of bread would not be enough for each of them to get a little." One of His disciples, Andrew, Simon Peter's brother, said to Him, "There is a boy here who has five barley loaves and two fish, but what are they for so many?" Jesus said, "Have the people sit down." Now there was much grass in the place. So the men sat down, about five thousand in number. Jesus then took the loaves, and when He had given thanks, He distributed them to those who were seated. So also the fish, as much as they wanted. And when they had eaten their fill, He told His disciples, "Gather up the leftover fragments, that nothing may be lost." So they gathered them up and filled twelve baskets with fragments from the five barley loaves left by those who had eaten. When the people saw the sign that He had done, they said, "This is indeed the Prophet who is to come into the world!" Perceiving then that they were about to come and take Him by force to make Him king, Jesus withdrew again to the mountain by Himself.*

1. In this Gospel, Christ once again teaches us faith, that we should not worry about our belly and nourishment, and He incites us [to faith] by a miracle. It is as if He would say with His deed what He says with His words: "Seek first the kingdom of God and His righteousness, and all these things will be added to you" (Matthew 6 [:33]). Here we see that when people follow Him because of God's Word and sign, and so seek God's kingdom, He does not forsake them but richly feeds them. He points out that before those who seek the kingdom of God would suffer need, the grass in the wilderness would become grain, a crumb of bread would become a thousand loaves, or a crumb would feed as well and as many as a thousand loaves. Thus He

confirms His words: "Man does not live by bread alone, but by every word that goes through the mouth of God" (Matthew 4 [:4]). To strengthen that point, He Himself begins and is concerned about what they will eat. He asks Philip, before they complain or ask about it [John 6:5], so that we will leave concern about ourselves to Him and know that He cares for us more and before we ourselves do.

2. Second, He gives an example of great love in various ways. First, He had this miracle with food benefit not only the godly, who followed Him because of His work and the Word, but also the belly-slaves, who seek from Him only food and drink and temporal honor. Afterward, [these belly-slaves] quarreled with Him at Capernaum about the food, and He said to them: "You are seeking Me because you ate" [John 6:26]. Likewise, they wanted to make Him into a king [John 6:15]. So also here He makes rain fall and the sun shine on the evil and the good [Matt. 5:45]. Second, He bears so kindly with His disciples' dull minds and weak faith. He tests Philip, who rushes in with his reason, and Andrew, who speaks childishly about it, to bring to light the apostles' imperfection [John 6:5–9]. On the other hand, His love and kind action with them shines all the more beautifully and delightfully, in order to incite us to faith in Him and to give us an example that we also should do the same. The members of our bodies and all creatures among themselves teach us that everything God has made is full of love, so that one bears with, helps, and preserves another.

3. When He takes the five loaves and gives thanks [John 6:11], He wants us to understand that nothing is too little for His own people, and He can indeed so bless their little that they have an abundance, while the rich in all their wealth do not have enough, as Psalm 34 [:10–11] also says, "Those who fear God have no lack; but the rich suffer want and hunger." Mary sings in her song of praise: "He has filled the hungry with good things, and the rich He has sent away empty" [Luke 1:53].

4. On the other hand, when He tells them to be diligent about picking up the fragments [John 6:12], He is teaching us to be prudent in retaining and using His good gifts so that we do not tempt God. Just as He wants us to believe when we have nothing, and to be certain that He will give it, so He does not want to be tempted or to have His good gifts be despised or left lying to spoil, while we wait for other gifts from heaven through miracles. Rather, whatever is there we should receive and use, and whatever is not there we should believe and wait for.

## The Allegories

5. The whole chapter demonstrates that Christ has stirred us up to spiritual feeding by this miraculous feeding, and intended that we would seek and

expect from Him nourishment of our souls. He calls Himself the heavenly bread and the true food [John 6:32] and points the Jews away from bodily food to Himself, saying: "Truly, I say to you, you are seeking Me not because you saw signs, but because you ate your fill of the loaves. Do not work for the food that perishes, but for the food that endures to eternal life, which the Son of Man will give to you" [John 6:26–27]. Accordingly, we also will seek this evangelical history in its hidden understanding and interpretation.

6. First, there was much hay or grass in the place [John 6:10]. The evangelist could not leave that out, even though it does not appear to be very necessary. However, it signifies the Jewish people, which sprouted and flourished like grass in their outward holiness, wisdom, honor, property, etc., as Isaiah says: "Surely the people are grass. All flesh is grass, and all its beauty is like the flower of the field. The grass withers, the flower fades, for the Spirit of the Lord blows on it" (Isaiah 40 [:6–7]). The Word of God sprouted among such people, and the true food was given to us, "for salvation is from the Jews" (John 4 [:22]). Now, since grass is nourishment not for people but for cattle, all the glory of the outward Jewish holiness is nothing other than fattening for beastly, carnal hearts, who neither know nor have anything of the Spirit.

7. That the people sit on the grass signifies the same thing, for the true saints despise outward holiness, as Paul does when he counts his former holiness to be rubbish and a loss (Philippians 3 [:8]). But it is only the simple and hungry people who receive the Word of God and are nourished by it. Here you see that neither Caiaphas nor Annas, neither the Pharisees nor the scribes follow Christ and see the miracle; rather, they despise it and are grass and eat grass.

This sign happened when "the Passover feast of the Jews was near" [John 6:4], for the true Passover, when Christ would be sacrificed, was near as He began to feed them with the Word of God.

8. The five loaves [John 6:9] signify the outward, bodily word expressed by the voice and understood by the senses, for the number five signifies the physical, outward things of a man on account of the five senses in which he lives, as shown by the five [wise] and five [foolish] virgins (Matthew 25 [:2]). These loaves are in the basket [John 6:13], that is, hidden in the Scriptures. A boy carries them [John 6:9], that is, the servile people and the priesthood among the Jews, who had the oracles of God, which were committed and entrusted to them (Romans 3 [:2]), though they did not enjoy them. That Christ took them in His hands, blessed, and increased them signifies that Scripture is opened, correctly understood, and preached through Christ's works and deeds, and not by our deeds or reason. Then He gave them to the disciples, and the disciples to the people [John 6:11; cf. Matt. 15:36], for Christ takes the Word from the Scriptures, and all the teachers receive it from

Christ and give it to the people. He did this to confirm His words: "You have one master, Christ" (Matthew 23 [:10]), who sits in heaven and alone teaches all of us with His Spirit through the mouth and words of the preachers. This is against the false teachers, who teach their own ideas.

9. The two fish which were also in the basket [John 6:9] are the example and witness of the patriarchs and prophets. Through them the apostles confirm and strengthen their doctrine and the believers, as St. Paul does when he refers to Abraham and David (Romans 4 [:1–12]). But there are two of them because the examples of the saints are full of love, which cannot be alone, as faith is, but must be applied to its neighbor. Moreover, [the fish] were broiled [cf. Luke 24:42?], for such examples are put to death by much suffering and torture, so that we find nothing carnal in them, and so that they do not comfort us with false faith in works, but point us always to faith [in Christ] and put works to death, along with confidence in them.

10. The twelve baskets full of fragments [John 6:13] are all the writings and books the apostles and evangelists left behind. For that reason, there are twelve of them, like the apostles, and these books are nothing else than what was left over, taken and developed from the Old Testament. For the same reason, the number five signifies that Moses has five books, as John says that the world could be written full of books about Christ (John 21 [:25]), even though everything was written and proclaimed about Christ previously in the Old Testament.

11. Philip advises on how to feed the people with so many denarii, and yet loses confidence in this [John 6:7]. That signifies human teachers who would gladly help souls with their teachings, but consciences sense that it does not help. The discussion that Christ holds with His disciples takes place so that they would see and understand that it is naturally impossible to feed these people with what they had, and the miracle would become all the more obvious. So He lets us wallow in and labor with human teachings, so that we would see and understand how necessary and precious God's Word is and that teachings without God's Word cannot at all help.

12. Andrew points out the loaves and the boy, and yet doubts all the more that it is enough [John 6:8–9]. That signifies the teachers who want to make the people godly and soothe them with God's laws. However, the conscience cannot have satisfaction or rest in them, but only becomes worse and worse until Christ comes with His Word of grace. He alone is and does enough, sets us free from sin and death, gives us peace and full joy, and does that of Himself, unasked, against and beyond all hope and expectation, so that we would know that the Gospel is intended and bestowed not through our merit but out of pure grace.

13. Finally, you see in this Gospel that Christ, though He had the highest regard for evangelical poverty and was not anxious about tomorrow, as He teaches (Matthew 6 [:34]), nevertheless had in reserve two hundred denarii, five loaves, and two fish. We are to learn from this that such poverty and freedom from anxiety does not consist in having nothing—as the sect of the barefooted [friars] and monks assert, and yet do not themselves keep. Rather, it consists in a free heart and a poor spirit. Abraham and Isaac had great possessions, and yet they lived without anxiety and in poverty, as the best Christians.

# GOSPEL FOR JUDICA SUNDAY [FIFTH SUNDAY IN LENT]

## John 8:46–59

*"Which one of you convicts Me of sin? If I tell the truth, why do you not believe Me? Whoever is of God hears the words of God. The reason why you do not hear them is that you are not of God." The Jews answered Him, "Are we not right in saying that You are a Samaritan and have a demon?" Jesus answered, "I do not have a demon, but I honor My Father, and you dishonor Me. Yet I do not seek My own glory; there is One who seeks it, and He is the judge. Truly, truly, I say to you, if anyone keeps My word, he will never see death." The Jews said to Him, "Now we know that You have a demon! Abraham died, as did the prophets, yet You say, 'If anyone keeps My word, he will never taste death.' Are You greater than our father Abraham, who died? And the prophets died! Who do You make Yourself out to be?" Jesus answered, "If I glorify Myself, My glory is nothing. It is My Father who glorifies Me, of whom you say, 'He is our God.' But you have not known Him. I know Him. If I were to say that I do not know Him, I would be a liar like you, but I do know Him and I keep His word. Your father Abraham rejoiced that he would see My day. He saw it and was glad." So the Jews said to Him, "You are not yet fifty years old, and have You seen Abraham?" Jesus said to them, "Truly, truly, I say to you, before Abraham was, I am." So they picked up stones to throw at Him, but Jesus hid Himself and went out of the temple.*

1. This Gospel reading teaches how the hardened become more raving, the more they are taught and kindly enticed. Here Christ asks them very kindly for the reason why they still do not believe, since they can find no fault either with His life or with His teaching. His life is innocent, for He defies them and says, "Which one of you can rebuke Me of a sin?" His teaching also [is innocent], for He says, "If I tell the truth, [why do you not believe Me]?" [John 8:46]. So He acts as He teaches.

2. Each preacher should demonstrate these two points. First, [he should demonstrate] an innocent life, so that he can defy [his opponents] and no one has a reason to slander his teaching. Second, [he should demonstrate] irreproachable doctrine, so that he misleads no one who follows him. In this way he would be in the right on both sides: with his good life against his

enemies, who look much more at his life than at his doctrine and despise the doctrine for the sake of the life; and with his doctrine among his friends, who pay much more attention to his doctrine than to his life and will bear with his life for the sake of his doctrine.

3. It is certainly true that no life is so good that it is without sin before God. For that reason it is enough that it be irreproachable before the people. But his doctrine must be so good and pure that it stands not only before people but also before God. Therefore, each godly preacher can indeed say: "Which one of you can find fault with me—among you, I say, who are human? But to God I am a sinner." Moses does that when he boasts that he had never taken anything or wronged anyone (Numbers 16 [:15]). Samuel (1 Samuel 12 [:3]), Jeremiah [Jer. 26:15], and Hezekiah [2 Kgs. 20:1–3; Isa. 38:1–3] also did that when they boasted about their innocence before the people in order to stop the mouths of the slanderers. But Christ does not speak that way about His doctrine. He does not say, "Which one of you can find fault with My doctrine?" Rather, [He says], "If I tell the truth" [John 8:46]. We must be certain that the doctrine is correct before God and is the truth, and accordingly pay no attention to how it is regarded by the people.

4. Thus the Jews have no reason for their unbelief other than that they are not God's children; therefore, He brings down the verdict on them and says: "Whoever is of God hears the words of God. The reason why you do not hear them is that you are not of God" [John 8:47]. That is nothing other than [to say], "You are of the devil."

5. The Jews could not tolerate this, for they wanted to be God's children and people; for that reason they now rage away and defame both His life and doctrine. [They defame] His doctrine by saying, "You have a demon" [John 8:48], that is, "You speak from the devil and Your doctrine is the devil's lie." [They defame] His life by saying, "You are a Samaritan" [John 8:48], which sounds worse among the Jews than any other vice.

So Christ teaches us here how things must happen with us and with His Word. Both our life and our doctrine must be condemned and defamed, and this will be done by the most distinguished, wisest, and greatest people on earth. We know the bad trees by their fruits [cf. Matt. 7:15–19] when they, under a good appearance, are so bitter, venomous, impatient, shameless, and mad to condemn and pass sentence, when they are really hit and what they do is rejected by means of God's Word.

6. What does Christ do here? He leaves His life stuck in shame and is silent and tolerates it when they call Him a Samaritan, but He defends His doctrine. The doctrine is not ours but God's, and He does not tolerate anything, for that is where patience ceases. But I ought to risk all I have for it, and suffer all they do, so that the honor of God and of His Word do not suffer.

If I perish, no great harm is done. But if I let God's Word perish and remain silent, then I do harm to God and to the whole world. Although I cannot restrain their mouths nor prevent their slander, nevertheless I ought not keep silent, as I do about my good life, nor let them be in the right, lest they be victorious. Although they do me injustice, yet it remains right before God.

So Christ defends Himself and says, "I do not have a demon" [John 8:49]—that is, My doctrine is not the devil's lies—"but I honor My Father." That is: "In My doctrine I preach the grace of God, through which He is to be praised, loved, and honored by believers. The evangelical preaching office is nothing other than God's glory. Psalm 19 [:1] says, 'The heavens declare the glory of God,' etc. But 'you dishonor Me,' that is, you call Me a devilish liar, who disgraces and dishonors God."

7. Why does He not say, "I honor My Father, and you do not honor Him"? Rather, He says, "You dishonor Me" [John 8:49]. In that way He secretly points out that His Father's honor and His honor are one and the same thing, just as He is one God with the Father. Yet at the same time He also wants [to point out] that if our preaching office, which praises God, is justly to be honored, then it must suffer disgrace. We are also to do the same against our princes and priests. When they impugn our life, we should tolerate it and repay them love for hate, good for evil.

But when they attack our doctrine, then God's honor is attacked, and then love and patience should be at an end and we should not keep silent but also say: "I honor my Father, and you dishonor me. Yet I do not care that you dishonor me, for I do not seek my own honor. But watch out! There is one who does investigate and judge it; that is, the Father will require it from you and will judge you and not let you go unpunished. He seeks not only His honor but also my [honor], because I seek His honor, as He says, 'Those who honor Me I will honor' (1 Samuel 2 [:30])." Our comfort is that we are happy, even though the whole world disgraces and dishonors us, because we are certain that God promotes our honor, and for that reason He will punish, judge, and take revenge. It will certainly come to anyone who believes and waits for it.

*Truly, truly, I say to you, if anyone keeps My Word, he will never see death. [John 8:51]*

8. Here He completely spoils it, because He not only defends His doctrine, which they attribute to the devil, as right and good but also ascribes such power to it that it becomes a queen over the devil, death, and sin, with the power to give and preserve eternal life. Look at how divine wisdom and human reason butt into each other. How can a human being grasp that one simple, oral word should redeem forever from death? But let blindness go away, for we will discuss this beautiful passage.

He is speaking here not about the word of the Law, but of the Gospel, which talks about Christ, who died for our sins, etc. God could not send Christ out into the world in any other way. He had to put Him into the Word, and thus spread and present Him to everyone. Otherwise Christ would only be for Himself and remain unknown to us. Then He would have died for Himself alone. But because the Word presents Christ to us, it presents Him to us as the one who has overcome death, sin, and the devil. For that reason, whoever grasps and holds onto [the Word] grasps and holds onto Christ—and through the Word is set free from death eternally. Consequently, it is a Word of life, and it is true: whoever keeps it will not see death eternally [cf. John 8:51].

9. From this we can easily understand what He means by "keeping" [John 8:51], [namely,] that it is not said about the kind of keeping we do when we keep the Law with works. This word of Christ must be kept in the heart by faith, and not with the fist or with works. The Jews here understand it [about works], and horribly rage against Christ that Abraham and the prophets died [John 8:52], but they do not know what "keeping," "dying," or "living" mean. It is not for nothing that He calls it "keeping," for it is a matter of struggling and fighting when sin bites, when death oppresses, and when hell pierces. Then it is called holding onto the Word and not being separated from it. Look at how Christ answers the Jews and praises His doctrine: "You say that My Word is of the devil and want to press it down to the bottom of hell. So I say again that it has divine power in it, and I exalt it above all the heavens and above all creatures."

10. How does it happen, then, that we do not see or taste death, and yet Abraham and all the prophets die, even though they had God's Word, as the Jews say? Here we must pay attention to the words of Christ, since He makes a distinction between death and seeing or tasting death. We must all go into death and die, but a Christian does not taste or see death; that is, he does not sense it, he is not terrified of it, and goes into it calmly and quietly, as if he were falling asleep, and yet he does not die. But a godless person senses it and is horrified of it forever. Thus "to taste death" can mean the power and might or bitterness of death; indeed, it is eternal death and hell.

The Word of God makes this distinction: A Christian has and keeps [the Word] in death, and for that reason he does not see death, but [he sees] life and Christ in the Word; for that reason he also does not sense death. But the godless person does not have the Word, and for that reason he sees no life but only death; so he also must sense [death], that is, bitter and eternal death.

11. Thus Christ means that whoever clings to His Word will, in the midst of death, not feel or see death, as He also says, "Whoever believes in Me, though he die, yet shall he live, for I am the life" (John 11 [:25]); that is, he does not sense death.

Here we see what a great thing it is to be a Christian, one who has already been eternally redeemed from death and can never die. His death or dying looks externally just like the dying of the godless, but inwardly there is as great a difference as between heaven and earth. The Christian sleeps in death and goes through [death] into life, but the godless goes from life and feels death eternally. We see how some tremble, doubt, despair, and become crazy and mad in their death throes.

For that reason, in Scripture death is called a "sleep" [cf. Ps. 13:3; Dan. 12:2; Matt. 9:24; John 11:11–14]. Just as anyone who falls asleep does not know what happens and wakes up in the morning unexpectedly, so we will suddenly rise on the Last Day and will not know how we came into death and through death.

12. Let us take a second example of this. When the children of Israel marched out of Egypt and came to the Red Sea, they were free and perceived no death, but only life. But when King Pharaoh came after them with all his forces, then they stood in the midst of death, and there was no more life in sight. In front of them was the sea through which they could not go, behind them was King Pharaoh, on both sides were high mountains. Everywhere they were captured and enclosed in death, so that they said to Moses: "Is it because there are not enough graves in Egypt," etc. [Exod. 14:11], so completely had they given up on life. Then Moses came and brought them God's Word, which comforted them in the midst of death and kept them alive, when he said, "Stand still and fear not, for you will see the great victory God will give, so that you shall never again see these Egyptians" [Exod. 14:13].

They clung to this Word and kept it. Through it life was seen in the midst of death, because they believed the Word, that it would happen, and so went into the middle of the Red Sea, which stood on both sides like two walls [Exod. 14:22]. Thus it happened that only life and safety were in the sea, where before there was only death and danger. They would never have been so bold as to go into the sea, even if it had been divided a hundred times, if God's Word had not been there to comfort them and promise them life. Thus man overcomes death through the Word of life, if he clings to it and believes it and goes into death with it.

13. So Christ also says here against the Jews that Abraham and the prophets are still alive and never died, but in the midst of death have life; they [only] lie down and sleep in death. "Abraham," He says, "saw My day, and was glad" [John 8:56]. So also the prophets saw it. Where and when did he see it? Not with bodily eyes, as the Jews understand it, but with the sight of faith in the heart; that is, he recognized Christ when it was said to him: "In your Seed shall all the Gentiles be blessed" (Genesis 22 [:18]). That is when he saw and understood that Christ, born of his seed through a pure virgin (so that

He would not be cursed with Adam's children but remain blessed), should suffer for the whole world, cause this to be preached, and so cover the whole world with blessing, etc.

This is the day of Christ, that is, the time of the Gospel, which is the light of this day, which gleams, shines, and enlightens the whole world about Christ, the sun of righteousness [Mal. 4:2]. It is a spiritual day, which nevertheless began at the time of Christ, as Abraham saw. However, the Jews understood none of this because of their carnal minds; for this reason they accuse Him of being a liar.

14. For this reason Christ goes further and establishes the basis and reason why it is just His Word and not the word of another which makes alive. He says it is because He was before Abraham, that is, because He is the one true God [John 8:58]. If the person who sacrificed Himself for us were not God, it would not help or avail before God at all if He were born from a virgin and suffered a thousand deaths. But what brings the blessing and the victory over all sin and death is that the Seed of Abraham is also the true God, who gives Himself for us.

Therefore, Christ is not speaking here about the human nature which they saw and experienced, for they could easily grasp that He was not yet fifty years old and had not been before Abraham [John 8:57]. With the same nature in which He was before Abraham so long ago, He was also before all creatures and before the whole world. According to His spiritual nature, He also became a man before Abraham; that is, through His Word and their knowledge of faith He was in the saints, for they all knew and believed that Christ, God and man, would suffer for us, as is written: "Christ [is the same] yesterday and today and forever" (Hebrews 13 [:8]) and "The Lamb who was slain from the foundation of the world" (Revelation [13:8]). Nevertheless, here He is speaking properly about His divine essence.

15. But here reason is terribly offended and becomes mad [at the idea] that man should be God, which makes no sense to them. This is the article at which the Jews to the present day take offense and cannot stop throwing stones and slandering. But, on the other hand, Christ also does not stop hiding Himself from them and going out of their temple [John 8:59], so that they can neither see nor find Him in the Scriptures, in which they search daily.

This history is not an insignificant terror to all who are presumptuous in Scripture and are not humble. At the present day it happens that many read and study in Scripture, and yet they cannot find Christ, for He has hidden Himself and gone out of their temple. How many there are who say with the mouth that God is man, and yet they are without the Spirit in their hearts! When things get serious, they will show that they never seriously meant it. This is enough on that.

# A SERMON CONCERNING MEDITATION ON THE HOLY SUFFERING OF CHRIST

*Written in [1519]*[1]

1. First, some reflect on the suffering of Christ in such a way that they become angry at the Jews, harp at and scold poor Judas, and let that be enough, just as they are accustomed to fault other people and condemn and disdain their adversaries. That could better be called reflecting not on Christ's suffering, but on the wickedness of Judas and the Jews.

2. Second, some have pointed out various benefits and fruits which come from meditating on Christ's suffering. Moreover, a saying attributed to Albert [the Great] is misleading; it says that it is better to consider Christ's suffering once superficially than to fast for a whole year, pray the Psalter every day, etc. Those who blindly follow him miss out on the true fruit of the suffering of Christ, for they seek their own things in it. For that reason they are busy with pictures and booklets, with letters and crosses; some even go so far as to imagine that they are safeguarded from water, iron swords, fire, and all kinds of danger. In that way Christ's suffering is supposed to work in them an absence of suffering, which is contrary to its nature and character.

3. Third, they take pity on Christ, mourning and lamenting for Him as an innocent man, just like the women who followed Christ out of Jerusalem, whom He rebuked and told to weep for themselves and for their children [Luke 23:27–28].

They are the ones who go far astray in the midst of the Passion, add a lot about the departure of Christ for Bethany [Matt. 21:17] and the sorrows of the Virgin Mary, but they do not get much farther. That is why they prolong [preaching on] the Passion for so many hours; God knows whether that was devised more for sleeping or for watching.

4. Fourth, people reflect on the suffering of Christ correctly when they look at it in such a way that they are frightened at heart, and their conscience

---

1 The 1540 *Winter Postil* mistakenly gave the date for this sermon as 1521. This sermon was reprinted frequently from 1519 to 1524, attesting to its popularity. Thereafter it found its permanent home in the *Winter Postil*, which spread its circulation even more widely. See WA 2:131–35; E² 11:151–54.

at once sinks into despair. This fright comes when we see the strict wrath and unwavering seriousness of God toward sin and sinners, since He even did not want to give His own dearest Son to free sinners unless He did full penance for them, as He said, "For the sin of My people I have struck Him" (Isaiah 53 [:8]).

What will happen to the sinner, when His dearest Son was struck in that way? An unspeakable and unbearable seriousness must be there when such an immeasurably great person goes to meet it, and suffers and dies for it. If you profoundly reflect on the fact that God's Son, the eternal Wisdom of the Father, Himself suffers, then you will indeed be frightened; the more [you reflect], the more profoundly [you will be frightened].

5. Fifth, you should deeply believe and not at all doubt that you are the one who tormented Christ, for your sins have certainly done it. So St. Peter struck and frightened the Jews as with a thunderbolt when he said to all of them in common: "You crucified Him" (Acts 2 [:36]). That same day three thousand were frightened and said to the apostles, trembling: "Dear brothers, what shall we do?" (Acts 2 [:37]). Therefore, when you see the nails piercing through Christ's hands, believe surely that that is your work. When you see His crown of thorns, believe that it is your evil thoughts, etc.

6. Sixth, where one thorn pricks Christ, there more than a hundred thousand thorns should justly prick you; indeed, they should prick you that way and much worse forever. Where one nail pierces Christ's hands and feet, you should have to endure even worse nails forever. That will also happen to those who let Christ's suffering have no effect on them. This severe mirror, Christ, will not lie or jest, for whatever He points out must abundantly happen.

7. Seventh, St. Bernard took such a fright from this that he said: "I thought I was safe and knew nothing about the eternal judgment that had come upon me in heaven, until I saw the only Son of God have mercy on me, step forward, and submit Himself to the same judgment for me. Alas, I can no longer play and be secure when there is such severity behind [His sufferings]."

So Christ commanded the women: "Do not weep for Me, but weep for yourselves and for your children" [Luke 23:28], and told them the reason for that: "For if they do these things when the wood is green, what will happen when it is dry?" [Luke 23:31]. It is as if He would say: "Learn from My torment what you deserve and what will happen to you." Here it is true that a little dog is hit in order to frighten a big one. So also, as said above,[2] they were frightened who said to the apostles: "Brothers, what shall we do?"

---

2 See above, paragraph 5.

(Acts 2 [:37]). Likewise, the Church sings: "I will diligently remember it, and my soul will faint within me" [Lam. 3:20].[3]

8. Eighth, in this point we must train ourselves well, for the benefit of Christ's suffering very much depends on one coming to know himself, being frightened for himself, and being battered. If he does not come to that point, the suffering of Christ is not yet truly beneficial for him. The proper, natural work of the suffering of Christ is that it makes us similar to Him, so that, just as Christ was miserably tormented in body and soul for our sins, so we also must like Him be tormented in our consciences by our sins. This does not happen with many words, but with deep thoughts about the seriousness of our sins.

Take an illustration: Suppose an evildoer were condemned for slaying the child of a prince or a king. You would be secure and sing and play as if you were entirely innocent, until someone frightfully laid hands on you and claimed that you were an accessory to the evildoer. Then the world would be too narrow for you, especially if your conscience deserted you. You should become much more anxious when you reflect on Christ's suffering. Although God has condemned and banished the evildoers, the Jews, they were nevertheless servants of your sins, and you are truly the one for whose sins God has slain and crucified His Son, as has been said.

9. Ninth, if anyone is so hard and dry that Christ's sufferings do not frighten him and do not lead him to confess it, he should be afraid. It will not turn out differently, for you must become similar to Christ's sufferings, whether that happens in life or in hell. At the very least, you must be frightened at death, tremble, quake, and sense everything Christ suffers on the cross. It is terrible to expect this on your deathbed; therefore, you should pray God to soften your heart and permit you fruitfully to reflect on Christ's suffering. It is impossible for us thoroughly to reflect on Christ's suffering ourselves, unless God sinks this into our hearts.

Neither this meditation nor any other teaching is given to you so that you should boldly take it on yourself to carry it out; rather, you are first to seek and desire God's grace so that you may carry it out through His grace and not through yourself. That is why the people mentioned above do not treat Christ's suffering correctly, for they do not call on God for this, but from their own ability they make up their own ways, and so deal with [that suffering] in an entirely human and unfruitful way.

10. Tenth, whoever reflects on God's suffering in that way for a day, an hour, or even for fifteen minutes—we would freely say that that is better

---

3 This text from Lamentations was used in a responsory at Matins for the Feast of Corpus Christi; see Barbara R. Walters, Vincent J. Corrigan, and Peter T. Ricketts, *The Feast of Corpus Christi* (University Park, PA: University of Pennsylvania Press, 2006), p. 277.

than if he fasts a whole year, prays the Psalter every day, or reads the Passion History a hundred times. This kind of reflection changes a man, and he is again born anew, almost as in Baptism. Then the suffering of Christ accomplishes its true, natural, and noble work; slays the old Adam; and banishes all the delight, joy, and confidence we can have from creatures, just as Christ was forsaken by all, even by God.

11. Eleventh, because this work is not in our hands, it happens that sometimes we pray and do not obtain it at once. Nevertheless, we should not despair or cease [praying]. Sometimes it comes when we do not pray for it, since God knows and wants it to be free and unconstrained. Then one becomes distressed in his conscience, wrongly displeased with his own life, and that can certainly be because he does not know that Christ's suffering is working this in him, which he perhaps does not think about. Similarly, others may think about Christ's suffering, and yet not arrive at knowledge of themselves through it. With the former, the suffering of Christ is secret and true; with the latter, it is a pretense and deceptive. In that manner, God often turns over the page, so that those who reflect on the suffering do not reflect on it.

## The Second Part, about Comfort
## from the Suffering of Christ

12. Twelfth, so far we have been in Holy Week and have celebrated Good Friday in the right way. Now we come to Easter and the resurrection of Christ. When one has become aware of his sins in this way and is completely frightened in himself, he must be careful that his sins do not remain in his conscience, or sheer despair will certainly result from it. Rather, just as [the sins] proceeded and were recognized from Christ['s suffering], so we should throw them back on Him and set our conscience free.

Therefore, see to it that you do not act like the wayward people do, whose sins bite and devour their hearts, and so they strive to run back and forth with their good works or satisfactions, or even [try to] work themselves out of it and get free of their sins by indulgences. That is impossible, but unfortunately this false confidence in satisfactions and pilgrimages has spread widely.

13. Thirteenth, you throw your sins away from yourself onto Christ when you firmly believe that His wounds and suffering are [for] your sins, so that He carries and pays for them. Isaiah says, "God has laid on Him the iniquity of us all" (Isaiah 53 [:6]). St. Peter writes: "He Himself bore our sins in His body on the tree" (1 Peter [2:24]). St. Paul says, "God made Him to be sin for us, so that in Him we might become the righteousness that avails before God" [2 Cor. 5:21].

You must rely on these and similar passages completely, and even more as your conscience torments you more severely. If you do not do this, but presume to quiet [your conscience] with your remorse and satisfactions, then you will never secure peace and must finally even despair. If we deal with our sins in our conscience, let them remain with us, and look at them in our hearts, then they are much too strong for us, and they live forever. But when we see that [our sins] lie on Christ, and He has overcome them through His resurrection, and we boldly believe this, then they are dead and come to nothing. They cannot remain on Christ. They are swallowed by His rising [cf. 1 Cor. 15:54], and now you can see no wounds, no pains in Him, that is, no sign that sin [still remains].

So St. Paul says that "Christ died for our trespasses and was raised for our justification" [Rom. 4:25]. That is, He made our sins known by His suffering and so slew them; but by His rising He justifies us and sets us free from all sins, if only we believe this.

14. Fourteenth, if you are unable to believe, then, as said before, you should pray to God for [faith]. This point is free in God's hand alone, and is given sometimes openly, sometimes secretly, as said in the point about suffering.

15. But you can stir yourself up to do the following: First, you can stop looking at the suffering of Christ (for that has done its work of frightening you), but press on through to look at His kind heart, how it is full of love toward you, love which compels Him to the difficult task of carrying your conscience and your sin. In that way your heart delights in Him, and the confidence of your faith is strengthened.

Then climb further through Christ's heart to God's heart, and see that Christ could not have shown love for you if God had not wanted to have [you] in eternal love; in His love toward you, Christ is obedient to Him. There you will find the divine, good, Father's heart, and, as Christ says, you will thus be drawn through Christ to the Father [John 6:44]. Then you will understand Christ's words: "For God so loved the world, that He gave His only Son," etc. [John 3:16]. Knowing God correctly means that we take hold of Him not in His power or wisdom (which are frightening), but in His goodness and love. There our faith and confidence can continue, and we are truly born anew in God.

16. Fifteenth, when your heart has thus been established in Christ, and you have become an enemy of sin out of love and not out of fear of pain, then the suffering of Christ should further be an example for your whole life, and you should reflect on [that suffering] in a different way. Previously we have reflected on [Christ's suffering] as a sacrament which works in us and which we suffer. Now we should reflect on the fact that we also work, namely, in this way:

If a time of pain or sickness burdens you, think about how insignificant that is compared to the crown of thorns and the nails of Christ.

When you must do or not do what you loathe, think about how Christ was led here and there, bound and captive.

If arrogance attacks you, then look at how your Lord was mocked and despised with the criminals.

If unchastity and lust are striking against you, think about how bitter it was for Christ when His tender flesh was flogged, pierced, and beaten.

If hatred and envy attack you or if you seek revenge, think about how Christ, who had much more reason to seek revenge, prayed with many tears and cries for you and all his enemies [Heb. 5:7].

If sorrow or any kind of adversity troubles you, whether bodily or spiritual, strengthen your heart and say: "Why should I not also endure a little sorrow when my Lord sweat blood in the garden [Luke 22:44] because of anguish and sorrow?" Only a lazy, despicable servant would lie in bed while his Lord must struggle in His death throes.

17. So, against all vice and depravity, we can find strength and comfort in Christ. That is the correct way to reflect on Christ's suffering, and those are the fruits of His suffering. Whoever trains himself in this does better than if he were to hear all Passion [sermons] or read all Masses. Those are true Christians who bring Christ's life and name into their own lives, as St. Paul says, "Those who belong to Christ crucify the flesh with its passions and desires" [Gal. 5:24].

Christ's suffering must be dealt with not in words and pretense, but in our lives and in truth. Thus St. Paul admonishes us: "Consider Him who endured from sinners such opposition against Himself, so that you may not grow weary and faint in your minds" (Hebrews 12 [:3]). St. Peter [writes]: "As Christ suffered in the flesh, arm yourselves with the same way of thinking" [1 Pet. 4:1]. This kind of meditation has fallen out of fashion and become rare, though the Epistles of St. Paul and St. Peter are full of it. We have changed the essence into a pretense and reflect on the suffering of Christ only in letters and as painted on the walls.

# GOSPEL FOR EASTER SUNDAY

## Mark 16:1–8

*When the Sabbath was past, Mary Magdalene, Mary the mother of James, and Salome bought spices, so that they might go and anoint Him. And very early on the first day of the week, when the sun had risen, they went to the tomb. And they were saying to one another, "Who will roll away the stone for us from the entrance of the tomb?" And looking up, they saw that the stone had been rolled back—it was very large. And entering the tomb, they saw a young man sitting on the right side, dressed in a white robe, and they were alarmed. And he said to them, "Do not be alarmed. You seek Jesus of Nazareth, who was crucified. He has risen; He is not here. See the place where they laid Him. But go, tell His disciples and Peter that He is going before you to Galilee. There you will see Him, just as He told you." And they went out and fled from the tomb, for trembling and astonishment had seized them, and they said nothing to anyone, for they were afraid.*

1. This Gospel reading is part of the history of Christ's resurrection and its first announcement. This was initially made by the angel to the women who went to the grave to anoint the dead body of the Lord, before Christ showed Himself to them and spoke with them. He first wanted to reveal His resurrection through the Word before they saw Him and learned the power of His resurrection.

2. Just as was said previously about the suffering and dying and other articles about Christ—that there is a twofold way of looking at it—so also there are two things to know and understand about the resurrection of the Lord.[1] First, there is the history which points out how things happened, with all the circumstances, how He revealed that He is alive through various demonstrations so that we would have a sure record and testimony about it as a foundation and support of our faith, because this article of the resurrection is the chief one on which our redemption and salvation finally stands, without which all the others would be futile and without any fruit.

Whatever else is to be known about the history—such as that both the angel's appearance (a part of which is reported in this Gospel) and the

---

1 See sermon for Meditation on the Holy Suffering of Christ.

appearance of the Lord occurred one after the other—should be treated when the whole history is put together in order from all the evangelists. For that reason, we will save the part this Gospel reports until then.

3. The second point, which is the chief and most necessary one, and on account of which the history happened and is preached, is about the power, benefit, and comfort of the joyous resurrection of the Lord and how we should use this through faith. St. Paul and all the apostles and all of Scripture teach and preach gloriously and abundantly about this as being the chief point of our faith; but the Lord Christ Himself does this most gloriously of all when He shows Himself especially to the women. So that we can hear and grasp something useful from this, too, let us take up the words which Christ spoke to Mary Magdalene, as the evangelist John records them in chapter 20.

> "Do not touch Me, for I have not yet ascended to My Father; but go to My brothers and say to them: 'I am ascending to My Father and your Father, to My God and your God.'" [John 20:17]

4. This is the first sermon which the Lord Christ preached after His resurrection, and without a doubt it is the most comforting, even though preached with few words, but with exceedingly kind and cordial words. He preached them first to His dear Mary Magdalene, and through her also to His disciples in order to comfort and gladden them about His resurrection after the severe distress, sorrow, and suffering which they experienced because of His departure and death. Because this Mary takes a much more ardent and fervent interest in the Lord than the others—she is the first at the grave to anoint the body of Christ with costly spices and, moreover, was frightened and dismayed when she did not find Him; she was deeply troubled and in tears, as if He had been taken away [John 20:1–2, 11]—therefore, He lets her enjoy this [evidence of His] love, that He appears to her first and preaches this beautiful sermon to her. Let us look at it.

5. First, when Jesus appears to her not far from the grave, before He speaks to her, she considers Him to be the gardener [John 20:14–15]. But when He calls her by her name and says, "Mary," she immediately recognizes His voice and at once also welcomes Him with the name which she (together with His other disciples) used to call Him in their language: "Rabboni" [John 20:16], that is, "O dear Master" or "dear Lord" (for among them "master" means the same as when we commonly say "dear sir"). She immediately falls at His feet, as she was accustomed to do, to touch Him. But He hinders her and says, "Do not touch Me" [John 20:17], as if He would say, "I certainly know that you love Me, but you cannot yet rightly look at or touch Me in the way that you should look at and touch Me."

She does not yet rejoice with a joy any higher or greater than bodily, fleshly joy, rejoicing only that she has her Lord alive again as she had Him before. So she continues to cling to the event and thinks that He will be among them again as before, eating and drinking with them, preaching and doing miracles. So she wants to show Him her love by serving Him, touching His feet, as before when she anointed Him both in life[2] and in death.

6. For that reason He now no longer wants to let her touch Him in that way. He gives her a reason so that she will keep quiet and listen and learn what she does not yet know, namely, that it is not His intention that He should be touched or anointed and waited on and served, as she had done for Him before. Rather, He says: "I will tell you something different and new. I rose not because I want to live and remain among you bodily and temporally, but so that I may ascend to the Father. For that reason, I do not need or want this service and work, and it is no longer right to look at Me as at Lazarus and others who still live this life, for this is not where I want to be and remain. Rather, believe that I am going to the Father, where I will rule and reign with Him eternally.

"Therefore," He means to say, "set aside now such bodily service and honor, and instead do this: Go and become a preacher and proclaim this (what I will tell you) to My dear brothers, that I will no longer be and remain here in a bodily way, but that I have gone out of this mortal life into another way of life where you will know and have Me no longer in a touchable and tangible way, but with faith."

7. Here He introduces an entirely new way of speaking when He says, "Go and tell My brothers," taken from Psalm 22 [:22]—which is completely about Christ—in which He is speaking about both His suffering and His resurrection when He says, "I will proclaim Your name to My brothers," etc. Previously He had never spoken in that way with His apostles, for at the supper He called them His "dear children" and His "friends" (John 13 [:33]; 15 [:14]). Now, however, He takes up the kindest and most glorious name that He can name and calls them "brothers." This was very important to Him; He does not delay for long, but, as soon as He has risen, His first concern is that they are told what He intends to do and why He rose.

8. This is certainly said in such an exceedingly pleasing and sweet way that whoever would believe has enough here to believe his whole life, as long as the world stands, that these things are true, as they (the dear apostles) also themselves had enough and more than enough to believe. The comfort is too great and the joy too high, and the heart of man too small and narrow, to attain it.

---

2 The sinful woman of Luke 7:36–50 who anointed Jesus' feet remains unnamed in Scripture but is often identified with Mary Magdalene.

9. The apostles were hiding behind locked doors, not only discouraged and fearful, like a scattered flock without a shepherd, but also with a bad conscience [John 20:19; cf. Matt. 9:36]. Peter had denied and renounced the Lord and cursed himself [Matt. 26:70–74]; the others had all run away and deserted Him [Matt. 26:56]. It certainly was a difficult and dreadful fall—they had to think that they would never again be forgiven for denying God's Son and for so shamefully abandoning their dear Lord and faithful Savior.

How could it ever enter their hearts that Christ would send such a friendly greeting and such a pleasing "good morning" to anyone who had deserted and denied Him, and would not only forgive and acquit everything but even call them His dear brothers? Who today can believe and grasp it? Sometimes I would gladly believe it, but I cannot get it into my heart so strongly that I would completely rely on it and regard it as genuine truth. If we could do that, we would already be in bliss[3] here and could not even be afraid of death or the devil and the world, but our heart would always have to leap and sing to God an eternal *Te Deum laudamus*.

10. But unfortunately it is not like that on earth, for our miserable beggar's sack—that is, our old hide—is too narrow. Therefore, here the Holy Spirit must come to our aid, who not only preaches the Word to us but also blows on and drives us inwardly; for this He uses the devil, the world, and all kinds of temptations and persecutions. Just as a pig's bladder must be rubbed with salt and thoroughly worked so that it becomes large, so our old hide must be thoroughly salted and afflicted so that we cry out and call for help, and so stretch and expand ourselves both through internal and external suffering that we may come up to and attain this kind of heart and spirit, joy and comfort from His resurrection.

11. Let us, then, look a little at what kind of words these are which Christ is speaking here and not run past them—as has previously happened and still happens in all the papacy, where we have read, heard, and sung them until we are bored, and yet have run past them as a cow passes by a relic.[4] It is a sin and a shame to hear and know such words, and then to let them lie cold and dead, without any heart, as if they were spoken and written completely for nothing. The Christians themselves, who do not despise them (as the others do) but are occupied with them daily, cannot regard them as so great and precious or believe them so firmly as they would like to.

12. Figure out for yourself (I say) what these words contain and express: "Go, My dear sister" (for without a doubt that is what He must have called the women, since He appeared to them first), "and say to the denying and deserting disciples that they are called and are 'My dear brothers.'" Does that

---

3 *selig*, elsewhere translated as "saved" or "blessed."

4 *wie die kue fur dem Heiligthumb*, that is, without understanding.

not, with one word, make us equally entitled and heirs with Christ of heaven and of everything Christ has [cf. Rom. 8:17]? They must truly be rich and blessed brothers and sisters who can boast of this Brother, who now does not hang on the cross or lie in the grave under death but is a powerful Lord over sin, death, hell, and the devil.

13. But how do these poor, frightened, discouraged disciples come to such honor and grace, and how is such brotherhood deserved? Was it deserved when Peter shamefully denied Christ and the others all were disloyal to Him? How have I and others deserved this (so that we speak also about ourselves)? It is truly a beautiful merit that I have celebrated the idolatrous Mass for fifteen years, slandered God, and daily helped crucify Christ anew! In the devil's service we rode to hell and sought other brotherhoods of the devil and his sects (under the names of the deceased saints, St. Anthony, Francis, St. Sebastian, St. Christopher, St. George, St. Anne, Barbara; about some of them it is unknown whether they were holy or even whether they ever lived). Shame on this sin and disgrace! We, who are called Christians and who hear this brotherhood of the Lord Christ so graciously offered to us, despise and abandon it and fall under such deep blindness that we let ourselves be enrolled in the roguish brotherhood of the shameful monks and of the whole papistic sect, and then preach and boast about it as if it were precious![5]

That is what should happen to the world. Why did we not want to esteem God's Word which has been written, painted, performed, sung, and rung before our eyes and ears? And now, moreover, when this is pointed out and rebuked through God's Word, people still do not cease to slander and persecute. But we should thank and praise God who so graciously has, without and even against our merit, snatched us from this blindness and slander and allowed us to know this.

14. Now whoever can believe it, let him believe it, for even if we do not believe it, it is still the truth. This brotherhood has been established here, and this brotherhood is not like our lax Calends brotherhood[6] and the brotherhood of the monks, but it is Christ's brotherhood in which God is our Father and His only Son is our Brother. This inheritance has been given to us, which

5 A "brotherhood" (also called a confraternity or sodality) was a religious association, often organized by a trade guild, whose members met for common prayer and celebration of the Mass by a chaplain. Like members of the monastic orders, members of brotherhoods were supposed to share in the merits of the works of all the other members. See also *The Blessed Sacrament and the Brotherhoods* (1519), LW 35:68–72.

6 Calends brotherhoods were usually groups of priests who assembled on the calends (first day) of the month. Over time they became noted more for their feasts of revelry than for their piety.

does not mean that we receive a hundred thousand gulden[7] or one or more kingdoms. Rather, we are redeemed from fellowship with the devil, from sin and death, and receive possession of the fief and inheritance of eternal life and eternal righteousness. Although we were in sin, guilty of death and eternal damnation, and are still stuck in it, yet we know that this brotherhood is greater, mightier, stronger, and more than the devil, sin, and all things. We have not fallen so deeply nor are things so evil and corrupted that this brotherhood cannot again restore and abundantly replenish everything, since it is eternal, infinite, and inexhaustible.

15. Who is the one who brings us this brotherhood? The only Son of God and the almighty Lord of all creatures, who has never been guilty of any sin. Isaiah 53 [:9] and 1 Peter 2 [:22–23] say that He for His own person did not need to suffer any agony or death, but "I have done this not for My own person or will," He says, "but as your Brother. I could not endure that you should be separated eternally from God and lost in misery under the devil, sin, and death. Rather, I stepped into your place and took your misery onto Myself, gave up My body and life for you so that you would be delivered. I rose again so that I could proclaim and ascribe this deliverance and victory to you and receive you into My brotherhood, so that you can have and enjoy with Me all that I have."

16. So you see that He does not want to stop with the fact that the history occurred and that He carried it out for His own person. Rather, He mingles among us and makes a brotherhood out of it, so that it is the common benefit and inheritance of us all. He does not place this in an "absolute category," but in a "category of relation";[8] that is, He has done this not for His own person, or for His own sake, but as our Brother and only for our good. And He wants to be regarded and known in no other way than as the one who is ours with all of this, and that we, on the other hand, are His. Thus we belong together most closely, so that we could not be more closely connected than those who have the same Father and sit in the same common and undivided possession. We can employ, boast of, and take comfort from all His power, honor, and benefit as our own.

17. Who can sufficiently comprehend this, and what heart can sufficiently believe that the dear Lord belongs to us so closely? It is something too great and inexpressible that we poor, miserable children of Adam, who were

---

7 A gulden was the most valuable gold coin in common circulation. Luther's salary was 100 gulden in 1524 (the first year it was granted), increased to 200 by Elector John of Saxony (r. 1525–32), then to 300 by Elector John Frederick, and finally to 400 in 1540. There was also an annual 100 gulden from the All Saints' Foundation, beginning in 1535.

8 *Nicht jnn predicamento absoluto, sondern Relationis.* "Absolute" here means "not having any relation to anything else, relationless, independent, or unconditional."

born and grew old in sin, should be the true brothers, fellow heirs, and fellow regents of the supreme Majesty in eternal life. St. Paul gloriously praises and extols this when he writes: "If we are children" (in Christ), "then we are also heirs, namely, heirs of God and fellow heirs with Christ" (Romans 8 [:17]; Galatians 3 [4:7]). All of this follows one from the other: if we are called God's children, then we must also truly be His heirs and brothers and fellow heirs of the Lord Christ (who is the only natural Son of God).

18. Therefore, whoever can learn, let them learn to begin to pray the Our Father correctly—what it means when I call God my Father and that I should truly and with certainty consider and think that I am His dear child and the Lord Christ's brother, who has shared all He has with me and made me equally entitled with Him to eternal benefits. Here search and ask your own heart whether you can say "Our Father" without doubting and wavering, from the bottom of your heart, take your stand on it, and conclude before God: "I regard myself to be Your dear child and You to be my dear Father, not because I merit or ever in the future could merit it, but because my dear Lord wants to be my Brother and has Himself told me this and invites me to regard Him as my Brother; and He, on the other hand, regards me as His brother."

Only begin this (I say) and see how you will succeed, for you will certainly find what an unbelieving villain is stuck in your breast, which your heart has a hard time believing. "I am a poor sinner!" nature says. "How can I exalt myself so highly, put myself in heaven, and boast that Christ is my Brother and I am His?" This greatness and glory is so exceedingly high, beyond the mind, heart, and thoughts of any man, that it cannot be comprehended. Even St. Paul himself confesses that he certainly grasps for it but has not yet comprehended it (Philippians 2 [3:12]). We are shocked and must ourselves be terrified to presume to claim such honor and glory.

19. What, then, should we do? We must indeed say—and it is the truth—that we are poor sinners and have denied our Lord with St. Peter. (I especially have done that above others.) But what can we make from that? What I have done against Him is enough and more than enough: I have fallen away from Him and made myself into a villain. Should I, then, make Him into a liar and a villain and deny and slander this comforting sermon? God forbid!

20. "Yes," says the devil through my flesh, "you are not worthy." That is unfortunately true. But if I do not believe and accept this, then I must call my Lord a liar and say that it is not true when He says that He is my Brother. May God keep me from that, for then I would have rejected and trampled underfoot God and all my salvation and blessedness.

21. Therefore, I will say: "I know very well that I am an unworthy man, worthy to be the devil's brother (not Christ's or His saints'). But now Christ has said that I (as the one for whom He died and rose again, as well as for

St. Peter, who was a sinner like me) am His brother, and in all sincerity He wants me to believe Him without any doubting and wavering. He does not want me to consider or pay attention to the fact that I am unworthy and full of sin." He Himself does not consider or remember, as He justly could do; He has sufficient cause to take revenge and punish His disciples for what they have merited from Him. Rather, everything is forgotten and blotted out of the heart [cf. Isa. 44:22; Acts 3:19]—indeed, [put to] death, covered, and buried. Now He can say nothing about them except everything delightful and good. He greets them and speaks with them as kindly as with His faithful, dearest friends and good children, as if they had done nothing wrong and had not troubled the water, but had done everything good for Him, so that they have no worry or care in their hearts that He would remember it and reproach them or take revenge on them.

Because He does not want to know about that, but has it [put to] death and covered up, why would I not let that be true and thank, praise, and love my dear Lord from my heart that He is so gracious and merciful? Even though I am burdened with sins, I still should not go ahead and call these kind words which I hear about Him a lie and arrogantly cast away the brotherhood He has offered. If I do not believe it, that is not good for me, but there is not for that reason anything false or lacking in Him.

22. If anyone now wants to burden himself with new sins and not let what He has forgotten be forgotten, he certainly will be sinning in a way which can no longer be forgotten or be helped. The Epistle to the Hebrews speaks about those who fell into sin by falling away from God's Word and calling it lies (Hebrews 6 [:6]; 10 [:26]). This is called the sin against the Holy Spirit,[9] which means holding the Son of God up to contempt, trampling Him underfoot, and profaning the Spirit of grace. May God preserve from this all who want to be Christians!

Unfortunately, there is too much of the former blindness and folly in which we have previously tarried, which ought now be gone and forgotten, since we have been made His brothers, if we will only accept it. If we cannot believe as strongly as we ought, then we should begin (like young children) to suck up at least a little spoonful of this milk [cf. 1 Pet. 2:2] and not at all push it away from us until we become stronger.

23. Therefore, even though your own unworthiness hits you in the head when you should pray, and you think: "My sins are too great! I worry that I cannot be Christ's brother," strike out and defend yourself as best you can from giving way to these thoughts. Here you are in great danger of the sin against the Holy Spirit. Confidently and boldly you should answer the devil's

---

9 Luther understood the sin against the Holy Spirit not just as despair of God's mercy but also as willful false teaching against the acknowledged divine truth. See LW 59:192–93 n. 31.

suggestions: "I know very well what I am, and you do not need to tell or teach me that, for it is not your business to judge about that. Therefore, go away, you lying spirit, for I should not and will not listen to you. But here is my Lord Christ, God's only Son, who died for me and rose from the dead. He tells me that all my sins are forgotten and that He now wants to be my Brother and that I in turn should be His brother. He wants me to believe this from my heart without any wavering."

24. Whoever will not accept this must be a villain and a miscreant, even the brother of the devil himself. If I am unworthy, I am certainly needy; and even if I were not [needy], yet God is worthy that I should give Him the honor and regard Him to be the truthful God. But if I would not believe, I would (beyond all other sins) be doing to Him the highest dishonor against the First Commandment[10] by regarding Him to be a liar and a worthless God. What greater wickedness and blasphemy can be heard or spoken of than this?

Much rather, when you feel that it is too hard for you to believe, do this: fall on your knees, tell Him your inability, and say with the apostles: "'O Lord, increase our faith' [Luke 17:5]. I would gladly from my heart regard You to be my heart's dear Father and Christ to be my Brother, but my flesh unfortunately will not follow; therefore, 'help my unbelief' [Mark 9:24], so that I can give honor to Your name and regard Your Word to be true."

25. See, in this way you will find from your own experience what a difficult struggle it is to believe these words and to pray the Our Father correctly. Not that these words are in themselves not certain, firm, and strong enough, but that we are so weak, even such hopelessly unstable quicksilver, that we cannot hold what is certainly worthy of being held with hands and hearts of iron and diamond.

26. Formerly, when we were led astray and deceived with lies and false worship, we could cling to all the saints and brotherhoods of monks, take comfort in firm (but false) faith, and boldly say, "Help, dear lord St. George, St. Anthony, and Francis, and let your intercessions benefit me." There was no temptation or obstacle; things succeeded well, and we had iron fists and strength to believe. But here where Christ, who is Himself the Truth [John 14:6], offers us His brotherhood—and moreover attracts and entices us in the kindest way: "Dear friend, accept Me as your Brother"—He cannot prevail on us to believe and accept Him, so very much do the flesh and the devil himself strive and fight against it.

27. Therefore, (I say) the best thing is for each one, when he goes into his room and begins to pray, to experiment and practice thinking about what he is saying, and put on the scales the words "our Father," [asking]: "Dear friend, what are you praying? What does your heart say about that? Do you truly

10 I.e., "You shall have no other gods before Me" (Exod. 20:3 ESV).

regard God as your Father and yourself as His dear child?" "No, indeed!" says the heart. "I do not know that. How can I attribute such a great and glorious thing to myself?" "Well, then, why do you not leave such a prayer aside, in which your mouth calls God a Father and your heart is calling yourself and Him a liar in His Word?" You should much rather confess your weakness [and say]: "I indeed call You my Father, and should call You that according to Your Word and command, but unfortunately I am worried that my heart is lying as a villain would. And the worst is not that I am lying for myself but that I am also calling You a liar. Help me, dear Lord and Father, not to make You into a liar, for I cannot become a liar myself unless I first make You into a liar."

28. Therefore, though I feel and experience that unfortunately I cannot say "our Father" with my whole heart (as no one on earth can say it completely—otherwise we would already be in perfect bliss), yet I will experiment and begin as a little child to suck at His breasts. If I cannot sufficiently believe it, I will still not let it be false or say no to it. Although I cannot play the game as it should be done, I will not promote the opposite (as the monks and despairing hearts do, who do not regard Christ as their Brother but as an enemy and a jailer), for that would be to turn Him into the devil. Rather, I will daily learn to spell, until I learn to repeat this Our Father and this preaching of Christ as well or as poorly as I can, no matter if it is stammered and stuttered or babbled, so long as I somehow accomplish it.

29. As already said, the sin above all sins is when God is gracious and wants to have all sins forgiven, but man through his unbelief rebukes God's truth and grace, throws it away, and refuses to let the Lord Christ's dying and rising avail. I cannot say that this brotherhood (which brings and gives us forgiveness of sins and all blessedness) is my work or activity or anyone else's, or that anybody has labored or searched for it. This resurrection happened and was accomplished before anyone knew about it, and its proclamation and preaching to us also is not human words but God's Word. For that reason, it cannot go wrong or tell lies. Because it is the truth and work of God alone, it is our duty, at the risk of incurring God's utter wrath and hostility, to accept it for God's sake and to cling to it with faith, so that we do not fall into the sin which cannot be forgiven.

30. Whatever other sins there are against God's command and Law (which consists of all that we should do and that God demands from us), they are all covered by forgiveness. For all our lives we are not completely free from them, and if God wanted to reckon with us according to our life and deeds, then we could never be saved. Whoever does not believe these words of Christ or will not accept His work sins a hundred thousand times more deeply and severely, for he strives against grace and robs himself of

forgiveness. It is grace that says, "The Law shall not harm you or condemn you," even if you have sinned greatly against it, but these sins are all forgiven and taken away through Christ. For just that reason He died and rose again for you and gives you this through this preaching about His brotherhood.

If you now do not want to believe or accept this, but ram your head against it and say, "I do not want grace," what will help you? Or what else will you seek in order to have forgiveness and be saved? "I will become a Carthusian[11] or run barefooted to Rome and buy an indulgence, etc. Well, then, run there if you want—not in God's name, but in the name of the devil himself, for in this way you have denied not only grace but also the Law and have fallen away from God completely, because you seek works and holiness which God has not commanded but has forbidden.

31. Should He not, then, become angry and rebuke us because we have daily prattled, sung, and read the Our Father and the Creed without understanding, faith, and heart and because we have considered not only Christ but also God's Law to be nothing? Rather, we have thought only about what we do and false spirituality; we have set these both above and against grace and command and placed them before God in order to reconcile Him and merit heaven. Since we have despised God's Word and this glorious, comforting sermon of Christ, what must happen is that we become shamefully blinded and deceived by the devil, and rebuked and afflicted by the pope, as if God were actually saying: "Very well, if you do not want My Son as your Brother and Me as your dear Father, then accept the pope with his monks, who point you away from the Gospel, the Creed, and the Ten Commandments to their shabby, stinking cowls and devil's brotherhood."

32. Because they do not want it to happen that Christ, who brings us God's grace and the forgiveness of sins, should be and remain our Brother without our merit and worthiness, what else is this but fundamentally and actually denying faith in God and His Son (as St. Paul says [Titus 1:16; 1 Tim. 5:8]), even if they confess Him with their mouths? I did the same thing in my former blindness, when I and others helped people to sing and read these words, and yet thought much more about my monkery and my own works.

If I had regarded Paul's words as true and certain when he says that "Christ died for our sins and rose for our justification" (Romans 4 [:25]) so that we would be His brothers, then I would have learned from this that my own works and my monk's cowl could not help me obtain it. Why else would Christ have needed to step up and take my sins and God's wrath onto Himself

---

11 Founded by Bruno of Cologne (ca. 1030–1101) in 1084 in Grand Chartreuse, France, Carthusians are a famously strict order that requires silence, labor, and contemplative prayer. Luther often referred to them as exemplars of the most intensive form of ascetic life. See Luther's preface to [George of Hungary], *On the Ceremonies and Customs of the Turks* (1530), LW 59:259; and LW 20:86 n. 4.

through His cross and death, and through His resurrection place me in the inheritance of the forgiveness of all sins, eternal bliss, and glory?

33. But now, because they cling to their monkery, seek God's grace through their own merits, and want in that way to lay aside sin and make amends for it, they testify against themselves that they believe none of what they say with their mouth: "I believe in Jesus Christ who died and rose for me," etc.[12] Rather, they believe the opposite: [they believe] in the cowl and cord of the barefooted monks,[13] in St. Anne and Anthony, and (pardon me!) in the devil's rear end. It is impossible for someone who knows Christ in this brotherhood to be occupied with such nonsense that is taught and adhered to not only apart from and against faith but also against the Commandments, and which are truly devilish sins above all other sins.

34. Therefore, if a Christian cannot speak a strong Our Father, he should again learn at least to make the sign of the cross and think: "Preserve me, dear God, from the sin against the Holy Spirit, so that I do not fall away from faith and Your Word and do not become a Turk, a Jew, or a monk and pope's saint, who believe, teach, and live against this brotherhood. Rather, let me retain a little corner of this brotherhood." Let it be enough that we have believed and lived so long against it; now is the time to ask God to make this faith sure and strong in us.

If we have that faith, then we are rescued and delivered from sin, death, and hell and can now judge all other spirits; recognize and condemn all error, deception, and false faith; and speak the verdict: "Whoever puts on a cowl and lets himself be shorn in order to become holy thereby—or buys his way into a brotherhood of monks—is a mad, stupid fool, a blind, miserable, wretched, desperate man, who tortures himself with much fasting and mortification like the Carthusians or Turkish saints. Such a one is already separated from God and Christ and condemned to hell."

All of this is nothing but slandering and contradicting the dear heavenly brotherhood of Christ. They can certainly pray and recite much about this, as Isaiah says, "These people draw near Me with their lips"; they step up under My very nose in the churches with singing and ringing, "but their hearts are the farthest of all away from Me" (Isaiah 29 [:13]). What great pleasure (do you think) is He to have in such saints? Outwardly they act as if they were the true children of God; they read and sing the Gospel, use the most beautiful words, and celebrate a glorious Easter festival and procession with banners and candles, yet they are not concerned to understand or believe it. No, they fight against it with their doctrine and life.

12 Cf. the Second Article of the Apostles' Creed (Kolb-Wengert, pp. 21–22; *Concordia*, p. 16).

13 I.e., the Franciscans.

35. If they did understand and believe it, they would not remain with their monkery and human inventions but would quickly trample their cowls and cords underfoot and say: "Shame on this despicable brotherhood! To the devil with it! It is not worth looking at or thinking about compared to this brotherhood that teaches me my Creed and Our Father."

Similarly, St. Paul passes a verdict on his holy life in Judaism and says: "I was a good, blameless man, not according to my own human inventions but according to the Law of Moses. When I came to know Christ, I regarded all my righteousness under the Law as a loss—not only a loss, but I regarded all of it as rubbish and filth" (Philippians 3 [:6–8]). "I certainly thought that I was a great saint and that I kept the Law strictly and diligently—and regarded that to be my highest treasure and greatest gain. But when I heard of this brotherhood and inheritance of the Lord Christ, how quickly my pride and bragging about my own righteousness left me! I now shudder at it and can no longer think about it."

36. See, this is how he praises the righteousness which this brotherhood brings us: in comparison he can belittle and despise the life and holiness of all people extremely, even when it is at its best according to God's commands (which should and must be kept—indeed, there is nothing more praiseworthy and better on earth). Because [that holiness] is still completely our activity and life, it cannot and should not have the honor and glory of making us God's children and of acquiring the forgiveness of sins and eternal life. Rather, that belongs to hearing the words of Christ, who says to you: "Good morning, My dear brother. Your sin and death have been overcome in Me, for what I have done, I have done for you," etc.

37. That is the source of St. Paul's defiance toward sin and death: "Death, where is your sting? Hell, where is your victory?" (1 Corinthians 15 [:55; Hosea 13:14]). It is as if he would say: "Formerly, you were strikingly frightful enemies, before whom all people, no matter how holy and godly they were, had to tremble and despair. Where are you now? How have I so completely lost you? Everything has been swallowed up," he says, "and completely drowned or flooded by a victory! Where is that victory, or who did it come from? Thanks be to God," he says, "who has given it to us through our Lord Jesus Christ" [1 Cor. 15:57].

38. Although that is a glorious, great defiance, no one can have it without the faith with which St. Paul believed. However, he himself laments that [his faith] was not as strong as he wanted it to be [cf. Rom. 7:24; Phil. 3:12; 2 Cor. 12:7–10]; yet he had it surely and could preserve it against the devil's wrath and power. The fact that we do not have that and are still so afraid and frightened of death and hell is a sign that we still have too little faith. Therefore, we have all the more reason to push ourselves to call out to God and to ask

Him, together with the help of our brothers' prayers, for that, and to push that Word daily into our hearts, until we also in some measure can obtain this defiance.

39. Our adversaries can scornfully laugh and mock that we do not know how to teach anything except faith; they can cry out that people must rise far higher and do much more. But if we only had enough faith, we would easily attend to the other things. The most important and necessary point (about which they know nothing) is how we become free from the terrors of sin, death, and hell and can obtain a cheerful conscience toward God, so that we can truly pray "our Father" from our hearts. Where that is not present, everything else is lost, even if we tortured ourselves to death with works. But because this is still lacking in all people, we need not be ashamed to learn it and to be occupied with it as we are with our daily bread and, in addition, to implore God for His power and strength. Amen.

# GOSPEL FOR EASTER
## MONDAY

*Luke 24:13–35*

*That very day two of them were going to a village named Emmaus, about seven miles from Jerusalem, and they were talking with each other about all these things that had happened. While they were talking and discussing together, Jesus Himself drew near and went with them. But their eyes were kept from recognizing Him. And He said to them, "What is this conversation that you are holding with each other as you walk?" And they stood still, looking sad. Then one of them, named Cleopas, answered Him, "Are you the only visitor to Jerusalem who does not know the things that have happened there in these days?" And He said to them, "What things?" And they said to Him, "Concerning Jesus of Nazareth, a man who was a prophet mighty in deed and word before God and all the people, and how our chief priests and rulers delivered Him up to be condemned to death, and crucified Him. But we had hoped that He was the one to redeem Israel. Yes, and besides all this, it is now the third day since these things happened. Moreover, some women of our company amazed us. They were at the tomb early in the morning, and when they did not find His body, they came back saying that they had even seen a vision of angels, who said that He was alive. Some of those who were with us went to the tomb and found it just as the women had said, but Him they did not see." And He said to them, "O foolish ones, and slow of heart to believe all that the prophets have spoken! Was it not necessary that the Christ should suffer these things and enter into His glory?" And beginning with Moses and all the Prophets, He interpreted to them in all the Scriptures the things concerning Himself.*

*So they drew near to the village to which they were going. He acted as if He were going farther, but they urged Him strongly, saying, "Stay with us, for it is toward evening and the day is now far spent." So He went in to stay with them. When He was at table with them, He took the bread and blessed and broke it and gave it to them. And their eyes were opened, and they recognized Him. And He vanished from their sight. They said to each other, "Did not our hearts burn within us while He talked to us on the road, while He opened to us the Scriptures?" And they rose that same hour and returned to Jerusalem. And they found the eleven and those who were with them gathered together, saying, "The Lord has risen indeed, and has appeared to Simon!" Then they told what had happened on the road, and how He was known to them in the breaking of the bread.*

1. This Gospel reading shows and teaches especially three points on the article of the resurrection of Christ. First, this history happened and was written, among others, as a sure testimony and proof for our faith concerning this article. First, these two disciples go away from the others and, with a very strong unbelief in the resurrection, talk with each other about these things as if they despaired of Christ. For them, He was completely dead and eternally buried in their hearts, no longer able to do anything. They themselves confess this with their words when they say, "We had hoped that He would redeem Israel, but now He has been dead for three days," etc. [Luke 24:21]. Although they have heard from the women that they had seen "a vision of angels who said, 'He has risen and lives'" [Luke 24:23], they neither saw nor found Him anywhere.

Second, the chief point is not only that here Christ shows Himself alive to the unbelieving disciples—so that they are certain of it and immediately return to proclaim it to the others, and then hear the same thing from them, so that this testimony agrees and is confirmed on both sides—but the chief point is also that Christ, before He was recognized by them, proved abundantly and clearly through the Scriptures that He had to do both, suffer and rise again from the dead [Luke 24:27]. For this reason He rebukes them for not believing, since they should know the Scripture about Christ, which He had spoken to them before His suffering.

2. The second point of this Gospel is an example of the power and fruit of the resurrection. This happened in these two disciples as they talked about Him and listened to His preaching, which is also a part of the proof of the true resurrection. Christ here proves as a matter of fact that He is not dead, as they regarded Him at first to be, but works in them and exerts His power through the Word even before they recognize Him. He causes them to believe and to have a different mind and understanding, heart and spirit than before, as they also themselves perceive and confess: "Did not our hearts burn while He talked to us?" [Luke 24:32], etc. He still does the same thing in all Christendom when He is not seen and yet carries on His work and dominion and proves that, as the living Lord, He enlightens, comforts, and strengthens them through the Word, defends them with His power, and preserves them against the wrath and raging of the devil and the world.

3. The third point here shows the way in which Christ reveals His resurrection and how it is recognized and apprehended, namely, first through the Word and faith before this happens through bodily vision or perception. For that reason He is at first hidden from them and unknown to them when He comes to them and walks with them—even though He is truly with them and is the same Christ whom they had so often seen and heard and knew very well. Yet now they do not at all know Him, nor can they imagine that

it is Him, because they know that three days previously He had died and was buried, and so they cannot think of Him otherwise than as a dead man. He has become to them so strange and hard to recognize that they would not have recognized Him no matter how long He had been with them, until He proclaimed to them this article of the resurrection and preached about it. The text says, "Their eyes were kept from recognizing Him" [Luke 24:16], not that He was different or would not let them recognize Him, but that their hearts and thoughts were so strange and far from Him. So also He was not recognized by [Mary] Magdalene or by the other disciples until they first heard the words about His resurrection [cf. John 20:14].

4. In this way He wants to teach and show us that the power of His resurrection and of His kingdom should work and show itself here on earth and in this life only through the Word and faith, which clings to Christ, whom it does not see, and thus conquers sin and death in Him, lays hold of righteousness and life, etc. That is a brief summary of the story or history of this Gospel (as much as it concerns the article of the resurrection generally), about which we heard more above.[1]

5. But this Gospel reading especially pictures for us the weakness of faith in the disciples and how Christ is and conducts Himself in His kingdom toward such weak believers. Thus we see in the whole history of the Gospel of the resurrection of Christ that first all the apostles, and then the other disciples, were all too weak to believe this article, even at His ascension when He had to rebuke them for their hardness of heart and lack of understanding "because they had not believed those who saw Him risen" (Mark 16 [:14]). Yet He had often Himself proclaimed to them from the Scripture that He must be crucified and rise again on the third day, etc. [e.g., Matt. 16:21].

6. From this we learn, first, that weakness and defects remain even in those who are now Christians and holy, especially in the high points of doctrine and faith, namely, that they cannot immediately understand or grasp them as firmly and strongly as they should. Faith is not such a trifling or easy matter as foolish and inexperienced spirits imagine and as our coarse blockheads, the pope's donkeys, assert. They think that faith is nothing other than having heard and knowing the story and history, and then they imagine that they have at once thoroughly understood and believed everything the Gospel says about Christ when they have heard or read it once, and that they no longer need to learn and believe it.

7. This is nothing other than a loose, futile thought, which is proved when they must confess that this knowledge of the history lies in their hearts still, cold, and idle, like a bare, empty husk, without moisture or strength, neither benefiting nor helping them, neither strengthening nor improving

---

1 See sermon for Easter Sunday on Mark 16:1–8.

them. Nevertheless, this great, high work of the resurrection of Christ happened and is to be preached, and thus heard and known, so that it produces fruit in us, awakens and kindles our hearts, and works in us new thoughts, understanding and spirit, life and joy, comfort and strength.

If that does not happen, then the history has been heard in vain; it is dead within you and is nothing more than it is in Turks and heathen who never knew anything about it or who by no means regarded it to be true. You cannot boast about your faith, even if you have retained from the history some froth on your tongue or some sound in your ears or a dream in your memory, of which your heart has experienced or tasted nothing. The Papists clearly show with all their doctrine and life that in their hearts they believe and hold nothing about this article. They show this since they teach people to seek and obtain the power and benefit (which the resurrection of Christ ought to accomplish) apart from Christ, in themselves, and through their own works and merit; they condemn, slander, and persecute the saving doctrine which points us away from these lying inventions to the power of His resurrection.

8. Christians and believers experience—both in others and in themselves—confess, and lament their weakness, that they cannot grasp this article and bring it into their hearts with as strong a faith as they ought. They have to fight and contend against their weakness all their lives, as Paul himself says that he has not laid hold of it but always strives and stretches for it so that he can lay hold of it, to know the power of Christ's resurrection, etc. (Philippians 3 [:12, 10]).

9. Although this article is in itself most delightful and comforting, pure joy and happiness, so that it ought calmly and easily to enter the heart, yet there are two great obstacles which make it difficult to believe. First, this work is in itself much too high and great for us ever sufficiently to comprehend in this life, even if our faith were completely strong and without weakness, for it is the kind of strength and power which we will first truly see and experience eternally in the next life. Second, our flesh and blood and the hearts of all people are by nature much too weak and fearful to believe God's Word; yet even apart from that, when we consider the greatness of this work and then look at ourselves and our unworthiness, we must be frightened and horrified.

10. God cannot overlook or tolerate the first cause and obstacle, for the work must and should remain as great as it is and not be diminished at all; it must be the strength and might to which all creatures, humans, angels, devils, and hell must yield and succumb, because it is necessary for our salvation and blessedness. If it were not true, then we would have to remain under sin, the eternal wrath of God, and death. However, with the second obstacle—that we are too weak to grasp this great work and strength by our faith—He can

be lenient and have patience. We see here that Christ does this with His disciples, who certainly had heard that He had risen and yet were in very great doubt, so that they almost completely despaired of Christ, because they said, "We hoped that He would redeem Israel" [Luke 24:21].

11. But look at how He intentionally accepts these two who are weak in faith, cares for them, and does everything to aid their weakness and to strengthen their faith. Because He sees and knows that they had gone away from the other apostles troubled and sad, not knowing what they should think or hope, He does not want to leave them stuck, remaining in such doubt and temptation. Rather, in order to help them out of it, He comes and joins them on the way. He leaves the other apostles all sitting together, even though they, too, were quite troubled and weak in faith.

But because these [two] are in great danger of unbelief, He soon shows Himself to them alone, as if He now after His resurrection has nothing else to do. He speaks and disputes with them from Scripture in a friendly way, and thus gives them a reason to stop Him and ask Him to remain with them and to eat and to drink with them long enough that their faith is again awakened and they get rid of doubt [Luke 24:29–30]. They become strong in faith so that they now recognize Him and see that He is the same Christ whom they had had living with them before and had seen crucified three days ago. Before this, they were unable to recognize Him on the way because of the doubt and weakness which was still in them.

12. Thus for our teaching and comfort He Himself wanted to depict and show here what kind of governance He should have in His Christendom after His resurrection. He does not want to reject or push away from Himself those who are weak in faith or who have erring, foolish, or otherwise frail, fearful, and discouraged hearts and consciences. Rather, on just these people He exerts and proves the power of His resurrection by attracting them to Himself in a friendly way, coming to them, associating with them in a most beautiful and easy way, chatting with them, teaching and instructing them, even eating with them, long enough that they become strong and certain in faith, and their hearts, which were so sad and troubled, are again gladdened.

Thus we also should know and confidently expect that in Him we have a Lord who can bear with our weakness and not hold it against us and who does not want to push us away from Himself and because of it condemn us, who cannot immediately live and believe as we ought to. If only we had hearts which would not despise and deny Christ and His Word but would delight in and love Him and gladly be strong and perfect in faith and life!

13. When we look at these disciples, weak and foolish as they are, we see that their hearts favored Christ, gladly and eagerly spoke about Him and listened to Him speak, and had no more delightful wish than that what they

heard about His resurrection would be true. But it was much too big for them to believe, so that they could not immediately regard it as certain and true, just as it is also much too high and too big for us. Our dear Lord knows and sees this very well; therefore, He can also be all the more patient with us. He is satisfied and pleased if only we listen to Him as His students, gladly wanting to be taught and instructed by Him.

14. He wants to teach us here how we are to act in His kingdom, especially toward those who are weak in faith and infirm. We also should not immediately condemn or reject those we see erring or even stumbling, but also have patience with them, just as Christ has done and must still daily do with us. Although in His own person through His resurrection He is Lord over heaven and earth in divine power and might, yet He rules His dear Christendom by exerting and proving the power of His resurrection on His poor, weak little flock and serving them with His power and might, to comfort and strengthen them.

15. According to this example, we, too, though being strong, should not take pleasure in ourselves and boast, but rather let our gifts and strength serve the weak. We should strive to support and improve them with instruction, comfort, strengthening, friendly admonition and rebuke, etc., just as people do with weak or frail children and the sick. We must act and deal with them in a careful and merciful way, care for them, carry them, and lift them until they are grown and can walk for themselves.

16. This is one of the chief points in the Gospel about the kingdom of Christ, from which we learn what it is like and what happens there. It is the kind of reign in which weakness, lack of understanding, and other sinful defects still remain among the Christians who have begun to believe and be holy. Nevertheless, He bears with them and overlooks it, yet in such a way that they will be corrected. We should not dream about a church on earth in which there are no defects or errors in faith, as the Papist crowd boasts that their churches and councils cannot err, etc.

In this passage we hear that not only these two disciples but also the other apostles all together erred in this chief and most necessary article and were stuck in unbelief until Christ Himself pulled them out of it through many and various sermons and revelations. Faith in the resurrection of Christ was completely extinguished from all hearts for three days after He was crucified. This light was retained almost nowhere except in Mary, His mother, who retained in her heart the Scripture she had heard from Him and elsewhere and through that was comforted and sustained in her great grief at her Son's suffering and dying.

17. Nevertheless, faith in Christ must always remain and be preserved somewhere in the Church, and there must be some who have and confess[2] the truth, even if there are few of them and the greater number err, as they erred here and it was preserved through no more than one Mary. He lets it happen that even many of the true saints err and stumble so that we will not rely on people, no matter how many, great, and holy they are, but look to the Word which is sure and cannot deceive, just as here He directs and leads these two and afterward all the others always into Scripture.

18. Besides this, the example of the Gospel is not to be forgotten; it urges and admonishes us to speak and hear about Christ gladly and to be occupied with Scripture and God's Word, even if we do not always immediately understand it or take it to heart as we should. The Gospel shows us what kind of power, benefit, and fruit it has when handled by a simple heart.

19. First, we see that even though these two disciples were still completely stuck in unbelief, nevertheless, because on the way they were each concerned about Christ, talking and disputing in all simplicity and almost for no reason, He will not and cannot remain away from them but immediately is present, joins them in a most friendly way, soon touches their hearts and thoughts, and begins to give them a beautiful, glorious sermon about just the article they were concerned about and doubting, the like of which they had not previously heard.

Second, they then immediately feel its power, so that their hearts no longer remain heavy, slow, and cold to believe as before, but are moved and kindled, even enlightened. They gain a new understanding, so that now they begin to understand the Scriptures correctly; what they had previously not understood becomes plain and clear to them.

Last, the mask and cover are taken away from their hearts and eyes so that they no longer regard Him to be a guest and a stranger but now correctly recognize Him and perceive that He is no longer far away from them but is Himself present and working in them. They are now completely certain in their faith, and henceforth no longer need the bodily, visible revelation, but can immediately begin to preach to others and to strengthen and help them against doubt and unbelief.

20. Therefore, we also should gladly hear God's Word according to their example and not become discouraged. This is not only a necessary training for both the weak and the strong, for the foolish and the learned, which abundantly teaches everything necessary for salvation and can never be completely learned, but it is also the means through which God wants to work in our hearts and to give us faith and the Holy Spirit, as St. Paul says, "Faith comes from hearing the Word" [Rom. 10:17]. There is surely fruit if this is

---

2 Luther's notes have: "preach" (WA 22:434).

done earnestly, even if the heart at first is cold and lazy about it. Yet if we only continue and persist, it will not be useless for bringing and correcting the foolish and erring, for strengthening the weak, and finally for warming and enlightening the heart, because Christ is best understood and recognized in Scripture.

21. If there were no other benefit to it, yet we should be stirred up and gladly be occupied with it because in that way we please God and the Lord Christ and worship our dear God. We know that then He is certainly not far from us, as He Himself promises and says, "Where three or two of you are together in My name, there am I among them" (Matthew 18 [:20]). Then the dear angels are certainly with Him around you and have delight and joy in this. On the other hand, the devil must be driven away and withdraw, as he had to withdraw from Christ when He opposed him with God's Word [Luke 4:13].

22. We have read an example of this involving an old father in the desert who had special visions and revelations from God: When he was among young people [and heard] what they said to each other, he saw that whenever they spoke about Scripture and divine things, beautiful youths joined them and smiled in a friendly and happy way. But, on the other hand, whenever they frivolously and idly gossiped, the same [beautiful youths] sadly turned away from them in displeasure, and filthy black pigs came and danced among them, etc.

23. That is enough about the chief points of the history of this Gospel. Beyond that, there is still the important point of Christ's sermon which He preached to the disciples from Scripture and in summary proved from it that Christ had to suffer and so enter into His glory, etc. [Luke 24:26]. The evangelist says about this sermon:

> *And He began with Moses and all the prophets and interpreted to them all the Scriptures which were spoken about Him. [Luke 24:27]*

24. This[3] was without a doubt a very beautiful, glorious sermon. Now it is true that we all—and each one of us—would like to know which Scriptures the Lord quoted which spoke about Him, by which they were kindled, strengthened, and convinced. We find very little—almost nothing, it would seem—in Moses which speaks about what He says: that He must suffer and rise on the third day and repentance and forgiveness be preached in His name [Luke 24:46–47], etc. The Jews had Moses at that time and long before, and

---

3 Paragraphs 24 through all but the last sentence of paragraph 41 (below, p. 56) are a free adaptation of Rörer's notes on Luther's sermon of April 6, 1534 (WA 37:363–67).

still to this day diligently read themselves full of him, and yet they have never observed something so great and unusual in him.

25. But the evangelist answers this and solves the problem in this way: their hearts were kindled when He explained the Scriptures to them [Luke 24:32]. Shortly afterward the Gospel says that He opened their understanding so that they understood the Scriptures [Luke 24:45]. It is established that Moses certainly writes about Christ and that He can be read about there, but what matters is that whoever reads also should understand what it says. Paul also says that the veil of Moses, which only Christ takes away (2 Corinthians 3 [:14]), remains before the face of the Jews when they read the Old Testament. He says to His apostles: "To you it has been given to know the secrets of the kingdom of heaven, but to the others that they see and hear it but may not understand it" [Matt. 13:11].

26. Therefore, Scripture is the kind of book which requires not only reading and preaching but also the true Exegete, namely, the revelation of the Holy Spirit. In our time we see in our own experience that, when we prove most clearly from Scripture the articles of pure doctrine and refute the errors of our opponents, it does not help them. There has never been any article of faith preached which was not more than once attacked and contradicted by the heretics, who, after all, read the same Scriptures that we have.

27. This revelation also requires true students who want to be taught and instructed (like these simple, godly disciples), not sophists and obstinate spirits and self-made masters who with their cleverness reach far above the heavens. This is the kind of doctrine which makes our wisdom into folly and puts out the eyes of our reason, if it is to be believed and understood. It does not come from human wisdom like other teachings and knowledge on earth, which have come from reason and can again be grasped by reason.

That is why it is impossible to grasp this [revelation] with our reason; and if you presume to measure and calculate how far [the revelation] agrees with [reason], you will not succeed. All heresies from the beginning have arisen from [reason], and both Jews, Gentiles, and now the Turks become frantic and wild about our doctrine and faith because it does not conform to reason and human wisdom. Only the godly, simple people who hold to this course and say, "God said it; therefore, I will believe it," can grasp and understand how Christ Himself speaks and thanks God from a happy heart that He "had hidden these things from the wise and understanding and revealed them to little children" [Matt. 11:25].

28. There is no help for it—we cannot instruct wise people and high reason in the wonderful things about Christ: that a natural man is God's Son from eternity and yet died and rose again and became Lord in heaven and earth in His human nature, and rules all creatures with divine power even

though no one sees Him; and that we are saved only for His sake, if we believe in Him, etc. Therefore, God had to set it up in this way: that whoever does not want to be a fool and a child and simply believe shall not grasp it.

29. Look at the kind of people to whom He first revealed and declared this highest work of His resurrection! The poor, foolish women came to the grave with useless and futile expense and trouble, since they had bought the costly ointment but did not consider that the grave was covered with a heavy stone, sealed, and secured by a guard [Matt. 27:66]. Yet these senseless and foolish women were the first to whom Christ revealed His resurrection, and He made them into preachers and witnesses [Matt. 28:10]. In that way He gave these disciples the understanding of Scripture which all the highly intelligent scribes did not have, so that now they looked at Moses with different eyes and had to say, "Look, I read and heard that a long time ago, but I never understood it."

30. It is as if God would in fact say, "Well, I see that it does not help even if everything were said and written as clearly as possible, just as all articles are set forth quite clearly and distinctly in Scripture." How the article about God and God's creation, which is certainly spoken and written most clearly, long ago produced a throng of heretics, such as Manichaeans, Valentinians, Marcionites, etc.![4] Likewise, what did it help when Christ Himself clearly and publicly corroborated His teaching among His own people with great miracles? Nothing other than that they went ahead and turned both His words and His works upside down and called them the words and works of the devil and of Beelzebub [Matt. 12:24].

God has to go ahead and say: "Because they do not want to have and accept it as I speak it to them, it will remain hidden and not understood by them. I will certainly have it written and preached in clear words, but I will arrange everything in the revelation for some few, simple people who inquire after My Word. For the others it will be a darkness which can be felt (as it was for the Egyptians [Exod. 10:21]), even though it shines and is preached most clearly; indeed, it will be nothing but an offense and poison over which they must stumble and fall with their slandering and contradicting, until they are wrecked."

31. Thus the Jews to the present day have had and read Moses, and yet they have altogether understood nothing that he says about Christ and even about other less important articles. So also their fathers understood nothing about this, except for some few who believed, such as the dear prophets and afterward the apostles, who spun their whole books out of one passage (as we

---

[4] Manichaeism, a third-century heresy, and second-century Valentinian Gnosticism and Marcionism insisted that the material world and the flesh are evil. Cf. Luther, *Sermons on John 1–2* (1537–38/1565), LW 22:22–23.

will hear). The revelation gives them such a sermon that everyone must say, "That is the truth."

32. How does Christ shut the mouths of the Sadducees (who did not believe the resurrection of the dead and retained no Scripture except Moses) and convince them of the resurrection of the dead? He takes the most common words they had in their whole religion, which were known to all Jews and were in daily use, when God says, "I am the God of Abraham, the God of Isaac, and the God of Jacob" [Exod. 3:6], etc. With these words He explains Moses and concludes: If you regard God to be a God of the dead, what kind of a God would He be—a God for those who are no more [Matt. 22:32]?

Therefore, if He is and calls Himself the God of Abraham, Isaac, and Jacob, then they must be alive, even though they are dead to this life and lie in the grave, for He cannot be a God of what is nothing. Therefore, Abraham (who is now under the ground) and all the saints must be alive before Him (He says), though they are dead before you. This is and remains His name in eternity, that He is the God of Abraham and of all who believe, as He promised him and all [believers], saying, "I will be your God" [Exod. 6:7], etc.

33. Now who would have thought that such short, simple, common words should contain so much and yield such a strikingly rich sermon, so that even a large, thick book could be made from it? They certainly knew this very well and yet thought that there was not one word to be found in all of Moses about the resurrection of the dead. For that reason they accepted only Moses and rejected the prophets, who nevertheless took all their sermons on the high articles of faith in Christ out of Moses.

34. So let us approach this sermon of Christ and look at one of the passages which He cited from Moses. Genesis 3 [:15] contains the first gracious word and promise of grace which God gave to Adam and Eve when He said to the serpent: "I will put enmity between you and the woman, and between your seed and her Seed; He will trample your head, and you will bite His heel." The Jew, Turk, heathen, and human reason read this passage, but it is only hard pebbles to them, even dead and useless words, from which they can squeeze or make nothing. But when the revelation comes, then they understand that it is saying: through sin the serpent (the devil) has worked death and the eternal wrath of God in Adam and Eve.

But so that they could again be helped out of this terrible downfall and misery, into which they were led by the devil, God Himself, out of unfathomable mercy, formed the plan that through the woman's Seed (that is, the natural fruit of a woman) this head of the serpent (that is, sin, death, and eternal wrath) would be trampled and its power taken away, so that he would no longer be the lord of death, nor could he keep people under sin or in God's wrath and damnation.

35. From this now comes an entirely new testament, all the sermons of St. Paul and the apostles, who do not tell much about the history and miracles of Christ, but wherever they can, from one such passage, as from a flower, they make a whole meadow, especially when the revelation is added together with the Holy Spirit, who knows how to mouth the words correctly and to press them so that they have and give juice and strength. First, it is pointed out that this Seed must be a natural child born from a woman, yet without sin, for Scripture testifies that whatever is born into this world from man and woman is born in sin and under God's curse, as David says, "Behold, I was begotten from sinful seed" (Psalm 51 [:5]), etc. This flesh and blood is completely permeated and corrupted with evil desires and disobedience toward God; therefore, since things are corrupted in father and mother, they also remain so in the children. Therefore, no one can be descended from man and woman without a sinful nature.

For that reason God came up with this solution: He took only a woman for the conception and birth of the promised Seed, Christ. She became the child's mother without a man through the Holy Spirit [Luke 1:35], who worked that conception and birth in her, so that He would nevertheless be a natural man, our flesh and blood, but without any sin and power of the devil, so that He could trample on his head.

36. Second, if He is to be the Lord over sin and death, subdue the devil, and snatch us from his power, then this requires divine, almighty power. Human strength and ability are not enough, even if He were completely pure and without any defect in body or soul (as Adam was created at first), if He is to take away this eternal, infinite misery and corruption and in place of it procure and give us eternal, imperishable benefits and life. Therefore, it follows that He must have greater power than any creatures or even all the angels. No one except God Himself can be the Lord over all creatures.

37. It further follows that if He is born of a human being, then He is also mortal and must, like the others, also die bodily. Because He was born a man for our sake, and was sent by God to help us out of sin and death, He had to take our place, become a sacrifice for us, and Himself bear the wrath and curse into which we have fallen and under which we lie and make satisfaction for it. But He did not have to remain under it; rather, because He was an eternal person, "He could not be kept by death" (as St. Peter says [Acts 2:24] also from this and similar passages); also with His body, before it was consumed and decayed, He had to press through [death] and again free Himself from it. Through His resurrection and eternal life He began to rule powerfully with eternal power and glory, so that He could finally bring His

people out of sin, death, and the devil and past these into eternal righteousness and life.

38. This alone is the one passage which Christ without a doubt did not
neglect as the first and chief passage from which later the others flow. He
explained it from His full spirit, so that we would see that these mere words
are actually miracles which cannot be comprehended or judged by reason. So
they are only understood when the Holy Spirit comes, preaches, and reveals
them to people who believe with simple hearts and persist in them. Then it
begins to taste good and to provide its juice and strength, so that they must
say, "This does it; it enlightens the heart and lights a fire there."

39. Thus the prophets looked into this passage of Moses and sucked
their glorious prophecies about Christ out of it. From this passage Isaiah
[7:14] states his prophecy about Christ's birth in clear words: "Behold, a
virgin is pregnant and will bear a Son," etc. Likewise, the entire fifty-third
chapter [prophesies] about His suffering and resurrection, how He would
give Himself as a sacrifice for our sins, etc. Without a doubt Christ also cited
these things in His sermon.

40. Thus the apostles, the unlearned fishermen, did not learn to understand the Scriptures in the schools of the great scribes but through the revelation through which Christ led them into Scripture. From one passage they
can make a book or a sermon which the world cannot understand. If I had
the same Spirit that Isaiah or Paul had, I could make out of this passage a
New Testament, if that were not made [already].

41. Where did St. Peter get it, or where is it written in Moses, when he
says, "The prophets who prophesied to you about the coming grace sought
and searched out this salvation, and searched out what person and what time
the Spirit of Christ in them was pointing to" (1 Peter 1 [:10–11])? Who told
him that the Spirit of Christ existed and prophesied about Christ before there
were prophets and above all before Christ and the Holy Spirit were present?
Are those the words of a fisherman or of an intelligent and wise scribe? No,
it is the revelation of the Holy Spirit who had revealed it first to the prophets.

Likewise, where is this written in Moses, what the Epistle to the Hebrews
says, that "Christ sat down at the right hand of the Father to be Lord over all
and became much higher and better than the angels," etc. (Hebrews 1 [:3–4])?
Obviously he took it out of the Old Testament; he learned it there not through
reason, but by revelation. Therefore, he reasons in this way: If Christ is a Son
of God and Lord of the angels, then He is certainly more and of a higher
being than the angels. Now every angel is more powerful than all the world
and all of human nature. If the natural child of this virgin is to be Lord not
only of the evil but also of the good and holy angels, then He must be of
one power and nature with God. Nobody can say or believe this except by

revelation. So I would like to take Moses, the Psalms, Isaiah, and also that same Spirit and make as good a New Testament as the apostles wrote. But because we do not have the Spirit as richly and powerfully, we must learn from them and drink from their spring.

42. That is enough about one point or passage of the sermon from Scripture which Christ preached to these disciples. With that He fully and richly earned, even paid and laid down His penny for, what He consumed with them at the inn. As far as the other passages from Moses and the prophets written about Christ and treated by Him—that would take too long to tell at one time and would make a book as large as the Bible. But without a doubt they were the same ones which the apostles later cited as they had heard them from Him here and later on Pentecost learned to understand better. A good number of them were quoted by them in their sermons, in the Acts of the Apostles, and in all the Epistles. They are commended to each Christian for his meditation as he studies and reads Scripture. Moreover, when we treat Scripture seriously and with simple hearts, the Holy Spirit is powerful and gives understanding (as we have heard) as the true Exegete. He produces this fruit: that we find Christ and learn to know Him correctly in Scripture, by which our hearts are awakened and kindled, comforted and made happy.

# GOSPEL FOR EASTER TUESDAY

*Luke 24:36–47*

*As they were talking about these things, Jesus Himself stood among them, and said to them, "Peace to you!" But they were startled and frightened and thought they saw a spirit. And He said to them, "Why are you troubled, and why do doubts arise in your hearts? See My hands and My feet, that it is I Myself. Touch Me, and see. For a spirit does not have flesh and bones as you see that I have." And when He had said this, He showed them His hands and His feet. And while they still disbelieved for joy and were marveling, He said to them, "Have you anything here to eat?" They gave Him a piece of broiled fish, and He took it and ate before them. Then He said to them, "These are My words that I spoke to you while I was still with you, that everything written about Me in the Law of Moses and the Prophets and the Psalms must be fulfilled." Then He opened their minds to understand the Scriptures, and said to them, "Thus it is written, that the Christ should suffer and on the third day rise from the dead, and that repentance for the forgiveness of sins should be proclaimed in His name to all nations, beginning from Jerusalem."*

1. First, this Gospel reading points out who hears about the resurrection of the Lord profitably and fruitfully, namely, those who sat there with the doors locked in fear and dread [John 20:19]. They are the proper ones to receive it, and they are the best students; we should preach only to such people, though it must be preached among all nations, as the Lord says at the end of this Gospel reading [Luke 24:47]. Therefore, let us first learn from this what kind of people hear the Gospel correctly.

2. The disciples sit there together secretly, afraid of the Jews; moreover, they have a bad conscience because they forsook and denied Christ. Thus they are despondent and terrified at sin and death. If they had been strong in faith, they would not have crawled into a corner in that way. Afterward they became courageous when the Holy Spirit came, strengthened, and comforted them, so that they stepped forth and preached publicly without fear.

This was written for us, so that we would learn that the Gospel of the resurrection of the Lord Christ is comforting only for those who are fearful and fainthearted, whose sins oppress them, who feel their weakness, who do not face death with gladness, and who are afraid and alarmed even at a rustling leaf [cf. Lev. 26:36]. The Gospel comes to comfort them, and they also relish it.

3. This can also be observed from the nature of the Gospel, for the Gospel is a message and a sermon which proclaims how the Lord Jesus Christ rose from the dead so that He might take away sin, death, and all misfortune from those who believe on Him. When I recognize that He is that kind of Savior, then I have truly heard the Gospel, and He has also truly revealed Himself to me. Now if the Gospel teaches nothing else than that Christ has overcome sin and death by His resurrection, then we must indeed confess that this preaching can help no one except those who perceive sin and death. It is of no benefit at all for the others, who do not perceive or regard their defects and sin; they also do not relish it. Even when they hear the Gospel for a long time, it produces nothing in them, except that they learn the words and speak about them, but it does not go into their hearts and gives them neither comfort nor joy.

4. Therefore, it would be good—if it could be that way—that we would preach the Gospel only in those places where there were fearful and frightened consciences; but because we cannot keep such people away from the multitude—and for that reason must preach it out in public, commending to God whom and at what time it will strike—that is why it happens that it does not produce fruit everywhere. For that reason people accuse us of wanting to preach many new things, and yet our doctrine improves no one. The fault is not in the Gospel but in the students who certainly all hear it, but they do not all sense their misery and distress; they go on, secure and heedless, like dumb animals.

For that reason no one should be surprised that the Gospel does not bring forth fruit everywhere. Beyond these righteous students of whom we have been speaking, there are many others who take no interest in it at all, who have neither conscience nor heart and think neither of death nor of their soul's salvation. We have to govern them like donkeys and dumb animals: with force, the coercion of the Law, and fear of punishment, for which the secular sword was instituted. Likewise, there are some who do not despise the Gospel and indeed understand it, but do not improve their lives and do not strive to live according to it. Rather, they can only produce words and chatter much about it, but no deeds or fruit follow. The third and smallest group, however, are those who receive it correctly so that it bears fruit in them.

5. So the conclusion of this point is that the Gospel is a preaching about the resurrection of Christ, which is to serve to comfort and refresh poor, distressed, and terrified consciences. It is beneficial and useful to know this, especially in death and every other need, so that we are prepared for it and can grasp and retain this comfort.

If a person knows and understands this and believes, then Christ is already in his heart and brings him peace so that he is confident and says, "If my Lord Christ has overcome my sin through His resurrection and trampled it underfoot, why would I be afraid and terrified?" However, no one perceives this comfort, peace, and joy of the heart except the few people who previously were so frightened and full of sorrow and sensed their defects. Therefore, the unbroken, coarse people understand neither this nor any other Gospel, for whoever has not tasted the bitter does not relish the sweet, and whoever has not had misfortune does not understand happiness. It naturally happens in the world that whoever strives for nothing nor attempts and suffers anything is worthless; it is even more true in spiritual matters that it is impossible for someone to comprehend the Gospel unless he has such a fearful and terrified heart.

6. Therefore, it is not surprising that not all who hear the Gospel comprehend it and act according to it. Everywhere there are many who despise and persecute it, whom we leave alone and to whom we are accustomed. Wherever the Gospel is preached, such people will certainly be found. Accordingly, there are also many who do not persecute it and yet also do not receive it, for they bring no fruit from it but lead the same life as before. In short, even when the Gospel is preached and promoted for a long time, the complaint always comes up: "No one wants it! Everything remains the way it was." Therefore, we must not be troubled and frightened by that.

7. Look at what happened at Jerusalem when the Gospel was first heard. People write that there were so many people there that in the city at the Easter festival[1] there were one million, one hundred thousand men.[2] How many of them were converted? When St. Peter stood up and preached, they made a laughingstock out of him and regarded the apostles as drunken fools [Acts 2:13]. When they had preached most vigorously, the best they could, they brought together three thousand men and women [Acts 2:41]. What were they compared to the whole city? Compared to the other crowd, it was as if no one could perceive that it had worked anything, for everything continued to be done and governed as it was before. No one saw any change, and almost no one was aware that there were Christians there. It always remains that way.

8. Therefore, we should not measure the Gospel according to how many hear it, but according to the small group who comprehend it. They have no glory, people have no regard for them, but God acts in them secretly.

9. At this point there is one thing which the Gospel strongly conceals, namely, the weakness of the believers, which is described in this history of the

---

1 *Osterlich fest*. But see Acts 2, which describes what happened at Pentecost.

2 See Josephus (ca. 37–ca. 101), *Jewish War* 6.9.3 (Loeb 210 [1997], pp. 298–301).

disciples and later remained in the apostles even after the ascension of Christ. For example, though Peter was full of faith and the Holy Spirit [Acts 4:8], nevertheless he fell and stumbled with many who were with him, so that Paul had to rebuke him publicly [Gal. 2:11–14]. Many great, holy people clung to him, and they all stumbled with him. Likewise, we read that Mark journeyed with Paul but then deserted and ran away from him [Acts 13:5, 13; 15:37–38]. Likewise, Paul and Barnabas quarreled with each other and sharply disagreed with each other [Acts 15:39]. We read in the Gospels how often the apostles, who were the best Christians, erred in weighty matters [e.g., Luke 22:24].

10. These defects in Christians and believers obscure the Gospel most of all, so that the people who want to be prudent and wise are offended and scandalized by them. There are few who truly know how to handle this so that they are not scandalized. Therefore, they say, "Yes, they brag about the Gospel and want to be good Christians, and yet are so foolish, angry, impatient," etc., and want to conclude from this that the Gospel is preached with no effect. Really that is taking offense at the weak and sick Christ.

11. This is what happened to the disciples too. At first, when Christ went about with bold and brave deeds in great honor, and no more began a work than it was finished, they clung to Him, though the high, great lords, the holy and the learned, were offended at Him because He would not side with them. On the other hand, the common man did improve, and the people clung to Him, because they saw that He did such miracles with great power, and also no one could find fault with His life, but everyone had to say, "He is a great and holy prophet!" [cf. Matt. 21:11]. But when it comes to His suffering, then they all stepped back and withdrew from Him, and not one of His disciples remained with Him [Matt. 26:56]. What was lacking in them? Only this: that they no longer saw in Him the strong but nothing other than the weak Christ, for He was now in the hands of the Jews, did no works or miracles, just as if He could no longer do them and was forsaken by God. His power and high name fell to the ground. Previously, they regarded Him as a prophet, the like of whom had never come; now they consider Him to be a murderer and a condemned man. Who could now see that this Christ was God's Son? Here all reason must fall, even the true, great saints. They thought that if He were the Christ, then the fruits must also be there by which they could perceive that it was He; but now they see nothing in Him other than weakness, sin, and death.

12. Therefore, it is the highest wisdom on earth, known to very few people, that we can regard the weak Christ. If I see a godly, holy man who already leads a holy life, does anyone thank me for praising him and saying, "There is Christ, who does things rightly"? Even though that troubles the bishops and great lords, the common man is still improved. But when he

becomes weak and stumbles, everyone immediately takes exception to him and says, "I thought he was a godly Christian, but I see that I was deceived!" However, when we look around, we will find none who are not weak. Indeed, everyone will notice this in himself, but still they will think that the Gospel is finished. They think that God is not clever enough to conceal it, drawing a veil over Christ and pulling death and powerlessness over Him while Christ is underneath. Because no one could see that, He also says to His disciples beforehand: "All, all of you will be offended because of Me, so that you will no longer believe that I am the Christ" [Matt. 26:31]. This is the very greatest hindrance, as I have said, at which people take exception, thinking that the Gospel is without power, when they look at the defects and weakness of Christians who occasionally stumble.

13. Therefore, whoever wants to know Christ correctly must not be troubled by the veil. Even if you see someone else stumble, you should not despair or think that it is finished, but rather you should think: "Perhaps God will deal with him by bearing with the weak Christ, just as another bears with the strong." Both must be and remain on earth, even though the greater part are weak, especially in our times. Nevertheless, when you penetrate through such weakness, you will see that Christ lies hidden under that weak person and at His time will come forth and let Himself be seen.

14. That is what Paul means when he says, "I did not represent myself among you as knowing anything except Jesus Christ, the Crucified One" (1 Corinthians 2 [:2]). What kind of boast is it when he writes that he knows nothing except the crucified Christ? It is something that reason and human wisdom cannot comprehend. Moreover, those who have already studied and learned the Gospel do not sufficiently know it. It is a wisdom which is mighty, secret, and hidden. It appears to be nothing at all, because it is concealed under weakness and folly, just as Christ, after He emptied Himself of all God's strength and power [Phil. 2:7], hung on the cross like a wretched, forsaken man; it seemed as if God would not help Him. "I know how to speak and preach only about Him," says St. Paul. Christ who publicly does miracles comes and breaks in with power, so that everyone sees who He is and soon learns to recognize Him. But to know the weak Christ who hangs on the cross and lies in death requires greater understanding. Whoever does not know Him in that way must take exception and be offended at Him.

15. Yes, there are even true Christians who know the Gospel but nevertheless are offended at their own life. They think that they would like to become good, that they want Christ to be strong in them and to reveal Himself in great deeds, but they feel they are not making any progress. They begin to be afraid and to think that they have lost because they do not feel the strength they ought to have. But our Lord God does this to humble us, so

that we see that we are such weak creatures, wretched, lost, and condemned people, if Christ had not come to help us with His righteousness and to carry our weakness with His strength. That is the high wisdom which we have and at which all the world is offended.

16. However, in saying this we are not giving permission for people to go and remain weak forever, for we do not preach that people should be weak, but that they should recognize and bear with the weakness of Christians. It was not because of weakness that Christ hung on the cross as a murderer and villain, but so that we would learn how deeply strength lies hidden under weakness and that God's strength is shown in weakness [2 Cor. 12:9]. Thus it is not praiseworthy that we are weak, as if we should be and remain that way. No, we should learn that those who are weak should not for that reason be regarded as non-Christians, and whoever senses his own weakness should not despair [cf. Rom. 15:1]. This is done so that we recognize our weakness and always strive to become stronger. Christ must not always lie dead in suffering and the grave, but again come forth into life.

17. Therefore, no one should think that this is the right way and condition. It is only a beginning, in which we should increase from day to day. But we should see to it that we do not slacken and despair because of weakness, as if all were lost. Rather, we should work at it until we become stronger and stronger, until God takes it away. Therefore, even if you see your neighbor weak and stumbling, do not think for that reason that he is finished. God does not want one to condemn another and be pleased with himself, since we are all sinners. Rather, each one should bear with another's defects (Romans 14 [:1; 15:1]; Galatians 5 [6:2]), and if you will not do that, then He can certainly let you fall, throw you down, and lift up the other.

18. We have been speaking about the weakness of Christians so that we would learn to regard it rightly, for there is a great need to know it, especially at this time. If our bishops, pastors, and prelates had had this wisdom, which they ought to have most of all, how good things would be in Christendom! But now it has become so bad that we never look at any except only strong Christians and cannot bear with the weak; rather, we deal harshly and proceed with force. Formerly, when conditions were still good, the bishops were greatly lacking in this point; although they were holy people, nevertheless they forced and oppressed consciences too much. That is not the way it happens among Christians, for Christ wants to be on earth and to be feeble for a while in His Church.

He points this out by saying to His disciples here in the Gospel reading: "Touch Me and see. For a spirit does not have flesh and bones as you see that I have" [Luke 24:39]. He wants to have both—not bones only or flesh only, but both together, as it must be in the natural body of a man. So we read that

Adam said about his Eve (who had been made from a rib out of his side): "This is bone of my bones and flesh of my flesh" (Genesis [2:23]). He does not say only flesh or only bones but also gives himself both because he says "of my bones and of my flesh."

As it is with Christ, so it is also with us, for which reason He says here: "I have both flesh and bones, and you will not find in Me only bones or only flesh," that is, "You will find both, that I am strong and weak.

19. "So I must also be among My Christians in such a way that some are strong and some are weak." Those who are strong go about, are vigorous and healthy, and must carry the others; they are the bones. The others are the weak who cling to the strong; that is the larger group, as we see that there is always more flesh than bones in a body. Therefore, Christ was both crucified and died, and also again made alive and glorified, because He is not a spirit as the disciples regard Him here to be a spirit, before whom they must be horrified, but a true, natural man and in every way like us according to the same flesh and blood, so that He may take up our weakness and carry it.

20. The apostles and Christ Himself greatly emphasized this wisdom, and besides this I know of no other book in which it is written. It is, indeed, occasionally touched upon, but nowhere emphasized. But this one book, the New Testament, always emphasizes it and is everywhere occupied with it, so that it may portray for the people both the weak and strong Christ. Thus St. Paul says to the Romans [15:1–3]: "We who are strong should bear with the failings of the weak and not please ourselves, etc. For even Christ did not please Himself." This should be the wisdom we learn from this.

21. All who are portrayed in the Gospel, whom Christ finds despondent and fearful, belong in this school. We can easily notice the others who do not belong here, since they completely ignore and despise the Gospel. Everyone can perceive in himself whether he is sincerely pleased with the Gospel. If you observe someone else acting in such a way that you can notice that he wants to be righteous, you should not despise him.

22. That is what this Gospel reading furnishes, one after another. First, the Lord stands among the disciples and is now strong, having overcome everything, sin, death, and the devil. They do not yet stand, but sit there, as He comes and stands among them. Where does He now stand? He stands among the despondent and weak group who are frightened and fearful. But He is strong and mighty, though it is not yet apparent to the world.

Second, He shows them His hands and feet, comforts them, and says: "See My hands and My feet, that it is I Myself. Touch Me, and see Me. For a spirit does not have flesh or bones as you see that I have" [Luke 24:39].

23. This is nothing else but the sermon which teaches that we should not be offended at the weak Christ. He does not speak angrily with the disciples;

He does not say: "Away with you! I do not want to have you. You should be strong and bold, but you sit there and are despondent!" Rather, He comforts them in a friendly way, so that He makes them strong and fearless. Therefore, afterward they have also become strong and fearless, and not only that but also happy and joyful. Therefore, we also ought not reject the weak but so deal with them that we may induce them to become strong and confident. This does not mean that it is proper for them to be weak and that they should remain that way, for Christ does not stand among them for that reason but so that they increase in faith and become fearless.

24. Something is also to be said here (because the Gospel reading mentions it) about appearing or wandering spirits. Here we see that the Jewish people and the apostles themselves held that spirits stray about and are seen at night and otherwise. When the disciples were in the ship at night and saw Jesus walking on the sea, they were frightened as of a ghost and cried out in fear (Matthew 14 [:24–26]). In this passage we hear that Christ does not deny it but confirms with His answer that spirits do appear, because He says, "A spirit does not have flesh or bones," etc. [Luke 24:39].

25. However, Scripture does not say or give any example that these are the souls of dead people and that they wander among people and seek help, as we believed previously in our blindness, deceived by the devil. Because of this the pope has invented purgatory and set up his shameful trafficking in Masses. We may easily regard this lying doctrine and abomination as the fruit, which is also the consequence of that on which it is built, namely, the wandering souls, which comes from the father of lies, the devil [John 8:44], who has deceived the people in the name of dead men.

26. We have reason enough not to believe such apparitions of spirits straying about under the name of souls. First, Scripture says nothing anywhere about the souls of dead men who have not yet risen going about among the people, though everything else we need to know is sufficiently revealed in Scripture. He wanted us to know not even one word (it is not even possible for us to grasp and understand) about what happens with spirits which have departed from the body before the resurrection and the Last Day, since they are now divided and separated completely from the world and from this time. Second, it is clearly forbidden in Scripture to ask anything of the dead or to believe them (Deuteronomy 18 [:10–12]; Isaiah 8 [:19–20]). It is pointed out in Luke 16 [:29, 31] that God does not want any to rise from the dead or to preach, because Moses and the Scriptures are present.

27. Therefore, we should know that all those ghosts and apparitions which are seen or heard, especially with rumbling and rattling, are not the souls of men, but surely devils who are playing either at deceiving the people with false claims and lies or at frightening and afflicting them in vain.

Therefore, a Christian should act toward these ghosts who pretend to be souls no differently than toward the real devil. He should be equipped with God's Word and faith so that he is not confused or frightened but remains with the doctrine he has learned and confessed from the Gospel about Christ and cheerfully despises the devil with his rattling. He also should not remain for long where he perceives that people trust in Christ and despise him. I say this so that we will be wise and not let ourselves be misled again by such deception and lies, since he previously deceived and fooled even excellent people such as St. Gregory by claiming to be a soul.

# ANOTHER SERMON
# [FOR EASTER TUESDAY]

*Luke 24:36–47*

*As they were talking about these things, Jesus Himself stood among them, and said to them, "Peace to you!" But they were startled and frightened and thought they saw a spirit. And He said to them, "Why are you troubled, and why do doubts arise in your hearts? See My hands and My feet, that it is I Myself. Touch Me, and see. For a spirit does not have flesh and bones as you see that I have." And when He had said this, He showed them His hands and His feet. And while they still disbelieved for joy and were marveling, He said to them, "Have you anything here to eat?" They gave Him a piece of broiled fish, and He took it and ate before them. Then He said to them, "These are My words that I spoke to you while I was still with you, that everything written about Me in the Law of Moses and the Prophets and the Psalms must be fulfilled." Then He opened their minds to understand the Scriptures, and said to them, "Thus it is written, that the Christ should suffer and on the third day rise from the dead, and that repentance for the forgiveness of sins should be proclaimed in His name to all nations, beginning from Jerusalem."*

1. In the first part of this Gospel, we are again presented with a comforting example and pattern of how Christ showed Himself and what attitude He had toward His dear disciples. He is present as soon as they speak about Him, comes among them, and speaks the friendly and cheerful words: "Peace to you" [Luke 24:36]. Yet the disciples were frightened at this and thought that they saw a spirit. But He will not tolerate such fright and rebukes them for letting such thoughts into their hearts [v. 38]. He shows them His hands and feet, so that they can see that He is not a ghost or a different Christ than He was before but has the same flesh and bones and nature as they. He does this so that they will not be afraid of Him, but rather be cheerfully comforted and expect good from Him.

2. This pattern and attitude is to serve as a comforting look or pattern for all frightened hearts, especially against the ghost which is called a false christ [Matt. 24:24]. The devil also can come to people, both in public and in private, either through false doctrine or through secret suggestions, and he even wants to be Christ Himself. He can begin with a friendly greeting and

offer a "good morning," but then he attacks the heart with fear and sorrow so that it does not know where Christ is.

3. He takes pleasure in deceiving us under the appearance and name of Christ. He always wants to be God's ape and imitate what he sees Him do. Now God's way of dealing with us is that He first frightens those who are not yet frightened, so that in addition naturally fearful hearts are always horrified at His words and works because of the timidity of their nature. However, He again soon comforts those who are now frightened and speaks to them in a friendly way. The devil certainly imitates this and also comes under the name and words of Christ, but with both false comfort and false frightening. He turns both upside down, so that he makes those who are in need of comfort frightened and despondent and, on the other hand, comforts and strengthens those who should fear and be frightened of God's wrath.

From this Gospel reading we should learn to make the correct distinction between the doctrine and thoughts that come to us, both the frightful and the comforting ones, which are from God and which are from the devil.

4. First, the lying spirit began already in Paradise with such sweet deception when he came to Eve with his friendly, sweet words: "There is no danger here! Why do you need to be afraid and horrified of eating from one single tree? Do you think that God would have forbidden you only this fruit and not allowed you to eat from this tree? Yes, He knows that if you eat from it you will become much wiser and will be like God" [cf. Gen. 3:1–5]. That was certainly a good comfort and a beautiful, sweet sermon, but it left behind an abominable stench and led the whole human race into the injury about which we all must still lament. For that reason there is a proverb among those who want to be devout and to distinguish the spirits that the devil always first comes with sweet, comforting words, and then leaves behind fright and evil consciences. The good Spirit, on the contrary, does the opposite.

5. It is true. One kind of villainy he practices is that he secretly sneaks in like a snake; at first he adorns and ingratiates himself, but before we have a chance to look around, he stings with his tail and leaves his poison behind. Therefore, we should not rely on it when a preacher comes sneaking in like an angel of God, speaks very well, swears that he seeks nothing else than to help souls, and says, "Peace to you" [Luke 24:36]. The devil does the same thing when he deceives the people with smooth words and through them gains the opportunity to preach and to teach so that he can then cause harm. If he accomplishes nothing else, he still confuses consciences and finally leads them into misery and despair.

6. He acts similarly with the thoughts which he drives into the heart, inwardly, by which he attacks people and entices them even to coarse sins. He always begins with the word "peace," so that he puts the fear of God out of

sight, makes the matter insignificant, and always with such thoughts preaches and writes: "Peace and security" [Isa. 39:8], "there is no danger." But he does this much more in high sins which concern faith and God's glory, in which he urges us toward idolatry and to trust in our own works and holiness. Then he first pretends to be holy and godly and gives the sweetest thoughts: "There is no danger! God is not angry with you." The prophets [Jer. 6:14, 17; Ezek. 33:30–32] speak similarly about such people: "They will listen to you and let you preach, but they will always take comfort and bless themselves and say: 'There is no danger! Hell is not so hot nor the devil so black as he is painted.'"

That is the devil's entrance and deception, even when he teaches peace and extends friendly greetings. Only afterward do we see what harm and misery he has caused, when we are already lying in it and can no longer get out. Experience teaches that a person comes into sin, shame, and punishment so easily that he himself does not know how, since he was drawn in by such sweet thoughts, as if by one hair or piece of straw.

7. That is one way in which he misleads many foolish, secure, and careless spirits, so that they imagine that they are sitting in God's lap and playing dolls with Him. They become so fully drunk with those thoughts and sweet devil's poison, so proud, obstinate, and stubborn, that they simply will not hear or follow anyone.

However, some God-fearing people have understood this and have warned others about how the devil sneaks in so sweetly and pretends that he has divine comfort but in the end leaves a stench behind, so that people see that he was there. But this is still a small matter, fitting for young students. Every Christian should learn to guard himself against such sweet poison. If we are first to experience this, it will require much loss before we learn to guard against it, and then we will still not fully learn his villainy.

8. The second way [of misleading people] is completely different, for he works with fright, even in insignificant matters, such as externally with his tricks and ghosts. Previously he has done much with rattling under the name of [dead] souls. In that way he afflicts and frightens timid and fearful hearts and manages to leave no comfort behind him. It is much worse, however, when he comes into the heart and there begins to debate and cite passages which Christ Himself spoke; in that way he so terrifies the heart that it thinks only that it is God and Christ Himself. When such thoughts gain the upper hand, the heart must in the end despair, for where else can it find comfort if it feels that God Himself, who should comfort it, is frightening it and shooting arrows at it?

Job (6 [:4]) laments this and says, "What should I do when He sticks His arrows in me, the arrows which suck out my life and consume all strength and might?" Nevertheless, that is done not by God but by the devil, who takes pleasure in thus piercing and spearing hearts (as also he did to Paul, 2 Corinthians 11 [12:7]). However, [the devil] had so captivated Job's heart that he could say or think nothing except "God is doing this."

9. It is a much higher and more dangerous deception of the devil when he comes and does not wish us "good morning" or "peace" but frightens and alarms the heart under the form and voice of God. The man who is oppressed and shattered cannot get up or think: "It is the devil." Because he thinks and feels in his heart that it is God (whom no one can withstand), heaven and earth are too narrow for him, all creatures are against him, and everything he sees and hears frightens him.

10. In opposition to this shameful, lying devil, Christ here has represented and painted Himself correctly as He truly is. Although it is true that He sometimes comes in a frightening way, sometimes in a comforting way, yet He comes only and finally for life and comfort and to gladden the heart. Yet the human heart is so foolish on both points that it does not recognize Him (the devil promotes this with his suggestions) nor think that He is Christ, or at once makes a false christ out of Him, just as the apostles here regard Him to be a spirit or a ghost [Luke 24:37]; their hearts do not at all think that it is Christ, even though they see Christ's form and appearance. Therefore, it requires great insight and understanding to tear the false christ out of our hearts and to learn to think of Him correctly, because we must consider (as has been said) that the devil depicts a false christ or even disguises himself in His form.

11. Thus this Gospel reading shows who the true Christ is and what His Word is. First, He says, "Peace be to you" [Luke 24:36], which is part of the comfort which He brings. Second, He rebukes them and will not allow them to have such false, frightened thoughts about Him; He says, "Why are you so frightened, and why do such thoughts arise in your hearts?" [Luke 24:38]. This text cannot be purchased with money or goods because a distressed heart can learn and conclude from it: even if the devil were to cite all the passages in the Bible in order to frighten the heart, if he does that too much and does not give comfort afterward, then it is surely the devil, even if you should seem to see the form of Christ hanging on the cross or sitting at the right hand of the Father. It may well be that Christ comes and frightens you at first, but that is surely not His fault, but the fault of your nature, because you do not correctly recognize Him. However, it is the devil himself who attacks you with fright and does not cease until he brings you into despair.

12. Therefore, you must here separate very far from each other the frightening of Christ and of the devil. Although Christ may begin with frightening, yet He surely brings along comfort and does not want you to remain in fright. The devil, however, cannot cease or desist from frightening, even

though at first he comforts and is pleasant. A Christian must know this and be acquainted with the devil so that, especially in high temptations, when he feels fright and anguish, he will think: "There must not be only fright, but it will also cease, and comfort will again follow."

13. "Yes," you say, "yet it is Christ and His Word, for He also preaches about God's wrath at sin when He says, 'Unless you repent, you will also all perish'" (Luke 13 [:3, 5]), etc. Answer: Yes, He can allow that, and it will happen that you become frightened because of your sins (if you were not frightened before). Yes, He must have this happen so that you (on account of your fearful nature) are also frightened of Him, as these apostles were. However, it is not His intention that you remain frightened; rather, He wants you to cease [being frightened]. Yes, He rebukes you because of your fright and says that you wrong Him with your thoughts when you attribute such things to Him. In short, He does not want you to be frightened of Him, but that you would lay hold of comfort and cheerful confidence in place of your fright.

14. If, from His words and works which He began in you, you now have thoughts which are frightful, then point Him away (where He intends to go) to those people who are still secure, obstinate, and hardened. He must cry out woe against them and threaten them with the eternal fire of hell. These are the people who are not at all afraid of God; on the contrary, when we want to frighten them with God's name and Word, they put on their horns,[1] defy Him, and become harder than an anvil and diamond. But when you feel that you are frightened (whether the true Christ does that or not), only have in mind to make an end of it and stop. If He is the true Christ, then He will not want this from you; if He is not [the true Christ], then much less should you do this.

15. Therefore, note and retain this text and example, that Christ does not want His own to be frightened, and He is not pleased when people are terrified of Him. Rather, He wants us to learn to know that when He sees you distressed and frightened, He is delighted to come to you, so that you also would become happy again and abandon your frightened thoughts. We should only learn that His style of speaking says: "Why are you frightened, and why do you let such thoughts arise in your hearts? [Luke 24:38]. You picture Me as a spirit and as someone who only wants to frighten you, but I come and want to comfort and gladden you."

16. Therefore, be wise and know that when you have such oppressive thoughts about Christ, they definitely do not come from Christ but from the devil; even if you are terrified of Him, a little sudden fright will not harm you. Our nature is such that it never thinks of anything good, especially when the heart is otherwise fearful or distressed and fainthearted. Let thoughts be

---

1 I.e., "they become belligerently obstinate in their point of view."

thoughts and come when they will. Think only that you hear Christ's words which do not want you to be frightened in His name and afraid of Him. Rather, He wants you to rejoice and receive Him as the one who wants to comfort your poor, sinful, distressed heart. Let the others—the obstinate, impenitent heads, pope, tyrants, and all His enemies and slanderers—be frightened. They need a thunderbolt to smash the iron cliffs and mountains.

17. Therefore, if He is a frightening Christ, then He is and wants to be this only for those hardened heads. They do not believe it, but arrogantly despise it until their hour and His time comes, when He, without any mercy, must trample them under His feet. But He does not want to be this toward His dear disciples and believers, who were previously too fearful and frightened, so that they easily become horrified even of their dear Savior. As St. Matthew [12:20] says from the prophet Isaiah [42:3], He does not at all intend wholly to break and quench the bruised reed and the smoldering wick (that is, the broken, distressed, humbled, and despondent consciences).

Now, if the infamous, arrogant, insolent devil's heads pay no attention anywhere to His frightening, for that reason should the fearful, timid hearts atone for that and have that fright come on themselves, whom He does not want to be frightened? If no frightening and threatening helps the former, for that reason should no comforting help the latter? Then Christ would be completely lost, and His kingdom could find no place or produce any fruit on earth.

18. Therefore, if you feel yourself frightened and despondent, let yourself be comforted until Christ finds His home in you. He does not find in you an arrogant, impenitent heart, which does not want to submit to Him. Otherwise you would have a reason and a need to be frightened of Him as the one who was appointed the Judge of the godless and the scorners. Rather, He comes to offer and bring you grace and peace, just as you desire and ask.

Here you should take care (I say) that you do not push away this friendly greeting and your own salvation and make this dear Savior into Satan—or, rather, instead of listening to Christ, listen to the devil (who is a liar and a murderer [John 8:44] and takes pleasure in afflicting weak, distressed hearts). It is his method that he does not cease, and if he cannot frighten enough with one saying,[2] he will come with ten or a hundred and oppress until he completely sinks and drowns the heart in sorrow.

19. On the contrary, as a Christian you can definitely conclude that such thoughts are not and cannot be from Christ. Yes, even if it were possible that it was Christ Himself, you still have His Word and true testimony here, which you should believe more than all apparitions. Instead of that, you should desire no secret revelation of Christ or of an angel from heaven, for these

---

2 *Spruch*, or "passage."

can be wrong and deceive and are nothing but mute pictures. Here, however, you have His living voice and words which He publicly speaks before all the disciples and rebukes them for such thoughts. From this we should know that He has no pleasure in those thoughts.

20. On account of that, He shows the very same thing by outward signs and works. He does not rebuke their thoughts only with words but also shows them His hands and feet so that they can see and feel that it is He Himself. It is as if He wanted to say: "Why would you still doubt Me and with your thoughts make a ghost out of Me? You have never yet handled or seen a devil or a spirit that has flesh and blood as I have, even though they sometimes assume such a form and deceive the senses."

21. Thus He adds to the words also a strong, definite sign and comforts them with the action, that they should not be afraid of Him. He shows them what He has done for them. It is a delightful, comforting, and cheerful picture to see this dear Savior's hands and feet which were pierced for my sake and with which my sins were also nailed to the cross. He shows me this as a token and testimony that He suffered, was crucified, and died for me, and certainly does not intend to be angry at me and shove me into hell.

22. Seeing His hands and feet really means that I recognize through His Word and faith that what He has done happened for my good, salvation, and comfort. Here I see no executioner, death, or hell at all, but only delightful, sweet grace toward all poor, distressed people. I cannot be afraid or terrified at this, even though this work is far too great for the heart sufficiently to comprehend and understand. Thus through both words and works He wants to free us from fear, even though at first we are frightened of Him.

23. On the other hand, the devil also finally shows his hands and feet, after he first comforts us; they are the hideous, abominable claws of the wrath of God and eternal death. At last he comes with only frightening, murdering, and slaying, which are his works, which he has done from the beginning. He can hold in front of the heart all the frightful pictures, examples, and histories of all the abominable sins, murders, and punishments which ever happened and how many great people he ever misled, blinded, and threw into damnation.

24. Now, where Christ is correctly recognized, there true joy begins, so that, as the evangelist says, "the disciples marveled for joy, and could not yet believe" [Luke 24:41]. This is a peculiar text and a strange saying. Before, their faith was hindered by fear and frightened thoughts; now what hinders it is their joy, which is much greater than was their previous fright. Now they are so full of joy, after the Lord reproaches them and shows them His hands and feet, that they still could not believe.

25. This is one of the temptations Christians face (of which we spoke before), that grace is too great and glorious when we look at our insignificance and unworthiness compared to Christ, and that the comfort is so very superabundant that our hearts are much too narrow to comprehend it. Who can comprehend in his heart that Christ is such a friendly Savior to me, a poor, sinful man, that He gives me for my own at once all that He has done? Must not the heart be frightened for itself and think: "Do you really believe it is true that the Majesty who created heaven and earth should take such a high interest in my misery and look at me so graciously? I have frequently sinned against Him and have a thousand times deserved and brought on myself wrath, death, and hell. How can such grace and treasure be understood by a human heart or by any creature?"

26. In summary, faith is attacked in the human heart on both sides and at both times, both in fright or sorrow and in joy. Either the scarcity or the abundance is too great, and there is too little or too much comfort. Before, when [the disciples] would gladly have had something great, all the treasures of God were too small and too insignificant to comfort their hearts, when Christ was still hidden from them. Now when He comes and is seen by them, it is much too great for their hearts, so that in their astonishment they cannot believe that He should be risen from the dead and alive with them.

27. At last He shows Himself to be still more friendly. He sits down with them at the table and eats some broiled fish and honeycomb with them [Luke 24:42]. He preaches to them a beautiful sermon to establish them in the faith, so that they would no longer be afraid or doubt but become strong in faith. Thus all their sorrow goes away.

28. Therefore, let us now learn from this to know Christ's property and manner, that when He comes and reveals Himself, He takes His leave with only comfort and joy. He must at last come with comfort, or He must not be Christ.

If, however, anguish and fright remain in the heart, then you can confidently conclude that it is not Christ (even though represented that way to the heart), but the devil. Therefore, pay no attention to such thoughts, but cling to the words He speaks to you: "See My hands and feet" [Luke 24:39], etc. Then your heart will again become cheerful, and the fruit will follow that you will correctly understand Scripture, relish His Word in your heart, and there will be nothing but honey and the sweetest comfort.

29. The main point of the second part of this Gospel reading is that after Christ explained the Scriptures to them and opened their understanding, He concludes and says:

*"Thus it is written, and thus Christ had to suffer and rise from the dead
and have repentance and forgiveness of sins preached in His name among
all nations." [Luke 24:46–47]*

30. Here you see how the Lord again points and leads His people into
the Scriptures and in that way intends to strengthen and confirm their faith.
Although He now reveals and shows Himself to them visibly, in the future,
when they will no longer see Him, He wants them to cling to the Word and
through the testimony of Scripture to make both their own and other people's
faith certain. The strength and comfort of the resurrection are not understood or received other than through faith in the Word, as we have heard.
Even when they see Him, nevertheless they do not recognize Him, but rather
are frightened of Him until He speaks to them and opens their understanding
through Scripture.

31. Second, He wants to teach them by this testimony of Scripture how
His kingdom on earth works and of what it consists, namely, that it is not to
be a new government or authority which deals with worldly and temporal
matters, but a spiritual, divine power in which He wants to rule invisibly in
the hearts of people everywhere through the Word or preaching office and to
work in them so that they come from sin, God's wrath, and eternal death to
grace and heavenly, eternal life. That was why He also suffered and rose again.

32. He points out and indicates all of this in these few words, and thus
includes the summary of the entire Gospel and the chief point of Christian
doctrine which we should always preach and emphasize in the churches,
namely, repentance and the forgiveness of sins. Therefore, we must also say
something about this.

33. Previously the entire papacy has not known how to teach about
repentance other than that it consists of three parts, which they call contrition, confession, and satisfaction—and yet they could instruct the people correctly about none of this. Specifically, to humor them we have let them have
the word *satisfactio*, "satisfaction" (in the hope that with gentleness we could
bring them to the correct doctrine). However, we have done that with the
understanding that it does not mean our satisfaction (since we in truth have
none), but Christ's satisfaction, through which He paid for our sin through
His blood and dying, and reconciled God.

However, since we have often previously experienced and still see before
our eyes that nothing is to be gained from them with gentleness—and they
only continue to oppose the true doctrine more and more—we will and must
cleanly peel and separate ourselves from them and know nothing more about
the invented words which they advance in their schools and with which they
now only seek to endorse their old errors and lies.

For that reason, this word "satisfaction" should from now on be nothing and dead in our churches and theology, and instead be commended to the office of judge and the schools of jurists (where it belongs and from which the Papists took it), who should be occupied with it in teaching the people how to make satisfaction and compensation when they have stolen, robbed, or possess goods acquired unjustly.

34. To be sure, the word "contrition" (*contritio*) is taken from Scripture, which speaks of a *cor contritum*, "a broken, distressed, and miserable heart" [Ps. 51:17]. However, the monks did not correctly understand or teach this word, for they called "contrition" the work which was forced from one's own thoughts and free will. They meant that a man should sit in a corner, hang his head, and with bitter thoughts contemplate the sins he committed. Yet no serious sorrow and displeasure with sin followed; rather, they flattered themselves all the more with such thoughts and strengthened their sinful desires. No matter how long they talked about it, they still could not decide how great the contrition ought to be so that it would be enough for the sin. They had to take comfort and make do with this patchwork: that whoever could not have truly perfect contrition should at least have "attrition" (as they called it), a half contrition, and be a little bit sorry for the sin.[3]

35. Then with "confession" they made for themselves intolerable torment and anguish, because they taught that everyone was bound at least once a year to count up all his sins with all the details, even those often forgotten which afterward are again remembered. Yet they gave the conscience no real instruction or comfort about absolution, but pointed the people to their own works, so that if they were sufficiently contrite, made a clean confession of sin (which according to their doctrine was impossible), and also made sufficient satisfaction for them, then their sins would be forgiven. There was not one word about Christ or faith, but the foolish, afflicted hearts who wanted to be free from sin and sought comfort had to hang and dangle on such an uncertain basis in eternal doubt.

36. The worst of it was that they did not teach correctly what sin is. They knew nothing more about it than what lawyers call sin and what belongs before the judge and secular penalties. They could say nothing about original sin or the inward impurity of the heart. They also alleged that human nature and the powers of free will were so perfect that a man could from his own strength bring it about that he fulfilled God's Law and thus earned God's grace; he could be without sin so much that he would not need repentance. Nevertheless, so that they would have something to confess, they had to invent sins where there were none (just as they also invented their own good

---

3 See *Smalcald Articles* (1537/1538) III III 16 (Kolb-Wengert, p. 314; *Concordia*, p. 273); for the later definition of "attrition" by the Council of Trent (session 14, chapter 4).

works). They regarded these to be the greatest and most serious sins, such as when a layman touched a consecrated chalice or, in the Mass, when a priest stammered over the canon[4] and similar foolishness.

37. We must not forget this futile, dreamed-up doctrine of the papacy concerning repentance, [first,] so that we can convince them of their error and blindness, because they are now everywhere embellishing and adorning themselves as if they had taught nothing wrong. Second, so that from the distinction (when we compare both to each other) we can understand the true Christian doctrine all the better. For that reason we want to speak according to Scripture about the nature of true Christian repentance and forgiveness of sins which Christ commands us to preach in His name.

38. First, in Scripture true contrition is not our own self-made thoughts which the monks call *contritio* and *attritio*, whole or half contrition. Rather, true contrition is when your conscience begins to sting and alarm you, and your heart is seriously frightened of God's wrath and judgment, not only because of obvious, coarse sins but also because of the truly strong, knotty doubts which you see and sense, which put in your flesh and blood nothing but unbelief, contempt, and disobedience for God and (as St. Paul says) "hostility against God" (Romans 8 [:7]). This makes itself felt with all kinds of evil lust and desires, etc., by which you have brought God's wrath on yourself and have deserved to be rejected eternally from His sight and to burn in hellfire.

Thus contrition does not apply piecemeal to some works which you have committed publicly against the Ten Commandments—that is where the dream and delusion of the hypocritical monkish repentance stays; they invent for themselves this distinction in their works and nevertheless find something good in themselves. Rather, contrition applies to the whole person with all his life and being, even to your whole nature, and shows that you are under God's wrath and condemned to hell. Otherwise the word "contrition" still sounds too juristic, the way people speak about sin and contrition in worldly matters as about something someone did and then thinks differently and wishes that he had not done it.

39. This contrition and serious fright does not come from our own human intentions or thoughts, as the monks dream, but it must be worked in man through God's Word, which points out God's wrath and affects the heart so that it begins to fear and tremble and does not know where it can stand. Human reason cannot see or understand by itself that all human strength and ability is under God's wrath and has already in His judgment been condemned to hell.

4 The eucharistic prayer of the Roman Mass, in which the priest is believed to transubstantiate bread and wine into the body and blood of Christ and to offer these as a sacrifice to God for sins.

40. Therefore, this must be preached and proclaimed (as Christ says here) so that people are directed and brought to true repentance. They must recognize their sins and God's wrath, and so first be thrown by the Word under God's wrath and condemnation, so that in turn, through the other preaching of the forgiveness of sins, they are delivered to true comfort, divine grace, and their salvation. Otherwise man would never recognize his misery and distress nor sigh for grace. Much less would he learn how he can come from God's wrath and condemnation to grace and the forgiveness of sins.

41. This preaching of repentance (He says) should go "among all nations" [Luke 24:47]. He truly reaches very far and at once includes everyone in the world, whether Jews, Gentiles, and whoever else. In short, nobody at all is excluded, but He puts all of them—as He finds and encounters them (apart from Christ)—under God's wrath and says, "You are all condemned, together with all that you do and are, no matter what, how much, how great, how high, how holy you are."

42. Indeed, He frightens and condemns most of all those who go about in their own holiness and do not imagine that they are sinners and need repentance. Among the Jews these could be the most holy Pharisees (before his conversion St. Paul was one of them [Acts 23:6; 26:5; Phil. 3:5]) who earnestly lived and walked according to the Law. Among the heathen they could be certain refined, highly intelligent, wise, and respectable people. Among us they could be the truly good monks, Carthusians, or hermits, who were seriously concerned about being righteous before God and lived in such a way that they did not think they were guilty of any mortal sin, and in addition castigated their bodies severely with fasting, vigils, hard beds, some even with bloody whipping, etc. Everyone—they themselves too—thought that because of their works and life they needed no contrition or repentance but would pay for their previously committed sins with the best, most meritorious works, that they honestly earned heaven from God by such a holy life and paid for it dearly enough.

Repentance should be preached most strongly against just such people, and as with a thunderbolt should knock to the ground and shove into hell and damnation all who are secure and arrogant and do not yet recognize their distress and God's wrath.

43. St. John the Baptist, who prepared the way for Christ, began such preaching publicly and applied this ax of thunder confidently and boldly to all Judaism; he attacked the holy Pharisees and Sadducees more harshly than the others and said, "You brood of vipers, how do you think of yourselves so securely and presume to flee from the wrath to come?" [Matt. 3:7].

Repentance is most necessary for these people, since also before God they merit greater wrath than other public sinners (who are rebuked by their own consciences). They lie in blindness and imagine that they have no sin. Yet before God they are full of filth and abomination and sin with real transgressions against God's Law, since without the fear of God and with contempt for His wrath they are haughty and proud with confidence in their works and holiness; they practice idolatry with their self-chosen worship. Moreover, despite that, their hearts are full of uncleanness and inward disobedience against God's Commandments, even though outwardly they refrain from evil works. Previously, even we who want to be the most righteous of people angered God extremely with the abominable idolatry of the Mass, the worship of the saints, and our own monkish holiness, by which we thought we could merit heaven instead of by the death and resurrection of Christ; we miserably misled both ourselves and others.

44. For this reason St. John continued his preaching of repentance and said to them: "See that you produce the righteous fruit of repentance" [Matt. 3:8], etc. That is: "Listen to my words and advice. Do not first become secure and proud, but recognize your sin and God's wrath on you. Humble yourselves before Him, and desire grace. If you do not, then judgment has already been passed on you, the ax is already at the tree, so that its trunk and roots will be cut down like a tree that produces no good fruit and is good for nothing except to throw it into the fire and reduce it to ashes—notwithstanding that it is tall, thick, and has beautiful leaves, just as you brag that you are Abraham's children," etc. [Matt. 3:9–10].

45. The apostles also carried on this preaching. On Pentecost and afterward St. Peter pointed out to the Jews what kind of godly children they were and what they had earned from God by denying His dear Son, fastening Him to the cross, and killing Him [Acts 2:23; 3:13–15]. St. Paul says, "God commands all people everywhere to repent, because He has fixed a day on which He will judge the whole earth" (Acts 17 [:30–31]), etc. That is, He wants all people on earth to learn to know themselves, to be frightened of God's wrath, and to understand that He will judge and condemn them, if they do not repent and obey this preaching.

46. So also Christ says, "The Holy Spirit will rebuke the world concerning sin" (John 16 [:8]) (through this preaching of repentance), etc. Reason (as said above) cannot teach such repentance, much less effect it by its own strength; rather, it must be preached (as Christ says here [Luke 24:47]) as a revelation which is above reason, understanding, and wisdom. Similarly, St. Paul calls it a heavenly revelation when he says, "God's wrath will become evident from heaven" (Romans 1 [:18]), etc. Neither reason nor any lawyer will say that I am a sinner and under God's wrath and condemnation if I do not steal, rob, commit adultery, etc. Rather, I am a godly, respectable man whom no one can rebuke or censure, and, besides, I am a holy monk.

Who would believe that I, with such a wonderfully respectable life (even if I am without faith), merit only God's wrath, and with such beautiful worship and strict training (which I have undertaken without God's Word, on my own) I am carrying on only abominable idolatry, and thus I condemn myself deeper into hell than other open sinners?

47. Therefore, it is unsurprising that, when the world hears this preaching of repentance and is rebuked by it, few accept it. Rather, most (especially the smart ones and the saints) despise it, lift their heads against it, and say: "Ha! How can that be true? Shall I let myself be called a sinner and a condemned man by these people who come here with an unknown, new doctrine? What have I done? With all earnestness I have refrained from sin and been eager to do good. Is that supposed to be nothing? Should, then, all the world before us, with all it did and lived, be in error and lost? How is it possible that God should give up the whole world and say they are all lost and condemned? The devil is telling you to preach that!" So they defend and strengthen themselves in their impenitence and only take more of God's wrath on themselves by slandering and persecuting His Word.

48. But, for all that, this judgment and preaching always continues penetrating, because Christ here commands them simply to preach among all nations, to tell everyone, wherever they go, to repent, and to say that no one who refuses this preaching can escape God's wrath or be saved. He rose in order to begin this kingdom. It must be preached, accepted, and believed by those who should and would be saved, even if it angers the world, the devil, or hell.

49. That is the first part of this sermon on true repentance, which rebukes not only a crowd of evildoers, whom even the world and the lawyers call sinners (though these, too, are to be earnestly rebuked), but attacks and condemns even those who are the most godly and holy in the eyes of the world (yet without knowledge of their sin and of Christ). This sermon does not make repentance our work, brought about by our own thoughts, extending only partially to some works—that man must first search long and ponder how, when, where, and how often he has sinned—though it is true that it can begin with one sin, as David was rebuked because of adultery and murder [2 Sam. 12:7–10]. Rather, this extends over your whole life, throws you down suddenly completely under God's wrath as by a thunderbolt from heaven, and tells you that you are a child of hell so that your heart is frightened and the world becomes too narrow for you.

50. Therefore, separate it this way: Direct the repentance which is still our work (our own contrition, confession, and satisfaction) to the schools of lawyers or children, where it may serve for discipline and bodily training. Keep that absolutely separated from the true spiritual contrition which works

through God's Word wherever and whenever it affects the heart, so that it must tremble and shake at God's serious and frightful wrath and in anguish does not know where it can stand.

51. Scripture shows this contrition and repentance with many examples, such as when St. Paul was converted and Christ Himself preaches repentance to him from heaven, saying, "Saul, Saul, why are you persecuting Me?" (Acts 9 [:4]), etc. Immediately the effect and the strength are there so that he suddenly falls to the ground, trembles, and says, "Lord, what do You want me to do?" (Acts 9 [:5]). This is true contrition. It did not come from his own thoughts, for he comes in the strong hope and confidence of his own holiness according to the Law. He knows of no sin with which he might have deserved God's wrath. But Christ suddenly shows him what he is, namely, a persecutor and murderer of Him and His Church. He had previously not seen this, but rather had regarded it as an excellent virtue and divine zeal. Now, however, he falls into such fright because he is shown that with all his righteousness according to the Law he is condemned before God. And He must rejoice when he hears these gracious words from Christ about how he should come to grace and the forgiveness of sins. Likewise, on Pentecost and afterward when Peter stepped forward with such thunderbolts, saying that the whole Jewish nation were betrayers and murderers of their promised Christ, the Son of God, the text says, "When they heard this, they were cut to the heart and said to the apostles: 'You men, brothers, what shall we do?'" (Acts 2 [:37]).

52. This is true contrition. It suddenly attacks the heart and makes it afraid and alarmed, so that it feels God's wrath and condemnation lying on it and begins to know the real, strong, hidden sins, of which it previously did not know. Such a heart must now say: "Alas! What shall I do? There is nothing but sin and wrath here, which—sadly!—I did not know or think about before," etc. St. Paul also speaks of the strength of the Word, which confronts us with God's wrath: "I was once alive apart from the Law" (Romans 7 [:9]); that is, I was arrogant and secure and knew neither sin nor God's wrath. But when the Law came and struck my heart, then sin became alive, so that only then did I begin to sense God's wrath, and so I died, that is, experienced trembling, anguish, and trepidation, which I could not endure. I would have had to perish in eternal death, if I had not again been delivered.

53. Then the second part follows, which Christ commands to be preached, namely, the forgiveness of sins. It is not enough to speak only about sin and God's wrath and frighten the people. Although it is necessary to begin in such a way that sin is recognized and sensed (so that they can also desire grace), yet it must not remain there, for otherwise there would be no Christ and salvation, but only death and hell. Christ's betrayer, Judas, began strongly enough with this first part of repentance, namely, contrition

and knowledge of his sin—yes, far too strongly, because no comfort followed, so that he could not endure it, but he plunged himself immediately into ruin and eternal death [Matt. 27:3–5], as did also King Saul and many others. But that is not the correct or complete preaching about repentance, as Christ wants to have it preached. The devil gladly lets himself be used to preach this part, even though it has not been committed to him, just as he always wants to cite God's name and Word, but only to deceive and harm. He turns both upside down—comforting where he should not comfort, or only frightening and leading to despair.

The Lord Christ's intention is not that repentance should be preached so that consciences are left in fright, but that those who recognize their sins and have a contrite heart should again be comforted and cheered. For that reason He immediately attaches the second part and commands that not only repentance but also the forgiveness of sins be preached. Thus (as He also says) He commands that this be preached in His name.

54. Therefore, when your conscience has been frightened by the preaching of repentance (whether that happened by word of mouth or otherwise in your heart), then you must know that you should also hear and comprehend the second part which Christ commanded to be spoken to you. Even though you certainly deserve eternal wrath and are guilty of hellfire, yet out of boundless goodness and mercy God does not want to leave you stuck or lost in your damnation but wants to forgive your sins, so that His wrath and your damnation are taken away from you.

55. This is the comforting preaching of the Gospel, which a man cannot understand of himself, as he does of himself understand the preaching of the Law (which was at first implanted in his nature [Rom. 2:15]) when his heart is affected by it. Rather, the Gospel is a special revelation and Christ's own true voice.

Human nature and reason cannot rise above the judgment of the Law, which concludes and says, "Whoever is a sinner is damned by God." Thus all people would have to remain eternally under wrath and damnation if a second, new preaching had not been given from heaven. God's Son Himself had to establish this preaching and command that it be spread into the world, in which God offers His grace and mercy to those who sense their sins and God's wrath.

56. But in order for this preaching to be grasped and considered certain, it must happen (as He here said) "in His name," that is, not only that sins are forgiven at His command but also for His sake and because of His merits. Thus we must confess that neither I nor any man (Christ excepted) have accomplished or merited this—nor could ever merit it. How should I be able

to merit it when I and all my life and whatever I can do is (by the terms of the first preaching) damned before God?

57. But if God's wrath is to be taken away from me and I am to obtain grace and forgiveness, then someone must merit this from Him, for God cannot be friendly or gracious to sin, nor put an end to punishment and wrath, unless sufficient payment is made for it. No one (not even an angel in heaven) could make compensation for the eternal, irreparable injury and eternal wrath of God which we merited by our sins except the eternal person, God's Son Himself, by taking our place, taking our sins onto Himself, and answering for them as being guilty Himself, etc.

Our dear Lord and only Savior and Mediator before God, Christ, has done this with His blood and dying, by which He became a sacrifice for us. Through His purity, innocence, and righteousness (which was divine and eternal) He surpassed all sin and wrath which He had to bear because of us; He completely drowned and swallowed it up. His merit is so great that God has now been satisfied and says, "Whomever He helps with it shall be helped." Christ also says about His Father's will: "This is the will of the one who sent Me, that whoever looks at the Son and believes in Him should have eternal life" (John 6 [:40]). Likewise: "All power in heaven and on earth has been given to Me" (Matthew 28 [:18]). In His prayer He says, "Father, glorify Your Son that Your Son may glorify You, even as You have given Him authority over all flesh, that He may give eternal life to all whom You have given to Him" (John 17 [:1–2]).

58. He has not only fulfilled this with His deeds, but also He has done it and accomplished it so that it would be preached and proclaimed to us—otherwise we would know nothing about it, nor could we obtain it. Therefore, it is completely unmerited on our part and is given to us entirely free of charge and only from grace. He did this just so that we can be certain of this grace and have no reason to doubt it. We would have to remain in eternal doubt if we were to look for our own merit and seek our own worthiness, until we had done so much that God would look at it and become gracious because of it. But now Christ commands that forgiveness of sins be preached in His name, so that I would know that it is definitely given to me for His sake, because He merited it and did it for me (since He had no need for it Himself); He shows this to me and imparts it to me through the Word.

59. So that I and everyone may take comfort for themselves in this, and no one may have any reason to be anxious and worried about whether he may claim this great grace for himself—for man's heart naturally doubts and disputes with itself: "Yes, I certainly believe that God chose certain great people such as St. Peter, Paul, etc., but who knows whether I, too, am one of those to whom He grants such grace? Perhaps I am not predestined to it"—Christ

wants and commands that this be proclaimed not in a corner or only to some special people, not only to His Jews or perhaps to a few more nations, but preached to the whole wide world or (as He says) "among all nations" [Luke 24:47], even as He says in Mark 16 [:15] "to all creatures."

He does this so that we know that He wants to have no one anywhere eliminated or excluded from this (if only they accept it and do not exclude themselves). Just as the preaching of repentance is to be a common preaching which goes against all people so that they recognize that they are sinners, so also the preaching of forgiveness is to be common and accepted by all, since all people from the beginning need it, and even to the end of the world. Why else would the forgiveness of sins be offered and preached to all if they did not all have sin? So what St. Paul says remains true: "God has shut them all up under sin, so that He might have mercy on all" (Romans 11 [:32; cf. Gal. 3:22]), etc.

60. Therefore, faith also belongs to this preaching, namely, that I conclude surely and undoubtedly that because of the Lord Christ forgiveness of sins is given to me. Through Him I have now been redeemed from the frightful wrath of God and eternal death. God wants to have me believe this preaching, so that I do not despise or reject the grace Christ offers nor call God in His Word a liar. Because He commands that this Word be preached in all the world, He also at the same time requires of everyone that we receive this preaching and regard and confess it to be divine, unchangeable truth, so that we definitely receive it for the sake of the Lord Christ. How unworthy I feel should not hinder nor frighten me away from this faith, if only my heart is sincerely displeased with my sins and would gladly be rid of them.

Just as this forgiveness is not offered and preached to me because of my worthiness—for I have not done or performed anything so that I should merit it and have it proclaimed to me—so also I neither pay anything nor am deprived of it because of my unworthiness, if only I desire it.

61. Finally, for our greater comfort, Christ here also institutes that this preaching of repentance and the forgiveness of sins should not be the kind of preaching which is carried out only for a while and at once, but should always go on and continue in Christendom without ceasing, as long as the kingdom of Christ continues. Christ established it so that it would be a continuous, eternal treasure and eternal grace, which always works and is strong. He does not want forgiveness applied only to that one moment when the Absolution is spoken and to past or previous sins (as was previously taught in papistic blindness), as if afterward we ourselves had to do so much that we would henceforth be completely pure and without sin.

62. In this life on earth it is impossible for us to live without any sin and defect (even if we have already received grace and the Holy Spirit) because

of our sinful, corrupt flesh and blood. This does not cease to be active in evil lusts and desires against God's Commandments until the grave, even in the saints, even though, after they have received grace, they refrain from and guard against sin and oppose the evil lusts, as repentance requires. Therefore, they also still daily need forgiveness, just as they also daily repent because of those remaining defects and weaknesses. They recognize that their life and works are still sinful and would merit God's wrath, if they were not forgiven and covered for Christ's sake.

63. For that reason Christ has established His kingdom on earth which should be called an eternal kingdom of grace and always remain under the forgiveness of sins. Upon those who believe it, it is so powerful that, even though sin is still stuck and so deeply rooted in their flesh and blood that it cannot at all be swept out in this life, nevertheless it shall do no harm but shall be forgiven and not imputed, as long as we remain in the faith and daily work at suppressing the remaining evil lusts until they are entirely blotted out through death and decay in the grave with this old maggot sack,[5] so that the man may rise completely new and pure to eternal life.

64. Yes, even if the man who now is under grace and holy would again fall away from repentance and faith and thus lose forgiveness, nevertheless this kingdom of grace stands firm and immovable, so that we can always come to it again, if we again cling to it through repentance and conversion. Similarly, the sun daily rises in the heavens and not only drives away the past night but always proceeds to illuminate the whole day, even when it is gloomy and overcast with thick clouds—yes, even when someone himself closes door and window against that light, yet it remains the same sun and again breaks through so that we can see it again and again.

65. This is the true doctrine of the Gospel concerning Christian repentance contained and included in two parts, namely, contrition, or earnest fright because of sin, and faith in forgiveness for Christ's sake. The entire papacy previously taught nothing about this, and especially did not want to say anything at all about faith in Christ (which should be the chief point of this preaching). Rather, they pointed the people only to their own works and pronounced the absolution on the condition of being truly contrite and confessing rightly. So Christ was completely forgotten and omitted, and the preaching which He commands here has been turned upside down and obscured, so that it was not repentance and absolution in His name but in our own names and because of our works of contrition, confession, and satisfaction. That is forcefully suppressing and even blotting out the faith and knowledge of Christ, taking comfort away from distressed consciences,

---

5 One of Luther's favorite colorful expressions for human mortality. See also LW 58:39 n. 10.

leading them out onto ice with that kind of absolution, and leaving them stuck to perish in doubt, since they are not to be certain of the forgiveness of sins until they have sufficiently afflicted and tortured themselves with their self-made and artificial contrition and confession.

66. The pope and all his rabble turn upside down the doctrine of Christian repentance and forgiveness of sin and corrupt it severely. By this one thing they have deserved, and still daily deserve, more severely to be cursed by all Christians to the depths of hell, as Paul curses all who teach a different gospel, etc. (Galatians 1 [:8–9]), because they still will not repent of all the error and misleading, which they themselves have to acknowledge, but instead slander and rage against the acknowledged truth.

67. Here we should also speak about confession, which we retain and praise as something useful and beneficial.[6] Although (properly speaking) it is not a part of repentance, nor is it necessary and commanded, yet it serves the purpose of receiving absolution, which is nothing other than the preaching and proclamation of the forgiveness of sins. Christ here commands that both be preached and heard. However, because it is necessary to retain this preaching in the churches, we should also retain Absolution. There is no other difference between them than that in Absolution the words (which otherwise in the preaching of the Gospel are proclaimed everywhere publicly to everyone together) are especially spoken to one or more who desire it. Christ ordered that this preaching of the forgiveness of sins should go and sound forth everywhere and at all times, not only in general to the whole group but also to individual persons (where there are the sort of people who need it). In next Sunday's Gospel reading, He says, "Whosesoever sins you forgive, they are forgiven to them" [John 20:23].[7]

68. For that reason we do not teach confession as the pope's theologians do, that we must count up our sins (this is the only thing the Papists call "confession") or that by doing so we obtain forgiveness and become worthy of absolution (as they say, "Because of your contrition and confession, I absolve you from your sins"). Rather, we teach that we should use confession in order to hear the comfort of the Gospel, and thus to awaken and strengthen faith in the forgiveness of sins (which is the true, chief part of repentance). Thus "to confess" does not mean (as it does among the Papists) to make a long list, counting up the sins, but to desire absolution, which is in itself confession enough, that is, that we acknowledge our guilt and confess that we are sinners. Nothing more should be demanded or imposed on us about counting up by name all or some, many or few sins. You yourself could then point

---

6 See AC XI 1 (Kolb-Wengert, p. 44; *Concordia*, pp. 35–36) and *Smalcald Articles* (1537/1538) III VIII 1 (Kolb-Wengert, p. 321; *Concordia*, p. 280).

7 See sermon for Sunday after Easter on John 20:19–31.

out something which especially burdens your conscience, for which you need instruction and advice or special comfort, as is often necessary for young, inexperienced people and also for others.

69. We praise and retain confession not for its own sake, but because of absolution. This is the golden treasure: that you hear proclaimed to you [individually] the words Christ commanded to be preached in His name to you and to all the world, so that even if you do not hear it in confession, yet you otherwise daily hear the Gospel, which is precisely the word of absolution. Preaching the forgiveness of sins means nothing other than acquitting or absolving from sins. This also happens in Baptism and the Sacrament, which were instituted in order to show us this forgiveness of sins and to make us sure of it. Since being baptized or receiving the Sacrament is also an absolution, in which forgiveness in Christ's name and at His command is promised and given to each one individually, you should hear this wherever and however often you need it; you should receive and believe it as if you were hearing it from Christ Himself. Since it is not our absolution but Christ's command and word, it is just as good and powerful as if it were heard from His own mouth.

70. So you see that everything that is taught according to Scripture about Christian repentance applies to the two points: contrition, or fright at God's wrath because of our sins, and, on the other hand, believing that our sins are forgiven for Christ's sake. There are no more than those two kinds of words instituted for us to preach, namely, the Law, which sets forth our sin and God's judgment, and the Gospel, which points us to Christ and points out in Him God's grace and mercy. In summary, all of repentance is just what Scripture says in different words in Psalm 147 [:11] and elsewhere: "The Lord has good pleasure in those who fear Him and who hope in His kindness." Those are the two points: the fear of God, which comes from knowledge of our sins, and trust in grace, which is presented to us in the promises about Christ, etc.

71. What the Papists say about their satisfaction is not at all to be tolerated (as said above). What was formerly called "satisfaction," and can still be read in the ancient teachers, was nothing other than an outward, public punishment of those who were guilty of public vices, which they had to endure in front of people, just as a thief or a murderer before the secular court pays with the gallows or the wheel. Scripture nowhere teaches anything about this, nor does it contribute anything to the forgiveness of sin; rather (as I have said), it can be committed to the lawyers as another bodily, worldly matter. But when they say that God punishes sins—sometimes even when they have been forgiven—with temporal punishment and affliction, that is true, but that is

no satisfaction or redemption from sin or a merit on account of which sin is forgiven, but God's fatherly rod provoking us to repentance.

72. Even if they wanted to retain the word "satisfaction" and explain it as meaning that Christ made satisfaction for our sins, nevertheless it is too weak and says too little about the grace of Christ. It does not sufficiently honor the sufferings of Christ, to which we must give higher honor, since He not only made satisfaction for sin but also redeemed us from the power of death, the devil, and hell. He established an eternal kingdom of grace and of daily forgiveness of the sins that remain in us. In this way He has become for us an eternal redemption and sanctification (as St. Paul says, 1 Corinthians 2 [1:30]; more was said of this above).

# GOSPEL FOR THE SUNDAY AFTER EASTER

## John 20:19–31

*On the evening of that day, the first day of the week, the doors being locked where the disciples were for fear of the Jews, Jesus came and stood among them and said to them, "Peace be with you." When He had said this, He showed them His hands and His side. Then the disciples were glad when they saw the Lord. Jesus said to them again, "Peace be with you. As the Father has sent Me, even so I am sending you." And when He had said this, He breathed on them and said to them, "Receive the Holy Spirit. If you forgive the sins of any, they are forgiven them; if you withhold forgiveness from any, it is withheld."*

*Now Thomas, one of the twelve, called the Twin, was not with them when Jesus came. So the other disciples told him, "We have seen the Lord." But he said to them, "Unless I see in His hands the mark of the nails, and place my finger into the mark of the nails, and place my hand into His side, I will never believe."*

*Eight days later, His disciples were inside again, and Thomas was with them. Although the doors were locked, Jesus came and stood among them and said, "Peace be with you." Then He said to Thomas, "Put your finger here, and see My hands; and put out your hand, and place it in My side. Do not disbelieve, but believe." Thomas answered Him, "My Lord and my God!" Jesus said to him, "Have you believed because you have seen Me? Blessed are those who have not seen and yet have believed."*

*Now Jesus did many other signs in the presence of the disciples, which are not written in this book; but these are written so that you may believe that Jesus is the Christ, the Son of God, and that by believing you may have life in His name.*

1. The first part of this Gospel reading is the same history which we heard in the Gospel for Easter Tuesday.[1] On the evening of Easter day (which the evangelists call "the first of the Sabbaths"[2] [Matt. 28:1; Mark 16:2; Luke 24:1; John 20:1]), Christ first appeared to His frightened disciples as they

---

1 See sermon for Easter Tuesday on Luke 24:36–47; and Easter Tuesday—Another Sermon on Luke 24:36–47.

2 That is, the first day of the week. The Greek word σάββατον, sometimes translated "Sabbath," can also mean "week."

were all together (except for St. Thomas), comforted them, and strengthened their faith in His resurrection. Thus we hear again what the power and benefit of His resurrection are, namely, that Christ, when He comes with this preaching, brings peace and joy, which are the true fruits of faith, as also St. Paul lists them among the other fruits of the Spirit (Galatians 6 [5:22–23]).

2. When He comes, He finds them still sitting in fear and fright, both outwardly because of the Jews and inwardly because of their consciences. Their hearts are still too weak and heavy to believe, even though they have heard from the women and some of the disciples that He had risen. While they were troubled about this and were talking with one another about it, He is there and bids them a friendly greeting in the manner of the Hebrew language: "Peace be with you" [John 20:19], which in our language would be: "All good wishes." They call it "peace" when it is going well and the heart is content and cheerful. Those are the friendly words which Christ always brings along, which He then in this history repeats a second and a third time [John 20:21, 26].

3. However, this peace of Christ is very secret and hidden from the eyes and the senses, for it is not a peace such as the world portrays it and seeks it, or such as flesh and blood understand. The situation of Christians is that for the sake of Christ they cannot have any peace or anything good from His enemies, the devil and the world. They must daily suffer misfortune and hostility. The devil alarms them, oppresses and afflicts them with fear of this sin and punishment for it; the world alarms them with its persecution and tyranny; and the flesh alarms them with its own weakness, impatience, etc.

Therefore, this is not a visible or tangible peace which is sensed externally, but internally and spiritually in faith, which grasps and lays hold of nothing but what it hears, namely, these friendly words of Christ which He speaks to all who are frightened and distressed: "*Pax tibi.* Peace be with you. Do not be afraid" [John 20:19], etc. So [the believer] is satisfied and content with the fact that Christ is his friend and God wants to offer him everything good, even though externally in the world he perceives no peace, but only its opposite.

This is the peace of which St. Paul says, "May the peace of God, which is higher than all reason, guard your hearts and minds in Christ Jesus" (Philippians 4 [:7]). Christ says: "I have said this to you that in Me you may have peace. In the world you have anxiety" (John 16 [:33]), etc.

4. The devil cannot bear to let a Christian have peace. Therefore, Christ must give peace in a different way than the world has and gives, namely, by soothing the heart, making it content, and inwardly taking away the fear and fright, even though outwardly hostility and misfortune remain.

You see here what happened to the disciples of Christ. They sit there, locked up because of their great fear of the Jews; they dare not go out, and they have death before their eyes. Even though they outwardly have peace and no one does anything to them, yet inwardly their hearts tremble, and they have no peace or rest. In this fear and anxiety the Lord comes, soothes their hearts, and sets them at peace—not by taking away the danger, but by their hearts being unafraid. The malice of the Jews was not taken away or changed, for they are angry and rage as before, and outwardly everything remains as it is. But they are inwardly changed, so that they are comforted and immovable and no longer care if the Jews are still raging.

5. The true peace that can soothe the heart is not the one at the time when there is no misfortune present, but the one in the midst of misfortune, when externally only hostility is visible. That is the difference between worldly and spiritual peace. Worldly peace means that the evil which causes hostility is taken away. For example, when an enemy is camped before a city, there is hostility, but when they go away, there is again peace. So when poverty and sickness oppress you, you are not at peace, but when they go away and you are freed from that misfortune, then there is again peace and rest externally. However, the one who endures this is unchanged; he remains just as despondent whether or not it is there, except that when it is present, he feels it and is anxious about it.

6. But Christian or spiritual peace turns that around, so that outwardly the misfortune remains, such as enemies, sickness, poverty, sin, devil, and death. They are present, do not cease, and are encamped all around; nevertheless, inwardly there is peace, strength, and comfort in the heart, so that it does not care about misfortune and even becomes more courageous and bold when it is there than when it is not. For that reason it is correctly called "the peace that is higher than reason and all understanding" [Phil. 4:7]. Reason understands and seeks no more than the peace that comes outwardly from the goods the world can give; it knows nothing about how to put the heart at peace and take comfort in times of need, when all of this is lacking.

When Christ comes, He lets the external adversities remain but strengthens the person. Out of timidity He makes a fearless heart; He makes a trembling heart bold; He makes a restless conscience peacefully quiet. Then the person is confident, courageous, and cheerful in the things in which otherwise all the world is frightened, that is, in death, fear of sin, and all distresses in which the world can no longer help with its comfort and goods. That is a true and lasting peace, which remains forever and is invincible as long as the heart clings to Christ.

7. So this peace means nothing else than that the heart is certain that it has a gracious God and the forgiveness of sins, for without that it cannot persist in any distress or be put at peace with any possession on earth.

8. However, this happens and comes only when Christ points us to His hands and side, that is, when He shows us through the Word that He was crucified for us, shed His blood and died, and thus paid for our sins and appeased and warded off God's wrath. That is the true sign which comforts frightened consciences and hearts and assures them of divine grace and the forgiveness of sins. He shows them this so that they will not doubt, but be certain that it is He Himself who is not angry with them but is their dear Savior. This peace is not so easy for them and all distressed consciences to lay hold of because they are alarmed and conflicted. Therefore, He comes and strengthens them both with the Word and with visible signs.

9. He still continues to do this after His resurrection, not visibly but through the preaching office (which we are to believe, even though we do not see Him, as He says at the end of this Gospel reading [John 20:29]), through which He also reminds us of how He shed His blood for us. It is enough that He showed this to His disciples once, to strengthen both their faith and ours, that He truly has risen and is the same Christ who for our sake was nailed to the cross and pierced.

10. The second point—that which follows the friendly greeting of Christ, or the offer of peace, and the showing of His hands and side (which were received by faith)—is joy, as the text says, "The disciples were glad when they saw the Lord" [John 20:20]. It is the greatest joy the human heart can feel, when it again sees and recognizes Christ who had previously been in death and with Him all comfort and joy were gone. But now it can cheerfully take comfort and know that in Him it has a dear and friendly Savior and, through Him, pure grace and comfort with God against all the fear of sin and death and against the power of the world and of hell. This is the same thing St. Paul says, "Since we have been justified by faith, we have peace with God through our Lord Jesus Christ, through whom we also have a cheerful admission or access in faith" (Romans 5 [:1–2]), etc.

11. We also sing about it at this time in the common, old Easter hymn about the resurrection of the Lord: "Christ is arisen from all His agony." It is not enough to be told the history of the resurrection; rather, the hymn brings it home to us and tells us that we are to be glad in our treasure and salvation, that we have peace and every good from God. Otherwise, how could we rejoice in Him if we had nothing from Him nor could accept as our own what He has done? Therefore, He also resolves to teach us that Christ wants to be our comfort, so that we may expect this with certainty. We can and should have no other comfort to which we would cling in every need.

Through His resurrection He has conquered everything and gives us as our own everything that He has done and suffered.

12. Christ came to the disciples through the closed door in order to point out that after His resurrection and in His kingdom on earth He will no longer be bound to a bodily, visible, tangible, and worldly way of life, to time, place, space, and the like. Rather, we should recognize and believe that He is present and rules through His power everywhere, in all places and at all times, when and where we need Him, and will be with us and help us, undetained and unhindered by the world and its power.

13. Second, He also shows that wherever He comes with His governance through the office of the Word, He does not come with bragging and blustering, with storming and raging, but very gently and slowly, so that He disturbs, breaks, and destroys nothing in outward human life and government. He lets them go and remain in the estates and offices in which He finds them, and so governs Christendom that orderly government on earth is not overthrown or destroyed. Thus He deranges and disturbs nothing inwardly in a man, neither a man's thinking nor his reason, but illuminates and improves his heart and understanding.

14. The devil, on the other hand, with his sectarian spirits, rumblers, bustlers, and disturbers, deranges and ruins everything, both in the external and worldly government and life and internally in people's hearts. He makes them very disturbed and gloomy with his false spirituality. We at this time have had much experience with this in his rebellious prophets, fanatics, and Anabaptists.[3]

15. That is the first part of this Gospel reading, as Christ again comforts His dear disciples through His resurrection and makes them cheerful and alive again, together with Him, from the oppressive death and misery of their hearts [when they thought] that Christ was now lost and eternally dead to them. Because they now have the profit and fruit of this, and so that He may now promote this same power and comfort of the resurrection [to others], He continues and gives them the command to spread this in the world through their office, as follows:

> *Then Jesus again said to them: "Peace be with you. As the Father has sent Me, so I am sending you." And when He had said that, He breathed on them and said to them: "Receive the Holy Spirit. Whosoever sins you*

3 For Luther's controversy with the Anabaptists, who rejected infant Baptism, see Luther's letter to Melanchthon, January 13, 1522, LW 48:364–72; and *Concerning Rebaptism* (1528), LW 40:225–62. Luther grouped Sacramentarians and Anabaptists together with radical spiritualists such as Thomas Münzer (ca. 1498–1525) under the epithet of "fanatics" [*Schwärmer*] or "Enthusiasts"—those who rejected the spiritual power of the external Word or Sacraments.

*pardon, they are pardoned to them; and whosesoever [sins] you retain, they are retained." [John 20:21–23]*

16. With these words the Lord points out what He has accomplished through His resurrection, namely, that He has established a government that does not have to do with and is not to handle money or gold and what concerns this temporal life, or how we are to acquire and keep them. That kind of kingdom already exists, established from the beginning of the world, subjected to human reason through God's Word when He said, "Rule over the fish in the sea and over the birds under heaven and over all the animals on earth" (Genesis 1 [:28]). This is the old government, with which the worldly government has to do and work, for which the Holy Spirit is not needed. We do not have much to teach about that in Christendom. Here lawyers can help and give advice about how it should work.

17. Alongside and above that is another government, which is over consciences and concerns the matters in which we deal with God. This government is twofold.[4] One was established through Moses. Here the Lord established the second when He says, "As the Father has sent Me, so I am sending you" [John 20:21], etc. Moses' government should serve to teach us what is sin and what is not sin and is necessary for those who do not yet know or perceive sin. For example, the Antinomians now are alleging that the Law should not be preached. It would be futile to preach much about grace among them, for where the Law is not preached, people cannot know about sin. St. Paul says, "Without the Law, sin is dead" [Rom. 7:8]. Likewise: "Where there is no Law, there is no transgression" [Rom. 4:15]. We recognize sin (no matter how great it is) and God's wrath only through the Law. Therefore, wherever this is not taught, the people will be very heathen; they will think that they are acting correctly when they are sinning abominably against God's Commandments.

18. Worldly government certainly restrains and punishes public sins, but it is far too insignificant to point out or teach what sin before God is, even if it were to take advice from all the books of the lawyers. Therefore, the Law was given so that people would learn from it what sin is. If sin remains unknown, then we cannot understand—much less desire—forgiveness and grace. Indeed, then grace is good for nothing, for grace must fight against and conquer in us the Law and sin, so that we do not despair.

A good physician must be experienced in his profession so that he first knows what kind of sickness it is. Otherwise, if he wants to help the

---

4 The distinction between two kingdoms [*Reiche*] or two governments [*Regimente*] was basic to Luther's understanding of God's work in the world and of human responsibility and freedom before God. See *Temporal Authority* (1523), LW 45:81–129, especially pp. 88–93; *Sermon on the Mount* (1530–32/1532), LW 21:5.

sick person but does not know the cause of the sickness, he would as soon give him dangerous poison as medicine. So sin must first and previously be known before grace is preached. The Law is necessary for that knowledge; so we must keep the catechism before people and diligently teach the Ten Commandments, for, as I have said, reason with its wisdom and the skill of all lawyers is too weak for this. Even though something from that knowledge is innate in you [Rom. 2:15; Jer. 31:33], yet it is too little and insignificant. For that reason, God established this preaching of the Law through Moses, which preaching he had previously received from the fathers.

19. Of course, Christ Himself ratified this preaching when He commanded His disciples, as we have heard in the previous Gospel reading,[5] first to preach repentance in His name [Luke 24:47], and when He said, "The Holy Spirit will rebuke the world about sin" (John 16 [:8]), etc. Although pointing out sin properly belongs to Moses' government, nevertheless, so that Christ can enter on His government and work, He must begin with the preaching of the Law where sin is not recognized. Where that does not occur, sin cannot be forgiven.

20. The other government is what the resurrection of the Lord Christ has established. Through this He wanted to set up a new kingdom that has to do and deals with sin (which was previously recognized through the Law) and with death and hell. This does not teach anything about becoming married; about managing house, city, and country; about keeping worldly peace; about cultivating, planting, etc. Rather, it is directed to where we will be when this temporal, perishable government and life cease, when we must leave goods, honor, house, farm, world, and everything on the earth, together with this life, as we are to expect every moment.

What is necessary here is this kingdom of Christ. He has been made an eternal King because He is Lord over sin and righteousness, over death and life. His kingdom has to do with ruling over these things.

This is what the Lord means when He says here: "Receive the Holy Spirit. Whosoever sins you pardon, they are pardoned to them; and whosoever [sins] you retain, they are retained" [John 20:22–23]. You can hear that He is occupied with delivering people from their sins or with leaving them stuck in them and pointing out that they are condemned.

21. Here we cannot say that by doing this He has established a worldly kingdom. The pope boasts about his binding key and loosing key, that he has the power to loosen and to bind even what is not sin—yes, even what Christ does not bind or loose; thus he makes a worldly power out of it. But Christ

explains here quite clearly what His Keys are: not to make laws and abolish them again, as the pope does, but to pardon or retain sins.

He means to say: "My kingdom is to consist of this, first, that the people recognize that they are sinners. I commanded Moses to teach and proclaim this not so that I would bind them, for they are already bound." He also does not want to make sins or to be occupied with manufacturing sins (as the pope does through his laws and with his binding key, making sin where there is no sin), but to work with those things which naturally are sins against God's Commandments, such as despising God and unbelief, slander of His name, despising His Word, disobedience, etc. These were not made sins by the pope's laws but are true [sins] which are stuck in flesh and blood and born with man, which cannot be absolved or taken away through the pope's loosing key, as he uses it, but which remain in man until the grave.

22. The goal of Christ's kingdom is that people know how they can become free from this. For that reason He everywhere calls it not a worldly or earthly kingdom, but the kingdom of heaven, for it is to begin just when this earthly [kingdom] ceases (through death), so that the people know then how they are to come into heaven. That is the way (He says) that His kingdom is to operate and consist.

*"As the Father has sent Me, so I am sending you." [John 20:21]*

23. With these words He first of all takes from them the fleshly opinion which the disciples had after His resurrection, that He would rule and govern like a worldly king and lord, with external, physical power. Therefore, He says: "You have now seen what kind of an office I have conducted on earth, for which I was sent by My Father, namely, that I should begin a spiritual kingdom against the power of the devil, sin, and death, and through this bring those who believe in Me to eternal life. I have done this and completed it as far as My person is concerned—and took for Myself nothing at all of the worldly life and government. Yes, I have even been killed by the world because of My office and service, and thus separated from you. But now through My resurrection I have entered into glory. There at the right hand of the Father I will govern all creatures forever.

"Therefore, I am also now sending you so that you will be My messengers, not occupied with worldly affairs, but conducting and working at the same office which I have so far done, namely, to preach the Word which you have heard and received from Me." This is an office through which people who sense sin and death and want to be delivered from them are delivered from sin and death.

24. With this the apostles and their successors to the end of the world are made lords and are given just as great power and might (with regard to

their office) as Christ, God's Son, Himself had, in comparison to which all the world's might and dominion are nothing (even though before the world it neither appears to be nor is called dominion). Nevertheless, [that office] should not and cannot go further than only over what is called "sin" before God, so that wherever [sin] begins or ends, their government should also both begin and end. Everything that lives on earth and is called "man"— whether emperor or king, great or small, no one excluded—is to be subject to this government. For that reason He says, "Whosesoever sins you pardon" [John 20:23]. This "whosesoever" means nothing else than "all together"— Jews, Gentiles, high and low, wise and ignorant, holy or unholy. No one will come to heaven and eternal life unless he receives this from you, that is, through your office.

25. With this word they are all together thrown under sin and locked up. Through this word He points out that on earth and in the world they will find nothing but sin. He pronounces the verdict that all people to whom the apostles and their successors were sent are sinners and condemned before God in their person and life. One of two things must happen: either their sins will be forgiven and pardoned when they recognize this and desire forgiveness, or they must remain eternally bound in sin for death and damnation.

26. Now, in order to use and carry out this authority and government, special power is required which is not human but divine. Therefore, He does not give them a sword and weapons for this; He does not equip them with armor and worldly power, but He breathes on them and says, "Receive the Holy Spirit" [John 20:22], namely, so that they would know that this office and work does not come from their own strength but from His power through the Holy Spirit, who will work through their office and words. So it is and is called the office of the Holy Spirit, who was given by Christ. Even though it seems to be weak preaching, nothing more than an insignificant breath out of a man's mouth, yet there is such power with and under it that sin, God's wrath, death, and hell must yield to it.

27. From this it is now also easy to answer people's question and quibbling: "How can man forgive sins, since this belongs only to God?" It is true that there is no human power or ability or merit and worthiness to forgive any sins, even if someone were as holy as all the apostles and all the angels in heaven. For that reason we ourselves also condemn the pope with his monks, who promise the people forgiveness of sins and pronounce absolution on the merit of their own works and holiness, so that the poor people who would gladly have true and sure comfort are shamefully and miserably deceived.

28. However, here we must have the true distinction—which the Papists and other sects do not know and cannot give—between what people do from their own initiative and on their own worthiness and that which Christ

commands us to do in His name and which He produces through His power. It is obviously of no value when a barefooted shorn head,[6] at his own audacity, comes and presumes to pronounce absolution and forgiveness to a poor conscience on the basis of his own remorse and repentance and the merit of the saints and his order, as their absolution reads (we can still convince them of that through the letters that are sold to people on the basis of their brotherhood): "The merit of the suffering of Christ and of Mary, the blessed Virgin, and of all saints; the merit of this stern and severe order; the humility of your repentance and remorse of heart and all good works which you have done or will do will be given to you for the forgiveness of your sins and eternal life," etc.

That is nothing other than abominable slander of Christ and turning true absolution upside down, for even though they mention His suffering, they are not serious about it, and do not regard it as good and powerful enough for the forgiveness of sins, but must have in addition the merit of Mary and all saints, and most of all of their own order and monkery, and make them equal to Christ. They do this without any command from Christ, even against His Word and command, not from the Holy Spirit, but from their own spirit, the devil, who is the father and author of such lying doctrine [John 8:44].

29. But if the absolution is to be true and powerful, then it must come from this command of Christ, so that it says: "I absolve you from your sins not in my name or in some saint's name, or for the sake of some human merit, but in the name of Christ and by the authority of His command, who has commanded me to tell you that your sins are forgiven. So it is not I but He Himself (through my mouth) who forgives your sins, and you are obliged to accept that and believe it firmly, not as the word of man, but as if you had heard it from the Lord Christ's own mouth."

30. Therefore, though the power to forgive sins is God's alone, we should nevertheless also know that He uses and distributes this power through this external office, to which Christ summons His apostles and commands them to proclaim forgiveness of sins in His name to all who desire it. It does not say that sins are forgiven from human will and power, but from Christ's command; moreover, He then also gives the Holy Spirit [to] forgive sins.

31. God does that also for our good, so that we do not need to gape at heaven in vain when we cannot obtain it and have to say (as St. Paul quotes from Moses): "Who can climb up to heaven?" etc. [Rom. 10:6; Deut. 30:12]. Rather, so that we would be certain of the matter, He has put the forgiveness of sins into the public office and Word so that we can always have it with us in our mouths and hearts. There we are to find absolution and forgiveness;

6 I.e., the Franciscans.

there we are to know when we hear this Word proclaimed to us by Christ's command that we are obliged to believe it as if proclaimed to us by Christ Himself.

32. This is the power which was given to the Church through this office of the apostles. This is far above all power on earth, for without it no one, no matter how great and mighty he is, shall or can come to God or have the comfort of conscience that he is free from God's wrath and eternal death. Even if all emperors and kings were to gather their might and power, their money and goods together, they could not deliver themselves or any person from even the least sin. If someone's heart is frightened, what does it help if he is a powerful king or emperor? This did not help the great and powerful King Nebuchadnezzar of Babylon when he became senseless, so that he was driven away from people, had to be with the irrational animals in the field and eat grass. He could not be helped in any other way than by the prophet Daniel absolving him from his sins [Dan. 4:25, 27].

33. But who can fully express what an unspeakable, mighty, and blessed comfort it is that one human being can with a word open heaven and lock hell for another? In this kingdom of grace which Christ has established through His resurrection, we do nothing other than open our mouths and say, "I forgive you your sins, not by myself or from my own power, but in the stead and in the name of Jesus Christ." He does not say, "You should forgive sins because of yourselves"; rather: "I am sending you as the Father has sent Me" [John 20:21]. I Myself have not done this by My own choice or counsel, but I was sent by the Father for this purpose. I am giving you this same command, even to the end of the world, so that you and all the world can know that this forgiving or retaining of sin does not happen by human power or might, but by the command of the one who sends you.

34. This is said not only to those who are preachers or pastors but also to all Christians. In the hour of death or in any other need, each one can comfort and speak absolution to another. Now, when you hear from me the words "Your sins are forgiven," then you are hearing that God wants to be gracious to you, deliver you from sin and death, justify, and save you.

35. "Yes," you say, "you certainly have spoken absolution to me, but who knows if it is certain and true with God that my sins are forgiven?" Answer: If I said and did that as a man, then you certainly can say, "I do not know whether your absolution is valid and effective or not."

However, so that you may be certain about this, you must be instructed from God's Word to say: "Neither the preacher nor any other man has absolved me; the pastor has not commanded me to believe that way. Rather, God has said and done it through him. I am certain of this, for my Lord Christ has commanded and said, 'As the Father has sent Me, so I am sending you'

[John 20:21]." Thus He makes those to whom He gives this command completely like Him in the sending, since they are sent by Him to do and accomplish exactly what He was sent by the Father to do, namely, to pardon and retain sins. Cling to that and do that; otherwise, without such a command, the absolution would be nothing.

36. Now, if you are sad and distressed because of your sins and horrified of death, with which God will eternally punish sin, and you hear from your curate[7] or (if you cannot have him) from your Christian neighbor who comforts you with these or similar words: "Dear brother or sister, I see that you are fearful and despondent, that you are afraid of God's wrath and judgment because of your sins, which you now sense, and are alarmed. Listen and let me say to you: Be of good cheer; have no fear, for Christ, your Lord and Savior, who came to save sinners, has commanded that both His called servants through the public office and in necessity each one individually is to comfort another for His sake and in His name absolve from sin."

When you hear this comfort (I say), then accept it with joy and thanksgiving, as if you heard it from Christ Himself. Then your heart will definitely be put at rest, cheered, and comforted, and you can then cheerfully say: "I have heard a man speaking with me and comforting me. I would not believe a word from him because of his person. However, I believe my Lord Christ, who has established this kingdom of grace and the forgiveness of sins and has given people this command and power to pardon or retain sins in His name."

37. Therefore, every Christian should become accustomed, when the devil attacks him and suggests that he is a great sinner and that he must be lost and condemned, etc., not to let himself be vexed by him for a long time or to remain alone, but to go to or summon his curate, or otherwise a good friend, tell him your trouble, and ask for advice and comfort from him. Rely on the fact that Christ says, "Whosesoever sins you pardon" [John 20:23], etc., and elsewhere: "Where two or three are gathered in My name, there am I among them" [Matt. 18:20]. Whatever he says to him in Christ's name from Scripture he should believe. It will happen as he now believes.

However, two or more come together in Christ's name when they are dealing with one another not concerning physical things, about how they can earn or obtain money and goods, but about what serves the salvation and happiness of their souls. For example, [this happens] when you in confession or otherwise point out your weakness and temptation, and the one to whom you are telling this observes that Moses with the Law has you between his spurs,[8] that sin is vexing and oppressing you, that death alarms and frightens

---

7  *Seelsorger*, that is, those to whom the care of souls has been committed.

8  *Zwischen die Sporn gefasset hat.* The reference is to a mounted rider equipped with spurs. Cf. below, sermon for Pentecost on John 14:23–31, paragraphs 87 and 100.

you, and that you sigh and lament about your own life and even utter the words: "If only I had never been born!" Likewise: "If only God would spare my life, I would improve," etc.

38. When your pastor or whoever it is begins to comfort you in a way that is not worldly, and also does not do that for the sake of money but because he sees that you are anxious and alarmed for fright of sin and death, he says to you: "Give up everything which is on earth—money, goods, the deeds and life of all people. But pay attention to this: your heart is in great anguish and thinks: 'How can I get free from my suffering, misery, and bad conscience? How can I escape from Moses with his thrusting horns?'"[9] Listen to him (I say) when he speaks to you in this way or similarly: "I say to you in the name of the Lord Christ, who died for your sins, that you should take comfort, believe, and be certain that your sins are forgiven and that death will not harm you."

39. "Dear friend," you say, "how will you prove that this is so?" Answer: Christ our Lord has said to His disciples and to all Christendom: "I command and bid you to forgive or retain sins. Whichever you do, you do it not of yourselves; rather, because you do it at My command and order, I also do it."

Therefore, the pastor or preacher as your curate, or even any Christian in such a case, is summoned and sent to comfort you. For that reason, because he seeks nothing other than your soul's salvation, you are just as obliged to believe him as if Christ Himself stood there, laid His hand on you, and spoke an absolution to you.

40. This is the way to deal with sins so that they are loosed and forgiven. Otherwise there is no remedy or relief for it—just as the pope alleges with his lying doctrine, pointing people to their own works or satisfactions, telling them to run into monasteries, to Rome, to the saints, to chastise themselves, build churches, donate to large institutions and monasteries, hold Mass, buy indulgences, etc. This is not the right way. You can better invest your running, money, and works elsewhere. This is what happens (as was said) when Moses puts on his horns and thrusts against you, that is, when through the Law he reveals and points out how great and many are your sins and so puts you into great fright and trepidation. Then you are no longer among the great, wicked, and hardened crowd, but rather among the little group that realizes and senses its distress and misery and, therefore, is even frightened at a rustling leaf [Lev. 26:36]. Then this is the only remedy: "I," says Christ, "I have established a kingdom of grace, which is to consume and slay sin and death, devour both of them, and bring righteousness and life."

9 In Western medieval art, Moses is often depicted with horns on his forehead, based on the Vg translation of the Hebrew word קָרַן, which can mean either "ray [of light]" or "horn" in Exod. 34:29: *ignorabat quod cornuta esset facies sua.*

41. Therefore, do not say: "Where will I find that? Shall I run after it to Rome or to Jerusalem?" No, for even if you could climb a golden ladder to heaven, if it were possible, nothing would come of it. Rather, it must happen in this way: look to His Word and command when He says, "I am sending you" [John 20:21], etc. It is as if He would say: I must first come to you, proclaim to you My Father's will through the Gospel, and institute the holy Sacraments and Absolution, if you are to come to Me. Now, though I cannot be bodily in all places in the whole world and will not always be visibly present with you, yet I will do as My Father has done. He took for Himself a small corner on earth—namely, Judea—and sent Me there to be a preacher. There I traveled through Galilee and Judea, as much as I could personally. I preached the Gospel for the comfort of the poor sinners among the Jewish people, healed the sick, raised the dead, etc.

That was the work He was commanded to do, for which He was sent by the Father. That was where He could be found—not at the court among the gluttons and pigs; not with Annas, Caiaphas, and other holy, rich, wise people; but among the blind, lame, leprous, deaf, dead, and misled, poor, distressed sheep. They are the ones He helps in body and soul. He brings them the most precious treasure of all, which no one has, much less can give, unless he receives it from Him, namely, righteousness and salvation.

"You should do this," He says, "in every place you come to. I am sending you for just this purpose, that you would run (as My messengers) throughout the whole world. Moreover, alongside of you and after you [I will] appoint and arrange others who will run and preach and do the same thing I was sent by My Father to do; and I have sent you to the end of the world. I will always be with you [Matt. 28:19–20], so that you will know that it is not you who are doing this, but I through you."

42. From this command we have the power to comfort distressed consciences and to absolve from sin, and we know that wherever we exercise this office not we but Christ Himself is doing these things. Therefore, each Christian, in this situation as well as from the pulpit, should listen to the pastor or preacher not as a man, but as God Himself. Then he can be certain and does not at all need to doubt that he has the forgiveness of sins. Christ has established through His resurrection that when a called minister—or whoever it is in time of need—speaks an absolution to his neighbor who is alarmed and desires comfort, it will avail just as much as if He Himself had done it, for it happens at His command and in His name.

43. Therefore, when two deal with each other in this way, then they are gathered in Christ's name, for (as said above) one is not seeking the other's money or goods, as the pope's shorn heads do, who speak to the sick in this way: "Dear man, the time is at hand for you to die. Where will your

goods be then? Think about your poor soul, and give us a share; then we will pray to God for you and do much other good with it," etc. Rather, [a Christian] says to the sick: "Now is not the time to be occupied with money and goods. Let others worry about that. I see that your heart is despondent and frightened. You are struggling with despair and cannot help or free yourself. However, Christ has established a comforting and blessed kingdom on earth. He says, 'As the Father has sent Me, so I am sending you' [John 20:21]. So He has consecrated us all as priests, so that one can proclaim the forgiveness of sins to another.

"Therefore, I come to you in the name of our Lord Christ and tell you not to quiver, tremble, or be afraid, as if there were no longer any comfort, help, and aid. Listen well, for Christ says that He came to save sinners (not the righteous) [Mark 2:17; Luke 5:32]. Therefore, be content, receive this cheerful message with joy, and thank Him from your heart for having me proclaim this to you without any trouble or expense to you and that He commands that your sins be pardoned. Therefore, I pronounce you free of all your sins in the name of the Father, Son, and Holy Spirit." To that you can cheerfully say, "I thank You, merciful God, heavenly Father, that You have forgiven my sins through Your dear Son, Christ," and then do not doubt that you are certainly absolved by God the Father Himself.

44. From this you can see that this section about the Office of the Keys does not at all confirm the pope's tyranny, for this is stated not so that you can make me rich, or I make you rich, or so that I can be your lord and you must be subject to me—as the pope, the chief villain and betrayer of God, wants to make worldly pomp and power out of it; but he is passing away. When I come to you in your need and anguish of conscience to advise and help you in your last hour or otherwise, I should say: "Power, money, honor, and goods should now all be neglected and wound up in a ball.[10] Now we are speaking about the kingdom of Christ, through which alone and through nothing else you must be delivered from sin and death."

45. That certainly does not mean an external and worldly dominion or power, but a service. I am seeking nothing from you, but I am serving and bringing you a great and precious treasure, not gold and silver. Rather, because your heart desires to be secure and confident and to have a gracious God in heaven, I come and bring you a cheerful message, not from my own choice or opinion, but from the command and commission of Christ who says, "Come to Me, all who labor and are heavy laden, and I will enliven you" [Matt. 11:28], etc. Likewise: "Whatever you loose on earth will be loosed in

10  *Auff ein Klewel gewunden.* The image is of wool wound up into a ball, that is, not currently being used.

heaven" [Matt. 18:18]; or, as He says here: "Whosesoever sins you pardon, they are pardoned to them" [John 20:23].

46. Is that not being served and freely being given an unspeakable, heavenly, eternal treasure which neither you nor the world can purchase with all its goods and riches? What are the treasures of all the world, the crowns of all kings, gold, silver, gems, and whatever the world esteems compared to this treasure called "the forgiveness of sins," through which you are liberated from the power of the devil, death, and hell and are assured that God in heaven wants to be gracious to you and is so gracious that, for Christ's sake, you are His child and heir, Christ's brother and co-heir? For that reason, it is impossible to sell such a precious treasure for money or to purchase it with money, as our Judas Iscariot, the pope, has done. It must only be given and received for free, or you are not improved by it, for God's gift is not obtained with money (Acts 8 [:20]).

47. However, I do not say this so that people would give nothing to the ministers who teach God's Word purely and faithfully. Unfortunately, people now would like to do that, and many are ready to count out every bite their pastors swallow. If they could snatch for themselves the property of the churches and pastors, and by doing so prove that they want to starve their pastors out and get rid of them, they are ready to do so. We would soon see what kind of savagery and misery would follow from this, if the government did not take notice. No, that is not at all my intention. They should be given support, for if they do not have food, drink, clothes, and other necessities, they will be unable to administer their office for long, but they will have to think about how else to support themselves. Then the Gospel will not remain for long, which is what the devil is seeking.

48. Christ Himself teaches that people are obliged to give them support when He says, "The laborer deserves his wages" (Luke 10 [:7]). St. Paul teaches: "The one who is taught the Word should share all good things with the one who teaches him" (Galatians 6 [:6]). He adds stern words: "Do not be deceived; God is not mocked" [Gal. 6:7]. Again: "Let the elders" (or priests) "who administer well be considered worthy of double honor, especially those who labor in the Word" (1 Timothy 5 [:17]).

If we take care of others who are in worldly offices, in which they serve the community, so that they can attend to their service, we are even more obliged to do this for the servants of the Word, for St. Paul says that, more than others, they are "worthy of double honor" [1 Tim. 5:17].

49. And if the doctrine of the Gospel is to remain pure in the pulpit in the future, so that our descendants can have and hear it, then we are obliged not only to care for the ministers, but we also are responsible to make very sure that the schools are supplied with qualified persons, whom we should

faithfully support. We should do this so that people can be trained who are not only simple, ordinary preachers, able to instruct the Christian community in the Word, but also especially learned people who can put a stop to the sects and false spirits and restrain them. Not only princes and lords should willingly and gladly give for that purpose but also townsmen and peasants.

50. From what has been said, everyone can ponder what a great and precious treasure it is to hear the Gospel or the Absolution with a correct understanding from the pastor or preacher. When he comes to you in your sickness and comforts you, then you should definitely think that Christ the Lord Himself is visiting and comforting you. Without His divine command, no one would ever dare come to you in this way, nor would he know how to help or aid you. However, because you hear that He Himself has commanded this, you can definitely and cheerfully say, "Christ Himself comes to me in my father confessor, for he does not speak his own words but God's Word, for which he was sent and has the command."

51. Here you have a sure comfort against fear and trepidation of conscience. You need not doubt or waver, as the pope's doctrine has taught us, where no one is absolved from sin unless he has sufficiently repented and purely confessed. Not the least word was mentioned about faith and the power of the Keys instituted by Christ, for this doctrine and knowledge was so completely unknown that I myself as a doctor (who should indeed have known better) held and taught nothing else than that if I was sufficiently contrite and did enough penance, my sins would be forgiven. However, if sins are not forgiven until they have been overcome by our contrition, penance, and good works, then we have no hope at all of forgiveness, for I could never come to the conclusion that my contrition and penance were sufficient. Therefore, on that basis no one can ever absolve or acquit me, whether he is called "pope" or anything else.

52. Thus, through the pope's lies, the conscience has been miserably led away from the Word of faith and the command of God to their uncertain contrition and penance. This has brought in a lot of money, and consequently many churches, monasteries, chapters,[11] chapels, and altars have been built and richly endowed. The pope's bulls and letters are still on hand which refer to and confirm these things, through which he has miserably deceived the whole world, so that no one can sufficiently ponder, to say nothing of fully describing, the harm and misery which has arisen from it.

That is why we faithfully and constantly admonish that whoever can should help to maintain schools, parishes, and pulpits, so that these errors or worse—which the devil definitely has in mind—may not prevail.

---

11  Associations of clergy (such as the canons of a cathedral chapter) endowed with corporate identity, property, and rights under church law.

53. This is the correct teaching and faith about the kingdom of Christ and the Office of the Keys. When we are guided by this, then we remain Christians and in all things can deal rightly with God and man. We will also thank God from the heart that He has delivered us from the pope's coercion and tyranny. He has made nothing but pomp and worldly dominion out of the power of the Keys, though they were established and arranged by Christ to bring the whole world to this treasure, which cannot be purchased with money or goods.

54. So let us be thankful to our dear Lord Christ, who through His resurrection established this kingdom of grace. Its purpose is that in every need and anxiety we should, without ceasing, find help and comfort in this kingdom. We do not need to go far away for this precious treasure nor run after it at great labor and expense. Rather, He has given the command and full power to His apostles and all their successors, and in case of need to every Christian, until the end of the world, that they should comfort and strengthen the weak and despondent and in His name pardon their sins, etc.

## THE SECOND PART OF THE GOSPEL, ABOUT ST. THOMAS[12]

1. The evangelist John further writes that Thomas was not there when the Lord first appeared to the disciples all together on Easter evening [John 20:24]. Now, it does not happen without a reason that the Lord first comes just when St. Thomas was not there, for He could certainly have come at the hour when he could find Thomas together with the other apostles. However, this happened both for our instruction and our comfort, so that the resurrection of the Lord would be witnessed and attested even more strongly. Now, on Easter He appeared to the Eleven[13] together; eight days later, that is today, He appears to them again and at the same time to Thomas, for whose sake alone this appearance and revelation happened. This one is more beautiful and glorious than the one eight days earlier.

2. First, we see here how poor the human heart is when it begins to become weak, so that it cannot be cheered up again. The other apostles and Thomas, during the time they were with the Lord, not only heard Him teach the people with great authority—and then also saw Him confirm His teaching with the great miracles He performed as He healed the blind, the lame,

12 The latter part of this sermon was considered a separate sermon in StL 11:770–79 and Lenker 2:403–12; therefore, our paragraph enumeration starts anew. See the introduction to the sermon for Easter 1, April 4, 1540, LW 69:424–25.

13 Previously, they were called "the Twelve" (John 20:24); now they are called "the Eleven" (Mark 16:14), even though only ten of them were present at Jesus' first appearance to the disciples.

the lepers, the deaf, etc.—but also [saw] that He raised three dead people,[14] especially Lazarus, who had already been in his grave four days. Among all of them it seems that St. Thomas was the most bold and courageous, for he is the one who says (when Christ wanted to go back into Judea to the dead Lazarus): "Let us go with Him, that we may die with Him" (John 11 [:16]). The apostles of Christ were fine people—and especially St. Thomas seems to have had a more valiant heart than the others. Besides this, he had recently witnessed Christ raise Lazarus, who had already lain in his grave for four days, and who ate and drank with Him [John 11:38–44; 12:1–2]. Yet they could not believe that the Lord Himself rose from the dead and was alive.

3. So we see in the apostles that we are nothing at all when He takes away His hand and we are left to ourselves. The women—[Mary] Magdalene and the others—and now the apostles themselves had proclaimed that they had seen the risen Lord. Still St. Thomas is obstinate and will not believe; he will not be satisfied even if he sees Him, unless he sees the nail marks in His hands and puts his fingers into the nail marks and his hand into His side [John 20:25].

So by refusing to believe, the dear apostle wants himself to be lost and condemned. There can be no forgiveness of sins or salvation if we do not believe this article of the resurrection of Christ, because all the strength of faith and of eternal life are in that article. St. Paul says, "If Christ has not been raised, then our preaching is in vain and your faith is also in vain." "Then you are still in your sins. Then also those who have fallen asleep in Christ are lost," etc. (1 Corinthians 15 [:14, 17–18]). St. Thomas wants to go away; he wants to be not saved but lost, because he refuses to believe that Christ has risen. He would have perished and been condemned in his unbelief if Christ had not delivered him out of it by this revelation.

4. So the Holy Spirit shows and teaches us with this example that without faith we are simply blind and completely hardened. Everywhere in Holy Scripture it can be seen that the human heart is the hardest thing, beyond all steel and diamond. On the other hand, when it is fearful, despondent, and weak, there is no water or oil as weak as the human heart [cf. Ps. 22:14].

5. You can find many examples and stories of this in Scripture. Moses did so many frightful signs and miracles before Pharaoh that he could say nothing against them, had to realize that it was God's finger [Exod. 8:19], and for that reason he also confessed that he had sinned against God and His people, etc. [Exod. 10:16]. Yet his heart became ever more hardened and obdurate, until the Lord cast him down together with all his might in the midst of the sea [Exod. 14:26–30].

---

14 The young man of Nain (Luke 7:11–17), Jairus's daughter (Matt. 9:18–19, 23–26; Mark 5:22–24, 35–43; Luke 8:41–42, 49–56), and Lazarus (John 11).

So also are the Jews. The more Christ powerfully proved by both word and deed that He was the one promised to their fathers to bless them and all the world, the more violently and bitterly they were enraged against Him. There was no measure or end to their hatred, slander, and persecution until they condemned their Lord and God to the most disgraceful death of all as a blasphemer and a rebel and crucified Him between two evildoers. Nothing could prevent it, even though Pilate himself, the judge, pronounced Him innocent in opposition to them [John 18:38; 19:4, 6]. Created things acted differently than usual and so testified that their Lord and Creator hung there on the cross, etc. [Matt. 27:45, 51–53]. Likewise, the thief frankly and publicly confessed that even though He was hanging there and dying, nevertheless He was a King who had an eternal, heavenly kingdom [Luke 23:42]. The heathen centurion publicly cried out: "Truly this was the Son of God" [Matt. 27:54], etc. All of this, I say, did not at all help to convert them.

6. This is the way the godless, condemned world always acts. The more God shows it grace and favor, the more unthankful and worse it becomes. Now it is right for us all to thank God from the heart that He has revealed His holy Word so purely and clearly before the Last Day. From it we learn what inexpressible benefits He has given us in Christ, namely, that through Him we are redeemed from sin and death and shall now be justified and saved, etc. What attitude does the world take to this? As usual, they cannot sufficiently profane, slander, and condemn this Word of grace and life; wherever they can, they persecute and slay those who confess it.

Even when they hear that God will severely punish such sin with the fires of hell and eternal damnation, they do not pay much attention to it, but go ahead securely and obdurately as if it were nothing at all, but only something to ridicule, as we now see in the pope and his crowd. Nevertheless, it is such horrible, frightful wrath, at which all creatures are horrified. Therefore, it is surely true that no stone, steel, diamond, or anything on earth is as hard as an impenitent human heart.

7. On the other hand, when a heart is despondent and frightened, it is weaker than any water or oil, so that (as Scripture says [Lev. 26:36]) it is afraid of a rustling tree leaf. When such a person is alone in a room and hears the rafters or joists crack a little, he thinks that lightning and thunder are striking him. He comes into such anxiety and fear (of which I have seen much) that no one can comfort or cheer him, and all sermons and comforting words are too few to calm him. So there is no middle ground at all with the human heart: either it is so hard like wood and stone that it cares nothing at all about God or the devil, or, on the other hand, it is despondent, fickle, and despairing.

8. Thus the apostles here are so scared and frightened by the scandal of seeing their Lord so miserably mocked, spit at, whipped, pierced, and finally crucified in the most miserable way of all that they no longer have a heart in their body. Previously, because they had Christ with them, they were so bold and courageous that James and John presumed to command fire to fall from heaven and consume the Samaritans who did not want to receive Christ [Luke 9:54]. Then they could grandly boast that even the devils were subject to them in the name of Jesus [Luke 10:17]. Thomas admonished the others and said, "Let us go with Him, that we may die with Him" [John 11:16]. Especially Peter, more than the others, quickly slashed with his sword among the crowd who wanted to lay hands on and capture Christ [John 18:10]. Now, however, they are locked up in great fear and fright and want no one to come to them.

For this reason they are also terrified of the Lord when He comes to them and greets them, but they think that they are seeing a spirit or a ghost (which is an indication that they are completely frightened and despondent) [Luke 24:36–37]. So quickly they have forgotten all the miracles, signs, and words they had seen and heard from Him. During the forty days after His resurrection, before He was separated from them, the Lord had enough to do with appearing and revealing Himself in many ways—now to the women, now to the apostles, both separately and together, even eating and drinking with them—all so that they would be certain that He had risen. Yet it was still difficult for them to accept this.

9. Likewise, during the forty days, He spoke with them from Scripture about the kingdom of God, which was now beginning and is the kind of kingdom in which repentance and the forgiveness of sins should be proclaimed in His name among all nations [Luke 24:47]. Beyond this, when He was about to be taken from them in a cloud, they began to ask Him: "Lord, will You now restore the kingdom to Israel?" [Acts 1:6]. They have completely different thoughts about the kingdom of Christ than the one of which He had been speaking. Here you can see how exceedingly difficult it is for fearful, despondent hearts to be comforted and cheered up, and then to be correctly instructed, so that they know what kind of a king Christ is and what He has accomplished by His death and resurrection.

10. So both the obduracy and the fearfulness of the human heart are inexpressible. When it is out of danger, it is beyond all measure hard and obdurate, so that it does not pay attention to God's wrath or threatening. Even after hearing for a long time that God will punish sin with eternal death and damnation, it goes on and is drowned in arrogance, greed, etc. On the other hand, if it begins to be afraid, it becomes so despondent that it cannot again be restored. It is a great misery that we are such abominable people.

If there is no trouble at the moment, then we live secure in sin without any fear and alarm; we even stiffen like a dead corpse, so that what is spoken to us does just as much good as if it were spoken to a rock.

On the other hand, if there is a change so that we feel our sins, then we are frightened of death, God's wrath, and judgment. We in turn are paralyzed by great anguish and sorrow, so that no one can again cheer us up. We even become frightened of what ought to comfort us, as the disciples were frightened of Christ, who came to them just so they would be confident and cheerful. Nevertheless, He does not immediately set them right, but has to patch them up throughout the forty days, as was said. He takes and uses all kinds of comfort and medicine and still He can hardly help them, until He at last gives them the truly strong drink, namely, the Holy Spirit, of which they become drunk and truly comforted so that they were no longer fearful and frightened, as before.

11. Finally, the power of Christ's resurrection is pointed out to us in St. Thomas. We heard above that he was so firm and even stiff-necked in unbelief that, even though the other disciples together testified that they had seen the risen Lord, he simply would not believe it. It seems that he was a fine, valiant man who had decided that he would not soon believe the others. He had seen the Lord nailed to the cross just three days before, with the nails going through both hands and feet and the spear piercing His side. That had impressed him so firmly that when the others said, "He is risen," he regarded it as nothing.

Therefore, he says very defiantly: "Unless I see in His hands the nail marks, and place my hand into His side, I will not believe" [John 20:25]. This is a strong hyperbole, that he will not believe his eyes alone but will also feel and grope with his hands. It is as if he would say: "No one will persuade me to believe, but I am so certain about this 'no' that I will not believe even if I see, as you say you saw Him. If I am to believe, then He must come so close to me that, if it were possible, I could touch His soul and look Him in the eye."

12. He is very firmly and rigidly stuck in unbelief. It is surprising that he should think of such an absurd thing as placing his hand and finger into the holes of the wounds. He should have been clever enough to figure out that if Christ was alive again, had conquered death, and was free from all the wounds from the scourging and the crown of thorns, then He would have healed and disposed of the five wounds.

13. The high apostles have to blunder and stumble as an example for us and for our comfort. In this we see how Christ treats and regards those in His kingdom who are weak. He can even endure those who are still so obstinate and stubborn (as St. Thomas is here), and He does not want to condemn or disown them for that reason, if only they want to remain His disciples and

do not maliciously slander Him or become His enemies. By doing this He teaches us not to be offended at them or despair of them, but, according to His example, to be gentle with them and serve their weakness with our strength, until they again are cheered up and even strong.

14. However (as I began to say), this serves not just to show us that the resurrection of the Lord was proved and attested by this unbelieving and stiff-necked Thomas—who was hardened and almost paralyzed for eight days in this unbelief—but also that its power becomes known and is applied to our benefit. This is to be seen in Thomas, who was brought from unbelief to faith, from doubt to certain knowledge and to a glorious and beautiful confession [John 20:18].

15. This did not happen (says the evangelist) until the eighth day after His resurrection, when Thomas had become strong in his unbelief, against the testimony of all the others, when He was dead and no one hopes that Christ will show Himself specially to him. Then He comes and shows him the same scars and wounds, as fresh as He had shown them to the others eight days before; He tells him to present his finger and hand and put them into the nail marks and into His side. He grants him so freely not only to see Him as the others but also to take hold of Him and feel, just as he had said, "Unless I see in His hands" [John 20:25], etc. He says in addition: "Do not be unbelieving, but believing" [John 20:27].

16. Here you can see that Christ does not leave it at the history. His concern is to make Thomas a believer and one who rises from his stiff-necked unbelief and sin, as indeed follows. St. Thomas soon begins to say to Christ: "My Lord and my God!" [John 20:28]. He is already a different person, not the old Thomas Didymus (which in German means "twin," not "doubter," as people have, without understanding, explained from this text), as he was just before when he was so paralyzed and dead in unbelief that he would not believe unless he put his finger into His wounds.

Rather, he suddenly began to make such a glorious confession and sermon about Christ—none of the apostles at that time preached so well— namely, that the person who rose is true God and man. He speaks very significant words: "My Lord and my God!" [John 20:28]. He was not drunk; he is not joking or jesting; he does not mean a false god. Therefore, he surely is not lying. Christ also did not rebuke him for this; rather, his faith is confirmed, and so it must be true and sincere.

17. So this is the power of Christ's resurrection: St. Thomas, who had been so deeply obdurate in unbelief above all others, was so suddenly changed and became an entirely different man. He now freely confesses that he not only believes that Christ has risen but is so enlightened by the power of Christ's resurrection that he also now believes it as certain and confesses that He, his

Lord, is true God and man. Just as he has now risen from unbelief, the chief source of all sin, through Him, so on the Last Day he will also arise from the dead and live eternally with Him in inexpressible glory and bliss. That is true not only of him but also of all who believe this, as Christ Himself further says to him: "Thomas, because you have seen you have believed. Blessed are those who have not seen and yet have believed" [John 20:29].

18. Finally, as far as putting his finger into the wounds is concerned, I will not contest whether Christ after His resurrection retained the wounds and nail marks, except that they were not hideous, as they would be otherwise, but beautiful and comforting. But whether they were still fresh, open, and red, as artists paint them, I will let others decide. Otherwise, what they represent for the common man is very fine, so that he can have a memorial and a picture which remind and admonish him about the suffering and wounds of Christ. It can certainly be that He retained the same signs or marks which will perhaps shine much more beautifully and gloriously on the Last Day than His whole body, and He will show them to all the world, as Scripture says, "They will look on Him whom they have pierced" [John 19:37; Zech. 12:10]. However, I will commend this to everyone's devotion, to ponder over.

19. However, the main point which we should learn and retain from this Gospel reading is this: we believe that the resurrection of Christ is ours and works in us so that we will be resurrected from both sin and death. St. Paul speaks abundantly and comfortingly about this everywhere, as does Christ Himself when He says here: "Blessed are those who do not see and yet believe" [John 20:29]. In the conclusion of this Gospel reading, St. John teaches and admonishes us about the use and benefit of the resurrection and says, "These are written so that you may believe that Jesus is the Son of God, and that through faith you may have life in His name" [John 20:31].

20. This is also a powerful, clear passage that gloriously praises faith and testifies that through it we surely have eternal life. This faith is not an empty, dead thought about the history of this Jesus, but it concludes and is certain that He is the Christ, that is, the promised King and Savior, God's Son, through whom we all are redeemed from sin and eternal death. He died and rose again so that we would obtain eternal life only for His sake. So it says "in His name," not in Moses' nor ours nor somebody else's name, that is, not because of the Law nor our worthiness and activity, but only because of His merit, as Peter also says, "There is no other name given to men in which we are to be saved" (Acts 4 [:12]), etc.

# GOSPEL FOR THE SECOND SUNDAY AFTER EASTER

*John 10:11–16*

*I am the good shepherd. The good shepherd lays down His life for the sheep. He who is a hired hand and not a shepherd, who does not own the sheep, sees the wolf coming and leaves the sheep and flees, and the wolf snatches them and scatters them. He flees because he is a hired hand and cares nothing for the sheep. I am the good shepherd. I know My own and My own know Me, just as the Father knows Me and I know the Father; and I lay down My life for the sheep. And I have other sheep that are not of this fold. I must bring them also, and they will listen to My voice. So there will be one flock, one shepherd.*

1. This Gospel reading, I think, is used on this Sunday because here Christ announces that He will give His life for His sheep, that is, suffer and die; and yet He also shows that He will rise again, because He says, "I have still other sheep, whom I must bring also" [John 10:16], etc. If He is to be and remain a Shepherd for His sheep, then He must not remain in death, as He Himself later explains and interprets in clear words: "I have the power to lay down My life and again to take it" [John 10:18].

2. Now, the Jews certainly heard this parable and sermon of Christ but understood none of it, as the text previously says [John 10:6]. It sounded altogether too strange in their ears that He alone would be the true Shepherd, and yet He was occupied with laying aside His life for His sheep. "What kind of a shepherd would that be," they think, "who dies and lays down his life for the sheep? Is that guarding and looking after the sheep?"

3. So it was also an intolerable preaching to them when He said that He has still other sheep which were not of this sheepfold (that is, they did not belong to the people who alone are called God's people), whom He would also bring to Himself. Those who were not of this sheepfold would become one flock under one Shepherd, no matter where they remained with their sheepfold and their sheep farm.

They understood very well what He meant by "Shepherd" and "sheep" (which was customary language for them, well-known especially from Scripture), namely, that He claimed to be a man who wanted to teach and rule the people, etc. However, because He is so absurd, as they thought, that

He wants to be the only Shepherd, and yet says that He will lay down His life for the sheep and that He has still other sheep whom He wants to bring and make one flock—even though they, the Jews, do not want to be His sheep— they are offended at Him and say, "He is insane and the devil is speaking from Him" [John 10:20].

Nevertheless, they did perceive this much: His intent was that their sheep farm—that is, their whole government which they had from Moses: the Law, the priesthood, circumcision, worship arranged for them by God Himself— would cease and no longer have any authority. He wants to make a new [government], in which He alone would rule, and would set up a new flock of both Jews and Gentiles (as He finds them) who would all cling to Him. He would pay no attention to the other, and Judaism with its government, glory, and existence can remain, stand, or fall, if it can.

4. He makes it still worse by saying, "I am the Good Shepherd" [John 10:11], by which He draws the people to Himself. He means to say, "Abandon whatever you have for teachers and rulers, and take Me for your Shepherd." He calls the best of all among them, those who teach and work with Moses and the Law, "hirelings," who are to be abandoned and not heard. And then there is the other group: "thieves and murderers" [John 10:1], that is, those who teach against God's Word and are public [persecutors. By that He fully] deserves that they should execute Him without any sentence and grace as a publicly cursed slanderer against God, God's Law, and God's people.

5. Without doubt, the great lords, high priests, Pharisees, scribes, and all who belonged to their spiritual government defiantly boasted and bragged: "We sit in the true office and priestly estate, instituted not by Moses but by God Himself (through Moses). How dare You, You rebellious scoundrel, open Your mouth before all the people and boast against God's institution and commandment that You want to be the Shepherd (and You alone)? You are not of the priestly tribe, to whom God committed what they were to do through Moses and commanded the people to listen to them. When did God speak publicly before all the people with You as He did with Moses? Who are You, then, or where do You come from, that You dare on Your own authority to let this be heard and to apply to Yourself alone everything that is said and commanded about the shepherd's office? By so doing, You are exalting only Yourself above and against Moses, God's Law, the priesthood, and the whole government! Does that not mean rebelliously intruding on the whole people's government and crown, and in addition slandering and sinning against the divine Majesty?"

6. What does it mean when He says, "I am the Good Shepherd," other than: "People should listen to Me alone. The whole flock of sheep—that is, all the people—belongs to Me alone. I alone am the Shepherd for them, the only

Good Shepherd who helps the sheep. You, on the other hand, are nothing but hirelings who do not care about the sheep, but seek only your own [advantage] in them and let them perish in their need." That means, in a word, making all the people disloyal to them and saying that they have no Good Shepherd or preacher who is faithful to them or can help them; they should not listen to them. ("My sheep," He says, "do not listen to a stranger's voice" [John 10:5]). But if they cling to Him, they will be helped.

7. Moreover (He says), He is not only the Shepherd of these sheep, but He also has still another group and people (who are not under Moses' government and are completely outside of this sheepfold) who also cling to Him and are all of equal value to Him—Gentiles like Jews, Jews like Gentiles. Now this is the most offensive thing of all: that He so humiliates God's people; and along with their Law, priesthood, and everything else makes them equal to the Gentiles; and, again, makes the Gentiles equal to them so that neither is better or has more than the other. In short, this is as much as saying that everything Moses instituted and ordered with the priesthood, temple, and worship should be finished and done with. Here begins a new priesthood and government, a new Shepherd, to whom alone the flock belongs and who alone does everything. This surely is knocking the bottom out of the barrel, cutting the head off of all Judaism, depriving it of all its glory, and telling them simply to cease being shepherds, to listen to Him alone, and to let Him be everything.

8. That had to be an offensive, slanderous preaching to them. In their minds they thought nothing was more certain than: "God through Moses put us into the priesthood, the teaching and ruling office of the whole nation. Whatever God has commanded and arranged must stand and not be changed by any creature. Therefore, our priesthood and Moses' government must remain eternally." If the Gentiles are to be brought and become God's people, that must not and cannot happen through this carpenter's apprentice from Nazareth (as they regarded and called Jesus [Matt. 13:55; Mark 6:3]), but through Moses, in that they are circumcised, accept his Law, visit the temple at Jerusalem, etc. At that time even the apostles themselves still thought that this must remain above all things as God's arrangement and command, given and instituted from heaven. In opposition to it, this Jesus of Nazareth dares to step forward and publicly say the opposite: "If you want to come to God and be saved, then you must finally abandon Moses, the Law, the temple, and the priesthood. None of these will in any way help you. All must cling to Me, whether they are Jew, Gentile, priest, layman, or whoever, even if it were Moses himself."

So the Jews stumbled over this preaching, and still stumble over it to this day. This offense against Moses and their Law is so much in their way that they cannot get over it.

9. It is no less offensive to our opponents, the pope and his crowd, to preach in this way against their government (as must be preached from this Gospel reading). Their government has been called the only government of the Christian Church in the world; in it was the regular power and everything that belongs to the Church, namely, Baptism, the Sacrament, the Keys, etc. These things were inherited from the apostles and have endured for a long time. For the sake of these they, just like the Jews, want alone to be God's people and the Church.

It is so very intolerable to them when, despite all that they assert, we on the contrary want to say that they are not the Church and that God cares nothing about their boasting, government, and all that, and when we separate from them, are disobedient, and teach this to others. We do this because, under the name of the Church of Christ and of faith, they have quite obscured this Shepherd, Christ, and (under the name of the church and Christian government) they have filled the church with their own worthless inventions. Yet they are not as good as hirelings, but are wolves and murderers, as they themselves prove by their public persecuting and murdering of Christians on account of this doctrine and confession about Christ. He is the only Shepherd. Through Him alone we have the forgiveness of sins and eternal life. He alone has also laid down His life for us.

10. I say that if the pope had it as good as the Jews did, who undeniably had Scripture and God's Word for them, then no one could have gotten along with them. The Jews had this great advantage for themselves: that their affairs were instituted at God's command through Moses, and then confirmed by miracles; it was so strictly arranged that whoever refused to listen to Moses had to be stoned at God's command and uprooted from His people [cf. Lev. 24:10–23; Num. 15:32–36; Deut. 13:6–11]. Our [opponents], God be praised, at least do not have the boast and testimony that their church government was commanded and confirmed by God. Now they act just like the Jews: no matter what is preached about Christ and the Gospel, they cry out against it that we must obey the church, listen to the fathers, keep the canons and decrees of the councils, etc. "How else," they say, "will anyone know what and where the Christians or the church are? There must be a set method and an established order, as that was beautifully arranged through the fathers and councils and as has happened for so long a time, that the church has a common head, the pope, and a regular government of bishops, and under these, the common priesthood, etc.; and over all of this there is a general council, whose judgment, conclusion, and verdict is to be followed

in all matters, etc. Whoever does not keep this beautiful arrangement and set method, or speaks against it and causes it to be divided, must be from the devil, an apostate, rebellious, cursed heretic."

11. We must open our mouths against this and say to everyone, along the lines of this sermon of Christ (since He has commanded to preach it to all creatures [Mark 16:15]): "Dear friend, you may certainly keep, brag highly, and elevate these human things, but you do not become a Christian with them, for that is not yet the true Shepherd and Master, who is called Christ. You must be led elsewhere so that you correctly know and listen to Him, or all of this will not at all help you to salvation." The Christian estate is something different from the pope's government, and also something different and higher than the fathers taught or the councils decreed. Although they did a good job, just as Moses also did a good (and even somewhat better) job, so that the Jews were circumcised, they sacrificed and observed their worship, or so that among us there is a beautiful arrangement of offices and estates, external discipline, and beautiful worship with fasting, praying, singing, etc.—all this is not yet what Christ says, "I am the true Shepherd" [cf. John 10:11].

12. We must carefully distinguish this Shepherd and His office from all other preachers, teachers, and whatever there may be which govern souls. (That is why He preaches this.) Let all of them do as good a job as they can, still none of them is a Good Shepherd. Moses certainly did not do a bad job; he set up a beautiful ordinance for spiritual and bodily government, both in external discipline and in worship. Nevertheless, his Jews had to hear that it does not in any way help them before God. Now, after it has lasted and endured so long, another will come who will strikingly brag and boast: "You do not yet have the true Shepherd you ought to have. I alone am the one whose voice you must listen to (provided that you want to be saved). I have still other sheep, that is, people who neither know nor observe anything at all about Moses and your whole government, and nevertheless they are all to be one flock. How will that happen? In this way: both of them will learn to know Me as their true Shepherd and to listen to My voice. Therefore, I let preach whoever preaches and leave it alone; but no one will find the Shepherd who can help the sheep unless he comes here and stays with Me."

13. Therefore, we should also conclude from this that there is nothing of value in what those shouters are asserting who still want to maintain the papacy with its episcopal masks and who blabber much about the church government which they want, where they sit together in the regularly inherited power as the heirs of the chairs of the first bishops, who were ordained by the apostles, etc. They say that the entire government of the church is to be bound to this, so that without it there can be no church. They alone have the

power to ordain (or consecrate) and confirm bishops. They persuade us that we should listen only to whatever they decide together and must receive from them everything that belongs to the office and government of the church, namely, the Sacraments, the preaching office, the consecration of priests, etc. They say that whoever has not been smeared and anointed by them are not true bishops or priests and cannot administer the Sacraments. For that reason they also rant and spit at us, saying that we have disobediently and rebelliously set ourselves against the regular power of the church and have separated from them, etc.

14. In opposition to this, Christ teaches us in this Gospel reading to look to Him alone as the true Shepherd, who is the only Founder, Lord, and Head of the Church, and thus says that His sheep listen to His voice and no other. By doing this, He shows that [His sheep] are the true Church, even if they are not under the pope and his bishops (not even under Moses). Along with His kingdom and Church He is bound neither to Moses nor to Judaism, even though they were ordered by God, much less to the pope's and bishops' government, which they themselves set up. He has not taken or received anything from them, but is the Lord over Moses and all creatures; all people should be obediently subject to Him.

15. Therefore, even though the Jews in the name of Moses, or our [opponents] under the name of the church and its power, venture to lead people away from Christ—that is, from His Word and the pure teaching of the Gospel—He says, "My sheep listen to My voice, but they do not listen to the voice of strangers and do not follow them" [John 10:3, 5]. Thus He gives us not only the power and right but also the earnest order and command not to listen or stay with such [strangers].

16. Now we see and comprehend that the whole papal crowd not only themselves keep, believe, and teach nothing about Christ but also are obvious persecutors of the Gospel, that is, wolves and murderers of Christ's sheep and His Church, and that they conduct and use a truly anti-Christian government. Therefore, we should and must, at Christ's command, thoroughly break away from their imaginary power and whatever they have, as from people already dismissed by Christ Himself. We are commanded to have nothing to do with them, but to avoid and flee from them as from the devil's church, as also St. Paul pronounces that verdict: "If anyone teaches a different gospel, even if it were an angel from heaven, let him be cursed" (Galatians 1 [:8]). That certainly means that all power in the church has been dismissed quite strongly, and we have been commanded to regard it as dismissed and condemned by God.

17. The chief point and summary of this Gospel reading is that Christ is called and alone is the Good Shepherd. It holds out to us the power and fruit

of the preaching of the Gospel and its office and distinguishes this from the office of Moses and the preaching of the Law. He states only the two (who guard and feed the sheep), the true Shepherd and the hireling. The wolf is nothing but a murderer, who only harms and ruins everything. To restrain it we must have shepherds. However, if we compare both the Shepherd and the hireling, then we find that Christ alone is the Shepherd who lays down His life for the sheep [John 10:11]. Neither Moses nor anyone who preaches the Law does that.

18. This is why He justly calls Himself alone the Good Shepherd, that is, the comforting and beneficial Shepherd. Although Moses, the prophets, and all other preachers who deal with the Law certainly preach and teach, they still cannot lay down their lives for the sheep and deliver them. They all must die for themselves and cannot deliver either themselves or others. However, "I alone am the one," He says, "who lays down His life for the sheep. Only My dying avails and delivers the sheep. Because this is what I am, I institute both this new preaching and a new flock and people."

19. In this way He draws the true Shepherd's office—that is, the authority to deliver consciences and souls—to His own person alone, as the one who alone has done and accomplished the work of our redemption, put down His body and life for His sheep, and instituted, promotes, and maintains the office through which He brings them to Himself, rules, and maintains them. So the whole preaching of the Gospel is included in this office wherever, whenever, and through whomever it is preached. They, too, are called "shepherds" after Christ, not with regard to their person (no one can be that except Christ Himself), but because they are in the office which belongs to Christ alone, and through them He is active and working in it.

20. That is the first point, about His person and office that He conducts in His Christendom. Afterward He Himself explains it further when He speaks about His sheep. But first He establishes the contrast with the hireling, saying:

> "But the hireling who is not the shepherd, to whom the sheep do not belong, sees the wolf coming and leaves the sheep and flees, and the wolf snatches and scatters the sheep. But the hireling flees because he is a hireling and does not care for the sheep." [John 10:12–13]

21. He names three kinds of persons or a threefold office which has to do with the sheep: the true Shepherd, which is He alone, as has been said; the hireling, that is, all besides Him who preach and teach from the Law how we ought to live and act but who do not point to Christ, such as the scribes and Pharisees among the Jewish people of that time; and, finally, the wolf, who also wants to be among the sheep and rule but only harms and ruins. That is

the devil himself; he also has his messengers and preachers who do not have God's Word (neither the Ten Commandments nor the Gospel) but mislead souls with false doctrine and heresy (which Paul also calls "the doctrines of the devil, of those who speak lies in hypocrisy," 1 Timothy 3 [4:1–2]). At the present time there are the pope's anti-Christian doctrines, the Turks' Koran, and other sects. These three teachers have always been in the world from the beginning. We should cling to the first alone, correct the second, and flee completely from the third. But no one does this except the true sheep, that is, the little flock which knows Christ.

22. Now He also shows what the situation is with the sheep and why He alone must be recognized and believed as the true Shepherd. The situation with the sheep is that they are in certain danger and peril (if they are apart from the Shepherd) of being snatched, torn to pieces, and murdered by the wolf, since by their own strength they can neither guard nor defend themselves against him. By nature the sheep is more weak and defenseless than all other animals and must live by the protection, defense, and help of another. The true shepherd must take an interest in them; be with them everywhere; watch over, deliver, and defend them whenever it is necessary, so that they do not perish. He does not do it (says Christ) with a paid hireling who is not their own, to whom the sheep do not belong, for even though he will lead and feed them for a while, he will not remain to the end. When the wolf comes, he takes to flight so that he himself can escape, and meanwhile he leaves the poor sheep stuck in peril and perishing.

23. So it also happens in this spiritual government of the conscience that, if Christ does not Himself guard, guide, and lead through His office as Shepherd, then no other preaching is helpful or beneficial, even if it is otherwise good and correct. It cannot stand the test in peril against the devil when he opens the jaws of hell through fright at sin and eternal death. When this happens, then the poor sheep stands there alone and forsaken, directed to himself and his own efforts through the doctrine of the Law and our works. He no longer has any help or assistance in which he can find comfort and deliverance.

24. We can find no better example of this than our own past (which we ourselves experienced) under the papacy. Then the most precious and pleasing sermon anyone could make (which, along with others, I sought to teach both to myself and to the people) sounded like this: "You must keep the Ten Commandments, love God with your whole heart and your neighbor as yourselves," etc. It was not and is not wrong to teach this, for the teaching of the Law should and must remain. However, in order to impress this upon the people, they added that we can certainly do this, for man has the natural light of reason given by God so that he can understand what he is to do and

not do. Moreover, he has the will, by which he can intend and begin to keep it. And if he diligently practices these things and does what is in his power, then God will look at it and be pleased and undoubtedly give him grace, etc.

25. On top of this comfort, they gave many more good suggestions (since they themselves noticed that what they taught about the Ten Commandments would not yet help). Everything they taught about separate, strict orders and life, mortification of the body, fasting, vigils, pilgrimages, etc., was to serve for escaping death and being saved. They regarded all of that as good and precious, and did it with good intentions, as if God would be pleased with it and regard it as fulfillment of His Commandments. However, when people had attempted all of this, and at the last the devil came when they were on their deathbed or with other difficult afflictions, then all this teaching and activity were of no help at all. The poor consciences were miserably led into the devil's sweat bath, in which they were alarmed and tormented themselves with despairing thoughts, words, and sighs, such as: "Lord God, if I could prolong my life, I would make amends for all my sins!" etc.

26. That was the benefit and fruit of the hirelings' doctrine, which pointed the poor people to their own doing and suffering, since they knew nothing at all about Christ and faith. This preaching can only comfort and sustain until the devil comes. He cares nothing about our works or satisfactions and life. Rather, if he does not find Christ, he has won the game, and continues to tear souls to pieces and devour them as much as he wants without restraint or hindrance. These teachers and masters cannot even help themselves. Together with the sheep, they are chased off and hunted down so that they cannot endure and finally themselves are lost to the enemy, if they do not learn of other help.

A common example of this is told about a hermit who once came to a sick man on his deathbed and wanted to comfort him so that he would die well. He admonished him (as such comforters—work-saints and monks—are accustomed to do) willingly to submit to death and patiently to suffer, since in that way he would obtain forgiveness for all sins from God. He would pledge his soul for that. Dear God! Here lies a poor sheep in peril, at its last gasp; it takes what it can and dies relying on that comfort. But what happens? Soon after the death of this poor man, remorse comes to the old hermit and makes him so anxious and alarmed that he becomes despondent (of just that comfort which he gave others), and no comforting would help him, until he also came into despair.

27. This is what must happen when nothing more than our works are preached or even only the Ten Commandments are proclaimed—even though we must have and proclaim this preaching, especially for the uneducated crowd. But if Christ Himself is not there, this accomplishes nothing

more than that the poor sheep wander and are scattered, and fall into fright and despair, until they finally perish, if they are not brought back by the true Shepherd.

28. When human nature and reason hear the preaching of the Law, even from those who proclaim the Law best, [but] do not know Christ, they fall into folly and imagine, when they have heard this preaching, that they can immediately do it. "They have," they say, "both the understanding and the will to do it." They think no further than that this is accomplished with their self-made thoughts and outward works. Then they go ahead and think that they must do whatever people say or assert about good works, as if these were commanded by God. They want to make amends for sin and to blot it out in that way. Yet God does not demand that we do good works for that reason or that sin can be blotted out with works. Then they go on from that erroneous delusion to gather and heap up all the works they can invent or hear about from others, which God has not commanded.

They are simply caught up in this syllogism: We are to do good works. This is a good work. Therefore, I am obliged to do it. So they go away and are always busy doing this, but never reach the point where they have finished. So they also cannot withstand the wolf. The more they do, the less they are satisfied, and the more they find to do. As soon as the devil comes and asserts: "Look, here is a good work which you have not done!" they cannot get over it and must let him tear them away.

29. Yes, even if they had done all that a man can do, yet they would still see, when the wolf comes before their eyes with his wide-open jaws of hell, that it will not pass the test against God's wrath and judgment. The devil blows all that away with one breath and says: "It is true that you have done much, but when did you finish doing what God commanded? He tells you to love Him with your whole heart above all things, to have no evil thoughts or lusts or desires in your heart, to speak no useless and futile words," etc. Then immediately both the doctrine which the hireling gave you and all your works and activities which you have carried out with such hard labor fall away, and you have no comfort or refuge against the devil. He always has the advantage of working on you through your own conscience and the testimony of your own deeds, to which you were directed by the hireling who only teaches you what to do but does not and cannot give you the ability to do it. So you are stuck in peril, vanquished by yourself, and trapped by the words: "We must do good."

30. In this way he (the devil) through the pope also introduced into the churches all his dirt and filth of human doctrines, which no one could prevent, for they all proceed from the basis: "We must do whatever is good." Therefore, people had to do whatever they called "good" and "worship of

God." They also do not cease to blabber against us that our doctrine of faith and love is a simplistic doctrine, since we do not know to preach anything more than the childish doctrine of the Ten Commandments. They say that we must go much higher and do much more, and not only teach what is in Scripture but also listen to what the church and the councils say, etc.

31. Therefore, everything any shabby, shameless beggar-monk dared to assert was forcibly confirmed, and it prevailed like a flood. We simpletons who were doctors of Holy Scripture could not restrain the wicked barefoot rabble from persuading the people that if they buried a dead man in their monk's cowl, he would be saved and the devil could not carry him off (unless he had already gotten him earlier).[1] We were all blinded and taken captive by the words: "We must do good works, and whoever does them will be saved."

32. To this day we could still not hold our own against the papacy or overthrow their least error if we had no more than this doctrine of our deeds and works. Even the holy martyr, John Hus, was shouted down and condemned by the devil at their hellish Council of Constance because he rebuked the pope and his crowd on account of their wicked, shameless life by which they did not even keep their own canonical laws.[2] They had this defense against it: even though the life was not right, the doctrine was right, that we should do and keep these things. So the papacy was not overthrown as long as its doctrine was regarded as right and remained unharmed.

33. Therefore, these two, the hireling and the wolf, are always together. The devil can easily tolerate such teachers, for (when the true Shepherd is not there) they serve him so that he can rend apart and wreak havoc among the sheep without any trouble, when and as he wants. There is no way to prevent it except Christ with His teaching and protection. He (as the only true Shepherd) does not let the sheep be slain by the wolf (for if that happens, then they are already in his jaws), but Himself stands against him, gathers us to Himself, and protects us so that the devil must yield. That means that we preach from Scripture that no human work or activity (no matter how good it is, even done according to the Ten Commandments), and nothing we can teach, helps at all to free from sin or to stand against God's wrath and the

---

1 The monastic orders could grant tertiaries or benefactors the privilege of being buried in the monastic habit, which was thought to confer participation in the good works of the order.

2 John [Jan] Hus (1369–1415), Czech theologian and rector of the University of Prague, criticized clerical immorality and the papal doctrine of the Church and was condemned by the Council of Constance and burned at the stake. Luther scandalized his opponents at the 1519 Leipzig Disputation by defending Hus (LW 31:315, 321). Luther frequently referred to Hus as evidence of the impossibility of suppressing the Gospel: *Commentary on Psalm 94* (1526), LW 14:253; *To the Christians at Halle* (1527), LW 43:146; *Lectures on Isaiah* (1527–30/1532–34), LW 17:44; *Commentary on Psalm 118* (1530), LW 14:88; *Sermon on the Mount* (1530–32/1532), LW 21:165; *Lectures on Genesis* (1535–45/1544–54), LW 8:226.

fright of death and hell, etc. Rather, the only thing that helps is that Christ has laid down His life for you and taken it up again in order to overcome the devil and death and subject them to Himself, so that you are preserved through His strength and power.

34. But where the voice of this Shepherd remains, the sheep can protect themselves from both the hireling and the wolf, saying: "You preach correctly that I should keep the Ten Commandments, but you do not tell me where that leaves me, because I have not fulfilled them. In this situation I will listen to my dear Shepherd who died for me; He did not die without reason or in vain, but just for this: to save me, who was such a poor, lost sheep without a Shepherd, in the power of the wolf." So also when the devil shows his teeth to your heart in order to slay and devour you and says, "You should have done or avoided this or that; you have not done or avoided it; therefore, you must be mine," then, as a lamb who knows its Shepherd, you can take refuge in Christ. You can tell the devil to stand against the one who died for you and rose again and see what victory he can have against Him.

35. You can even more beat back the others who are not as good as hirelings but are the slaves and servants of the wolf (who come with their goose sermon[3] about our own invented works). You can say to them: "I will not know or hear anything about that, for I have something much different and greater to do: learning the Ten Commandments. And yet I cannot keep them. Why, then, should I afflict myself with such useless works, which only harm and hinder me from looking at the Ten Commandments correctly?" It has happened that the world was so full of human doctrines and commands that no bishop, not even a doctor, correctly understood or taught the Ten Commandments.

36. We have not rebuked and attacked the papacy because they live wickedly and shamefully (which they themselves also must confess). Rather, we say to them that, even if they led holy, angelic lives (which they have never done and never will do) and kept not only their own law but also Moses' Law (both of which are impossible), we would still regard them not as hirelings but as wolves themselves because they teach nothing except what kills souls. That which is not the doctrine of Christ cannot feed or give life to the souls. Also, even though the hireling does not himself slaughter and kill, still he does not restrain the wolf. Therefore, because you do not point out or teach this Shepherd, but do the opposite, we should not and will not listen to you, but rather flee from you as from the wolf.

37. With this argument we overthrow the entire papacy and everything that leads us away from this doctrine. Otherwise (as was said) it is impossible

---

3 *Gens Predigt.* That is, a sermon delivered to simple people, perhaps for the purpose of misleading them.

to rebuke even the least error which is advanced under the form of a holy life. There is no doctrine so foolish or shameful that does not find hearers and students, as we have had to experience in so many heresies and schisms in the church. We read that the heathen (who were at least sensible and highly intelligent people) nevertheless worshiped not only cats and storks but also cabbages and onions, and even the male member. All of this has the name and delusion of being a good work and of serving God, and the one who preaches this has the reputation and pretense of being a shepherd who wants to counsel souls and show them how to come to God, etc.

38. We have so far been unable to rebuke or prevent the shameful lies and fables of the monks concerning the rosary of Mary (this was fifty *Ave Maria*s and five Our Fathers, which were spoken to Mary the virgin). The popes gave many indulgences to it, and the preacher monks[4] smeared large books full of invented and stinking lies about the powerful miracles done by this prayer, which they had first invented. There were innumerable lying inventions of this sort devised by others, such as the barefooted monks[5] with Mary's crown and psalter,[6] etc., about which they themselves must now be silent and ashamed. Yes, at the present day nobody in the papacy could refute or resist the Turkish or Jewish religion, for they have neither the true Master nor the true, fundamental doctrine of this Shepherd. Therefore, the devil has power and authority over them, even through the Ten Commandments, for he always has the advantage of convincing you by your own conscience that you have not kept them—even more if you have spent your entire life only with the works of human doctrine.

39. However, if you know this Shepherd, you can defend yourself against the devil and death, saying: "Sadly, I have not kept God's Commandments, but I crawl under the wings of this dear hen (my dear Lord Christ [Matt. 23:37; Luke 13:34]) and believe that He is my dear Shepherd, Bishop, and Mediator before God, who covers and defends me with His innocence and gives me His righteousness. Whatever I have not kept, He has kept; what is more, whatever I have sinned, He has paid for with His blood," etc. He died and rose again not for Himself but for me, since He says here that He gives His life not for Himself but for His sheep [John 10:11], that is, as St. Peter says, "The righteous died for the unrighteous" [1 Pet. 3:18], etc. So, then, you are secure, and the devil along with his hell must leave you alone, for he certainly

4 *Prediger Mönche*, that is, the Dominicans.

5 *Barfusser*, that is, the Franciscans.

6 "Mary's crown and psalter" were forms of prayer centered on the repetition of the Lord's Prayer and especially of the *Ave Maria*, a prayer that had arrived at its expanded form (with the petition for Mary's intercession) only at the beginning of the sixteenth century and was not officially approved until 156.

cannot get anything from Christ, who has already overcome him. He defends and keeps you, if you believe in Him as His lamb. (As a faithful Shepherd, He does not leave you but stands by you.)

40. If you are now secure under this Shepherd against the wolf, the hireling correctly comes and becomes a good teacher of how you should live according to God's Commandments and do good works. He leads you where you yourself can now go (since it is apart from the struggle of the conscience against sin and death) in such a way that you are first in the protection and pasture of this Shepherd and do not depart from Him.

41. These three kinds of preaching are always current in the world. The first [is the preaching] of the great crowd, who do not advance God's Word but human doctrine. These are wolves, such as the pope with his decrees, the Turk with his Koran, the Jews with their Talmud, and other sects against the correct, pure doctrine of Scripture. The second [is the preaching] of the hirelings, who preach only the Ten Commandments. There are few of these, since without the Gospel they do not remain pure for long. The third are those who purely and rightly point and lead to Christ. Although these are the fewest of all, they must still be found somewhere until the Last Day, as we say in the creed: "I believe in the holy Christian Church," etc.[7]

42. These are the true shepherds, because they preach not themselves but Christ and so are the Lord Christ's mouth, as He Himself says, "You are not the ones speaking, but your Father's Spirit speaks through you" (Matthew 10 [:20]). Again: "I will give you a mouth and wisdom" (that is, "It will not be your mouth, but I will so prepare your mouth that it will be a mouth full of wisdom given by Me and speaking about Me") "which all your adversaries will not contradict or withstand" (Luke 21 [:15]).

This is the thunderbolt by which everything that is not of this doctrine and stamp is put down, because it gives no benefit or help for the life to come, even though it may otherwise be good for keeping discipline among people or for bringing them to a knowledge of their weaknesses. What is everything that a man, a pope, or a Turk can do against eternal death and hell?

43. This storms and overthrows the pope's government and all human doctrines. We do not challenge them for failing to keep their own commandments and doctrine, for they always have a defense against this, that even though their life is culpable, yet their doctrine is right and good. They forcibly retain their government from Christ's words: "The Pharisees sit on Moses' seat. All they tell you to keep, you should keep and do, but do not do according to their works, for they say, and do not do" (Matthew 23 [:2–3]), etc. That is why, before we had the Gospel, we could do nothing against

---

7 I.e., in the Third Article of the Apostles' Creed (Kolb-Wengert, p. 22; *Concordia*, p. 16).

them. Now that we know Christ, we can condemn their doctrine along with all their deeds.

44. So now you have the distinction that Christ shows between His preaching and government and that of all others, who want to govern consciences and hearts without or apart from Him. With these many words about the hireling He depicts the danger, even the harm and destruction, which must follow if He is not heard and recognized as the only Shepherd, since the wolf will not be kept away no matter how many hirelings we have. With their doctrine none of them can give counsel or help about how we are to be freed from sin and death or oppose the devil. In short, the poor sheep must be eternally lost and perish, if they do not come to this Shepherd. That is why He repeats again what He said at the beginning, in order to impress on us that we must cling only to His protection and pasture (that is, to His Word and preaching office). He says:

> *"I am the Good Shepherd. I know My own and am known by My own, just as My Father knows Me and I know the Father. I lay down My life for the sheep." [John 10:14–15]*

45. "There are many of you—unfortunately, all too many—who are called shepherds and undertake the governance of feeding and leading souls, but I alone am the one," He says again, "who is called and is the Good Shepherd." That means in plain words: "Apart from Me they all are not good, but pitiless, cruel shepherds, because they leave the poor sheep in the jaws of the wolf! You should learn to know Me as your dear, faithful, good, kind, sweet, and comforting Shepherd. Your heart should laugh and be certain that through Him you are redeemed from every burden, fear, trouble, and danger and that He will not and cannot let you perish. I am proving this," He says, "by laying down My life for the sheep. Therefore, cheerfully cling to Me, and let no one else rule in your consciences. Rather, listen to Me speak comforting words and demonstrate by deeds that I do not want to force, afflict, or burden you as Moses and others, but want to lead and guide, defend and help you in the dearest way."

46. So He always emphasizes this one doctrine as the chief point of our salvation, that apart from this Shepherd, Christ, apprehended through this faith—that He alone rescues us through His death from the power of death and the devil—there is no deliverance or help. This is the most necessary doctrine that must be proclaimed in Christendom. The devil is hostile to it and cannot tolerate it when we remain with this Good Shepherd and in a pure understanding and mind. Therefore, he is always raging against it through his "scales," both with cunning and villainy, persecution and slander, in order to tear the people away from it, just as he also did through the Jews

against this preaching. On the other hand, as His good sheep we should hold to the Shepherd's voice and know that, when all things fail and the aid and help of all men is nothing, we are secure and are preserved through faith in this Shepherd who laid down His life for us.

Therefore, He makes a conclusion about His sheep—that is, about all of Christendom—about how He knows them and they, in turn, know Him: "I know My own and am known by My own" [John 10:14].

47. This is certainly strange language, and by all means peculiar and ridiculous to the Jews, as much as when He said that He alone is the Shepherd. Without a doubt they scornfully shook their heads at Him and said: "You talk much about Your Shepherd's office and Your sheep. Friend, where do You have Your sheep, and where are they to be found? We have a nation and a flock who cling to the temple and the worship instituted by God, who cling to the Law of Moses. Thus they are contained in a sheepfold, so that we can know and name them. But where are Yours? How are they known? What are their features? Give them a name and sign." "No," He says, "you will not and should not know them as you presume. Your sheep have their sign by which they are known and distinguished, in that they are circumcised, come to the temple at Jerusalem, etc. My sheep have a different mark, but not painted or marked with red ochre and dyes so that it can be seen on the forehead or on the clothes." The pope, following the Jews, also makes and paints such a church and Christians who act and live externally so that everyone can recognize them.

"No," He means to say, "what does it is not that you portray them with the mark and seal which you draw on them or which Moses paints on them. Rather, they are so painted and drawn that no one knows them except I alone."

48. Although Christians also have external signs given by Christ—namely, Baptism, the Sacrament, and the preaching of the Gospel—these can certainly fail (if we are to judge each person in particular). Many have Baptism, hear the Gospel, and go with others to the Sacrament and nevertheless are evil and not Christians. [Christ's sheep] are to be recognized only where they have in their hearts the faith that regards Christ as its Shepherd. But who knows this? You will not see that in me, nor I in you, for no one can look into another's heart. Therefore, it is still true that no one knows these sheep and this flock, or can describe them, except this Shepherd, Christ alone. "So, in turn, only My sheep know Me," He says, "so that they do not let themselves be sent away or torn from Me, but remain with this faith, confession, and preaching: that I am the Shepherd and lay down My life for them against the devil, the world, death, and hell."

49. By doing this, He once again drives out Judaism with its Law and priesthood and, even more, our papacy with all its conduct and takes from all of them the power to rule and judge His flock. He simply will not let them be His and His Church's master. He rejects and condemns all the judgments they want to pass, according to their Moses or another external ordinance and government, on who are Christians or not Christians, and God's people. On the contrary, He tells them that they shall not and cannot know His sheep. Nevertheless, He will have and preserve His Church, even though they do not know or accept either the Shepherd or the sheep, but reject and condemn them as separated from God's people.

50. He then tells us how we are to distinguish the true Church and God's people from that which has the name and reputation but in truth is not the Church. He teaches us that the Church is not and should not be a group which must be formed by external government and ordinance, like the Jewish people by Moses' Law. It does not continue and rule by external human power, nor is it preserved thereby; it is not at all bound to a regular succession or a government of bishops or their successors, as the papacy asserts.

Rather, it is a spiritual assembly which listens to this Shepherd, believes in Him, and is ruled by Him through the Holy Spirit. It is recognized externally only by having His Word, that is, the preaching of the Gospel and His Sacraments. But it is known inwardly only by Him, as in turn it also knows Him through faith and clings to Him when it hears His Word—regardless of whether it observes or even knows anything about that external, Jewish or papistic government and ordinance, or whether it is scattered here and there in the world without any organized, external government. That is the way it was at the time of Christ and the apostles, when they believed in Christ and confessed Him apart from and in opposition to the regular power of the whole priesthood.

51. Therefore, if you really want to know and find and give the definition of what a Christian is or why a man is called a Christian, then you must not gape or look to Moses' Law, the pope's government, or the life and holiness of all people (even the saintliest of them). Rather, you must look only at these words of Christ, where He says: "My sheep know Me" and "My sheep hear My voice" [John 10:27]. Then you can say that a Christian is not someone who lives as a very strict and serious Carthusian or as a hermit, for even Jews and Turks can do that (some of whom live even more strictly). In short, nothing that is in us or can be done by us makes us Christian. What does? Only that we know this man, entrust ourselves to Him, and regard Him as He wants to be regarded, namely, as the Good Shepherd who lays down His life for His sheep and knows them.

52. This knowledge is nothing else than faith, which follows from the preaching office of the Word. The preaching office is derived not from our own thoughts or from people but was brought and revealed through Christ Himself from heaven, as He says to Peter: "Flesh and blood has not revealed this to you" (Matthew 16 [:17]), etc. These two, His Word and our faith, must always agree and be together, for if He did not reveal Himself through the Word or let His voice be heard, then we would know nothing about the Shepherd. In this way and in no other do we become Christians: by hearing this voice alone and knowing no other shepherd nor imagining any other, no matter what it is called or how it glitters, but grasp this image alone in our hearts. So they are all at the same time the sheep of Christ without any distinction. Some have color and form by which they are recognized, but are similar to each other by believing together in this Shepherd and confessing His Word, even though otherwise they differ externally in many ways, and are even scattered here and there throughout the world without order, and cast among other people.

53. From this we have the comfort that whoever knows Christ in this way is surely one of His sheep, already known by Him and chosen as a sheep. He ought not and need not seek or gape further about how he may become a sheep, nor alarm and torment himself with vain thoughts about whether he is predestined or how he can be certain of salvation. Rather, he should cheerfully take comfort and be sure that when he hears Christ's voice, he has Him as the dear Shepherd who knows him, that is, who receives him as His lamb, cares for him, and will protect and deliver him, so that he need have no fear of the devil, hell, and death. He then later further explains this knowledge of His sheep and its power with comforting words, saying, "My sheep hear My voice, and I know them, and they follow Me, and I give them eternal life, and no one will snatch them out of My hand" [John 10:27–28], etc.

54. For greater comfort He adds: "just as the Father knows Me and I know the Father" [John 10:15]. It is a glorious, comforting knowledge through which the Father knows His dear Son with inexpressible, unfathomable, eternal love, as He also publicly testified by the voice from heaven and said, "This is My beloved Son" [Matt. 3:17; 17:5]. For His sake He has shown mercy to the human race and received them into grace, since they had fallen into eternal wrath and damnation and would have been eternally lost, as St. Paul says, "He has been gracious to us in the Beloved" (Ephesians 1 [:6]), etc. So Christ also knows us with a similar inexpressible love, since from the beginning He loved the human race and, therefore, most deeply humbled Himself beneath all men, and even beneath sin and death, and bore God's wrath for us, since He could not tolerate that the devil should keep us in bonds and eternal damnation [cf. Phil. 2:5–8].

55. Because the Father now knows Christ in this way, and Christ knows us, His sheep, in that way, too, there is one kind of knowledge which reaches from the Father through Christ even to us, through which we in turn are to know the Father's heart toward us through Christ. In other words, just as He loves Christ, His Son, so for His sake He bears toward us (who as lambs know Christ, our Shepherd) true fatherly love, so we would know that, because He has given us His Son, He does not want us to be lost or condemned, if only we believe in Him. He cannot hate His Son, but has sent Him from heaven so that He would save us from sin through His blood and death.

56. This is a strikingly high comfort but also a very spiritual comfort, that is, a knowledge secret and hidden from our eyes and minds—believing that both Christ and the Father know us in this way. This has been totally concealed from all human eyes by all kinds of offenses, weakness, and the offensive attitude of the world and of our flesh and blood. It is not only before the world that they take offense at this kingdom of Christ and His Church, because it is not governed, formed, or ordered according to their wisdom as they think it should be, if it were God's government and work. Because it is even completely against their reason, understanding, and thoughts, they both regard the doctrine to be pure folly and deception, and they condemn and persecute all who cling to it and will not follow their judgment.

But it is still more difficult when Christ hides Himself from His Church and acts as if He has forgotten it—or even completely forsaken and condemned it. He leaves it lying oppressed under the cross, subjected to all the cruelty of the world, while its enemies boast, brag, and gloat against it (as we will hear in the next Gospel reading).[8] Moreover, they must tolerate having the devil severely torment them in particular, being frightened within their hearts at their sin and God's wrath, and thus enduring every misfortune and all of hell. Moreover, they must otherwise sense and see weaknesses and defects in both faith and life in themselves and among their people, and whatever other offense the devil can cause.

57. Who is there, now, who knows the sheep or regards them as sheep? They are so deeply buried and overwhelmed with suffering, shame, disgrace, death, scandal, etc., that they are even hidden from themselves. Obviously, no one except Christ alone comforts them and tells them that, irrespective of all this that scandalizes the world and our own flesh and blood, He nevertheless knows His lambs and does not forget or forsake them, as it appears.

58. In order to impress this all the more strongly on us, He adds the comparison and says, "As My Father knows Me" [John 10:15]. It is obviously a high, hidden knowledge with which God the Father knows His dear, only-begotten Son, since He must lie in the manger like the child of the most

8 See sermon for Third Sunday after Easter on John 16:16–23.

miserable beggar, not only unknown by all His people but also cast off and rejected—yes, since He hangs in the air most shamefully and disgracefully, naked and uncovered, between two murderers, as the worst blasphemer and rebel, cursed by God and all the world, so that He Himself must shout out to Him the great, anguished cry: "My God, My God, how have You forsaken Me?" [Matt. 27:46]. Nevertheless, He says here: "My Father knows Me" (even in this suffering, disgrace, and offensive form) as His only Son, sent by Him, "so that I would be the sacrifice and lay down My soul for the salvation and redemption of My sheep. So I know Him in return, and I know that He has not forgotten nor forsaken Me but will lead Me through and out of the shame, cross, and death to eternal honor, life, and glory.

"So My lambs should and will learn to know Me in their misery, disgrace, suffering, and death as their dear, faithful Savior, who has suffered similarly and even laid down My life for them. They will expect of Me, in certainty, that in their troubles they are not forsaken or forgotten by Me (as reason and the world imagine), but that in all this I will wonderfully preserve them and bring them through it to eternal victory and glory."

59. The true knowledge of Christ is that He knows us and we are known to Him. This is a very high wisdom, too far and too deeply covered and hidden from the reason and thinking of the world. It is apprehended only in faith, which must here struggle and strive to preserve this knowledge and increase in it, so that it is not led away from Christ by the great scandal that appears, as He Himself says about this: "Blessed is the one who is not offended at Me" (Matthew 11 [:6]).

60. From this we should also learn (as I have often said) not to judge the kingdom of Christ and His Church by the outward appearance and the judgment of reason and human wisdom. Here you are told that this knowledge of the sheep belongs to Christ alone and that it is as much hidden to reason under the greatest offense as He Himself was when hanging on the cross.

61. For that reason the boldness of the mad, arrogant saints and foolish sophists is to be rebuked; with their impudent opinions they are quick to fault and condemn the Christians who still have the doctrine of the Gospel and faith in purity, if they see any weakness or defect in them somewhere. In their heads they picture a church which must have only perfect, heavenly saints, without any blemish, flaw, or offense—which cannot be in this life.

Even apart from the fact that the devil is always sowing his seed among the true flock with the help of his sects and false saints, there are also many among the Christians who are still weak in faith and have many defects in their lives. Yes, even the greatest saints, who are pure in faith and blameless in life, find and sense in themselves many a weakness and residual, sinful inclinations, at which they themselves lament and have plenty of struggling in order to overcome this offense in themselves. Christ (as the only one who knows His sheep) wants us not to condemn these people, as St. Paul also admonishes: "Who are you to pass judgment on another's servant?" (Romans 14 [:4]), etc.

62. Those who are in the office of the Church—that is, preachers and pastors—especially should learn here how they should act toward the weak and infirm. They are to learn to know them as Christ knows us, that is, not to be bitter and harsh toward them with carrying on and blustering or condemning if everything is not always rigorously correct, but gentle and cautious as they deal with them and bear with their weaknesses until they become stronger. Therefore, the prophet Ezekiel also harshly rebukes the priests and those to whom God committed the office of shepherd because they domineered strictly and harshly over the sheep and did not tend to the weak, did not heal the sick, did not bind up the wounded, did not bring back the straying, and did not seek the lost [Ezek. 34:4]. He says: "I Myself will feed My sheep. I will again seek the lost, bring back the straying, bind up the wounded, and tend to the weak" (Ezekiel 34 [:15–16]), etc.

This shows that among His little flock God also has those who are weak, wounded, straying, and even lost, whom He nevertheless recognizes as His sheep; He does not want them to be rejected, but rather tended, bound up, healed, and brought back. Because they did not do this, but only wanted to rule harshly and strictly according to Moses' government and by the compulsion of the Law, He makes this promise about the kingdom of Christ, in which through the Gospel He will Himself rule and feed His sheep through the true Shepherd, Christ.

> "I have still other sheep that are not of this fold. I must bring them, and they will hear My voice. There will be one flock and one Shepherd." [John 10:16]

63. We spoke about these words above, at the beginning. With them Christ dismisses the Jews who cling to Moses, along with their synagogue, nation, and priesthood. He tells them that, even though they do not accept Him and cling to Him as their Shepherd (which He was made by God and by the testimony of Moses), He would still find sheep both among them and among others (because they were unwilling) who are not yet called God's people and do not know about Moses—that is, the Gentiles. He proclaimed earlier through the prophets: "I will call them My people who are not My people" (Hosea 2 [:23; Rom. 9:25]), etc. And: "I will make you angry with those who are not a nation" [Deut. 32:21; Rom. 10:19].

"These," He says, "I will bring," not so that they have to hear Moses and you, but so that they hear My voice and so through My Word become My sheep, even if they do not come here nor receive circumcision and Moses' government nor even have Me bodily and visibly with them. So they all will become one flock in one Word, faith, and Spirit, under Christ, the only Shepherd, and subject to no one else. This began with His ascension and is being fulfilled daily until the Last Day.

# GOSPEL FOR THE THIRD SUNDAY AFTER EASTER

*John 16:16–23*

*"A little while, and you will see Me no longer; and again a little while, and you will see Me." So some of His disciples said to one another, "What is this that He says to us, 'A little while, and you will not see Me, and again a little while, and you will see Me'; and, 'because I am going to the Father'?" So they were saying, "What does He mean by 'a little while'? We do not know what He is talking about." Jesus knew that they wanted to ask Him, so He said to them, "Is this what you are asking yourselves, what I meant by saying, 'A little while and you will not see Me, and again a little while and you will see Me'? Truly, truly, I say to you, you will weep and lament, but the world will rejoice. You will be sorrowful, but your sorrow will turn into joy. When a woman is giving birth, she has sorrow because her hour has come, but when she has delivered the baby, she no longer remembers the anguish, for joy that a human being has been born into the world. So also you have sorrow now, but I will see you again, and your hearts will rejoice, and no one will take your joy from you. In that day you will ask nothing of Me. Truly, truly, I say to you, whatever you ask of the Father in My name, He will give it to you."*

1. This Gospel reading presents and also pictures for us the high and excellent work that God accomplished when Christ, His only Son, died for us and rose again from the dead. Much has been said about this, and much more could be said. For myself, I feel that the more I study this, the less I understand it. However, because God wants us to remember Him, praise His works and grace, and thank Him for them, it is proper that we speak about this and listen to it as much as we can.

2. The Lord speaks here to His disciples in obscure and veiled words, which they do not understand. Without a doubt He chiefly does this to admonish them and impress on them these words; they sound so unusual so that they will not be forgotten. We retain words which are spoken in a somewhat unusual way much better than those that are spoken in ordinary usage.

3. That is why they repeat it two times ["a little while," John 16:17–18] and ask each other what it must mean. He also repeats it Himself a fourth time [John 16:19], and yet it remains obscure, incomprehensible words to them, until He afterward reveals what He meant. When He rose from the

dead and gave them the Holy Spirit, then they clearly understood it. So we also now understand it, insofar as we hear and read it. However, as for understanding it completely, none of that will happen in this life. Rather, as I said, the longer and the more we learn it, the less we understand, and the more we must learn.

4. God's Word is a different government, and the Holy Scriptures are a different book than human speech and writings. St. Gregory said it well (and found a good proverb): Scripture is the kind of water in which a large elephant must swim, but a lamb can walk through on foot. It speaks clearly and brightly enough for the common people but, on the other hand, so profoundly to the wise and very intelligent that they cannot comprehend it. St. Paul makes this confession about himself (Philippians [3:12]).

5. St. Peter says what was asserted and written in [Scripture] was so great that even the angels have more than enough to do in looking at the great work [1 Pet. 1:12], that Christ, God's Son, became man, suffered death on the cross, but rose again, and now sits at the right hand of the Father as Lord over all, also according to His human nature, and governs and preserves His Church against the devil's wrath and the power of the whole world. We certainly listen to the words about this, but they (the angels) see and understand it and have their eternal joy in it. Just as they in eternity cannot look at it enough, much less can we understand it enough, for it is a work that is imperishable, inexpressible, immeasurable, and inexhaustible.

6. We are speaking here about *cognitio obiectiva*,[1] that is, as it is seen with a glance, as the angels look at it, and as we in the life to come will see it. But in this life we must have a different understanding of it, which is called *cognitio practica*,[2] that we learn to recognize what the power of this work is and what it can do. That happens through faith, which will cease in the life to come, where we will fully know it.

7. So we need to learn here what it means when the Lord says in this text: "A little while, and you will not see Me; and again a little while, and you will see Me" [John 16:19], etc.; and that this means: "You will be sorrowful, and the world will rejoice" [John 16:20], etc., "but your sorrow will become joy." This is an unusual way of speaking: "For a little while you will not see and be sorrowful, and then in a little while you will again see and be cheerful."

8. According to the letter and the history, it is easy to understand what these words mean (especially now). In the confession of our faith, even the children say, "I believe in Jesus Christ, etc., crucified, dead, buried, and risen

---

1 Literally, "objective awareness" or "knowledge of an object."

2 Literally, "practical knowledge."

again from the dead on the third day."[3] These are the two "little whiles" He is talking about here.

But when the matter is dizzying, and we are to test and taste and bring it into life or experience, it becomes very hard to understand, if in ourselves we lose Christ, whom we believe to be God's Son died and risen for us, etc.—that He should be dead for us, as the apostles experienced it during the three days. It is a miserable crucifixion and dying when Christ dies in me and I also die in Him. He says here: "You will not see Me, for I am going away from you"; that is, I am dying, and you will also die because you do not see Me. Thus I will be dead to you and you will be dead to Me. That is an especially high and difficult sorrow.

9. Here on earth there are various kinds of sorrow (just as, in turn, there are various kinds of joy). For example, someone is robbed of his money and goods, is insulted and reviled when innocent, loses father and mother, child and dearest friends, etc. Likewise, the devil distresses someone's heart and torments him with depressive thoughts (as he certainly can), so that he does not know why or how.

However, the true, high sorrow above all sorrow is when the heart loses Christ, so that He is no longer seen and there is no hope of further comfort from Him. There are few who are tested so highly. Not even His disciples were all tested in that way, such as perhaps St. Thomas, Andrew, Bartholomew, etc., who were such good, plain, and simple people. But the other tender hearts—St. Peter, John, Philip, etc.—were affected by these words, when they heard that they would lose Christ and not see Him.

10. This had been preached to these disciples more than to the others, who certainly also believed and knew that Christ died and afterward rose again. For them also it was "a little while," but in a common, insignificant, and childlike way; and it was only a bodily sorrow. But these disciples truly had to feel and put to the test what it meant to lose Christ out of their sight, when He was taken from them not only bodily but also spiritually, and so also to have at the same time twofold distress and sorrow.

They had had not only the bodily joy in Him—that He was with them so long, cared for them, ate and drank with them, and enjoyed delightful, sweet acquaintance and fellowship [with them]—but also He had especially dealt with them in such a pleasant way, borne their weaknesses, and spent time with them more pleasantly and delightfully than any father with his child. He also often let them run on coarsely and even speak nonsense. For that reason it pained them to lose such a pleasant Lord.

11. But [their sorrow] was much greater because they had set their hearts on Him becoming a mighty Lord and King and setting up a government in

---

3 I.e., the Second Article of the Apostles' Creed (Kolb-Wengert, p. 22; *Concordia*, p. 16).

which they together with Him would also become lords and never die. That had so far been the sincere joy and confidence they had in this Savior.

12. Now, however, they lose both completely at once, not only the pleasant association with the Lord but also this beautiful, glorious confidence. Suddenly they fell into the abyss of hell and eternal sorrow. Their Lord was most shamefully put to death, and they themselves must now expect every hour that because of Him they will be seized in the same way. They must now sing the dirge: "How completely is our confidence now lost! We hoped through this man to become great lords and to have all the joy we desired. Now He lies in the grave, and we have fallen into the hands of Caiaphas and the Jews. There are no more miserable and unhappy people on the earth than we."

13. This is the true grief and sorrow about which Christ is properly speaking here, into which God does not lead everyone, and no one easily; but then He gives the comfort to which He points in this Gospel reading. Other bodily suffering and danger can also be called "sorrow," such as when we suffer persecution, prison, and misery for the sake of Christ and must lose goods, honor, and even our lives.

But the greatest of all [sorrows] is when Christ Himself is lost. Then all comfort is gone, and all joy is at an end, and neither heaven nor sun and moon, neither angel nor any creature, not even God Himself, can deliver. Apart from this Savior (Christ), there is no other in heaven or on earth. If He is gone, then all salvation and comfort are gone, and the devil has acquired the opportunity to afflict and alarm the distressed heart. He wants to do this, even under God's name and person, at which he is a master.

14. On the other hand, the joy that is greater than all others is what a heart has in the Savior, Christ. It is also, to be sure, called "joy" when we rejoice in great prosperity, money and goods, power, honor, etc.; but that is all still only childish and foolish joy. Then there is also the shameful, devil's joy which rejoices at another's harm and misfortune. About that Christ says here: "The world will rejoice and laugh up its sleeve at your crying and weeping when they kill Me and afflict you with all misfortune."

Also, in other worldly affairs, there are many who cannot be happy unless they have done harm or seen things go badly for their neighbors. They are just like the poisonous animal, the salamander, which is so cold that it can even live and protect itself in fire.[4] So these people live and thrive on other people's harm. It is the beautiful fruit of the devil when a wonderfully

---

4 "The salamander ... is so intensely cold as to extinguish fire by its contact, in the same way as ice does" (Pliny ["The Elder," 23–79], *Natural History* 10.86 [Loeb 353 (1956), pp. 412–13]). Pliny also offers an entire section on the salamander, which begins "Of all venomous creatures the salamander is the most wicked" and continues with an extensive description of the poisonous character of the salamander (*Natural History* 29.23 [Loeb 418 (1963),

envious person is sad that things go well for someone else and would be glad to lose an eye if that meant that his neighbor would have none.

15. But all this is still nothing compared to the joy which the world (urged on by the devil) has against Christ and His Christians. It rejoices most at the great harm when Christ is crucified, all the apostles are driven out, the Church is knocked to the ground, His Word is silenced, and His name is completely blotted out. This also is a spiritual joy (just as, on the other hand, great sorrow is spiritual)—however, it is not from the Holy Spirit, but from those who belong to the devil in body and soul, and yet are called the wisest, the most learned, and the holiest on earth. In the Jewish nation, these were the high priests, Pharisees, and scribes, who had no peace and knew no joy so long as they heard the name of Christ spoken and His Word resounding, or saw one of His disciples still alive.

As [the godless] say, "It is intolerable to us to hear or to see Him" (Wisdom of Solomon 2 [:15]), etc. When He hangs on the cross, they slander and revile Him with great joy: "If He is God's Son and the King of Israel, let Him climb down from the cross. He trusted in God; let Him deliver Him now" [Matt. 27:40, 42–43], etc. How their hearts leap with joy—what a paradise, what a heavenly kingdom they have, when they see the dear Lord reviled on the cross and put to death. That they themselves have done this is to them only sugar and malmsey.

16. Christ gives this joy to the world, and, on the other hand, He gives His Christians the great sorrow of having to see, hear, and endure that which permeates their hearts, bodies, and lives. Thus He truly pictures the world in an abominable and frightful way as a child of the devil which has no greater joy than to see Christ annihilated and His Christians shamefully condemned and lost.

17. We see just this now in our dear squires, the pope, cardinals, bishops, and their scum, who delight and rejoice when they sense that it is going somewhat badly with us, and would gladly have that fact not hidden but resounding even into the abyss of hell. Dear God, what have we done to them? Do they not have goods and money, power and everything in abundance, of which we have scarcely a crust of bread? Is it not enough that they prevail over us with everything they desire, and we are otherwise afflicted and miserable? Must they be so bitterly hostile to us besides, that they do not want us to have God's grace but want us to burn in the deepest fire of hell?

18. This is a horrible picture and the true fruit of the hellish spirit. They cannot rejoice so greatly over the good nor over worldly or human joy; they do not love gold or silver so much, no string music sounds so good, no

pp. 230–33]). For proverbial reference to the salamander's poison, cf. *Confession concerning Christ's Supper* (1528), LW 37:269 (WA 26:402); *Table Talk* no. 4790, WA TR 4:512.

drink tastes so sweet as when they see the misfortune and distress of righteous Christians. They are so inflamed with hatred and revenge that they enjoy no really happy hour until they can sing: "Praise be to God, the evildoers are at last gone! Now we have rooted out the Gospel." Meanwhile, they have no rest and taste no joy until they have brought this about.

So far they have attempted this and in part accomplished it by all kinds of clever artifices, machinations, and tricks, and God has allowed them to have a little fun with some of them; they labored away slowly on each of them and removed them. But that was still far from cooling their rage, as they had desired.

19. Therefore, Christ now means to say here: "You have now heard both what kind of joy the world will have and what kind of sorrow you will have. Therefore, learn and remember this, so that when it happens and you experience it, you can have patience and lay hold of true comfort in this suffering. So I must let you be tested so that you taste what it means for Me to be lost and dead in your hearts, so that you learn to understand this mystery and secret a little. Otherwise you will not finish studying Me, for it will be too high for you to finish learning the high work that God's Son goes to the Father, that is, dies for you and rises, so that He also brings you to heaven. If I do not have you tested now and then, you will remain foolish and finally become good for nothing.

20. "Therefore," He says, "you must agree and submit to being tested about what this *modicum* ('a little while' [John 16:16–19]) is, and yet not despair and perish. That is why I tell you ahead of time that it must happen. You must have and suffer such sorrow (both inwardly and outwardly, that is, in body and soul). However, when it happens and the little hour begins when you have nothing more with which to sustain yourself, but have lost both Me and God, then remember My words, which I am now speaking to you: 'It is only a little while.' If you can only learn this saying and remember these words—'a little while' and 'again a little while'—then there will be no danger.

21. "Of course, the first *modicum* ('a little while'), when you now see that I am still with you until I go away from you, is still to be suffered and overcome. But the second 'little while' until you see Me again will be especially long and difficult. It is the true hour of sorrow, when for you I will be dead, along with all the joy, comfort, and confidence you had from Me, and you yourselves will be totally lost.

"However, dear little children, only remember and do not at all forget what I am telling you now: 'It will not last forever.' I must be lost and unseen for a little while. You must now experience and learn this. But remember only this much, that I have called it 'a little while,' and in My eyes it is only a little, short hour, even though in your hearts and feelings it is not a little while, but a great while, even an eternal, great while and a great, eternal while. According to your feelings you will be unable to think differently than that I have been taken away from you and that you have lost everything, because I am the eternal good and the eternal comfort. When that is gone, then there is only an eternal and no longer a little while, namely, eternal sorrow and death."

22. So He preaches here for the comfort of His disciples and Christians when they are tested by God with this temptation, whether it happens inwardly or outwardly, bodily or spiritually, especially in the highest point which is called losing Christ from the heart. They are to learn this passage, and if they can do no more, retain this drop of lavender water to refresh and strengthen their hearts: "My Lord Christ has said it will be only a little while."

Even if I now have lost Him and know no joy at all, but lie languishing in sheer sorrow, yet I will use that drop and retain this tonic: that He will not remain lost to me. He says, "It will only be a little hour," even though it seems to me to be great, long, and eternal. He will return, as He says here and in John 14 [:18]: "I will not leave you as orphans; I will return to you," etc., so that I am to have in Him eternal comfort and joy instead of this little hour of sorrow.

23. On the other hand (Christ goes on to say), you must allow the world to rejoice over your suffering and sorrow, even though it has no reason for it except sheer devilish jealousy, by which it is so highly blinded, embittered, and soured that it has no joy until it sees you stumble and perish. That is their heart's joy and delight—they regard it as a heavenly, eternal joy—as they then say: "Let us now see if God will deliver Him. If He is God's Son, then let Him come down from the cross" [Matt. 27:42–43], etc. It was as if they would say, "He is now gone, and He is at His end, forever!"

24. But look at what follows after this. "Just as," He says, "you shall not be eternally deprived of seeing Me, nor remain in your sorrow, so they also shall not eternally rejoice at your misfortune; rather, it shall also be for them only a short hour and (as they say) 'like a dance at high Mass.' I will return to you soon and make it worse and more bitter for them than it has ever been before." This was fulfilled in them after the resurrection of Christ, since the Jews had no more bitter suffering than that they must hear of our Lord Christ and see Him. Apart from that, it pleases them somewhat to slander Christ and His mother, Mary, and us Christians most shamefully. But they can never again have true joy, even though they would like to have it and still always hope that their messiah will come and root out all Christians.

25. So also our Caiaphas and Judas, the pope with all his rabble, continually take comfort in the hope that we will be rooted out. However, they cannot be happy, because we live and the Gospel spreads. Nothing in which people take delight helps them at all. Some are so depraved that they cannot

cease their raging and raving until we are all dead. When that happens, they will for once be happy, but it will still not be the kind of joy they want. Even though we are dead, the Gospel will still remain [cf. Isa. 40:8], and others will come in our place, and that will again be new grief for them.

26. The Turk also intends to root out Christ and to set up his Mohammed in all the world; he rejoices whenever it starts to happen. However, the joy for which he strives will never happen. This, our Lord (whom [the Turk] himself nevertheless highly exalts and must regard to be a great prophet), will keep this [joy] from him and finally make it salty and quite bitter for him through the great work of His death and resurrection, by which He tramples underfoot sin, death, and the devil. God accomplished this through Him and announced it previously in the Scriptures; on that basis the dear prophets and fathers died in this joy, as Christ says about Abraham (John 8 [:56]).

27. If [Abraham] received this when it had not yet happened, but was only in the Word and promise, how much more can and will he receive it in the future after it has happened and has been spread in the world and even in heaven by the angels! Neither the pope nor the Turk will and can suppress and blot that out. They can certainly suppress it and think that they are tasting sugar when they do Christendom a little harm, but they shall never obtain the joy for which they hope and thirst.

28. They can rejoice for a while (Christ says [John 16:20]), but not longer than while you are in sorrow. That is an especially brief joy, just as your sorrow is brief and is only a little while. It will soon be changed into joy, and into the kind of joy that no one will take away from you. Without a doubt, their joy will also become sorrow which will not end.

29. However, you will be unable to have enough of your joy here on earth, nor will it be of full measure, enough to quench your thirst. Rather, you will have only a sample, a taste, or a sip. [This joy] is too great and can never be exhausted, just as the work that produces this joy is far too great for us to finish learning it. God mingles and mixes things on the earth so that those who should by right rejoice must have much suffering and sorrow, while, on the other hand, those who should be sorrowful have joy and good days.

Yet this happens in such a way that their outward joy becomes salty. They cannot acquire the true inner joy that they desire, and so they also lose their outward joy. They cannot take joy in their goods, power, honor, pleasure, and luxury, and they cannot lay their heads down in rest until they see that Christ is dead and His Christians are exterminated. They are always poor, miserable people whom we can easily pity. The worst is that, because of their jealousy and hatred, they cannot have their temporal joy pure as they would like. Through themselves we have already been avenged far too much toward them, for how could they have more misfortune and do themselves greater harm than that they themselves lose and destroy their joy?

30. On the other hand, we also have sorrow, both outwardly and inwardly (when Christ hides Himself from us), but not, like them, because of jealousy and hatred toward our neighbor, but because we do not have the highest good, Christ. But then sugar is already mixed into the sorrow, for Christ says: "Dear friend, only wait a little while. It will not be an eternal sorrow, but only a brief sorrow, and soon it will be better. We are only dealing with a little hour."

31. I hear these words, but the sorrow (when it is there) so deeply oppresses my heart that I do not feel this comfort, and I think that it is impossible that it should cease. Nevertheless, I am kept from falling away from Christ to that crowd. Although I still have trouble and danger, yet the sorrow must not be completely filled with bitterness, just as, on the other side, their joy is not completely filled with sweetness and sugar. Rather, just as their joy is always corrupted by wormwood and gall, so this sorrow still has sugar and honey with it.

32. Therefore, let us listen to Christ and learn to understand His language, so that we do not judge according to our feelings, as if we were eternally lost and it would never end. "You feel and think that way," He says, "I certainly know it. But listen to what I say to you and learn only this word *modicum*, 'a little while.' You must feel this, but it will not harm you and will not last long." In that way sorrow has already been covered over with sugar and alleviated.

Afterward, when the little hour is past and has been overcome, then we experience what He says, "Your sorrow will become joy" [John 16:20]. Then a true, heartfelt joy begins, and the heart sings an eternal "alleluia" and "Christ is arisen," which will be completely perfect only in the life to come, without any lack and without end.

33. Thus this Gospel reading presents to us both the articles of the death and resurrection of Christ and how these must be learned and used "practically," in our work and experience, not only heard with the ears and spoken with the mouth. So when we feel this power working in us, then both body and soul are changed through it.

Namely, when Christ dies in me and I in Him, that is a great change of life into death. However, then I must learn to cling with faith to the words Christ says—"a little while"—and not only hear but also take to heart that it will not last forever. Rather, there will be a change from death to life when Christ again rises and lives in me and I become alive in Him. Then it is said, "I will see you again, and your heart will rejoice, and no one will take your joy from you" [John 16:22], etc. Every Christian should be equipped for this when it is necessary, for he must experience something of this either in life or at the hour of death. He is to be equipped so that then he can remember these words of Christ and not let this comfort be torn from his heart. Amen.

34. Whatever more is to be said about the text of this Gospel reading you can read for yourself in the explanation of the three chapters of John, the sermons Christ preached to His disciples at the Last Supper, in which this and the following Sunday's Gospel reading are treated at length.

# GOSPEL FOR THE FOURTH SUNDAY AFTER EASTER

*John 16:5–15*

*But now I am going to Him who sent Me, and none of you asks Me, "Where are You going?" But because I have said these things to you, sorrow has filled your heart. Nevertheless, I tell you the truth: it is to your advantage that I go away, for if I do not go away, the Helper will not come to you. But if I go, I will send Him to you. And when He comes, He will convict the world concerning sin and righteousness and judgment: concerning sin, because they do not believe in Me; concerning righteousness, because I go to the Father, and you will see Me no longer; concerning judgment, because the ruler of this world is judged. I still have many things to say to you, but you cannot bear them now. When the Spirit of truth comes, He will guide you into all the truth, for He will not speak on His own authority, but whatever He hears He will speak, and He will declare to you the things that are to come. He will glorify Me, for He will take what is Mine and declare it to you. All that the Father has is Mine; therefore I said that He will take what is Mine and declare it to you.*

1. We have often heard the meaning of this Gospel reading elsewhere. The problem is that people do not always understand the words as speaking about things we know. Therefore, we will explain it a little, so that people see that the very same things are in these words which nearly all other Gospel readings contain.

2. This is a part of the beautiful sermon that the Lord Christ preached after His Last Supper with His disciples. He especially wants to comfort His dear disciples about His departure, because He is now about to die and to leave them alone in danger and distress, in the hostility of the world, in persecution, and in death for His sake. He Himself announces to them with many words that they would be excommunicated, and those who killed them would boast that they were serving God [John 16:2]. It was very difficult and frightening for them to hear this, and they became distressed on account of it, both because they were about to lose their dear Lord and because they would be left in such misery and distress.

Therefore, it was necessary for them to be comforted about this, as Christ then did through these three chapters [John 14–16] of His last sermon with all diligence and faithfulness. The summary of it is that, in place of the loss from His departure, He promises to send the Holy Spirit, who will both comfort and strengthen their hearts, and then set up the kingdom of Christ and extend it throughout the world. He tells them plainly what His kingdom is all about, what it consists of, and what the Holy Spirit will accomplish in the world through them.

3. That is why He first says: "I know and plainly see, dear disciples, that you are very frightened and distressed because I told you that I am going away. My going away should abundantly delight you, for in place of Me you will have the consolation of the Holy Spirit and in addition the power by which He will accomplish through you what I cannot do now while I am present with you. By this bodily mission I am required to suffer and die, and so make My way to the Father. Afterward I will send the Holy Spirit. Through you He will do many greater things than can now happen through Me. He will place on you a great and excellent office and work, through which My kingdom will be spread in the world."

4. He first points out what His kingdom on earth shall be, in order to take away from them their old deeply rooted delusion about the external, worldly dominion and government over the Jewish people and all the world in this life. Against this He has said plainly enough and in many words that He would go away, leave the world, and no longer be seen, etc. However, if He dies and leaves the world, He cannot ever in a worldly way govern and rule externally and visibly, like a king and emperor on earth.

Likewise, He made this still clearer when, with so many words both before and after this text, He announced to them how things would be for them after His departure, namely, that they will be hated, persecuted, excommunicated, and even killed by their own people [John 16:2]. Likewise, they will mourn and howl and be afraid in the world; and the world, on the other hand, will be confident and cheerful [John 16:20]. This does not at all agree with their hope for a worldly kingdom on earth; rather, they should expect just the opposite. Nevertheless, they must know that He wants to have and preserve His kingdom in the world; for that purpose, then, He promises the Holy Spirit.

5. What kind of a kingdom is it, and how is it ruled? He shows this in the words He speaks: "The Holy Spirit will rebuke the world" [John 16:8]. It is not to be a government conceived and organized in a worldly way by human wisdom, power, might, law, and order, but a government of the Holy Spirit, or a spiritual kingdom, in which Christ rules invisibly and not with external, bodily power, but only through the Word, which the Holy Spirit will preach and through which He will work in people's hearts. "The Holy Spirit," He says, "will rebuke the world." This does not mean compelling the world with armor and weapons and worldly power, but using an oral word or preaching

office. That means that the Word of God, or of the Holy Spirit, sent by Christ, should go through the world and attack it, so that it is proper to say that the world has been rebuked, that is, not only some people, one or two races or countries, but both Jews and Gentiles, the learned, the wise, the saints, who have conceived their government most beautifully and laudably.

6. By "the world," He does not mean the ordinary common crowds and mobs, but the best and most laudable part in the world, whose external government has nothing to be rebuked. He means especially those who want to be holy above all [others], such as the Jews, who were called God's people and had Moses' Law. About them Christ said previously that they hate Him and His people without cause, as is written in their Law [John 15:25].

7. So Christ gives His apostles power and might, and even a mandate over all the world, which is to be exposed to their preaching and must listen to the apostles. He strengthens them and comforts them for this, because their office is despised by the world and not respected, since they are plain, ordinary people. Moreover, even apart from that, they are hated, oppressed, and must suffer in the world, when their reprimands run counter to the world. Nevertheless, their office will have power, force, and vigor, so that the world must listen to them and leave them alone, not abolished, and unrestrained— irrespective of how they are angry and storm against them with persecuting, banishing, and killing, with all the power and might not only of the world but also of the whole kingdom of hell.

8. "Therefore," He says, "you really should not be frightened of this and distressed that I am going away from you bodily. By doing this I will give you something much better than you had before while you were with Me. Then you will accomplish much greater and more glorious things than can now happen, namely, the Holy Spirit will accomplish through you what belongs to My kingdom much more gloriously and strongly than you now think. Then you will not, as now, think and strive for how you may become lords on earth and have great kingdoms under you. All of that is transitory. That is of no interest to God; it has always produced more evildoers than godly people. Rather, He will put you into such a government that you will judge all people's consciences, and what is highest in the world (that is, all its wisdom and holiness) will be subject to you. You will pass judgment on it, rebuke, and condemn, so that no one who does not want to listen to your words and obey them will be able to escape sin, death, and hell, nor come into heaven."

9. So He will also give you this comfort and courage, so that you will not, as now, be frightened or afraid to death of the threats, anger, and bluster of the world against your preaching, but confidently continue to rebuke, irrespective of what both the world and the devil can do and are doing against it with persecution, murder, and all the power of hell.

10. This is the promise about the work which the Holy Spirit will begin in the kingdom of Christ. It is the teaching office of the apostles; its character is that it must rebuke the world however it finds it (outside of Christ), no one excepted, great, small, learned, wise, holy, of high or low estate, etc. This means, in short, to invite the world's wrath onto themselves and to begin the quarrel and to be punched in the mouth for it. The world, which has the government on earth, will not and cannot tolerate it when people will not let their ideas be right. That is why there must be persecution, and one part must yield to the other, the weakest to the stronger. However, because the office of the apostles is to be nothing but a teaching office, it cannot operate with worldly might and power, and the world retains its external kingdom and power against the apostles. But, on the other hand, the apostles' office of rebuking the world, because it is the office and work of the Holy Spirit, will not be suppressed, but will overcome and pierce through everything, as Christ has promised: "I will give you a mouth and wisdom, which all your opponents will not withstand" [Luke 21:15].

11. The Holy Spirit has certainly previously rebuked the world through preaching, ever since its beginning (for Christ always rules and "is the same Christ yesterday and today and forever," Hebrews 13 [:8]). He did this through the holy fathers, Adam, Noah, Abraham, Moses, Elijah, Elisha, and John the Baptist. This rebuke is still preserved by divine power.

However, now is when it will really begin. Christ wants to institute a public rebuke, which will happen not only among the Jewish people but also over all the world until the Last Day. This will be much more powerful and piercing, and hearts will be struck and wounded. (It was said about the first sermon of St. Peter on Pentecost that the apostles' sermon pierced their heart, Acts 2 [:37], and so they were enlightened from their blindness and were converted.) However, if they will not accept this preaching, then it will have the effect of condemning and offending them, so that they fall and are hurled into eternal ruin. So it is a power unto life and salvation for the believers, but a preaching and power unto death for the others, as St. Paul says (2 Corinthians 3 [:6; 2:16; 1 Cor. 1:18]).

12. Now, what will the Holy Spirit rebuke, or about what will He teach? He tells us this plainly in the words He speaks:

*"And when He comes, He will rebuke the world concerning sin and concerning righteousness and concerning judgment." [John 16:8]*

13. This means taking a lot in one bite and loading plenty [of trouble] onto themselves: the poor beggars, the apostles, will interfere in the world and severely scold everything it does. Obviously, they must have a large back and strong supports. He shows that this rebuking is not to be a joke, nor is

it concerning frivolous, insignificant matters—not even concerning government, land, people, money, and goods—but concerning the highest thing by which the world's government exists, which is its reputation for wisdom, justice, and its judgment or punishment, especially in the high matters that concern worship and what avails before God.

14. Whatever concerns the earthly government over house and home, money and goods has nothing to do with the Holy Spirit and Christ. He lets their wisdom, rights, and order go and remain as they are, for the world has the command to rule and judge what is to be praised or rebuked in such things. So also He does not rebuke the offices and various estates of the world, which are God's creation and order. Rather, the reason He rebukes the world (that is, the people who rule in their government most laudably) is that they want to interfere in God's matters and government with their reason and wisdom, and they presume to find and judge how people are to serve God. They think that God must let whatever they assert be right and pleasing to Him.

15. The Holy Spirit's rebuking is against this, and it does not happen piecemeal regarding certain works and activities, but He destroys and condemns everything that reason and worldly wisdom undertake. In summary, He rebukes and faults them just for that point where they refuse to be rebuked, but instead want to praised and glorified for teaching and acting correctly. He accuses them of sin and shame with all their glory, and openly blames them for knowing nothing at all about these things and being unable to teach people how to recognize sin, how to be freed from it, how they are to be helped to righteousness, and how wrong is to be rebuked. What good can any longer be left when they boastfully knock down all of this as with a thunderbolt? He Himself explains what each of these three points means and how we are to preach them. First, He says:

*"Concerning sin, because they do not believe in Me." [John 16:9]*

16. The world itself must confess that it does not understand anything Christ says about these three points. Who of all the wise and learned on earth has ever heard this before? What reason has produced this? And in what books is it written that "sin" means not believing in this Jesus of Nazareth? Does not Moses himself and all the world call "sin" that which happens against the Law, whether it deals with doing or refraining, in words or deeds or even thoughts? Now the baby has been named, and the article has been decided and fixed by the Holy Spirit: the sin of the world is that it does not believe in Christ—not that there is no sin against the Law except this, but that this is the true chief sin which condemns all the world, even if it could be charged with no other sin.

17. So now this reprimand begins, which is to bring people to the true knowledge of salvation. The first [point] is that it makes all people—learned, high, and wise—into sinners: sinners because they do not believe in Christ. So even those who are blameless before the world and also seriously strive to live according to the Law and the Ten Commandments are subjected to God's wrath, and the verdict of damnation and eternal death is pronounced on them (for that is what it means to "rebuke concerning sin"). Such were Paul before his conversion and Nicodemus at first and similarly many others among the Jews. St. Paul testifies that they have zeal to serve God and followed righteousness, and yet they did not obtain righteousness [Rom. 10:2; 9:30–31]. Thus this word "sin" briefly and simply includes however people live and whatever they do without faith in Christ.

18. Here you will say: "How does this happen? Is it, then, sin to live obediently, honorably, and chastely according to the Ten Commandments, as well as not kill, not commit adultery, not steal, not lie and deceive?" Answer: Surely not! However, it is still not enough, and the Ten Commandments still have not been kept, even if externally in works we do not act against them. God's commandment not only demands external conduct and appearances, but it also lays hold of the heart and demands its perfect obedience. Therefore, it also judges a person not only according to his external life and behavior but also according to his innermost heart. However, the world does not understand and pay attention to that, for it knows nothing more than public, external sins, such as murder, adultery, theft, and whatever the lawyers label as "sin" and rebuke. But it does not know and does not see the true problem and its root, such as despising God; the innate, inward impurity of the heart; disobedience toward God's will; etc. These things are and remain in all people who are not sanctified through Christ.

Everyone finds this in himself, if he will confess it, no matter how good he is (even the true saints ardently lament about this). Even if he wanted to keep God's Law, his flesh and blood—that is, his whole nature, with heart and all members—strive against it. St. Paul says, "I find another law in my members, which struggles against the law of the mind and takes me captive in the law of sin" (Romans 7 [:23]), etc. This happens much more in those who are without grace and the Holy Spirit, who outwardly live blamelessly only from fear of punishment or because of boasting and vainglory, and yet would rather do the contrary if they did not fear hell or punishment and shame. The heart always remains hostile to the Law and strives against it with inward disobedience.

19. Now, because no one fulfills God's Commandments and can be without sin before God, and so all people through the Law are condemned under God's wrath to eternal damnation, God found a remedy for this evil.

He decided to send His Son into the world so that He would become a sacrifice for us, atone for our sins by shedding His blood and dying, take away from us God's wrath (which otherwise no creature could appease), and bring us the forgiveness of sins. Moreover, He would give us the Holy Spirit, so that we could get and receive this, begin to become new people, and so come out of sin and death into righteousness and eternal life.

20. This is what He now has done, and He has commanded us to preach it through the Gospel. He requires from all people (as we heard in the Easter sermons[1]) repentance (that is, true knowledge of their sins and serious fright before God's wrath) and faith that in this repentance God wants to forgive their sins for the sake of His Son. Whoever now believes this preaching has forgiveness of sins through this faith and is in God's grace. Even though he does not satisfy the Law, yet his remaining sin is not reckoned to him but is under forgiveness. Together with this faith the Holy Spirit is also given to him, so that he acquires love and the desire to do good and to resist sin, etc. So he is no longer condemned by the Law (as a sinner), even though he does not fulfill the Law completely. Rather, he is accepted and kept before God through grace and forgiveness as if he had no sin.

21. But, on the other hand, whoever does not have faith cannot be freed from sin nor escape God's wrath. He has no forgiveness and remains under damnation, even if to the utmost he seeks to live according to the Law. He cannot fulfill it, and in addition he does not accept Christ, who brings forgiveness and gives the fulfillment [of the Law] to believers and who, moreover, gives them the power to begin to keep the Law from the heart.

22. Therefore, wherever this preaching is not accepted, sin and damnation must certainly remain there. Yes, then this unbelief becomes the true chief sin. If faith in Christ were present, then the sins would all be forgiven; but now, since they do not want to accept this Savior by faith, they are justly condemned in their sins. It does not help them at all if they observe many works of the Law and outward worship, reasoning that if they sinned with works, then they will pay for them with works or put away sin and merit God's grace. By doing that, they do nothing else than either presume to blot out sin with sin, even to atone for big sins with little ones, or commit big [sins] in order to put away the others.

They go on in disobedience and sins against God's Commandments and are in such blindness that they neither see nor pay attention to it. Without repentance and fear of God's wrath, they still have the audacity and arrogance of wanting to please God with their own works and merits. Besides all that, they go on not only to despise this preaching about Christ, which admonishes

---

1 See sermon for Easter Tuesday on Luke 24:36–47; and Easter Tuesday—Another Sermon on Luke 24:36–47.

to repentance and faith, but even to persecute it. That alone would be enough (even if they had no other sins and fulfilled the whole Law) to bring eternal wrath and damnation on them.

23. So the Holy Spirit rightly and justly rebukes as sinners and condemned people all who do not have faith in Christ. If [faith] is not present, then other sins in abundance must follow, so that people despise and hate God and so are fully disobedient to the entire First Table [Exod. 20:3–8]. Whoever does not know God in Christ cannot expect anything good from Him nor call on Him from the heart nor honor His Word. Rather, he holds to the devil's lies, persecutes and slanders true doctrine, and continues in obstinacy and defiance, so that he even reviles the Holy Spirit. Accordingly, he is also disobedient to the other commandments in his station and life, so that he does to no one what he should do, has no true, sincere love, kindness, gentleness, patience, desire for chastity and righteousness, faithfulness, and truth in his heart, but only works at the opposite, except where he has to fear disgrace or punishment.

24. Look at how unbelief must be followed by the dragon's tail of the devil and all of hell [Rev. 12:9]! The reason is that whoever does not believe in Christ has already turned away and completely separated from God. Therefore, he cannot have the Holy Spirit nor conceive any good thoughts nor have a true, sincere desire to live according to God's will, even if he outwardly pretends like a hypocrite, behaves and acts differently, so that he is not reproached or rebuked. He is like an evil, badly behaved household servant who is hostile to his master and only does what he does not want to do because he must. When he gets the opportunity, he does nothing good. Those are the excellent, beautiful fruits that all come from this source and root, when people will not accept and listen to Christ as the Savior given to us by God to blot out our sins and take God's wrath away from us.

25. So here you can see depicted what the world is like, namely, nothing other than a great crowd of such wicked, stubborn people who will not believe Christ but despise God's Word, praise and accept the devil's temptation, and defiantly run against all the Commandments of God. They take all God's benefits and blessings, and then repay Him with ingratitude and slander. Yet in all of this they want to escape being rebuked or reproached; instead, they want to be called laudable, good, holy people. They are like the Jews who crucified Christ and persecuted His apostles, and then wanted to have the glory of having done God a great service. Therefore, against this, the Holy Spirit must oppose the world and always use and work at His rebuking office through His divine power and might until the Last Day.

26. He has not begun to rebuke with the intention of ceasing and letting His mouth be plugged. Rather, He must continue rebuking in the devil's

kingdom, since there is nothing good there, and knock all of it under God's wrath and damnation, irrespective of how the world is angry and blusters about it. Some might be brought by this rebuking to repentance and faith, which is why this preaching was begun. However, the others, who do not want to be rebuked, must nevertheless be convicted and condemned by this preaching. All flesh and blood must be rebuked, either unto salvation or unto damnation. The verdict which Christ commanded to be preached to all creatures must stand: "Whoever believes will be saved, but whoever does not believe will be condemned" [Mark 16:16], etc.

That is enough about the first point of the Holy Spirit's preaching. The second point follows:

*"Concerning righteousness, because I am going to the Father, and from this time you do not see Me." [John 16:10]*

27. The world is rebuked not only because it has sin but also because it does not know how to become righteous[2] and what justice or righteousness is. However, He is not talking here about the justice of which the philosophers and lawyers speak, by which they mean keeping the civil or imperial laws and doing what reason teaches. Rather, He is talking about the righteousness that avails before God or that He regards as righteousness. Now, what kind of righteousness is this? Of what does it consist? "It is," He says, "that I am going to the Father, and from this time you do not see Me." The world regards this as unintelligible and ridiculous speech. If the first statement was strange and obscure (that the world's sin is that it does not believe in Him), then this one sounds much more peculiar and unintelligible (that this alone is righteousness: that He is going to the Father and will not be seen).

28. What should all the world say about this—the world that strives for justice and wants to be righteous before God? They are Jewish, Turkish, and papistic saints, who stumble against this as an offensive, even a foolish, doctrine. How can it be that all good works, devotion, good intentions, fine obedience, and the serious and strict life of many people are nothing at all before God? Why does He give such a peculiar and absurd definition, that we should be righteous before God because He is going to the Father and we will not see Him? How does it harmonize to be justified from what we cannot see or feel?

29. Well, you hear how strongly and powerfully He concludes that this alone is the righteousness that He calls "righteousness," and the world is rebuked because it does not have this. It is as if He would say: "Why are

---

2 *from*, sometimes translated "pious" or "godly." In Luther's usage it usually means simply "good" or "righteous."

you disputing so long and so much about good works, holy living, and what you think about how we are to be justified? If you do not grasp that I am going to the Father, then all of this is and counts for nothing before God. If you strive to death and invent, think and study, and live and strain for righteousness with all your powers, you will still not think it out or hit on it. There must be another righteousness than what you understand and undertake, namely, that you should undertake to be obedient to the Law and live according to it. It must be far and high above all of that, where there is no law or commandment at all, or any human work and life, but only what I do, namely, that I am going to the Father," etc.

30. How does that happen? Answer: In the previous section, we heard that all people are rebuked concerning sin. From this it follows (as was explained) that no one fulfills the Law or the Ten Commandments. If someone did fulfill them, then he would obviously not be rebuked as a sinner and would be called and be righteous through this obedience or fulfilling of the Law, as St. Paul says: "If a law had been given which could give life, then righteousness would truly come from the Law. But Scripture has enclosed all under sin" (Galatians 3 [:21–22]), etc. Because no one can fulfill the Law, we have no righteousness from the Law in and of ourselves with which we can stand before God against His wrath and judgment. Rather, if we are to come before God, then we must have a different righteousness, the righteousness of another, which God regards and which is pleasing to Him.

31. The rebuke concerning sin applies to all human life and conduct on earth, so that even the saints and Christians must still let this rebuke apply to their best life and work and confess that they have sin that would still be wrong and damnable if it were judged according to God's commandment and before His judgment seat. The prophet David, who was holy and full of good works, prays and says, "Enter not into judgment with Your servant, for no one living is righteous before You" (Psalm 143 [:2]); and St. Paul says, "I am unaware of anything against myself, but I am not for that reason righteous" (1 Corinthians 4 [:4]). The only reason that they are not condemned like the others is that they accept this rebuke, confess and lament that they have sin, believe in Christ, and seek the forgiveness of sins through Him. In this way they have the righteousness of another, which is entirely the Lord Christ's own work, power, and merit. This is what He calls "going to the Father."

32. These words—"because I am going to the Father"—contain the whole work of our redemption and salvation, for which God's Son was sent from heaven and which He did for us and still does until the end, namely, His suffering, death, resurrection, and His whole reign in the Church. This "going to the Father" means nothing else than that He surrenders Himself as a sacrifice by shedding His blood and dying in order to pay for sin. Afterward He again

conquers through His resurrection; brings sin, death, and hell under His power; and, alive, sits down at the right hand of the Father, where He invisibly rules over everything in heaven and earth and gathers and extends His Christendom through the preaching of the Gospel. As an eternal Mediator and High Priest, He intercedes and prays to the Father for those who believe, because they still have weakness and sin remaining in them. Moreover, He gives the power and strength of the Holy Spirit to conquer sin, the devil, and death.

33. The Christians' righteousness before God means and is that Christ goes to the Father, that is, suffers for us, rises, and so reconciles us to the Father that for His sake we have the forgiveness of sins and grace. That is not at all because of our work or merit, but only because of His going, which He does for our sake. That is the righteousness of another (for which we have done or merited nothing nor can merit anything), presented and given to us as our own to be our righteousness, by which we please God and are His dear children and heirs.

34. But it is only through faith that this righteousness, which was presented to us, is in us and that we can take comfort in it as our treasure and chief possession. It must ever be received and accepted by us. Now, it cannot be grasped other than with the heart, which clings to the "going" of Christ and firmly believes that for His sake it has forgiveness and redemption from sin and death. It is not something external that we can accomplish with human works, ordinances, or exercises, but a high, hidden treasure which cannot be observed with the eyes or comprehended by our senses (as He also Himself says, "Because from this time you do not see Me" [John 16:16]), but it must only be believed.

35. So now, all at once, what all the world seeks, disputes, and asks without end—namely, how we can become righteous before God—is ended and cut off. Each one says something different; one teaches to do this, another that; and yet none has ever attained it, even if they have heard, learned, and practiced every doctrine of the Law and good works. We justly should ask this Master Christ and listen to what He says about it (as each one should wish to do; if this preaching were not present, they would gladly run to the ends of the world for it). Of course, everyone hopes that He will add something to it that we must do, something much higher and better than all others have taught.

36. But what does He say? Not one word about our deeds and life. Rather, He says: "All of that is still not the righteousness that avails before God. But if you want to be righteous before God, then you must have something else, namely, what neither you nor any people are or can do, which is this: that I am going to the Father. This means that no one will be justified before God

except by and on account of this, that I die and rise again." It is the "going" which alone accomplishes that God graciously accepts a man and regards him as righteous, if he clings to Christ with faith.

37. Therefore, these words are to be carefully noted, in which Christ is such an astonishing man speaking against the understanding and ideas of all people, especially of the wise and holy. All of them, when they speak with each other about what it means to be righteous, can talk about nothing else than what they call *justitia formalis*, that is, the sort of virtue that is in ourselves or which we ourselves do or which is called our work and obedience.

38. Then again you say: "What about the doctrine of good works? Is this, then, to be nothing? Is it not beautiful and laudable when someone seeks to keep the Ten Commandments and is obedient, chaste, honorable, and truthful?" Answer: Yes, indeed! We should do all of this, and it is also a good doctrine and life, but only if we leave it in its place where it belongs and keep the two doctrines distinct, about how we become righteous before God and how and why we should do good works. Although the doctrine of good works must be proclaimed, yet alongside of it and even before it we must also carefully teach (so that the doctrine of the Gospel and of faith remains pure and unadulterated) that all our works, no matter how good and holy they may be, are not the treasure or merit because of which we become acceptable and pleasing to God and obtain eternal life. Rather, it is this alone: that Christ is going to the Father, and through His "going" acquires this for us, and gives and shares with us His righteousness, innocence, and merits. Thus He begins His kingdom in us so that we (who believe in Him) are redeemed by His power and Spirit from sin and death and shall live with Him eternally, etc. It is not the kind of righteousness that only remains here on earth and then ceases, but a new righteousness that lasts forever in the life to come with God, just as Christ lives and rules above eternally.

39. For this reason I have often said, in order to speak and judge correctly about these matters, that we must carefully distinguish between a good man (what the philosophers call *bonus vir*) and a Christian. We also praise being a good man, and there is nothing more laudable on earth. It is God's gift just as much as sun and moon, grain and wine, and all creation. However, we do not mix and brew those things into each other, but let a good man have his praise before the world, and say: "A good man is certainly an excellent, precious man on earth, but he is not for that reason a Christian." He could even be a Turk or a heathen (as formerly some were highly renowned). It cannot be otherwise than that among so many wicked people a good man must at times be found. However, no matter how good he is, despite that goodness he still is and remains Adam's child, that is, an earthly man under sin and death.

40. However, when you inquire about a Christian, then you must go much higher, for he is a different man. He is not called Adam's child and does not have father and mother on earth, but is God's child, an heir and nobleman in the kingdom of heaven. He is called a Christian because he clings with his heart to this Savior who has gone up to the Father, and he believes that for His sake and through Him he has God's grace, eternal redemption, and life. This is neither captured nor seized, attained nor learned by our life, virtue, and work (from which we are called good people on earth), nor by righteousness according to the Law and the Ten Commandments. As has been said, these things are also necessary and are found in every Christian, but they are far from obtaining this chief point and righteousness about which Christ is here speaking and which He calls "righteousness."

41. Even if a man his whole life long did these things and did everything he could more and more, he still could not arrive at the point that he could be certain that God is pleased with these things and is truly gracious to him. So in all of life the heart always remains uncertain and in doubt, as all experienced consciences must testify. Even the monks testify with their books, in which they publicly taught that we should doubt, for no person can know whether he is in grace or not, and it would be great audacity for someone to try to make this boast about himself, etc.

42. From this it must follow that, because the man is in such doubt, he can have no true heart toward God nor turn to Him and call on Him from his heart. Rather, he is fearful and flees from God and must at last fall into hatred of God and despair. When the real struggle comes and he must stand before the tribunal, he feels and sees that with his life and works he cannot withstand God's wrath, but sinks into the abyss with all of it.

43. If now in such dangers we are to withstand and overcome despair, then we must have another basis than our righteousness or the Law's righteousness, namely, this eternal righteousness of Christ, which stands at the place (the right hand of the Father) where the devil cannot overthrow it and can bring no accusation against it before God's tribunal. The devil can overthrow me whenever he wants, along with all my life and works, by presenting God's tribunal and wrath and by blowing away all [my life and works] as the wind blows a little down feather. However, when I point him away from me and my works to the right hand of the Father where my Lord Christ sits, who gives me His righteousness (that is why He went to the Father), he will certainly be unable to overthrow Him—yes, even to attack Him.

44. Therefore, Christ is acting like a faithful, good Savior when He takes all of this away from us and all people, and takes it to Himself alone, and establishes and builds our righteousness only on His "going" to the Father. Thus we should know where we can remain secure against every onset and

storming of the devil and his gates of hell [Matt. 16:18]. If it depended on us and on our worthiness—that we had done penance purely enough and had done enough good works—then our hearts would never have any rest and finally could not endure.

45. From this we see how shamefully cursed has been the doctrine of the monks and of the whole papacy. With it they have misled the world. They taught not a word about Christ and faith—and not only that, they have also shamelessly asserted that their monasticism is a much higher, nobler, and more perfect estate than that of ordinary Christians. Hearing this should be an abomination to all Christians. No matter how highly one might want to put and exalt the life and goodness of all people, the chastity of virgins, the discipline and mortification of hermits, the laudable deeds and virtues of great, excellent, godly lords and regents, and whatever may be called "good people," yet it can never equal a Christian, that is, one who has this Lord sitting at the right hand of God and His righteousness. We will gladly let that [life] remain in its honor and praise it as a precious gift. But we should exalt a Christian as a lord far and high above all of that, as one who has this eternal benefit and inheritance in the kingdom of heaven at the right hand of God with Christ, his Brother.

46. Whoever understands and can distinguish these things can also teach and judge correctly about all of life, act correctly in all matters, and guard against all error, for he judges and measures everything according to the rule and standard which Christ teaches here. The Christian's righteousness is not the kind of righteousness that has grown in us (like the other righteousness, which is called the righteousness of the Law or human righteousness), but it is a completely heavenly and divine righteousness apart from and beyond us.

47. Therefore, if someone comes and wants to deceive you and put great illusions and miracles before your eyes concerning great, special holiness, directing you to live up to the example of this or that great saint so as to please God and become a Christian, then you can say in reply: "My friend, I will let all of that be good; I want to be righteous, live according to God's Commandments, be on my guard against sin, etc. However, you must not teach me that in this way I am to become a Christian or attain to something greater and higher. Those people did not become Christians by fasting, working, and suffering so much.

"That would insult my dear Lord Christ and would mean that His going away was in vain and equal to human works. Rather, I want to be called a Christian from clinging to this Savior—as He has taught me and as all saints who wanted to stand before God have had to do. As St. Paul says, I am 'found not having my righteousness according to the Law' [Phil. 3:9], but His righteousness, which He gained for me by this going away, by which He overcame my sin and death, and which He proclaims and gives to me through the preaching of the Gospel." When you have that, then go ahead and do as many good works as you can, but do them in accordance with God's command. Without this and before this you can do nothing good, because you are still in unbelief, do not have or know Christ, and therefore are under sin with all that you do, as we have heard in the first part.

48. This is what it means to speak in Christ's way and with His words about the righteousness that He regards as righteousness. It is not an external, human way of life on earth, but one that is incomprehensible and invisible in this life. It is not found on earth among us people nor attained through people but is a new, heavenly righteousness that He alone has made and established by His death and resurrection. We now must grasp it in faith (because we do not see it). It is prepared as an eternal, endless way of life where He rules in a new, heavenly way.

49. This does not happen with this life, because all of this has been ruined by sin and death and will finally come to nothing. For that reason the Son of God from heaven has instituted a kingdom that does not have to do with external, worldly affairs and government (as the Jews and the apostles imagined about His kingdom [Luke 19:11; Acts 1:6]), nor with the poor, beggarly righteousness of this life. Rather, He makes a new, eternal righteousness, by which all of nature is changed and renewed, so that there is no longer any sin or death, but only perfect, divine works and life. This is the work that He has begun through "going to the Father" and has already fully accomplished in His person. He always promotes this kingdom in this life through the preaching of the Gospel and the work of the Holy Spirit in the hearts of believers until the Last Day. However, in the life to come it will completely and perfectly live and be found in us.

50. "That is," He wants to say here, "what the words mean: 'I am going to the Father, and from this time you do not see Me' [John 16:10]. I am not speaking about this temporal way of life on earth, which in this corrupt nature cannot be without sin and death. Therefore, there can be no perfect righteousness and life there. My kingdom does not have such a transitory existence. Rather, it must become something different; what must happen is that you no longer see Me when I rule eternally apart from this bodily, visible existence. I will also bring you there, where there is only the new, perfect righteousness and eternal life, which I am now beginning in Christendom by the preaching and work of the Holy Spirit."

*"Concerning judgment, because the prince of this world has been judged."*
*[John 16:11]*

51. In the previous two points, He spoke about doctrine and summarized the whole Gospel. First, everything which is human nature, ability, activity, and life is sin and under God's wrath, because they do not believe in Christ. Second, we are justified—that is, are redeemed from sin and death, please God, and have eternal life—only because He goes to the Father. The third point follows, both how the world acts toward this preaching and, on the other hand, how the Holy Spirit will press on through His preaching.

52. About it He says that He will go on to rebuke the world concerning judgment. That sounds somewhat strange and obscure in our ears, since we are unaccustomed to the Hebrew language. The word "judgment" means nothing else than (as we also say about it) that we deal with and pass sentence on which of two disputing parties is right or wrong. At the same time it includes the two points which must always be present in a lawsuit, namely, grace and wrath, help and punishment. The one is present so that the innocent party is acquitted and helped to his rights. Yet the second point of judgment or verdict is used most often, namely, for condemnation and its consequence or execution.

53. That is what Christ is speaking about here. He points out that when the Holy Spirit proclaims the two points of His preaching in the world and rebukes it concerning sin and righteousness, the world will not receive this, nor does it want to be rebuked for being in sin and without righteousness, nor is it moved by being offered the righteousness of Christ. Rather, it opposes this teaching and rebuking of the Holy Spirit, condemns it, and persecutes it. The world alleges that it is right and must not suffer its wisdom, righteousness, etc., to be nullified, which it regards as divine gifts and worship; rather, it forcibly resists this. On the contrary, the Holy Spirit must once more proceed to rebuke the world concerning judgment and in turn urge the sentence of condemnation, telling it that it and its verdict are condemned, together with its prince and head, the devil.

54. This is where strife arises and begins, with one judgment running against another. The world puts its verdict and its wisdom against this and despises this teaching, not only because it does not come from its wisdom or from the great, excellent people of the world but also because it is preached by poor, unimportant people. It opens its mouth wide against this and says: "What else is this but some worthless beggars revolting against established authority? They want to reject and do away with everything previously observed by everyone and even established by God Himself." It condemns, bans, and curses both the doctrine and the preachers. It proceeds to shut their mouths with powerful threats and takes up severity and the sword. It simply refuses to let its error and idolatry be attacked or rebuked, and even

maintains and defends it against God and Christ as wisdom and holiness. It wants to have the preaching of the Gospel rooted out and abolished.

55. But then Christ says that the Holy Spirit will retain the supreme judgment and continue rebuking this verdict of the world until the Last Day. However, in this matter Christians get pinched between the door and the hinge, when the cross and persecution begin. Because the kingdom of Christ (as we have heard) is not of the world, but spiritual and invisible now on earth, the might and power that the world has on earth are directed against Christendom by means of condemning, persecuting, tormenting, harassing, killing, and murdering with sword, fire, water, and whatever it can. Moreover, the world is also egged on and strengthened by the devil's sharply furious wrath and hatred against Christ, as he desires and strives completely to abolish and root out Christendom. The result is that it appears to the eyes of the world and of Christians that the Church must completely perish because they exert such persecution, cruelty, and murder on the Christians who confess and conduct this preaching of the Holy Spirit.

56. So, with this point, Christ first gives the prophecy of how this preaching will be received by the world and what will happen to the apostles because of it. The world will despise them because they come without any public authority and command and bring a new doctrine against the established government, priesthood, and teaching office that were ordained by God, rebuking and faulting all they do as if it counted for nothing before God— and not only because of that, but also because they continue to preach and will not cease. So the world will go ahead and issue the verdict and its consequence against them, as against people who are not sent by God and do not preach God's Word but must be the devil's messengers and slanderers of God. They are seen as disobedient and insubordinate to God's Law, God's people, and the worship of God and are declared to be deserving of death and should not be allowed to live. This is what the Jews cried out regarding St. Paul: "It is not right to let such a man live" (Acts 22 [:22]); and they gave the reason: "This man does not cease to speak against the nation, against the Law, against the temple and the holy city" [Acts 21:28], etc.

57. Second, against this scandal of judgment or persecution of the world, Christ gives this comfort: they should know that by His divine power and strength He will maintain His preaching and preserve His Church against the wrath and raging of the world and the devil. Then the devil with his kingdom, being conquered by Him, will have to yield to Him and must not carry out against His Church what he wants according to his fierce, furious wrath and hatred. For that reason, even though the Christians must suffer from the devil and the world because of this preaching, this Word shall nevertheless not be overthrown but shall finally be victorious and hold its

ground and make it plain before all the world that their verdict against the Gospel is unfair. Finally, they will have to be ashamed of it themselves and in fact confess about themselves that they have condemned and persecuted the Gospel unjustly and unfairly. Similarly, when Christ was suffering, His judges and even His betrayer themselves had to testify about His innocence [John 18:38; 19:4, 6; Matt. 27:4].

The reason (he says) is that this King Christ by His going to the Father has already overcome both the world and the devil. He now sends the announcement that He is the Lord over all and has the power and might to condemn and to punish with eternal hellfire whatever opposes Him, together with the devil and his angels.

58. What He says means that this punishment will continue against the world which persecutes the Gospel, and finally maintain the victory against it, so that He overpowers its verdict and condemnation and in turn condemns and puts it to shame—not only the world but also its god, the devil himself (who urges the world against Christ). He is (He says) already judged [John 16:11], the verdict of condemnation has already been spoken against him, and the only thing still lacking is its *executio*, that the punishment be carried out on him in eternal hellfire. Similarly, when a thief or a murderer has been convicted by his judge, after wrath and the court have already proceeded and death has been pronounced, he is simply led away and receives justice.

59. So this judgment proceeds from the power and might of the Lord Christ sitting at the right hand of the Father, and this verdict is publicly proclaimed through the preaching office, namely, that the prince of the world and his adherents are already finally condemned and can do nothing against Christ. Rather, he must let Him remain the Lord and lie under His feet eternally and let his head be trampled [Gen. 3:15]. He sends this preaching into all the world, that whoever does not want to believe in this Lord will be condemned together with the devil, no matter how high, mighty, learned, or holy he may be—irrespective of how he tries to condemn this doctrine or to suppress and abolish it, no matter if he is called the Roman or Turkish emperor, king, and lord over all.

60. Even if the world meanwhile goes away and despises and makes fun of this verdict, which has already been spoken on the devil and all his members, because it does not see it happening before its eyes—just as it also despises the first and second parts of this preaching—Christ still proceeds against it and confidently lets Himself be despised. However, He shows the devil and the world that He is the Lord, who can break and put a stop to the devil's wrath and raging and overthrow His enemies (as Psalm 110 [:1] says about Him), "until He makes all of them His footstool." The ax has already been laid to the tree [Matt. 3:10; Luke 3:9], and chains and ropes have already

been thrown on him (as St. Peter says [2 Pet. 2:4]), with which the devil is bound for eternal darkness in hellfire. No one will believe this except the Christians, who regard their Lord's Word as true, recognize His power and kingdom, and take comfort in their King and Lord. The others will have no other reward than what they seek with their lord, the devil, so that in eternal darkness they must sink into the abyss of hell, overthrown and perishing because of their raging against the Christians.

That is the first part of this Gospel about the kingdom of Christ and the preaching of the Holy Spirit in the world. Now follows:

## The Second Part

*"I still have many things to say to you, but you cannot bear them now. But when the Comforter, the Holy Spirit, comes, He will guide you into all truth." [John 16:12–13]*

61. This part also belongs to the promise about the Holy Spirit and His office in Christendom. However, He breaks off here from what He had begun to say about the doctrine and what the Holy Spirit will preach, which He had summarized in a few words. He points them instead to the fact that the Holy Spirit Himself will come and teach them these things, so that they will understand them and in fact experience them. "It is not now the time," He means to say, "to speak much about doctrine," since He is saying farewell and comforting them about His departure. Moreover, even if He were to speak long and much about it, they are not yet ready to grasp and understand correctly how it will be in His future kingdom.

They are still so deeply drowned in the thoughts and hopes of an external, bodily kingdom and worldly glory that they cannot conform and take into their hearts what He is saying to them about His spiritual kingdom and office, which He will perform through the Holy Spirit. They cannot think otherwise than that, if He is to be a King, then He must Himself be present and either bring the world to Himself with His preaching and miracles, so that it is willingly obedient to Him and accepts Him as its Lord, or, if it will not voluntarily do that, then compel it by external force and punishment.

However, if it is to happen (as He has now said) that He will go away from them and no longer be seen—that is, die—then it is no longer to be hoped that He will become a king and carry out such great things. So they are and remain very confused until after His resurrection, because they do not at all understand what He told them earlier, except that they sense the beginning of the misery, sorrow, and persecution of the world which He here announces to them.

62. This is what He says, "I still have many things to say to you, but you cannot bear them now" [John 16:12]. What has been said and is yet to be said about this is still much too difficult for you to grasp, for it all goes completely against your thoughts and hopes. If you understood it, you would receive comfort and a cheerful heart from it, as He also said previously: "If you loved Me, you would have rejoiced when I said, 'I am going to the Father,' etc. [John 14:28]. Now, however, what I am telling you for your comfort about My glorification, ascension, and the glorious kingdom which I will begin through you only makes you frightened and distressed, etc. It is obviously correct that 'you cannot bear them now.' Therefore, I must also defer it until the time comes when these things (what I am telling you now beforehand) begin and the Holy Spirit comes. He Himself must teach it to you and lead and guide you out of your present erroneous thoughts and misunderstandings into the truth and correct knowledge."

63. His office, then, is (He says) that "He glorifies Me" [John 16:14], that is, gives the revelation and testimony about Me that, raised out of suffering and death into glory and seated at the right hand of the Father, I am reigning Lord over all. He is to proclaim in all the world that this has been the Father's plan. The Holy Spirit will be sent so that the world may know this and be brought to My kingdom, etc. Now, when it happens that I am taken from you and the Holy Spirit comes, that itself will teach it (much differently than you now think and understand). So you will yourselves experience everything I have now said to you and much more that I still must say (to explain and amplify it further).

It is with just this thought that He later concludes this chapter (as we will hear in next Sunday's Gospel reading[3]) and says, "I have spoken these things through a proverb" [John 16:25]; that is, what I have so far said to you about My suffering, resurrection, and your suffering, and how in the midst of them you are to ask the Father in My name, are now only strange, dark, and hidden sayings to you, which you do not understand. "However, the time is coming when I will no longer speak with you through parables, but will tell you plainly about My Father" [John 16:25], namely, when I have ascended to heaven and will send you the Holy Spirit. Then you will experience what I am telling you, which now are only proverbs.

This is the true, simple meaning of the text "I still have many things to say to you" [John 16:12].

64. However, these words have suffered and still must suffer from our Papists. These words must let themselves be distorted and interpreted to strengthen their worthless inventions and to be the basis for their alleging

---

3 See sermon for Fifth Sunday after Easter on John 16:23–30; and sermon On Prayer on John 16:23–30.

and babbling that we must believe and hold much more than the Gospel and the Scriptures teach, namely, what the councils and the fathers have said and ordered. For, they say, Christ promised here that the Holy Spirit will say much more to them than He has said and will guide them into all truth, etc. It is just as if the apostles had understood very well what Christ says to them here, though they themselves testify the opposite by the fact of their unbelief about His suffering and resurrection. Or it is again as if this were so easy to understand that we had no need of the Holy Spirit for it, though to this day no Papist understands anything of it. I know this from experience, for I also learned what they know. The books they write make it clear that they still understand nothing of this. Therefore, we must answer these fools in order to do away with their lying inventions.

65. First, you hear that He says, "I still have many things to say to you" [John 16:12]. Who is this "you," or to whom is He talking? Without a doubt He is talking to the apostles, to whom He also says: "You cannot bear them now" and "The Holy Spirit will guide you into all truth." Therefore, if Christ did not lie, then these words must have been fulfilled at the time when the Holy Spirit came. In them and through them He must have carried out everything of which the Lord here speaks and must have guided them into all truth. How, then, can we conclude from this that Christ did not say everything to the apostles, nor did the Holy Spirit, but left behind much that the councils are supposed to teach and decide? Nevertheless, according to their assertions, the opposite was supposed to follow, that the Holy Spirit has said everything to the apostles, and Christ is emphasizing that He will explain everything to the apostles and will bring into the world through them what they have learned from the Holy Spirit. How, then, does this agree with their trickery, that what we are to know, believe, and do in Christendom will first be spoken, taught, decided, and arranged after the apostles, at the end of the world?

66. Likewise, if what the councils taught and established after the apostles must be regarded as truth (as having been revealed anew by the Holy Spirit), then the apostles themselves did not come into the truth—much less did those to whom they preached. Together with them the Church would have been fully deceived by Christ, since He promised them that the Holy Spirit would guide them into all truth.

67. Second, Christ plainly says, "I still have many things to say to you." With those words He is not saying, "I have something far different to say to you, and the Holy Spirit will teach and explain something different to you than what I have said to you." That is their addition, which they smear on the words of Christ, and so distort the words that teaching "many things" (*multa*) is supposed to mean teaching "other things" (*alia*). We would certainly grant them the word *multa*, if only they had the grace from the Holy Spirit to

teach "many things." However, it is not to be tolerated when with the word "many" they want to introduce and have power to teach "different" things. For example, they again shamelessly assert that by inspiration of the Holy Spirit the church has established and arranged many things after the apostles which must be observed, such as, among others, the article about one kind in the Sacrament, the prohibition of the marriage of priests, and the like.

That is not teaching "more" or "further," but something completely different and even contrary, against the clear ordinance and command of Christ, as they themselves must confess is correct. Yet it is supposed to be heresy and wrong when we act according to Christ's command against their law, for "the church," they say, "has ordered it differently." If you ask, "On what basis?" they answer, "Christ says, 'I still have many things to say to you'"—yes, even what is contrary to His own words and command!

68. That would truly be an excellent church: one that would take for itself the power (as the anti-Christian church of the pope does) to teach whatever it wants against Christ and to change His ordinance, and then would want to make it good and confirm it with the words "I still have many things to say to you"! Nevertheless, Christ clearly says about the Holy Spirit, establishing His limits and goal, that He will glorify Him and not speak about Himself, but will take and proclaim His things, that is, Christ's words and command [John 16:13–14]. Therefore, the crowd that teaches differently must not be from the Holy Spirit or Christ's Church, but the rabble of the devil.

69. The Christian Church and the Holy Spirit Himself remain only with what Christ has said and commanded. They certainly increase it—that is, amplify it in length and breadth—but they do not make it different. This "many things to say" means that even though one thing is proclaimed in many ways, yet always the same thing is being proclaimed. For example, John the evangelist could have written many more things than Christ said here [John 20:30; 21:25], but he always remains with the one point, thoroughly proclaiming the article about the person, office, and kingdom of Christ (about which Christ Himself also speaks), and always has his *scopus* or "main point" pointing at this Lamb of God [John 1:29]. Similarly, St. Paul in the letter to the Romans and almost throughout Galatians repeatedly stresses and repeats the one point of the righteousness of faith [Rom. 1:16–17; 3:21–24; Gal. 3:6–9, 22].

70. Now, that is what it means to preach "many things" and say more than Christ does with these few words, but yet to preach the same one thing and nothing different. A good preacher has the ability to take up a matter and briefly grasp it and bring it to a close in two or three words, and then, if it is necessary, also amplify and explain it with sayings and examples, and thus make a whole meadow out of one flower. Similarly, a goldsmith can beat one

piece of silver close and thick on top of itself into one ingot, and then again beat it flat, curly, curved, and into a thin sheet. So a sermon can be long or short, but it is always the same one thing and not contradictory. "God's Word should dwell in us richly," says St. Paul [Col. 3:16], so that we are powerful in Scripture and can demonstrate the true doctrine from it.

This is what the Epistle to the Hebrews does. The greater part of it speaks about the priesthood of Christ and develops a long sermon from the passage "You are a Priest forever" (Psalm 110 [:4]), to which it adds many other passages, texts, and examples. Yet when we look at the summary of it, all of it is nothing more than the one point that Christ is the only eternal Priest. That is certainly "saying much more" than David did in that psalm, but still saying nothing different. So, since the beginning of Christendom, much more has been taught and preached (through the Holy Spirit) than Christ did, and still more may be taught each day, and it may be amplified most abundantly and in every way, since more is revealed to one than to another, or more is more abundantly allotted or given to one to speak than to another. However, this happens in such a way that when it is all finally brought together, it all refers to one Christ. How many illustrations we can cite from the entire Bible, and even from all creatures, which all agree in the doctrine of the Gospel, none of which He taught or said, and yet it is the same doctrine!

71. St. Paul also talks about this when he speaks about the gift of prophecy or interpreting Scripture and gives this limit and rule by which it is to be judged: "If anyone has prophecy, it should be in conformity with the faith" (Romans 12 [:6]); that is, it must agree and be in keeping with the doctrine of faith. For example, someone might want to introduce the example of Abraham, who led his son Isaac up the mountain to sacrifice him there but left his servants and the donkey at the base of the mountain [cf. Gen. 22:1–5]. Such an example can be explained for faith and as agreeing with the faith, or also against faith. The Jewish preachers and teachers asserted that whoever would let himself similarly be sacrificed and slain would do the very highest work and go immediately to heaven. For that reason, kings who wanted to be excellent saints sacrificed their own children alive to God and burned them up. Our monastic saints explain it the same way, that if we want to come to God, then we must leave the servants and the donkey at the base of the mountain, that is, stamp out the five senses and have nothing to do with any external, worldly concerns or matters, but, separated from all of this, live in spiritual contemplation. This is not "explaining and teaching in keeping with and in conformity to faith," but against faith.

But you can explain it this way: Whoever wants to come to God must go above human understanding and thoughts, so that he has God's Word through which he learns to recognize and lay hold of God. There he must bring the sacrifice before Him—that is, Christ, God's Son, who was given as a sacrifice to God for us—bringing forth this sacrifice through faith (so that the conscience can stand before God). Meanwhile, we can leave our donkey with the servants below, that is, whatever is our own work and activity, etc. I have adduced this example in such a way that it is just the same as the Gospel teaches everywhere, not against faith but for it—even if this does not correctly explain the actual, sure meaning of this history.

72. Our papistic donkeys, swine, and fools pay no attention to this. Rather, they want to persuade us to accept anything they assert and teach in the name of the church or the councils as if the Holy Spirit had taught it, without any regard for whether or not it agrees or harmonizes with the doctrine of the Gospel. All of this is supposed to be confirmed by the words "I still have many things to say to you" [John 16:12]. No, dear friend, even if He has more to say, it is wrong for you to say whatever you please or what each monk has dreamed or what an insolent Papist wants observed. I will gladly allow you to amplify these words of Christ and be a fertile preacher, making a thousand words out of one, in order to make it beautiful, clear, distinct, and bright so that everyone can understand it—as long as you remain with the one genuine and pure doctrine.

But if instead you bring forth a new doctrine and assert that whoever becomes a monk has a new baptism and becomes as pure as a young child, just baptized—the Holy Spirit has not told you to say that, but the devil! That is not teaching more, but something completely different and the opposite of what Christ says. For that reason a Christian must be wise and, as St. John teaches, be able to distinguish the spirits [1 John 4:1; cf. 1 Cor. 12:10] (according to God's Word), so that he does not let someone tell him something different (whether much or little is preached) or point him and lead him on a different path.

73. Third, He says, "You cannot bear them now" [John 16:12]. Here He is speaking about very great matters that are too difficult for them, and only for this reason does He not want to say more about them now: because they are too imperfect and weak. This is, of course, nothing else than what He had begun to speak about, namely, His kingdom, what its course in the world will be, how He must die the most shameful death and be cursed, and yet that people would believe in Him as the Savior, God's Son and Lord over all. Likewise, He was saying that they will be persecuted and killed by the world, and nevertheless the Gospel will continue, and because of it the whole Jewish people, along with their priesthood, temple, worship, and all their glory, will fall to the ground, etc. At that time they could understand none of this, even if He had preached to them about it for many years, until the Holy Spirit would teach it to them through experience in their preaching office.

74. But tell me, instead of this, what has been further arranged and established after the apostles by the councils or the popes? Would it be a difficult thing which they could not understand or endure (without the special revelation and power of the Holy Spirit) to grasp which rules should be observed in this or that monastic order, or whether black or gray cowls should be worn, or that meat is not to be eaten on Fridays, or that only one kind is to be used in the Sacrament? Should not the apostles have been able to understand and bear those things, which every unlearned, godless evildoer can easily understand and do?

There are much higher matters which the apostles could not bear and higher skills than these useless gossips dream about! I consider it certain that what the apostles could not understand and handle you also could not easily understand or endure without the enlightenment of the Holy Spirit. The doctrine of faith is very difficult to grasp and is not so easily understood as these inexperienced spirits dream. A person must step outside of himself—that is, out of his own life and works—and cling with all his confidence to what he does not see or feel in himself, namely, that Christ is going to the Father. It is a difficult skill to despair so much of himself that he abandons whatever he has of both good and bad life and clings only to the words of Christ, and because of them parts with body and soul. What power of reason could fathom or teach this, even if we searched the whole world? Just give it a serious try with a real conflict of conscience, and you will learn! The devil and our own nature, along with many sects and false doctrines, will strive harshly against it.

Let that be enough against the Papists' lying babble and asinine skill with which they defile and smear this beautiful text in order to confirm their lies.

75. However, as for what it means when Christ calls the Holy Spirit "the Spirit of truth" [John 16:13], this will be discussed in the other Gospel readings, and it is abundantly explained elsewhere [John 14:17; 15:26].[4] It is intentionally stated here "the Spirit of truth" and "He will guide you into all truth" (that is, into the true, pure, clear doctrine that preaches about Me and, as He says right after that, "glorifies Me" [John 16:14]). Here He is looking very far ahead to how the lying spirit, the devil, will be active and show himself in the church and assert his ideas with great pretense and commotion. He would gladly say, "How many sects will arise, who will all brag about their great spirit, and yet they will only lead people away from Christ and the truth into error and ruin."

76. For that reason He also describes the Holy Spirit and gives Him His true sign, by which He is to be known and tested: "He will glorify Me, for He

---

4 See sermon for Sunday after Ascension on John 15:26–16:4, paragraph 1; and sermon for Pentecost on John 14:23–31.

will take from what is Mine" [John 16:14]. He alone is the one who explains Christ as He has made Himself known through His Word, so that we would know that whoever teaches something different and claims to be and decks himself out as a spirit is not Christ's Spirit. He will teach nothing different but will remain with the same doctrine of Christ, except that He expands it further and makes it clearer and brighter. That is why He says, "He will glorify Me."

77. Likewise, He says, "He will not speak about Himself" [John 16:13]. Here He again distinguishes the false [spirits] and this true Spirit, for the others all come from themselves and speak what they have invented about themselves. Now, He says, that is not a property of the Holy Spirit, but of the devil. "When he speaks lies, he speaks from his own self, for he is a liar and a father of them" [John 8:44], etc. Therefore, He wants to say that if you hear a spirit who talks about himself, he is surely a liar. The Holy Spirit will not speak about Himself, but what He receives from Me and what He hears Me and the Father speaking with each other, etc.

78. This is certainly an astute text on the article of the three persons in the divine Being. The Son of God is the Word of the Father in eternity, which no one hears speaking except the Holy Spirit. He not only hears it but also testifies and proclaims it in the world. In summary, it all is aimed at this: God has resolved that the Holy Spirit alone is to proclaim and teach the article of Christ (how we are justified before God for His sake). That is why He concludes: "He will glorify Me, for He will take what is Mine" [John 16:14]. This means that He will certainly produce more than I and speak more plainly and bring to light; but He will only take what is Mine and speak about Me, and not about people's own holiness and works. This shall be His true office and work by which He will be known, which He will proclaim without ceasing until this Christ is well-known. When you have finished learning this completely, then you can seek a different Holy Spirit. However, we will, I hope, all remain students of this Master and Teacher until the Last Day.

# GOSPEL FOR THE FIFTH SUNDAY AFTER EASTER

*John 16:23–30*

*"In that day you will ask nothing of Me. Truly, truly, I say to you, whatever you ask of the Father in My name, He will give it to you. Until now you have asked nothing in My name. Ask, and you will receive, that your joy may be full. I have said these things to you in figures of speech. The hour is coming when I will no longer speak to you in figures of speech but will tell you plainly about the Father. In that day you will ask in My name, and I do not say to you that I will ask the Father on your behalf; for the Father Himself loves you, because you have loved Me and have believed that I came from God. I came from the Father and have come into the world, and now I am leaving the world and going to the Father." His disciples said, "Ah, now You are speaking plainly and not using figurative speech! Now we know that You know all things and do not need anyone to question You; this is why we believe that You came from God."*

1. We are accustomed to use this Gospel reading on this Sunday because it teaches about prayer, and this week is called Cross Week, in which people are accustomed to pray and to go about with crosses.[1] Those who first instituted it perhaps meant well, but it turned out poorly. In the processions many unchristian things took place up until now, while nothing at all or very little was prayed, so that they were rightly abolished and discontinued. I have often admonished that we should continue praying, for there is great need of it. However, now that the outward babbling and muttering of prayers have ended, we no longer pray at all. From that we can also become conscious that previously, among so many prayers, we prayed nothing at all.

---

1 The three Rogation days (Monday, Tuesday, Wednesday) after the Fifth Sunday after Easter and before Ascension Day on Thursday were called "Cross Days," and the week as a whole was called "Cross Week." Prior to the Reformation, it was customary for ecclesiastical processions and blessings of cultivated fields to take place on these three days. As early as 1519 Luther criticized the practice and wanted the days to be dedicated to true prayer. See *On Rogationtide Prayer and Procession* (1519), LW 42:85–93; Brecht 1:353.

2. The Lord points out five things here that are necessary for true prayer.[2] The first is God's promise, which is the basis, power, and chief thing in every prayer. He promises here that what we pray for will be given to us. He takes an oath on that and says, "Truly, truly, I say to you, if you ask the Father for something in My name, He will give it to you" [John 16:23], so that we should be certain that we are heard in prayer. He even reprimands them for being lazy and not having prayed at all. It is as if He wanted to say, "God is ready to give more quickly and much more than you ask; He even offers His benefits if we will only take them." It is truly a great shame and a harsh punishment among us Christians that He should still reproach us for our laziness in prayer and that we do not let such rich and excellent promises incite us to pray. We leave this precious treasure lying there and do not attempt or use it to experience the power in such promises.

3. So God Himself now bases our prayer on His promise and so entices us to pray, for if there were no promise, who would dare to pray? We have in the past used various ways of preparing ourselves for prayer, of which the books are full. But if you want to be well prepared, then take for yourself this promise and hold God to it, for then your courage and desire to pray will quickly grow—courage you could never get in any other way. Those who pray without God's promise devise for themselves the idea of how angry God is and hope to appease Him with their prayer. In that situation there is neither courage nor desire to pray, but only uncertain opinion and a depressed spirit. Then the prayer is unheard, and both prayer and labor are lost.

4. With these words He is now rebuking the unbelief of those who have a foolish idea about their own unworthiness to pray. They are gauging the worthiness of their prayer according to themselves and their own ability, and not according to the promise of God. That must result in nothing but unworthiness. However, you should be utterly certain of your worthiness, not from what you do but from the promise of God, so that even if you were alone and no one in the world was praying, yet you would pray because of this promise. You cannot point out to me any saint who has prayed depending on his own worthiness and not only on God's promise, whether it is Peter, Paul, Mary, Elijah, or whoever else—they were altogether unworthy. I would not give one penny for all the prayers of a saint who prayed because of his worthiness.

5. The second point which belongs to this promise is faith, namely, that we believe that the promise is true and do not doubt that God will give what He promises, for the words of the promise require faith. However, faith is a firm, undoubting confidence that God's promise is true, as James says: "If anyone lacks wisdom, let him ask God, who gives in simplicity and

---

2  The sermon On Prayer on John 16:23–30 also mentions five things that are necessary for prayer. Although the lists overlap, they are not the same.

reproaches no one, and it will be given to him. But let him ask in faith and not doubt, for whoever doubts is like the waves of the sea, driven and tossed by the wind. Such a person should not think that he will receive anything from God" (James [1:5–7]). Whoever doubts in his heart and yet prays tempts God, for he doubts God's will and grace. Therefore, his prayer is nothing, and he gropes for God like a blind man gropes for the wall [Isa. 59:10].

John also speaks about this certainty of faith in his Epistle: "This is the boldness that we have toward Him, that if we ask anything according to His will He hears us. And if we know that He hears us in whatever we ask, then we know that we have the requests that we have asked of Him" [1 John 5:14–15]. With these words St. John is describing how a right-believing heart is prepared for prayer, namely, that nothing else is on its mind except that its prayer is heard and that it has already obtained its requests, which is also true. Since the Holy Spirit must give this faith and sure certainty, no prayers are really prayed without the Holy Spirit.

6. Try it now and pray in this way, and you will experience the sweetness of God's promise, that is, what courage and cheerful heart it produces for praying for all kinds of things, no matter how great and high the request may be. "Elijah was a man, weak like us; yet when he prayed, it did not rain for three years and six months, and when he again prayed it rained" [James 5:17–18]. Here you see the prayer of one man, and with his prayer he rules over clouds, heaven, and earth. So God lets us see what might and power one true prayer has, namely, nothing is impossible for Him.

7. Let each one now ask his heart how often he has prayed during his life. Singing psalms and reading the Lord's Prayer is not praying.[3] These were instituted for the sake of children and uneducated people, in order to train them and give them experience in the Scriptures. No one, however, sees and feels your prayer except you alone in your heart, and you will certainly know when it hits the mark.

8. The third point is that we must name something for which we are asking God, such as when you ask for strong faith, love, peace, and consolation for your neighbor. We must point out the needs, just as the Lord's Prayer presents seven needs. This is what Christ means with the words "if you

3 Luther rejects the view that the act of prayer, performed without attention and considered apart from faith, is truly prayer. Yet elsewhere Luther approves of using written, prescribed prayers, especially the Lord's Prayer, the Commandments, and the Creed. See *Exposition of the Lord's Prayer* (1519), LW 42:21–22; *Sermon on Worthy Reception of the Sacrament* (1521), LW 42:173–74; *Personal Prayer Book* (1522), LW 43:12–13; *Sermon on Prayer* (1528), LW 51:169–71; *Commentary on Psalm 117* (1530), LW 14:8; *Table Talk* no. 122 (1531), LW 54:17; *Simple Way to Pray* (1535), LW 43:200; the *Church Postil*, sermon for Epiphany 2 on Rom. 12:6–16, paragraph 45 (LW 76:225). See also the prayers that Luther provides in the *Small Catechism* (1529) (Kolb-Wengert, pp. 363–64; *Concordia*, pp. 344–45).

ask for something" [John 16:23]—"something," that is, something you need. Likewise, He Himself explains this "something" and says "that your joy may be perfect" [John 16:24]. That is, pray for all kinds of necessities, until you have obtained everything and have full joy. This prayer will first be fulfilled completely on the Last Day.

9. The fourth point is that we must desire or wish that it happen, which is nothing other than asking as Christ says, "Ask." Others have called this *ascensus mentis in Deum*, that is, the heart rises and soars up to God, and desires something from Him, and for that reason sighs and says, "If only I had this or that!" St. Paul highly praises this sighing and says that it is "an inexpressible sighing" of the Spirit (Romans 8 [:26]); that is, the mouth cannot speak as sincerely and mightily as the heart wishes. The yearning exceeds all words and thoughts. Therefore, it also happens that a person does not himself feel how deep is his sighing or desire. When Zacchaeus desired to see the Lord, he himself did not feel that his heart wished that Christ would speak with him and come to his house. However, when it happened, he was very happy, for he had succeeded according to all his wishes and requests, more than he had dared to ask or desire with his mouth [Luke 19:2–6]. Moses cried out so that God said to him: "Why do you cry to Me?" (Exodus 14 [:15])—he was silent with his mouth, yet his heart sighed deeply in its need, and that is what God then called "a cry." So St. Paul also says, "God is powerful to do more and higher than we ask or understand" (Ephesians 3 [:20]). Now this sighing is assisted by temptations, anxiety, and danger, which teach us true sighing.

10. The fifth point is that we ask in Christ's name, which is nothing other than that we come before God with faith in Christ and confidently take comfort that He is our Mediator, through whom all things are given to us and without whom we deserve nothing but wrath and enmity. Paul says, "Through Him we have access into this grace in which we stand, and we boast in the hope of the coming glory which God will give" (Romans 5 [:2]). We truly ask in Christ's name when we rely on Him that we are being received and heard for His sake, and not for our sake. Those, however, who ask in their own name—such as those who think that God will hear or regard them because they say so many, so long, so devout, and so holy prayers—will deserve and obtain only wrath and enmity. They want to be the people for whom God should have regard without any means, so that Christ is of no value or use.

11. Here we see that all five points in prayer can certainly happen in the heart, without any oral babbling, though what the mouth says is certainly not to be despised but is necessary to kindle and incite inner prayer in the heart. However, the additions [to prayer], of which I have written enough elsewhere, should and must be set aside; namely, we are not to specify for

God the time, speed, person, place, and limit, but confidently leave all of that to His will. We are only to cling to asking, and not doubt that the prayer is heard and that it is already arranged that what we asked for will be given, as certainly as if we already had it. This is pleasing to God, and He wants to do as He here promises: "Ask, and you will receive" [John 16:24]. Those, however, who set the time, speed, place, and limit tempt God and do not believe that they are heard or that they have obtained that for which they asked. Therefore, nothing will be given to them. The Gospel reading continues further:

*"Until now you have asked nothing in My name," etc. [John 16:24]*

12. That amounts to saying that they as yet knew nothing about this prayer and name. Besides, they felt no need which would urge them to ask. They imagined that because Christ was with them, they needed nothing and had enough of everything. But now that He is to go away and leave them, the needs begin. These will give them sufficient reason to pray.

*"I have said this through a proverb," etc. [John 16:25]*

13. When He says "this," He means what He said before: "A little while, and you will not see Me, and again a little while, and you will see Me, for I am going to the Father" [John 16:16]. Likewise, [He means what He said] about the anguish of a woman giving birth [John 16:21]. These were nothing but proverbs, that is, dark, obscure sayings which they did not understand. John calls these dark, hidden words "proverbs," even though in German they are not called that, but rather "riddles" or "hidden words." We are accustomed to say about someone who speaks garbled words: "That is a covered dish," since there is something else behind the way the words sound; it is nimble and clever speech which not everyone understands. All the words that Christ spoke on the evening of His departure and going to the Father were like that, for they could understand nothing of them. They did not think about His dying and coming into another existence, but going for a physical walk and returning, as we travel to another country and return. Even though He spoke out bright and clear, yet His going and departure were "a covered dish" to them. Therefore, He further says:

*"But the time is coming when I will no longer speak with you in proverbs but will tell you plainly about My Father." [John 16:25]*

14. That is, what I now physically speak with you—and you do not understand My proverbs—I will certainly explain to you through the Holy Spirit. I will plainly tell about My Father, so that you will certainly understand what

"the Father" is and what "My going to the Father" means. That is, you will see clearly that I am ascending through suffering into the Father's kingdom and kind of existence, and that I am sitting at His right hand, representing you and being your Mediator. You will see that I have done all of this for your sake, so that you also can come to the Father. This "telling about His Father" is not to be understood to mean that He will tell us much about the divine nature, as the sophists invent, for that is pointless and incomprehensible. Rather, [He will tell us] how He goes to the Father, that is, how He receives the kingdom and government of the Father, just as a king's son comes to his father to receive the kingdom. He further says:

*"On the same day you will ask in My name." [John 16:26]*

15. Then you will not only have reasons to ask in various difficulties, but you also will know and recognize what My name is and how you should regard Me. Then the asking itself will teach you what you now do not at all understand and for which you have so far never prayed. Therefore, He further says:

*"And I do not say to you that I will ask the Father for you; for He Himself, the Father, loves you, because you love Me and believe that I came from God." [John 16:26–27]*

16. How is that? Does He not want to be a Mediator? Are we not to ask in His name? Are we to come to the Father through ourselves? How delightfully and sweetly the Lord can speak and entice us to Himself and through Him to the Father! Here He Himself explains what must happen when we want to ask in His name. "You have loved Me," He says, "and believe that I came from God," etc. That is, "You know Me and love Me. Thus you have Me and My name and are in Me as I am in you." Christ dwells in us, not because we can think, speak, sing, or write much about Him, but because we love Him and believe in Him, that He has come from God and returns to God, that is, that in His suffering He emptied Himself of all divine glory and again went to the Father in His kingdom for our sake [cf. Phil. 2:5–11]. This faith brings us to the Father, and thus everything happens in His name.

17. Here we are certain that Christ does not need to ask for us, for He has already prayed for us. We ourselves can now come through Christ and ask. We no longer need another Christ who asks for us, but this one Christ who has prayed for us and brought us [to the Father] is enough. That is why He says, "The Father loves you" [John 16:27]. "It is not your merit, but His love. However, He loves you for My sake, because you believe and love Me; that is, He looks at My name in you. Therefore, I have carried out My office, and you

have been brought through Me [to the Father]. Just like Me, you yourselves can now come before Him and ask. There is no need for Me to ask for you again." Those are strikingly great words, that through Christ we have become like Him as His brothers and can boast of being His Father's children, and that His Father loves us for Christ's sake. He says above: "From His fullness we have all received grace upon grace" (John 1 [:16]); that is, God is gracious to us because He is gracious in Christ, who is in us and we in Him.

18. Here we also see that "believing in Christ" does not mean believing that Christ is one person who is God and man, for that helps no one.[4] Rather, it means believing that this same person is Christ, that is, that He came from God for our sake and came into the world, and again leaves the world and goes to the Father [John 16:28]. That is as much as to say, "Here is Christ, who became man for us and died, rose again, and ascended into heaven." Because of this office, He is called Jesus Christ, and believing that this is true means being and remaining in His name. There follows further in the Gospel reading:

> His disciples said to Him: "Now You are speaking plainly, and not speaking proverbs." [John 16:29]

19. Here you see that "speaking plainly" or "speaking clearly" is the same as speaking without proverbs or without dark and hidden words. The good disciples think that they understand very well what it means that Christ comes from the Father and goes to the Father. However, they do this as good children of Christ, as if they could easily understand, and they tell Him this to please Him. Good, simple people sometimes tell each other yes or no, and one will speak up and tell another that it is true and he understands it when he is still far from understanding it. That can happen without any hypocrisy, in true simplicity. The evangelist points out here what a beautiful, simple, pleasant, and delightful life Christ led with His disciples, that they could understand Him so easily. Therefore, they further say:

4 Luther accepted the ancient dogma of the person of Christ and often emphasized its importance, but he also wanted it to be connected with faith in Christ's saving work. On the connection of Christology with soteriology as the "chief article" of the Christian faith, see *Sermons on John 17* (1528/1530), LW 69:69–70; *Freedom of a Christian* (1520), LW 31:351–52; *Smalcald Articles* (1537/1538) II I (Kolb-Wengert, p. 301; *Concordia*, p. 263); and the *Church Postil*, sermon for Third Day of Christmas on Heb. 1:1–12, paragraphs 11–140 (LW 75:259–316), and sermon for Sunday after Christmas on Gal. 4:1–7, paragraphs 56–61 (LW 75:382–83).

*"Now we know that You know all things and do not need anyone to question You; this is why we believe that You came from God." [John 16:30]*

20. That is, "You anticipate and explain Yourself and no longer speak in proverbs, about which we would have to question You. You already know where we are lacking in understanding." All of this refers to their question about what the "little while" meant [John 16:16]. He notices this and says that He must go to the Father. They still did not understand it, but it was clearer than when He said, "A little while, and you will not see Me" [John 16:16]. Now, when He saw from their thoughts that they wanted to question Him, they then confessed that He came from God and knows all things, so that they do not need to question Him, for He Himself sees very well where the trouble is.

# ANOTHER SERMON,
## ON PRAYER

*John 16:23–30*

*"In that day you will ask nothing of Me. Truly, truly, I say to you, whatever you ask of the Father in My name, He will give it to you. Until now you have asked nothing in My name. Ask, and you will receive, that your joy may be full. I have said these things to you in figures of speech. The hour is coming when I will no longer speak to you in figures of speech but will tell you plainly about the Father. In that day you will ask in My name, and I do not say to you that I will ask the Father on your behalf; for the Father Himself loves you, because you have loved Me and have believed that I came from God. I came from the Father and have come into the world, and now I am leaving the world and going to the Father." His disciples said, "Ah, now You are speaking plainly and not using figurative speech! Now we know that You know all things and do not need anyone to question You; this is why we believe that You came from God."*

1. In order for a prayer to be truly good and be heard, note first that five things are necessary. The first is that we have a promise or pledge from God, which we keep in mind and of which we remind God, and thus cheerfully move ourselves to ask Him. If God had not commanded us to ask, and pledged that He would hear, all creatures with all of their asking could not obtain even one kernel. From this it follows that no one obtains anything from God because of his worthiness or the worthiness of his prayer, but only from divine kindness, which anticipates every request and desire. Through His gracious pledge and command He moves us to ask and desire, so that we learn how very much more He is concerned about us and how much more He is ready to give than we are to receive and to seek. So we can become confident in asking, since He offers everything and more than we can ask.

2. Second, it is necessary that we not doubt the pledge of the true and faithful God. He has pledged to hear and even commanded us to ask for the very reason that we would have a sure and firm faith that He will hear. He says in Matthew 21 [:22] and Mark 11 [:24]: "Everything you ask for in prayer, if you only believe, you will receive." He says: "And I also tell you: Ask, and it will be given to you; seek, and you will find; knock, and it will be opened to you. For whoever asks receives, and whoever seeks finds, and whoever

knocks, to him it will be opened. Where among you is a son who asks his father for bread, and he offers him instead a stone; and if he asks for a fish, he offers him a snake instead of a fish; or if he asks for an egg, he will offer him a scorpion instead? So, then, if you who are evil know how to give good gifts to your children, the Father in heaven will much more give the Holy Spirit to those who ask Him" (Luke [11:9–13]). We must confidently proceed with this and similar pledges and commands and ask in true confidence.

3. Third, if anyone asks in such a way that he doubts that God will hear, and only bases his prayer on the chance that it will happen or not happen, he does two bad things. The first is that he himself ruins his prayer and labors in vain. James says that whoever wants to ask from God should "ask in faith and not doubt, for whoever doubts is just like a wave of the sea which is driven and tossed by the wind. Such a man should not think that he will receive anything from the Lord" (James [1:6–7]). He means that this man's heart does not keep still, and for that reason God cannot give him anything. Faith, however, keeps the heart still and makes it receptive to divine gifts.

4. The second bad thing is that he regards his utterly faithful and truthful God, who is more faithful than anyone, as a liar and a loose, unreliable man— as someone who cannot or will not keep His pledges. Thus, by his doubt, he robs God of the honor and the name of "faithful" and "true."

This is such a weighty sin that through just this sin a Christian becomes a heathen, denying and losing his own God. If he remains in it, he must be eternally condemned without any relief. However, if something is given to him for which he asks, it will be given to him not for salvation but for his harm temporally and eternally. It is given to him not for the sake of his prayer, but from the wrath of God, as a reward for the good words that were spoken in sin, unbelief, and divine dishonor.

5. Fourth, some say, "Yes, I would certainly trust that my prayer would be heard, if I were worthy and did it well." I answer: "If you do not want to ask until you know or feel that you are worthy and capable, then you must never again ask." As was said before, our prayer must not be based or dwell on our worthiness or the prayer's worthiness, but on the unwavering truth of the divine promise. If it is based on itself or on something else, it is false and deceives you, even if the heart is breaking because of its great devotion and weeps nothing but drops of blood. We ask because we are unworthy to ask. We become worthy to ask and be heard just through believing that we are unworthy and confidently trusting only in the faithfulness of God.

No matter how unworthy you may be, look at this and observe it with all seriousness: a thousand times more depends on honoring God's truth and not making His faithful pledge a lie with your doubt. Your worthiness does not help you at all, and your unworthiness does not hinder you at all.

Mistrust is what condemns you, but confidence makes you worthy and keeps you safe.

6. Therefore, beware all your life of ever thinking that you are worthy or capable to ask or to receive, unless you happen to be risking your neck on the true and certain promise of your gracious God. He wants to reveal to you His mercy and goodness, so that just as He has promised to you, unworthy as you are, an unmerited and unasked hearing out of pure grace, so He also wants to hear your unworthy prayers out of pure grace, to the honor of His truth and promise. Then you can give thanks not for your worthiness, but for His truth with which He fulfills His promise and for His mercy that made the promise.

The words in Psalm 25 [:10] are true: "The ways of the Lord are goodness and truth for those who keep His covenant and testimony." Goodness or mercy is in the promise; faithfulness or truth is in the fulfilling and hearing of the promises. In Psalm 85 [:10] he says, "Goodness and faithfulness meet each other; righteousness and peace kiss." That is, they come together in every work and gift that we obtain from God through asking.

7. Fifth, in this trust we should act in such a way that we do not set a limit for God, determine the day or place, or fix the manner or measure of His hearing. Rather, we should leave all of that to His will, wisdom, and omnipotence. We should just await His hearing boldly and cheerfully, and not want to know how and where, how soon, how long, and through whom. His divine wisdom will find a superabundantly better manner and measure, time and place than we could think of. Perhaps even miracles will happen. For example, in the Old Testament, the children of Israel trusted that God would rescue them, even though there was no possible way before their eyes nor in all their thoughts. Then the Red Sea opened and gave them a way through, and all their enemies drowned at once [Exodus 14].

8. This is what Judith, the holy woman, did when she heard that the citizens of Bethulia would surrender the city in five days if in the meanwhile God did not help them. She rebuked them and said: "Who are you that you tempt God? That is not the way to acquire grace, but rather to provoke disfavor. Are you trying to fix a time for God to have mercy on you and determining a day at your own caprice?" [Judith 8:12, 16]. That is why God helped her in an unusual way, so that she struck off the head of the great Holofernes and the enemies were driven away [Judith 13:6–8; 15:1–5].

9. Similarly, St. Paul also says that God's ability is so great that He does superabundantly higher and better than we ask or understand [Eph. 3:20]. Therefore, we should know that we are too insignificant to be able to name, describe, or identify the time, place, manner, measure, and other circumstances for what we ask from God. Rather, we should leave it all completely to Him and immovably and firmly believe that He will hear us.